Pillar II in the New Basel Accord

Pillar II in the New Basel Accord

The Challenge of Economic Capital

Edited by Andrea Resti

Published by Risk Books, a Division of Incisive Financial Publishing Ltd

Haymarket House
28–29 Haymarket
London SW1Y 4RX
Tel: +44 (0)20 7484 9700
Fax: +44 (0)20 7484 9797
E-mail: books@incisivemedia.com
Sites: www.riskbooks.com
www.incisivemedia.com

ISBN 978-1-906348-15-1

British Library Cataloguing in Publication Data
A catalogue record for this book is available from the British Library

Publisher: Nick Carver
Managing Editor: Jennifer Gibb
Production Editors: Lucie Carter and Sarah Hastings
Copy Editor: MFE Editorial Services
Typeset by Mark Heslington Ltd, Scarborough, North Yorkshire

Printed and bound in the UK by Printondemand-worldwide

Contents

PART 2: THE MAIN RISK TYPES TO BE ASSESSED UNDER PILLAR II

PART 3: RISK INTEGRATION AND CAPITAL MANAGEMENT

List of Figures

List of Tables

About the Editor

Andrea Resti is a professor of financial markets and institutions at Bocconi University, Milan, where he holds courses on "credit risk measurement and management", "risk and value management in banks", "private banking and institutional money management", as well as in several short courses for bank executives. He heads Bocconi's Carefin, Centre for Applied Research in Finance, a think tank producing books, conferences and research papers.

Andrea has been active in the financial sector for about 20 years. After working for seven years in the research and planning department of a major Italian bank, Andrea moved to academia, first at Bergamo University and then at Bocconi, the leading Italian university in business and economics. In the last few years he has been in charge of risk management education projects for the Italian Bankers' Association and the Bank of Italy, including a number of courses on Pillar II and economic capital. Formerly, he has served as managing director of FinMonitor, a research institute on bank M&As in Europe, as well as "senior rapporteur" for the Basel II Task Force promoted by the Centre for European Policy Studies in Brussels and "economic advisor" to Assogestioni, the association of Italian fund managers.

His books in English include *Recovery Risk: the Next Challenge in Credit Risk Management* (co-editors: Ed Altman and Andrea Sironi) and *Risk Management and Shareholders' Value Creation in Banking* (co-authored with Andrea Sironi). His articles have been published in several scientific journals, including the *Journal of Business, Journal of Banking and Finance, Journal of Financial Intermediation* and others.

Andrea acts as a consultant to major banking institutions and as an independent expert for the Italian magistrates on crimes arising from complex financial transactions. His main research areas are credit risk management and regulation, with a special focus on the Basel Accord, risk measurement for managed portfolios and quantitative measures of bank efficiency (including post-merger efficiency increases).

About the Authors

Carlo Acerbi currently heads the financial engineering department of Abaxbank in Milan. He holds a PhD in high energy physics from the International School for Advanced Studies (ISAS-SISSA, Trieste, Italy). He turned from physics to mathematical finance in 1997 and ever since he has worked for several financial institutions as a risk manager and quantitative analyst. His research activity focuses in particular on the pricing on financial derivaties and on the foundations of the theory of financial risk. He collaborates on this field with several leading universities around the world.

Patrick Acx, economic capital programme director at Fortis, holds an engineering degree, which he completed with a MBA at Vlerick Ghent Leuven Management School. After military service he joined the former Generale Bank as a management trainee. He worked for several years in the credit department, at local level as well as central level, in Belgium and in the Netherlands. In his previous job as director credit analytics he was responsible for the development of the various Basel II credit risk models for all Fortis portfolios. In October 2006 he joined the integrated risk department where he is now responsible for the overseeing of Fortis' economic capital.

Mario Anolli is a professor of financial markets and institutions in the School of Banking, Finance and Insurance of the Università Cattolica del S. Cuore, Milan. There, he teaches courses in portfolio management and risk management and serves as the dean of the school. He has been teaching and researching for more than 15 years about banking and finance subjects (mostly on risk management, banking and securities markets microstructure) and authored publications in academic journals, books and book chapters both in Italy and internationally. He acts as a consultant to large financial institutions and sits on the Risk Management Scientific Committee of the Italian Bankers' Association.

Martina Bignami. After graduating in economic and social disciplines at Bocconi University in Milan, she worked as a researcher in the department of economics for a couple of years, dealing mainly with international monetary economy topics. She joined Bank of Italy in 1991. Since then she has been working in the banking supervision area. She spent the first five years in the Milan branch of the Italian Central Bank, performing off-site technical reviews as well as on-site examinations of local banks. Martina moved in 1996 to the head office in Rome, where she joined the division in charge of setting methodologies and procedures to be applied by the Bank of Italy staff in assessing banks' performance. In this capacity she has dealt mainly with the development and maintenance of the credit, market and liquidity risk analysis methodologies. In this respect she has taken part in several national and international supervisors working groups. In 2004 she was appointed member of the Conglomerates Technical Group (a forum for the implementation of supplementary supervision on financial conglomerates established among the three Italian financial sectors supervisors). She is a member of the Interim Working Committee on Financial Conglomerate established in 2005 by CEBS and CEIOPS. Martina's main duties in 2005, 2006 and 2007 have been linked to the coming into force of the Basel II prudential framework: she is the head of the validation team in charge of the supervisory assessment of the IRB system developed by a primary Italian banking group, she has been working on the transposition of the Basel II directives concerning Pillar II in the banking regulation issued by Banca d'Italia and she has contributed to the drafting of the new Supervisors' Guide, which aligns the Bank of Italy intermediaries' Risk Assessment System to the CEBS guidelines on SREP. In 2008 she was appointed head of the Risks Review Support Division within the Banking Groups Supervisory Department.

Klaus Böcker works as a senior risk controller in UniCredit Group and is team head of "Risk Analytics and Methods", which is based in Munich, Germany. In this capacity, one of his primary responsibilities is overseeing all quantitative aspects of UniCredit Group's economic capital model, in particular business risk, real estate risk, financial investment risk, and risk aggregation. Klaus holds a university degree in theoretical physics and a PhD in mathematics. He is also research fellow at the Center for Mathematical Sciences at the Munich University of Technology. Klaus is doing research in various fields of finance where he authored and co-authored several articles that have been published in recognised finance and mathematical journals. Klaus is also a frequent speaker at international risk conferences and at seminars about risk management and quantitative finance. In 2007 and 2008 he won the PRMIA Institute's Award for New Frontiers in Risk Management related to his research in multivariate operational risk using Lévy copulas and the interaction of market and credit risk. In August 2007, Klaus was inducted by his peers as a charter member of the international Risk Who's Who honour society.

Thomas Breuer is director of the PPE Research Centre at FH Vorarlberg. He did undergraduate and graduate work at ETH Zürich and Princeton, and holds a Cambridge PhD. At the Austrian Central Bank he led on-site teams supervising market risk models. Thomas was a Humboldt Fellow at the University of Köln. His research focus is on stress testing, the integration of market and credit risk models, and multi-period risk.

Brian Dvorak is a managing director in the Credit Strategies Group of Moody's KMV. He joined KMV as client solutions director in 1998 and moved to London in 2000. Named head of Europe, Middle East and Africa in 2003, he went on to lead the Global Account Solutions team in 2005. Before joining KMV in 1998, Brian was vice president of product marketing and technical support at CATS Software Inc. Previously, he was executive vice president and chief operating officer of LOR/Geske Bock Associates, Inc. and LORGB Investment Advisors, Inc. Brian received both his BA in economics with highest honours and his MBA in finance from the University of California, Berkeley. Brian is also a frequent speaker at international risk management conferences and seminars.

Andrea Enria is now deputy head of regulation and supervisory policy at Banca d'Italia. He has written his contribution while Secretary General of the Committee of European Banking Supervisors (CEBS), which is mandated to advise the European Commission on technical aspects of EU banking legislation, to enhance convergence in supervisory practices within the EU and to facilitate the exchange of information between supervisory authorities. Andrea previously held the position of head of the financial supervision division at the European Central Bank, where he also served as a secretary of the ESCB Banking Supervision Committee. Before joining the ECB he worked for several years in the research department and in the supervisory department of Banca d'Italia, covering issues like competition policy, bank ownership and group structures, implementation of community legislation, supervisory co-operation, analytical issues on banking supervision and financial stability.

Thierry Grunspan started his career as an economist in the Monetary Policy Research Unit at the Bank of France, before joining the inspection teams of the French Banking Commission in charge of validating internal models for credit and market risks (2003). In 2007, he joined Standard & Poor's as a director in the Financial Institutions Department of the Paris office, working on the capital project team and serving as an analyst on French financial institutions. Thierry is a graduate from Ecole Nationale de la Statistique de l'Administration Economique (ENSAE) and from the Institut d'Etudes Politiques de Paris. He holds a PhD from Columbia University (US).

Élie Hériard-Dubreuil is a director in the Financial Institutions department of Standard & Poor's Ratings Group. He focuses as a specialist on projects related to quantitative risk analysis, Basel II and economic capital. In particular, Élie coordinates at a global level the development of Standard & Poor's new risk adjusted capital framework for financial institutions. Prior to joining Standard & Poor's, Élie was in charge of Basel II preparation and economic capital modeling at IXIS and the Group Caisses d'Épargne. He was involved in the validation of models and methodologies related to investment banking, as well as in the development of benchmark risk modelling tools. Previously, Élie worked in structured finance ratings on various asset classes and credit risk modelling for another rating agency. Élie is a graduate engineer from the École Nationale de la Statistique et de l'Administration Économique (ENSAE).

Martin Jandačka is a junior researcher in the PPE Research Centre at FH Vorarlberg. He did graduate work at the Faculty of Mathematics, Physics and Informatics of Comenius Univestity in Bratislava. His research focus is on the integration of market and credit risk models and pricing of financial derivatives.

Ahmet E. Kocagil is a MD and global head of the Quantitative Analytics and Advisory Services Groups at Fitch Solutions, managing teams in New York, London, and Hong Kong. Ahmet was earlier a senior director at Moodys KMV where his responsibilities included being in charge of the Default Risk Group and being the developer and leader of Moody's RiskCalc Suite of Default Probability Models globally. Prior to that, he was an assistant professor with The Pennsylvania State University, a research assistant with the National Bureau of Economic Research (NBER) and a research assistant with Columbia University - Center for the Study of

Futures Markets. Ahmet has published papers in refereed journals and contributed a chapter to a book. His current areas of research interest are focused on single-name and portfolio level credit risk modelling. He serves on the editorial boards of *The Journal of Credit Risk*, programme committee of *Journal of Investment Management*, and is leading the Fitch Academic Advisory Board (FAAB). Ahmet holds a BS in economics from Bosphorus University and a MPhil/PhD in financial economics and econometrics from City University of New York.

Jing Liu is an analyst in Fitch Solutions Quantitative Analytics and Advisory Services group. Her primary areas of expertise are structured finance pricing models and bank rating models. Jing was previously commodities risk management intern of global procurement at Kraft Foods. She also worked as a finance, marketing and business analyst intern at MSTRS Technologies, and finance and accounting intern at O'Halloran International. Jing earned a BA in economics from Renmin University of China and a PhD in economics from Iowa State University, with specialisation in financial economics, applied econometrics and industrial organisation.

Bernard de Longevialle, managing director, has been working for Standard & Poor's since 1998. For the past three years he has been responsible for leading a global capital task force in charge of Basel II analysis as well as of the development of an enhanced Standard & Poor's risk adjusted capital framework for banks. He is also heading the Paris based team of analysts in charge of rating banks in Benelux, France and French speaking cantons in Switzerland. Between 2000 and 2003 he spent three years in Milan, where he set up a team of bank analysts responsible for Italian banks ratings. Prior to that, he worked for five years with the Commission Bancaire, the French banking supervisory authority, where his responsibilities included serving as head of the foreign bank department and French representative on the European Central Bank sub-group on financial fragility. He also spent two years at UCB, a subsidiary of group Paribas, including a year and a half in Italy. He has a master degree from the Institut d'Etudes Politiques de Paris (IEP), and also completed a three-year legal studies programme at the University of Nanterre (*Licence en droit*). From October 1997 until June 2000 he was *Maître de Conference* (lecturer) in economics at IEP. He speaks French, English and Italian.

Cécile Meys joined the CEBS Secretariat mid February 2007. Prior to joining the CEBS Secretariat Cécile worked as a policy officer and an on-site examiner at De Nederlandsche Bank in The Netherlands. Before joining De Nederlandsche Bank, Cécile worked as an attorney-at-law in The Netherlands. At the CEBS Secretariat Cécile is responsible for a wide range of issues in the area of convergence of supervisory practices and cooperation at the EU level, including the strengthening supervisory cooperation for cross-border banking groups in the EU.

Laetitia Mouquot works at the International Affairs department of the French Commission bancaire. Her areas of responsibility include hybrid capital issuances and liquidity. She joined the CEBS Secretariat in London in 2004, where she was in charge of supporting the Expert Group on Capital Requirements, which promotes the convergent implementation of Basel II in Europe and prepares the CEBS regulatory advice to the European Commission. Laetitia was also involved in the issues related to the Lamfalussy review. From 2000 to 2004, she was an off-site examiner at the French Commission bancaire. Laetitia is a graduate from ESSEC (Ecole Supérieure des Sciences Economiques et Commerciales) and from Sciences Po Paris (Institut d'Etudes Politiques de Paris).

Ruben Olieslagers, head of R&D for credit portfolio management in the merchant banking business of Fortis, has a Master of Science degree in applied engineering (KU Leuven), a postgraduate degree in finance (Solvay Business School) and a MBA in financial services and insurance from Vlerick Ghent Belgium/St. Gallen Switzerland. He has been active for more than 10 years in risk management at Fortis and is closely involved in the development and the implementation of credit risk and economic capital models within Fortis. Furthermore, he represented Fortis in several national and international banking and insurance associations in order to safeguard the interests of financial institutions in respect of the Basel Committee and the European Commission. Ruben regularly lectures at universities (in Belgium, the Netherlands, Germany, Switzerland, Austria and Italy) on financial topics related to risk management and regulation.

David Palmer is a senior supervisory financial analyst in the credit risk section of the division of banking supervision and regulation at the Federal Reserve Board. He focuses primarily on supervisory evaluations of banks' internal processes to assess capital adequacy, under US requirements for

Pillar II of Basel II and Federal Reserve expectations contained in SR letter 99–18. David leads the Federal Reserve System's Pillar II qualification team, which assists onsite examiners in making their assessments of banks' ability to meet Pillar II requirements. He specialises in analysing banks' assessments of credit risk for internal assessments of capital adequacy. His work includes evaluating the use of economic capital as one among several tools used by banks to estimate capital needs. David has a Bachelor's degree from Oberlin College and a Master's degree from Georgetown University.

Andrea Pilati holds a degree in banking and economics. In 1982 he joined the Bank of Italy, achieving the role of senior manager before leaving. For many years he supervised large Italian banking groups and subsidiaries of foreign banking groups, covering many areas that concerned Italian and international banking systems: privatisation; concentration and mergers; analysis and interventions on weak banks; validation of internal models for measuring market risks; and progressive moves of large banking groups to "Basel II". Since 2006, he has been working on methodologies and procedures: this has included implementing the New Capital Accord in the Italian regulatory framework and coordinating a project on the New Supervisory Guidance for banks, investment firms, asset management companies and non-banking financial intermediaries. Alongside his duties at the Bank of Italy, Andrea joined a working group of experts, who were given the job of drafting the Capital Adequacy Directive (CAD1), and other technical groups set up by the Basel Committee to deliver a supervisory framework aimed at measuring risks that arise from off-balance sheet items. Currently, he is a member of the Accord Implementation Group; this was established by the Basel Committee to promote consistency in applying the New Basel Accord. He is also a member of the working group focusing on liquidity that is responsible for revising sound practices for managing and controlling liquidity risk. He is the author of many articles and papers on questions concerning the banking system and risk measurement and control processes.

Klaus Rheinberger is research assistant and lecturer at the PPE Research Centre at the University of Applied Sciences Vorarlberg. He studied theoretical physics at the University of Innsbruck where he also attained a PhD. His research focus is on the integration of market and credit risk models.

Francesco Saita is full professor and head of the department of finance at Bocconi University, where he has also previously been the director of the MSc in finance and vice director of the Research Center on Financial Innovation. His main research interests are related to risk management and capital allocation in banks, asset-liability management and risk management in life insurance companies and derivatives. His recent publications include the book *Value at Risk and Bank Capital Management*. He has often been involved in risk management courses and seminars for bankers and regulators by SDA Bocconi Business School and is a member of the Scientific Committee of the review of the Italian Financial Risk Managers' Association. He has also served as a consultant for banks and life insurance companies on risk measurement and risk management projects.

Oleg Shmeljov is a member of the CEBS Secretariat, where he is involved in a wide range of technical issues including crisis management, operational risk and Pillar II. Oleg is seconded to the CEBS Secretariat by the Estonian Financial Supervisory Authority, where he held a position of a financial auditor, being involved in on-site and off-site supervision, Basel II implementation and validation, Pillar II and EU cooperation. Previously he was employed by the Estonian subsidiary of the SEB, where he worked in the risk management area. Oleg holds a MSc degree in economics from Tallinn University of Technology (Estonia) and is currently working at the same university on his PhD thesis in the field of risk management and supervision.

Andrea Sironi is professor of banking and finance at Bocconi University, where he has also been dean for international affairs. He has held visiting positions at the research and statistics department of the Federal Reserve Board of Governors, and at the Salomon Brothers Center (Stern School of Business, NYU). He is a member of the Fitch Academic Advisory Board and has previously been a financial analyst at The Chase Manhattan Bank in London. Andrea's research interests include financial risk management and international banking supervision. He has published and edited many books and papers in international refereed journals on these subjects.

Martin Summer is head of the economic studies division at the Austrian Central Bank (OeNB). Before he joined OeNB in 2000 he worked as a lecturer at University of Vienna, University of Birmingham and the University of Regensburg. He has also worked as a visiting researcher at the Bank of England and the Financial Markets Group of the London School of

Economics in 2004. His research interests are banking regulation and systemic risk, financial stability and financial economics.

Nikola Tarashev is a senior economist at the Bank for International Settlements. He holds a PhD degree in economics from Princeton University. His PhD thesis, entitled "Information Heterogeneity and Currency Crises" and written under the supervision of Pierre-Olivier Gourinchas, applies techniques from the global games literature to the theoretical and empirical analysis of speculative attacks on currency regimes. Nikola joined the Research and Policy Analysis division (Monetary and Economic Department) of the BIS in August 2002. Part of his current research extends his thesis work in order to study the design of policy institutions in the context of time-varying strategic uncertainty and analyse the social value of public information. In addition, he has worked on measures of investors' risk aversion, on the empirical evaluation of structural credit-risk models and on the pricing and measurement of portfolio credit risk. Nikola also contributes to the BIS Quarterly Review, mainly with articles analysing the BIS international banking statistics, and to projects of the Research Task Force of the Basel Committee on Banking Supervision.

Dirk Tasche is head of modelling in the Corporate Markets Rating Systems department of Lloyds TSB Bank. He oversees the development and maintenance of Basel II compliant internal rating systems for the estimation of PDs, LGDs, and EADs. Before joining Lloyds TSB Bank, Dirk was a senior director in the Quantitative Financial Research department of Fitch Ratings in London. His work there focused on credit portfolio risk modelling and risk scoring models. From 2002 to 2006, Dirk was a risk analyst in the banking and financial supervision division of Deutsche Bundesbank, where he was involved in the European and German legal implementation of the Basel II internal ratings based approach and was charged with research on economic capital models. Before 2002, Dirk worked in the corporate credit risk management of HVB, Munich, and as a researcher in the mathematics departments of Munich University of Technology and the Federal Institute of Technology (ETHZ) in Zürich. He has published a number of papers on measurement of financial risk and capital allocation, including "On the Coherence of Expected Shortfall" (with Carlo Acerbi) and "Thinking positively" (with Katja Pluto). Dirk holds a PhD in mathematics from Berlin University of Technology.

Preston Thompson is an assistant vice president of the Federal Reserve Bank of Boston. Preston is currently the Federal Reserve System's Basel II risk coordinator where he is responsible for overseeing all aspects of Basel II implementation and qualification in the US. Preston works closely with supervisory teams and their respective Reserve Bank management to develop overall strategies to assess each individual bank's progress towards meeting the various requirements of the Basel framework. Preston also coordinates interactions between supervision, policy, and research staff as well as between the Federal Reserve and other US regulators. Finally Preston is responsible for coordinating discussions and interactions between the Federal Reserve and foreign supervisors for home/host related issues. He is involved in a number of ongoing projects that support research, policy, and exam work related to Basel II, economic capital, and risk management. Preston is a regular speaker at conferences and seminars related to operational risk management, capital adequacy, and Basel II. He has authored or contributed to a number of papers on these issues as well. Preston serves on the editorial board of the *Journal of Securities Operations and Custody* and is a member of a number of professional risk management organisations. Prior to his current responsibilities, Preston was involved in efforts to develop an overall approach to supervision at many of the largest banks operating in the US. Preston's efforts were centred on operational risk measurement, management, and quantification. Before joining the Federal Reserve, Preston worked for a large regional bank in a number or positions including retail lending and internal audit. He holds an undergraduate degree from the University of Alabama and a MBA from the Edinburgh Business School at Heriot-Watt University in Edinburgh, Scotland.

Haibin Zhu is a senior economist in the Research and Policy Analysis group of the Monetary and Economic Department of the Bank for International Settlements (BIS). He joined the BIS in 2001 after receiving his PhD in economics at Duke University. His research agenda falls into the areas of credit risk and credit derivatives, bank regulation and financial stability issues, and real estate cycles. His work has been published in the *International Journal of Central Banking*, *Journal of Financial Services Research*, *Journal of Financial Stability* and *Journal of Fixed Income* as well as publications by the BIS. He is also responsible for monitoring the developments of global real estate markets and the financial sector in the Asia-Pacific area.

Preface

Rarely does a book make a more timely appearance. As *Pillar II in the New Basel Accord* goes to print, bankers and regulators are grappling with the most severe and widespread financial crisis since the Great Depression. It is in the midst of this maelstrom that Basel II makes its debut. The crisis has magnified uncertainty over parameter inputs to the formulas of Pillar I, and market volatility and illiquidity can render the market discipline of Pillar III rather less constructive than usual. Under such circumstances, weight shifts to the remaining pillar of the Basel II edifice, that is, to the qualitative aspects of risk management and of regulatory supervision that comprise Pillar II.

There is an ancient Indian parable about four blind men who touch an elephant to learn what it is like. One touches its leg, another its ear, the third its trunk and the fourth its belly. When they are asked to describe the animal they have touched, the four are in complete disagreement.[1] Pillar II is something like an elephant in its complexity and in the weight of its implications. And, like the elephant in the parable, its shape and nature depend on the vantage point of the beholder.

To a quant immersed in models of economic capital, Pillar II might be seen as compensation for the limitations of Pillar I. The formulas of Pillar I emerge from a special case of the class of structural models of portfolio credit risk. In the design and negotiation of Basel II, this model served as a useful organising principle. It imposed order and parsimony on an undertaking of otherwise unmanageable complexity, and also ensured a modicum of internal consistency to the treatment of different instruments. By necessity, however, this model is a highly stylised representation of the multifaceted reality of financial risk, a Mies van der Rohe glass box standing in for a Baroque cathedral. To achieve better alignment with economic capital, Pillar II requires banks and supervisors to assess the impact of factors left out of the model, including single-name and sectoral credit risk concentrations and interest-rate risk in the banking book. More generally, the text of Pillar II prominently and unambiguously calls for banks to assess their own capital adequacy using quantitative methods such as value-at-risk and stress tests.

The quant's boss, the chief risk officer, might view Pillar II as the "principles-based" complement to the "rules-based" framework of Pillar I. The expectations for sound capital assessment cannot be satisfied with equations alone, but demand disciplined internal processes and managerial oversight. Furthermore, Pillar II calls for a comprehensive assessment of risks (eg, liquidity risk) for which quantitative models are not yet satisfactory. In his excellent Introduction, Andrea Resti views Pillar II first and foremost in this light. He invites bank management to embrace Pillar II as an opportunity to make strategic investments in risk-management processes and tools that can deliver value to shareholders, rather than as an exercise in regulatory compliance.

To a corporate finance theorist, the crux of Pillar II is the authority it grants to supervisors to audit more intrusively than could arm's-length market participants and to intervene in a troubled institution before the hard requirements of Pillar I are breached. Loosely speaking, this is the role of Pillar II in the theoretical exploration of the three pillars by Decamps, Rochet and Roger (2004).

Viewed as an international agreement, Pillar II represents a milestone in efforts to harmonise supervisory principles and practice across jurisdiction. Broadly speaking, the goals and methods of supervisory audit were not addressed within the first Basel Accord of 1988. In practice, the resources available to supervisors varied enormously from country to country. In the late 1980s, this heterogeneity was tolerable and perhaps even desirable in adapting Basel rules to markets with very different regulatory environments and organisation. The risk weights of Basel I were simple enough to audit, and the complexities of securitisation and credit derivatives were as yet unimagined. As markets evolved, simplicity had to be sacrificed for risk-sensitivity. The most effective way to achieve risk-sensitivity is to draw on the bank's own internal assessment of risk. Once bank inputs are admitted into the capital rule, credible validation of these inputs by supervisors becomes indispensable to upholding competitive equity across countries. Furthermore, it became increasingly obvious over time that the expanding international span of the largest banks demanded better cross-border cooperation among supervisors. Pillar II fosters the pursuit of common goals by providing a common language for discussing differences in supervisory philosophy and practice.

Finally, for economists who are concerned by the potential effects of Basel II on macro stability, Pillar II is welcomed as a way to offset the potentially procyclical effects of minimal capital requirements. The explicit intent of the

Basel Committee is that large, internationally active banks will choose for their own competitive reasons a level of creditworthiness that exceeds the standard implicit in Pillar I. As embodied in Principle 3 of Pillar II, "supervisors should expect banks to operate above the minimum regulatory capital ratios and should have the ability to require banks to hold capital in excess of the minimum." Borio, Furfine and Lowe (2001) and Estrella (2004), among others, argue that supervisors can and should use these discretionary powers to require banks to hold a buffer of excess capital in good times that can be drawn upon in a downturn.

All these perspectives and more are represented in the chapters of this volume. The coverage here is remarkable not only for its breadth, but also for its depth. Andrea Resti observes that "Pillar II" generates a bounty of hits in a Google search. True, but far too few of these hits lead us to substantive analysis. Remarkably little has been published on Pillar II in the leading academic journals, and even in the practitioner literature a disproportionate share has come from the regulatory agencies. This volume fills a large and glaring gap on the Basel II bookshelf.

In his previous book, *Risk Management and Shareholders' Value in Banking* (with Andrea Sironi), Andrea Resti gave us a comprehensive, coherent and up-to-date treatment of the science and practice of risk management in banking. This new volume is another unique contribution, and should be required reading for both bankers and supervisors involved in the implementation of Basel II.

Michael B. Gordy[2]
Federal Reserve Board
Washington, DC

1 For more on the origins and interpretation of this tale, see http://en.wikipedia.org/wiki/Blind_Men_and_an_Elephant.

2 This Foreword reflects the personal views of its author and does not represent an endorsement by the Board of Governors of the Federal Reserve System.

REFERENCES

Borio, C., C. H. Furfine and P. Lowe, 2001, "Procyclicality of the financial system and financial stability: Issues and policy options", BIS Working Paper No 1.

Decamps, J.-P., J.-C. Rochet and B. Roger, 2004, "The three pillars of Basel II: Optimizing the mix", *Journal of Financial Intermediation* 13(2), pp. 132–55.

Estrella, A., 2004, "The cyclical behavior of optimal bank capital", *Journal of Banking & Finance* 28(6), pp. 1469–98.

Introduction

Andrea Resti

Bocconi University

At the outset of 2008, a Google search for the words "Pillar 2" would produce 88,000 results (plus another 25,000 for "Pillar II", plus all translations into languages other than English). As a matter of comparison, "Caesar Augustus" would get slightly more than 450,000 (including, truth to say, a number of holiday resorts). However, it could be noted that, while the founder of the Roman Empire (born 63 BC) has been around for a couple of thousand years, the words Pillar 2 were introduced by the Basel Committee only in 1999. Should we then use, as a crude (but impartial) impact index, the number of Google results per year, then Pillar 2 (9,800 results per year versus 225) would score definitely better than the inventor of the "Pax Romana" …

How can we explain such a vast and quick popularity? The first, and possibly most important, reason is that Basel's Pillar II represents an intersection between compliance needs and management opportunities. In fact, on one hand Pillar II involves a number of compulsory steps, so that all banks adopting Basel II are required to develop and implement a given set of risk management tools; on the other hand, those very tools, if conceived and used correctly, may significantly increase the quality of corporate strategies in an area – value and risk planning – that is quite vital and compelling to shareholders and supervisors alike. In this sense, as will be better explained below, Pillar II is seen as a unique opportunity to narrow the gap between two different definitions of capital (regulatory and economic capital), mitigating the "managerial squint" of bankers, having to keep under control two different targets at the same time: the capital constraints imposed by regulators, and the risk-taking capacity shareholders are providing to the bank (and that the managers are expected to reward).

Another reason for the popularity of Pillar II hinges on the delay experienced by many banks (including a number of large institutions) in tackling Pillar II issues, investing in know-how, databases, models and procedures. For a long while, the new Basel Accord has been identified mostly with Pillar I, that is, with the set of rules aimed at quantifying a bank's capital requirement through a system of parameters and algebraic functions. Indeed, banks were anxious to produce, within an acceptable timeframe, the quantitative estimates required to "feed" the supervisory formulas (for example, in the case of credit risk: probability of default, loss-given default, exposure at default); and the Basel Committee, too, seemed to give priority to Pillar I parameters when subjecting them to a number of impact studies where financial institutions were not required to produce details on Pillar II risks (say, interest rate risk on the banking book or liquidity risk), nor on the way they intended to aggregate capital figures relative to different risk types. As Pillar I models have started to be established and validated, banks have become increasingly conscious of the strategic relevance of Pillar II, starting projects and investments with alacrity and haste, because they were aware of the considerable backlog they had to cope with.

A third reason is that Pillar II is sometimes seen as a threat that could bring forth corrective actions by supervisors, including an additional capital requirement; such an extra capital cushion might offset any capital saving achieved under Pillar I, thereby disproving the assumption – shared by financial institutions during the last ten years – that banks investing into sophisticated, state-of-the-art rating systems would be "rewarded" by some kind of capital relief.

The fourth and last driver of this revived interest in Pillar II originates from the market events of the last 12 months. Liquidity shortages on financial and interbank markets have shown clearly that banks' uncertainty sources go beyond the "classic" credit, market and operational risks. Namely, the sudden peak in liquidity risk – both in terms of funding risk and market liquidity risk[1] – has made bankers aware of the need to have in place robust risk management systems, encompassing all material loss events and complemented by tools and procedures (for example, contingency funding plans, disclosure channels, internal checks and balances) that go beyond the availability of an adequate amount of shareholders' capital.

For all these reasons, Basel's Pillar II is today seen as a vital and promising area for research, both from an academic and a bank management point of view. This has led me – together with the other authors and Bocconi University's Centre for Applied Research in Finance (CAREFIN) – to promote and produce the contributions published in this book.

In this Introduction, we first quickly review the origins and the basic principles of Pillar II; we then look at the objectives of Pillar II and at the instruments used to achieve them; we therefore try to figure out how Pillar II will change bank management (and, indeed, already has started to change it); finally, we introduce the structure of this book and preview the content of the various parts and chapters in it

PILLAR II: HOW IT ALL BEGAN

The presence in Basel II of a second pillar, based on supervisory review, was first announced in a preliminary document entitled "A New Capital Adequacy Framework", released in June 1999 (Basel Committee on Banking Supervision 1999).

That was the very first draft of the future Basel II Accord, and was going to undergo many deep changes in the following five years. Nevertheless, as far as Pillar II is concerned, the guidelines and principles stated in the 1999 paper were already quite similar to those approved in 2004, when the final agreement was reached on the new Accord. Namely, the 1999 document had already introduced four complementary principles: first, the possibility that supervisors require banks to operate with an amount of capital greater than the minimum level stated in Pillar I; second, the request that banks have in place an internal process to assess their capital adequacy relative to the risks faced, and to preserve such adequacy through time; third, the provision that such an internal process be formally verified by supervisors; fourth, the faculty, for supervisors, to act promptly, before a bank's capital becomes inadequate.

None of those four key elements has been removed (or even significantly amended) in the final Accord. The subsequent drafts, as well as the European directives implementing the Accord's provisions, have only stated in greater detail how those four principles must be enacted in practice (mostly focusing on the actual contents of the internal capital adequacy assessment process)[2]. Throughout the five years between 1999 and 2004, the scope of Pillar II has never been reduced; instead, it was increased, for example, to accommodate for risks that were originally intended to be part of Pillar I (such as name-concentration risk). This suggests that, while other portions of the Accord were lively debated and required fine-tuning and compromise, a high degree of consensus existed, among supervisors (and supervised entities), on the objectives and instruments of supervisory review. Those objectives and instruments are briefly reviewed below.

OBJECTIVES AND INSTRUMENTS OF PILLAR II

We know that capital represents a "cushion" aimed at absorbing losses and protecting a bank's creditors. A larger amount of capital makes it possible to take on larger risks for the bank, without increasing risk for its counterparties. Such an increase in the bank's risk-taking capacity must obviously be accompanied by a rise in its profits, in order for the shareholders' investment to be adequately rewarded.

The concept of capital therefore plays a key role for both supervisors and banks (namely, for bank managers and shareholders). For all these parties it is crucial to know with adequate confidence the amount of capital that is actually available, as well as the optimal capital that is required to meet the risks implied by the bank's investments (capital-at-risk).

In the past, such an optimal capital was quantified by the supervisors through a set of simplified rules; namely, since 1988, capital-at-risk was computed as a simple percentage of the various asset classes in the bank's balance sheet: 4% of mortgage loans, 8% of loans to private customers and non-financial companies, 1.6% of the exposures to Organization for Economic Co-operation and Development (OECD) banks, etc. This simple scheme was increasingly at odds with the sophisticated models used by banks for internal purposes. In 2004, to reduce the gap between the amount of capital imposed by supervisory rules (regulatory capital) and that suggested by internal risk-management models (economic capital), Basel II promoted a set of more realistic and flexible criteria.

This reform notwithstanding, there are still differences between the capital indicated by the computation rules in Basel's Pillar I and that estimated by financial institutions; accordingly, the Basel II accord introduced a "Pillar II", where the regulatory capital charge must be integrated and amended to become more similar to the bank's "true" economic capital.

This goal is effectively stated in Article 123 of the EU Directive 2006/48 (European Union 2006), which affirms that credit institutions must have in place sound, effective and complete strategies and processes to assess and maintain on an ongoing basis the amounts, types and distribution of internal capital that they consider adequate to cover the nature and level of the risks to which they are or might be exposed. Through this requirement the quantification of economic capital, an eminently managerial task, also becomes a regulatory obligation. In Article 123, regulators acknowledge that Pillar I rules may not be enough to quantify comprehensively all actual outstanding risks, and require banks to provide an independent estimate of capital-at-risk based on their internal models (which are expected to be more sophisticated than the computation rules imposed by the regulation).

Figure 1 summarises the relationship between Pillars I and II within the new Basel Accord.

- Under Pillar I, the banks' risk management systems are used to quantify some risk types (mainly credit, market and operational risk) through the estimation of a set of (more or less sophisticated) risk parameters; these could, for example, be ratings, loss-given default rates, the net position in debt securities across maturity bands, the gross income earned by different businesses. Such risk parameters are subsequently transformed into a capital charge through a number of standard devices (risk weights, coefficient schemes or mathematical functions). Compared with the capital charge originated from 1988 rules (Basel I), the result can be greater or smaller; in the latter case, the bank enjoys some "capital relief", leverage increases and return on equity improves, for any given return on assets.
- Under Pillar II, national supervisors are entitled to complement Pillar I capital ("regulatory capital" in a narrow sense) with an additional capital requirement. Such an extra requirement is due mainly to risks that were not included in Pillar I, risks quantified under Pillar I in a

Figure 1 The relationship between Pillars I and II

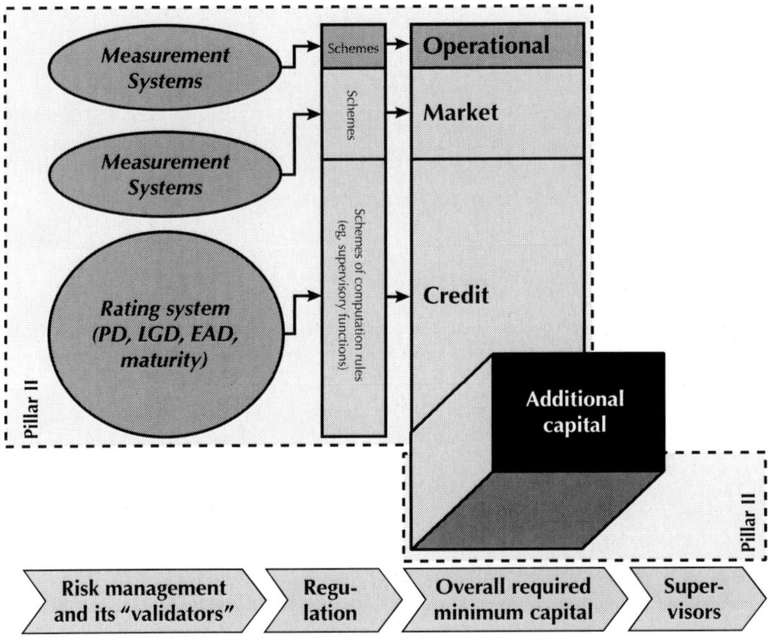

simplistic way, inadequacies in the bank's ability to manage risks and capital in an active and timely way. Note that supervisors play an indirect role, as they act only once the bank has already carried out its own risk management and capital adequacy analyses.

The internal evaluation process carried out by the bank is called ICAAP (internal capital-adequacy assessment process, see Figure 2) and its structure, as we just mentioned, must independently be decided by each bank. Regulators do not impose any specific methodology, although of course they have a say in the *ex post* validation of the procedures put in place by the bank:[3] such an *ex post* evaluation is known as SREP (supervisory review and evaluation process).

If the supervisors' evaluation leads to a negative assessment, then supervisors may take corrective steps and request the bank to improve its risk management systems, to refrain from putting in place businesses or deals for which it is deemed ill-equipped, to hold an additional capital cushion above the Pillar I charge and so on. Note that a request for additional capital may seriously affect the shareholders' return on equity; this explains why, as mentioned in the first part of this introduction, bank managers are now striving to implement adequate ICAAPs.

The ICAAP (and the SREP, insofar it is aimed at checking and validating the ICAAP) should perform the following main tasks (see Figure 3):

Figure 2 The link between ICAAP and SREP

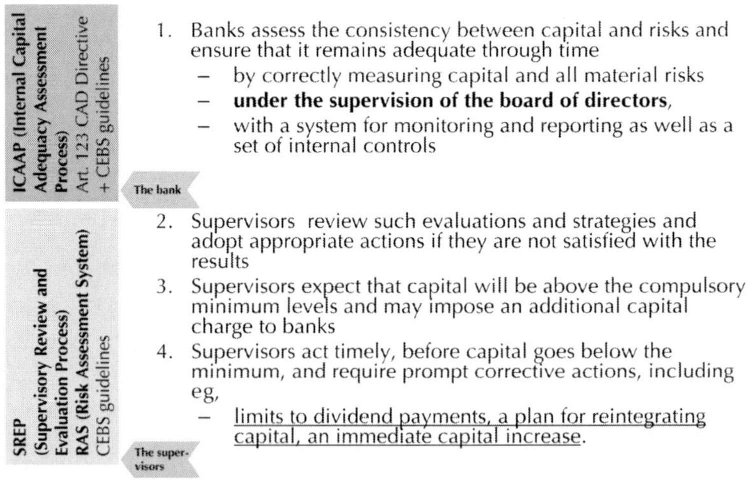

- verify that the risk management systems developed under Pillar I are consistent with the requirements dictated by that part of the Basel Accord (eg, in terms of minimum length of the time series used for parameter calibration, the minimum number of rating buckets and so forth);
- measure those risks that are already covered in Pillar I, but that Pillar I quantifies in an imprecise and oversimplified manner (eg, concentration risk on credit exposures);
- assess risk factors not included in Pillar I (eg, interest rate risk on the banking book, reputational risk or strategic risk); and
- evaluate the influence of factors that, while being outside the bank's control, might significantly affect its capital adequacy (eg, technological changes, the economic cycle).

To address these objectives, a sound ICAAP should include four phases.

1. The risks to be assessed should be listed, and such a list should include, at least, credit risk, market risk and operational risk (as far as they are not satisfactorily covered under Pillar I), concentration risk, interest rate risk on the banking book, liquidity risk, any residual risk due to imperfect risk mitigation techniques, risks arising for securitisations, strategic risk and reputation risk.
2. Individual risks should be measured, also through stress-testing exercises.

Figure 3 The four main areas covered by the ICAAP

1. A **compliance check** of the requisites set out in Pillar I
   - e.g. the depth of the time series used, the number of rating buckets, etc.
2. A more accurate estimate of risks mapped under Pillar I, but **in an over-simplified way**
   - eg, concentration risk
3. **Risks not mapped** under Pillar I
   - especially interest rate risk on the "banking book"
4. Impact of **factors outside the bank's control**
   - eg, technological progress, economic cycle

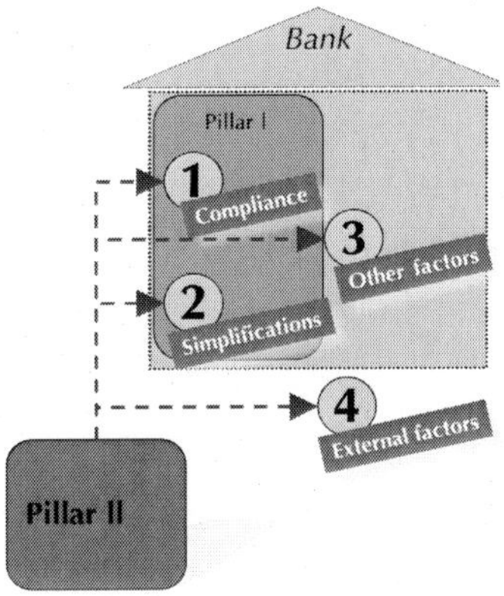

3. Individual risks should be aggregated into a measure of overall economic capital, accounting for any diversification effect across risks.
4. Overall economic capital should be compared with regulatory capital, and any differences should be reconciled and/or explained.

In the design of an appropriate ICAAP (and in its assessment through the SREP) a key role is played by the concept of proportionality: in short, proportionality requires that the risk measurement solutions implemented by a financial institution be proportionate to its size and to the complexity of its business. This suggests that the most sophisticated and complex options may not always be the best ones in the eyes of the supervisors; the need for transparency and accountability may make a simple risk management system preferable to a "black box" developed by a few risk management rocket scientists but inadequately understood by the bank's top managers.

HOW PILLAR II WILL CHANGE BANKS (AND HAS CHANGED THEM)

The new framework summarised above has several significant implications for bank risk management, as well as for bank management as a whole.

1. First, we mentioned that the ICAAP provides banks with an important opportunity to narrow the gap between regulatory and economic capital (a gap that was only partially filled by the shift from Basel I to Basel II). We saw that Article 123 of the EU Directive requires banks to assess the capital that they consider adequate to cover risks: regulation is therefore asking banks to carry out a practice that should already be in place, out of a duty towards the shareholders. This suggests that Pillar II will not become just another piece of paperwork to be filed with regulators but will, instead, provide (a) the basis for a structured dialogue between the top managers, the bank's owners and the other investors, and (b) the benchmark against which expectations will be formed and verified.
2. This leads us to our second remark: the ICAAP is not just a technical, methodological issue to be addressed mostly by the risk management and planning department. Instead, the main "owner" of such a process should be the bank's top management. This is true for at least two reasons: first, an inadequate assessment of risks and a faulty capital planning, leading to an unfavourable outcome of the SREP, might bring about supervisory actions that limit the bank's ability to do business and dilute its shareholders' profitability; second, the tools

developed for the ICAAP build the backbone of a modern value-based performance measurement system.

3. The innovation triggered by Pillar II, in terms of information quality and managerial decisions' quality, is bound to go beyond the scope originally envisaged by the supervisors, prompting new processes and tools that are not strictly part of the tasks imposed by Basel regulation. Think, for example, of capital allocation policies, that is, of all tools and models required to allocate the bank's overall capital to different business lines and operating units. Capital allocation is not part of the compulsory steps required under Pillar II; nevertheless, it is needed to make the economic capital estimates derived under Pillar II both more useful and more reliable. Through capital allocation, economic capital estimates become more useful because, when the bank's total capital is distributed across all risk-taking businesses and units, it is easier to check whether each of them adequately rewards shareholders' capital (closing down or restructuring units that do not contribute to the bank's overall performance); economic capital will also become more reliable because the managers of those business units for which it suggests an unsatisfactory performance will try to spot all fallacies and inconsistencies in the process through which it has been estimated, thereby contributing to make it sounder and more realistic.

While these three characteristics of Pillar II are somewhat unprecedented, it is important to emphasise that Pillar II will not mark a clean break as compared with previous banks' practices. Rather, by asking banks to compute and plan the amount of capital needed to cover all their risks, Pillar II will turn the banks' best practices into a regulatory requirement. In fact, most large international financial institutions already have in place some systems and algorithms to compute economic capital, and use them as a tool to manage their internal processes, as well as to improve communication with external stakeholders (including shareholders, rating agencies, supervisors).[4]

This clearly emerges by the survey of 17 large universal banks (in Europe, the US and Asia) carried out in 2006 by the Institute of the Chief Risk Officers, together with the Chief Risk Officer Forum (Institute of the Chief Risk Officers – Chief Risk Officer Forum 2007). The survey results can be compared with those gathered in 2000 by a similar study by Mercer Oliver

Wyman, to see how large banks have changed their attitude towards economic capital.

The share of respondents who think they own a "mature" system for the estimation of economic capital has remarkably increased (41% versus 21%); the same happens for banks responding that they have an internal system that is "comprehensive" and used in association with some process to report information to outsiders (35% versus 21%). On the other hand, the share of banks that have not developed any system or prototype for economic capital estimation has now fallen to zero (it used to be 14% in 2000).

Survey participants also state that their economic capital estimation systems are such that they will be used as a key tool to comply with Pillar II requirements; in fact, half of the respondents indicate they will not have to make significant changes to those systems in order to make them "Basel-compliant".

THIS BOOK

This book aims to provide a better understanding of the key issues in Pillar II through contributions from a number of prominent scholars, regulators, bank managers and rating specialists; this ensures that the perspective is kept as broad as possible, and encompasses different views and professional profiles. While some contributions are rather advanced, a number of more introductory chapters are also provided on topics – such as liquidity risk or credit risk correlations – where banks are still implementing (or deeply restructuring) their measurement and management systems, also due to the 2007–08 turmoil.

The book is structured into three parts: Part 1 provides a complete and updated picture of the regulatory framework in which Pillar II processes and models have to be implemented; Part 2 discusses a number of individual risk types that have to be addressed under Pillar II (concentration risk, business risk, liquidity risk and interest rate risk on the banking book); Part 3 deals with risk integration and capital management. Details on the structure and contents of the three parts are provided below.

Part 1

While the reasons to develop a system for measuring and monitoring economic capital go beyond mere regulatory compliance, a bank facing the considerable investments required by this type of tools and procedures clearly wants to make sure that they satisfy all requirements and expectations set out by supervisors. For this reason, Part 1 of our book presents the regulatory perspective.

Chapter 1, by Martina Bignami and Andrea Pilati, summarises and discusses the Pillar II rules introduced by the Basel Accord and the European Directives, highlighting the real innovations brought forth by the new regulatory framework. The authors argue that, while Pillar II actually involves a number of dramatic novelties (as it extends the range of risks to be considered when evaluating a bank's capital adequacy and links this analysis to the evaluation of the bank's internal control systems), the ICAAP and SREP processes in themselves are not really innovative, but rather give a more formal structure to supervisory practices that are far from unprecedented. According to Bignami and Pilati, what is really new is not the content of ICAAP and SREP, but rather the idea that banks and supervisors must engage in a constant and structured dialogue on risks, capital and internal controls. The chapter also mentions a number of open issues that will require further work in the coming years: among them, the debate surrounding the so-called "Available Financial Resources" (AFR), that is, the reconciliation of capital items eligible to satisfy Pillar I requirements from a strictly supervisory perspective with those (facing both Pillar I and Pillar II risks) that banks deem adequate to cover their internal economic capital estimates.

The AFR is not the only issue that will need further discussions if Pillar II rules are to be implemented effectively. Indeed, since those rules have been written – both in the Basel Accord and in the EU Directives – in a very high-level style, their practical application is going to raise a number of complex choices. Also, to avoid that the wide margins of flexibility left to national supervisors in defining the contents and timing of ICAAP and SREP become a source of arbitrariness and give rise to unjustified differences across different countries, patient and careful work will be required of supervisory forums to ensure that their enactment in different jurisdictions is grounded on a common set of principles and practices. Accordingly, Chapters 2 and 3 are dedicated to the foreseeable implementation of Pillar II rules, in the US and the EU respectively.

In the US, Pillar II requirements will be an extension of longstanding supervisory expectations for banks to look beyond minimum regulatory capital requirements established using existing risk-based capital guidelines. Hence Chapter 2, by Preston Thompson and David Palmer, starts by discussing the rules governing supervisory review practices before Basel II (including the Federal Reserve's Supervision and Regulation Letter 99–18).

Moving then to the new elements laid down by Basel's Pillar II, the authors emphasise that, while the estimation of economic capital is likely to be a key input for the ICAAP process, the latter goes beyond the mere measurement of capital-at-risk, and involves a much more holistic view of capital adequacy (determining the overall level of capital and ensuring that capital is adequate at all times), as well as a capital planning process and an oversight/governance element. Based on this framework, the chapter discusses the expectations of US supervisors regarding the various elements that constitute a bank's ICAAP.

In the EU, the uniform cross-country implementation of Pillar II has been one of the supervisors' main concerns, not just to avoid improper competitive advantages among intermediaries based in different jurisdictions, but also to ensure that the supervision of large multinational banking groups remains feasible, consistent and effective. The Committee of European Banking Supervisors (CEBS) has played a key role in this effort towards a uniform application of Pillar II principles, producing consultative documents, surveying practices and promoting instruments (eg, colleges of supervisors and joint examinations) through which common criteria can be agreed and controversies among national supervisors can be solved when necessary. In Chapter 3, Andrea Enria, Cécile Meys and Oleg Shmeljov, of the CEBS Secretariat, review the CEBS guidelines on Pillar II (including those on home–host cooperation) and the way they have been transposed into national regulations. The chapter also explores a range of practices that have been agreed among supervisors to ensure a smooth and fair implementation of the SREP (eg, regarding information flows and the division of responsibilities) and a consistent, balanced structure of the banks' ICAAPs (eg in terms of scope and timing) across countries.

Part 2

The second part of the book addresses several risk types that either have not been dealt with under Pillar I (business risk, liquidity risk and interest rate risk on the banking book) or have been covered there in an oversimplified way (credit concentration risk), and therefore have to be addressed again in a bank's ICAAP.

Three chapters of Part 2 deal with credit concentration risk; in fact, credit plays a key role in the business mix of most banking institutions, so that a proper understanding of the diversification benefits enjoyed by their credit portfolios is likely to prove crucial in assessing their overall capital adequacy.

Chapter 4, by Andrea Resti, provides a complete framework – based on the works by Gordy, Pykhtin, Martin and Wilde and others – to bridge the gap between Pillar I capital against credit risk and the true amount of economic capital that a bank needs when the actual characteristics of its loan portfolio (in terms of correlation, name concentration, industry concentration, etc.) are measured and accounted for. In fact, while it is comparatively easy for a bank to set up a value-at-risk (VaR) model on its credit portfolio and to estimate the losses associated with some worst-case scenario (in order to decide how much capital has to be held), a much more difficult step is to reconcile this economic capital with the regulatory capital dictated by Pillar I. Chapter 4, using a step-by-step example, shows how the gap between those two measures of capital can be quantified and explained; the last part of the chapter also shows how this methodology can be used to spot "regulatory arbitrages" based on name and industry correlation, that would otherwise go unnoticed if banks and supervisors were to rely exclusively on Pillar I capital requirements.

Chapter 5, by Nikola Tarashev and Haibin Zhu, also provides an analysis of the possible gaps between the capital requirement set out in Pillar I and the actual economic capital of a credit portfolio. While the key assumptions of the regulatory model (such as infinite granularity) are not found to create a substantial difference between the two measures (at least for large, well-diversified portfolios), serious biases can arise from an inaccurate calibration of the correlation estimates used to capture diversification effects (especially when those are based on small samples and therefore are affected by random noise) or from non-normal tails in the distribution of asset value returns.

As indicated by Tarashev and Zhu, the estimation of correlations is a very sensitive step in the implementation of a model for concentration risk. Accordingly, a whole chapter of this book (Chapter 6, by Ahmet Kocagil and Jing Liu) is specifically dedicated to the empirical assessment of asset correlations. In the first part of the chapter, the main approaches to correlation estimation are reviewed, including methodologies based on stock market prices, default time series and rating up/downgrades. In the second part, some of these methodologies are used in a practical exercise, to derive asset correlations from a wide sample of real-life data. A comparison of the estimates obtained through different approaches reveals that all default correlation-based methods produce similar results, which are broadly in line with the parameters devised by Basel Committee (for inter-industry correlations) or somewhat lower (in the case of the intra-industry estimates.

Chapter 7, by Klaus Böcker, presents a thorough treatment of business risk, that is, of the risk linked to the uncertainty of specific earnings components that are not associated with traditional risk types such as market or credit risk. Business risk is usually measured in terms of earnings-at-risk (EaR), that is, the drop in yearly earnings associated with an especially adverse scenario; however, if they are to be fully understood in their implications for bank capital, EaR must be converted into a measure of VaR that is conceptually homogeneous with (and therefore can safely be aggregated with) the economic capital measures used for risk types. The shift from EaR to VaR is far from being trivial and represents the main focus of Böcker's contribution. By introducing a number of different assumptions on the shape of the stochastic process followed by corporate earnings, the chapter shows how the EaR–VaR link can be modelled in practice.

Liquidity risk has been one of the key elements in the market crisis of 2007–08: the fragility shown by markets and intermediaries when confronted with this type of risk suggests that it is still poorly understood and managed by many financial institutions. Accordingly, this book includes two chapters on this topic: an advanced and rigorous framework for liquidity risk measurement, as well as a more introductory presentation, where many well-known (and often forgotten) facts on liquidity risk are discussed.

The introductory chapter (Chapter 8), written by Mario Anolli and Andrea Resti, presents liquidity risk in both its meanings, that is, funding risk and market liquidity risk. The former is the risk that a financial institution may not be able to face expected and unexpected cash outflows without jeopardising its orderly operations; the latter is the risk that the quick liquidation of a large amount of assets ends up affecting the price in a considerable (and unfavourable) manner, because of the limited depth (or momentary disruption) of the market where those assets are traded. As shown in the chapter, funding risk is usually measured through liquidity gaps and ratios, and managed through contingency funding plans that ensure that the bank has access to enough funds in the event of a liquidity shortage; although simple in principle, the management of funding risk is made complex by the presence of assets and liabilities with a *de facto* maturity that is different from their contractual duration; such items (non-maturing assets and liabilities) are carefully discussed in the chapter. Market liquidity risk requires that market risk VaR be adjusted to account for adverse price reactions and/or that the market VaR time horizon be extended, to allow for a gradual liquidation of the tradable portfolio; several formulas for this adjustment are proposed in the chapter.

Overall, Chapter 8 shows that liquidity risk management still is, to a large extent, a qualitative discipline with limited quantitative tools to support the intuitions and beliefs of bank managers. Chapter 9, by Carlo Acerbi, tries to fill this gap by proposing a rigorous mathematical framework which – relaxing the infinite-liquidity assumption on which standard portfolio models are based – reconsiders the most basic concepts of risk and investments (such as "asset", "portfolio", "price") and extends their notation to the case where markets are not perfectly liquid. The author's opinion, widely discussed in the chapter and effectively supported by several introductory examples, is that, once such a richer, more general framework has been introduced, there is no need at all to use specific liquidity risk measures, as liquidity risk will automatically be captured by traditional risk (and return) measures. A key role in this more general framework is played by the concept of "liquidity policy": this captures the personal attitude towards liquidity of the investor holding a given asset or portfolio, and makes it possible two explain why two similar assets may bring forth substantially different levels of liquidity risk (and hence should be assigned different values) when held by different financial institutions.

Chapter 10 (by Andrea Resti and Andrea Sironi) closes Part 2 by providing a basic framework for the measurement of interest rate risk that is consistent with the provisions of Pillar II. To that end, the chapter first describes how interest rate risk on the banking book is regulated in the new Basel Accord and in other Basel Committee documents; it then presents the main approaches used to measure interest rate risk in banks, distinguishing between methods that rely on the EaR paradigm and the VaR perspective, and showing how they can be used to quantify the effect, on the bank's value, of a 2% shift in market rates (as required by Pillar II). The chapter also extensively discusses the treatment of non-maturing assets and liabilities, that is, of balance-sheet items that, while being formally on demand, react to market rate changes only partially and with delay, and provides a general framework for dealing with the indirect effects of interest rate risk on the banking book.

Part 3

The third part deals with more advanced topics, ranging from risk aggregation to capital management. The idea is to provide the reader with a string of selected issues that are likely to play a major role in Pillar II implementation and day-to-day management.

Risk aggregation is the most complex step in the estimation of economic capital, and is likely to become the area in which the dialogue between banks and supervisors proves most lively. On the one hand, as far as risk aggregation methods are concerned, the state of the art is still patchy, as banks and scholars have only a limited knowledge of the mechanisms and parameters needed to merge capital requirements on individual risks into one overall capital estimate (where diversification benefits across risks are properly recognised). On the other hand, the benefits (in terms of capital relief) expected by banks from the risk aggregation step are vast, compared with the regulatory approach where capitals are simply summed across individual risks and no diversification among risks is acknowledged.

Risk aggregation is covered in four different chapters of this book. First Chapter 11, Francesco Saita introduces a number of basic principles for risk aggregation. The chapter starts by asking what risk measures should be aggregated and what risk types should be included in a bank's overall economic capital. It then discusses how different VaR measures should be harmonised before they can be aggregated. In fact, VaRs computed for different risks (eg, market, credit, operational) often incorporate different assumptions as far as the confidence level and the time horizon are concerned, so they have to be made homogeneous before starting the actual aggregation exercise. The next part of the chapter deals with the main techniques used by banks when aggregating capitals-at-risk and covers in detail three of them: the variance–covariance approach, copulas and the multi-factor simulation approach. Finally, a brief survey is provided of how aggregated capital is disclosed in the financial statements of some large international banking groups.

Chapter 12, by Klaus Böcker, presents in detail several key issues in risk aggregation. The chapter starts by discussing some fallacies of linear correlation that may call for the use of alternative dependence measures, such as tail dependence or copulas; the last part shows how copulas can be used to aggregate credit risk and market risk in a way that is both well grounded and tractable. The chapter also investigates how the estimation of inter-risk correlations can be supported by expert judgements, and provides a comprehensive numerical example of a typical aggregation problem as it may occur in a bank.

Chapter 13 further discusses risk aggregation by introducing a state-of-the-art case study based on the methodology recently developed by Fortis, a large European banking and insurance conglomerate. Ruben Olieslagers and Patrick Acx, both with Fortis, first describe a multi-year project for economic capital estimation recently developed by the Group, then provide an empirical test for the various approaches introduced by Saita and Böcker in the previous two chapters. Olieslagers and Acx compare the risk aggregation technique used by Fortis with a number of more complex alternatives, based on comonotonicity, copulas and Monte Carlo simulations. Their results also show how the ranking among different measures of economic capital is affected by assumptions regarding correlations among risk types.

The last chapter in the block dedicated to risk aggregation is Chapter 14, by Thomas Breuer, Martin Jandačka, Klaus Rheinberger and Martin Summer. The authors challenge the conventional wisdom on risk aggregation, according to which aggregated risk capital can never exceed the sum of the capitals associated with individual risks. In fact, they show that, for portfolios that are jointly affected both by market and credit risk, a "compounding effect" may be present, that is, an interaction between different risk types that drives total economic capital above the sum of single-risk capitals. As an example, they discuss the case of foreign-currency-denominated loans and provide a numerical example based on a G-VaR framework. Remarkably, their key result holds not just for VaR, but also for expected shortfall (that is, for a strictly subadditive risk measure).

Stress testing is going to play a key role in Pillar II, as it will be extensively used by banks to verify that capital remains adequate over time, notwithstanding an adverse macroeconomic scenario. However, stress testing poses a series of challenges not only from a methodological standpoint, but also from a conceptual one. In a sense, all VaR measures represent a stress test, since they estimate the unexpected losses associated with an especially unfavourable state of the world; before further models are developed and implemented, it is therefore necessary to understand how stress tests are related to percentile-based risk measures. This is one of the issues discussed by Brian Dvorak in Chapter 15, where stress testing is discussed in the context of credit risk; the chapter also includes some "practical recommendations", such as the need to use stress-scenario analysis as a tool for communication within the bank and externally (eg, with regulators).

While Pillar II is going to make a bank's capital more realistic and bring it more closely into line with internal economic capital estimates, this greater flexibility will make it harder to compare capital figures across different banks and different countries. In this sense, Pillar II will somehow blur the picture of risks and capital that banks are going to disclose to the market under Pillar III. This possible decrease in the readability of capital figures clearly represents a danger for investors and market analysts; unsurprisingly, large rating agencies have already developed methodologies to restore comparability across different capital estimates. Chapter 16, by Bernard De Longevialle, Thierry Grunspan and Élie Hériard-Dubreuil, presents in detail the risk-adjusted capital framework developed by Standard & Poor's; while the scope of this methodology is quite wide, a section in the chapter is specifically dedicated to Pillar II risks, including adjustments for industry diversification, name granularity, interest rate risk on the banking book and more.

Chapter 17, by Dirk Tasche, focuses on capital allocation. As noted above, capital allocation is not strictly called for by Pillar II. In other words banks, after having aggregated individual risks into one overall capital estimate, are not required to split it back across business units or subportfolios. Nevertheless, as argued above in this Introduction, by allocating capital to individual units a better insight can be gained of how risks are originated and rewarded inside the bank; this makes capital allocation a very attractive area for research and for advanced implementations. Tasche's contribution focuses on a sound and rigorous criterion to apportion risk capital within the bank, based on Euler's theorem for linearly homogeneous functions; such an approach can prove useful in many risk allocation problems, including issues (such as the decomposition of risks across CDO tranches) that go beyond the scope of Pillar II.

Finally, Pillar II is not just about risk measurement, but also requires that banks have in place sound capital management policies; hybrid capital instruments are going to represent a key tool in this effort to plan and maintain capital adequacy. Indeed, while such securities – which combine features of both equity and debt – have experienced a strong growth over the last 15 years, regulators in the main advanced financial systems still have not ensured a uniform and unambiguous framework for their recognition as bank capital. In Chapter 18, Laetitia Mouquot first draws an updated picture (based on a recent CEBS survey) of the amounts of hybrid capital used by banks in the main European countries; then presents the characteristics of the various types of hybrid capital (highlighting differences and commonalities) and discusses how such characteristics could be used to improve the consistency and effectiveness of the European regulatory framework (which today relies on separate national regulations inspired by a set of common principles).

This concludes our "guided tour" of the various parts and chapters; this Introduction should have highlighted the importance of Pillar II and explained the way this book aims to contribute to a lively and complex debate. The last, pleasant task for me before I leave the reader to the pages that follow is to thank a few people who have significantly contributed to this book. Clare Beesley, Steve Fairman and Jennifer Gibb at Risk Books, for supporting this project and helping me to make it real with their vision and professionalism; my colleagues at Bocconi's Centre for Applied Research in Finance (CAREFIN) for the many useful discussions on Pillar II issues that we had during the last months; my wife Luciana for the time this book stole from our happy life together and my 10-month-old son Davide for screaming just a bit more softly when Daddy needed to concentrate. Finally, and above all, I thank the authors who participated in this book, for providing me with a state-of-the-art collection of rigorous and enjoyable pieces of research and for giving me the opportunity to work closely with an outstanding group of passionate risk management experts.

1 See Chapter 8 for further details.
2 See Chapter 2 for a detailed discussion of the provisions in the final Accord and in the EU Directives.
3 "Institutions should 'own', develop and manage their risk management processes – the ICAAP belongs to the institution and supervisors should not dictate how it is applied" (Committee of European Banking Supervisors 2005, p. 2).
4 The way economic capital is disclosed in the financial statement of some large financial institutions is briefly discussed in Chapter 11 of this book.

REFERENCES

Basel Committee on Banking Supervision, 1999, "A new capital adequacy framework", Bank for International Settlements.

Committee of European Banking Supervisors, 2005, "Application of the Supervisory Review Process under Pillar II – CP03 revised", consultation paper, Committee of European Banking Supervisors.

European Union, 2006, "Directive 2006/48/EC of the European Parliament and of the Council of 14 June 2006 relating to the taking up and pursuit of the business of credit institutions (recast)", *Official Journal of the European Union* L 177, pp. 1–200.

Institute of the Chief Risk Officers – Chief Risk Officer Forum, 2007, "Insights from the joint IFRI/CRO Forum survey on Economic Capital practice and applications" IFRI Foundation, Geneva.

Foreword

Professor Dr Frank De Jonghe

Deloitte Partner and EMEA Quant Initiative Leader

This book is dedicated to Pillar II in the new Basel Accord and to the internal capital adequacy assessment process (ICAAP) that banks have to put in place according to this new piece of regulation. This foreword benefits from several exchanges of views with partners in the European member firms of Deloitte, where I serve as a partner, and contributions from Joerg Engels (Germany), Martin Flaunet (Luxembourg), Paolo Gianturco (Italy) and Sandro Schmid (Switzerland) are gratefully acknowledged.

The ICAAP is more than just another regulatory compliance challenge. First, it includes several areas (eg, business risk, risk aggregation) for which no market standard has yet emerged, and therefore is less prescriptive than other risk regulations. Second, it touches the core of being a financial institution, by providing an answer to the question "How much capital does it need to protect all its debtors while at the same time achieving an adequate return on equity for the shareholders?"

In this context, any Pillar II implementation project should pay particular attention to the following points.

- While the risk quantification is an important aspect, it is not the only one. Risk management processes and the treatment of risks that are hard to measure deserve particular attention.
- The ICAAP is evolutionary by nature. The institution's business mix, the business environment and the market's best practices change continuously, and so does the scope of risks that can be accurately measured.
- The risk assessment derives its relevance from the fact that it is actually used in management's decision process on a regular basis.
- Contrary to many controlling processes, the ICAAP is by its very nature forward looking.
- To avoid the impression that absence of evidence is interpreted as evidence of absence, it is important that the entire ICAAP be well documented.

Obviously, these points are not independent of each other, as we will highlight below.

Let us first zoom in on the inherent limitations of the quantitative approach to measuring risks and how they can be accommodated in the ICAAP process. Not only are there several risk categories for which we have not yet developed a tried and tested benchmark model (eg, business risk, liquidity risk – and even operational risk), there is also the mathematical challenge of integrating them all at the company level. In order to make progress in the quantification of some of the more evolved risk categories, we have to think of the capital needed not only in order to absorb realised losses, but also to cover the incremental costs that the entity can incur to avoid the risk. For instance, a business risk consisting of a significant decrease in client volumes could be avoided by spending more on marketing to strengthen the market recognition of the company. Another example is liquidity risk: while it cannot be avoided at any incremental cost under certain circumstances, the illiquidity of the markets recently provides some idea of the increased cost of funding, if available.

On the mathematical modelling side, diversification is at present a key point of attention. The Committee of European Banking Supervisors (CEBS) made it clear that institutions cannot profit from reduced capital requirements due to risk diversification unless they can convincingly argue that the diversification effect is genuine. Obviously, the stakes are high for the institutions in this domain. However, even if we were to agree on a mathematically correct and economically sensible approach such as those presented in Part 3 of this book (for example, copulas), one would still be confronted with the daunting task of feeding these models with meaningful inputs.

Clearly, being unable to measure accurately a specific risk does not exempt institutions from implementing sound risk management practices, such as defining a risk appetite, assigning risk management responsibilities, taking risk-mitigating actions, and so on. Similarly, a first argument on diversification benefits should consist of a qualitative understanding of why one business activity or risk provides an offset for another.

Regardless of these obstacles, in order to get a rough idea of the potential losses and hence capital requirements linked to risks that are hardly measurable with (statistical) models, we can always turn to scenario analysis. Scenario analyses and stress tests that assess the impact of highly improbable yet very adverse events and that are performed with the active collaboration of senior management have proven to be an effective instrument in helping organisations better understand their risk exposures. As part of this analysis the likelihood and severity of extreme events need to be assessed, ie, the distribution assumptions regarding the tails should be determined and stressed.

Obviously, the outcome of the ICAAP is the answer to the question of whether the organisation has enough capital to support its business. However, the process by which the company arrives at that number is as important, if not more so. By involving people at different layers, including board members and members of the senior management and of all entities of the organisation, head office and subsidiaries, we increase the risk awareness of the entire organisation, and protect against dogmatic thinking by letting employees in the field contribute to risk identification and assessment.

The ICAAP is not a one-off process. Its evolutionary nature is driven by changing practices in risk-measurement techniques observed in the industry. For instance, whereas in 2007 many banks defended the view that liquidity risk did not require any capital, this consensus could change over the next few years given that the renewed focus on liquidity risk will most probably lead to improved methods for quantifying such risks.

The periodic updates in the ICAAP also relate to changes in existing risks (identification through risk mapping) and their potential impact. Indeed, the organisation's business mix and business environment are constantly evolving. New products launched with small volumes in one year, and therefore probably considered immaterial in the global context of ICAAP, can grow into significant risks a few years later. We need look no further than the recent problems with structured credit that underscore the need to follow up closely any new product. It also shows that changing market expectations on solvency levels can seriously impact a bank's capital planning. Currently, investors demand a much higher excess of capital relative to the regulatory requirements than they did a year ago.

As the events of the last few years have shown, even when the sky is blue and sailing is easy, we constantly need to identify and analyse the smallest cloud that appears on the horizon. Only by constantly challenging the status quo in the light of newly available information does a company become a risk-intelligent organisation. Being a risk-intelligent organisation can be the factor that makes the difference between a financial institution merely incurring damage, and having its continued existence called into question. Risk and return are constantly to be balanced in the management of the institution. Decisions at all levels should take into account the risks involved, across all risk categories. Moreover, the ICAAP analysis that is prepared for the regulator should not consist of analyses made for that purpose, but should be building on risk analyses that are available and that support the business on an ongoing basis. This idea is often captured under the term "use test".

One practical way to do this is to incorporate the riskiness of the activity in the pricing of the services. The well-known underlying basic principle is that expected losses are incorporated in the pricing of any of the services, while the unexpected losses, the fluctuations that can happen from year to year, are to be supported by sufficient capital. The target return on this capital is then also contributing to the pricing of the services. While the principle is easy in theory, the maturity in this area is different for different risk categories and banking products or services.

Furthest advanced in this domain is credit risk pricing, since it was, so to speak, the area in which it was invented. Processing activities, like custody, asset management and payment services, which are predominantly exposed to operational risk, are not often priced with an eye on the capital requirements that come from this operational risk. Finally, liquidity risk is currently a key attention point in this context. In particular, institutions are rethinking how to transfer the true cost of the risks incurred to the entities that use the liquidity, in order to give the desired incentives to the management.

A second approach to achieve the same objective, not unrelated to the previous point, is to look at the performance of a given activity or business unit, in the light of the capital needed to support that business. It complements the previous point, in the sense that the pricing is more forward-looking, while a risk-based performance analysis is more retrospective in nature. Again, progress along this path is being made, albeit at different speeds in different institutions. A major obstacle for significant breakthroughs in this direction is the required data/information backbone for the entire organisation, which is supporting both the finance and risk organisation. Many institutions are struggling to come to a common vocabulary for both departments, which inhibits making progress on this trajectory. This is the first example of how the challenge of aligning finance and risk is linked to embedding the ICAAP process in the organisation.

As indicated before, the ICAAP is not only about quantifying the risks: it is also, and foremost, about systematically identifying, assessing and monitoring them. A typical example of how risk monitoring and assessment should be interwoven into the operations of the institution is the New Products Approval Committee. New products, particularly if they are as revolutionary as the structured credit products of the last decade, require dedicated risk analyses and the build-up of knowledge and infrastructure. Some investors, but probably also some structurers, evidently seem to have dabbled in the field of structured credit products without performing an initial risk analysis on them; or, if they did, it may not have been done as thoroughly as it should have been, given the perhaps spurious distinction between holding such assets in the trading book and holding them in the banking book.

Another example is the fact that many institutions were caught out by the current crisis in the middle of uncompleted transactions, be they securitisations or underwritings of buy-out deals or even full-blown takeovers of their own. Deciding to proceed with any transaction should be based on an analysis of the risks involved and the ensuing capital requirements, even if the transaction stalls for one reason or another. Again, we do not need to have a fully accurate risk quantification to incorporate these considerations into the decision-making process.

In many banks the ICAAP can be seen as an opportunity to improve management processes for enabling business goals. It forces banks to think at the same time about capital, risk, performance and their planning processes – thus improving awareness of the interconnections among all those elements. Being able to demonstrate to regulators and stakeholders a strong commitment to capital and risk management processes will generate support both for model design and for a better definition of business goals, risk exposure, commercial objectives. The ICAAP implementation has helped create the momentum to look at the business and risks in a more holistic way. Obviously, all the above points linking capital management with performance assessment are complicated by the challenge of demonstrating any diversification benefits, allocating them to the different businesses, and so creating the right incentives.

Another essential ingredient of the ICAAP lies in its forward-looking nature. It is not sufficient to take into account the present exposures, but also how they are expected to evolve over time. As such, the ICAAP exercise becomes intimately related to the medium-term business plans that are periodically performed in financial institutions. Some risk categories that are only recently receiving more attention, such as business risk and strategic risk, naturally fit into this periodic business-plan exercise. For example, you may have had over the years a stable margin on the funding, derived from the deposits of retail clients, but recent rediscovery of such deposits as a strategic funding source may call this historic fact into question.

This forward-looking character is sometimes another source of confusion between finance and risk functions, since the former has by its very mission, a more backward-looking view, and feels sometimes less at ease with the type of what-if questions that risk has a habit of raising. Yet, any good forward-looking analysis should build on the solid ground of reliable information of past performance and current exposures.

Clearly, increasing the available capital of an institution, and therefore its risk-bearing capacity, does take time. Typically, by setting volume and risk limits a bank can ensure that its risk taking does not lead to capital requirements that exceed available capital, ie, its risk-bearing capacity. Dealing rooms get VaR limits, even on a book/product level; credit departments get volume limits etc. Calibrating such limits is often a challenge, in particular if they are not directly based on the actual risk measures, but on more manageable or more readily computed indicators such as notional volume and credit rating. Moreover, limits may have evolved over time, based on criteria other than allowing an optimal return while staying within the boundaries of the available capital. Evaluating now and then the limit system with an eye on optimising performance, given the risk-bearing capacity of the organisation, is sometimes a useful exercise. In fact, these limits present yet another example of how the ICAAP is embedded in a bank's organisation.

While it may sound obvious coming from a Big Four firm, we strongly believe that it is of the utmost importance that all the activities performed in terms of risk identification, risk measurement and assessment, mitigating actions and so forth in the context of the ICAAP process be well documented. Not only is it in the spirit of the current times to consider "absence of evidence" as "evidence of absence" but there are numerous aspects in any ICAAP analysis that are requiring significant judgement and, sometimes implicit, assumptions. In order to be able to backtest the analyses and to create accountability, these judgements and assumptions need to be documented. In fact, these assumptions will often also underlie other management decisions (general market conditions, client behaviour and so on), making this documentation part of the effort to embed the ICAAP within the overall business organisation. But, given that the ICAAP should be based to a large extent on pre-existing risk practices, this documentation requirement should not present a significant extra operational burden.

Another question that arises in this context is whether the ICAAP is a centralised or decentralised process. In fact, given that operational entities in different jurisdictions – belonging to the same multinational financial conglomerate – will often be subjected to ICAAP reporting on a standalone basis, the most obvious approach is that a central team provides the group methodology and guards over compliance with the instructions, while the local entities take up ownership and responsibility for the analysis at the local level. Again, ICAAP is not just a reporting flow in the organisation: it is to be rolled out with responsibilities given at different levels. The work done at each of these levels needs to be documented.

As mentioned at the outset of this presentation, the ICAAP process is part of Pillar II in the Basel Accord, dedicated to the supervisory process. Therefore, the regulators will first want to see evidence that the process was organised, with sufficient executive involvement, and will then enter into a dialogue with the institutions on the assumptions, models and analyses performed by the institutions. We would not be surprised if through this process, over the years, the bar is raised little by little by the regulators, based on their perception of best market practice for specific risk classes.

The ICAAP philosophy chimes in well with Deloitte's view on risk modelling and risk management in general. In fact, impenetrable though risk modelling and valuation sometimes seem, a calculation makes sense only in a context that can be defined either by the governance structure of the organisation or by the regulation. This context is what ultimately justifies the simplifications made, and the assumptions taken. Nevertheless, we are equally devoted to making sure that our experts are knowledgeable in best practices in the domains of risk modelling and risk management. This is why we are particularly proud to be able to present this volume, including contributions by several leading experts in the field. We wish you interesting and challenging reading.

Part 1

The Regulatory Framework

1

Pillar II in the New Basel Accord and in the New European Directives

Martina Bignami, Andrea Pilati[1]

Bank of Italy

It is a widely shared opinion – endorsed also by the authors of this chapter – that the Second Pillar is the real innovation in the new prudential framework known as "Basel II".

By introducing a Second Pillar, the Basel Committee recognises that the new Pillar I rules for determining regulatory capital requirements for credit, counterparty, market and operational risks are inadequate to get a comprehensive view of a bank's risk profile, even if they are much more accurate than the previous ones in measuring the level of the different risks faced by intermediaries.

The Committee has acknowledged that there is still a long and winding road ahead towards a synthetic measure of the intermediaries' risk profiles. This is the reason why the Pillar I "calculator" of regulatory capital requirements has been supplemented with a more flexible and customised Pillar II Supervisory Review Process (SRP).

The SRP is a twofold process: it asks banks to design a formalised, documented and comprehensive process for determining their optimal capital level (the so-called Internal Capital Adequacy Assessment Process, ICAAP); and it asks supervisors to review and evaluate the ICAAP (the so-called Supervisory Review and Evaluation Process, SREP) within the broader context of assessing risk profiles as well as internal risk management and control systems.

The dialogue between supervisors and intermediaries is therefore crucial to settle the dispute over what level (and composition) of capital is deemed adequate to sustain growth and to face risks.

If we consider that the ultimate objective of the new prudential framework is the creation – both inside and outside national borders – of a competitive financial market, governed by regulations promoting fair competition, the Second Pillar is thus the true challenge that supervisory authorities and intermediaries are facing. This holds true for two reasons.

First, ensuring a harmonised implementation of the principles and guidelines underpinning the SRP is much more complex then giving a uniform interpretation of the quantitative Pillar I provisions. As a matter of fact, the SRP has not only to verify that Pillar I calculations are performed properly (for example, in the internal system validation process), but also to determine a level of capital such as to take into account:

- risks investigated in Pillar I but not adequately measured;
- non-Pillar I risks;
- interactions among different risks;
- adverse market conditions that each intermediary may face;
- risk management and internal control systems;
- risk aversion and strategic objectives; and
- risk-mitigation procedures and techniques.

The challenging nature of the goals the Committee assigns to the SRP is thus self-evident. In addition, it must be considered that the practical means by which the above-mentioned issues can be treated may vary significantly across intermediaries and across countries.

Second, the constant dialogue between banks and supervisors does represent a significant novelty for several countries. It must also be considered that the Second Pillar urges authorities – even in those countries where the dialogue with the supervised entity seems a consolidated feature in the supervisory approach – to review and update methodologies used to supervise bank risks, to revamp examination and evaluation schemes, to fine-tune the interaction with supervised entities, to refine laws and regulations in order to entrust supervisors with appropriate intervention instruments and sanctioning powers, and to strengthen the supervisory teams by providing them with specific methodological skills. In a nutshell, SRP asks for a non-trivial change in the supervisory culture and approach.

An additional factor must be considered. Financial market globalisation, together with the growing number of international players on the European market, has dramatically amplified both the need for convergence of the secondary regulations – which each member state has tailored in implementing the CRD provisions – and the importance of identifying a set of practices that are shared among supervisors while conducting the SREP.

This latter issue is particularly relevant for the definition of the future institutional setting of the European Supervision, with particular reference to the survival of the ongoing model of local supervision of large cross-country groups licensed in a Member State. The Committee of European Banking Supervisors is now focusing on this topic,[2] given that the work towards the convergence of supervisory practices on Pillar I issues has already been set up and that the ICAAP implementation and its review process are beginning to rank high on banks' and supervisors' agendas alike.

This chapter deals with Pillar II from a regulatory perspective, presenting innovations and rules introduced by the Basel Accord and the new European Capital Adequacy Directives. It discusses what parts of Pillar II are just a confirmation of previous supervisory practices and what portions, instead, represent a true novelty. Later we review and explain the main rules on the Second Pillar set out, respectively, in the new Basel Accord and in the European Capital Adequacy Directive. We conclude by discussing a number of open issues for bankers and regulators.

WHAT IS REALLY NEW IN PILLAR II?

The real innovation of Pillar II rests with having extended the range of risks to be considered when evaluating a bank's capital adequacy, with having linked this analysis to the evaluation of the internal control system, and, above all, with having set up a constant dialogue on these topics between the authorities and the supervised entities. On the contrary, the ICAAP and SREP processes do not appear in themselves to be extremely innovative. When dealing with ICAAP, the Committee states that "… the analysis of a bank's current and future capital requirements in relation to its strategic objectives is a vital element of the strategic planning process. The strategic plan should clearly outline the bank's capital needs, anticipated capital expenditures, desirable capital level, and external capital sources".[3] It seems out of question that such a statement could be easily endorsed by the vast majority of middle to large corporations operating in different sectors of the economy. That is to say that best practices in banking are the same as in other sectors and that banking today requires a cautious management of the causal relationship between corporate strategies and the capital structure of the bank, an old saw in corporate finance.

On the other hand, if banking means delivering an ICAAP as defined above, then supervision cannot refrain from evaluating such a process: "The supervisory authorities should regularly review the process by which a bank assesses its capital adequacy, risk position, resulting capital levels, and quality of capital held. Supervisors should also evaluate the degree to which a bank has in place a sound internal process to assess capital adequacy".[4] This means that there is nothing dramatically different between the tasks that have to be performed by supervisors while conducting a SREP and what they have been doing under the previous prudential framework. Review of risks faced by intermediaries, analysis of internal controls, check of the compliance with capital-adequacy requirements and prudential rules, comprehensive assessment of the supervised entity performance, identification of any weaknesses or inadequacies, and adoption of supervisory measures if necessary have always been the instruments of the risk-based supervision model prevailing in the countries where the 1988 Accord was implemented.

In conclusion, the Pillar II framework does not innovate the content of either the ICAAP or the SREP processes, but it does introduce a new approach in asking banks and supervisors to enter a framework of constant and structured dialogue, which should encompass[5] at least Pillar I risks, risks not fully captured under Pillar I (for instance residual risk), Pillar II risks (for instance interest-rate risk in the banking book, concentration risk, liquidity risk) and external factors (for instance, IRB stress testing, impact of economic cycles). The dialogue should, on the one hand, truly test and challenge an institution's ICAAP and on the other hand it should not necessarily result in automatic capital add-ons. Furthermore, it should be tailored to an institution's standing, in accordance with a fully proportional supervisory approach.

The idea that the new elements in the Pillar II framework are basically hinged on the need to establish a structured dialogue between supervisors and institutions seems to be supported by the evidence that almost all the supervisory bodies endorsing the Basel II prudential framework have initiated a revision of their Risk Assessment Systems. Such revision is aimed not only at strengthening the methodological foundations of these systems, but also at transposing the need for interaction with supervised entities into their internal guidelines and, what is more, into their ongoing practices.

THE SECOND PILLAR IN THE BASEL II ACCORD

Pillar II is defined and structured in the "International Convergence of Capital Measurement and Capital Standards (a revised framework, comprehensive version)", published by the Basel Committee in June 2006.[6]

The Basel Committee acknowledged that the revised Framework is designed to establish minimum levels of capital for internationally active banks. As under the 1988 Accord, national authorities were left free to adopt arrangements that would set a higher level of minimum capital. Moreover, they were free to put in place additional capital charges for the individual banking organisations to which they issue a banking charter. Additional capital charges may be used – for example, in order to address the potential uncertainty in the accuracy of the risk measure underlying any capital rule or to limit the extent to which an organisation may be funded with debt. More generally, under the Second Pillar, supervisors should expect banks to operate above the minimum regulatory capital levels.

The Second Pillar is specifically explained in paragraphs 719–907. Sections 720–4 explain why the supervisory review is important.

First of all, the Supervisory Review is intended not only to ensure that banks have adequate capital to support all the risks in their business, but also to encourage them to develop and use better risk management techniques in monitoring and managing those risks. It is widely recognised that there is a relationship between the amount of capital held by the bank against its risks and the strength and effectiveness of the bank's risk management and internal control process. In any case, the Committee stresses the importance of the following points:

- capital must not be viewed as the only option for addressing increased risks confronting the bank;
- other means of addressing risk must be considered; they encompass: strengthening risk management, applying internal limits, increasing the level of provisions and reserves, improving internal controls; and
- inadequate controls or risk management processes should require countervailing actions in the control and mitigation factors: capital should not be regarded as a substitute for a sound management and adequate controls.

Four key principles of supervisory review are identified.

1. Banks should have a process for assessing their overall capital adequacy in relation to their risk profile as well as a strategy for maintaining their capital levels.
2. Supervisors should review and evaluate banks' internal capital adequacy assessments and strategies, as well as their ability to monitor and ensure their compliance with regulatory capital ratios.

Supervisors should take appropriate supervisory actions if they are not satisfied with the results of this process.
3. Supervisors should expect banks to operate above the minimum regulatory capital ratios and should have the ability to require banks to hold capital in excess of the minimum requirements
4. Supervisors should seek to intervene at an early stage to prevent capital from falling below the minimum levels required to support the risk characteristics of a particular bank and should require rapid remedial actions if capital is not maintained or restored.

Principle 1 stresses banks' responsibilities: they must be able to demonstrate that the internal capital targets they choose are well founded and consistent with their overall risk profile and with the current operating environment. The primary responsibility for ensuring adequate capital to support risk lies with the bank management.

The main features of a rigorous capital-adequacy valuation process are the following: (a) board and senior management oversight; (b) sound capital management; (c) comprehensive assessment of risk, taking into account particular stages of the business cycle and including forward-looking stress testing; (d) monitoring and reporting; (e) internal control reviews.

The capital assessment process is not simply based on a calculation model: capital must be strictly interlinked with a sound risk management process that must include all significant and material risks a bank is exposed to. This requires: setting the bank's tolerance for risk; identifying, measuring, managing and controlling risks; drafting the strategic plan to outline the capital needs, relating risk to capital; adopting strong internal controls, written policies and procedures, internal reporting; communicating the procedures and the results to the whole organisation.

As for risks, banks should address all material risks. First, Principle 1 focuses on the Pillar I risks: credit, counterparty,[7] market and operational risks. Given that Pillar I credit risk capital requirements for banks using IRB methodologies entail the assumption of perfect granularity in the banking book portfolio, Principle 1 points out the importance of taking into consideration the risks involved in managing credit concentration.

Internal policies should cover the different forms of concentration to which a bank may be exposed: (a) significant exposures to an individual counterparty or a group of related counterparties, considering legal and/or financial links; (b) counterparties in the same economic sector or geographic region; (c) indirect credit exposures arising from a bank's credit risk mitigation activities (exposures to a single collateral type or to credit protection provided by a single counterparty).

Among the risks mentioned in Principle 1, interest-rate risk in the banking book and liquidity risk are not Pillar I risks.

As far as interest-rate risk is concerned, the Committee is convinced that it is a potentially significant risk, which requires capital support. Given the heterogeneity across internationally active banks in terms of the nature of the underlying risk and the processes for monitoring and managing risks, it was finally decided to treat interest-rate risk in the banking book as a Pillar II risk.[8] Liquidity risk is recognised as crucial to the ongoing viability of any banking organisation. Therefore, each bank is required to have an adequate system for measuring, monitoring and controlling liquidity risk. Banks should also evaluate the adequacy of capital given their own liquidity profile and the liquidity of the markets in which they operate.[9]

As for other risks, such as reputational and strategic, even though the Committee acknowledges that they are not easily measurable, it expects the industry to further develop techniques for managing all aspects of these types of risk.

Finally, the importance of having in place strong and robust stress-testing procedures is emphasised.

Within the IRB approach to credit risk, the Committee expects banks to operate with a level of capital sufficient to meet the Pillar I requirements as well as the results of the credit risk stress test performed in compliance with the IRB minimum requirements. If this is not the case, supervisors are expected to take the appropriate actions (requiring banks to reduce their risks and/or to hold additional capital/provisions).

The same expectations are being voiced with reference to counterparty and market risks. In this case, appropriate risk management strategies could involve hedging against stress-test results, reducing the size of the firm's exposure and holding an additional amount of capital.

Also in concentration risk, periodic stress tests should be conducted with reference to major credit risk concentrations. The results of those stress tests should be reviewed in order to respond to potential changes in market conditions that could adversely impact the bank's performance.

The other three principles point out the supervisory authorities' duties and responsibilities.

First, supervisory authorities are required to review regularly the process through which a bank assesses its capital adequacy, risks and the quality of the capital it holds. The assessment must refer not only to quantitative variables (risk assessment, capital adequacy) but also to qualitative requirements (sound risk management process, robust internal control systems, control environment, compliance with minimum standards provided for by Pillar I).

Therefore, the Committee stresses the importance of carrying out specific analyses on the following aspects: risk measures used in assessing internal capital adequacy; the comprehensiveness of chosen target levels of capital; composition of capital; and the extent to which these measures are used operationally (use test). Finally, the results of sensitivity analyses and stress tests conducted by the bank and their impact on capital plans must be specifically reviewed. Following the results of the analysis, it is up to supervisors to decide whether and how to take appropriate actions.

The Committee stressed the importance of having higher capital levels than those required under Pillar I. In fact, bank-specific uncertainties are not treated under Pillar I, and other risks (apart from credit, market and operational risks) may be significant. These and other reasons[10] may induce banks to maintain a buffer of capital above the Pillar I minimum requirements.

Among the other methods that can be used by supervisors, reference is made to "target" and "trigger" ratios. In a target-ratios system, supervisors establish the level of capital banks must reach in a planned period of time (usually, in the short to medium term) taking into account also the bank's strategy. Trigger ratios are specific thresholds, above the minimum requirements but below the target ratios, below which banks should not fall. When deemed necessary supervisors undertake specific actions to keep a bank's capital level above those thresholds.

However, higher capital is not always the solution: intensifying the monitoring of the bank, restricting the payment of dividends and improving systems and controls are among the range of measures supervisors could adopt. In some cases, increased capital is seen as an "interim" step until "permanent" measures to improve the bank's position become effective.

The Committee points out that the presence of discretionary elements in the supervisory review process is necessary. However, supervisors must ensure transparency and accountability in carrying out their task. This concerns the criteria used in the review of banks' internal capital assessments and in the setting of target or trigger ratios. Any request for additional capital as well as any corrective measure should be justified in the light of the risk-profile characteristics or of other specific features.

Finally, the Committee devotes one whole section (from 784 to 807) to the supervisory review process for securitisation. Credit risk arising from structured products is considered a Pillar I risk and, accordingly, is subject to detailed capital computation rules. However, regulators acknowledge that the economic essence of securitisations can be very hard to assess analytically for capital-adequacy purposes. Hence, sometimes Pillar I capital could not reflect the real risk taken by the bank and implied by the characteristics of the contract. This is particularly relevant when structured products make up the bulk of a bank's portfolio.

The main concern of the Committee concerns the so-called "implicit support". The Committee stresses that in case of a traditional securitisation the provision of implicit support undermines the "clean-break criteria", which allow banks to exclude securitised assets from the capital-requirements calculation. In more general terms, by providing implicit support, banks send a signal to the market that risk has not been transferred, so that capital requirements are likely to be understated.

For all those reasons, the Committee's stance on this issue is very conservative. In principle, when a bank is found to have provided implicit support to a securitisation (supporting it beyond contractual obligations), all the underlying exposures associated with the structure must be treated as if they had not been securitised. In this case banks are required to disclose publicly that they were found to have provided non-contractual support as well as the resulting increase in their capital charge. In case such a behaviour occurs more than once, the range of supervisory actions increases progressively and includes: preventing banks from gaining favourable capital treatment on securitised assets for a period of time to be determined by the national supervisor; requiring banks to hold capital against all securitised assets by applying a conversion factor to the risk weight of the underlying assets; requiring banks to treat all securitised assets as if they remained on the balance sheet; requiring banks to hold regulatory capital in excess of the minimum risk-based capital ratios; pending further investigation, prohibiting banks from any capital relief for planned securitisation transactions (moratorium).

Further specific recommendations are provided on credit risk mitigation in structured products (Section 795), call provisions (Sections 796–800), early amortisation (Sections 801–7) and the impact it could have on capital requirements.

THE SECOND PILLAR IN DIRECTIVE 2006/48/CE

The principles set forth in the new Basel Accord have been enacted in the EU through the Directive 2006/48/CE (usually referred to as CRD, Capital Requirements Directive).

To begin with, the room devoted to Pillar II by the Directive is remarkably limited: the topics treated in detail in almost a hundred paragraphs by the Basel II Revised Framework are dealt with in five articles (22, 123, 124, 136 and 144) and in two brief enclosures (Annex V and Annex 12) of the CRD. Such discrepancy can be easily explained if we consider the different aims of the two texts. The former is a technical document that delivers the supervisory perspective about the principles to be adopted for a sound risk and capital management in banks, together with the operating guidelines that supervisors should follow in reviewing its soundness. The latter transforms the Basel principles into stylised rules that have to be applied by all Member States and, most importantly, by all banks licensed in Member States, thus greatly enhancing the scope of application of Pillar II measures set by the Basel Committee, which were meant to be applied to internationally active banks.

This wider scope of application explains the central role assigned by the CRD to the concept of proportionality.

The proportionality principle is affirmed in Recital 41 of the CRD, which states that the Directive has "regard in particular to the diversity in size and scale of operations and to the range of activities of credit institutions". This principle affects the ICAAP, which according to Article 123 has to be "proportionate to the nature, scale and complexity of the activities of the credit institution concerned", as well as the SREP, whose frequency and intensity should be determined, pursuant to Article 124, "having regard to the size, systemic importance, nature, scale and complexity of the activities of the credit institution concerned ..."

Coming back to the comparison between the Basel II text and the CRD, it must be noted that other major differences – apart from the obvious different degree of technicality and scope of application – lie in the different perspective from which the two texts look at the "desirable level of capital" of an institution.

The Revised Framework conveys the supervisors' view, so that it expects "banks to operate above the minimum regulatory capital ratios" and authorities to "have the ability to require banks to hold capital in excess of the minimum".

The Directive follows a partly different approach: Article 136 states the supervisory measures that can be implemented in case of noncompliance with the prudential regulation. If a bank's ICAAP is deemed unsatisfactory or, more generally, if the SREP leads to an unfavourable outcome, then "a specific own funds requirement in excess of the minimum level laid down in Article 75 shall be imposed by the competent authorities … if the sole application of other measures is unlikely to improve the arrangements, processes, mechanisms and strategies sufficiently within an appropriate timeframe". In other words, the CRD, does not openly endorse the Basel supervisors' expectations concerning the "desirable" capital endowment. On the contrary, it regulates cases when the application of additional capital requirements is necessary (because other organisational measures are not effective) for banks that work, on a going concern basis, with own funds that never fall below total Pillar I capital requirements (Article 75 of the CRD). The CRD approach is clearly simplistic compared with the Basel one, since it represents the outcome of a compromise between supervisors and financial institutions. Therefore, most issues investigated by the Basel Committee that voice the concerns of supervisors (for instance, target and trigger ratios – see previously) are not present in the CRD.

OPEN ISSUES FOR BANKS AND REGULATORS

The reticence of the CRD about the banks' "optimal" capital structure has led to a number of controversial issues that still have not found a definite settlement, among neither supervisors nor bankers.

The first one relates to the definition of capital used in the CRD articles devoted to Pillar II, but is only apparently nominal in nature. The words "internal capital" are used in Article 123, referring to the ICAAP, while the words "own funds" are used in Article 124, devoted to the SREP. This difference has generated an intense debate in almost all member states, usually referred to as the "Available Financial Resources", or AFR, issue. This issue mainly concerns the reconciliation of the items eligible to satisfy Pillar I capital requirements from a supervisory perspective, with those (covering both Pillar I and Pillar II risks) that banks deem adequate to cover internal capital requirements.

The AFR debate is centred on the reconciliation of the supervisors' and bankers' views on the capacity to absorb losses of different "capital" items, but involves also the gap that supervisors are willing to accept between supervisory capital requirements and the capital estimates stemming from internal calculations.

In a nutshell, the AFR debate is more wide-ranging than its label would suggest: it looks as a methodological dispute, but more importantly asks for the definition, across EU Member States, of clear-cut prudential policies regarding the maximum acceptable gap between internal capital and own funds on the one hand, and between supervisory capital requirements and internal capital needs on the other.

The reasons behind this latter gap are widely known: first, a given risk can be faced not only through capital, but also by putting in place mitigating measures; second, for each Pillar I risk, confidence intervals (and/or holding periods) may have been defined that are different from those set by the supervisory rules; third, the internal modelling of intra-risk correlation may generate outcomes that differ from the correlation hypotheses embedded, for instance, in the credit risk supervisory formula. This last topic seems second only to the overdebated issue concerning the most appropriate measure of the correlation among risks, that is to say the recognition of diversification benefits.

All the above-mentioned topics, together with the crucial issue of the smoothing of the cyclical behaviour of the new prudential framework, are being analysed in depth in the supervisory cooperation forums, the banking associations and the risk managers' committees across Europe. The so-called "Pillar II Convergence Network" within the Committee of European Banking Supervisors has taken the lead in coordinating the debate, implementing stocktaking of national approaches and promoting the convergence of national practices. CEBS has also launched a programme of Pillar II onsite examinations, where the ICAAPs implemented by the top-ranking European cross-border groups are investigated by international teams of experts, representing the supervisory bodies participating in the groups' supervisory colleges.

Such open issues are now ranking high on the supervisors' and intermediaries' agenda. The need to speed up the convergence towards a shared approach among European regulators should be top of the list. What is at stake is not only – as mentioned at the beginning of this chapter – the survival of the current institutional setting of European banking supervision, but (more importantly) the strengthening of capital standards and the preservation of a level playing field in the European banking system.

1 The views expressed in this chapter are those of the authors and do not involve the responsibility of the Bank of Italy. Although this chapter is the outcome of a joint work, paragraphs 1, 2 and 4 have been drafted by Martina Bignami, paragraph 3 by Andrea Pilati. The authors wish to express their gratitude to Franca Rosa Congiu for proofreading the first English draft.

2 See Chapter 4.

3 See Paragraph 729 in "International Convergence of Capital Measurement and Capital Standards – A Revised Framework – Comprehensive Version", Basel Committee on Banking Supervision, June 2006.

4 See *ibid.*, paragraph 736.

5 See Chapter 4 in *CEBS, Guidelines on the Application of the Supervisory Review Process under Pillar II*", January 2006.

6 The document is a compilation of the June 2004 Basel II framework, the items of the 1988 Accord that were not revised during the Basel II process, the 1996 "Amendment to the Capital Accord to incorporate Market Risk", and the 2005 paper on the "Application of Basel II to Trading Activities and the Treatment of Double Default Effect".

7 Specific references to counterparty risk were introduced in the last version of the paper, as a result of the application of Basel II to the trading activities (points from 777i to 777xiv).

8 Nevertheless, evidence of the importance attributed by the Committee to interest-rate risk in the banking book is found in the specific reference to the possibility, for supervisors, to establish a mandatory minimum capital requirement and in the identification of a specific threshold – 20% of the sum of Tier 1 and Tier 2 capital, as a result of a standardised interest rate shock (200 basis points) or its equivalent – above which "outlier banks" should be closely monitored.

9 However, the most widespread practices showed that banks tend to estimate the "expected cashflow" on the basis of some specific assumptions concerning on- and off-balance items, rather than on an internal capital measure. Moreover, while higher levels of capital may give some sort of insurance to market participants, they do not prevent banks from experiencing severe liquidity problems. This demonstrates the importance for banks to have in place strong liquidity risk management systems, which include stress-testing procedures and contingency plans.

10 Most international banks prefer to be highly rated by internationally recognised rating agencies; the type and volume of activities and the risk exposures normally change, causing fluctuations in the overall capital ratio; it may be costly for banks to raise additional capital especially in particular environments and market conditions; it is a serious matter for banks to fall below minimum regulatory capital requirements.

2

The Capital Adequacy Assessment Process: a Supervisory Perspective[1]

Preston Thompson; David Palmer[2]

Federal Reserve Bank of Boston; Federal Reserve Board, Washington

Around the world, banks[3] in many countries have begun, or will soon begin, the process of implementing the Basel II capital rules. A key element of these rules is the bank's own assessment of its capital adequacy – the so-called internal capital adequacy assessment process or ICAAP articulated in Pillar II of the Basel II framework. For many banks this may well be the first time that they have gone through a thoughtful process of evaluating capital adequacy in relation to their overall risk profile rather than relying on supervisory minimums or guidelines, or on external factors such as rating agency recommendations. For others, however, the ICAAP will be just an incremental step in how they evaluate capital adequacy and communicate such information to their supervisors.

In the US, Pillar II requirements will be an extension of longstanding supervisory expectations for banks to look beyond minimum regulatory capital requirements established using existing risk-based capital guidelines. These expectations were predicated, in part, on the view that the evolution of banking products and services made existing regulatory measures of capital adequacy less reflective of actual risk undertaken. The reader need look no further than the securitisation market, certain investment activities (eg, in structured securities) or custody operations to understand that the existing Basel I capital guidelines – using calculations based largely on on-balance-sheet credit exposures (or their equivalent) – were missing potentially large segments of a bank's risk profile. While we recognise that the Pillar I minimum capital requirements under Basel II offer significant advancements for the evaluation of regulatory capital, we believe that Pillar II requirements are of equal or greater importance in determining overall capital adequacy and conveying that analysis both internally as well as to supervisors.

SUPERVISORY EXPECTATIONS PRIOR TO BASEL II

US supervisors have long believed that it is important for all banks to have a process for evaluating their capital needs, with the supervisory expectations for the rigor and structure around that evaluation increasing with the size and complexity of the bank in question. As noted, the Basel I risk-based capital guidelines offer a one-size-fits-all approach to calculating regulatory capital needs and do not incorporate overarching issues that affect capital adequacy such as plans for growth, the quality of risk management and management's own capital goals. In 1999 the US Federal Reserve issued guidance to examiners and certain banks to address these elements. The Federal Reserve's Supervision and Regulation Letter 99–18 (SR99–18) entitled "Assessing Capital Adequacy in Relation to Risk at Large Banking Organizations and Others with Complex Risk Profiles" emphasised the need for certain banking organisations to take greater efforts to ensure that their capital was not only sufficient to meet formal regulatory standards, but also fully sufficient to support their underlying risk positions and strategic goals. Further, SR99–18 recognised the diminishing usefulness of regulatory measures for those institutions. The letter directed banks to develop internal capital management processes and supervisors to evaluate those processes to determine whether they meaningfully tie the identification, measurement and management of risk to the determination of capital needs.

Among the key elements of the guidance is the need for fundamental risk measurement and management practices to accompany the bank's own evaluation of its capital adequacy. This element builds on the notion that, without a sound risk management and governance framework, internally derived capital measures may lose some of their relevancy. The concept here is fairly straightforward – no amount of capital is sufficient to offset weak risk management or oversight. Supervisors also expect the sophistication of risk measurement and management to increase commensurate with the size and complexity of the institution. Another key element is the need for capital to relate explicitly to the level of risk. In doing so, the bank's capital should reflect the perceived level of precision in the risk measures used, include a "cushion" to take into account uncertainties in risk measurement, and reflect the fact that historical measures of dependency among exposures can change rapidly. In linking capital to risk exposure, we again see the importance of a robust risk measurement foundation, as the absence of credible risk parameters used as inputs to the capital attribution process may mean that capital adequacy assessments are no longer tied to risk and therefore will have little meaning.

Of course, some risks may not readily lend themselves to quantification or be suitable for direct capital attribution. On one hand, credit and market risks have a fairly long history of quantification and it would be difficult to argue that a specific amount of capital should not be held against those risks for most banks. Liquidity risk,[4] on the other hand, may not have a commonly accepted approach to quantification, at least in terms of capital attribution, and many have argued that capital for liquidity risk should not be held. In this case, liquidity risk may be considered a second-order risk, in that it results from problems with other risk types – creditworthiness of assets, broad market disruptions, etc. As such, liquidity risk may be more appropriately viewed and managed in conjunction with other risk types. Whether liquidity risk is treated explicitly as a standalone risk type or implicitly in the measures of other risks, a bank should be able to understand the impact of liquidity risk on capital adequacy. Similar approaches should be taken with other risks that currently do not have a commonly accepted method of quantification or direct capital attribution. Regardless of how risks are measured – quantitative or qualitative, explicit or implicit – the ultimate goal is to ensure there is adequate capital to support all risks. In every case there is the need for sound judgement to accompany the measurement of risks and the evaluation of capital adequacy.

The final two elements of the Federal Reserve's 1999 guidance include the requirement to set specific capital goals and assess conformity with the stated objectives of the entire process, including the ability to meet capital goals. In setting capital goals, management should consider how they want to express their assessment of capital adequacy – such as an implied target debt rating, at a specific confidence level, or a level of loss coverage. While these measures have some common elements, they are not perfect substitutes for one another. For example, a number of banks have chosen for economic capital purposes to target an implied AA debt rating, using a 99.97% confidence level. While that confidence level may reflect the current implied default probability, the AA default probability has changed over time. In communicating their capital goals, management should understand the possible divergence in these measures across a longer time horizon. In assessing conformity with the stated objectives for capital adequacy, the board of directors and management should ensure that there is a robust governance framework and proper controls over the entire capital adequacy process, which include documentation of the process and validation of its component pieces. Assessing conformity also includes the ability to differentiate between short and long-term capital goals. In setting short-term goals, management should consider the costs and implications of rapidly changing capital levels and balance that with long-term goals and needs.

CAPITAL ADEQUACY ASSESSMENTS AND ECONOMIC CAPITAL

A common misperception among many banks is that their economic capital practices alone will provide an assessment of overall capital adequacy. It is important to note that neither SR99–18 nor Basel II specifically requires banks to use economic capital as part of their evaluation of capital adequacy. For purposes of this chapter, we define economic capital (sometimes called risk capital) as those methods or practices that allow a bank to attribute capital to cover the economic effects of risk-taking activities. These methods may be used for a variety of objectives, including limit setting, performance analysis, and pricing.[5] In addition, these methods are often associated with an allocation of capital to a particular product or activity – that is, they sometimes are more focused on dividing up an existing capital "pie", rather than focused on how to determine the overall size of the capital "pie" in the first place. An internal process for assessing capital adequacy, on the other hand, offers a much more holistic view of capital adequacy that should help determine the overall level of capital and ensure that capital is adequate at all times. Thus, capital adequacy assessments are more closely associated with capital attribution rather than allocation. As noted above, a capital adequacy assessment includes capital planning (both short and long-term) and an oversight or governance element. Capital adequacy also incorporates those risks that do not fit well in an economic capital construct. A rigorous process to assess capital adequacy will also consider both the capital needs implied by the risk profile as well as the actual supply of capital available to meet potential capital needs. In determining capital adequacy, many banks choose to hold additional capital at the top of the house as unallocated capital that represents risks that management chooses not to include in an economic capital figure or for other strategic purposes. Similarly, management may choose to hold capital for goodwill or other intangibles that are not included in allocated economic capital. This is not to suggest that economic capital could not be an important input into capital adequacy assessments, but it should not be seen as the end state. The diagram in Figure 2.1 attempts to demonstrate how economic capital measures can be

Figure 2.1 Uses of economic capital

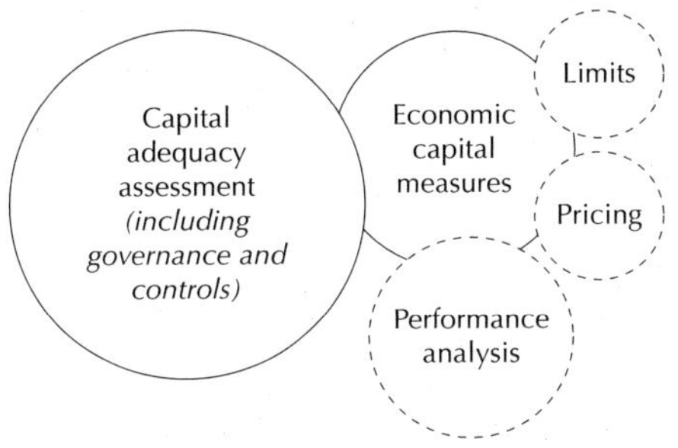

used for a number of purposes, but by themselves are not sufficient to assess capital adequacy.

One final distinguishing difference between economic capital and internal assessments of capital adequacy is that the former is a model or collection of models that tends to focus on a single output to determine a hurdle rate or other performance measure. On the other hand, an internal assessment of capital adequacy is a process, and that process generally includes consideration of a number of outcomes, reflecting the uncertainty of any one particular outcome, as well as incorporating elements such as plans for future capital needs, sources of capital, explicit capital goals and a process to evaluate the success in meeting those goals. In evaluating banks' capital adequacy assessments, supervisors will focus less on a single number or output and more on the overall process by which the bank arrived at their estimate, including such elements as sensitivity analysis, stress testing, and scenario analysis.

US APPROACH TO PILLAR II

US bank supervisors consider Pillar II an integral part of the Basel II framework. In implementing Pillar II – also known as supervisory review – US supervisors are continuing their longstanding approach to assessing overall capital adequacy at each individual banking organisation, and ensuring that capital levels are reflective of an institution's risk profile and appropriately above minimum regulatory measures. As noted above, US supervisors have been promoting a process similar to Pillar II for some time and, to a considerable extent, have already adopted the four key principles of Pillar II outlined in the international Basel framework, either through supervisory programmes or the US Prompt Corrective Action framework:

- Principle 1: banks should have a process for assessing their overall capital adequacy in relation to their risk profile and a strategy for maintaining their capital levels;
- Principle 2: supervisors should review and evaluate banks' internal capital adequacy assessments and strategies;
- Principle 3: supervisors should expect banks to operate above minimum capital ratios; and
- Principle 4: supervisors should seek to intervene at an early stage to prevent capital from falling below the minimum levels required to support the risk characteristics of a particular bank.

As noted above, since 1999 the Federal Reserve has set forth expectations for certain large, complex banking organisations to have a more structured and rigorous internal process for assessing capital adequacy. In this manner, we believe that US supervisory expectations for the ICAAP in Pillar II of the Basel framework are similar to expectations set forth in the Federal Reserve's SR99–18.[6]

The Pillar I minimum regulatory capital measures in Basel II are indeed considerable improvements over Basel I-based measures for large, complex banking organisations and provide greater risk sensitivity. But Pillar I measures constitute only a minimum level of capital. In their final rule for Basel II, the US agencies state, "A bank should be particularly mindful of the limitations of regulatory risk-based capital requirements as a measure of its full risk profile – including risks not covered or not adequately quantified in the risk-based capital requirements."[7] These limitations are essentially unavoidable given that a primary purpose of Pillar I capital measures is to establish a regulatory minimum that is also relatively comparable across institutions. By design, Pillar I contains numerous simplifying assumptions to apply to a broad spectrum of international institutions. These include:

- risk coverage under regulatory capital requirements that includes only credit, operational and market risk (through the market risk rule[8]);
- supervisory-determined asset value correlations, which in most cases do not correspond to each bank's individual risk profile;
- portfolio invariance, meaning that no single credit exposure has a greater contribution to the overall portfolio's riskiness than another exposure;
- infinite granularity, meaning that all credit exposures are assumed to be of the same size and therefore do not present any single-name concentrations;

- solvency standard that is calibrated around 99.9%; and
- inputs that are based on the long-run average, not conditioned on the current state.

In general, Pillar I is not tailored to an individual institution's business mix, strategies, risk appetite or true risk profile. Thus, Pillar II is needed so that banking organisations have an internal process, tailored to their risk profile, to determine whether their overall capital is adequate and demonstrate such to their supervisors.

US EXPECTATIONS FOR ICAAP

The US final rule for Basel II has a firm requirement for Pillar II: "A bank must have a rigorous process for assessing its overall capital adequacy in relation to its risk profile and a comprehensive strategy for maintaining an appropriate level of capital."[9] Despite its brevity, the requirement for banks to have an ICAAP is considered a very important and significant piece of the US final rule. Indeed, the US agencies emphasise the rigor, depth and comprehensiveness needed for a credible ICAAP in their supervisory guidance on Pillar II.[10,11]

At its most basic, an institution's ICAAP should:

- identify and measure material risks;
- set capital adequacy goals that relate to risk; and
- ensure the integrity of internal capital adequacy assessments

Each of these three elements must be completed in full and all should be consistent with each other, since together they comprise an integrated process.[12] Additionally, the supervisory review process emphasises that an institution's overall capital should remain adequate on an ongoing basis, as underlying conditions change. In general, the capital levels prescribed by the ICAAP should exceed the level required by its minimum risk-based capital requirements, and should be adequate to address all material risks.

Within each of the three broad elements of the ICAAP, US supervisors have expectations for US banking organisations. For one, institutions should ensure that they are capturing material risks that can affect capital adequacy, which can include not just credit, market and operational risks, but also interest-rate risk, liquidity risk, reputational and strategic/business risk – or other risk types. Naturally, not every institution is equally exposed to all these risk types, and – as noted above – some risks are more easily measured and/or quantified than others. Nevertheless, banking organisations should have a good understanding of how all risks affect capital adequacy, even if direct capital attributions are not possible. This includes latent risks that may become apparent only in times of stress. A bank should assess whether its capital is sufficient to absorb any losses that may arise from activities that expose the bank to multiple risks within and across business lines, and recognise that losses could arise in several risk dimensions at the same time, stemming from the same event or a common set of factors. In short, all relevant factors that present a material source of risk to capital should be incorporated into a well-developed ICAAP.

It is quite important that institutions not immediately assume they already meet the expectations for the first element of their ICAAP, identifying and measuring material risks. In other words, if an institution is not first able to determine its overall level of risk, its ICAAP will not be meaningful and it will not be able to demonstrate that capital is adequate. Accordingly, the first thing US supervisors will evaluate in an institution's ICAAP is the fundamental risk management infrastructure that allows it to appropriately identify risk and the more advanced practices that allow the institution to measure and quantify risk. For example, an institution planning to calculate capital attributions for wholesale credit risk should first have in place a credible and robust credit risk rating system, with reliable risk parameters for use as inputs to its capital attributions. Proper risk identification and measurement also should capture both on and off-balance-sheet positions, as well as effects arising from provisions of explicit or implicit support. Material risks can include those that in isolation do not appear to be material at first, but when combined with other risks can lead to material losses.

There are also some clear objectives for the second element of the ICAAP, setting and assessing capital adequacy goals with respect to risk. The most fundamental objective is to relate capital to identified risks, in order to determine how those risks affect the bank's overall capital adequacy. An institution should be able to demonstrate that its approach to relating capital to risk is conceptually sound and that results are reasonable given the risk profile of the organisation. The chosen target capital level is likely to reflect either the desired level of risk coverage or, alternatively, a desired credit rating for the institution that reflects a desired degree of creditworthiness and thus access to funding sources. Whatever the source of the target capital level, it should have strong analytical grounding and should be consistently applied across the enterprise. Through the ICAAP, a bank should ensure that adequate capital is held against material risks, and that it remains adequate not just at a point in time, but over time, to account for evolving economic conditions, volatility in the financial environment and changes in a bank's strategic direction. It is important to note that this expectation does not preclude a bank's internal measure of capital adequacy from temporarily falling below internal targets (as long as it remains above regulatory minimums), but that the ICAAP would address strategies for returning to internal solvency targets.

Ensuring the integrity of the ICAAP means that there should be a credible and robust governance process and proper validation around the ICAAP and its results that includes board and senior management oversight, policies and procedures, and effective monitoring and management information systems. As noted above, the ICAAP should be a process, not simply a model or set of models. Importantly, the board of directors and senior management have certain responsibilities in developing, implementing and overseeing the ICAAP. They should ensure that proper controls exist around and within the ICAAP. The board or its appropriately delegated agent should approve the ICAAP and its components, review them on a regular basis and approve any revisions. On top of that, the board or its delegated agent should determine that, consistent with broad safety and soundness expectations, the bank's capital adequacy assessment takes into account material risks and the level of capital is appropriate for its risk profile, business environment and strategic direction.

Management is responsible for ensuring that the ICAAP is fully consistent with the overall risk management framework of the bank, including a process to identify and discuss current and emerging risks across business lines as well as risk management, finance and other control functions. One aspect often overlooked is that the ICAAP should also be fully supported by comprehensive and clearly written policies and procedures that adequately describe the ICAAP process, document lines of responsibility and authority, and detail a formal review process for continually ensuring that the ICAAP is functioning effectively and as intended. Management reports should be developed for monitoring the effectiveness of the ICAAP.

Validation in the context of an ICAAP should encompass both the overall process for assessing capital adequacy and the individual components within the ICAAP (eg, risk parameters and other types of input). In validating the ICAAP, institutions should ensure that validation is objective, and that validation provides a description of the overall process, lists the responsibilities of various committees/individuals involved, demonstrates that all aspects of the process are properly documented and analyses ICAAP output. When significant issues are identified, management should ensure that the impact of the issues on the results of the ICAAP is well understood and addressed in a timely manner. Additionally, each model or process that feeds into the ICAAP should be subject to proper validation, regardless of whether the model or process is developed internally or provided by a third party. Validation at these lower levels is essential so that firms can identify the potential vulnerabilities in their ICAAP.

SOME KEY CHALLENGES IN DEVELOPING A SOUND ICAAP

As noted, Federal Reserve supervisors have considerable experience in evaluating internal processes to assess capital adequacy. In conducting those assessments, supervisors have identified some areas that pose particular challenges for banking organisations as they try to assess capital adequacy – challenges that most institutions will face in trying to meet US Pillar II expectations. One area mentioned above relates to risk infrastructure or "building blocks" for capital attributions. Credible inputs, such as probabilities of default or market values, are vital. Unfortunately, the shortage of quality data can often be a problem, particularly if an institution is trying to estimate the impact on capital adequacy during stress events when, arguably, capital is most needed. Institutions may also have recently introduced new products with a limited history. Another related challenge is the ability to ensure appropriateness of techniques or models to produce capital attributions. For example, given the difficulty in estimating capital needs for certain exposures and risks, practitioners sometimes "borrow" techniques from other risk areas. This practice is not inherently flawed, but should be done with considerable care. For example, using a model to measure retail credit risk that was originally developed for wholesale credit risk can present problems, because risk associated with exposures in those two areas may behave quite differently. Similarly, utilising a data series that may not be appropriate for the assessment or quantification of risk may also lead to incorrect assessments of capital adequacy.

In a broad sense, institutions may realise that proper validation is a considerable challenge that requires substantial time and resources. As noted above, validation should include underlying risk models, data sources, risk parameters that feed into the capital attribution process, the processes for attributing capital, and ICAAP output. Validation should highlight that institutions need to be very aware of limitations in models and other quantitative tools because of their inherent assumptions and biases, particularly when data is scarce or of poor quality. In some cases, proper validation of quantitative estimates may indicate that banking organisations need to rely on more qualitative estimates. In these cases, banks should be aware that those qualitative estimates have their own biases and assumptions. Stress-testing exercises can be a useful complement to an institution's more formal approach to assessing risk and estimating capital attributions, by gauging the consequences of outcomes that are less likely but of high severity. These exercises should include sensitivity analysis at underlying levels of the ICAAP (where risk inputs are estimated), as well as broader scenario analyses to see the range of potential overall capital needs. In general, institutions should be very mindful of the unavoidable uncertainty embedded in capital attribution estimates and understand that greater uncertainty in estimates should normally lead to higher capital needs.

One of the areas presenting a significant challenge for banks is estimating dependencies within and across risk types. Many institutions assume that their business lines are "naturally diversified" but may not have necessarily explored that assumption in detail. For one, they may not have an extended data series that includes periods of stress to see how individual portfolios, business lines and risk types behave in various environments. Dependencies among credit risk exposures, which can result in credit risk concentrations, are one area clearly identified by the Basel framework as needing attention in Pillar II, since they are not addressed in Pillar I and have the potential to dramatically affect the distribution of losses, especially during economic downturns or periods of financial stress. Institutions should treat the potential for credit concentrations with great care, and understand that, even though credit concentrations may not manifest themselves in one period (such as concentrations of counterparty credit risk), they may arise during subsequent periods.

Aggregation across risk types also presents certain challenges, perhaps even greater than aggregation within risk types. Choices about aggregation and diversification can have a very material impact on the overall assessment of capital needs. For example, institutions should consider the various interdependencies among risk types, the different techniques used to identify such interdependencies, and the channels through which those interdependencies might arise. It is evident that high-quality data about risk dependencies is not always in adequate supply, and that cross-risk concentrations may remain latent and unrecognised, particularly in good times. The relationship among risk types and the potential for seemingly unrelated business lines to realise losses at the same time is still a relatively new field of study. Accordingly, banking institutions should understand the limitations of their quantitative estimates and not necessarily believe that those estimates fully capture all potential outcomes. In general, banks should consider a wide range of possible adverse outcomes that have the potential to affect multiple risks at the same time and have the potential to limit assumed diversification benefits among risk types.

Banking institutions may not always consider the full potential of all risk types to have an impact on capital adequacy, particularly when, for certain risk types, direct capital attributions are difficult or not applicable. For example, a bank involved in securitisation activities should consider the capital adequacy implications of relying on market liquidity to distribute warehoused assets, including the potential for unexpected onboarding of assets to create pressures on capital ratios even if the level of capital remains stable. During times of financial turbulence, an institution may experience pressures in a number of areas of its balance sheet simultaneously, possibly impairing its capital adequacy. In short, institutions should not just focus on whether capital is a good mitigant for certain risks. They also need to understand more broadly how all risks can affect capital adequacy.

Another area in which institutions can face challenges is in developing a robust capital plan that is tied directly to estimates of risk-sensitive capital needs. That is, institutions should understand the connection between "capital demand" (the capital prescribed by the risk profile) and "capital supply" (the capital actually held by the institution). Capital demand and capital supply may not always be viewed together by banking institutions, meaning that those institutions are not truly analysing their capital adequacy in a risk-sensitive fashion. Such analysis is necessary and should include the time period over which the institution is assessing capital adequacy, as well as the expected solvency standard, credit rating, or loss coverage ratio established by the board and senior management. Even if an institution does analyse capital demand and capital supply together, it should monitor that relationship and run exercises to assess the impact of adverse outcomes. For example, it should evaluate whether all supposed capital resources have the same ability to absorb loss, particularly during stressful periods.

The chart in Figure 2.2 is a very simple illustration of the potential impact of stressful situations on capital demand and capital supply and the resulting effect on overall capital adequacy. The initial assumptions include diversification benefits in overall risk capital (affecting capital demand), as

Figure 2.2 Comparing capital demand and capital supply

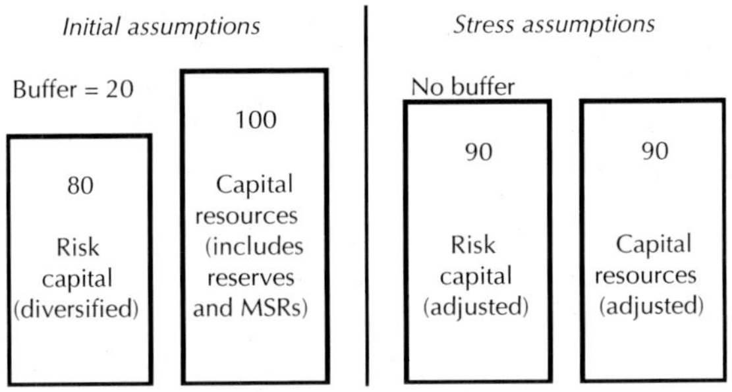

well as the ability to draw on many types of capital resources (affecting capital supply). Under stress situations, assumed diversification benefits may be considerably lower than expected, thereby increasing capital demand, and certain capital resources may not have a full capacity to absorb unexpected loss – such as reserves or mortgage servicing rights (MSRs) – thereby decreasing capital supply. As a result, the assumed capital "buffer" may erode just when the institution finds itself needing to rely on its capital base.

CONCLUDING THOUGHTS

The Federal Reserve, along with the other US banking agencies, understands the importance of Pillar II in the Basel II framework and will work to ensure that banks develop sound ICAAPs. Fortunately, many large, complex banking institutions in the US are already familiar with Pillar II-type reviews conducted by US supervisors. For the proper implementation of Pillar II in the US, supervisors will focus on the full ICAAP and its results, and how the different pieces of the ICAAP interrelate. US supervisors will also ensure that banking institutions know that the ICAAP is a distinct and comprehensive process that produces its own assessment of capital adequacy with respect to all risks, particularly those not covered or fully addressed in Pillar I. There are a number of challenges associated with developing a credible ICAAP of which bankers should be keenly aware, such as proper risk identification and measurement, aggregation and validation. Proper governance and oversight, senior management involvement, and use of information from the ICAAP process in day-to-day business and strategic decisions are tangible evidence that the ICAAP is an important tool that has relevance to senior management and is not simply done as a compliance mechanism. Finally, it is very important to remember that, while capital is needed to support risk taking and ensure solvency of a banking institution, it is not a replacement for sound risk management. Strong capital levels and good risk management are both integral to safety and soundness of banking institutions.

1 We would like to thank Jeff Samuel, Doug Mandel, Steven Fay, Karen Schneck and Sabeth Siddique for their valuable comments and contributions. Any errors are those of the authors.
2 The views expressed here are those of the authors and not of the Federal Reserve Bank of Boston, the Federal Reserve Board, or the Federal Reserve System.
3 For purposes of this chapter, we use "bank", "institution" and "banking organisation" interchangeably.
4 In this example, liquidity risk is defined in the context of market liquidity risk defined as: the potential for a bank to encounter market constraints in its effort to convert assets into cash, or to access financial market sources of funds. Of course, banks also face liquidity risk as it relates to their ability to match sources and uses of funds and that should be taken into account in capital adequacy assessments as well.
5 Other techniques include RAROC, EVA, etc.
6 Indeed, if an institution meets the expectations for ICAAP, it is generally expected that it would meet SR 99–18 expectations. Although SR99–18 and ICAAP are similar, the latter has higher expectations in some areas and is embedded in US regulation.
7 Section III. B. 1 of preamble to US Basel II final rule, page 69303.
8 Appendix E to Federal Reserve's Regulation Y (12 CFR 225).
9 Section 22(a)(1) of the Basel II final rule, page 69407.
10 The US agencies have issued supervisory guidance on US Pillar II, including supervisory standards for what should be included in an ICAAP (see http://www.federalreserve.gov/newsevents/press/bcreg/20080715a.htm).
11 The US agencies also note that supervisory review under Basel II includes compliance with Pillar I requirements; while that is an important aspect of supervisory review, the main focus of this chapter is on the ICAAP portion of US Pillar II implementation.
12 Notably, the US agencies are taking a somewhat different approach to Pillar II from those of some other countries, in that the agencies do not plan to take an institution's Pillar I measures and "add on" additional charges under Pillar II for risks not covered or appropriately addressed in Pillar I. Instead, the US agencies are asking banking organisations to develop an entire process (the ICAAP) under Pillar II that addresses all material risks and then the agencies will review the level of capital that process produces. The ICAAP, where appropriate, may draw upon work the institution has conducted to meet Pillar I requirements (for example, the advanced measurement approaches (AMAs) for operational risk or the rating system used in the internal ratings-based (IRB) approach).

REFERENCES

Federal Reserve, 1999, "Assessing Capital Adequacy in Relation to Risk at Large Banking Organisations and Others with Complex Risk Profiles", Supervision and Regulation Letter 99–18 (SR99–18). URL: http://www.federalreserve.gov/boarddocs/srletters/1999/SR9918.htm

Federal Reserve, "Bank Holding Companies and Change in Bank Control (Regulation Y)", Title 12 U.S. Code of Federal Regulations, part 225, URL: http://ecfr.gpoaccess.gov/cgi/t/

text/text-idx?c=ecfr&sid=635f26c4af3e2fe4327fd25ef4cb5638&tpl=/ecfrbrowse/Title12/12cfr225_main_02.tpl.

OCC, Federal Reserve, FDIC, OTS, 2007, "Risk-Based Capital Standards: Advanced Capital Adequacy Framework — Basel II; Final Rule", Federal Register/Vol. 72, No. 235/Friday, December 7/Rules and Regulations, URL: http://edocket.access.gpo.gov/2007/pdf/07–5729.pdf.

3

The International Coordination of the Supervisory Activity under Pillar II

Andrea Enria, Cécile Meys and Oleg Shmeljov

Committee of European Banking Supervisors[1]

The implementation of the Basel II framework in the European Union has been one of the main challenges for both bankers and supervisors. With the Capital Requirements Directive (EU/2006/48) (CRD), which has transposed Basel II into community legislation, supervisory requirements have moved towards a growing reliance on the internal measures and safeguards developed by the banks themselves for controlling risks, thus providing a more risk-sensitive framework. The new capital-adequacy framework is expected to evolve with industry practices; it provides incentives for improving, refining and innovating in risk management. At the same time it is a window of opportunity for the Committee of European Banking Supervisors (CEBS) to promote convergence in supervisory practices.

The first priority both for bankers and supervisors lately was getting the Pillar I models for credit and operational risk up and running and approved by supervisors. The CEBS was supporting these efforts by working on common guidelines for the implementation of the CRD.

Now that supervisors are in the process of completing the regulatory approvals of advanced Pillar I models, both bankers and supervisors are turning their attention to other components of the new regulatory framework, in particular the requirements set under Pillar II.

The current market turmoil underlines the importance of Pillar II both from the institutional and supervisory points of view, and calls for scrutiny of banks' internal risk management processes and supervisory review processes.

The aim of this chapter is to introduce the cross-border perspective of the implementation of Pillar II. The requirements mentioned in the CRD for Pillar II leave room for divergences in the supervisory practices, which pose challenges for the supervision of cross-border banking groups. Close cooperation and coordination between home and host supervisory authorities is therefore essential.

First a brief overview of the European supervisory framework will be given, highlighting the role and work of the CEBS with respect to Pillar II and cross-border supervisory cooperation. Then we turn to broader aspects of home–host supervisory cooperation, including the work undertaken by the CEBS to foster convergence of supervisory practices through supporting the framework of colleges of supervisors for cross-border banking groups. Finally, we deal with some practical tools for achieving convergence at the EU level: joint examinations, delegation of tasks, peer review and mediation.

EU SUPERVISORY FRAMEWORK AND ROLE OF THE CEBS

The European banking sector is increasingly integrated. The adoption of the single currency in most Member States has led to the amalgamation of payment infrastructures and to a common framework for accessing central bank liquidity, thus affecting the scope for systemic risk. The wave of consolidation driven by mergers and acquisitions has increased the concentration of cross-border business, where 46 banking groups with significant cross-border business account for two-thirds of the EU banking market and the 17 truly pan-European players for more than one-third. The integrated banking sector calls for a shift in the supervisory paradigm. Approaches based on diverse national legislative and administrative tools and preserving longstanding supervisory traditions will no longer cope with an integrated market. Without close cooperation and exchanges of information between the supervisory authorities responsible for the various components of a cross-border group, the effectiveness of supervision would be impaired. Likewise, differences in the requirements and the supervisory processes stemming from the same EU-wide rules would generate inefficiencies, unduly inflating the compliance costs for cross-border players.

Community legislation generally provides *de minimis* criteria, but Pillar II is only briefly mentioned in both international (Basel II) and European (CRD) regulatory frameworks, leaving room for flexibility in interpretations and implementation.[2] Therefore the risk of divergence in national approaches is very high and calls for a major effort of supervisors in the EU.

To address the changes in the banking landscape and find ways for better regulation, EU institutions set up in 2000 the Committee of Wise Men on the

Regulation of European Securities Markets, chaired by Alexandre Lamfalussy. In its final report, the Committee of Wise Men called for the establishment of a new regulatory framework to make the regulatory process for securities legislation more flexible, effective and transparent. The so-called Lamfalussy approach was established in 2001, then extended to other financial services sectors in 2003. The CEBS is part of the Lamfalussy framework together with its sister committees CESR in the securities markets and CEIOPS in the insurance and occupational pension sectors.

CEBS brings together all the banking supervisory authorities and central banks of the 27 EU countries, including the European Central Bank. Supervisors from the European Economic Area (EEA) sit in the CEBS as observers.

CEBS is formally charged with promoting convergence of banking supervisory practices and supervisory cooperation in Europe. The role of the CEBS is threefold:

- advise the Commission as regards the preparation of drafts implementing measures in the field of banking activities; this can be done either at the Commission's request (within a time limit set by the Commission according to the urgency of the matter) or on the CEBS's own initiative;
- contribute to the consistent implementation of Community Directives and to the convergence of Member States' supervisory practices throughout the Community; and
- enhance supervisory cooperation, including the exchange of information.

During the first years of activity, the main priority for the CEBS has been to develop common guidelines related to the implementation of the CRD. The overall framework for supervisory convergence and cooperation in CRD-related matters has been completed and is now compiled in a comprehensive guidebook published on CEBS's website.[3] Now that the policy framework is in place, the focus of the CEBS is gradually shifting to monitoring the progress achieved and making sure that convergence is effectively achieved in day-to-day supervisory practices. Particular attention is being devoted to the supervision of cross-border banking groups, without neglecting the level playing field for smaller locally operating banks.

CEBS's objective is not to create additional levels of regulation but rather to reflect the common understanding of supervisors. The current priorities include Pillar II issues and enhancing the functioning of colleges of supervisors.

CEBS SUPERVISORY GUIDELINES REGARDING CROSS-BORDER ISSUES AND PILLAR II

EU supervisors observe large and complex cross-border banking groups increasingly centralising key functions, in particular in the area of risk management, while at the same time retaining presence in existing host markets through local subsidiaries. As a result, misalignments emerge between legal structures of the groups, on the basis of which supervisory competences are allocated, and operational structures through which risks are measured and managed. These trends emphasise the importance of effective coordination and cooperation of the authorities in planning and conducting of their supervisory tasks, as well as agreeing on a joint and coordinated approach to the supervisory review process under Pillar II.

To foster convergence, enhance the cooperation between EU supervisors and promote a coordinated approach to the supervisory review and evaluation process (SREP), the CEBS has developed a set of guidelines. For the purposes of this chapter we will concentrate on the CEBS guidelines and other publications directly related to the cross-border implication of Pillar II and the SREP in particular.

CEBS guidelines on Pillar II

The underlying aim of the Pillar II processes is to enhance the link between an institution's risk profile, its risk management and risk mitigation systems, and its capital. Institutions should themselves develop sound risk management processes that adequately identify, measure, aggregate and monitor their risks. Institutions are expected to have an adequate assessment process that encompasses all the key elements of capital planning and management and generates an adequate amount of capital to set against those risks (internal capital-adequacy assessment process – ICAAP). The ICAAP is the institutions' internal responsibility and process. The task of supervisors is to review and evaluate (under the framework of the SREP) the ICAAP and the soundness of the internal governance processes within which it is used.

The cornerstone of the supervisory review process is a structured dialogue between institutions and supervisors (so-called ICAAP–SREP dialogue). In its "Guidelines on the Application of the Supervisory Review Process under Pillar II" (hereinafter Pillar II Guidelines), published in January 2006, the CEBS presented a common understanding between EU supervisors on how this dialogue should be conducted and clarified the supervisory expectations for the process (including on internal governance standards).

When developing its Pillar II Guidelines, the CEBS has been in close dialogue with the industry, through public consultations, hearings and dialogue with dedicated structures of the CEBS's Consultative Panel. Industry representatives stressed that Pillar II should remain in the ownership of the banks and advised the CEBS against issuing specific requirements in this area. Concerns were raised also with reference to an excessively burdensome process for smaller banks, stressing the importance of applying the principle of proportionality. Finally, banks stressed that the possible application of additional capital requirements should not give rise to an interpretation of Pillar II as a process for defining automatic capital add-ons.

CEBS has addressed these concerns to a large extent. The Pillar II Guidelines point out that the ICAAP is the responsibility of the bank, but stress that the supervisors should form a view of the internal governance of the process and of the adequacy of capital *vis-à-vis* the risks taken by the bank in the SREP and challenge the banks' assessment in the ICAAP–SREP dialogue. With respect to proportionality, it is duly stated that the intensity and depth of the ICAAP–SREP dialogue should be proportionate to the nature, scale, complexity and systemic importance of the institution. For example, a small noncomplex institution would not be expected to have a sophisticated ICAAP, and its supervisor should not necessarily subject it to an intense and comprehensive dialogue. Finally, the Pillar II Guidelines state that capital is one among several instruments supervisors can activate to correct shortcomings identified in the Pillar II process.

Main Pillar II components

The Pillar II Guidelines cover five major components of Pillar II.

1. Supervisory review process, which is aimed at ensuring that institutions have sufficient capital to support all material risks to which their business exposes them. It should therefore reinforce the link between risk and capital, so that the institution's risk management strategy, approaches and systems are integrated with its capital planning.
2. Internal governance, which aims at ensuring that an institution's management body (including the supervisory function) is explicitly and transparently responsible for its business strategy, organisation and internal control.
3. ICAAP, which being a part of the institution's internal governance framework aims at ensuring that both supervisory and management

functions (a) adequately identify, measure, aggregate and monitor the institution's risks; (b) hold adequate internal capital in relation to the institution's risk profile; (c) use sound risk management systems and develop them further.

4. SREP,[4] aiming at the evaluation by supervisors of ICAAP, including the adequacy of capital held by an institution. The supervisory authority must review the institution's exposure to all material risks (its risk profile), the adequacy and reliability of its internal governance and ICAAP, the adequacy of its own funds and the internal capital mitigants it has set against its risks. The supervisor must also assess whether capital is the correct means of addressing the institution's vulnerabilities.
5. RAS (risk-assessment system), which is the supervisor's tool for organising (planning, prioritising and allocating) the use of supervisory resources, and performing and managing the supervisory risk assessment. It provides structure and a practical step-by-step guide to the first phase of the SREP.

SREP and ICAAP dialogue

The SREP should be structured with a view to ensuring consistency of treatment across institutions, keeping in mind that institutions differ in risk profile, strategy and management. Supervisors should have arrangements in place for the collection and verification of relevant information. Supervisors should also have procedures in place to maintain the quality and consistency of risk assessments. An essential element of the SREP (and of the RAS) is the ability to assess qualitatively each type of risk and its management, within the overall context of the institution's internal governance. Panel 3.1 includes the high-level principles of SREP as laid down in the CEBS Pillar II Guidelines.

As for the ICAAP, it is the responsibility of the institution to define and develop its ICAAP. During the dialogue with its supervisor the institutions will be expected to demonstrate that its internal capital assessment is comprehensive and adequate to the nature of risks posed by its business activities and its operating environment. Thus, the principles applied to ICAAP–SREP dialogue are of the utmost importance. The CEBS's understanding of the dialogue under the supervisory review process is represented in Figure 3.1.

The banking groups will be required to submit ICAAP-related information (ICAAP submission or reports) both to the home (group ICAAP report)

PANEL 3.1 THE CEBS'S GUIDELINES ON SREP

SREP 1: The SREP should be an integrated part of the authority's overall risk-based approach to supervision.

SREP 2: The SREP should apply to all authorised institutions.

SREP 3: The SREP should cover all the activities of an institution.

SREP 4: The SREP should cover all material risks and internal governance.

SREP 5: The SREP will assess and review the institution's ICAAP.

SREP 6: The SREP will assess and review the institution's compliance with the requirements laid down in the CRD.

SREP 7: The SREP should identify existing or potential problems and key risks faced by the institution and deficiencies in its control and risk management frameworks; and it should assess the degree of reliance that can be placed on the outputs of the institution's ICAAP.

SREP 8: The SREP will inform supervisors about the need to apply prudential measures.

SREP 9: The results of the SREP will be communicated to the institution at the appropriate level (usually the management body) together with any action that is required of the institution and any significant action planned by the supervisory authority.

SREP 10: The supervisory evaluation should be formally reviewed at least on an annual basis, to ensure that it is up to date and remains accurate.

and the host's supervisors (subsidiaries ICAAP reports), and will be subject to multilevel ICAAP–SREP dialogues.

To tackle the issue of cross-border complexity, the CEBS is working on fostering convergence of supervisory practices and outcomes (supervisory response) in the EU (see "Home–host supervisory cooperation and colleges of supervisors" further on).

Transposition of the CEBS Pillar II guidelines into national regulations

Establishing common EU guidelines is only the first step to coordination of supervisory approaches. The guidelines provide a ground for supervisory convergence, when implemented in the national environment.

An internal research performed by the CEBS indicates that all the CEBS members have transposed the CEBS guidelines on Pillar II into their national

Figure 3.1 ICAAP–SREP dialogue under supervisory review process[5]

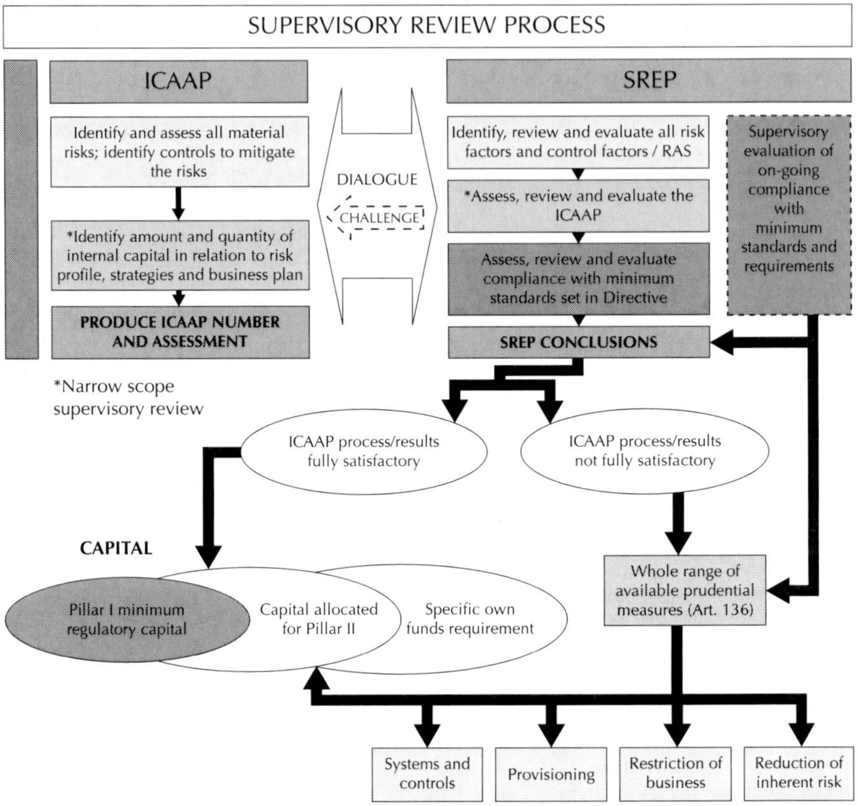

regulations. The form of transposition varies per country: some countries have incorporated the CEBS guidelines into their national legislation (legal texts); however, most of the countries have issued national guidelines (mostly not legally binding) on Pillar II, building on the provisions mentioned in the CEBS guidelines. Many EU supervisors have also incorporated the SREP section of the guidelines into their internal handbooks and manuals.

As regards the guidelines for market participants, all EU supervisors agree that the ICAAP section of the supervisory review process is the full responsibility of banks. It is commonly accepted that given the overall objective of the ICAAP – to assess internally one's own capital adequacy – it is the banks' full responsibility to define and implement most appropriate processes and methodologies for the ICAAP. However, most of the EU supervisors have provided banks operating in their jurisdictions with indications of their (supervisory) expectations, aiming at ensuring that all aspects deemed to be relevant are covered by the ICAAP, and subsequently enabling comparability of the ICAAP submissions across institutions. Almost all EU supervisors have issued national ICAAP guidelines. A few countries issued specific ICAAP guidelines for smaller institutions, but also those who do not distinguish between small and large institutions in their guidelines have applied the principle of proportionality to treat smaller institutions differently.

Home–Host cooperation guidelines

In January 2006 the CEBS published the "Guidelines for cooperation between home supervisor and host supervisors" (hereinafter "Home–Host Guidelines"), which set an enhanced framework for cooperation and exchange of information between home and host supervisory authorities. The Home–Host Guidelines are the starting point for substantial developments in the supervision of cross-border groups.

In the Home–Host Guidelines the CEBS has tackled the practicalities for assessing the significance of an entity within a banking group entity, by providing specific criteria and procedures that allow to graduate the intensity of cooperation and the exchange of information with the different competent authorities involved. The Home–Host Guidelines also provide a broad framework for organising cross-border cooperation and exchange of information with clear examples of the types of information that could be exchanged, differentiating between subsidiary and branch structures.

The Home–Host Guidelines intend to provide a practical reference point for supervisors and also contain practical examples to structure the cooperation process for a general SREP and for the validation of advanced models for credit and operational risk. Typical processes are defined, dividing them into standard steps, and then, for each step, the respective roles of home and host authorities are sketched, by identifying actions that should be undertaken by each party, two-way information flows and possible consideration for the delegation of tasks between home and host authorities.

Following the principles laid down in the Home–Host Guidelines, European banking supervisors have developed and put into practice group-specific arrangements for cooperation and information sharing between home and host supervisors. The need for further sharpening home–host cooperation processes and for coordinating supervisory processes and actions has called for establishment of new and closer forms of cooperation within the so-called colleges of supervisors (see "Home–host supervisory cooperation and colleges of supervisors" further on).

Supervisory disclosure framework and Pillar II

The overarching nature and light degree of regulation of Pillar II, as well as the principles-based nature of the CEBS's guidelines, leave some room for interpretation for both banks and supervisors. An additional tool to drive towards convergence of supervisory approaches is an enhanced transparency of supervisory practices in the application of the CRD and the CEBS guidelines. In fact, greater transparency could trigger peer and market pressure towards common approaches.

According to Article 144 of the CRD, EU supervisory authorities are required to disclose under the supervisory disclosure framework certain information on the national implementation of the CRD. For our interest, authorities are also required to disclose the general criteria and methodologies used in the SREP.

Supervisory disclosure aims to make information related to prudential supervision available in a timely manner to all interested parties, including credit institutions, investment firms, other market participants, other supervisors, and consumers. The framework for supervisory disclosure is meant only to provide information, not to limit in any way the ability of individual national supervisors to act in a flexible, timely and independent manner.

To support the functioning of the supervisory disclosure principles, the CEBS has created a data repository on its website, where national supervisory authorities feed in information on their regulations and practices.[6] The CEBS website provides an overall compilation of the information across the EU, while more detailed information can be obtained in "clone" websites of national supervisors, linked to the CEBS hub. This is intended to provide easy access to more detailed information and to permit meaningful comparison of the approaches adopted by the supervisory authorities in different Member States.

It should be noted that the supervisory disclosure framework and supporting technological solutions are currently being rolled out and updated. Therefore the data available on the CEBS website is not yet complete and should be considered as work in progress. At the same time, individual disclosures are rather general and may not have sufficient information to understand and compare national approaches to SREP. Once the framework is fully tested, an extension may have to be considered.

SUPERVISORY PRACTICES WITH RESPECT TO PILLAR II

Supervisory convergence could be described as a multi-tiered process, the starting point being regulatory convergence and the end point convergence of supervisory practices and outcome. In the long term, credit institutions with similar profiles (such as risk profiles, business strategies, internal governance and control framework, capital composition, and market position) should receive a broadly similar supervisory response, whatever their domicile within the EU. The first step of convergence can be found in common legislation – this is definitely the case for the EU, where the CRD is transposed into national legislation of its Member States. The second step is a common set of supervisory guidelines, enriching and clarifying the legislation. As mentioned, the CEBS has developed its set of Pillar II guidelines, which are transposed into Members' national supervisory guidelines. The third step in the converging process is developing a common (to the extent possible) approach to the implementation and application of these guidelines.

The cornerstone of the supervisory review process under Pillar II is the dialogue between the credit institution and its supervisor. In most of the cases in the EU this SREP–ICAAP dialogue will be based on periodic ICAAP submission (ICAAP report) from the supervised institutions – or in some cases the external auditor – covering both quantitative and qualitative issues. However, in some countries ICAAP information will be required upon request. Some countries have previously established requirements on reporting on internal control and risk measurement, which could be seen largely as a part of future ICAAP reporting.

The following subsections will address the work done by the CEBS on several issues related to Pillar II raised by an industry platform of cross-border groups.[7]

Level of application of Pillar II

The starting point of Pillar II implementation is the CRD, which sets the scope of application of Pillar II not only at a consolidated level, but also at a solo/sub-consolidated level. All EU member states require ICAAP to be performed by banks operating in their respective countries on a consolidated/sub-consolidated level. In a great number of cases, the ICAAP is required from all individual institutions irrespective of whether they belong to a group or not (including application on consolidated, solo/sub-consolidated level for subsidiaries of EU and third countries' cross-border banking groups). However, quite often waivers for domestic subsidiaries of domestic banking groups are introduced.

In theory, the level of application of SREP and the allocation of responsibilities between home and host authorities should mirror the level of application of ICAAP. Therefore, it is expected that home and host supervisors conduct SREP on group and individual legal-entity levels respectively, and all those assessments (both at consolidated and solo levels) are expected to be fully coordinated.

A consistent approach to SREP does not necessarily mean there is a consistent approach from the institutions' side to ICAAP. CEBS internal research indicated that, in case the solo and consolidated ICAAPs are not consistent, in most cases it would be the responsibility of the home supervisor to achieve consensus within the college of supervisors. However, some supervisory authorities believe that solo and consolidated ICAAP need not be consistent, as each is separately valuable. There is general agreement that in case of inconsistency it would be the responsibility of the institution to explain the reasons behind this.

In order to better exploit supervisory resources and minimise the burden for cross-border banking groups, supervisors are currently exploring two main directions: (i) information flow between home and host supervisors, and (ii) proportionality.

Information flow and division of responsibilities regarding SREP

The information flow and division of responsibilities between home and host authorities is of the utmost importance in order to have effective and efficient cross-border supervision. The CEBS Pillar II Guidelines envisage the following.

- The consolidating (home) supervisor will conduct the SREP for the group as a whole, assess the internal governance and the group ICAAP, have the dialogue with the key staff of the group, and draw conclusions from the SREP. The consolidating supervisor should initiate on a timely basis a process of consultation with the individual supervisors involved and take the lead in establishing cooperative arrangements based on the SREP.
- The host supervisor will perform the SREP at local level in order to assess internal governance and the ICAAP at subsidiary level (sub-consolidated as appropriate). In doing so, the host supervisor will be able to take into account the dimension of the SREP/ICAAP at group level, within the context of the cooperative arrangements.
- The supervisory review will take into consideration the degree of inte-

gration of the banking group and its internal organisation. It is recognised that banking groups may be centralising certain activities such as their risk management functions, and that consequently there may be a need to develop a more integrated and coordinated approach to supervision. In such cases the coordinating role of the consolidating supervisor will be more important, in view of the need to reach a coordinated and efficient supervisory review.

- The cooperative framework should contribute to enhancing the consistency of supervisory assessment throughout the whole group and should make clear which tasks are best carried out respectively by each supervisor. The consolidating supervisor may allocate, where appropriate, some tasks to the host supervisor. The host supervisor may also allocate some tasks to the consolidating supervisor or even delegate full supervision over subsidiaries in accordance with Article 131 of the CRD. The consolidating supervisor will take due account of the local SREP in the evaluation of the whole group.

For efficient and smooth cross-border cooperation in the supervisory review process, authorities should exchange information and assessments. This is vital both for the coordination of activities and for reducing the supervisory burden on institutions, but it also allows supervisors to see the big picture of risks and controls in the institutions.

The common practice in the EU is for home supervisors to share Pillar-II-related information with relevant host supervisors directly and/or upon request.

Information flows from the home to the host supervisors are very important, especially if the subsidiary's ICAAP is based on the parent's ICAAP. From the host supervisor's perspective it is essential to know how local specificities have been taken into account by the group ICAAP. To the extent that the ICAAPs in subsidiaries rely upon central/group-wide processes, the home supervisors are expected, as in case of Pillar I advanced methods' validations, to provide assurance to the host supervisors that the central processes are sound and robust. This assurance would allow the host supervisor to rely upon the assessment done by the home supervisor, thus preventing a duplication of supervisory work and reducing supervisory burden for institutions.

However, no matter how well ICAAP and SREP processes are coordinated inside the cross-border banking group and between home and host authorities, there still may be inconsistencies and divergences. The predominant approach is to solve any divergences on a case-by-case basis and colleges of supervisors are a good platform for that.

The principle of proportionality

Proportionality is another key element in the application of the supervisory review process in a domestic and cross-border setting. Overall, proportionality is one of the cornerstones of the new Basel II prudential framework. Most of the EU supervisors agree that the application of Pillar II principles and the supervisory approach should be proportionate to the nature, size, systemic significance and risk profile of the institution.

A proportionate approach to the ICAAP and SREP has been adopted in most cases in Europe, reflecting the scale and nature of the institution's activities. In some cases an explicit classification of institutions has been introduced in the national regulations, according to banks' size and/or the methodologies adopted for risk measurement purposes under Pillar I.

In general, institutions with simple operations will not be expected to implement extensive processes (such as development and implementation of sophisticated economic capital models) to meet their ICAAP obligation, and will be subject to a less pervasive and extensive SREP review.

At the same time supervisors will seek to rely on the ICAAP implemented at a group level to the extent possible. This will depend on the scale and nature of the institution's operations as well as the extent to which the group ICAAP adequately addresses the risk and control profile of the institution at local level.

Scope of the ICAAP report requirements

The scope of the ICAAP report requirements differs across countries. Some authorities require compulsory information from all groups, regardless of their size. A small number of authorities require compulsory ICAAP submissions from large institutions and will rely on voluntary information submissions for smaller banks. In those countries where there is a formal requirement to present an ICAAP report, the minimum content of these reports is often defined. The content of ICAAP reports is largely debatable; however, a commonly accepted practice is to include information on at least the following topics: risk identification and capital adequacy; governance structure; systems and controls; risk measurement methodologies; stress testing; definition of internal capital used for covering risks; capital allocation; contingency planning.

Supervisors not requiring institutions to present formal ICAAP reports often base their assessment on the information that banks themselves believe necessary to allow full assessment of their risk profiles and internal capital adequacy.

As a part of its work on operational networks the CEBS is currently working on how to streamline the broad setting for ICAAP requirements.

Timing of ICAAP submissions

The timing of ICAAP submissions is another crucial aspect with respect to the ICAAP reports, especially for banks operating in a cross-border context. The majority of EU supervisors plan to assess ICAAPs with annual frequency. Some authorities request additional information on ICAAP on a more frequent basis – quarterly or monthly. In some countries authorities will apply a flexible schedule for ICAAP submissions, depending on the risk profile of an institution, and specific parts of the ICAAP report could be submitted only when relevant and significant changes occur. In a few cases the ICAAP submission document is sent upon explicit request of supervisors or when material information has changed and/or onsite examinations are carried out.

The different timing of submitting ICAAP reports poses certain problems for cross-border banking groups, when ICAAP reports covering group and subsidiaries are to be provided to home and host supervisors based on a different time schedule.

Through its work on operational network the CEBS is looking into this issue and encourages its members to work on synchronisation of ICAAP submission schedules. Most colleges of supervisors are currently discussing the possibility of synchronising the timing of their request for the ICAAP submission.

Performing the SREP

As regards the SREP, the common approach can be described only in general terms, since at the current stage of development not all EU supervisors have gained practical experience in ICAAP–SREP dialogues.

Most of the supervisors will use a mixture of on-site and off-site methods for assessing ICAAPs. In their ICAAP assessments authorities will concentrate on qualitative and quantitative factors covering internal governance, risk management and control processes, risk profile, capital planning and capital numbers. However, in some countries the main considerations will be given to documentation, governance system and controls. With respect to the capital aspect of the ICAAP, during the assessments supervisors will compare the generated capital number to the regulatory capital requirements and in some countries the generated capital numbers will be also compared with peer institutions.

At this early stage of the SREP application, the CEBS's involvement in the actual supervisory review and evaluation processes of its member authorities is rather limited. The role of the CEBS is to act as a facilitator for exchanging information and practices, providing a forum where authorities present their practices and discuss with peers, thus contributing to achieving further convergence of supervisory practices and outcome.

HOME–HOST SUPERVISORY COOPERATION AND COLLEGES OF SUPERVISORS

Cooperation between home and host supervisory authorities has been high on the CEBS agenda since its establishment, and remains one of its top priorities for 2008 and beyond. As mentioned, the CEBS has issued guidelines setting out the general framework for home–host cooperation and has then focused its attention on enhancing the cooperation and information exchange among supervisors, through a bottom-up approach. In accordance with its charter, the CEBS developed operational network mechanisms facilitating the exchange of information in normal times and at times of stress, and enhancing day-to-day consistent supervision and enforcement in the single banking market.

The CEBS's efforts centre on the working of colleges of supervisors, which are permanent, although flexible, structures for cooperation and coordination among authorities responsible for, and involved in, the supervision of the different components of cross-border banking groups.

The CEBS is actively working to enhance the role of colleges of supervisors in coordinating supervisory activities and decisions, as well as enhancing information sharing. This work, launched in mid-2006, represents the farthest-reaching cross-border cooperation exercise between European supervisors. The CEBS's contribution focuses on the organisation and working practices of colleges of supervisors and on practical issues arising in the implementation of European Community legislation and of the CEBS guidelines.

The aim of work on colleges of supervisors

The CEBS intends to create a stable connection between colleges of supervisors, providing a multilateral setting for identifying and addressing in a coordinated way concrete supervisory issues throughout the EU.[8] In order to fulfil this task, a specific working group has been established, providing an interface with the colleges of supervisors in charge of supervision of a number of selected cross-border banking groups. The work is conducted following a bottom-up approach to:

- identify issues stemming from the day-to-day implementation of the Community legislation and the CEBS guidelines and in the conduct of supervisory tasks with reference to cross-border groups;
- develop a catalogue of pragmatic supervisory approaches to address the identified issues, which are effective from both the home and the host points of view and which may help in streamlining the supervisory practices, processes and tools and reducing the compliance burden for cross-border groups;
- interact with the industry and other the CEBS working groups by activating the appropriate groups of experts when needed; and
- act as a hub in facilitating and enhancing the functioning of colleges of supervisors and act as a catalyst so that information is exchanged and home–host issues are effectively addressed and coordinated within the colleges of supervisors.

Interaction between the CEBS and industry regarding work on colleges of supervisors

The test phase of the work on colleges of supervisors focused its attention on a narrow sample of 10 cross-border banking groups, identified by taking into consideration criteria such as size, relevance of cross-border business, specific European focus, balance between different nationalities, different types of banking organisation and different organisational structures. The test phase ended in December 2007, and the CEBS has decided to expand the set of banking groups involved in this work to 18 of the largest cross-border banking groups.[9] The work on colleges of supervisors provides an opportunity for the cross-border banks involved to contribute to the development of cross-border supervisory cooperation. A proactive attitude from the banks involved is encouraged, with a view to bringing to the attention of supervisors implementation issues that should be addressed with high priority to favour a smooth conduct of cross-border business throughout the EU market.

As a response to the work performed by the CEBS, the industry established a platform at the beginning of 2007. The Industry Platform on Operational Networks, consists of the same banks represented in the work of the CEBS, and acts as a counterpart and sounding board for the CEBS's work relating to the functioning of colleges of supervisors. The dialogue has resulted in several meetings during 2007 and 2008 with the industry representatives. The industry representatives have also participated in seminars and workshops concerning the functioning of colleges, and more technical issues such as Pillar II. The interactions with the industry have resulted in a fruitful exchange of views on different issues of interest.

An example is the "issues list" that the industry provided to the CEBS. This list highlights various issues relating to cross-border implications relating to the implementation of the Basel II implementation framework, which need further consideration. The concerns mentioned in the "issues list" have been incorporated into the work programme of the CEBS for 2008. They encompass issues relating to Pillars I, II and III of the Basel II framework, which form pressure points for the industry. The issues have been allocated to the respective expert group within the CEBS for further consideration. The main issues in the list relating to Pillar II were described earlier in this chapter.

Objectives and functioning of colleges of supervisors

The CEBS work on enhancing the functioning of colleges has resulted in defining the concept of a college of supervisors as well as summarising its overall objectives.[10]

In a college there are different levels of association of supervisors, depending on their specific situation *vis-à-vis* the banking group. The CEBS has identified two different levels, referred to as (i) the General College and (ii) the Core College.

The General College involves all the relevant authorities and is normally used to share information on a group-wide basis, for the general discussion of the overall supervisory policy and planning, or for projects interesting a large number of authorities, with their frequency to be determined on a case-by-case basis, but normally on an annual basis. The Core College involves a limited number of authorities involved in the supervision of the main activities of the group, aiming at a more structured approach to cooperation.

The college may also involve authorities of systemically relevant branches and supervisors of non-EEA countries. It can also be extended to involve non-banking supervisory authorities (eg, insurance authorities) for banking groups that are financial conglomerates. Any time when it is necessary and appropriate for financial stability and crisis management purposes, central banks and other relevant authorities can be involved in the work of colleges. Therefore, the exact composition of a college will vary depending on the nature of the meeting and the issues to be discussed.

The organisation of a specific college will depend on various factors such as: structure of group, concentration in certain geographic areas, systemic relevance of individual entities, types of operations, services or products of the group, and original agreements among supervisors. The structure and organisation of a college of supervisors will vary depending on the banking structure. Therefore, there is no "blueprint" for the organisation and structure of a particular college of supervisors.

There is, however, a common denominator for the overall objective of a college of supervisors. The CEBS has summarised the overall objectives of a college of supervisors into the following elements.

- Facilitate exchange of information, views and assessments among supervisors in order to allow for a more efficient and effective consolidated and solo supervision and timely action in going concern and emergency situation.
- Enable supervisors to develop a common understanding of the risk profile of the group as the starting point for risk-based supervision at both group and solo levels.
- Achieve coordination of supervisory review and risk assessment, establishing supervisory plans, arrange any division of tasks and joint onsite visits.
- Coordinate major decisions taken by individual authorities as far as possible and practicable, and to strive to reach consensus where appropriate.

The use of colleges of supervisors will increase consistency of supervisory processes and outcomes. Therefore, the college is a good forum to discuss, for example, ongoing cooperation, delegation of tasks and joint inspections, cooperation in the process of joint model validation of IRB and AMA models and in SREP.

Template for written agreements and Pillar II

Building on the practices of supervisory colleges identified through its work, in December 2007 the CEBS published a template for a multilateral cooperation and coordination agreement on the supervision of a banking group (hereinafter "the Template"). According to Article 131 of the CRD, the home authorities and the other competent authorities will have written coordination and cooperation arrangements in place, facilitating and establishing effective supervision. The Template is a common operational document, which aims at fostering consistency across EU banking supervisors, while keeping enough flexibility to be adapted to the specific organisation, circumstances of each college and banking group, and legal frameworks of participating authorities.

The Template is to be used as a model by supervisory authorities when drafting and signing the agreements concerning specific banking groups. In designing the Template, two goals have been borne in mind. On the one hand, the Template has to retain enough flexibility to be adapted to the specific organisation of each college and of the banking group. On the other hand, it should represent a common operational guidance to supervisors, resulting in group-specific written agreements that are consistent across colleges. The Template should be able to narrow the gap between the high-level principles issued by the CEBS so far, and the actual supervisory practices.

It also attempts to address operational aspects of cooperation between home and host authorities in the conduct of the SREP on consolidated and solo/sub-consolidated levels. According to the Template, authorities in the college of supervisors led by the home supervisors are encouraged to agree on coordinating and synchronising, to a degree possible, SREP process, including:

- development of efficient and effective cooperative arrangements;
- risk identification and assessment;
- planning of supervisory actions;
- performance of tasks;
- timing of ICAAP submissions;
- follow-up actions towards the banking group in question and its legal entities; and
- monitoring the progress on achieving the agreed objectives.

The Template also encourages authorities to cooperate within the supervisory college on the ICAAP review, including sharing of available information and synchronisation of the information exchange. The Template envisages that the home supervisor will be responsible for ICAAP–SREP dialogue on the group level, and host authorities on domestic levels. Each authority's review and evaluation of the fulfilment of ICAAP requirements feeds into the overall SREP process. In performing the SREP at local level, the host supervisors should take into account the characteristics of the framework under which the SREP at group level has been developed. The supervisory activities at local level are taken into consideration in the supervisory plan at consolidated level.

For the successful cross-border implementation of Pillar II the CEBS expects local bank management to be adequately involved and empowered to discharge their duties in relation to the ICAAP. However, it is not required from the cross-border banking group to develop standalone quantitative capital models for each foreign subsidiary, provided that the subsidiary's business and risks are taken into account in the group-wide model and assumptions in a prudent and sound way. According to the CEBS's recommendations, the assessment of capital adequacy for each foreign subsidiary of the EU cross-border banking group by host supervisory authorities should not be different from that for local banks, but foreign subsidiaries may place greater reliance on global measurement and management tools in a manner appropriate and consistent with local market characteristics.

TOOLS FOR ENHANCING SUPERVISORY COOPERATION

Joint examinations

Complexity of business structures, models, IT systems, control environments of cross-border banking groups, centralisation of numerous business and support functions and the increased level of sophistication of banks, their business and risk management processes pose new challenges for supervisors.

Cross-border banking groups, like all major international corporations, have access to the pool of technological and human resources from all entities belonging to the group. Our observation is that in practice banks have established competence centres that centrally address issues of importance to the whole group or particular business entity. For example, there are cases where a central modelling unit located in one country (not necessary home country of the banking group) develops a risk measurement model for specific use in the legal entity located in another country. Another example, perhaps even more appropriate, would be the use of group-wide solutions and for all business entities across different jurisdictions.

It is the responsibility of each national supervisor to be sure that all risk management tools used by the bank operating in their countries (including subsidiaries of cross-border banking groups) are valid and adequate for the particular institutions, and take into account all specificities of local market conditions. In case of a group-wide approach and use of a group model on a level of a local entity, it is rather difficult for the host supervisor to assess adequacy of a group-wide model. Usually, host supervisors can assess how the model is implemented locally, but have rather limited possibilities to asses the model itself.

In this case host supervisors can rely on the assessment done by the home supervisor or participate in the process leading to this assessment, that is, participate in joint assessment and examination. If banks use internal pooling of resources, why not use the same approach to their supervision?

Most of the EU supervisory authorities have discovered joint examinations as a form of intensive and fruitful cooperation in the process of validation and approval of advanced models for credit (IRB models) and operational (AMA models) risks of cross-border banking groups.

For the model approval/validation purposes, many authorities have established well-structured joint validation teams supported by written technical agreements (joint approval process plan). A joint model approval agreement describes the division of roles and responsibilities between the home and host supervisors with respect to the model approval of a particular cross-border banking group setting forth provisions for coordination of the application process, completeness check of the application package, offsite and onsite reviews, decision-making process and practicalities related to the communication with the banking group.

In its turn, the CEBS supported the model-approval process by issuing guidelines on the implementation, validation and assessment of advanced measurement approach (AMA) and internal ratings-based (IRB) approach (hereinafter "Guidelines on Validation") and clarifying the home–host model validation related cooperation procedures in the Home–Host Guidelines discussed earlier in this chapter.

From the cross-border cooperation and coordination perspective, the implementation of the CEBS Guidelines on Validation and Home–Host Guidelines, as well as the practical experience from actual joint approval/validation work, provides a valuable impetus for cooperation between authorities. The networks of experts established for conducting joint onsite or offsite analysis, channels for communications and personal contacts are likely to be further enhanced and used for ongoing supervisory review process under Pillar II.

What already proved to be useful should definitely be continued and improved. At the CEBS we agreed that joint examinations will play a key role in supervisory review process under Pillar II.

A pilot cooperation project was launched in 2008 to assess economic capital models in a small sample of cross-border banking groups. The project involves six major pan-European cross-border banking groups, whose economic capital models will be assessed by joint examination teams consisting of home and host supervisors of each group. At the end of each individual examination, joint examination teams will present detailed results and assessments to the home supervisors, which will be consequently shared and discussed within the supervisory college of each banking group. At the end of all individual examinations of the project, a global report containing anonymised and aggregated information will be presented to the CEBS. The aim of this global report is to identify possible supervisory issues calling for further analysis by the CEBS and to provide a valuable input to the CEBS's work on Pillar II issues.

However, under the current legislative framework, joint examinations are confronted with a number of obstacles that need to be addressed if their potential is to be fully exploited. In particular, secrecy laws in some Member States prevent full roll-out of pan-European joint examination teams, as they prevent a full multilateral exchange of information beyond the narrow set of competent authorities directly responsible for entities included in the group. This means that the CEBS cannot establish a single, common team of examiners to run an analytical part of the assessment and allow for peer comparisons and consistency across groups.

Delegation of tasks

Besides joint examinations, a further step is delegation of tasks. Article 131 of the CRD stipulates that "in order to facilitate and establish effective supervision, the competent authority responsible for supervision on a consolidated basis and the other competent authorities shall have written coordination and cooperation in place". Under these arrangements, additional tasks may be entrusted to the competent authority responsible for supervision on a consolidated basis and for procedures for the decision-making process and for cooperation with other competent authorities.

In 2006 the EU Financial Services Committee (FSC) suggested that supervisors should explore the preconditions for the use of delegation of tasks. The CEBS is currently performing work on delegation and is of the view that delegation can take place in a variety of forms. Joint examination is an example of cooperation between supervisors in which no tasks are delegated, but knowledge and skills are being shared. The CEBS also recognises that delegation can be used in two directions: from the home to the host supervisor, and vice versa. Often it is thought of only as a means to delegate tasks to the home authority; however, it may be more efficient and cost-effective to delegate to the host supervisor and thus take advantage of its local knowledge.

The CEBS is looking for a delegation framework that can be applied in a consistent and convergent way, by analysing the current assignment of responsibilities to home and host supervisors and identifying their different tasks, and by assessing any possible obstacles for delegation.

The college of supervisors is a good forum in which supervisors can discuss and agree which tasks will be shared and delegated, as well as the processes involved in the sharing and delegation of tasks. In order to facilitate effective supervision, authorities should discuss which authority is best placed to conduct a task, taking into account issues such as technical skills and local market knowledge. Once the tasks have been identified, delegation arrangements should be put in place.

Peer-review mechanism

The CEBS's view is that the expectations about the desired degree of convergence have changed over time. There has been a shift from the original objective of enhanced consistency in national approaches and a level playing field, to the request of some market participants that the same business be subject to exactly the same supervisory treatment throughout the EU, so that country-neutral arrangements could allow cross-border groups to operate as if they were subject to a single supervisor.

Taking into account the higher expectation towards convergence of supervisory practices and outcome, internal monitoring and "peer pressure" mechanisms play an important role in the work of the CEBS. We see peer review as an important tool to assess the desired degree of convergence.

In October 2007 the CEBS published its "Protocol and Methodology" for a peer-review mechanism and established a review panel. As set out in the rules and related procedures, the review panel is mandated to assess the degree of convergence reached by the CEBS members in the implementation of a given supervisory provision or practice. To do so, the CEBS relies on self-assessments conducted by its members against clear and objective implementation criteria, and independent reviews conducted by the review panel. Consistent with the so-called "comply or explain" approach, should a member not have implemented a given supervisory provision or practice, it will have to explain why.

The credibility and the effectiveness of the mechanism are assured by the independence of the review panel, by a clear and objective methodology, and by the transparency of the process.

The peer-review mechanism is currently being tested in a pilot exercise: the national implementation of the CEBS Guidelines on validation. In the first half of 2008 the Review Panel completed the first part of the exercise (self-assessments done by members), results of which have been published on the CEBS website. The second part – challenging the results of the self-assessments through review by peers – is being done during the second half of 2008.

Mediation

Following the blueprint developed by CESR and as recommended by the ECOFIN Council, the CEBS has also established a mediation mechanism, which aims at helping to solve supervisory disputes among peers as they arise in a cross-border context. The objective is to support the application of the already existing cooperation tools among supervisors such as the CEBS Guidelines on validation and on home–host cooperation. Mediation will prove useful only when all other cooperation mechanisms have been exhausted.

The mediation protocol could be used to settle disputes between the CEBS members concerning cross-border aspects of (a) processes for consultation between the CEBS authorities; (b) processes for exchange of information; (c) processes for a joint agreement or for decision taking among the CEBS authorities; and (d) other potential general cases relating to cooperation between the CEBS authorities.

Up to now the CEBS members were able to solve any emerging issues/potential problems in a spirit of mutual understanding and cooperation, so there was no need to activate a formal mediation procedure. However, and despite the fact that the outcome of the mediation procedures is not legally binding, we believe that this instrument can support the enhancement of day-to-day cooperation between authorities and strengthens supervisory convergence.

1 The views presented in this chapter are the views of authors and do not necessary represent the views of the Committee of European Banking Supervisors or its members.

2 Pillar II issues in the context of the Basel II Capital Accord and EU Directives are discussed in Chapter 1.

3 CEBS guidelines and standards are collated into CEBS Electronic Guidebook, which can be found on the CEBS website: http://www.c-ebs.org/ElectronicGuidebook.htm.

4 Note that SREP and ICAAP are both part of the SRP (Supervisory Review Process). See also Figure 3.1 in this chapter.

5 CEBS Guidelines on the Application of the Supervisory Review Process under Pillar II.

6 See the supervisory-disclosure section of the CEBS website: http://www.c-ebs.org/sd/sdtf/htm.

7 The subsection "Interaction between the CEBS and industry regarding work on colleges of supervisors" further elaborates on the Industry Platform on Operational Networks.

8 According to the current Commission's proposal for the changes of the CRD, colleges of supervisors, which are envisaged for all cross-border banking groups, will be required to agree on certain home–host issues – for instance, capital add-on on subsidiaries and reporting requirements – and CEBS is expected to elaborate guidelines for the operational functioning of colleges.

9 As of September 2008, the following banking groups are involved: Erste Bank, Raiffeisen Zentralbank, Fortis, KBC, Dexia, Commerzbank, Intesa Sanpaolo Group, Deutsche Bank, Banco Santander, BNP Paribas, Crédit Agricole, Unicredit, National Bank of Greece, ING, SEB, Nordea, Société Générale and Royal Bank of Scotland.

10 CEBS published two documents in December 2007 on colleges of supervisors, which can be found on the CEBS website: range-of-practices paper and template for written agreements.

REFERENCES

EU Financial Services Committee Report on Financial Supervision, URL: http://www.minfin.nl/binaries/minfin/assets/pdf/dossiers/financi-le-markten/fsc-report-on-financial-supervision—februari-2006-.pdf (February 23, 2006).

EU Commission White Paper on Financial Services Policy 2005–2010, URL: http://eur-lex.europa.eu/LexUriServ/site/en/com/2005/com2005_0629en01.pdf (December 1, 2005).

EU Commission decision establishing CEBS, URL: http://www.c-ebs.org/documents/CommissionDecision.pdf.

ECOFIN Council, conclusions of May 5, URL: http://www.consilium.europa.eu/ueDocs/cms_Data/docs/pressData/en/ecofin/89449.pdf (May 5, 2005).

CEBS Template for a Multilateral Cooperation and Coordination Agreement, URL: http://www.c-ebs.org/press/documents/CEBS%202007%20177%20rev%202%20(template%20for%20written%20agreements)%20final%202.pdf.

CEBS Mediation Protocol between Banking Supervisors, URL: http://www.c-ebs.org/documents/ProtocolonMediation20070925.pdf.

CEBS Guidelines on the Implementation, Validation and Assessment of Advanced Measurement (AMA) and Internal Ratings Based (IRB) Approaches // CEBS Electronic Guidebook, pp. 107–270, URL: http://www.c-ebs.org/EGB2008_02_29.pdf.

CEBS Guidelines on the Application of the Supervisory Review Process under Pillar II // CEBS Electronic Guidebook, pp. 317–62 URL: http://www.c-ebs.org/EGB2008_02_29.pdf.

CEBS Guidelines on Supervisory Disclosure // CEBS Electronic Guidebook, pp. 30–66, URL: http://www.c-ebs.org/EGB2008_02_29.pdf.

CEBS Guidelines on Guidelines on Supervisory Cooperation for Cross-Border Banking and Investments Firms Groups // CEBS Electronic Guidebook, pp. 67–106, URL: http://www.c-ebs.org/EGB2008_02_29.pdf.

CEBS Contribution to Lamfalussy review, URL: http://www.c-ebs.org/LamReview/documents/CEBSpaperonLamfalussyreview.PDF (2007).

CEBS Charter // CEBS Electronic Guidebook, pp. 17–23, URL: http://www.c-ebs.org/EGB2008_02_29.pdf.

CEBS Annual reports for 2005, 2006 and 2007.

Part 2

The Main Risk Types to be Assessed under Pillar II

4

Concentration Risk in the Credit Portfolio

Andrea Resti

Bocconi University

Portfolio models for measuring credit risk, including value-at-risk (VaR) models, are now a well-known tool, thoroughly presented in most risk management handbooks for practitioners and students. Approaches such as CreditMetrics and Creditrisk+ are well understood and have represented, for at least 10 years, a common ground for professionals in risk measurement and management.

During recent years, rather than focus on making such models even more complex and realistic, one lively stream of research has looked for ways to make them more effective from a computational standpoint, cutting unessential steps and improving our knowledge of the "hard core" of hypotheses and results on which credit portfolio models are based. In this perspective, a fundamental contribution has come from Gordy (2003) where, based on Vasicek (1984), some usual assumptions of credit VaR models were suitably simplified, thereby providing the new ratings-based bank capital requirements in Basel II with a robust, transparent and relatively simple theoretical background.

The same author, being aware of the simplifications introduced to derive his model, subsequently proposed a set of extensions (Gordy 2004), to enable his original scheme to account for some characteristics of real-life portfolios (namely, a "granularity adjustment" through which idiosyncratic risk can be measured). This effort to bridge the gap between the simplified regulatory model and more realistic portfolio models based on more complex approaches (like the above-mentioned CreditMetrics and Creditrisk+) was continued by Martin and Wilde (2002) and Pykhtin (2004), where the original Gordy model was increasingly enhanced to account for the characteristics of real-life credit portfolios, while preserving most of the advantages of the simplified model in terms or rigour and computational efficiency.

Being based on the same conceptual backbone as the regulatory model, such enhancements provide an ideal set of tools to quantify and motivate gaps between regulatory capital and actual economic capital against credit risk, mostly due to concentration risk. However, their statistical and mathematical sophistication may have slowed their understanding by practitioners and bank managers, who are more interested in the practical application of the models than in their mathematical structure.

In this chapter we offer a thorough presentation of the above-mentioned literature, including the Taylor-series approximation proposed in 2004 by Michael Pykhtin. Such a procedure provides a useful tool to bridge (or, at least, to considerably narrow) the gap between Pillar I capital and the more advanced measures used by large, sophisticated banks. That gap is less and less acceptable in the light of Pillar II, where banks are invited to quantify and explain any risk factor that may require a different capital amount from the one suggested by the supervisory formulas in the Basel II Accord.

This chapter is structured as follows. First we review the conceptual and regulatory framework, which introduces the differences between regulatory and economic capital and the provisions of Basel's Pillar II. In the following section, a broad introduction to concentration risk is provided, as well as to the main approaches used to face it. Following this, a sample portfolio is introduced, which will be used as a reference to illustrate the techniques presented in the whole chapter. The following section goes back to the regulatory model used in Pillar I for banks having an internal rating system, showing why it cannot account for concentration risk. We then introduce a set of more realistic models, whereby concentration can be appropriately measured; and then we illustrate how the gap between the bank capital measures generated by the approaches in previous sections can be explained. This also introduces a third, intermediate measure called "calibrated regulatory capital". The following section shows how economic capital can be measured through the approach proposed by Pykhtin (2004), which is both more efficient and more transparent than traditional Monte Carlo simulations. We then present a sensitivity analysis to show how the tools presented in the previous sections may be used to quantify any improvements/deteriorations of concentration risk that would not be captured by regulatory capital alone. This is followed by our conclusions. A few technical issues are covered in the Appendixes.

PUTTING THINGS IN PERSPECTIVE: ECONOMIC CAPITAL, PILLAR II, CONCENTRATION RISK

Notwithstanding the many improvements that occurred with the new Basel II Accord, there are still differences between the capital indicated by the computation rules in Basel's Pillar I and that estimated by financial institutions; accordingly, the Basel II Accord introduced a "Pillar II", where the regulatory capital charge must be integrated and amended to become more similar to the bank's "true" economic capital.[1]

Pillar II requires, among other things, the measurement of concentration risk, that is, of the risk due to the presence, in a bank's credit portfolio, of a number of individual borrowers or groups (including countries and industries) that represent a considerable share of the bank's total exposure. This includes name concentration (when large exposures refer to individual companies or conglomerates) and industry concentrations (when a large portion of the credit portfolio insists on a single industry, area, or – more generally speaking – on a group of companies that depend on the same macroeconomic risk factors).[2]

Concentration risk is a component of credit risk (just like default risk, downgrade risk, counterparty risk on over-the-counter (OTC) products, recovery risk, exposure risk), which, being quantified in an unsatisfactory way under Pillar I, requires a more careful and realistic measurement under Pillar II. It surely does not comprise all risks that are to be tackled in a bank's ICAAP; nevertheless, given the key role played by credit risk among typical banking risks, it should be expected that its assessment will strongly affect the overall "capital consumption" of the whole bank. The concept of concentration risk is further outlined in the next section, where some facts on its management in large international banks are quickly surveyed.

CONCENTRATION RISK IN LARGE INTERNATIONAL BANKS

In late 2006 a group from the Research Task Force of the Basel Committee, including experts from the main supervisors worldwide, released a working paper (Basel Committee on Banking Supervision 2006) on concentration risk. The paper also includes the main results of an informal survey carried out among a number of large international banks, regarding the tools used to account for credit risk concentration. This shows that, generally speaking, banks mainly adopt three types of approach (sometimes jointly).

- Simple measures of name and industry concentration (sometimes associated with exposure limits) are widely used. The most common one is likely to be the Hirschmann–Herfindahl (HH) index, given by the sum of the squares of the portfolio shares associated with individual obligors (or industries); the HH index goes to zero for highly diversified portfolios, while it takes a value of one in case of perfect concentration.

- A less widespread class of tools are portfolio models that compute economic capital on the credit portfolio by removing the simplifying hypotheses used in the supervisory formulas dictated by Pillar I; such models, often purchased from external vendors,[3] are based on a multi-factor representation of systemic risk and include a number of macroeconomic factors (eg, combinations of countries and industries) that goes from seven to 110.
- Even less frequent are pricing algorithms that calibrate the bank's lending rates depending on the concentration risk originated by the single borrowers (that is, rewarding with lower rates the borrowers producing high diversification effects, due to their low correlation with the bank's pre-existing credit portfolio).

The survey produced by the Basel Committee also notes that the quantification of the capital increase, relative to Pillar I requirements, due to concentration risk, remains a challenge even for the most sophisticated banks. In other words, even those banks producing an estimate of economic capital on credit risk by means of a sound portfolio model are still striving to create a link (from both a logical and an algebraic point on view) between that measure and regulatory capital.

A SAMPLE PORTFOLIO

A sample portfolio will be used, throughout this chapter to show how the various models and techniques work in practice. The portfolio includes 1,000 corporate exposures and, while being based on mock data, has been created in such a way that it reasonably mirrors a typical real-life portfolio of bank exposures.

The frequency distribution of PDs looks clustered on low values (Figure 4.1, left), although with a few cases above 10% (customers experiencing a distress, but not yet in default). Expected LGDs (Figure 4.1, right) take the usual bimodal shape, with a large share of exposures for which either a full or a zero recovery is expected.

EADs (Figure 4.2, left) suggest some name concentration, given that most exposures account for less than 0.01% of the total portfolio, while only 25 loans exceed 1%.[4] As we see from the right panel in Figure 4.2, the latter are

Figure 4.1 The distribution of PD (left) and LGD (right) in the sample portfolio

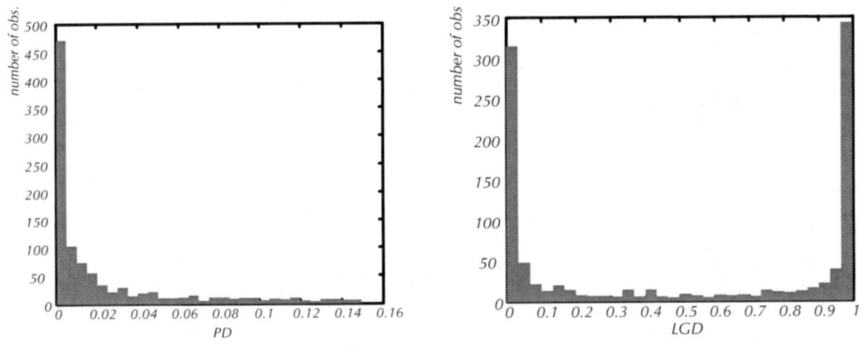

Figure 4.2 Distribution of EAD (left) and the EAD/PD relationship (right)

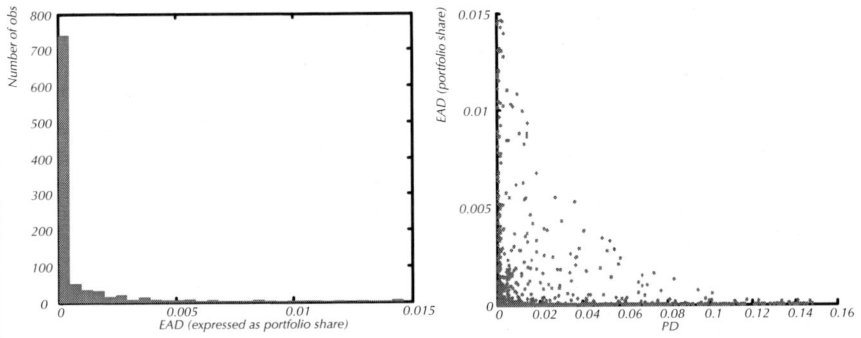

mostly associated with high-rating customers (having an average PD of 0.24%).

REGULATORY CAPITAL ON CREDIT RISK AND ITS LIMITS

The computation of regulatory capital on credit risk is based on different procedures depending on the approach followed by the bank (standardised versus internal ratings-based). In the former case, a simplified algorithm is used, based on the number of risky assets and on a number of risk weights; in the latter case, a formula is used ("supervisory function" or "supervisory formula") derived from Gordy's simplified portfolio model.

We now analyse the supervisory function, first recalling the main hypotheses and implications of the model through which it was derived, then discussing it in a more formal way.[5]

Gordy's model assumes the following:

- Credit risk arises from two different components: idiosyncratic risk, which is specific to each individual borrower and uncorrelated to the other ones; and systemic risk, due to macroeconomic aspects and therefore common to all obligors.
- Systemic risk is represented through a single factor (say, "the economic cycle as a whole") without introducing a set of diversified factors (which could be associated, for example, with different macro variables such as inflation, interest rates, GDP growth, to which individual obligors respond in a different way); the model is therefore called a "single factor" model.
- A borrower's sensitivity to the single systematic factor (their "factor loading") does not depend on their industry or geographic area; in other words, there are no industries or countries that are more vulnerable to economic cycles, but all share the same degree of "cyclicality".
- The credit portfolio of a bank may be reasonably described as including a very high number of very small exposures (that is, as an "infinitely granular" portfolio); in this way, idiosyncratic risk can be ignored, as the specific risks of individual borrowers tend to offset one another asymptotically, and all that matters in the end is systemic risk. For this reason, the model is usually called "asymptotic" (or ASRF, which stands for asymptotic single risk factor).

Under the above-mentioned assumptions, the amount of capital and reserves needed to cover a given (extreme) percentile of the loss distribution (namely, the 99.9th percentile) can be computed with a simple closed-form formula (the supervisory formula), which requires the knowledge only of PD, LGD and EAD (estimated by the bank), as well as of the factor loading (set by the Basel Committee).

We now provide a more formal representation of the model outlined above. Consider a portfolio including M small exposures, where M is a very high number and each exposure represents an equally small portion of the total. The "health" of the i-th obligor is indicated by a stochastic variable x_i. In turn, x_i is a linear combination of a systematic risk factor $\tilde{y}$, and of an idiosyncratic factor, $\tilde{\varsigma}_i$, which is specific of obligor i.[6] Formally

$$\tilde{x}_i = a_i\tilde{y} + \sqrt{1-a_i^2}\tilde{\varsigma}_i \tag{4.1}$$

A possible economic interpretation of Equation 4.1 is that it represents the percentage growth rate of the value of i's corporate assets (asset value return), standardised in such a way that it has zero mean and unit variance.

If the company's assets increase in value, the risk that i will not be able to pay back their loan becomes smaller; if, instead $\tilde{x}_i$, takes strongly negative values, then the asset value could drop below a minimum threshold that triggers i's default ("default threshold", which obviously depends on the obligor's unconditional PD[7], p_i), and a default would occur. More precisely, obligor i defaults if

$$\tilde{x}_i < N^{-1}(p_i) \tag{4.2}$$

where $N^{-1}(.)$ is the inverse of the standard normal cdf (cumulative density function).

From Equation 4.1, it follows that the correlation between the asset value returns of any two obligors i and j (henceforth: the "asset correlation") is[8]

$$\alpha_{i,j} = a_i a_j \tag{4.3}$$

Of course, for two obligors having the same factor loading, that is $a_i = a_j = a$, asset correlation is simply a^2.

If we assume that both risk factors $\tilde{y}$ and $\tilde{\varsigma}_i$ follow a standard normal distribution, then it is easy to show[9] that the PD for i, conditional on given value of the macroeconomic risk factor y, can be computed as

$$p_i|_y = N\left[\frac{N^{-1}(p_i) - a_i y}{\sqrt{1-a_i^2}}\right] \tag{4.4}$$

For an infinitely granular portfolio, including a high number, M, of very small exposures (so that idiosyncratic risk becomes fully diversified), the *ex ante* conditional PD given by Equation 4.4 also represents the actual *ex post* default rate. The value of the loss suffered by the bank[10] following a given value of y can then be computed by multiplying this default rate by the exposure w_i and the loss-given default rate μ_i (that is, by EAD and LGD).[11] Summing across all obligors, we get

$$L^*(y) = \sum_{i=1}^{M} w_i \mu_i p_i|_y = \sum_{i=1}^{M} w_i \mu_i N\left[\frac{N^{-1}(p_i) - a_i y}{\sqrt{1-a_i^2}}\right] \tag{4.5}$$

Note that Equation 4.5 is a strictly decreasing function of y. Hence, if we are interested in the qth percentile $t^q(L^*)$ in the distribution of losses, we simply substitute the generic y with the 1-q^{th} percentile of the distribution of the systemic factor. Since $\tilde{y}$ follows a standard normal distribution, such a percentile is given by $N^{-1}(1-q)$ and the formula for the qth percentile of the losses is

$$t^q(y) = \sum_{i=1}^{M} w_i \mu_i p_i \,|_y = \sum_{i=1}^{M} w_i \mu_i N\left[\frac{N^{-1}(p_i) - a_i N^{-1}(1-q)}{\sqrt{1-a_i^2}}\right] = EL + RC \quad (4.6)$$

Equation 4.6 is the supervisory function used by the computation of regulatory capital under Pillar I – leaving out, for the sake of simplicity, the so-called maturity adjustment.[12] Namely, it gives the overall capital requirement, to be covered through actual shareholders' capital and, as far as expected losses are concerned, with reserves. We therefore have indicated that Equation 4.6 provides the sum of *EL* (expected loss) and *RC* (regulatory capital).

As mentioned above, the values for p_i, μ_i and w_i (that is, PD, LGD and EAD) can be estimated by each bank based on its internal evidence, while the value for a_i was set by the supervisors and depends on a number of borrower characteristics (for example, on the fact that it is a sovereign state, a company with a given turnover and PD, an individual and so on), which, however, do not include the industry and/or geographic area.

For example, for non-financial companies with a total turnover above €50 million, a_i has been defined as the following decreasing function of the borrower's PD, p_i

$$a_i = \sqrt{0,12 \cdot \frac{1-e^{-50 \cdot p_i}}{1-e^{-50}} + 0,24 \cdot \left(1 - \frac{1-e^{-50 \cdot p_i}}{1-e^{-50}}\right)} \quad (4.7)$$

Since a_i is the same for all industries or countries, a bank with a high degree of diversification in its portfolio would be given no incentive, in terms of lower regulatory capital, by the supervisory formula and by Pillar I in general. Similarly, since the model assumes, for the sake of simplicity, that each obligor represents an infinitely small share of the overall portfolio and that idiosyncratic risk is totally diversified, Equation 4.6 does not "discipline" with a larger capital requirement, those banks where risks are concentrated on a small number or large exposures.

Let us now go back to the example data of the previous section. Based on that data, Figure 4.3 shows the factor loadings, a_i, computed through Equation 4.7. The left panel reports the frequency distribution of the loadings, the right one illustrates the relationship between loadings and PDs, as dictated by Equation 4.7.

Using these a_is, the PDs, LGDs and EADs of the sample portfolio and a conventional maturity of one year, Equation 4.6 yields the regulatory capital requirement associated with our sample portfolio. It amounts to 4.19% (RC)

Figure 4.3 Regulatory factor loadings: frequency distribution and relationship with PD

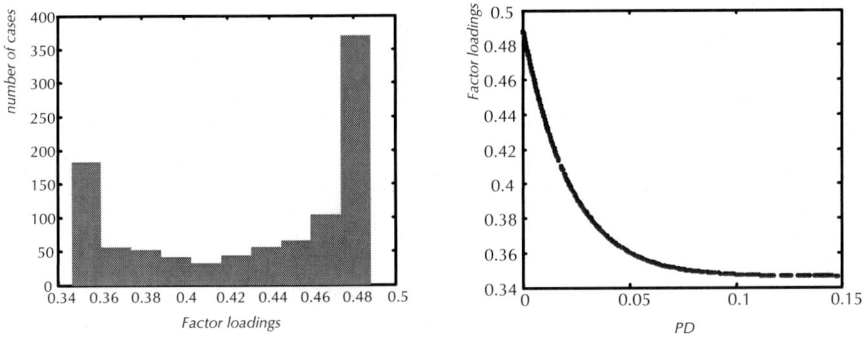

of the portfolio value, plus another 0.36% due to expected losses (EL, that can be covered also through reserves), leading to a total of 4.55%.

A FINITE-GRANULARITY, MULTIFACTOR MODEL

To get a more realistic model for the estimation of the "true" economic capital on a credit portfolio (finite-granularity, multifactor model), the simplifying assumptions used in the previous section must be overcome and we must start from three more realistic hypotheses (see Figure 4.4 for a comparison of the two models):

- the portfolio may include single large exposures, giving rise to an idiosyncratic risk due to the default of individual obligors;
- each obligor faces a different systemic risk, because "semi-specific" risk factors must be accounted for (eg, area- or industry-specific factors), as well as the single risk factor y representing the macroeconomic cycle as a whole; and
- the relevance (now indicated as r_i) of systemic risk could differ, in real-life portfolios, from the factor loadings chosen by the Basel Committee (a_i) and considered appropriate, on average, for any bank in the world.

If these more realistic assumptions are accepted, then the level of capital and reserves that is needed to cover a given, extreme percentile of the loss distribution (eg, the 99.9th percentile) can no more be computed through a closed-form formula (such as the supervisory function). Instead, Monte Carlo simulations must be resorted to, and a number of scenarios generated that is high enough to provide a good empirical approximation for the loss distribution associated with the portfolio.

Such a Monte Carlo approach is followed by some of the most widespread portfolio models used by banks for credit risk, including CreditMetrics, some versions of CreditRisk+ and KMV Portfolio Manager. Those models are computationally heavy; furthermore, it may be difficult to create a link between the economic capital measures generated with those models and the regulatory capital dictated by Pillar I.

In the remainder of this section, we provide a more formal treatment of a finite-granularity, multifactor model; this will help us understand the model's peculiarities and to draw a conceptual "bridge" between it and the supervisory function.[13]

We start by assuming that the asset value return of borrower i is given by

$$\tilde{x}_i = r_i \tilde{y}_i + \sqrt{1 - r_i^2}\,\tilde{\xi}_i \tag{4.8}$$

where $\tilde{\xi}_i$ is an idiosyncratic term and $\tilde{y}_i$ is a risk factor that is systematic but also specific of borrower i. Namely, $\tilde{y}_i$ is the result of N systemic factors,[14] gathered in vector $\tilde{\mathbf{z}}$, that are weighted in a different way for each borrower:[15]

Figure 4.4 The main differences between the ASRF model and a finite-granularity, multifactor model

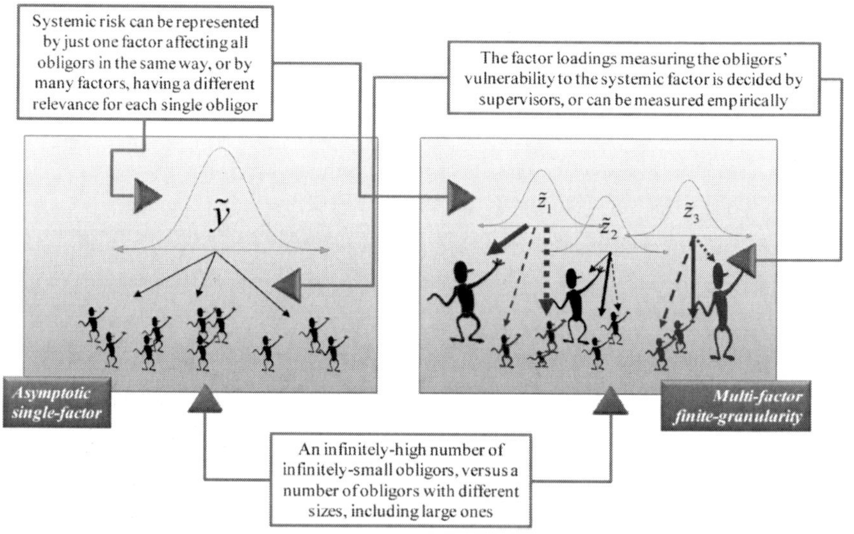

$$\tilde{y}_i = \alpha_{i1}\tilde{z}_1 + \alpha_{i2}\tilde{z}_2 + \ldots + \alpha_{iN}\tilde{z}_N = \boldsymbol{\alpha}_i'\tilde{\mathbf{z}} \tag{4.9}$$

Given Equation 4.8, the asset correlation between any two obligors i and j is

$$\rho_{ij} = r_i r_j \boldsymbol{\alpha}_i' \boldsymbol{\alpha}_j \tag{4.10}$$

which becomes $\rho_{ij} = r_i r_j$ (similar to Equation 4.3) if and only if the two obligors depend exactly on the same combination of systemic risk factors ($\boldsymbol{\alpha}_i = \boldsymbol{\alpha}_j$). Otherwise, we get $\rho_{ij} < r_i r_j$.

For a portfolio including a finite number M of exposures (of any amount), the total loss for the bank, $L(\mathbf{z})$, following a given value of the systemic risk factors $\mathbf{z}$, can be computed by summing the individual losses associated with defaulted borrowers; each of those losses is in turn given by the product between the exposure at default and the loss rate (EAD and LGD); if the portfolio is large enough, we can replace EAD and LGD with their mean values w_i and μ_i,[16] getting

$$L(z) = \sum_{i=1}^{M} w_i \mu_i 1_{\{x_i(z) \leq N^{-1}(p_i)\}} \tag{4.11}$$

where $x_i(\mathbf{z})$ has been defined in Equation 4.8, and $1_{\{\ldots\}}$ represents a binary variable taking a value of 1 if the condition in braces is true (in this case, if the asset value return falls below the default threshold), zero otherwise.

We can now sample from N standard normals a high number of values for $\mathbf{z}$ and then compute, for each one (using Equation 4.11), the associated value for L; in this way, we approximate empirically the desired percentile $t^q(L)$ of the loss distribution. Such a percentile represents the volume of reserves (associated with the expected loss, EL) and economic capital required by the portfolio's credit risk.

Let us now apply this finite-granularity, multifactor model to our sample portfolio. We first need to specify the number and structure of the systemic factors that drive the borrowers' health. For the sake of simplicity, we will use three systemic factors ($N = 3$); to make things more understandable, they can be thought of, for example, as the economic cycle of three different geographic areas (say, US, Europe and Asia); in practice they could be industries, combinations of areas and industries, or any other segmentations based on macroeconomic variables that significantly affect the performance of the obligors.

The pairwise correlation matrix between our systemic factors – that we assume to have already estimated[17] – is the following

$$\mathbf{F} = \begin{bmatrix} 1 & 0.5 & 0.2 \\ 0.5 & 1 & 0.3 \\ 0.2 & 0.3 & 1 \end{bmatrix}$$

Note that, as indicated in Equation 4.9, a given obligor can depend on more than one macroeconomic factor. For example, the first borrower, a US firm mainly serving US customers, depends on the economic cycle in the US, Europe and Asia according to the following loadings

$$\mathbf{h}_1 = \begin{bmatrix} 0.9887 \\ 0.1473 \\ 0.0271 \end{bmatrix}$$

The vectors of loadings $\mathbf{h}_i$ are shown in Figure 4.5: note that the sample portfolio has been constructed in such a way that 33% of the borrowers (including borrower 1) depend mostly on the US economy, another 33% are mainly exposed to Europe and the last 33% are prevalently affected by Asia.

Note that the factors referred to in matrix **F** and vector $\mathbf{h}_1$ are not, yet, the z_k mentioned above. In fact, the latter are orthogonal (ie, have the identity matrix as a variance–covariance matrix). We therefore must transform each vector $\mathbf{h}_i$ into the corresponding

$$\boldsymbol{\alpha}_i = \mathbf{B}\mathbf{h}_i \,/\, \sqrt{\mathbf{h}_i'\mathbf{F}\mathbf{h}_i} \tag{4.12}$$

Figure 4.5 Factor loadings of the 1,000 obligors in the sample portfolio

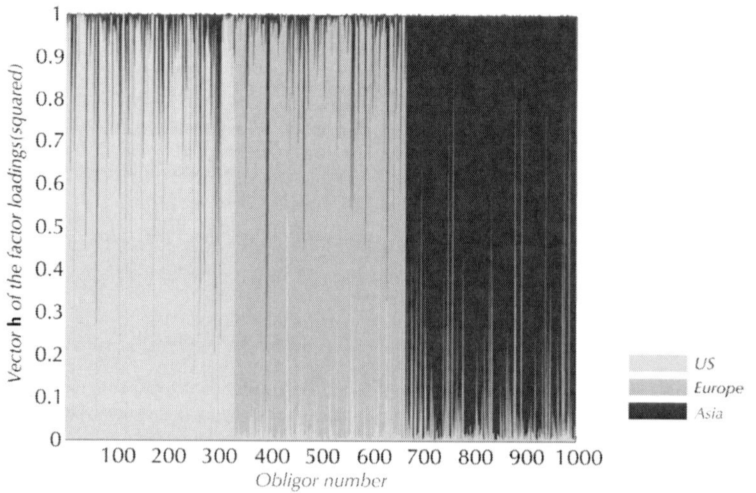

that is, a vector of weights associated with orthogonal factors. In our case we get

$$\mathbf{B} = \begin{bmatrix} 1 & 0.5 & 0.2 \\ 0 & 0.8660 & 0.2309 \\ 0 & 0 & 0.9522 \end{bmatrix}$$

Applying Equation 4.12, we can then, for example, compute the loadings of the first obligor with reference to the orthogonal factors in $\tilde{\mathbf{z}}$

$$\boldsymbol{\alpha}_1 = \begin{bmatrix} 0.9920 \\ 0.1243 \\ 0.0240 \end{bmatrix}$$

and similarly for all other obligors.

The last step in parameterising the model is the specification of the relative weight of systemic and idiosyncratic risk; to do that, for every obligor we must choose a value for r_i in Equation 4.8. Figure 4.6 shows the values used for our portfolio: we chose to use a roughly uniform distribution bounded between 0.4 and 0.8 (see left panel), with values associated randomly to the obligors (see right panel).

Of course, in practice a correct estimation of the r_is represents a critical step in implementing a reliable portfolio model for credit risk (be it single-factor or multifactor). Here, for simplicity, we assume that such values have already been estimated with an acceptable accuracy; interested readers are referred to Resti (2008) and to the references provided in endnote 17.

Figure 4.6 Values of the r_i (coefficients indicating the overall dependence on systemic factors)

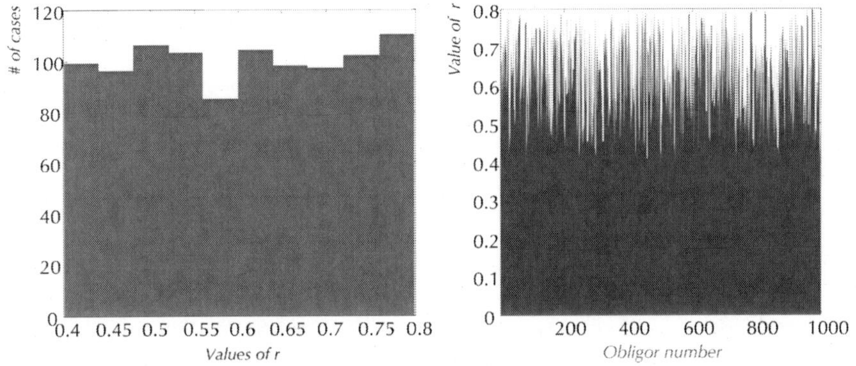

Having specified how obligors depend on macroeconomic factors, we can now compute economic capital through Monte Carlo simulation. We generate 500,000 scenarios and for each of them:

- we sample three values for the (orthogonal, standard normally distributed) macroeconomic factors z_1, z_2 and z_3;
- for each obligor, we compute her y_i through Equation 4.9, then sample a (standard normally distributed) value for idiosyncratic risk, and finally compute x_i according to Equation 4.8; we then compare that x_i to the borrower's default threshold to find out whether a default has occurred; and
- using Equation 4.11, we sum losses across obligors and quantify the loss L associated to each scenario.

Finally, the 500,000 losses are ranked in increasing order and the 99.9th percentile is selected; this gives us the total expected and unexpected loss with a 99.9% confidence.

On a PC with an Intel Pentium M processor at 1.73 GHz and one megabyte of RAM, the generation of the 500,000 scenarios requires 18,732 seconds (about five hours and 10 minutes). Figure 4.7 shows the frequency distribution of the losses generated by the simulation (the right panel is a magnified image of the upper tail). We see that, to find a value leaving beyond it (on its right) 0.1% of all scenarios (500 scenarios) it is necessary to move to rather high values, that is, to a loss rate beyond 5%.

More precisely, the 99.9th percentile of the distribution is 6.97%; this is the loss rate that must be covered with reserves (up to the expected loss, EL = 0.36%) and economic capital (EC = 6.61%). Note that the expected loss is the

Figure 4.7 The distribution of loss rates obtained through a Monte Carlo simulation

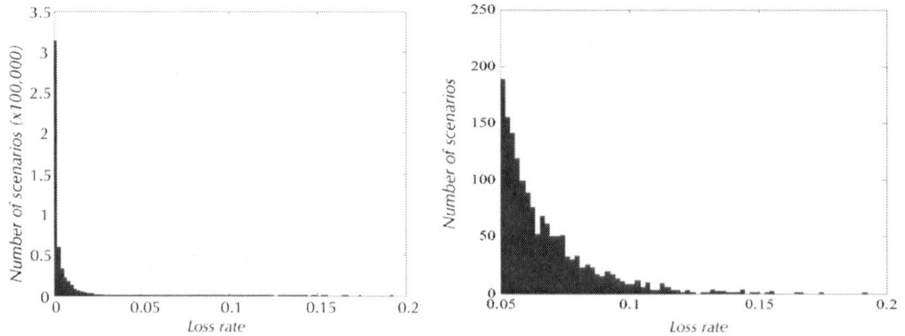

Figure 4.8 The gap between regulatory capital and economic capital for the sample portfolio

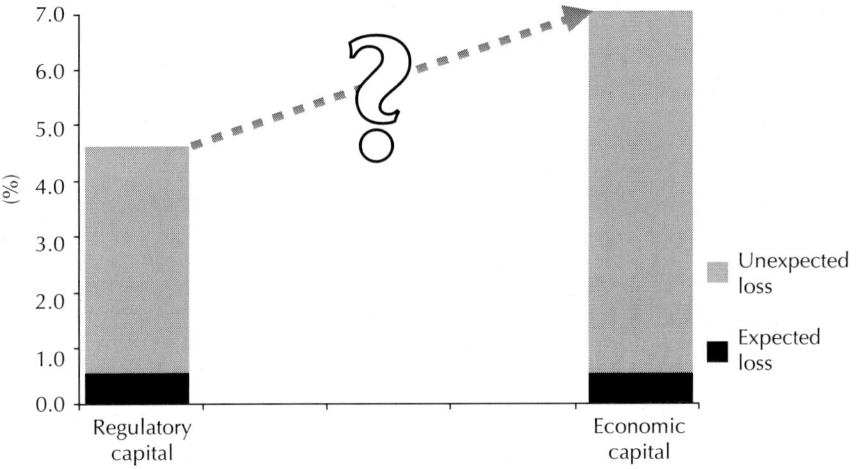

same as in the regulatory model. In fact, the expected value of the total losses on a portfolio is simply the sum of expected losses on individual exposures, and does not depend on diversification. Unexpected loss, instead, is impacted by the portfolio's name and industry concentration. It is therefore understandable that different models come to different results. The situation is portrayed in Figure 4.8. Note that economic capital, which in this example is higher than regulatory capital, might also be lower, depending on input data.

EXPLAINING THE GAP BETWEEN REGULATORY AND ECONOMIC CAPITAL

Banks have to comply with a regulatory capital constraint but, in the meantime, need to measure the economic capital associated with actual outstanding risks. It is not enough for them to be able to compute those two measures separately: a link must be established, both from a logical and algebraic point of view, in order to explain and manage the gap. The example in the previous section has shown that the difference between regulatory and economic capital can be substantial; in this section we develop a framework to understand and quantify the drivers of that gap.

The model used for computing economic capital (see Equation 4.11) and that used for computing regulatory capital (Equations 4.5 and 4.6) lead to different results because, among other things, the former depends on a single factor while the latter involves a vector $\tilde{\mathbf{z}}$ of N systemic factors. To compare the two models, we must therefore cast a "bridge" between $\tilde{y}$ and $\tilde{\mathbf{z}}$. To that aim, let us go back to the multifactor model and try to write it in a different way.

To begin with, we rewrite Equation 4.9 as follows

$$\tilde{y}_i = \boldsymbol{\alpha}_i'\tilde{\mathbf{z}} = \rho_i \mathbf{b}'\tilde{\mathbf{z}} + \sqrt{1-\rho_i^2}\tilde{\eta}_i = \rho_i \tilde{y} + \sqrt{1-\rho_i^2}\tilde{\eta}_i \tag{4.13}$$

In practice, we have replaced the N factors $\tilde{z}_k$ with a single factor $\tilde{y}$, defined as a linear combination of the N original factors (with weights $\mathbf{b}$ that are constant for all obligors and such that $\mathbf{b}'\mathbf{b} = 1$,). However, since systemic risk used to be different for each obligor (being a linear combination of the systemic factors based on a borrower-specific $\boldsymbol{\alpha}_i$), in order to get $\tilde{y}_i$, we have to combine the single systemic factor $\tilde{y}$ with a factor η_i that accounts for the share of systemic risk not captured by $\tilde{y}$ (that is, for the "semi-specific" risk to which the i-th borrower is exposed).

The quantity ρ_i, that is the weight with which the single systemic factor $\tilde{y}$ is "diluted" in Equation 4.13 to get $\tilde{y}_i$, is also the correlation coefficient between $\tilde{y}$ and $\tilde{y}_i$ (hence the choice to call it *rho*). Since the $\tilde{z}_k$ s are orthogonal by construction (so that their correlation matrix is the identity matrix), we note that such a correlation is by definition equal to

$$\rho_i = \rho(\tilde{y}, \tilde{y}_1) = \rho(\mathbf{b}'\tilde{\mathbf{z}}, \boldsymbol{\alpha}_i'\tilde{\mathbf{z}}) = \boldsymbol{\alpha}_i'\mathbf{I}\mathbf{b} = \boldsymbol{\alpha}_i'\mathbf{b} < 1 \tag{4.14}$$

Given $\mathbf{b}$, ρ_i is therefore uniquely defined, for each obligor, by its $\boldsymbol{\alpha}_i$. Furthermore, from Equation 4.14 we have that

$$\tilde{\eta}_i = \frac{[\boldsymbol{\alpha}_i' - \rho_i \mathbf{b}']}{\sqrt{1-\rho_i^2}}\tilde{\mathbf{z}} \tag{4.15}$$

is also standard normally distributed. In fact

$$\frac{[\boldsymbol{\alpha}_i' - \rho_i \mathbf{b}']}{\sqrt{1-\rho_i^2}}\frac{[\boldsymbol{\alpha}_i' - \rho_i \mathbf{b}]}{\sqrt{1-\rho_i^2}} = \frac{\overbrace{\boldsymbol{\alpha}_i'\boldsymbol{\alpha}_i}^{1} - 2\rho_i \overbrace{\boldsymbol{\alpha}_i'\mathbf{b}}^{\rho_i} + \rho_i^2 \overbrace{\mathbf{b}'\mathbf{b}}^{1}}{1-\rho_i^2} = \frac{1-2\rho_i^2+\rho_i^2}{1-\rho_i^2} = 1 \tag{4.16}$$

Having so redefined $\tilde{y}_i$, we can plug Equation 4.13 into Equation 4.8 and get

$$\tilde{x}_i = r_i\rho_i\tilde{y} + r_i\sqrt{1-\rho_i^2}\tilde{\eta}_i + \sqrt{1-r_i^2}\tilde{\xi}_i = r_i\rho_i\tilde{y} + \sqrt{1-(r_i\rho_i)^2}\tilde{\varsigma}_i \tag{4.17}$$

with

$$\tilde{\varsigma}_i \equiv \frac{r_i\sqrt{1-\rho_i^2}\tilde{\eta}_i + \sqrt{1-r_i^2}\tilde{\xi}_i}{\sqrt{1-(r_i\rho_i)^2}} \tag{4.18}$$

Note that Equation 4.17 is similar to Equation 4.1 in the ASRF model if the following consistency condition is verified

$$a_i = r_i\rho_i = r_i\boldsymbol{\alpha}_i'\mathbf{b} \tag{4.19}$$

Such a condition is far from trivial: in fact, it requires the actual factor loadings to match the regulatory ones. Namely, the regulatory weight a_i must equate the actual loading r_i, diluted by a suitable $\rho_i < 1$, which in turn is derived from vector $\boldsymbol{\alpha}_i$ (the vector showing how a customer depends on the N systemic factors). Such a condition may not hold in real life, for those banks having portfolios not in line with the "average" systemic risk that the Basel Committee had in mind when calibrating a_i.

Furthermore, even if the consistency condition holds, then Equations 4.17 and 4.1 are similar, but still not equal. Looking at Equation 4.18, in fact, it can be seen that $\tilde{\varsigma}_i$ is not perfectly idiosyncratic but instead includes a "semi-specific" risk component $\tilde{\eta}_i$ (relating to industry risk, regional risk and the like). This introduces an important difference compared with the Vasicek–Gordy model used for regulatory capital, where all risk that is not in $\tilde{y}$ is assumed to be merely idiosyncratic. As a consequence, for any two obligors i and j, $\tilde{\varsigma}_i$ and $\tilde{\varsigma}_j$ will not necessarily be uncorrelated.

To sum up, even if Equation 4.19 were to hold, when moving from the multifactor, finite-granularity model (used for economic capital estimates) to the asymptotic single-factor one (used for regulatory purposes) we would still experience two important changes:

- the weight of the systemic factor decreases, from r_i to a_i; and
- the systemic risk factor becomes "monolithic" in nature, meaning that it entirely depends on a single factor $\tilde{y}$, constant for all obligors, while all remaining risk is to be considered strictly idiosyncratic.

Based on Equation 4.17, Equation 4.11 – expressing losses associated with any given value of $\mathbf{z}$ – can be rewritten as

$$L(\mathbf{z}) = \sum_{i=1}^{M} w_i\mu_i 1_{\left\{r_i\rho_i y + \sqrt{1-(r_i\rho_i)^2}\varsigma_i \le N^{-1}(p_i)\right\}} \tag{4.20}$$

where both y and the ζ_is follow univocally from $\mathbf{z}$.

Consider now the expected value of Equation 4.20 conditional on a given value y of $\tilde{y}$. This is[18]

$$E\left[L|y\right]=\sum_{i=1}^{M}w_i\mu_i E\left[1_{\left\{r_i\rho_i y+\sqrt{1-(r_i\rho_i)^2}\varsigma_i\le N^{-1}(p_i)\right\}}\right]=\sum_{i=1}^{M}w_i\mu_i p_i\,|_y=$$
$$=\sum_{i=1}^{M}w_i\mu_i pr\left[\varsigma_i\le\frac{N^{-1}(p_i)-r_i\rho_i y}{\sqrt{1-(r_i\rho_i)^2}}\right]=\sum_{i=1}^{M}w_i\mu_i N\left[\frac{N^{-1}(p_i)-r_i\rho_i y}{\sqrt{1-(r_i\rho_i)^2}}\right] \quad (4.21)$$

This is similar to Equation 4.5, but has a different meaning. In fact, the quantity in Equation 4.5 is known with certainty, as it is a deterministic function of the exogenous variable y. Instead, Equation 4.21 gives an expected value and the actual loss could deviate from it because of two factors.

1. Idiosyncratic risk, affecting any portfolio that is not infinitely granular, may cause the *ex post* actual loss rate to be different from the *ex ante* loss probability.
2. Semi-specific risk due to the various systemic risk mixes that might hide behind a given value of y. In fact, since by construction we have $\tilde{y} = \mathbf{b}'\tilde{\mathbf{z}}$, there exist infinitely many vectors $\mathbf{z}$ generating the same y; depending on the bank's actual exposure to the various systemic factors z_k (say, to the different regions, or industries), each one of these $\mathbf{z}$ may bring about losses above or below the mean, as it may prove more or less favourable for the mix of semi-specific factors to which the bank is exposed. The single risk factor y in the regulatory model is therefore intrinsically unable to account for this semi-specific risk.

Accordingly, even if the consistency condition in Equation 4.19 holds, so that Equation 4.21 leads to the same result as Equation 4.5 for any value of y, the latter equation nevertheless underestimates the true loss volatility, as it overlooks idiosyncratic and semi-specific risk. Hence, even if $a_i = r_i\rho_i$, the percentile found with Equation 4.6 ($EL + RC$) still is lower than the one based on economic capital ($EL + EC$), as it implies an "average" configuration for idiosyncratic and semi-specific risk, rather than an extreme one (as required by the logic of percentile-based risk measures).[19]

Of course, it is certain that $RC < EC$ only if, for any obligor, $a_i = r_i\boldsymbol{\alpha}_i'\mathbf{b}$ (that is, if the regulatory factor loadings have been set in a way that is fully consistent with the "true" factor loadings r_i and the true vectors $\boldsymbol{\alpha}_i$ expressing dependences on the N systemic factors). Consequently the Basel Committee (which assumes to have correctly calibrated its factor loadings, so that Equation 4.19 holds "on average")[20] expects that, moving from regulatory to economic capital, banks should face an increase in capital, in order to account for semi-specific and idiosyncratic risks (that is, for sector and name concentration) that were left out of the ASRF model. In this perspective, concentration risk becomes an additional source of risk to be covered with an extra capital cushion.[21]

On the other hand, banks expecting some diversification benefit[22] when moving from regulatory capital (Equation 4.5) to a proper economic capital model (Equation 4.11) are assuming – possibly implicitly – that the regulatory a_is are greater than the "consistent" loadings $r_i\rho_i \equiv r_i\boldsymbol{\alpha}_i'\mathbf{b}$. In fact, as mentioned above, the values for the a_is in the supervisory formulas of Pillar I were set by the Basel Committee based on empirical studies that draw on average data for world bank loans; they may therefore not be appropriate (and Equation 4.19 may not hold) for individual banks and credit markets.

Equation 4.21 can be seen as a special case of Equation 4.5, obtained by calibrating the regulatory model and substituting the "Basel" factor loadings a_i with the values $r_i\rho_i$ that are consistent with the actual characteristics of systemic risk of the portfolio. We call $\bar{L}$ the losses generated by this "hybrid" model (that is, by the ASRF model used for regulatory capital, calibrated with the empirical factor loadings)

$$\bar{L}(y) = l(y) = \sum_{i=1}^{M} w_i\mu_i p_i\,|_y = \sum_{i=1}^{M} w_i\mu_i N\left[\frac{N^{-1}(p_i) - r_i\rho_i y}{\sqrt{1-(r_i\rho_i)^2}}\right] \tag{4.22}$$

(where we use $l(y)$ to emphasise that the loss is a deterministic, monotonically decreasing function of y). Furthermore, we call

$$t_q(\bar{L}) = \sum_{i=1}^{M} w_i\mu_i p_i\,|_{y=N^{-1}(1-q)} = \sum_{i=1}^{M} w_i\mu_i N\left[\frac{N^{-1}(p_i) - r_i\rho_i N^{-1}(1-q)}{\sqrt{1-(r_i\rho_i)^2}}\right] \equiv EL + RC^* \tag{4.23}$$

the q-th percentile of the loss distribution derived with this hybrid model. Note that RC^* represents our new measure of "hybrid", calibrated regulatory capital.

Let us now go back to our sample portfolio to show the practical meaning of the consistency condition (Equation 4.19) and of Equation 4.20.

To apply Equation 4.19, vector $\mathbf{b}$ must be specified. The only constraint imposed up to now is that it must have unit norm. Hence there are still infinitely many candidates. Pykhtin (2004) suggests to choose $\mathbf{b}$ in such a way as to maximise the weighted average correlation of the factors $\tilde{y}_i$ with the single risk factor $\tilde{y}$ (in order to minimise the impact of semi-specific risk $\tilde{\eta}_i$). Formally

$$\max_{\mathbf{b}}\left[\sum_{i=1}^{M} c_i \rho_i\right] = \max_{\mathbf{b}}\left[\sum_{i=1}^{M} c_i \boldsymbol{\alpha}_i' \mathbf{b}\right] \tag{4.24}$$

As concerns the weights c_i, Pykhtin uses the following criterion, based on the results of a series of numerical tests

$$c_i = w_i \mu_i N\left[\frac{N^{-1}(p_i) - r_i N^{-1}(q)}{\sqrt{1-r_i^2}}\right] \tag{4.25}$$

By applying the above procedure to the sample portfolio, we get

$$\mathbf{b}' = \begin{bmatrix} 0.6930 & 0.5018 & 0.5176 \end{bmatrix}$$

Although the borrowers in our portfolio are evenly distributed across regions, the vector clearly gives more weight to the first factor. This could look surprising. However, recall that the weights in the $\boldsymbol{\alpha}_i$s refer to a set of orthogonal macro factors, $\tilde{\mathbf{z}}$. From Equation 4.12 we get

$$\boldsymbol{\alpha}_i'\mathbf{b} = \frac{\mathbf{h}_i'}{\sqrt{\mathbf{h}_i'\mathbf{F}\mathbf{h}_i}}\mathbf{B}'\mathbf{b}$$

Hence, to see how real, non-orthogonal factors are combined, the following vector must be looked at

$$\mathbf{b}'\mathbf{B} = \begin{bmatrix} 0.6930 & 0.7811 & 0.7174 \end{bmatrix},$$

where, as we see, the three factors have more similar weights.

Given this **b**, the two sides of Equation 4.19 can be compared to see if, in the case of the sample portfolio, regulatory loadings (a_i) are in line the actual ones ($\rho_i r_i$). The result is shown in Figure 4.9: while the former are constrained within a rather narrow "corridor" (since Equation 4.7 only generates values between $\sqrt{0.12}$ and $\sqrt{0.24}$), the latter span a wider interval; furthermore, the average for $\rho_i r_i$ (50.7%) is higher than for a_i (43.3%) and this helps explain why, in our example, economic capital exceeds the regulatory one. Finally, in our case the two parameters are basically uncorrelated, as shown by the left-hand panel in Figure 4.9.

We can now compute the percentile in Equation 4.23, that is *EL* + *RC**, which includes calibrated regulatory capital.[23] The result is 6.10% (including, as usual, an expected loss *EL* of 0.36%) and looks considerably closer to the value estimated through the multifactor, finite-granularity model (*EL* + *EC* = 6.97%), although it still is somewhat lower. To see the reasons for such a difference remember that, as noticed previously, Equation 4.21 in the economic capital model does not generate a deterministic value, but rather an expected value around which some volatility persists because

Figure 4.9 Comparison between regulatory and empirical factor loadings

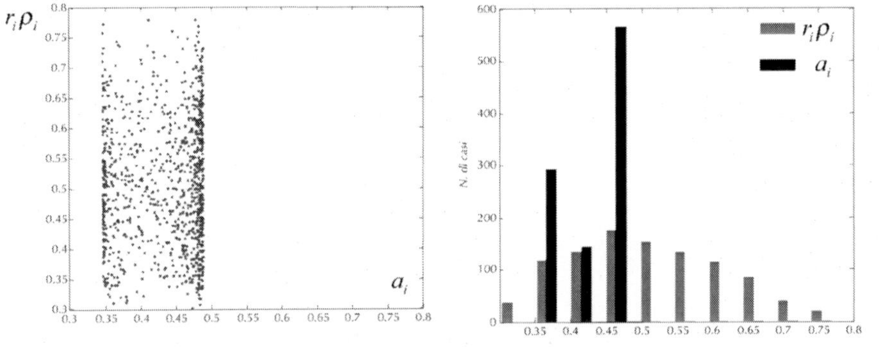

of industry and name concentration. To appreciate such a volatility we can do the following:

- we set the single systemic risk factor (y) to a value corresponding to the 99.9th percentile of losses, that is to $y = N^{-1}(0.1\%) \cong -3.09$;
- we sample from a standard normal distribution 50,000 scenarios for z_1, z_2 and z_3, chosen in such a way that $\tilde{y} = \mathbf{b}'\tilde{\mathbf{z}} = N^{-1}(0.1\%) \cong -3.09$[24] (see the result in Figure 4.10);
- for each scenario, we compute with Equation 4.11 the loss associated with the vector **z** generated above (**z** conditional on y, that is $\mathbf{z}\,|\,y$); and
- we compute the mean of all losses associated with the 50,000 scenarios (see Figure 4.11), getting 6.10%, that is, the value obtained above from Equation 4.21.

Figure 4.10 values of z_1 z_2 and z_3 constrained to a specific value of y.

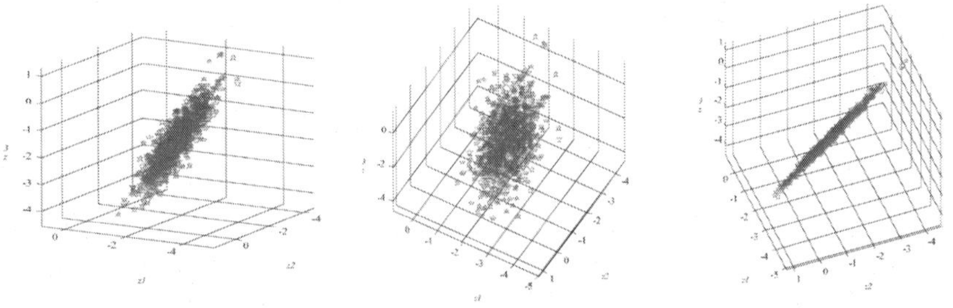

(note: the image was repeated from three different perspectives to help visualise the result)

Figure 4.11 Loss distribution conditional on $y = -3.09$

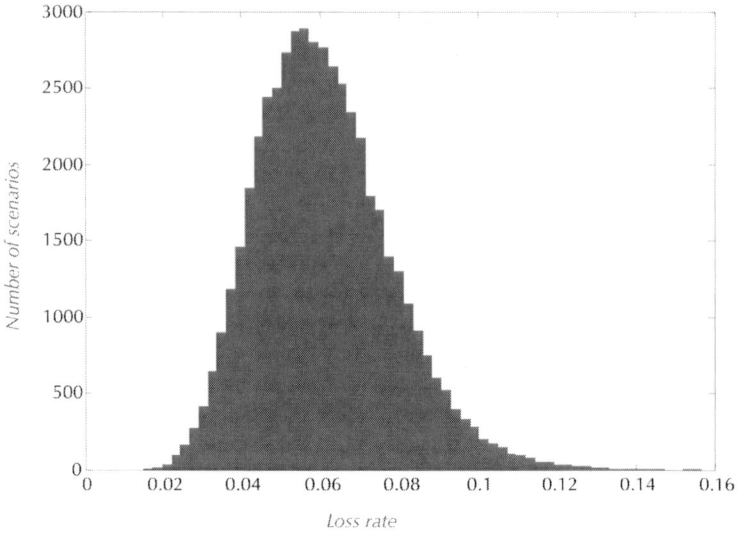

Note that this mean (conditional on $y = N^{-1}(0.1\%)$) is only one of the many values that could occur. In fact, as shown in the figure, 50,000 scenarios, all based on the same y, give rise to different losses on the sample portfolio. This is because each scenario involves different values for the three risk factors (z_1, z_2 and z_3, see again Figure 4.10) to which individual borrowers in the portfolio are exposed; hence, it generates a greater loss if $\mathbf{z}$ is especially negative for the industries where the bank is mostly involved and/or for its largest exposures. If, instead, $\mathbf{z}$ entails bad values for industries where the bank is only marginally present (and for smaller exposures), then the loss decreases as indicated by the left tail.

The single-factor model, even in the calibrated version where actual factor loadings ($r_i\rho_i$) are used instead of regulatory ones (a_i), can only estimate the mean of this distribution, as it cannot "see" the risks underlying different losses in Figure 4.11, that is industry and name concentration. It therefore provides only a partial solution, both from an algebraic and from a logical point of view (see Figure 4.12), to the problem of reconciling regulatory and economic capital.

PYKHTIN'S MULTIFACTOR ADJUSTMENT

To complete the transition from regulatory to economic capital, we must describe our problem in more formal terms. We know the q-th percentile (t_q)

Figure 4.12 Explaining the gap between regulatory and economic capital (Part I)

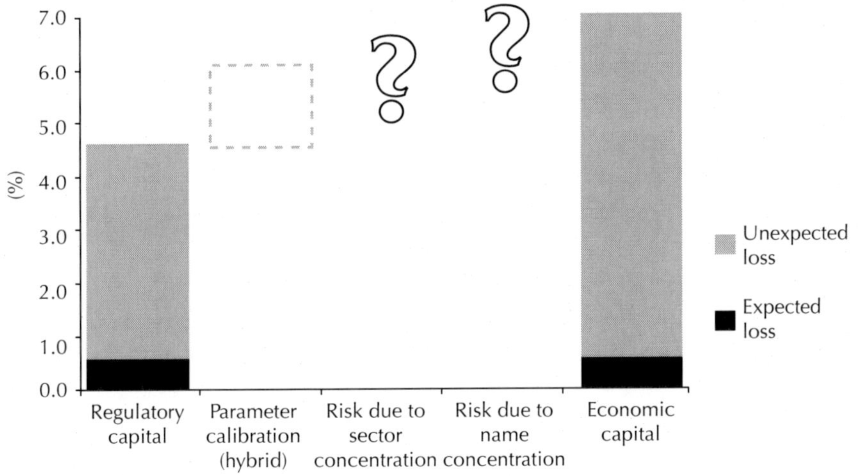

of a stochastic variable $\bar{L}$ (losses computed with the hybrid model, Equation 4.22) and would like to switch to the q-th percentile of another stochastic variable, L, that is losses generated with the multifactor finite-granularity model (Equation 4.11) which embeds the "true" economic capital. Let us then consider the following function of an auxiliary variable ε

$$L(\varepsilon) = \bar{L} + \varepsilon \cdot u \tag{4.26}$$

where u is the difference between the loss quantified with Equation 4.11 and that quantified with Equation 4.22, that is

$$u \equiv L - \bar{L} \tag{4.27}$$

Obviously, given Equation 4.26, we have $L(0) = \bar{L}$ and $L(1) = L$.

As mentioned above, we are interested in reaching a given quantile t_q of L (that is, of $L(\varepsilon)$ when $\varepsilon = 1$), starting with the same quantile t_q of $\bar{L}$ (that is, $L(\varepsilon)$ when $\varepsilon = 0$). Let $t_q(L_\varepsilon)$ be the q-th quantile of a generic $L(\varepsilon)$ and assume we know its derivatives: then we can approximate the quantile of L using Taylor's formula around $\varepsilon = 0$. For example, we can use the following second-order Taylor expansion

$$t_q(L_\varepsilon) \cong t_q(L_\varepsilon)\Big|_{\varepsilon=0} + \frac{dt_q(L_\varepsilon)}{d\varepsilon}\Bigg|_{\varepsilon=0} \cdot \Delta\varepsilon + \frac{1}{2}\frac{d^2 t_q(L_\varepsilon)}{d\varepsilon^2}\Bigg|_{\varepsilon=0} \cdot (\Delta\varepsilon)^2 \tag{4.28}$$

and set $\Delta\varepsilon = 1$ to move from the quantile of $L(0) = \bar{L}$ to that of $L = L(1)$. That gives

$$t_q(L) \cong t_q(\bar{L}) + \left.\frac{dt_q(L_\varepsilon)}{d\varepsilon}\right|_{\varepsilon=0} + \frac{1}{2}\left.\frac{d^2 t_q(L_\varepsilon)}{d\varepsilon^2}\right|_{\varepsilon=0} \tag{4.29}$$

Obviously, Equation 4.29 can be used in practice only if we know how to compute the first and second derivative of a quantile. This was studied by Gourieroux, Laurent and Scaillet (2000) and by Martin and Wilde (2002), who showed that such derivatives can, generally speaking, be computed as follows

$$\left.\frac{dt_q(L_\varepsilon)}{d\varepsilon}\right|_{\varepsilon=0} = E\left[u \mid \bar{L} = t_q(\bar{L})\right] \tag{4.30}$$

and

$$\left.\frac{d^2 t_q(L_\varepsilon)}{d\varepsilon^2}\right|_{\varepsilon=0} = -\frac{1}{f_{\bar{L}}(l)}\frac{d}{dl}\left\{f_{\bar{L}}(l)\cdot \mathrm{var}\left[u \mid \bar{L} = l\right]\right\}\Big|_{l=t_q(\bar{L})} \tag{4.31}$$

where $f_{\bar{L}}(l)$ denotes the probability density function of $\bar{L}$.

Note that those two formulas are quite general and involve the computation of the conditional expected value and the conditional variance of u. How to do this, in practice, depends on the shape of $\bar{L}$. Let us begin with the first derivative. We know (see for example Equation 4.23) that $\bar{L} = l(y)$ reaches its q-th quantile when $y = N^{-1}(1 - q)$. We can therefore rewrite Equation 4.30 as

$$\begin{aligned}\left.\frac{dt_q(L_\varepsilon)}{d\varepsilon}\right|_{\varepsilon=0} &= E\left[u \mid y = N^{-1}(1-q)\right] = E\left[L - \bar{L} \mid y = N^{-1}(1-q)\right] = \\ &= E\left[L \mid y = N^{-1}(1-q)\right] - t_q(\bar{L})\end{aligned} \tag{4.32}$$

This may appear complex at first sight, but becomes simpler if we consider Figure 4.13. Here we see that each state of the world (described by **z** in the multifactor model and by the associated y in the ASRF model) affects the state variables $\tilde{x}_1, \tilde{x}_2, \ldots, \tilde{x}_M$ driving the possible default of the obligors and thereby causing a given loss. Depending on the model used, for each state of the world we have a loss L (measured with the "true" multifactor finite-granularity model), a loss $\bar{L}$ (approximated with the hybrid model) and the difference u between the two. Now, consider all values for **z** associated with the $(1 - q)$th quantile of $\tilde{y}$ (in practice, the infinitely many values that, in the previous section's example, had been approximated through 50,000 scenarios). For each of them, compute L, (which will stay constant for any given y) and the difference u. Then, consider the mean of all the values of u (that is, the mean conditional on $y = N^{-1}(1-q)$). That conditional expected value, as indicated in Equation 4.32, is the first derivative of the percentile of $L(\varepsilon)$.

From Equation 4.32 we see that the first derivative can be computed as the difference between two components: the expected value of L conditional on $y = N^{-1}(1-q)$ and the (fixed) value of $\bar{L}$ when $y = N^{-1}(1-q)$ (that is, $t_q(\bar{L})$). The former can be found with Equation 4.21, by setting $y = N^{-1}(1-q)$; the latter is given by Equation 4.23. Since the two are the same, the first derivative is zero. Equation 4.29 therefore simplifies to

$$t_q(L) \cong t_q(\bar{L}) + \frac{1}{2}\frac{d^2 t_q(L_\varepsilon)}{d\varepsilon^2}\bigg|_{\varepsilon=0} \tag{4.33}$$

and the quantity

$$\frac{1}{2}\frac{d^2 t_q(L_\varepsilon)}{d\varepsilon^2}\bigg|_{\varepsilon=0}$$

is the only adjustment (known as the multifactor adjustment, MFA) required to move from one percentile to another, that is from RC^* to EC.

Figure 4.13 Multifactor model (left) and hybrid model (right)

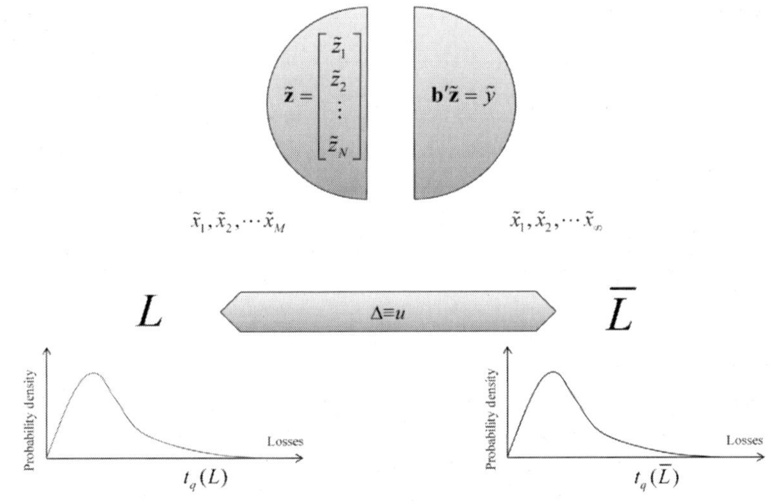

As far as the second derivative is concerned (Equation 4.31), in our case it can be computed as[25]

$$\left.\frac{d^2 t_q(L_\varepsilon)}{d\varepsilon^2}\right|_{\varepsilon=0} = -\frac{1}{l'(y)}\left[v'(y) - v(y)\left(y + \frac{l''(y)}{l'(y)}\right)\right]\Bigg|_{y=N^{-1}(1-q)} \tag{4.34}$$

Two terms in Equation 4.34 deserve a brief comment. First, $l(.)$ is the function (see Equation 4.22) that gives the loss in the hybrid model for any given value y of the systemic factor; such a function, as mentioned above, is deterministic and monotonically decreasing. Its first- and second-order derivatives – $l'(y)$ and $l''(y)$ respectively – can easily be computed as

$$l'(y) = -\sum_{i=1}^{M} w_i \mu_i \frac{r_i \rho_i}{1-(r_i\rho_i)^2} n\left[\frac{N^{-1}(p_i) - r_i\rho_i y}{\sqrt{1-(r_i\rho_i)^2}}\right] \tag{4.35}$$

$$l''(y) = -\sum_{i=1}^{M} w_i \mu_i \frac{(r_i \rho_i)^2}{1-(r_i\rho_i)^2} \frac{N^{-1}(p_i) - r_i\rho_i y}{\sqrt{1-(r_i\rho_i)^2}} n\left[\frac{N^{-1}(p_i) - r_i\rho_i y}{\sqrt{1-(r_i\rho_i)^2}}\right] \tag{4.36}$$

Second,

$$v(y) \equiv \operatorname{var}[u \mid y] \tag{4.37}$$

denotes the variance of the error u conditional on a given value of y. Unlike the conditional mean, this is not equal to zero. It can be seen as a function of y for which, in general, a first and second derivative can be computed. Namely, since for any $y\bar{L}$ is constant, we get that

$$v(y) = \operatorname{var}[L - \bar{L} \mid y] = \operatorname{var}[L \mid y] \tag{4.38}$$

so that $v(y)$ is equal to the variance of the losses in the multifactor, finite-granularity model conditional on a given value of y (in practice, to the variance of the losses in Figure 4.11). This is the risk missing from the hybrid model, that must be captured in order to fill the gap between calibrated regulatory capital and economic capital (see again Figure 4.12).

To compute $v(y)$ and to fully appreciate its economic meaning, the following variance decomposition rule proves useful. Given a random variable h, which is a stochastic function[26] of another random variable, k, then the variance of h can always be written[27] as

$$\operatorname{var}(h) = \operatorname*{var}_k\left[\operatorname*{E}_h(h \mid k)\right] + \operatorname*{E}_k\left[\operatorname*{var}_h(h \mid k)\right] \tag{4.39}$$

that is, as the sum of the following two components:

- $\underset{k}{\text{var}}\left[\underset{h}{E}(h|k)\right]$, the variance of the expected values for h conditional on all possible values for k; and
- $\underset{k}{E}\left[\underset{h}{\text{var}}(h|k)\right]$, the mean of the variances of h conditional on all possible values for k.

In the case of Equation 4.11 we have that the loss L is a stochastic function of the N random variables in vector **z**. In practice, we have L instead of h and **z** instead of k.

However, when computing Equation 4.38 we are not interested in any possible value for **z**, but only in the values $\mathbf{z}\,|\,\mathbf{b}'\mathbf{z} = y$.[28] Hence we look for var(L), with $L = L(\mathbf{z})$, constrained to $\mathbf{z}\,|\,\mathbf{b}'\mathbf{z} = y$; in short, for var($L\,|\,y$). By applying Equation 4.39, we can compute var($L\,|\,y$) as the sum of the two components seen above, that is

$$v(y) = \underset{\mathbf{z}}{\text{var}}\left[\underset{L}{E}(L\,|\,\mathbf{z})\right]\Bigg|_{\mathbf{b}'\mathbf{z}=y} + \underset{\mathbf{z}}{E}\left[\underset{L}{\text{var}}(L\,|\,\mathbf{z})\right]\Bigg|_{\mathbf{b}'\mathbf{z}=y} \equiv v_{\infty}(y) + v_{GA}(y) \tag{4.40}$$

where:

1. $v_{\infty}(y) = \underset{\mathbf{z}}{\text{var}}\left[\underset{L}{E}(L\,|\,\mathbf{z})\right]\Big|_{\mathbf{b}'\mathbf{z}=y}$ gives the variance of the expected losses that can occur for a given value of y.

Figure 4.14 The economic meaning of the two components in the loss variance

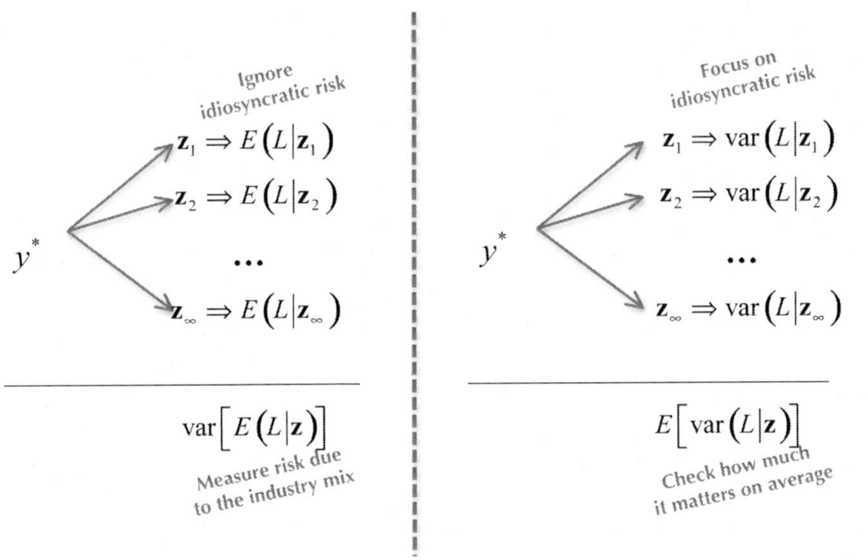

2. $v_{GA}(y) = \underset{\mathbf{z}}{E}\left[\underset{L}{\text{var}}(L \mid \mathbf{z})\right]\Big|_{\mathbf{b}'\mathbf{z}=y}$ gives the mean of the loss variances conditional on all possible values of **z** consistent with a given y.

Let us now explain in detail the economic meaning of those two terms (see also Figure 4.14). The former entails the variance of a set of expected values: it considers all values for **z** consistent with a given y and for each of them computes the expected loss. This expected loss is not computed across all possible **z**s consistent with y (as this would lead to $\bar{L}(y)$, given that Equations 4.21 and 4.22 are equivalent): instead, each expected value is conditional on a given **z** and the uncertainty around the mean only arises from the variables $1_{\{\ldots\}}$ in Equation 4.11. Those variables, which account for the possible defaults within a given macroeconomic scenario, are here replaced with their expected values, that is, the *PD* conditional on **z**. Such conditional *PD* can be computed, similarly to Equation 4.4, as

$$p_i\big|_{\mathbf{z}} = N\left[\frac{N^{-1}(p_i) - r_i \boldsymbol{\alpha}_i' \mathbf{z}}{\sqrt{1 - r_i^2}}\right] \tag{4.41}$$

so that $E(L \mid \mathbf{z})$ becomes

$$E(L \mid \mathbf{z}) = \sum_{i=1}^{M} w_i \mu_i p_i\big|_{\mathbf{z}} = \sum_{i=1}^{M} w_i \mu_i N\left[\frac{N^{-1}(p_i) - r_i \boldsymbol{\alpha}_i' \mathbf{z}}{\sqrt{1 - r_i^2}}\right] \tag{4.42}$$

Interestingly, the result in Equation 4.42 can be seen as the loss experienced, for a given value of **z**, on an infinitely granular portfolio (in short: $L^\infty(\mathbf{z})$). In fact, if the granularity were infinite, then the idiosyncratic risk associated with individual obligors could be ignored and the actual loss (for any **z**) would converge to the expected loss.

After computing the values of $E(L \mid \mathbf{z}) = L^\infty(\mathbf{z})$, we compute their variance by integrating over all the values of **z** that are consistent with y. This is the variance of the expected losses, that is, of the losses an hypothetical infinitely granular portfolio: accordingly, the first addendum in Equation 4.40 is called $v_\infty(y)$. It accounts for the fact that, for any value of y, there exist, in practice, infinitely many values for **z**, each of which leads to different losses because the credit portfolio differently affected by the various combinations of the z_k hidden behind the same level of y; however, it does not account for portfolio granularity as it is based on a loss measure (Equation 4.42) where infinite granularity is assumed. Hence, it captures industry concentration but ignores name concentration.

The second addendum in Equation 4.40 involves first the computation of a variance, then the computation of an expected value. This means that, for any value of **z** (consistent with a given y), we compute the variance in losses due to the limited granularity of the names. Such a variance accounts for the fact that, if the number M of obligors is finite and their exposures are not all equally small, then the loss rate on the portfolio may prove different from expected, even if the *PD*s conditional on a given **z** are univocally given (by Equation 4.41). To see how much this idiosyncratic risk matters, we compute the expected value of all conditional variances, integrating over all the **z** vectors consistent with a given y. As each variance is computed assuming that a specific value of **z** is known, this term is not affected by industry concentration (IC), but only by the name concentration, ie, granularity of the portfolio. Accordingly, Pykhtin calls it $v_{GA}(y)$, where GA stands for granularity adjustment.

The first derivative of Equation 4.40 can obviously be decomposed in a similar way

$$v'(y) = v'_{\infty}(y) + v'_{GA}(y) \tag{4.43}$$

so that we can rewrite the multifactor adjustment as follows

$$MFA = \frac{1}{2}\frac{d^2 t_q(L_\varepsilon)}{d\varepsilon^2}\bigg|_{\varepsilon=0} = ICA + NCA$$

where ICA and NCA are the industry-concentration adjustment and the name-concentration adjustment, defined as

$$ICA = -\frac{1}{2\cdot l'(y)}\left[v'_{\infty}(y) - v_{\infty}(y)\left(y + \frac{l''(y)}{l'(y)}\right)\right]\Bigg|_{y=N^{-1}(1-q)} \tag{4.44}$$

$$ICA = -\frac{1}{2\cdot l'(y)}\left[v'_{GA}(y) - v_{GA}(y)\left(y + \frac{l''(y)}{l'(y)}\right)\right]\Bigg|_{y=N^{-1}(1-q)} \tag{4.45}$$

The formulas for the computation of $v_{\infty}(y)$, $v_{GA}(y)$, $v'_{\infty}(y)$ and $v'_{GA}(y)$ are reported in Appendix 4.3. Leaving technicalities aside, it is worth noting that by Equations 4.44 and 4.45 we can describe and compute the gap between calibrated regulatory capital and economic capital. Economic capital can now be approximated as follows

$$t_q(L) \equiv EL + EC \cong t_q(\bar{L}) + ICA + NCA = EL + RC + \left(RC^* - RC\right) + ICA + NCA \tag{4.46}$$

We can therefore explain (apart from a small approximation error due to the use of Taylor's expansion) the gap in Figure 4.12.

Let us then go back to our sample portfolio to see how the approximation in Equation 4.46 can be used in practice.

By computing Equation 4.44 for $y = N^{-1}(0{,}1\%) \cong -3{,}09$, we get an *ICA* of about 0.14%; this is rather low and follows from the fact that the portfolio is well diversified across the three systemic risk factors (see again Figure 4.5). By replacing $y \cong -3{,}09$ in Equation 4.45, we then get the name concentration adjustment (NCA), which takes a value of 0.61%. This means that the assumption of infinite granularity in the Gordy–Vasicek model leads to an underestimation of capital of approximately 60bp. Together with the parameter calibration introduced with the hybrid model, these two adjustments explain most of the gap between regulatory and economic capital (see Figure 4.15).

The approximation error is about 0.1%; however, as mentioned by Pykhtin and confirmed by a number of simulations carried out by ourselves, the approximation quality might further improve as the number of obligors in the portfolio increases. Furthermore, the approximation in Equation 4.46 looks quite effective also in computational terms: the time required to compute capital and reserves with the hybrid model, adjusted with the ICA

Figure 4.15 Explaining the gap between regulatory and economic capital (Part II)

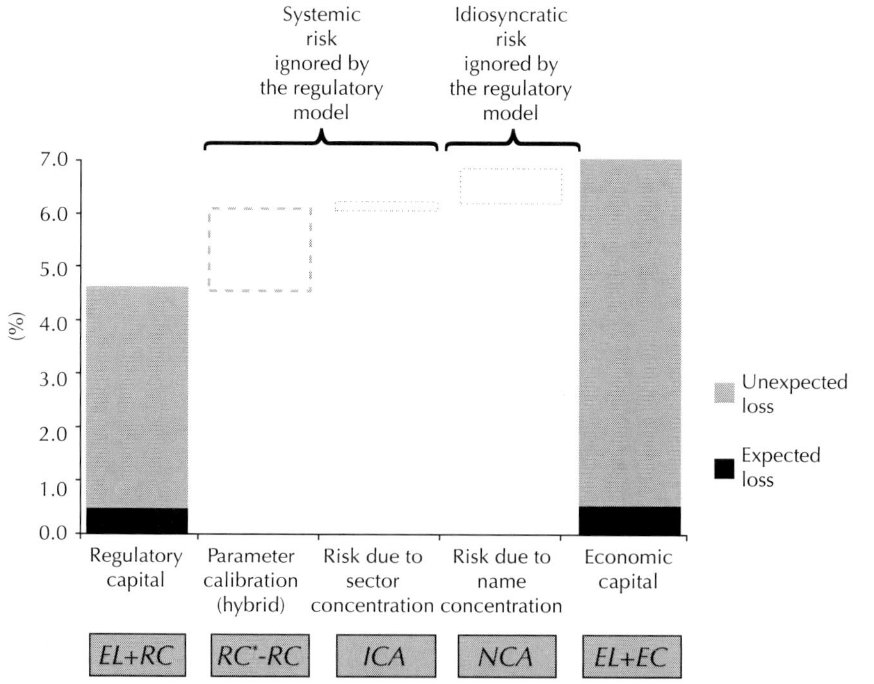

and NCA, is about 10 seconds, as opposed to more than five hours for the Monte Carlo simulation mentioned earlier.

Summing up, the gap between regulatory and economic capital for the sample portfolio is explained (see the top of Figure 4.15):

- by an exposure to systemic risk significantly above the one implied by the supervisory formula; this greater systemic risk is captured in two ways: first, by calibrating upwards the factor loadings in the ASRF model (getting an increase equal to $RC^* - RC$, see Figure 4.9); second, by introducing the *ICA*; the sum of those two adjustments is 1.69%;
- by an exposure to idiosyncratic risk that is not negligible (while in the asymptotic model this source of risk is deliberately ignored) and is accounted for by the *NCA* (0.61%); and
- by an approximation error of 0.1%.

AN APPLICATION TO TWO SPECIAL PORTFOLIOS

In this section we show how the approach outlined above (based on the hybrid model and on Pykhtin's approximation) performs in the case of two special portfolios where name and industry concentration are especially high, to capture risk profiles that would be simply ignored by regulatory capital.

The first portfolio is obtained by increasing the name concentration of the sample portfolio and will therefore be called HNC (high name concentration) portfolio. To generate it, we multiplied by three the portfolio share associated with the 10 largest exposures, while proportionately reducing the remaining 990 loans.

Figure 4.16 shows the new frequency distribution of the weights w in the portfolio (left panel); recalling Figure 4.2, 10 exposures that are significantly larger than those in the sample portfolio can easily be spotted, each of which accounts for about 4–4.5% of the total. Still in Figure 4.16 (right panel) we can see how these very large exposures tend to be associated with very low estimated PDs.

This is a realistic assumption, as a bank may try to reduce its regulatory capital burden by increasing exposures associated with low-PD large customers. In fact, while regulatory capital is inversely related to PDs, it does not capture the risk associated with an increase in name concentration (although, as seen above, it assumes higher factor loadings for low PDs).

Figure 4.17 shows regulatory and economic capital (the latter computed through Pykhtin's approximation) for the HNC portfolio. Results are also shown in Table 4.1, where the values for the "basic" sample portfolio are

Figure 4.16 Frequency distribution of EADs (left) and the EAD/PD relationship (right) for the HNC portfolio

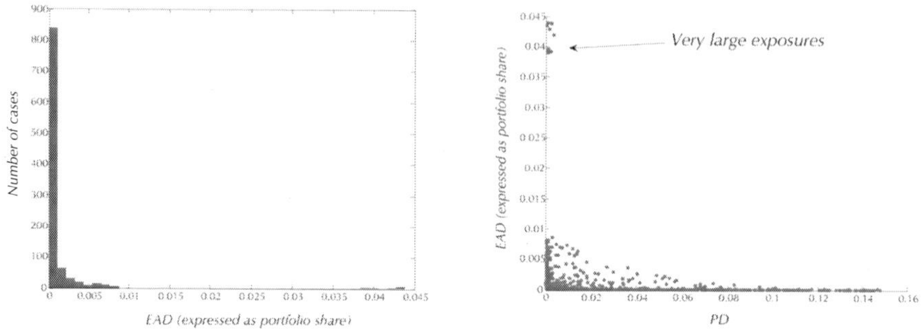

included, as well as those for a high industry concentration (HIC) portfolio that will be introduced later on.

Compared with the sample portfolio, the increase in the portfolio share associated with the 10 largest exposures brings about a decrease in regulatory capital (in terms of both expected loss and unexpected loss). However, in terms of economic capital the change is close to zero, since the improvement due to a lower average PD (from 0.81% to 0.60%, exposure-weighted) is offset by a worse granularity (the HH index goes from 0.69% to 1.97%). The latter effect, however, is by definition overlooked by the ASRF model

Figure 4.17 Regulatory and economic capital for the HNC portfolio

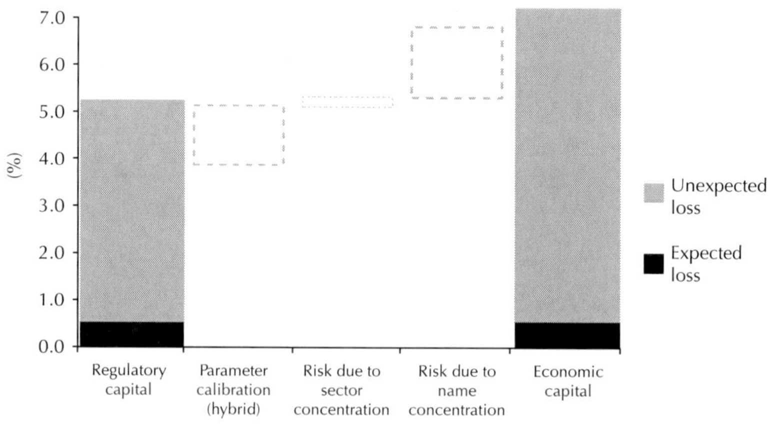

Table 4.1 A comparison of the results for three portfolios

	(a) Sample portfolio (%)	(b) HNC portfolio (%)	(b)–(a) (%)	(c) HIC portfolio (%)	(c)–(a) (%)
Regulatory requirements					
Expected loss (EL)	0.36	0.27	–0.09	0.36	0.00
Regulatory capital (RC)	4.19	3.63	–0.56	4.19	0.00
Systemic risk					
Parameter calibration (RC*–RC)	1.55	1.23	–0.32	2.18	0.63
ICA	0.14	0.19	0.05	0.11	–0.03
Idiosyncratic risk					
NCA	0.61	1.49	0.88	0.57	–0.04
Expected loss plus estimated economic capital (EL+EC)	6.85	6.81	–0.04	7.41	0.56

and would go unnoticed if we had not developed a suitable algorithm to measure economic capital and link it to the results obtained under Pillar I.

Note that systemic risk, too, is slightly affected when moving from the sample portfolio to the HNC one. On one hand, the hybrid model produces a lower adjustment (RC*–RC) for the HNC portfolio (+1.23% instead of +1.55%); on the other hand, however, the ICA is slighted higher (+0.19% instead of +0.14%).

The first effect can be explained as follows: while the average distance between regulatory and calibrated factor loadings is approximately the same for the two portfolios (moving from a_i to $r_i\rho_i$, the weighted average increase is 5.26% for the HNC portfolio, 5.29% in the base case), the larger dependence on systemic risk implied in the calibrated loadings is "less dangerous" for the HNC case, because the average PD is closer to zero and hence losses are expected to be lower for any given amount of systemic risk.

The second effect accounts for the fact that the 10 largest obligors in the portfolio are on average more exposed to factor z_2 (Europe) and less exposed to factor z_1 (US) than the remaining obligors; accordingly, as we increase loans to those 10 obligors, industry concentration grows more significant (see the weighted average values for the borrowers' $\mathbf{h}$ in Table 4.2). This larger exposure to a single systemic factor increases industry concentration. This effect is partly captured by the hybrid model, through an adjustment of

Table 4.2 Systemic risk of two portfolios (HNC and "base case" sample portfolio)

	Weighted average h				B′b weights	
	Largest 10 (%)	Other 990 (%)	Sample portfolio (%)	HNC portfolio (%)	Sample portfolio (%)	HNC portfolio (%)
US	23.6	35.8	34.1	30.7	69.3	68.3
Europe	54.2	46.6	47.7	49.8	78.1	82.9
Asia	42.8	41.8	42.0	42.2	74.7	71.1

the **b** vector leading from the z_k to the single risk factor y. The adjustment is shown in Table 4.2, where – to increase readability – we reported the version of **b (B′b)** for not-orthogonal risk factors (US, Europe and Asia). We see that the single factor for the HNC portfolio is more affected by Europe, while the role of the US is reduced. Since the new industry concentration is accounted for by the calibrated model, the ICA shows only a minor increase.

We now introduce another special portfolio (high industry concentration, HIC) where industry concentration (rather than name concentration) is shocked, by increasing the weight of the US.

Figure 4.18 Factor loadings for the 1,000 obligors in the HIC portfolio

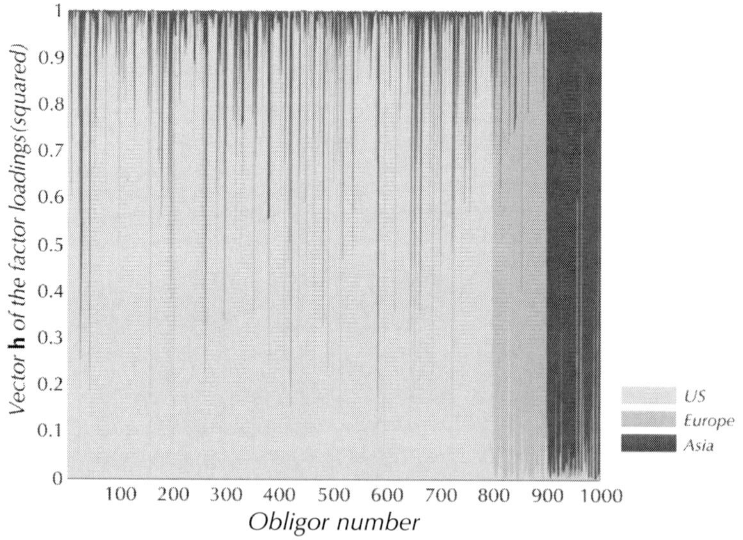

Table 4.3 Systemic risk of two portfolios (HIC and "base case" sample portfolio)

	Weighted average h		B'b weights	
	Sample portfolio (%)	**HIC portfolio (%)**	**Sample portfolio (%)**	**HIC portfolio (%)**
US	34.1	77.4	69.3	92,6
Europe	47.7	22.3	78.1	69,3
Asia	42.0	25.1	74.7	50,3

Figure 4.18 shows the new structure of the *h* coefficients. Recalling Figure 4.5, we see that the share of obligors mainly dependent on the US, which used to be approximately one-third, is now 80% (with another 10% mostly depending on Europe and another 10% mostly affected by Asia); the change in the average **h** is also reported in Table 4.3.

Note that such a portfolio mix is far from being unlikely. A bank tends to specialise in those areas and/or industries where it can better know and control the market, so that its dependence on systemic risk cannot be expected to be uniform across risk factors. However, if industry concentration is not carefully monitored under Pillar II, the regulatory model in Pillar

Figure 4.19 Regulatory and economic capital for the HIC portfolio

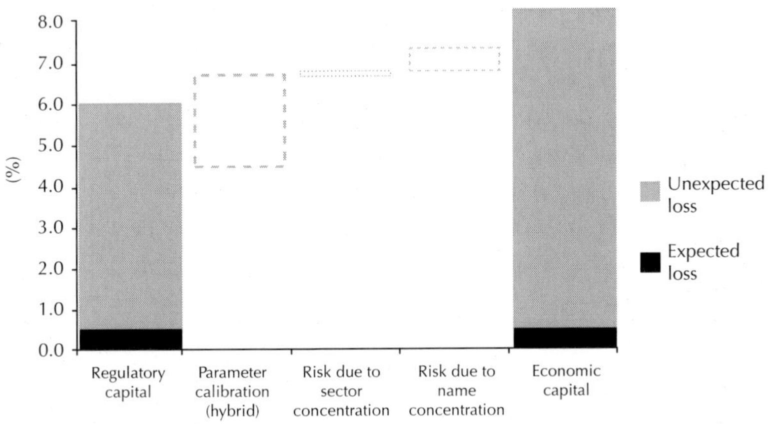

I will not be able to capture this behaviour and to impose a higher capital requirement.

This lack of sensitivity to industry concentration is confirmed, as far as the HIC portfolio is concerned, by the results in Figure 4.19 and Table 4.1: compared with the sample portfolio, the overall requirement on EL and UL remains unchanged, as though no increase in risk had taken place.

Economic capital, instead, rises from 6.85% to 7.41%, mainly because of the systemic risk component (parameter calibration and ICA); namely, most of the adjustment occurs when moving from regulatory capital to the calibrated ASRF model. This may look counterintuitive at first sight: the hybrid model, in fact, is a single-factor model (although it is "calibrated" in such a way as to account better for systemic risk). The reader could therefore wonder how it can be affected by a portfolio's industry mix, that is, by the different relevance of the individual systemic factors.

Recall, however, that the factor loadings in the calibrated model are the product of two components, r_i and $\rho_i = \boldsymbol{\alpha}_i'\mathbf{b}$; the former accounts for the overall weight of systemic risk and is clearly unaffected by the relevance of the individual *z*s; the latter, instead, measures the correlation $\rho(\tilde{y}, \tilde{y}_i)$ between the single macroeconomic factor and the systemic factor of the *i*-th

Figure 4.20 Coefficients ρ_i for the sample portfolio and the HIC portfolio

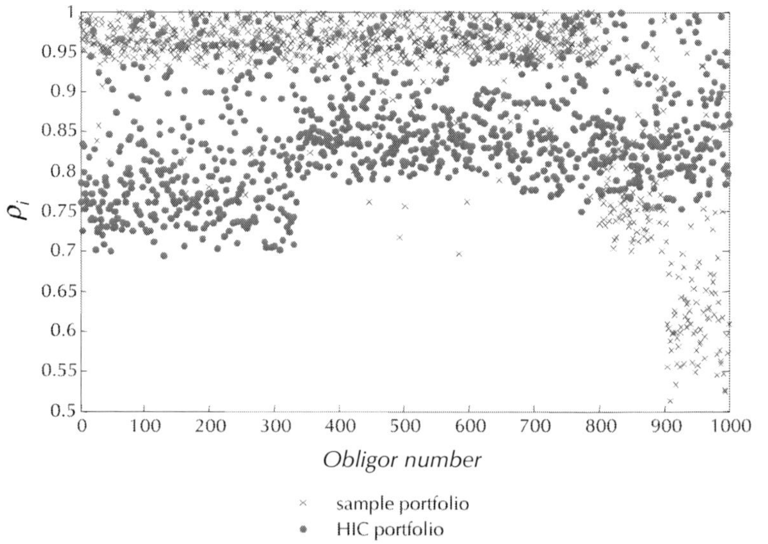

obligor (a linear combination of the z_k that is explicitly specified only in the multifactor model), and is therefore affected by industry risk.

In fact, as seen above, the single risk factor for the hybrid model had been generated, in the case of the sample portfolio (where the three macro factors were equally important) by combining the US, Europe and Asia with three roughly equivalent weights (see vector **B′b** reported on Page 82 and in Table 4.3). That single risk factor was therefore only partially correlated with the individual y_is of the 1,000 obligors, each of which was exposed mainly to one of the three z_ks: the correlation coefficients ρ_i were therefore significantly below one (see Figure 4.20), with an average of 84.6%.

This is different for the HIC portfolio. As 80% of the obligors are mainly affected by factor 1 (US), then the single risk factor $\tilde{y} = \mathbf{b}'\tilde{\mathbf{z}}$ is built by assigning a high weight to the first factor (see the second **B′b** shown in Table 4.3). Accordingly, for that 80% of the portfolio that mostly depends on the US, the correlation coefficient is close to 1 (see again Figure 4.20) and the average ρ_i is higher (91.21%) than in the base case.

Figure 4.21 compares them with the calibrated loadings of the sample portfolio: we see that most exposures (80%, see the dots above the 45° line on the right) experience an increase in the loadings. Loadings are now more dispersed (see the bars on the left) and, on average, higher (the weighted average being 55.4% for the HIC portfolio, as opposed to 51.3% for the base case).

By recalibrating vector **b**, the ρ_is and the factor loadings, the hybrid model is capable of capturing the increase in risk due to a higher industry concen-

Figure 4.21 Calibrated factor loadings ($r_i\rho_i$) for the sample portfolio and the HIC portfolio

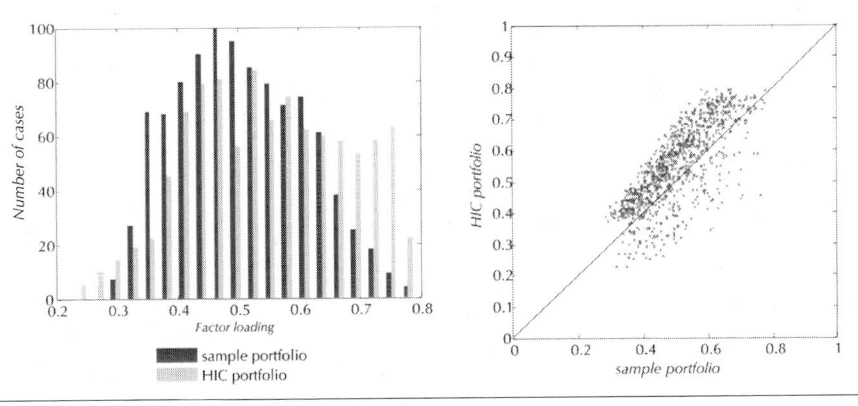

tration; in fact, it is through this recalibration that the increase in industry risk is accounted for, while the ICA stays basically unchanged. Actually, the ICA captures the volatility of losses around their expected value conditional on $y = N(0.1\%)$ or, more precisely, that share of volatility that is due to the presence of many $\mathbf{z}$ consistent with that y. Once the conditional mean has been recalibrated (to account for the different industry mix of the HIC portfolio), the mere volatility of losses around it (captured by the ICA) remains almost unaffected (0.11% instead 0.14%).

The same applies for that share of loss volatility that depends on idiosyncratic risk (the NCA). As we can see from Table 4.1, the risk due to name granularity remains basically unchanged (0.57% instead of 0.61%).

In this section, we saw how the hybrid model and Pykhtin's approximation can capture the risk increases due to different changes in a bank's portfolio mix. Namely, it can quantify the additional capital required, above and beyond Pillar I, to account for name and industry concentration risks, highlighting the causes behind those risks and quantifying their effects. Last but not least, it makes it possible to estimate economic capital in a quite acceptable way from the computational point of view: for both portfolios seen in this section, the results in Table 4.1 were computed in less than 11 seconds.

Note that the two examples presented above give a simplified representation of two typical "regulatory arbitrages" to which Pillar I in the 2004 Accord is exposed.

A regulatory arbitrage is a deal aimed at changing a bank's balance sheet in such a way that, while complying with all supervisory rules, it can reduce capital requirements without reducing risk, or leave the capital charge unchanged while making the portfolio riskier.[29] Under Basel I, since all loans to corporates were subject to the same 8% capital charge, arbitrages occurred mainly on PDs, as banks could increase loans to riskier obligors (earning higher spreads) without incurring any increase in capital requirements. The new Basel II Accord, setting higher capital charges for high-PD exposures, makes such arbitrages less feasible; however, as Pillar I does not include the actual portfolio concentration among the drivers of capital requirements, it paves the way to a new generation of concentration-based (rather than PD-based) arbitrages. This type of arbitrage can indeed be exemplified by the two simple examples presented in this section. In the former, Pillar I capital is reduced without actually decreasing the portfolio overall risk, but rather by "shifting" risk from default risk (the average PD decreases) to name concentration (the HH index increases); in the latter, portfolio risk is increased by strongly specialising on a single industry/area, a policy that that cannot be detected by the "sensors" of the Gordy–Vasicek model.

FINAL REMARKS

This chapter has thoroughly discussed a methodology – based on the results in Pykhtin (2004) – for quantifying and decomposing the gap between regulatory and economic capital on credit risk. Such a methodology, while being computationally very effective, can prove of great help to banks trying to assess concentration risk on their loan portfolios and to address the requirements set out by Pillar II. This approach entails two steps: calibrating regulatory capital with a hybrid model (shown in the section "Explaining the gap between regulatory and economic capital") and introducing two adjustments (industry concentration adjustment and name concentration adjustment) based on Taylor's expansion (see "Pykhtin's multifactor adjustment" above).

Using a sample portfolio, we have shown how this methodology can be used in practice, highlighting and quantifying the various factors that can create a gap between Pillar I capital requirements and the actual amount of capital at risk. By introducing two more portfolios, we also saw how the same approach can be helpful to spot and offset some regulatory arbitrages on concentration risk.

Those examples show that the first step (computing calibrated regulatory capital, RC^*) can capture most of the gap between regulatory capital and economic capital without the need to introduce the complex formulas of Pykhtin's multifactor adjustment (as the regulatory model is kept unchanged). Of course, in order to calibrate the factor loadings, a bank must estimate the key elements of the multifactor model ($\mathbf{h}$, $\mathbf{F}$, r_i), as well as the vector $\mathbf{b}$ linking the borrower-specific y_is to the single risk factor y.

Also, it is worth emphasising that, while the *ICA* and *NCA* are necessarily greater than zero, and therefore involve an increase in the capital charge, the shift from regulatory to calibrated capital may cause both a rise and a decrease in capital; in other words, the difference ($RC^* - RC$) can be either positive or negative. Accordingly, for portfolios where credit risk is mainly idiosyncratic in nature and/or industry diversification is stronger than expected by the Basel Committee, the calibration in factor loadings – and even the shift from regulatory capital to economic capital – could imply a reduction in the overall capital requirement. The use of Pillar I capital as a floor might prove inappropriate. Supervisors will hopefully be willing to discuss this with banks, should such situations arise.

APPENDIX 4.1: COMPUTING THE SECOND-ORDER DERIVATIVE OF A QUANTILE

To compute the second-order derivative of a quantile (Equation 4.31), two preliminary remarks are helpful:

1. Since we know the probability density function (pdf) of y (a standard normal, $n(y)$) and we know the function $l(y)$ linking and y, it must be possible to work out the pdf for $\bar{L}$ by applying the rule for the pdf of the function of a variable with a known pdf. Such a rule, in general terms, is the following

$$f_k \left| \frac{d}{dk} g^{-1}(k) \right| \cdot f_h\left[g^{-1}(k) \right]$$

   where f_v is the pdf of v and $k = g(h)$ is the function linking h (the pdf of which is known) with k (the pdf of which we would like to know). In our case the rule becomes

$$F_{\bar{L}} = \left| \frac{d}{d\bar{L}} l^{-1}(\bar{L}) \right| \cdot n\left[l^{-1}(\bar{L}) \right] = \left| \frac{d}{d\bar{L}} l^{-1}(\bar{L}) \right| \cdot n(y)$$

2. It is now useful to recall a theorem concerning the derivative of the inverse function: given $y = g(x)$, with derivative $g'(x)$, and given its inverse $x = g^{-1}(y) = h(y)$, then the derivative of the latter, $h'(y)$, is given by $1/g'(x) = 1/g'(h(y))$. In our case, given $y = l^{-1}(\bar{L})$, its derivative is $\frac{d}{d\bar{L}} = \frac{d}{d\bar{L}} l^{-1}(\bar{L})$ given by $1/l'(y)$, and the expression above simplifies to

$$f_{\bar{L}} = \left| \frac{1}{l'(y)} \right| \cdot n(y)$$

   Finally, as the link between $\bar{L}$ and y is monotonically decreasing (hence the derivative is bound to be negative), we have

$$f_{\bar{L}} = -\frac{n(y)}{l'(y)}$$

We now rewrite Equation 4.31 conditioning it on a percentile of y, rather than of $\bar{L}$; this is correct, since the two quantities are connected by a one-to-one correspondence, and gets

$$\left.\frac{d^2t_q}{d\varepsilon^2}\right|_{\varepsilon=0} = -\frac{1}{f_{\bar{L}}(l)}\frac{d}{dl}\left\{f_{\bar{L}}(l)\cdot \mathrm{var}\left[u \mid \bar{L}=l\right]\right\}\Big|_{l=t_q(\bar{L})} =$$

$$= -\frac{l'(y)}{n(y)}\frac{d}{dy}\left\{-\frac{n(y)}{l'(y)}\cdot\underbrace{\mathrm{var}\left[u \mid y\right]}_{\equiv v(y)}\right\}\frac{dy}{d\bar{L}}\Bigg|_{y=N^{-1}(1-q)} =$$

$$= -\frac{l'(y)}{n(y)}\frac{d}{dy}\left\{-\frac{n(y)\cdot v(y)}{l'(y)}\right\}\frac{1}{l'(y)}\Bigg|_{y=N^{-1}(1-q)} =$$

$$= -\frac{1}{n(y)}\frac{d}{dy}\left\{\frac{n(y)\cdot v(y)}{l'(y)}\right\}\Bigg|_{y=N^{-1}(1-q)} =$$

$$= -\frac{1}{n(y)}\frac{\left[n'(y)\cdot v(y)+n(y)\cdot v'(y)\right]l'(y)-n(y)\cdot v(y)\cdot l''(y)}{\left[l'(y)\right]^2}\Bigg|_{y=N^{-1}(1-q)}$$

Recalling that

$$n'(y) = \frac{d}{dy}\left(\frac{1}{\sqrt{2\pi}}e^{-\frac{y^2}{2}}\right) = n(y)(-y)$$

we finally get

$$\left.\frac{d^2t_q(L_\varepsilon)}{d\varepsilon^2}\right|_{\varepsilon=0} = -\frac{v'(y)-y\cdot v(y)}{l'(y)}+\frac{v(y)\cdot l''(y)}{\left[l'(y)\right]^2}\Bigg|_{y=N^{-1}(1-q)} =$$

$$= -\frac{1}{l'(y)}\left[v'(y)-y\cdot v(y)-\frac{v(y)\cdot l''(y)}{l'(y)}\right]\Bigg|_{y=N^{-1}(1-q)} =$$

$$= -\frac{1}{l'(y)}\left[v'(y)-v(y)\left(y+\frac{l''(y)}{l'(y)}\right)\right]\Bigg|_{y=N^{-1}(1-q)}$$

which is Equation 4.34 in the chapter.

APPENDIX 4.2: DECOMPOSING VARIANCE

Given a random variable h, which is a stochastic function of another random variable, k, we compute the sum of the following two terms:

- $\underset{k}{\mathrm{var}}\left[\underset{k}{E}(h \mid k)\right]$, that is, the variance of the expected values for h conditional on all possible values for k; and
- $\underset{k}{E}\left[\underset{h}{\mathrm{var}}(h \mid k)\right]$, that is, the mean of the variances for h conditional on all possible values for k.

That will give

$$\underset{k}{\text{var}}\left[\underset{h}{E}(h|k)\right]+\underset{k}{E}\left[\underset{h}{\text{var}}(h|k)\right]=\underset{k}{E}\left\{\underset{h}{E}(h|k)-\underbrace{\underset{k}{E}\left[\underset{h}{E}(h|k)\right]}_{E(h)}\right\}^2+\underset{k}{E}\left\{\underset{h}{E}\left[(h|k)-\underset{h}{E}(h|k)\right]^2\right\}$$

$$=\underset{k}{E}\left\{\left[\underset{h}{E}(h|k)\right]^2-2\underset{h}{E}(h|k)E(h)+\left[E(h)\right]^2+\underset{h}{E}\left[(h^2|k)-2(h|k)\underset{h}{E}(h|k)+\left(\underset{h}{E}(h|k)\right)^2\right]\right\}=$$

$$=-2\left[E(h)\right]^2+\left[E(h)\right]^2+\underset{k}{E}\left\{\left[\underset{h}{E}(h|k)\right]^2+\underset{h}{E}\left[(h^2|k)\right]-2\underset{h}{E}(h|k)\underset{h}{E}(h|k)+\left[\underset{h}{E}(h|k)\right]^2\right\}=$$

$$=-\left[E(h)\right]^2+\underset{k}{E}\left\{\underset{h}{E}\left[(h^2|k)\right]\right\}=E\left[h^2\right]-\left[E(h)\right]^2=\text{var}(h)$$

Accordingly, the variance of h can be decomposed as

$$\text{var}(h)=\underset{k}{\text{var}}\left[\underset{h}{E}(h|k)\right]+\underset{k}{E}\left[\underset{h}{\text{var}}(h|k)\right]$$

which is Equation 4.39 in the chapter.

APPENDIX 4.3: FORMULAS FOR COMPUTING v(y) AND ITS FIRST DERIVATIVE

Below we report the formulas for the computation of the two components of $v(y)$ and of their first derivatives. For further details, see Pykhtin (2004).

First component (v_∞)

$$v_\infty(y)=\sum_{i=1}^{M}\sum_{j=1}^{M}w_iw_j\mu_i\mu_j\left\{N^2\left[N^{-1}\left(\bar{p}_i|_y\right),N^{-1}\left(\bar{p}_j|_y\right),\rho_{ij}^{Y}\right]-\bar{p}_i|_y\cdot\bar{p}_j|_y\right\}$$

with

$$\rho_{ij}^{Y}=\frac{r_ir_j\left(\sum_{k=1}^{N}\alpha_{ik}\alpha_{jk}-\rho_i\rho_j\right)}{\sqrt{\left[1-(r_i\rho_i)^2\right]\left[1-(r_j\rho_j)^2\right]}}\text{ and }\bar{p}_i|_y=N\left[\frac{N^{-1}(\rho_i)-r_i\rho_iy}{\sqrt{1-(r_i\rho_i)^2}}\right].$$

Derivative of v_∞

$$v'_\infty(y)=2\sum_{i=1}^{M}\sum_{j=1}^{M}w_iw_j\mu_i\mu_j\bar{p}'_i|_y\left\{N\left[\frac{N^{-1}\left(\bar{p}_j|_y\right)-\rho_{ij}^{Y}N^{-1}\left(\bar{p}'_j|_y\right)}{\sqrt{1-\left(\rho_{ij}^{Y}\right)^2}}\right]-\bar{p}_j|_y\right\}$$

with

$$\bar{p}'_i|_y-\frac{r_i\rho_i}{\sqrt{1-(r_i\rho_i)^2}}n\left[\frac{N^{-1}(p_i)-r_i\rho_iy}{\sqrt{1-(r_i\rho_i)^2}}\right].$$

Second component (v_{GA})

$$v_{GA}(y)=\sum_{i=1}^{M} w_i^2\left\{u^2\left[\bar{p}_i\,|_y - N^2\left(N^{-1}\left(\bar{p}_i\,|_y\right),N^{-1}\left(\bar{p}_i\,|_y\right),\rho_{ii}^Y\right)\right]+\sigma_i^2\bar{p}_i\,|_y\right\}$$

where σ_i^2 denotes the variance (around the mean μ_i) of the loss-given default for obligor i.

Derivative of v_{GA}

$$v'_{GA}(y)=\sum_{i=1}^{M} w_i^2\bar{p}'_i\,|_y\left\{\mu_i^2\left[1-2N\left(\frac{N^{-1}\left(\bar{p}'_i\,|_y\right)-\rho_{ii}^Y N^{-1}\left(\bar{p}'_i\,|_y\right)}{\sqrt{1-\left(\rho_{ii}^Y\right)^2}}\right)\right]+\sigma_i^2\right\}$$

1 See the Introduction of this book for further details.

2 The phrase "industry concentration" is somewhat imprecise, given that this risk can arise by the portfolio's country mix (geographic concentration), and more generally by the fact that different groups of obligors depend on different sets of macroeconomic factors (factor concentration). Nevertheless, such a phrase is widely used in practice, also with reference to geographic and/or factor concentration. Accordingly, in this chapter we will use the words "industry concentration", or "industries", having in mind any type of semi-specific risk due to the dependence of a group of exposures on the same set of macroeconomic factors.

3 Alternatively, models provided by external vendors can be used as a benchmark to assess the performance of internal models.

4 The Hirschmann–Herfindahl (HH) index takes a value of 0.7%; as a benchmark, portfolio made up of 1,000 equally-sized corporate exposures would have an HH of 0.1%.

5 For further details, see Gordy (2004), Vasicek (1984) or Resti and Sironi (2007).

6 Throughout this chapter we indicate by $\tilde{x}$ a random variable and by x the specific value it may take.

7 By unconditional PD we mean a probability of default that is estimated without exactly knowing what the macroeconomic cycle will be during the following 12 months (the risk horizon usually associated with bank PDs).

8 By a^2 we mean the regulatory asset correlation, decided by the Basel Committee, while by ρ_{ij} we indicate (see Equation 4.10) the empirical asset correlation, used by a bank to estimate its own economic capital.

9 For further details, see Resti and Sironi (2007).

10 We indicate this loss as L^*. The asterisk underlines that it is different from the one (L) measured with a multifactor model with finite granularity, like the one presented in the section on "A finite-granularity, multi-factor model", and from the one ($\bar{L}$) obtained with a calibrated asymptotic single-factor model ("hybrid model", see the section on "Explaining the gap between regulatory and economic capital").

11 More precisely, w_i and μ_i represent expected values for EAD and LGD conditional on the value y of the systemic factor (and since we are especially interested in extreme, unfavourable values for y, they represent a downturn EAD and a downturn LGD). For the sake of simplicity, we will assume that EAD and LGD do not depend on y (in other words, we will assume that exposure risk and recovery risk are totally idiosyncratic in nature and therefore 100% diversifiable), in which case w_i and μ_i can be seen as unconditional expectations; a nice discussion of the case in which μ_i depends on y is presented in Pykhtin (2003). Also, we will express w_i as the share of the total portfolio exposure associated with obligor

i; hence, an exposure with an EAD of €1 million within a portfolio with a total value of €1 billion will have $w_i = 0.1\%$.

12 The maturity adjustment is intended to calibrate the regulatory model (or any of the other models presented in this chapter, as they all adopt a binomial approach to credit risk) for the risk due to a possible downgrading of a bank's exposures; note that this aspect has proved crucial in the 2007–08 banking crisis, where rating cuts to asset-backed securities (especially in the real-estate and venture-capital sectors) have played a major role. However, downgrade risk goes beyond the scope of this chapter. For the sake of simplicity, we are also omitting the so-called "scale factor", that is, the fact that supervisors currently require banks to multiply the result in Equation 4.6 by 1.06, to make it more conservative.

13 To make it easier for the reader to follow the further results presented in the sections "Explaining the gap between regulatory and economic capital" and "Pykhtin's multifactor adjustment", we will use the same notation as in Pykhtin (2004).

14 For the sake of simplicity, we will assume that the factors $\tilde{z}_k$ in vector $\tilde{\mathbf{z}}$ are orthogonal. The vector $\mathbf{h}_i$ of the weights associated with real-world systemic factors (eg, areas or industries) will therefore have to be transformed (based on the factors' correlation matrix, $\mathbf{F}$) into a vector of weights associated with the orthogonal factors, as explained later in this paragraph.

15 As we assume that the $\tilde{z}_k$s follow a standard normal distribution, it has to be imposed that $\boldsymbol{\alpha}_i$ has unit norm, in order to ensure that $\tilde{y}_i$ also is standard-normally distributed.

16 As in Endnote 11, here, too, we can think of w_i and μ_i as the expected values for EAD and LGD conditional on the actual combination $\mathbf{z}$ of systemic factors for which we are computing losses. Or we can, for simplicity's sake, assume that EAD and LGD only depend on idiosyncratic elements, and treat w_i and μ_i as unconditional means.

17 The estimation of asset correlations and the association of borrowers with one or more macroeconomic risk factors goes beyond the scope of this chapter, although its importance for the quality of the results generated by an economic capital model can hardly be overstated. See Chapter 7, Akhavein, Kocagil and Neugebauer (2005) or Chernih, Vanduffel and Henrard (2006) for an introduction to the main approaches. More details on the estimation techniques that use default correlation as a means to estimate asset correlation can be found also in de Servigny and Renault (2004), Dietsch and Petey (2003), Nagpal and Bahar (2001) and Lucas (1995).

18 Although the ζ_is are not mutually independent, the computation of the expected value in Equation 4.21 does not change: the mean of a sum, in fact, is the sum of the means, regardless of any correlation existing across the variables being summed.

19 In other words, Equation 4.21 is just the mean of a distribution, due to the possible shocks on η_i (the share of systemic risk which is borrower-specific) and ξ_i (the pure idiosyncratic component). Two extra risk factors must be accounted for when picking the loss percentile associated with optimal capital: accordingly, economic capital will be higher than the value found with Equation 4.6 and the gap will be larger when the ρ_is are small (so that η_i and ξ_i increase in importance).

20 "The asset correlation parameters were chosen to match the economic risk in a credit portfolio that is very well-diversified across sectors" (Basel Committee on Banking Supervision 2006).

21 "Name concentration could add anywhere between 2% and 8% to the credit value-at-risk while sector concentration can increase economic capital by 20–40%" (Basel Committee on Banking Supervision 2006).

22 "Banks perceive that sector concentration (often referred to, with a positive connotation, as 'diversification') warrants capital relief relative to Pillar 1" (Basel Committee on Banking Supervision 2006).

23 As mentioned, this is a hybrid measure, as it combines the regulatory ASRF model and a set of factor loadings that are calibrated on our sample portfolio.

24 To do that, it is enough to remember (Greene 2003; Mina and Xiao 2001) that for a normally distributed vector $\mathbf{x}' = [\mathbf{x}_1' \;\; \mathbf{x}_2']$, with means $\boldsymbol{\mu}' = [\mu_1' \;\; \mu_2']$ and variance–covariance matrix $\Sigma = \begin{bmatrix} \Sigma_{11} & \Sigma_{12} \\ \Sigma_{21} & \Sigma_{22} \end{bmatrix}$, the conditional distribution of $\mathbf{x}_1 \,|\, \mathbf{x}_2$ is also normal, with mean $\mu_{1,2} = \mu_1 + \Sigma_{12}\Sigma_{22}^{-1}\Sigma_{21}(\mathbf{x}_2 - \mu_2)$ and variance $\Sigma_{11.2} = \Sigma_{11} - \Sigma_{12}\Sigma_{22}^{-1}\Sigma_{21}$. In our case, $\mathbf{x}' = [\mathbf{z}' \;\; y]$, $\mu = 0$ and $\Sigma = \begin{bmatrix} \mathbf{I} & \mathbf{b} \\ \mathbf{b}' & 1 \end{bmatrix}$.

25 See Appendix 4.1 for details.

26 This means that the link between h and k is not deterministic, but instead affected by some further source of uncertainty. For example, it could be $h = k + \varepsilon$, where ε is a random noise.

27 See Appendix 4.2 for proof.

28 In fact, we know that, for any given value of y, there is not just one value of the loss (as in the hybrid model), but instead there are infinitely many values for $\mathbf{z}$ consistent with y, each of which causes a different loss, as seen in Figure 4.11.

29 For more details see Resti and Sironi (2007).

REFERENCES

Akhavein, J. D., A. E. Kocagil, and M. Neugebauer, 2005, "A Comparative Empirical Study of Asset Correlations", Quantitative Financial Research Special Report, Fitch Ratings, New York.

Basel Committee on Banking Supervision, 2006, "Studies on credit risk concentration", working paper 15, Bank for International Settlements.

Chernih, A., S. Vanduffel and L. Henrard, 2006, "Asset Correlations: a Literature Review and Analysis of the Impact of Dependent Loss Given Defaults", unpublished manuscript.

Committee of European Banking Supervisors, 2005, "Application of the Supervisory Review Process under Pillar 2", Consultation paper, Committee of European Banking Supervisors, London.

De Servigny, A. and O. Renault, 2004, *Measuring and Managing Credit Risk* (New York: McGraw-Hill).

Dietsch, M., and J. Petey, 2003, "Should SME exposures be treated as retail or corporate exposures? A comparative analysis of probabilities of default and assets correlations in French and German SMEs", mimeo, University Robert Schuman, Strasbourg.

European Union, 2006, "Directive 2006/48/EC of the European Parliament and of the Council of 14 June 2006 relating to the taking up and pursuit of the business of credit institutions (recast)." *Official Journal of the European Union*, L 177/1–200.

Gordy, M. B., 2003, "A Risk-Factor Model Foundation for Ratings-Based Bank Capital Rules", *Journal of Financial Intermediation* 12, pp. 199–232.

Gordy, M. B., 2004, "Granularity adjustment in portfolio credit risk measurement", in di G. P. Szegö, *Risk Measures for the 21st Century* (Chichester: John Wiley & Sons).

Gourieroux, C., J-P. Laurent, and O Scaillet, 2000, "Sensitivity analysis of Values at Risk", *Journal of Empirical Finance*, pp. 225–45.

Greene, W., 2003, *Econometric Analysis* (Upper Saddle River: Prentice-Hall).

Lucas, D., 1995, "Default correlation and credit analysis", *Journal of Fixed Income* 9(4), pp. 76–87.

Martin, R., and T. Wilde, 2002, "Unsystematic Credit Risk", *Risk*, November, pp. 123–8.

Mina, J., and J. Yi Xiao, 2001, *Return to Riskmetrics: the Evolution of a Standard* (New York: RiskMetrics Group).

Nagpal, K., and R. Bahar, 2001, "Measuring Default Correlation", *Risk* 14(3), March, pp. 129–32.

Pykhtin, M., 2004, "Multifactor adjustment", *Risk*, March, pp. 85–90.

Pykhtin, M., 2003, "Unexpected Recovery Risk", *Risk* 16(8), pp. 74–8.

Resti, A., 2005, "Il nuovo accordo di Basilea sul capitale: genesi, contenuti, impatti", working paper, Newfin Università Bocconi, Milan.

Resti, A., 2008, "Il rischio di concentrazione sul portafoglio crediti", in A. Resti, *Il Secondo Pilastro di Basilea and la sfida del capitale economico* (Rome: Bancaria Editrice).

Resti, A. and A. Sironi, 2007, *Risk management and Shareholders' Value Creation in Banks* (Chichester: John Wiley & Sons).

Vasicek, O. A., 1984, *Credit Valuation* (San Francisco: KMV Corporation).

5

*Specification and Calibration Errors in Measures of Portfolio Credit Risk**

Nikola Tarashev, Haibin Zhu[1]

Bank for International Settlements

Assessments of portfolio credit risk have attracted much attention in recent years. One reason is that participants in the increasingly popular market for structured finance products rely heavily on estimates of the interdependence of credit risk across various exposures.[2] Such estimates are also of principal interest to financial supervisors who, in enforcing new standards in the banking and insurance industries, have to ensure that regulatory capital is closely aligned with credit risk.

This chapter investigates the well-known asymptotic single-risk-factor (ASRF) model of portfolio credit risk, which underpins the internal-ratings-based (IRB) approach of the Basel II framework (Basel Committee on Banking Supervision 2005). The popularity of this model stems from its implication that the contribution of each exposure to the credit value-at-risk (VaR) of the portfolio – defined as the maximum default loss that can be incurred with a given probability over a given horizon – is independent of the characteristics of the other exposures. This implication has been derived rigorously in Gordy (2003) and is known as portfolio invariance of marginal credit VaR contributions. The implication has been interpreted as alleviating the data requirements and computational burden on users of the model. Indeed, portfolio invariance implies that credit VaR can be calculated solely on the basis of exposure-specific parameters, including individual probability of default (PD), loss given default (LGD), and dependence on the common factor.

Its popularity notwithstanding, the "portfolio invariance" implication of the ASRF model hinges on two strong assumptions that have been criticised as sources of specification errors. Namely, the model assumes that the systematic component of credit risk is governed by a single common factor and that the portfolio is so finely grained that all idiosyncratic risks are diversified away. Violations of the "single-factor" and "perfect-granularity" assumptions would translate directly into erroneous assessments of portfolio credit risk.

Moreover, putting specification issues aside, a practical implementation of the ASRF model may be quite challenging. An important reason is that the portfolio invariance implication does not allow a user of the model to consider any particular exposure in isolation. Namely, estimates of exposure-specific dependence on the common factor, which are required for a calibration of the ASRF model, hinge on information about the correlation structure in the portfolio or about the common factor itself.[3] When such portfolio- or market-wide information is imperfect, the user will implement a flawed calibration of the model, which will be another source of errors in measured portfolio credit risk.

A contribution of this study is to develop a unified method for quantifying the importance of model specification and calibration errors in assessments of portfolio credit risk. In order to implement this method, we rely on a large data set that comprises Moody's KMV estimates of PDs and pairwise asset return correlations for nearly 11,000 nonfinancial corporations worldwide. We use these estimates as the actual credit-risk parameters of hypothetical portfolios that are designed to match the industrial-sector concentration of typical portfolios of US wholesale banks. For each hypothetical portfolio, we derive the "true" probability distribution of default losses and then condense this distribution into unexpected losses, which are defined as a credit VaR net of expected losses. This summary statistic is equivalent to a "target" capital measure necessary to cover default losses with a desired probability.[4] Target capital can be compared directly to a "shortcut" capital measure, which relies on the ASRF model and incorporates a rule-of-thumb calibration of the interdependence of credit risk across exposures.

We decompose the difference between the target and shortcut capital measures into four non-overlapping and exhaustive components. Two of these components, which we attribute to a "multifactor" effect and a "granularity" effect, relate to misspecification of the ASRF model. The other two components, which we derive after transforming the correlation structure to be consistent with the ASRF model, relate to errors in the calibration of the interdependence of credit risk across exposures.[5] Specifically, the calibration errors we consider arise either from an overall bias in the measured correlations of firms' asset returns – which gives rise to what we dub a "correlation level" effect – or from noise in the measured dispersion of these correlations across pairs of firms – a "correlation dispersion" effect.

Another contribution of this study is that it provides two additional perspectives on flaws in the calibration of the ASRF model. First, we calculate deviations from a desired capital buffer that arise not from the adoption of rule-of-thumb parameter values but from plausible small-sample errors in asset return correlation estimates. Second, motivated by the analysis in Gordy (2000) and Frey and McNeil (2003), we examine the importance of errors in the calibration of tail dependence among asset returns. The impact of such errors on capital measures is similar to but materialises independently of the impact of errors in estimated asset return correlations.

Our conclusion is that errors in the practical implementation, as opposed to the specification, of the ASRF model are the main sources of potential miscalculations of credit risk in large portfolios. Specifically, the misspecification-driven multifactor effect leads a user of the model to underpredict target capital buffers by only 1%. This is because a single-factor approximation, if chosen optimally, fits well the correlation structure of asset returns in our data. In addition, the granularity effect results in a 5% underprediction of the target level. In comparison, assessments of portfolio credit risk are considerably more sensitive to possible miscalibrations of the ASRF model. The correlation dispersion effect, for example, leads to capital measures that are 12% higher than the target measure. In turn, the correlation level effect causes a roughly 8% overprediction (underprediction) of the target measure for each percentage point of positive (negative) error in the average correlation coeffcient. Furthermore, plausible small-sample errors in correlation estimates – arising when users of the model have five to 10 years of monthly asset returns data – translate into capital measures that may deviate from the target level by 30% to 45%. Finally, data on asset returns are at odds with the conventional multinormality assumption. Specifically, this assumption implies tail-of-distribution dependence among asset returns that is too low and translates into an underestimation of the target capital by 22% to 86%.

Among the four effects on capital measures, only the granularity effect is sensitive to the number of exposures in the portfolio. When this number decreases, the portfolio maintains a larger portion of idiosyncratic risks.

Thus, we are not surprised to find that the granularity effect leads to a 19% underestimation of target capital in typical small portfolios.

To the best of our knowledge, this is the first effort to develop a unified framework for analysing a wide range of errors in assessments of portfolio credit risk. Most of the related literature has focused exclusively on misspecifications of the ASRF model and has proposed partial corrections that do not impair the model's tractability. Empirical analyses of violations of the perfect granularity assumption include Martin and Wilde (2002), Vasicek (2002), Emmer and Tasche (2003), and Gordy and Lütkebohmert (2007). For their part, Pykhtin (2004), Düllmann (2006), Düllmann and Masschelein (2006), and Garcia Cespedes *et al* (2006) have analysed implications of the common-factor assumption under different degrees of portfolio concentration in industrial sectors. In addition, Heitfield, Burton, and Chomsisengphet (2006) and Düllman, Scheicher, and Schmieder (2006) have examined both granularity and sector concentration issues in the context of US and European bank portfolios, respectively.[6] A small branch of the related literature, which includes Loeffler (2003) and Morinaga and Shiina (2005), has considered only calibration issues and has derived that noise in model parameters can have a significant impact on assessments of portfolio credit risk.

The remainder of this chapter is organised as follows. The next section outlines the ASRF model and the empirical methodology applied to it. Following this, we describe the data and then report the empirical results. Finally, we conclude.

METHODOLOGY

In this section, we first outline the ASRF model. Then, we discuss how violations of its key assumptions or flawed calibration of its parameters can affect assessments of portfolio credit risk. Finally, we develop an empirical methodology for quantifying and comparing alternative sources of error in such assessments.

The ASRF Model[7]

The ASRF model of portfolio credit risk – introduced by Vasicek (1991) – postulates that an obligor defaults when its assets fall below some threshold. In addition, the model assumes that asset values are driven by a single common factor

$$V_{iT} = \rho_i \cdot M_T + \sqrt{1-\rho_i^2} \cdot Z_{iT} \tag{5.1}$$

where V_{iT} is the value of assets of obligor i at time T; M_T and Z_{iT} denote the common and idiosyncratic factors, respectively; and $\rho_i \in [-1,1]$ is the obligor-specific loading on the common factor. The common and idiosyncratic factors are independent of each other and scaled to random variables with mean 0 and variance 1.[8] Thus, the asset return correlation between borrowers i and j is given by $\rho_i \rho_j$.

The ASRF model delivers a closed-form approximation to the probability distribution of default losses on a portfolio of N exposures. The accuracy of the approximation increases when the number of exposures grows, $N \to \infty$, and the largest exposure weight shrinks, $\sup_i(w_i) \to 0$. In these limits, in which the portfolio is perfectly granular, the probability distribution of default losses can be derived as follows. First, let the indicator I_{iT} equal 1 if obligor i is in default at time T and 0 otherwise. Conditional on the value of the common factor, the expectation of this indicator equals

$$\begin{aligned} E(I_{iT} \mid M_T) &= \Pr\left(V_{iT} < F^{-1}(PD_{iT}) \mid M_T\right) \\ &= \Pr\left(\rho_i \cdot M_T + \sqrt{1-\rho_i^2} \cdot Z_{iT} < F^{-1}(PD_{iT}) \mid M_T\right) \\ &= H\left(\frac{F^{-1}(PD_{iT}) - \rho_i M_T}{\sqrt{1-\rho_i^2}}\right) \end{aligned}$$

where PD_{iT} is the unconditional probability that obligor i is in default at time T; the cumulative distribution function (CDF) of Z_{iT} is denoted by $H(\cdot)$; and the CDF of V_{iT} is $F(\cdot)$, implying that the default threshold equals $F^{-1}(PD_{iT})$.

Second, under perfect granularity, the law of large numbers implies that the conditional total loss on the portfolio, $TL \mid M$, is deterministic for any value of the common factor M

$$\begin{aligned} TL \mid M &= \sum_i w_i \cdot E(LGD_i) \cdot E(I_i \mid M) \\ &= \sum_i w_i \cdot E(LGD_i) \cdot H\left(\frac{F^{-1}(PD_i) - \rho_i M}{\sqrt{1-\rho_i^2}}\right) \end{aligned} \tag{5.2}$$

where time subscripts have been suppressed. In addition, the loss given default of obligor i, LGD_i, is assumed to be independent of both the common and idiosyncratic factors.[9]

Finally, the conditional total loss $TL \mid M$ is a decreasing function of the common factor M and, consequently, the unconditional distribution of TL can be derived directly on the basis of Equation 5.2 and the CDF of the common factor, $G(\cdot)$. Denoting by $TL_{1-\alpha}$ the $(1-\alpha)^{th}$ percentile in the distribution of total losses, ie, $\Pr(TL < TL_{1-\alpha}) = 1 - \alpha$, it follows that

$$TL_{1-\alpha} = \sum_i w_i \cdot E(LGD_i) \cdot H\left(\frac{F^{-1}(PD_i) - \rho_i G^{-1}(\alpha)}{\sqrt{1-\rho_i^2}}\right) \qquad (5.3)$$
$$= TL \mid M_\alpha$$

where $M_\alpha \equiv G^{-1}(\alpha)$ is the αth percentile in the distribution of the common factor. The magnitude $TL_{1-\alpha}$ is also known as the credit VaR at the $(1-\alpha)$ confidence level.

The capital buffer that covers unexpected (ie, total minus expected) losses on the entire portfolio with probability $(1-\alpha)$ equals[10]

$$K = TL_{1-\alpha} - \sum_i w_i \cdot E(LGD_i) \cdot PD_i$$
$$= \sum_i w_i \cdot E(LGD_i) \cdot \left[H\left(\frac{F^{-1}(PD_i) - \rho_i G^{-1}(\alpha)}{\sqrt{1-\rho_i^2}}\right) - PD_i\right] \qquad (5.4)$$
$$\equiv \sum_i w_i \cdot K_i$$

As implied by this equation, the capital buffer for the portfolio can be set on the basis of exposure-specific parameters, which comprise the exposure's weight in the portfolio, as well as its LGD, PD, and loading on the common factor. The flip side of this implication is that the portion of the capital buffer attributed to any particular exposure is independent of the rest of the portfolio and, thus, is portfolio invariant.[11]

In practice, an implementation of the ASRF model requires that the distribution of the common and idiosyncratic factors of asset returns be specified. It is standard to assume normal distributions and rewrite Equation 5.4 as

$$K = \sum_i w_i \cdot E(LGD_i) \cdot \left[\Phi\left(\frac{\Phi^{-1}(PD_i) - \rho_i \Phi^{-1}(\alpha)}{\sqrt{1-\rho_i^2}}\right) - PD_i\right] \qquad (5.5)$$

where $\Phi(\cdot)$ is the CDF of a standard normal variable. Equation 5.5 underpins the regulatory capital formula in the IRB approach of Basel II, in which $E(LGD_i) = 45\%$ and $\alpha = 0.1\%$.

Impact of model misspecification

The portfolio invariance implication of the ASRF model hinges on two key assumptions – ie, that the portfolio is of perfect granularity and that there is a single common factor. In light of this, we examine at a conceptual level how violations of either of these assumptions – which give rise to "granularity" and "multifactor" effects – affect capital measures. For the illustrative examples in this section, we use the ASRF formula in Equation 5.5 and set $\alpha = 0.1\%$.

Granularity effect

The granularity effect arises empirically either because of a limited number of exposures or because of exposure concentration in a small number of borrowers. In either of these cases, idiosyncratic risk is not fully diversified away. Therefore, the existence of a granularity effect implies that capital measures based on the ASRF model would be insufficient to cover unexpected losses.

The top-left panel in Figure 5.1 provides an illustrative example of the granularity effect. This example focuses on a homogeneous portfolio, which gives rise to a desired capital level that decreases with the number of exposures (solid line).[12] The figure also plots the capital measure obtained under the ASRF model and, thus, incorporates the assumption that there is an infinite number of exposures (dotted line). The difference between the dotted and solid lines equals the magnitude of the granularity effect. As expected, the granularity effect is always negative and decreases when the number of exposures increases.

Gordy and Lütkebohmert (2007) derive a closed-form "granularity adjustment," which approximates (the negative of) the granularity effect. When the portfolio is homogeneous, the approximation is linear in the reciprocal of the number of exposures, which is largely in line with the properties of the granularity effect plotted in Figure 5.1.[13]

Multifactor effect

The impact of various macroeconomic and industry-specific conditions on portfolio credit risk may be best accounted for by generalising Equation 5.1 to incorporate multiple (potentially unobservable) common factors. Multiple common factors affect the likelihood of default clustering (ie, the likelihood of a large number of defaults occurring over a given horizon), which influences the tails of the probability distribution of credit losses.[14] In line with our empirical results (reported later in this chapter), we treat a fattening of these tails (reflected in greater kurtosis) as implying unambiguously a higher level of the desired capital buffer.[15]

Importantly, the existence of multiple common factors of credit risk would violate the single-factor assumption of the ASRF model, leading to what we call a multifactor effect in capital measures. Depending on the characteristics of the credit portfolio, the multifactor effect could be either negative – ie, implying that the ASRF model underestimates the desired capital – or positive. To illustrate the two possibilities, we generalise Equation 5.1 to

$$V_i = \rho_{1,i} \cdot M_1 + \rho_{2,i} \cdot M_2 + \sqrt{1 - \rho_{1,i}^2 - \rho_{2,i}^2} \cdot Z_i \tag{5.6}$$

where M_1, M_2, and Z_i are mutually independent standard normal variables.

In our first example, we consider a portfolio in which all exposures have equal weights, have the same PD, and are divided into two groups according to their dependence on the common factors. For exposures in the first group, $0 < \rho_{1,i} = \rho < 1$ and $\rho_{2,i} = 0$, while $\rho_{1,j} = 0$ and $0 < \rho_{2,j} = \rho < 1$ for exposures in the second group. Thus, the common factors are group specific and underpin positive and homogeneous within-group pairwise correlations and zero across-group correlations. The solid line in the top-right panel of Figure 5.1 plots the desired capital measure for such a portfolio as a function of the relative weight of exposures in group 1.[16] This measure is lowest when the portfolio is most diversified between the two groups of exposures and, thus, the probability of large default losses is minimised. In addition, the dashed line in the panel plots an alternative capital measure, which is based on the ASRF model and, thus, incorporates a single-factor structure of the asset return correlations. We choose this structure optimally in order to provide the ASRF model with as much information about the true correlations as possible, subject to the single factor constraint (see Appendix 5.3). As it turns out, the single-factor approximation matches extremely well the true average asset return correlation but approximates only roughly the dispersion of correlation coefficients in the cross-section of exposures.

The difference between the dashed and solid lines equals the multifactor effect. This effect is negative because the single-factor assumption of the ASRF model ignores the fact that the common factors are two independent sources of default clustering, which leads to an underestimation of the desired capital. The underestimation is largest when the two groups enter the portfolio with equal weights, in which case the role of multiple factors is greatest.

It is possible, however, to construct another example, in which imposing an erroneous single-factor structure on portfolio credit risk distorts the interaction between asset return correlations and individual PDs in a way that leads to a positive multifactor effect. Consider a portfolio comprising two

Figure 5.1 Four sources of error in capital measures

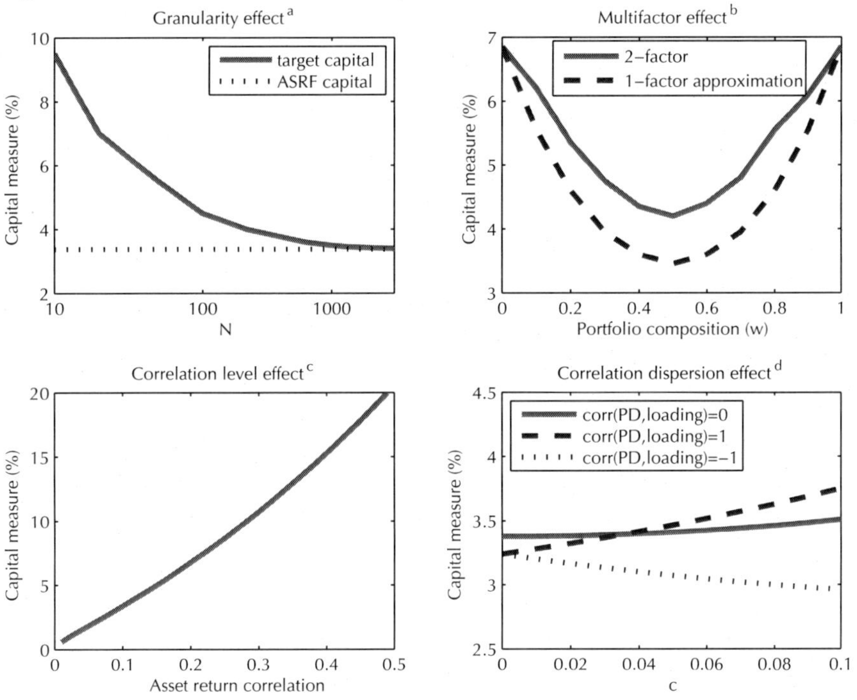

Note: Capital measures, in percent and per unit of aggregate exposure, are shown on the vertical axes. For each panel (unless noted otherwise), PD = 1% and LGD = 50% are the same across exposures.
[a]The solid line plots target capital for a portfolio in which all pairwise asset return correlations equal 10%. The number of exposures in the portfolio (N) varies across the horizontal axis. The dotted line plots the corresponding capital estimate when $N \to \infty$. [b]The portfolio consists of 1,000 exposures that are divided into two groups, with w denoting the weight of the first group. Within each group, the asset return correlations equals 20% for all exposure pairs. Intergroup correlations are zero. The solid line plots the target capital level, which incorporates the two common factors in the simulated data. The dashed line plots the capital calculated under a one-common-factor approximation of the correlation structure (see Appendix 5.3). [c]Capital measures are shown for different levels of homogeneous pairwise asset return correlations. [d]The solid line plots capital measures under the assumption that PD = 1%, there is a single common factor, and the loadings on this factor are distributed uniformly in the cross-section between $\sqrt{0.1} - c$ and $\sqrt{0.1} + c$. For the other two lines, PDs are distributed uniformly in the cross-section between 0.5% and 1.5% and have a positive (dashed line) or negative (dotted line) linear relationship with the common-factor loadings.

groups of exposures, with the exposures in the first group being individually riskier but less correlated among themselves than the exposures in the second group. In terms of Equation 5.6, this can be formalised by postulating that firms with high PDs feature $0 < \rho_{1,i} = \rho < 1$ and $\rho_{2,i} = 0$, whereas firms with low PDs feature $0 < \rho_{1,j} = \rho_{2,j} = \rho < 1$. A single-factor approximation to this correlation structure would match the average correlation coefficient but would also imply too high a correlation among riskier exposures. Raising the probability of default clustering, this would lead to a capital buffer that is larger than desired.

Impact of calibration errors

Errors in the calibration of the ASRF model will affect assessments of portfolio credit risk even if this model is well specified. In this chapter, we focus on errors in the calibration of the interdependence of credit risk across exposures, which can be driven by noise in the adopted values of asset return correlations or by a flawed assumption regarding the distribution of asset returns. When analysing the consequences of such errors, we maintain our earlier practice and treat fattening of the tails of the loss distribution as implying unambiguously a higher 99.9% credit VaR and, thus, a higher desired level of the capital buffer. In this way, we sharpen the conceptual analysis and keep it in line with our empirical findings.

We study two general types of errors in calibrated asset return correlations: errors in the average correlation coefficient and errors in the dispersion of correlation coefficients across exposure pairs. It is important to keep in mind how these calibration-driven errors relate to errors induced by the two misspecification effects that we examined earlier. First, given that they occur within the constraints of the ASRF model, calibration errors are independent of the granularity effect. Second, given the properties of the one factor approximation that underlies the extraction of the multifactor effect, this effect is effectively separated from errors in the average correlation (see above). By contrast, errors in the calibrated dispersion of asset return correlations could arise either as a result of ignoring the importance of multiple factors or as a result of noise in the estimated factor loadings when there is a single common factor. In this section, we are concerned with the second case, as it is consistent with a correct specification of the ASRF model and refers only to calibration errors.

The two types of errors in calibrated asset return correlations have various potential sources. One possibility is that a user of the ASRF model relies entirely on rule-of-thumb values, which may simply be correlation estimates for a popular credit index. Such estimates will lead to a discrepancy between desired and calculated capital to the extent that the popular index is not representative of the user's own portfolio. Alternatively, a user of the model may have access only to short time series of data on the assets of the obligors in its portfolio, which would lead to small-sample estimation errors in asset return correlations. Indeed, this second source of error is likely to be important in practice because (i) asset value estimates are typically available at low (ie, monthly or quarterly) frequencies and (ii) supervisory texts require that financial institutions possess only five years of relevant data.[17]

A positive error in the average level of asset return correlations leads to a capital measure that is higher than the desired one (Figure 5.1, bottom-left panel). This result reflects the intuition that inflating asset return correlations increases the likelihood of default clustering, which fattens the tails of the loss distribution. In the remainder of this chapter, the impact of errors in the average correlation on capital measures is dubbed the "correlation level" effect.

In turn, the effect of noise in the estimated dispersion of correlation coefficients can be seen in the following example. Suppose that all firms in one portfolio have homogeneous PDs and exhibit homogeneous pairwise asset return correlations. Suppose further that a second portfolio is characterised by the same PDs and average asset return correlation but includes a group of firms that are more likely to default together. The second portfolio, in which pairwise correlations exhibit dispersion, is more likely to experience several simultaneous defaults and, thus, has a loss distribution with fatter tails. Consequently, of the two portfolios, the second one requires higher capital in order to attain solvency with the same probability. This is portrayed by the upward slope of the solid line in the bottom-right panel of Figure 5.1 and is a particular instance of what we dub the "correlation dispersion" effect, which arises in the context of a single common factor.

This result can be strengthened (dashed line in the same panel) but also weakened or even reversed if PDs vary across firms. To see why, consider the previous example but suppose that the strongly correlated firms in the second portfolio are the ones that have the lowest individual PDs. In other words, the firms that are likely to generate multiple defaults are less likely to default. As a result, greater dispersion of asset return correlations may lower the probability of default clustering in the second portfolio to an extent that depresses the desired capital level below that for the first portfolio. This is illustrated by the negative slope of the dotted line in the bottom-right panel of Figure 5.1.

Even if asset return correlations were known with certainty, a flawed calibration of the overall distribution of asset returns would still drive errors in the calibrated interdependence of credit risk across exposures. Although the ASRF model imposes quite weak restrictions on asset return distributions, it is common practice to adopt distributions whose main advantages stem not from realistic features but from operational convenience. In particular, the consensus in the literature is that asset returns have fatter tails than those imposed by the conventional normality assumption. To the extent that the fatness of the tails reflects the distribution of the common factor, the probability of default clustering and, thus, the desired capital level would be higher than those derived under normality (Hull and White 2004; Tarashev and Zhu 2006). We study this issue by considering Student-*t* distributions for both the common and idiosyncratic factors of asset returns.

Evaluating various sources of error

An important contribution of this study is to present a unified empirical method for quantifying the impact of several sources of error in model-based assessment of portfolio credit risk. In particular, we focus on the difference between target capital measures and shortcut ones, the latter of which are based on the ASRF model and probable erroneous calibration of its parameters. We dissect this difference into four non-overlapping and exhaustive components, attributing them to the multifactor, granularity, correlation level, and correlation dispersion effects. In order to probe further the likely magnitude of the last two effects, we derive plausible small-sample errors that could affect direct estimates of asset return correlations. Finally, we also examine the implications of erroneous assumptions regarding the distribution of asset returns.

Baseline method

The baseline empirical method consists of two general steps. In the first step, we construct a hypothetical portfolio that is either "large"-consisting of 1,000 equal exposures – or "small" – consisting of 200 equal exposures.[18] The sectoral composition of such a portfolio is constrained to be in line with the typical loan portfolio of large wholesale banks in the US.[19] Given the constraint, the portfolio is sampled at random from the entire population of firms in our data set. Since each simulated portfolio is subject to sampling noise, we examine 3,000 different draws for both large and small portfolios.

For a portfolio constructed in the first step, the second step calculates five alternative capital measures, which differ in the underlying assumptions regarding the interdependence of credit risk across exposures. Each of these alternatives employs the same set of PD values and assumes that asset returns are normally distributed. In addition, each alternative incorporates random LGDs that are independent of all random variables driving defaults. The LGD distributions are symmetric, triangular, peak at 50%, have a continuous support on the interval [0%,100%], and are identical and independent across exposures.[20]

Each measure differs from a previous one owing to a single assumption:

1. The target capital measure incorporates data on asset return correlations, which are treated as representing the "truth." Using these correlations, we conduct Monte Carlo simulations to construct the "true" probability distribution of default losses at the one-year horizon. The implied 99.9% credit VaR minus expected losses equals target capital (see Appendix 5.2 for further detail).[21]
2. The second capital measure differs from target capital only owing to a restriction on the number of common factors governing asset returns. In particular, we adopt a correlation matrix that fits the original one as closely as possible under the constraint that correlation coefficients should be consistent with the presence of a single common factor (see Appendix 5.3). The fitted single-factor correlation matrix is used to derive the one-year probability distribution of joint defaults on the basis of the so-called Gaussian copula method (see Appendix 5.1). This distribution is then mapped into a probability distribution of default losses and, finally, into a capital measure.
3. The third capital measure differs from the second one only in that it assumes that all idiosyncratic risk is diversified away. This assumption allows us to use the fitted single factor correlation matrix, which underpins measure 2 in the ASRF formula (Equation 5.5).
4. The fourth capital measure differs from the third one only in that it is based on the assumption that loading coefficients on the single common factor are the same across exposures. The resulting common correlation coefficient, which is set equal to the average of the pairwise correlations underpinning measures 2 and 3, is used as an input to the ASRF formula (Equation 5.5).
5. Finally, the shortcut capital measure differs from the fourth one only in that it incorporates alternative, rule-of-thumb, values for the common correlation coefficient.

The three intermediate measures lead to a straightforward dissection of the difference between target and shortcut capital.[22] Specifically, the difference between measures 5 and 1 is the sum of the following four components: (i) the difference between measures 2 and 1, which equals the multifactor effect; (ii) the difference between measures 3 and 2, which equals the granularity effect; (iii) the difference between measures 4 and 3, which equals the correlation dispersion effect; and (iv) the difference between measures 5 and 4, which equals the correlation level effect.

The specific ordering and choice of the three intermediate capital measures is a result of the following reasoning. As far as measure 2 is concerned, it is determined by the necessity to extract the multifactor effect first. The reason for this is twofold. First, deriving a capital measure that assumes an infinite number of exposures but allows for multiple factors (ie, extracting the granularity effect before the multifactor effect) is subject to approximation errors (Pykhtin 2004). Second, it is possible to isolate calibration errors (via measures 4 and 5) only after the extraction of the multifactor effect (via measure 2) has modified the original correlation matrix so that it is consistent with the ASRF model. Likewise, an application of this model for the extraction of calibration errors requires the assumption of infinite granularity, which explains why measure 3 is calculated before measures 4 and 5.[23] Finally, modifying measure 4 by preserving the cross-sectional distribution of the single-factor correlation coefficients but changing their average level would reverse the order in which the correlation level and dispersion effects are extracted. An important problem with this procedure is that it would allow only for an imperfect estimate of the correlation level effect because this estimate would be influenced by changes in the structure of the single-factor correlation matrix.

Two extensions

In an attempt to delve further into the impact of plausible calibration errors on capital measures, we conduct two additional exercises. Each exercise focuses on a specific type of error in the calibrated interdependence of defaults and incorporates the assumption that the true PDs are identical across exposures. This assumption insulates capital measures from the impact of interaction between heterogeneous PDs and errors in the calibrated interdependence of defaults.

In the first exercise, we derive the extent to which plausible limitations on the size of available data can affect assessments of portfolio credit risk by affecting the estimates of asset return correlations. Specifically, we draw time series of asset returns from a joint distribution in which all pairwise correlations equal the correlation underpinning measure 4. Then we use the sample correlation matrix of the simulated series, a typical value for the probability of default, and the ASRF formula in Equation 5.5 in order to derive a capital measure.[24] The difference between this measure and the desired capital, which employs the exact correlation structure, is driven by small-sample noise in the estimates of asset return correlations.

In our second exercise, we examine how measure 4 would change if the common and idiosyncratic factors of asset returns are in fact driven by Student-*t* distributions. The results of this exercise reveal how flawed calibration of the tail-of-distribution dependence among asset returns affects capital calculations. In order to carry out the exercise, we use the general ASRF formula in Equation 5.4 and make two technical adjustments to the empirical setup. The first adjustment rescales the common and idiosyncratic factors to random variables with a unit variance.[25] The second adjustment addresses the fact that the generalised CDF of asset returns, $F(\cdot)$, does not exist in closed form. In concrete terms, we calculate the default threshold $F^{-1}(PD)$ on the basis of 10 million Monte Carlo simulations.

DATA DESCRIPTION

This section describes the two major blocks of data that we rely on: (i) credit risk parameter estimates provided by Moody's KMV and (ii) the sectoral distribution of exposures in typical portfolios of US wholesale banks.

Credit-risk parameters

Our sample includes the universe of firms covered in July 2006 by both the expected default frequency (EDF) model and the global correlation (GCorr) model of Moody's KMV. These two models deliver, respectively, estimates of one-year physical PDs and physical asset return correlation coefficients for publicly traded companies. We abstract from financial firms and work with 10,891 companies.

The sample covers firms with diverse characteristics. Specifically, 5,709 of the firms are headquartered in the US; 4,383 in Western Europe; and the remaining 799 in the rest of the world. Further, the distribution of the 10,891 firms across industrial sectors is reported in the last column in Table 5.1, with the largest share of firms (10.4%) coming from the business service sector. Importantly, only 1,434 (or 13.2%) of the firms have a rating from either S&P or Moody's, which matches the stylised fact that the majority of bank exposures are unrated.

There are several reasons why EDFs and GCorr correlations are natural data for our exercise. First, the two measures are derived within mutually consistent frameworks, which build on the model of Merton (1974) and are in the spirit of the ASRF model (see Das and Ishii 2001, Crosbie and Bohn 2003, and Crosbie 2005 for detail). Second, in line with their role in this chapter, Moody's KMV EDFs have been widely used as proxies for actual default probabilities (Berndt *et al* 2005 and Longstaff, Mithal, and Neis 2005). Third, the GCorr correlations are underpinned by a multifactor structure, which is crucial for our study of the multifactor effect. In particular, this model incorporates 120 common factors that comprise two global economic factors, five regional economic factors, seven sector factors, 61 industry-specific factors, and 45 country-specific factors.

Table 5.2 and Figure 5.2 report summary statistics of the Moody's KMV one-year PD and asset return correlation estimates. The cross-sectional distribution of PDs has a long right tail and, thus, its median (0.39%) is much lower than its mean (2.67%). In addition, the favourable credit conditions in July 2006 resulted in 1,217 firms (ie, about 11.2% of the total) having the lowest EDF score (0.02%) allowed by the Moody's KMV empirical methodology. At the same time, the upper bound on the Moody's KMV PD estimates (20%) is attained by 643 firms. For their part, GCorr correlations are limited between 0 and 65%. Clustered mainly between 5% and 25%, these correlations average 9.24%.[26]

Characteristics of hypothetical portfolios

The portfolios we simulate match the sectoral distribution of the typical portfolio of US wholesale banks. Specifically, to construct a large portfolio (1,000 exposures), we apply the forty nonfinancial sector weights reported by Heitfield, Burton, and Chomsisengphet (2006) (see Table 5.1). For a small portfolio (200 exposures), we rescale the 10 largest sectoral weights so that they sum to unity, and we set all other weights to zero. Within each sector, we draw firms at random.[27] All firms in a portfolio receive equal weights (up to a rounding error) and, thus, there is a one-to-one correspondence between the number of firms in a sector and that sector's weight in the portfolio.

The sector and name concentration indexes, reported at the bottom of Table 5.1, provide justification for our design of large and small portfolios. Calculated as the sum of squared sectoral (name) weights, the sector (name) concentration index of the large portfolios studied equals 0.0432 (0.001). This belongs to the range of concentration indexes [0.03, 0.045] ([0.000, 0.003]) reported in Heitfield, Burton, and Chomsisengphet (2006) for large portfolios of US banks. For small portfolios, the analogous indexes and ranges are 0.1135 (0.005) and [0.035, 0.213] ([0.001, 0.008]), respectively.

Table 5.1 Sectoral composition of simulated portfolios

	Large portfolio		Small portfolio		*Memo:*
Sector	**Number of names**	**Exposure weight (%)**	**Number of names**	**Exposure weight (%)**	**Number of firms in the sample**
Aerospace and defence	31	3.1			105
Agriculture	9	0.9			56
Air transportation	4	0.4			83
Apparel, footwear, and textiles	17	1.7			357
Automotive	51	5.1	19	9.5	198
Broadcast media	43	4.3	16	8.0	191
Business services	23	2.3			1132
Chemicals	42	4.2	15	7.5	940
Computer equipment	10	1.0			746
Construction	43	4.3	16	8.0	277
Electric, gas and sanitary	107	10.7	39	19.5	335
Electronics and electrical	18	1.8			693
Entertainment and leisure	33	3.3			294
Fabricated metals	17	1.7			146
Food, beverages and tobacco	63	6.3	23	11.5	490
General retail	31	3.1			133
Glass and stone	6	0.6			149
Health care	38	3.8	14	7.0	178
Legal and other services	16	1.6			452
Lodging	22	2.2			70
Machinery and equipment	36	3.6	13	6.5	645
Medical equipment	10	1.0			334
Mining	6	0.6			486
Miscellaneous manufacturing	18	1.8			130
Non-defence trans. and parts	2	0.2			130
Oil and gas exploration	55	5.5	20	10.0	458
Oil refining and delivery	24	2.4			100
Other trans. services	22	2.2			108
Paper and forestry	23	2.3			172
Personal services	7	0.7			31
Primary metals	11	1.1			188
Printing and publishing	28	2.8			186
Repair services and rental	13	1.3			37
Restaurants	9	0.9			141
Rubber and plastics	18	1.8			120
Semiconductors	2	0.2			177
Telecommunications	69	6.9	25	12.5	177
Trucking and warehousing	5	0.5			68
Water transportation	5	0.5			104
Wood, furniture and fixtures	13	1.3			151
Total	1000	100	200	100	10891
Sector concentration index	0.0432		0.1135		
Name concentration index	0.0010		0.0050		

Note: A concentration index equals the sum of squared weights, set either at the firm or sector level.

Table 5.2 Summary statistics (%)

	Mean	Std. dev.	Skewness	Median	Minimum	Maximum
One-year PDs	2.67	5.28	2.49	0.39	0.02	20.00
Pairwise correlations	9.24	3.86	1.87	8.45	0.29	65.00

Note: The sample includes 10,891 nonfinancial firms.

EMPIRICAL RESULTS

We implement the empirical methodology described earlier in order to quantify the impact of various sources of error in ASRF-based assessments of portfolio credit risk. Before reporting our findings, it is useful to highlight several aspects of the methodology.

First, as far as calibration of the model is concerned, our analysis focuses exclusively on errors in the values of parameters that relate to the interde-

Figure 5.2 Distribution of individual PDs and pairwise correlations

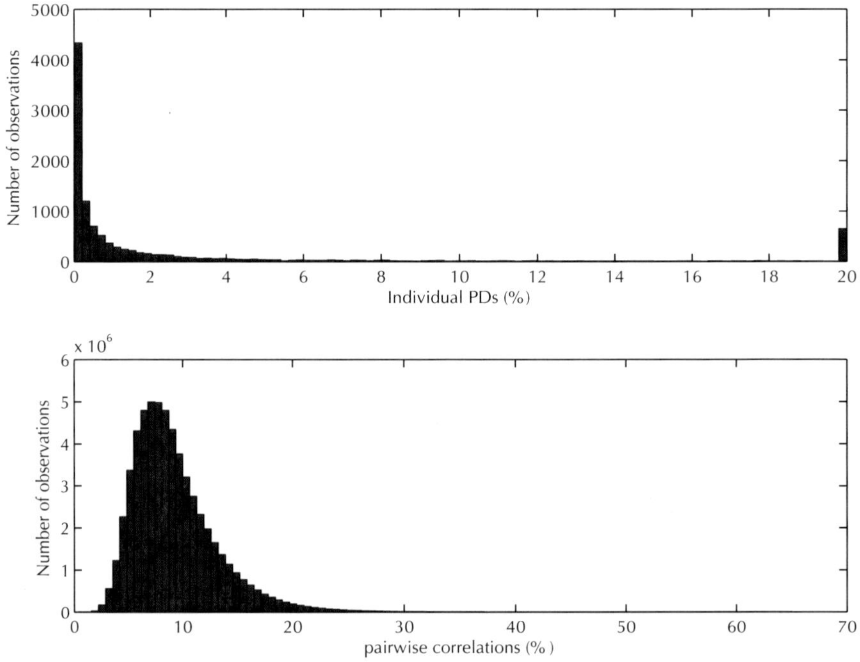

Note: The parameter estimates relate to 10,891 nonfinancial firms in July 2006.
Source: Moody's KMV

pendence of credit risk across exposures. Considering the impact of noise in PD and LGD estimates would make it extremely difficult to isolate the correlation level and dispersion effects we focus on. This is because noise in PDs and LGDs would interact with noise in correlation inputs in a highly nonlinear fashion.

Second, we make the stylised assumption that portfolios consist of equally weighted exposures. Considering disparate exposure sizes would require considering an additional dimension of portfolio characteristics, as it will no longer be the case that the granularity of a larger portfolio is necessarily finer. In addition, lower granularity that results from higher concentration in a small number of borrowers would also have a bearing on the number and importance of common factors affecting the portfolio and on the overall correlation of risk across exposures. This would make it impossible to isolate the granularity effect from the other three effects we consider.

Finally, our analysis treats the correlation matrix provided by Moody's KMV as revealing the "true" correlation of asset returns. Of course, this matrix is itself an estimate that is subject to errors. Nevertheless, the Moody's KMV correlation matrix provides a reasonable benchmark to work from. In addition, we have verified that results regarding the relative importance of alternative sources of error depend only marginally on the accuracy of the GCorr estimates, even though the absolute impact of alternative sources of error does change with the benchmark correlation level.

Various errors in shortcut capital measures

To study various sources of error in assessments of portfolio credit risk, we calculate the five capital measures (listed on page 121) for 3,000 large and as many small hypothetical portfolios. Even though they have the same sectoral composition by construction, the simulated portfolios differ from each other with respect to the individual constituent exposures and, thus, with respect to the underlying risk parameters (see Table 5.3).

Table 5.4 reports summary statistics of the target and shortcut capital measures (ie, the two extremes described earlier). For large portfolios, the target capital averages 3.31% (per unit of aggregate exposure) across the 3,000 simulated portfolios. The corresponding shortcut level (based on a rule-of-thumb asset return correlation of 12%) is 81 basis points (bp) higher.

Decomposing the difference between target and shortcut capital for large portfolios reveals that errors caused by model misspecification play a minor role. In qualitative terms, the multifactor effect can be of either sign (fourth

Table 5.3 Characteristics of simulated loan portfolios (%)

	A. Large portfolios (1000 firms)				
	Mean	**Std. dev.**	**Median**	**Minimum**	**Maximum**
Average PD	2.42	0.19	2.42	1.79	3.12
Std. dev. of individual PDs	5.16	0.26	5.16	4.25	6.14
Median PD	0.26	0.03	0.26	0.18	0.36
Average correlation	9.78	0.22	9.77	9.14	10.73
Std. dev. of loadings	9.33	0.31	9.32	8.33	10.47
Corr (PD, loadings)	–20.00	2.04	–20.10	–26.70	–12.80
	B. Small portfolios (200 firms)				
	Mean	**Std. dev.**	**Median**	**Minimum**	**Maximum**
Average PD	2.28	0.36	2.26	1.24	3.68
Std. dev. of individual PDs	5.05	0.53	5.06	3.01	6.89
Median PD	0.24	0.05	0.23	0.11	0.55
Average correlation	10.49	0.44	10.48	8.99	12.00
Std. dev. of loadings	10.54	0.70	10.55	7.80	12.79
Corr (PD, loadings)	–19.80	4.59	–20.20	–31.80	–1.20

Note: The results are based on 3,000 simulated portfolios and are obtained in two steps. First, portfolio-specific characteristics (specified by row headings) are calculated for each simulated portfolio. Second, summary statistics (specified by column headings) are calculated for each of the characteristics obtained in the first step. "Loadings" are estimated under a one-common-factor approximation of the correlation structure and refer to the firm-specific loadings of asset returns on the single common factor.

column in Table 5.4) but is more likely to be negative (fourth and fifth columns in Table 5.4). In light of an earlier discussion, imposing a single-factor framework is more likely to lead to too low a capital buffer because such a framework ignores the existence of multiple sources of default clustering. In quantitative terms, however, the multifactor effect entails an average discrepancy that amounts to less than 1% of the average target capital level.[28] This is because the single-factor approximation fits closely the raw correlation matrix. Indeed, our single-factor approximation matches almost perfectly the level of average correlations (with a maximum discrepancy across simulated portfolios of less than 4bp) and explains on average 76% of the variability of pairwise correlations in the cross-section of exposures.[29,30]

Similarly, the granularity effect is with the expected negative sign but, for large portfolios, leads to a small deviation from target capital. With an average of –16bp (or roughly 5% of target capital), this deviation is nonetheless significantly higher than that induced by the multifactor effect. Not surprisingly, the granularity effect we calculate is approximated extremely well by (the negative of) the closed-form granularity adjustment of Gordy and Lütkebohmert (2007), which averages –17 basis points for large portfolios in our sample. In addition, the correlation between the granularity effect and the granularity adjustment across large simulated portfolios is 66%.

By contrast, erroneous calibration of the ASRF model leads to much greater deviations from target. For large portfolios, the correlation dispersion effect raises the capital measure by 39 basis points, which amounts to roughly 12% of the target level.[31] The sign of this effect reflects the fact that, in our data, exposures with higher PDs tend to be less correlated with the rest of the portfolio (see the last row in each panel of Table 5.3).[32] The shortcut capital measure ignores this regularity and, in line with intuition provided on page 119, overshoots the target.

The correlation level effect has a similarly important implication. Specifically, this effect reveals that raising the average correlation coefficient from 9.78% (the one observed in the data) to a rule-of-thumb value of 12% leads to an 18% overestimation of the target capital level. The sign of the deviation is not surprising in light of the earlier discussion. Importantly, the shortcut measure drops (rises) by roughly 8% with each percentage point decrease (increase) in the homogeneous correlation coefficient. Thus, using a rule-of-thumb correlation of 6% leads to a 32% underestimation of the target level.[33]

Turning to small portfolios, the decomposition results are qualitatively the same, with the notable exception of the granularity effect. In these portfolios, a much smaller portion of the idiosyncratic risk is diversified away and the granularity effect equals –73 basis points, which implies a 19% underestimation of the target capital. This underestimation is approximated well by the Gordy and Lütkebohmert (2007) granularity adjustment, (the negative of) which averages –86 basis points for small portfolios and exhibits an 89% correlation with the corresponding granularity effect.

Regression analysis of calibration errors

Given the dominant role of correlation level and dispersion effects as determinants of model-based assessments of portfolio credit risk, we investigate the sources of these two effects via a regression analysis. The regressions – run on the cross-section of simulated portfolios – are simple linear models

Table 5.4 Capital measures and four sources of errors (%)

	A. Large portfolios (1000 firms)				
	Mean	**Std. dev.**	**Median**	**95% interval**	**50% interval**
Target Capital[a]	**3.31**	**0.18**	**3.30**	**[2.97, 3.67]**	**[3.19, 3.42]**
Deviation from target due to:[b]					
Multifactor effect[c]	–0.03	0.02	–0.03	[–0.08, 0.01]	[–0.05, –0.02]
Granularity effect[d]	–0.16	0.004	–0.15	[–0.16, –0.15]	[–0.16, –0.15]
Correlation dispersion effect[e]	0.39	0.05	0.39	[0.30, 0.48]	[0.36, 0.42]
Correlation level effect[f]	0.61	0.06	0.62	[0.49, 0.73]	[0.57, 0.66]
Shortcut capital (corr=12%)	**4.12**	**0.20**	**4.12**	**[3.75, 4.51]**	**[3.99, 4.25]**
Correlation level effect if:					
corr=6%	–1.06	0.08	–1.06	[–1.23, –0.92]	[–1.11, –1.01]
corr=18%	2.24	0.10	2.24	[2.05, 2.43]	[2.17, 2.30]
corr=24%	3.86	0.14	3.86	[3.59, 4.14]	[3.77, 3.95]

	B. Small portfolios (200 firms)				
	Mean	**Std. dev.**	**Median**	**95% interval**	**50% interval**
Target Capital[a]	**3.86**	**0.32**	**3.85**	**[3.25, 4.55]**	**[3.64, 4.07]**
Deviation from target due to:[b]					
Multifactor effect[c]	–0.04	0.04	–0.04	[–0.12, 0.04]	[–0.07, –0.01]
Granularity effect[d]	–0.73	0.03	–0.73	[–0.79, –0.67]	[–0.75, –0.71]
Correlation dispersion effect[e]	0.42	0.12	0.42	[0.19, 0.65]	[0.34, 0.50]
Correlation level effect[f]	0.40	0.13	0.40	[0.16, 0.67]	[0.32, 0.48]
Shortcut capital (corr=12%)	**3.91**	**0.38**	**3.90**	**[3.17, 4.70]**	**[3.64, 4.16]**
Correlation level effect if:					
corr=6%	–1.19	0.13	–1.19	[–1.46, –0.95]	[–1.28, –1.10]
corr=18%	1.95	0.21	1.94	[1.57, 2.38]	[1.81, 2.08]
corr=24%	3.50	0.30	3.49	[2.94, 4.12]	[3.30, 3.70]

Note: Results relate to the simulated portfolios underpinning Table 5.3. The column entitled "95% interval" reports the 2.5th and 97.5th percentiles of the statistics specified in the particular row heading. The column entitled "50% interval" reports the corresponding 25th and 75th percentiles. In all calculations, LGD_i has a symmetric triangular distribution between 0 and 1. [a] Target capital is based on Moody's KMV estimates of PDs and asset return correlations and a Monte Carlo procedure for calculating the probability distribution of default losses. [b] Four sources of deviation from the target capital level are shown; a negative sign implies underestimation. The sum of the target capital level and the four deviations equals the shortcut capital level. Each deviation is based on the assumptions underlying previous deviations plus one additional assumption. [c] For the multifactor effect, the correlation matrix underpinning the target capital level is approximated under the assumption that there is a single common factor. [d] For the granularity effect, there is the additional assumption that the number of firms is infinite. [e] For the correlation dispersion effect, the additional assumption is that the loadings on the single common factor are the same across exposures. [f] For the correlation level effect, the additional assumption imposes a different, shortcut level on the constant pairwise correlation.

of calibration-driven capital discrepancy, which is defined as shortcut capital (based on a correlation of 12%) minus target capital net of the multifactor and granularity effects.

We consider two blocks of explanatory variables. The first block comprises the average level and the dispersion of the asset return correlation coefficients underlying each simulated portfolio.[34] These variables are natural drivers of the correlation level and dispersion effects and would explain the two effects completely if assessments of portfolio credit risk did not depend on the interaction of asset return correlations with PDs. In order to account for such interaction, we include a second block of explanatory variables, which comprises average PDs and the cross-sectional correlations between PDs and single-factor loading coefficients. Recall that the PDs underlying target capital are identical to those underlying the shortcut measure. Thus, the regression coefficient of the first variable in the second block reflects how a general rise in single-name credit risk interacts with the different average correlations and correlation structures behind the two capital measures. In turn, the coefficient of the last explanatory variable captures the component of the correlation dispersion effect that is driven by

Table 5.5 Explaining calibration-driven capital discrepancies

	Regression 1			Regression 2		
	Large portfolio	**Small portfolio**	**Pooled sample**	**Large portfolio**	**Small portfolio**	**Pooled sample**
Constant	3.01 (65.6)	3.00 (53.0)	3.29 (111.6)	2.58 (129.6)	2.40 (84.0)	2.46 (159.8)
Average corr.	–0.24 (34.8)	–0.23 (31.5)	–0.24 (48.8)	–0.28 (95.6)	–0.26 (74.4)	–0.27 (114.5)
Std. dev. of loading coefficients	0.037 (7.5)	0.022 (4.8)	0.010 (3.1)	0.031 (14.6)	0.029 (13.9)	0.028 (19.9)
Average PD				0.21 (86.2)	0.19 (61.6)	0.19 (94.2)
Corr (PD, loading coefficient)				–0.018 (80.5)	–0.019 (79.5)	–0.019 (113.9)
Adjusted R^2	0.39	0.33	0.56	0.89	0.86	0.91

Note: *t*-statistics are shown in parentheses. The regression is based on 3,000 simulations for each portfolio size. The dependent variable equals shortcut capital (based on asset return correlation of 12%) minus target capital, net of the granularity and multifactor effects (see Table 5.4). Loading coefficients are estimated under a one-common-factor approximation of the correlation structure of asset returns. The last regressor equals the Kendall rank correlation between PDs and loading coefficients.

a systematic relationship between individual firms' riskiness and their dependence on the common factor.

The regression results, reported in Table 5.5, reveal that the correlation level and dispersion variables have strong explanatory power. Depending on the portfolio size, these variables explain one-third or more of the variation in calibration-driven capital discrepancies across simulated portfolios and enter the regressions with statistically significant coefficients of the expected signs. First, given that the correlation underpinning the shortcut measure stays constant across simulated portfolios, the positive impact of a higher average correlation on target capital translates into a negative impact on capital discrepancy. Second, the correlation dispersion variable enters with a positive coefficient because – given that the empirical relationship between PDs and asset return correlations is negative and that the shortcut capital measure abstracts from correlation dispersion – shortcut capital overpredicts the target level by more when correlation dispersion is greater. In order to visualise this phenomenon, refer back to the dotted line in the bottom-right panel of Figure 5.1, which represents the case of a negative correlation between PDs and common-factor loadings. In this plot, shortcut capital appears at zero correlation dispersion ($c = 0$), and a rise in correlation dispersion (ie, a rise in c) translates into a downward movement of target capital along the dotted line.

The second part of the analysis reveals that the main driver of the correlation level and dispersion effects is the interaction between correlation coefficients and PDs in assessments of portfolio credit risk. In particular, adding the second block of explanatory variables to the regression raises the goodness-of-fit measures (adjusted R^2) by 50 percentage points (to 89%) for large portfolios and by 53 percentage points (to 86%) for small portfolios. In addition, the positive statistically significant coefficient of average PDs indicates that, although an increase in this variable raises both the target and shortcut capital measures, the effect is stronger under the higher (homogeneous) asset return correlation, underpinning the latter measure. Finally, the statistically significant coefficient of the correlation between PDs and common-factor loadings is with the expected negative sign. This is because target capital tends to increase in the correlation between PDs and loadings on the single factor – as illustrated by an upward movement across the lines in the bottom-right panel of Figure 5.1 – whereas the shortcut measure abstracts from this correlation.

Importantly, the regression results are extremely robust across portfolio sizes. The robustness can be seen in that the values of the goodness-of-fit measures, as well as the coefficient estimates and *t*-statistics, obtained in the context of large portfolios match almost exactly their small-portfolio counterparts. In a further test of the robustness of the regression results, we pool observations across the two portfolio sizes and observe that all estimates change only marginally, leaving the message of the regression analysis intact.[35]

Estimation errors

The above results show that capital measures based on shortcut input estimates can deviate substantially from the target level. In practice, shortcut measures are likely to be adopted by less-sophisticated users of the ASRF model who face severe constraints in terms of data and analytical capacity. By contrast, larger and more-sophisticated users are likely to construct their own estimates of asset return correlations on the basis of in-house data. This section demonstrates that, for realistic sizes of such data, small-sample estimation errors in the correlation parameters are likely to lead to large flaws in assessments of portfolio credit risk.

In order to quantify plausible estimation errors, we consider a portfolio whose "true" credit-risk parameters match those of the "typical" portfolio in our data set. For this portfolio, we impose the simplifying assumption of homogeneous PDs (1%), LGDs (50%), and pairwise asset return correlations (9.78%) and consider different numbers of underlying exposures (see Table 5.6). Abstracting from issues related to granularity and multiple factors, this assumption allows us to use the ASRF model, which implies that the desired capital buffer, dubbed "benchmark," equals 3.31% for each portfolio size. Referring to Table 5.4, this is recognised as the average value of the target capital buffer examined earlier.[36]

Then, we place ourselves in the shoes of a model user who does not know the exact asset return correlations but estimates them from available data.[37] Specifically, we endow the user with 60, 120, or 300 months of asset returns data – drawn from the true underlying distribution – and calculate the sample correlation matrix. In order to quantify a plausible range of errors in the estimate of the correlation matrix, we repeat this exercise 1,000 times. As reported in panels A and B of Table 5.6, the sample correlations contain estimation errors that are likely to be substantial even for 300 months (or 25 years) of data.

Part C of this table reveals how estimation errors in correlation coefficients translate into deviation from the desired benchmark capital buffer. First, these deviations are affected little by the number of exposures in the

Table 5.6 Impact of estimation errors (%)

	A. Sample average of pairwise correlations			
	N=100	**N=200**	**N=500**	**N=1000**
T=60	9.72 [6.5, 13.3]	9.67 [6.4, 13.3]	9.64 [6.6, 13.0]	9.63 [6.9, 12.7]
T=120	9.77 [7.4, 12.4]	9.77 [7.6, 12.1]	9.76 [7.6, 12.1]	9.72 [7.7, 12.0]
T=300	9.75 [8.3, 11.3]	9.79 [8.3, 11.3]	9.74 [8.4, 11.2]	9.77 [8.4, 11.25]
	B. Sample standard deviation of loading coefficients			
	N=100	**N=200**	**N=500**	**N=1000**
T=60	12.1 [10.3, 14.1]	11.8 [10.5, 13.2]	11.6 [10.8, 12.5]	11.6 [10.8, 12.2]
T=120	8.50 [7.4, 9.8]	8.34 [7.5, 9.1]	8.17 [7.6, 8.8]	8.13 [7.7, 8.6]
T=300	5.35 [4.6, 6.2]	5.24 [4.7, 5.7]	5.16 [4.8, 5.5]	5.12 [4.9, 5.4]
	C. Estimated capital, based on one-factor loading structure			
	N=100	**N=200**	**N=500**	**N=1000**
T=60	4.87 [2.8, 5.1]	3.83 [2.8, 5.0]	3.80 [2.8, 4.9]	3.79 [2.9, 4.8]
T=120	3.59 [2.9, 4.4]	3.58 [2.9, 4.4]	3.56 [2.9, 4.3]	3.54 [2.9, 4.3]
T=300	3.41 [3.0, 3.9]	3.42 [3.0, 3.9]	3.40 [3.0, 3.9]	3.41 [3.0, 3.9]
Benchmark	3.31	3.31	3.31	3.31

Note: Results are based on 1,000 simulations of the asset returns of *N* firms over *T* months, with the true pairwise correlation, PD, and LGD fixed at 9.78%, 1%, and 50%, respectively. Each cell contains the mean and the 95% confidence interval of the average of sample estimates of pairwise correlations (A), the standard deviation of the loading coefficients in a one-factor approximation (B), and the implied capital measure (C). The "Benchmark" row in C refers to the level of the capital measure obtained on the basis of the true risk parameters.

portfolio. Second, at standard confidence levels, the deviations decrease in the size of the available time series of asset returns but remain substantial even if this size is assumed to be unrealistically large. For example, if a portfolio comprises 1,000 exposures and a user has 120 months of data, estimated capital buffers can deviate from the benchmark level by as much as 30% with a 95% probability. For longer time series, covering 300 months, the 95% confidence interval does become much tighter but remains consistent with errors as high as 18% of the benchmark capital level. Third, estimated capital buffers exhibit a positive bias relative to the benchmark level; ie, their average level is invariably higher than 3.31%. This is because the true correlation structure is assumed to be homogeneous, while small-sample errors introduce dispersion in estimated correlation coefficients. As discussed previously, this dispersion raises the implied capital buffer in the presence of homogeneous PDs.

Alternative asset return distributions

There is general consensus in the literature that the distribution of asset returns have tails that are fatter than the tails of the convenient normal distribution. Importantly, an erroneous normality assumption tends to bias capital buffers downward to the extent that the empirical distribution of asset returns is driven by fat tails in the distribution of the common factor.[38] Such a distribution of the common factor implies great tail dependence among asset returns, which leads to a large probability of default clustering.

In order to quantify the impact of alternative asset return distributions on capital measures, we consider a homogeneous portfolio in which all PDs equal 1%, all LGDs equal 50%, and all asset return correlations equal 9.78%. Given these risk parameters, we follow the literature on the pricing of portfolio credit risk (see Hull and White 2004; Kalemanova, Schmid, and Werner 2007) and consider the case in which both the common and idiosyncratic factors of asset returns have the same Student-*t* distribution. Experimenting with different distributional specifications, we do see that fatter tails of the distribution of the common factor (ie, fewer degrees of freedom) translate into larger deviations from a capital buffer derived under the normality assumption (Table 5.7, left panel).

In order to examine which distributional specification is supported by the data, we rely on time series of asset returns estimated by Moody's KMV. For each of the 10,891 firms in our sample, we use the available 59 months of estimated returns (from September 2001 to July 2006) to calculate the sample kurtosis, which is the standard measure of tail fatness. The mean and median of this statistic across firms equal 7.96 and 5.28, respectively. Then, on the basis of 10,000 Monte Carlo simulations, we derive the distributions of the estimators of these mean and median when (i) the data size matches the size of the Moody's KMV data on asset return estimates and (ii) both the common and idiosyncratic factors of asset returns follow the same Student-*t* distribution. As revealed by the confidence intervals for these estimators, the Moody's KMV data support only the "double-*t*" specification with three degrees of freedom for each factor (Table 5.7, centre and right panels).

If the asset returns are indeed driven by such distributions – which would be in line with findings in Kalemanova, Schmid, and Werner (2007) – then a normality assumption will lead to tremendous underpredictions of the desired capital buffer. Specifically, we find that a double-*t* specification with three degrees of freedom implies a capital buffer of 6.17% per unit of aggregate exposure. This buffer is 86% higher than the capital buffer calculated under a normality assumption.

Even though this result may be undermined by probable errors in the Moody's KMV estimates of asset returns, alternative double-*t* specifications studied in the related literature also lead to capital measures that are significantly higher than those implied by a normal distribution. Indeed, given that the available time series of Moody's KMV asset return estimates are short, plausible systemic errors in these estimates across firms might affect substantially the cross-sectional mean and median of the sample kurtosis. This casts doubt on the validity of the double-*t* specification with three degrees of freedom and prompts us to consider alternative specifications, with four degrees of freedom (which is recommended by Hull and White 2004) and five degrees of freedom (which is reportedly a market standard). As revealed in Table 5.7, these alternatives imply capital measures that are, respectively, 39% and 22% higher than the measure incorporating normal distributions.

CONCLUDING REMARKS

In this chapter, we have quantified the relative importance of alternative sources of error in portfolio credit risk measures based on the popular ASRF model. Our data has revealed that violations of key modelling assumptions-namely, that granularity is perfect and that there is a single common risk factor – are likely to have a limited impact on such measures, especially for large, well-diversified portfolios. By contrast, erroneous calibration of the ASRF model – driven by flaws in popular rule-of-thumb values of asset return correlation, plausible small-sample estimation errors, or a wrong assumption regarding the distribution of asset returns – has the potential to affect substantially measures of portfolio credit risk.

Given these results and the fact that we have abstracted from several additional sources of error in portfolio credit risk measures, the task of risk managers and supervisors appears challenging. In particular, we have assumed that PDs and LGDs are free of estimation noise. However, such noise is likely to be sizable in practice and to interact with noise in correlation estimates in generating errors in measured portfolio credit risk. In

Table 5.7 Alternative distributional assumptions

Degrees of freedom[a]	Capital measure[b] (%)	Mean Kurtosis[c]		Median Kurtosis[c]	
		Mean	95% interval	Mean	95% interval
(3, 3)	6.17	7.83	[7.30, 8.27]	5.54	[5.11, 6.54]
(4, 4)	4.59	5.72	[5.47, 5.92]	4.43	[4.25, 4.59]
(5, 5)	4.03	4.79	[4.64, 4.93]	3.96	[3.85, 4.06]
(6, 6)	3.81	4.31	[4.19, 4.40]	3.70	[3.63, 3.78]
(7, 7)	3.67	4.02	[3.93, 4.10]	3.55	[3.49, 3.60]
(8, 8)	3.59	3.83	[3.76, 3.89]	3.44	[3.39, 3.49]
(9, 9)	3.53	3.70	[3.64, 3.75]	3.36	[3.32, 3.40]
(10, 10)	3.49	3.60	[3.55, 3.65]	3.30	[3.26, 3.34]
(∞, ∞)	3.31	3.00	[2.99, 3.01]	2.89	[2.88, 2.90]

[a] This panel shows the degrees of freedom of the Student-*t* distribution of asset returns' common and idiosyncratic factors, respectively. The last row refers to a Gaussian specification. [b] Obtained by applying the general ASRF formula (Equation 5.4) to a homogeneous portfolio, in which PD = 1% and LGD = 50% for each exposure and asset return correlations equal 9.78% for each pair of exposures. The default boundary for such exposures is calculated on the basis of 10 million simulations. [c] This panel shows the means and the 95% confidence intervals (based on 10,000 Monte Carlo simulations) of the estimators of the cross-sectional mean and median of the kurtosis of asset returns when (i) the marginal Student-*t* distributions of the common and idiosyncratic factors have the degrees of freedom specified in the row heading and asset return correlations equal 9.78%, and (ii) the available data comprise time series of 59 returns for 10,891 firms.

addition, there may be time variation in credit-risk parameters that relate to the likelihood and severity of default losses as well as to the correlation of the occurrence of such losses across exposures. Such time variation, which could be due either to cyclical developments or to structural changes in credit markets, would impair the useful content of the available data and, thus, would make it even more difficult to measure portfolio credit risk.

That said, the ASRF model is by no means the only way to measure portfolio credit risk (see Gordy 2000). It is, thus, important to study the degree to which specification and calibration errors affect implications of alternative models as well. Such a generalisation of the analysis in this chapter would be valuable to risk managers and supervisors.

APPENDIX 5.1. GAUSSIAN COPULA

The Gaussian copula is an efficient algorithm for measuring portfolio credit risk when a portfolio consists of a finite number of exposures, the correlation matrix is driven by a common-factor loading structure, and underlying distributions are normal. The efficiency of the algorithm stems from the fact that, conditional on the realisation of the common factor(s), default occurrences are independent across exposures. This allows for a closed-form solution for the conditional probability of joint defaults. The corresponding unconditional probability is then derived by integrating over the probability distribution of the common factor(s). For further detail, see Gibson (2004).

APPENDIX 5.2. MONTE CARLO SIMULATIONS

Monte Carlo simulations deliver the target capital level. This method can be applied to any portfolio comprising N equally weighted exposures, provided that the exposure-specific probabilities of default, PD_i; the distribution of LGD_i; and the correlation matrix of asset returns, R; are known.

Given that LGD_i is assumed to be independent of the factors underlying PD_i, and that the distribution of LGD_i is identical across exposures, the simulation of portfolio credit losses can be divided into two parts. The first part calculates the probability distribution of joint defaults. Given this distribution, the second part incorporates the LGD distribution to derive the probability distribution of portfolio losses.

Specifically we estimate the probability of joint defaults as follows:

1. Using the vector $\{PD_i\}_{i=1}^{N}$ and the assumption that asset returns are distributed as standard normal variables, we obtain an $N \times 1$ vector of default thresholds.
2. We draw an $N \times 1$ vector from N standard normal variables whose correlation matrix is R. The number of entries in this vector that are smaller than the corresponding default threshold is the number of simulated defaults for the particular draw.
3. We repeat the previous step 500,000 times to derive the probability distribution of the number of defaults, $\Pr(nd = k)$, where nd refers to the number of defaults and $k = 0, 1, \ldots, N$.

Then, we estimate the probability distribution of portfolio credit losses as follows:

1. For a given number of defaults, k, we draw LGDs for the defaulted exposures 1,000 times and calculate the conditional loss distribution, $\Pr(TL \mid nd = k)$.
2. We conduct the above exercise for each $k = 1, \ldots, N$, and then calculate

the unconditional probability distribution of portfolio credit losses. Specifically, $\Pr(TL) = \sum_k \Pr(TL \mid nd = k) \cdot \Pr(nd = k)$.

Finally, we set the capital measure to equal $TL_{1-\alpha} - \sum_{i=1}^{N} E(PD_i) \cdot E(LGD_i)$.

APPENDIX 5.3. FITTING A SINGLE-FACTOR CORRELATION STRUCTURE

A single-factor approximation of an empirical correlation matrix is obtained as follows. Denote the empirical correlation matrix by Σ and its elements σ_{ij}, for $i, j \in \{1, \ldots, N\}$. The single-factor loading structure $\rho \equiv [\rho_1, \ldots, \rho_N]$ that minimises the discrepancies between the elements of Σ and their fitted counterparts are given by

$$\min_{\rho} \sum_{i=1}^{N-1} \sum_{j>i} \left(\sigma_{ij} - \rho_i \rho_j\right)^2$$

Andersen, Sidenius, and Basu (2003) propose an efficient algorithm to solve this minimisation problem. The fitted correlation matrix $\hat{\Sigma}$ has elements $\rho_i \rho_j$.

We also construct a measure that reflects the "explanatory power" of the single-factor approximation

$$\text{Goodness-of-Fit Measure} \equiv 1 - \frac{\text{var}(\in)}{\text{var}(\sigma)}$$

where σ is a vector of all pairwise correlation coefficients σ_{ij} $(i, j = 1, \ldots, N, i < j)$ and $\in$ is a vector of the errors $\sigma_{ij} - \rho_i \rho_j$ $(i, j = 1, \ldots, N, i < j)$. This measure reflects the degree to which the cross-sectional variation in pairwise correlations can be explained by common-factor loadings in a single-factor framework.

1 We are indebted to Michael Gordy and Kostas Tsatsaronis for their encouragement and useful comments. We thank Klaus Düllmann, Wenying Jiangli, and participants at a BIS workshop, the 3rd international Conference on Credit and Operational Risk at HEC Montréal, and the 17th Annual Derivatives Securities and Risk Management Conference at the FDIC for insightful suggestions. We are also grateful to Marcus Jellinghaus for his valuable help with the data. The views expressed here are our own and do not necessarily represent those of the Bank for International Settlements.

2 Examples of structured finance products are collateralised debt obligations (CDOs), *n*th-to-default credit default swaps (CDSs), and CDS indexes.

3 The IRB capital formula of Basel II abstracts from this calibration issue by postulating that firm-specific dependence on the single common factor is determined fully by the level of the corresponding PD.

4 In this chapter, we use the terms "assessment of portfolio credit risk" and "capital measure" interchangeably. Importantly, our capital measures do not correspond to "regulatory

capital," which reflects considerations of bank supervisors, or to "economic capital," which reflects additional strategic and business objectives of financial firms.

5 In order to sharpen the analysis, we do not analyse the implications of errors in the estimates of PDs and LGDs.

6 Basel Committee on Bank Supervision (2006) provides an extensive review of these articles.

7 This section provides an intuitive discussion of the ASRF model. For a rigorous and detailed study of this model, see Gordy (2003). In addition, Frey and McNeil (2003) examine the calibration of the ASRF model under the so-called Bernoulli mixture representation.

8 The ASRF model can accommodate distributions with infinite second moments. Nonetheless, we abstract from this generalisation in order to streamline the analysis.

9 The ASRF model does allow for interdependence between asset returns and the LGD random variable. Such interdependence leads to another dimension in the study of portfolio credit risk, which is explored by Kupiec (2008). We abstract from this additional dimension in order to focus on the correlation of default events.

10 In line with the IRB approach of Basel II, this study effectively incorporates a one-period model, in which a default occurs only at the end of the horizon (in our case, T). In contrast, Gupta *et al* (2005) consider obligors that default if their assets are below the default threshold at any one of multiple dates over the horizon. We do not consider such a multiperiod variant of the model because one of its key inputs is the term structure of asset return correlations, which cannot be estimated on the basis of our data set. Importantly, abstracting from "multiperiod" considerations is unlikely to influence our conclusions. Gupta *et al* (2005) find that switching from a one-period to a multiperiod setup lowers a 99.93% credit VaR by roughly 5%. Although not trivial, this magnitude is several times smaller than the magnitude of errors we identify and analyse in this chapter.

11 Given portfolio invariance, the contribution of each exposure to portfolio credit risk is simply $w_i K_i / K$. Ordovas and Thompson (2003) develop a procedure for deriving this contribution in a more general setting.

12 The calculation of the desired capital level uses a Gaussian copula (see Appendix 5.1).

13 Further comparison between the granularity effect and the granularity adjustment of Gordy and Lütkebohmert (2007) is reported later in this chapter.

14 These losses were denoted by TL earlier in the chapter.

15 Note that, depending on the confidence level of the targeted credit VaR, a fattening of the tails of the probability distribution of credit losses may either raise or lower the desired capital buffer. Fatter tails of the loss distribution translate into a higher desired level of the capital buffer only if the value of α in Equation 5.4 is sufficiently close to zero.

16 The desired capital buffer is calculated on the basis of Monte Carlo simulations (see Appendix 5.2) for a portfolio consisting of 1,000 exposures.

17 Data limitations are likely to be important irrespective of how a user of the model estimates asset return correlations. Such estimates may rely on balance sheet information and stock market data. Alternatively, as derived in Tarashev and Zhu (2006), asset return correlations can be extracted from the CDS market.

18 The distinction between what we dub large and small portfolios does not reflect the size of the aggregate exposure but rather different degrees of diversification across individual exposures.

19 Such a portfolio does not incorporate consumer loans and, thus, may not be representative of all aspects of credit risk.

20 The LGD specification warrants an explanation. The independence between the incidence of defaults and LGDs implies that, in the absence of simulation noise, only the mean of the LGD distribution enters (as a multiplicative factor) capital measures. However, the entire LGD distribution affects measures obtained from Monte Carlo simulations. Importantly, assuming a continuous distribution for LGDs smoothes the derived probability distribution of joint defaults, which improves the robustness of simulation-based capital measures.

21 In order to reduce simulation errors to levels that do not affect our conclusions, we estimate

each portfolio loss distribution on the basis of 500,000 draws. Alternatively, it is possible to circumvent the use of Monte Carlo simulations by approximating loss distributions analytically, on the basis of the so-called saddle-point method of Browne, Martin, and Thompson (2001).

22 Importantly, the method also applies to alternative definitions of target and shortcut capital, so long as the true correlation structure and shortcut correlation estimates chosen by the user are well defined.

23 Despite this observation, we have also experimented with imposing the infinite granularity assumption only after we calculate the correlation dispersion and level effects (ie, deriving measure 3 after measures 4 and 5). This modifies the meaning of these two effects but alters negligibly their magnitudes, as well as the magnitude of the granularity effect.

24 This measure abstracts from the granularity and multifactor effects.

25 A Student-*t* variable with $r > 2$ degrees of freedom has a variance of $\frac{r}{r-2}$.

26 The GCorr correlation estimates are quite in line with correlation estimates reported in other studies. For instance, Lopez (2004) documents an average asset correlation of 12.5% for a large number of US firms and Düllman, Scheicher, and Schmieder (2006) estimate a median asset return correlation of 10.1% for European firms.

27 Within each industry sector, we draw randomly with replacement. If the same firm is drawn twice, the corresponding pairwise correlation is set equal to the average correlation for the sector. Drawing randomly without replacement does not affect materially the results.

28 A similar result is obtained by Düllmann and Masschelein (2007), who rely on Pykhtin (2004) to approximate the multifactor effect in loan portfolios of German banks.

29 The goodness-of-fit measure for the one-factor approximation is described in Appendix 5.3. Across the 3,000 simulations of large portfolios, this measure ranges between 67% and 85%. For small portfolios, the range is between 63% and 86%.

30 Principal-component analysis confirms this result. Specifically, the portion of the total variance of asset returns explained by the first principal component is at least ten times larger than the portion explained by the second principal component.

31 On the basis of a hypothetical portfolio of US firms, Hanson, Pesaran, and Schuermann (2007) also demonstrate the importance of accounting for cross-sectional heterogeneity in credit risk parameters.

32 The negative relationship between PDs and correlations (or loading coefficients in a single-factor setting) is likely to be a general phenomenon. See, for example, Lopez (2004), Arora, Bohn, and Korablev (2005), and Dev (2006), who find that global factors often play bigger roles for firms of better credit quality.

33 The rule-of-thumb asset return correlations reported in the literature range between 5% and 25%.

34 The correlation dispersion variable is calculated as the standard deviation of the common-factor loading coefficients, which are obtained from the single-factor approximation of the correlation matrix.

35 Background checks reveal that the residuals of the full regressions can be attributed to a large extent to interactions among PDs and asset return correlations that are non-linear and difficult to pin down.

36 Given that we abstract from model misspecification in this subsection, the benchmark capital measure is conceptually equivalent to what we earlier called target capital.

37 In order to focus on issues in the estimation of the interdependence of credit risk across exposures, we assume that the user knows the true PD and LGD.

38 For existing theoretical and empirical analysis of the treatment of tail dependencies by credit-risk models, see, for example, Gordy (2000), Lucas *et al* (2002), and Frey and McNeil (2003).

REFERENCES

Andersen, L., J. Sidenius and S. Basu, 2003, "All Your Hedges in One Basket", *Risk*, November, pp. 67–72.

Arora, N., J. Bohn and I. Korablev, 2005, "Power and Level Validation of the EDF™ Credit Measure in the U.S. Market", Moody's KMV White Paper.

Basel Committee on Banking Supervision, 2005, "An Explanatory Note on the Basel II IRB Risk Weight Functions", BCBS Technical Note, Bank for International Settlements.

Basel Committee on Banking Supervision, 2006, "Studies on Credit Risk Concentration: An Overview of the Issues and a Synopsis of the Results from the Research Task Force Project", BCBS Research Task Force Working Paper, Bank for International Settlements.

Berndt, A., R. Douglas, D. Duffie, M. Ferguson and D. Schranz, 2005, "Measuring Default Risk Premia from Default Swap Rates and EDF5", BIS Working Paper No. 173.

Browne, C., R. Martin, and K. Thompson, 2001, "Taking to the Saddle", *Risk*, June, pp. 91–94.

Crosbie, P., 2005, "Global Correlation Factor Structure: Modeling Methodology", Moody's KMV Documents.

Crosbie, P. and J. Bohn, 2003, "Modeling Default Risk", Moody's KMV White Paper.

Das, A. and S. lshii, 2001, "Methods for Calculating Asset Correlations: A Technical Note", KMV Documents.

Dev, A., 2006, "The Correlation Debate", *Risk*, October.

Düllmann, K., 2006, "Measuring Business Sector Concentration by an infection Model", Deutsche Bundesbank Discussion Paper Series 2, No. 2006/03.

Düllmann, K. and N. Masschelein, 2006, "Sector Concentration in Loan Portfolios and Economic Capital", Deutsche Bundesbank Discussion Paper Series 2, No. 2006/09.

Düllmann, K. and N. Masschelein, 2007, "A Tractable Model to Measure Sector Concentration Risk in Credit Portfolios", *Journal of Financial Services Research* 32(1), pp. 55–79.

Düllmann, K., M. Scheicher and C. Schmieder, 2006, "Asset Correlations and Credit Portfolio Risk: An Empirical Analysis", Working Paper.

Emmer, S. and D. Tasche., 2003, "Calculating Credit Risk Capital Charges with the One-Factor Model", *The Journal of Risk* 7(2), pp. 85–101.

Frey, R. and A. J. McNeil, 2003, "Dependent Defaults in Models of Portfolio Credit Risk", *The Journal of Risk*, 6(1), pp. 59–92.

Garcia Cespedes, J. C., J. A. de Juan Herrero, A. Kreinin and D. Rosen, 2006, "A Simple Multifactor 'Factor Adjustment' for the Treatment of Credit Capital Diversification", *The Journal of Credit Risk*, 2(3), pp. 57–85.

Gibson, M., 2004, "Understanding the Risk of Synthetic CDOs", Finance and Economics Discussion Series, No. 2004-36, Board of Governors of the Federal Reserve System.

Gordy, M. B., 2000, "A Comparative Anatomy of Credit Risk Models", *The Journal of Banking and Finance*, 24(1–2), pp. 119–49.

Gordy, M. B., 2003, "A Risk-Factor Model Foundation for Ratings-Based Bank Capital Rules", *The Journal of Financial Intermediation*, 12(3), pp. 199–232.

Gordy, M., and E. Lütkebohmert, 2007, "Granularity Adjustment for Basel II", Deutsche Bundesbank, Discussion Paper No. 01/2007.

Gupta, S., A. McLeod, P. Teklos, and K. Thompson, 2005, "Time for MultiPeriod Capital Models", *Risk* October, pp. 74–78.

Hanson, S. G., M. H. Pesaran and T. Schuermann, 2007, "Firm Heterogeneity and Credit Risk Diversification", Forthcoming in *Journal of Empirical Finance*.

Heitfield, E., S. Burton, and S. Chomsisengphet, 2006, "Systematic and Idiosyncratic Risk in Syndicated Loan Portfolios", *The Journal of Credit Risk*, 2(3), pp. 3–31.

Hull, J., and A. White, 2004, "Valuation of a CDO and an n-th to Default CDS without Monte Carlo Simulation", *The Journal of Derivatives* 12 (Winter), pp. 8–23.

Kalemanova, A., B. Schmid and R. Werner, 2007, "The Normal Inverse Gaussian Distribution for Synthetic CDO Pricing", *The Journal of Derivatives* 14 (Spring).

Kupiec, P., 2008, "A Generalized Single Common Factor Model of Portfolio Credit Risk", *The Journal of Derivatives* 15 (Spring), pp. 25–40.

Loeffler, G., 2003, "The Effects of Estimation Error on Measures of Portfolio Credit Risk", *The Journal of Banking and Finance* 27(8), pp. 1427–53.

Longstaff, F. A., S. Mithal and E. Neis, 2005, "Corporate Yield Spreads: Default Risk or Liquidity? New Evidence from the Credit Default Swap Market", *The Journal of Finance*, 60(5), pp. 2213–53.

Lopez, J. A., 2004, "The Empirical Relationship between Average Asset Correlation, Firm Probability of Default and Asset Size", *Journal of Financial Intermediation*, 13(2), pp. 265–83.

Lucas, A., P. Klaassen, P. Spreij and S. Straetmans, 2002, "Extreme Tails for Linear Portfolio Credit Risk Models", in *Risk Measurement and Systemic Risk: Proceedings of the 3rd Joint Central Bank Research Conference* (Basel, Switzerland: Bank for International Settlements).

Martin, R., and T. Wilde, 2002, "Unsystematic Credit Risk", *Risk* November, pp. 123–28.

Merton, R. C., 1974, "On the Pricing of Corporate Debt: The Risk Structure of Interest Rates", *The Journal of Finance* 29(2), pp. 449–70.

Morinaga, S. and Y. Shiina, 2005. "Underestimation of Sector Concentration Risk by Mis-assignment of Borrowers", Working Paper.

Ordovas, R. and K. Thompson, 2003, "Credit Ensembles", *Risk*, April, pp. 67–72.

Pykhtin, M., 2004, "Multi-factor Adjustment", *Risk*, March, pp. 85-90.

Tarashev, N. and H. Zhu, 2006. "The Pricing of Portfolio Credit Risk", Bank for International Settlements, Working Paper No. 214.

Vasicek, O., 1991, "Limiting Loan Loss Probability Distribution", KMV, Working Paper.

Vasicek, O., 2002, "Loan Portfolio Value", *Risk*, December, pp. 160–62.

6

Empirical Assessment of Asset Correlations

Ahmet E. Kocagil, Jing Liu

Fitch Solutions

This chapter empirically estimates and compares several default correlation-based and rating transition-based methodologies with the asset correlation formula that is recommended by Basel Committee (BIS, 2005, p. 62, paragraph 283). In doing so, it follows up the framework of a prior paper (Akhavein, Kocagil and Neugebauer 2005) but extends the time period of evaluation to an observation window that is spun from 1970 to the end of 2007.

The next section discusses the role of correlations in credit risk analysis and outlines the main approaches through which they can be estimated. We then describe how rating agency data can be processed based on the so-called "static-pool methodology", before going on to present in detail a number of techniques for the estimation of asset correlations though default correlations, including the formulas proposed by De Servigny and Renault; Frey and McNeil; and Gupton, Finger and Bhatia.

The following section shows how asset correlations can be derived from rating transition data (based on the so-called "Directional Rating Transition Matrixes"). We then report the results of our empirical test, comparing them to those obtained by Akhavein, Kocagil and Neugebauer (2005) and analysing several hypotheses by means of statistical tests. We then present our conclusions.

Consistent with the previous study, we find that the average asset correlation estimates are close among different models, except for the rating transition model, which is much smaller than any other models. Similarly, as expected, the intra-industry average asset correlation is always larger than the inter-industry asset correlation estimates. In addition, average asset correlation estimates of the De Servigny and Renault, the adjusted Frey and McNeil, the RACM and the adjusted Gupton, Finger and Bhatia methodologies fall into each other's 95% confidence interval, except for the adjusted Gupton, Finger and Bhatia results on inter-industry average asset correlations. The intra-industry average asset correlation estimates of Akhavein, Kocagil and Neugebauer (2005) fall into the 95% confidence interval of current estimates, except for the De Servigny and Renault. All of the previous inter-industry average asset correlation estimates fall below the 95% confidence interval of current estimates. This indicates that, while intra-industry asset correlation estimates remained statistically unchanged, inter-industry asset correlations have demonstrated an increase since 2004, which can be interpreted as an enhanced systematic interdependency across different sectors in the economy.

More granular industry-level mean and distribution tests between previous and current asset correlation estimates reveal that most of the models have somewhat different estimates for different time periods, except for the RACM, the Basel II formula and the rating transition model. Nevertheless, these tests should be treated with caution, as they may be notably affected by small sample issues in individual industry buckets.

Previous studies' findings regarding the comparison between estimates of the De Servigny and Renault and the adjusted Frey and McNeil during 1970 and 2004 showed that, for a majority of industries, the Frey and McNeil asset correlation estimate is above the De Servigny and Renault. This is also in line with the current results that span the period between 1970 and 2007.

Finally, a comparison of the magnitudes of the inter- and intra-asset correlations across different estimates reveal that, while inter-industry correlations devised by the Basel Committee are in the ballpark with the estimates all of the default correlation-based methods, it is somewhat lower for the intra-industry estimates. As previously noted, rating-transition-based correlations produce notably lower correlations in both categories, which probably reflects rating agencies' emphasis on rating stability as an objective.

WHY CORRELATIONS MATTER AND HOW THEY CAN BE ESTIMATED

In general, credit risk evaluation can be thought of as a portfolio-loss risk-analysis exercise. Accordingly, basic laws of statistics suggest that an increase in the average default probability shifts the entire portfolio-loss distribution to the right or left (depending on the direction of the move), whereas an increase (decrease) in correlation between the individual assets within the portfolio fattens (thins out) the tail of the loss distribution by transferring some of the risk from the mean towards the tail (see Figure 6.1).

Figure 6.1 Effect of correlation on loss distributions

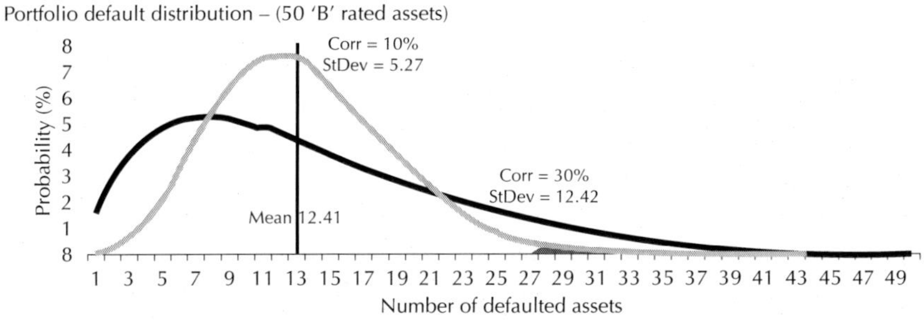

Given that credit risk analysis is concentrated on the tail behaviour, it is clear to see the importance of correlations since a variation in the level of correlation may have very profound impacts on the riskiness of the portfolio and/or any particular tranche of it.

Default and asset correlation estimation methodologies generally fall into three categories. A first approach employs historical credit default information (by rating categories) for the estimation of default correlations. A second alternative method uses historical rating transitions to deduce asset correlations based on the joint upward/downward movements of ratings. The first two methodologies yield more stable and time-invariant measures of asset correlations. Other methodologies utilise market information from equity or debt markets, which extract correlation information based on market prices. The advantages and disadvantages of each of these approaches are discussed below.

Default and asset correlations can be estimated using historical rating and default information. The advantage of using agency ratings is that they are widely available and acceptable benchmarks and cover a reasonable period of time. There are also disadvantages to using agency rating information for default and asset correlation measurement. The primary disadvantage is that defaults are rare events, thus making inferences difficult across a wide range of industries and geographies. In addition, the majority of agency-rated entities belong to North American institutions, thereby making it very difficult to extend inferences globally. Due to these disadvantages of historical rating information, methodologies based on historical rating and default data require some aggregation, either by rating class or industry, and thus categorically do not permit estimation at more granular levels.

Correlations based on market information have a number of advantages when compared with historical rating information. In the case of equity prices the main advantage is that they have wider coverage, in terms of both industry and geography. Thus, nuances between firms on a global basis can be empirically observed. With this methodology, however, there is a concern that equity prices reflect – in addition to credit-related information – information that is unrelated to credit. Credit default swap (CDS) spreads are also readily available in the marketplace, and can be an alternative to equity prices. The main drawback of this approach, however, is that the universe spanned by these instruments is considerably smaller than the equity-traded universe. Moreover, this methodology, as any other market-price-driven measure, is likely to yield estimates that are time-variant.

Considering the pros and cons above, particularly the availability of good historical data, we see two feasible alternatives to pursue for the broad and systematic measurement of asset correlations that are not highly time-variant, so they can be compared and contrasted with Basel II correlations:

- asset correlations based on default correlation estimates; and
- asset correlations based on rating transitions.

For asset correlations based on default correlations, we use historical agency ratings to calculate intra-industry and inter-industry default correlations, then translate these default correlations to asset correlations using a bivariate Gaussian copula. For rating transitions, the intra-industry and inter-industry asset correlations are measured directly using the co-movement of ratings. These two approaches are explained in detail later. Before that, we will briefly explain the static-pool methodology that will be used to process the historical agency ratings used in the following.

THE STATIC-POOL METHODOLOGY

We use the static-pool methodology in forming cohorts for the purpose of correlation calculation. This method is commonly used by rating agencies for default and rating transition studies. "Pools" were formed by grouping issuers by Fitch Industry groups in January of each year. Each static pool was followed for T years, depending on the chosen time horizon, and default and rating transitions were calculated. In this study, we concentrate on the five-year horizon, though for completeness we perform all calculations for the one-, three-, five-, and seven-year horizons. Since we have historical data from 1970 to 2004, we form 31 five-year cohorts for each of the 25 Fitch industries (see Table 6.1).

Figure 6.2 shows an example of one such cohort for the utilities industry.

Table 6.1 Industries and cohorts

Industry name	Industry	Cohort 1 1970–4	Cohort 2 1971–5	… ⇨ …	Cohort 33 2002–6	Cohort 34 2003–7
Aerospace and defence	1					
Automobiles	2					
⇩						
Transportation	24					
Utilities	25					

The 1970 utilities static pool or cohort consists of all companies that were in the utilities industry and rated as of January of 1970. These issuers were followed for five years through December of 1974 and their rating was recorded.

When calculating default and asset correlations from historical rating information, the statistics that are needed on a cohort level are the number of defaulted and non-defaulted issuers, and rating migration information on issuers to calculate upgrade, no-movement, and downgrade (1, 0, –1) statistics over a specified time horizon.

In our example, we started with 16 issuers in the utilities industry in January of 1970 and followed them until December of 1974. During this period three firms defaulted and two firms had "withdrawn ratings" or

Figure 6.2 An example of cohort for the utilities industry

	Jan - 1970	Dec - 1974	Upgrade / Downgrade
Firm 1	AA	NR	
Firm 2	AA	NR	
Firm 3	A	A	0
Firm 4	A	AA	1
Firm 5	A	A	0
Firm 6	BBB	BB	-1
Firm 7	BBB	BBB	0
Firm 8	BBB	BBB	0
Firm 9	BBB	D	-1
Firm 10	BBB	D	-1
Firm 11	BB	BB	0
Firm 12	BB	BB	0
Firm 13	B	BBB	1
Firm 14	B	B	0
Firm 15	CCC	D	-1
Firm 16	CCC	CCC	0

"NR" (not-rated). As we will demonstrate below, the method by which "withdrawn ratings" are treated may lead to notably different default and rating transitions rates, which in turn have an impact on the resulting default and asset correlations.

The withdrawn-rating or not-rated category corresponds to cases where the issuer's public rating has been withdrawn. Typically, this occurs when an issue has matured or has been called. For an overwhelming majority of withdrawn ratings, this simply indicates the issuer's exit from the public market and does not carry any negative credit connotations. Two important trends regarding withdrawn categories are (1) the likelihood of a withdrawn-rating increase as credit quality decreases and (2) the likelihood of a withdrawn-rating increase as the time horizon increases. On average, over a one-year horizon, 3% of AAA-rated firms and 8% of BB firms have withdrawn ratings. Over a five-year horizon, these statistics rise to an average of 16% for AAA-rated firms and 33% for BB-rated firms.

We calculate the default rate as the number of defaults divided by all firms that were initially in the cohort, or the number of rated firms at the end of the time horizon of interest plus the number of non-rated firms plus the number of defaulted firms. If we omit the "NR" from the denominator the default rate will naturally rise

$$\frac{D_{i,t}}{N_{i,t}} = \frac{D_{i,t}}{R_{i,t} + NR_{i,t} + D_{i,t}}$$

Given the above formula and our utilities example, we can calculate two default rates – the adjusted default rate of $3/14$ or 21.43%, and the unadjusted default rate of $3/16$ or 18.75%. Adjusting the default rates by the withdrawn category inflates the default rate of the pool. For some cases, such as lower-quality credits over a five-year time horizon, the adjustment can be more substantial than warranted. The default rate has a direct impact on default correlations and in turn on asset correlations. In this study, we use the unadjusted default rate for our calculations.

Withdrawn ratings also impact on rating migrations. The method used to calculate asset correlation directly from historical ratings relies on the tabulation of the upgrade, no-movement, and downgrade statistics on a cohort level. Suppose you have a BBB-rated pool or cohort, historically more than 25% of the portfolio with have withdrawn ratings after five years. This means that, in effect, 25% of the portfolio will be excluded in the calculation of asset correlation. We use two different methods for the treatment of withdrawn ratings. The first method simply assigns the letter grade of the issuer at the beginning of the analysis period. In our example on the previous page, Firm 1 and Firm 2 had withdrawn ratings as of December 1974. For asset correlation purposes, we replace the NR rating with their rating as of January of 1970. The second method replaces the NR rating with the last available rating available. For example, if Firm 1 transitioned to letter rating A in October of 1972 and remained an A until the rating was withdrawn, we would replace NR with A as of December of 1974 for asset correlation calculation purposes.[1]

ASSET CORRELATIONS BASED ON DEFAULT CORRELATION ESTIMATES

Defining default and asset correlations

In this section we briefly review the concept of default correlation and the relationship between default and asset correlations under a bivariate Gaussian assumption.

Let p_i denote the marginal default probability of obligor i and p_j denote the marginal default probability of obligor j. The joint probability that obligor i and obligor j both default by some time horizon T is denoted as p_{ij}. Let X_i and X_j denote the asset values for obligors i and j. Therefore

$$p_i = P\left(X_i \leq DT_i\right)$$

which simply states that marginal default probability of obligor i is equal to the probability that the asset value for obligor i falls below some default threshold DT_i. This can similarly be defined for the joint probability of default as

$$p_{ij} = P\left(X_i \leq DT_i, X_j \leq DT_j\right)$$

Using the notation above we write the linear default correlation coefficient as

$$\rho_{ij}^D = \frac{p_{ij} - p_i p_j}{\sqrt{p_i\left(1-p_i\right)p_j\left(1-p_j\right)}}$$

Standard models usually assume that the asset values $(X_1, X_2, \ldots, X_m)$ follow a multivariate normal distribution, therefore (X_i, X_j) are bivariate normal. Let ρ_{ij}^A denote the asset correlation between asset values X_i and X_j and let $f_\alpha(u,v)$ denote the standard normal bivariate density function with correlation coefficient of α. Then, by the distributional assumption on the asset values and the marginal and joint probabilities defined above, the joint default probability of obligor i and obligor j is defined as

$$p_{ij} = \int_{-\infty}^{DT_i} \int_{-\infty}^{DT_j} f_{\rho_{ij}^A}(u,v)\,du\,dv$$

where ρ_{ij}^A is the asset correlation. From above we see that the asset correlation affects the default correlation through the joint default probability. In the case of the bivariate Gaussian copula, the above can be written as

$$p_{ij} = \frac{1}{2\pi\sqrt{1-\rho_{ij}^{A^2}}} \int_{-\infty}^{DT_i} \int_{-\infty}^{DT_j} \exp\left[-\frac{1}{2(1-\rho_{ij}^{A^2})}\left(s^2 - 2\rho_{ij}^A st + t^2\right)\right] ds\,dt$$

Given the above, we can see that when asset correlations are computed based on default correlation estimates, we estimate ρ_{ij}^D, p_i, p_j, DT_i, DT_j on the intra-industry and inter-industry level using historical agency default information then calculate ρ_{ij}^A using the bivariate Gaussian copula. Conversely, when asset correlations are based on rating transitions (see the section "Asset correlations based on rating transitions" below), we estimate ρ_{ij}^A directly from historical agency rating information through the co-movements of ratings.

Estimating default correlations: an example

As mentioned above, in order to calculate default correlation ρ_{ij}^D, we need the joint default probability p_{ij} and the marginal default probabilities p_i and p_j. Since we are using historical agency default and rating information, we use the cohort methodology to calculate these statistics on an aggregate industry level.

The general specification for the joint default probability can be defined as

$$p_{ii} = \frac{D_{i,t}\left(D_{i,t} - 1\right)}{N_{i,t}\left(N_{i,t} - 1\right)}$$

where p_{ii} is the intra-industry joint default probability and is defined as the default probability for a company in industry i and another company in industry i jointly defaulting over a specified time horizon T.[2] Note that joint default probabilities are calculated on a cohort level; these are then aggregated to the industry level by averaging using either a simple or weighted method.

This formula is relatively intuitive, as it represents the number of pairs in industry i migrating to default over the total number of migrating pairs. This result comes directly from the fact that, given a group of N_i elements, there will be $N_i(N_i - 1)/2$ different pairs. There has been some criticism regarding this estimator by De Servigny and Renault (2002). They showed that, under default sparse environments, the above estimator could lead to negative spurious correlation. They illustrated this with the following example.

Suppose we have a sample of 10 firms, of which one defaulted. According to the formula above, the joint default probability would be zero, but the marginal default probability would be ⅒ or 0.1, which would lead to negative correlation. Instead, they proposed using the following estimator

$$p_{ii} = \frac{D_{i,t} D_{i,t}}{N_{i,t} N_{i,t}}$$

which would ensure that the correlation is zero for the given example. They compared the two estimators by simulating default for varying levels of default correlation. The proposed estimator outperformed the other in the 1–10% default correlation range, which is the typical region for default correlation. For this reason, our proposed estimator is based on the De Servigny and Renault (2002) definition, and a more recent study by Frey and McNeil (2003), the details of which are mentioned below.

We provide an explicit example of how to calculate intra-industry correlations using the cohort method. In essence, we need to calculate the joint default probabilities and marginal default probabilities on the cohort level, then aggregate them to the industry level by averaging over all cohorts.

Specifically, we rely on two statistics derived from the cohort methodology for the calculation of default correlation. These are (see Figure 6.3): $N_{i,t}$ the total number of firms that were rated in industry i at the beginning of the t-th year, and $D_{i,t}$ the total number of firms that had default within T years.

To help understand this process, we have created a hypothetical example below using the estimator of De Servigny and Renault (2002). For each of the 34 cohorts, we count the total number of firms and the number of defaulted firms over a five-year horizon. These are recorded as columns D and N in Table 6.2. We also create columns DD and NN, which correspond to the

Figure 6.3 Examples of cohort data

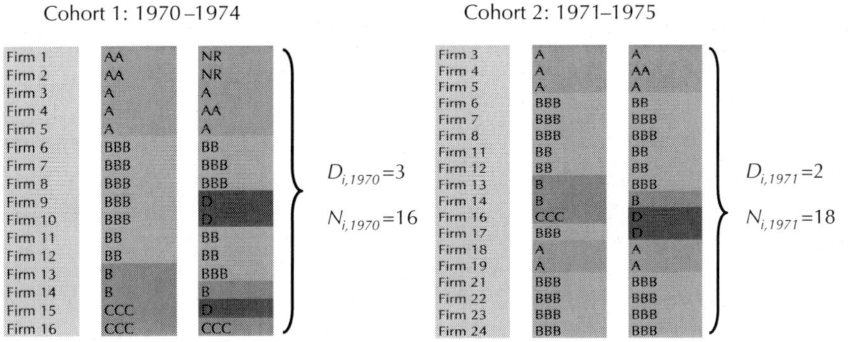

Table 6.2 A hypothetical example

From	To	Cohort	D	N	D*D	N*N
1970	1974	1	5	98	25	9,604
1971	1975	2	2	96	4	9,216
1972	1976	3	1	101	1	10,201
1973	1977	4	2	96	4	9,216
1974	1978	5	0	113	0	12,769
1975	1979	6	0	110	0	12,100
1976	1980	7	0	110	0	12,100
1977	1981	8	0	112	0	12,544
1978	1982	9	0	114	0	12,996
1979	1983	10	1	107	1	11,449
1980	1984	11	2	100	4	10,000
1981	1985	12	0	101	0	10,201
1982	1986	13	0	102	0	10,404
1983	1987	14	0	98	0	9,604
1984	1988	15	0	100	0	10,000
1985	1989	16	0	103	0	10,609
1986	1990	17	0	102	0	10,404
1987	1991	18	0	101	0	10,201
1988	1992	19	0	105	0	11,025
1989	1993	20	2	106	4	11,236
1990	1994	21	3	107	9	11,449
1991	1995	22	5	110	25	12,100
1992	1996	23	2	112	4	12,544
1993	1997	24	0	109	0	11,881
1994	1998	25	2	110	4	12,100
1995	1999	26	3	103	9	10,609
1996	2000	27	3	106	9	11,236
1997	2001	28	9	106	81	11,236
1998	2002	29	3	98	9	9,604
1999	2003	30	2	97	4	9,409
2000	2004	31	1	96	1	9,216
2001	2005	32	3	99	9	9,801
2002	2006	33	5	101	25	10,201
2003	2007	34	4	100	16	10,000
SUM			60	3529	248	367,265

$\boldsymbol{p_i}$ = 1.70%
$\boldsymbol{p_{ii}}$ = 0.07%
Default correlation = 2.33%

numerator and denominator of the joint default probability. We then aggregate across all cohorts using the formula of De Servigny and Renault (2002)

$$p_{ii} = \sum_{t=1}^{T} \frac{N_{i,t}}{\sum_{t=1}^{T} N_{i,t}} \frac{D_{i,t} D_{i,t}}{N_{i,t} N_{i,t}}$$

The marginal default probability can be aggregated in the following way

$$p_i = \sum_{t=1}^{T} \frac{N_{i,t}}{\sum_{t=1}^{T} N_{i,t}} \frac{D_{i,t}}{N_{i,t}}$$

Once we obtain our joint default probability and marginal default probability measures we simply invoke the default correlation formula

$$\rho_{ii}^{D} = \frac{p_{ii} - p_i p_i}{\sqrt{p_i (1 - p_i) p_i (1 - p_i)}}$$

to calculate our default correlation ρ_{ij}^{D}. We can then obtain the asset correlation measure by using the bivariate Gaussian copula.

Alternative formulas for default correlation estimation

The De Servigny–Renault formula for intra-sector correlations used in the example above is not the only one that we are going to use in our empirical analysis. Hence, in the section below, we present several alternative approaches that can be implemented (and will be implemented in the following) to estimate default correlations.

De Servigny and Renault (2002): This estimator averages the joint default probability by weighing it by the number of obligors in each cohort.[3] In the example in the previous section we have already seen the formula for intra-industry joint default probability

$$p_{ii}^{SR} = \sum_{t=1}^{T} \frac{N_{i,t}}{\sum_{t=1}^{T} N_{i,t}} \frac{D_{i,t} D_{i,t}}{N_{i,t} N_{i,t}}$$

The formula for inter-industry default probability is the following

$$p_{ij}^{SR} = \sum_{t=1}^{T} \frac{N_{i,t} + N_{j,t}}{\sum_{t=1}^{T} N_{i,t} + N_{j,t}} \frac{D_{i,t} D_{j,t}}{N_{i,t} N_{j,t}}$$

and is used to estimate joint default correlation in a similar way as the intra-industry one.

Frey and McNeil (2003): Frey and McNeil (2003) use a similar estimator except that the joint default probabilities are aggregated using a simple average over all of the cohorts.

$$p_{ii}^{FM} = \frac{1}{T}\sum_{t=1}^{T} \frac{D_{i,t}\left(D_{i,t}-1\right)}{N_{i,t}\left(N_{i,t}-1\right)}$$

$$p_{ij}^{FM} = \frac{1}{T}\sum_{t=1}^{T} \frac{D_{i,t}D_{j,t}}{N_{i,t}N_{j,t}}$$

As already mentioned, there has been some criticism by De Servigny and Renault (2002) regarding the intra-industry estimator above. They showed that under default sparse environments, the estimator could lead to negative spurious correlation.[4] Therefore, we modified the Frey and McNeil estimator in the spirit of De Servigny and Renault to get

$$p_{ii}^{FMA} = \frac{1}{T}\sum_{t=1}^{T} \frac{D_{i,t}D_{i,t}}{N_{i,t}N_{i,t}}$$

$$p_{ij}^{FMA} = \frac{1}{T}\sum_{t=1}^{T} \frac{D_{i,t}D_{j,t}}{N_{i,t}N_{j,t}}$$

which we call adjusted Frey and McNeil.

RACM or Robust Average Correlation Measure: The difference between the adjusted Frey and McNeil (2003) and De Servigny and Renault (2002) estimators is the fact that one utilises a simple average of all cohorts, and the other uses a weighted average by the number of obligors. There is no theoretical justification for using one or the other; moreover, there is no *a priori* reason to expect one to exceed the other measure in magnitude, and thus it is purely an empirical issue. Therefore, the range between the two estimates can be thought to provide us where the true estimate is likely to be located. Therefore, we create a robust estimator as the average of the adjusted Frey–McNeil and De Servigny–Renault and call it robust average correlation measure (or RACM). The RACM estimator is defined in the following way

$$p_{ii}^{RACM} = MEAN\left(p_{ii}^{SR}, p_{ii}^{FMA}\right)$$

$$p_{ij}^{RACM} = MEAN\left(p_{ij}^{SR}, p_{ij}^{FMA}\right)$$

Gupton, Finger, and Bhatia (1997): Finally, we implement Gupton, Finger and Bhatia (1997) for calculating default correlations. Given two sectors i and j the average default correlation can be expressed as

$$\bar{\rho}_{ij} = \frac{Cov\left(p_i, p_j\right)}{\sqrt{p_i\left(1-p_i\right)}\sqrt{p_j\left(1-p_j\right)}}$$

where the average default rates for industry i and industry j can be expressed as

$$p_i = \frac{1}{N}\sum_{n=1}^{N} D_{i,n} \text{ and } p_j = \frac{1}{N}\sum_{n=1}^{N} D_{j,n}$$

It is interesting to note that the method of Gupton, Finger and Bhatia (1997) does not explicitly use timing of the defaults. However, synchronicity may be introduced into the calculations by using estimates for finer time segments. For example, this can be achieved by applying the cohort methodology. In order to make this estimator compatible with the others, we apply the cohort methodology and call it Gupton, Finger and Bhatia Adjusted.

ASSET CORRELATIONS BASED ON RATING TRANSITIONS

This paragraph explains the methodology based on rating-transition-based methodology implemented in the analysis. This framework focuses on the directions of rating changes, and is based on the so-called directional rating transition matrix (DRTM).

The DRTM is similar to the traditional joint rating transition matrix in that it measures the size and direction of typical rating changes. The DRTM, however, considers only three states: upward, downward and no-movement. In this framework, by observing the co-movement of ratings, Kendall's τ-statistic can be calculated. Asset correlation is then inferred from Kendall's τ-statistic using Greiner's equality.

Creating DRTMs

As before, our main focus is on the intra- and inter-industry correlations. Hence, again we employ the cohort methodology but this time only to track the upgrades, downgrades, and no movements.

Figure 6.4 An example of rating transitions

Cohort 1 – Industry 1: 1970–1975

	Year 1	Year 5	Movement
Firm 1	AA	AA	0
Firm 2	AA	AA	0
Firm 3	AA	AA	0
Firm 4	AA	AA	0
Firm 5	AA	AA	0
Firm 6	BBB	AA	1
Firm 7	BBB	AA	1
Firm 8	BBB	BB	1
Firm 9	BBB	BB	-1
Firm 10	BBB	BB	-1

Assume we have Cohort 1 in Industry 1, as in Figure 6.4, and we are interested in five-year transitions. We compare the initial rating of each obligor with their final rating for all obligors in Industry 1 and Cohort 1 and assign a 1, –1 or 0, depending on whether the obligor was upgraded, downgraded, or had no movement.

In order to calculate a DRTM we need to construct a table of all possible pairs of obligors and their movements for each cohort and then aggregate this across all cohorts. We illustrate this in detail by following example.

Assume you have rating transition information for two cohorts in two industries. The possible movements that can be observed are:

Industry 1:
Cohort 1: 0,0,0,0,0,1,1,1,-1,-1
Cohort 2: 0,0,0,0,0,0
Industry 2:
Cohort 1: 1,1,1,1,1,0,0,0,0,0
Cohort 2: 0,0,0,0,0,0

In the case of inter-industry DRTM, we construct a table of all possible pairs of obligors in Industry 1 and Cohort 1 with obligors in Industry 2 and Cohort 1. In our example, that is 10 x 10 = 100 possible pairs. We repeat this exercise for Industry 1 Cohort 2, and Industry 2 Cohort 2, and then count the number of pairs for each cell of the matrix below:

		Industry 2		
		1	0	-1
Industry 1	1	(1,1)	(1,0)	(1,-1)
	0	(0,1)	(0,0)	(0,-1)
	-1	(-1,1)	(-1,0)	(-1,-1)

The (1,1) cell is joint movement of obligors in say Industry 1 / Cohort 1 that were upgraded with obligors in Industry 2 / Cohort 1 that were upgraded. Since we have two cohorts and two industries in our example, we need to construct two such matrices.

For Cohort 1: Industry 1 → Industry 2 the complete matrix would equal:

		Industry 2		
		1	0	-1
Industry 1	1	15	15	0
	0	25	25	0
	-1	10	10	0

For Cohort 2: Industry 1 → Industry 2 the complete matrix would equal:

		Industry 2		
		1	0	-1
Industry 1	1	0	0	0
	0	0	36	0
	-1	0	0	0

We then add the matrices element by element and divide by the total number of combinations to arrive at the inter-industry DRTM. If we had 31 cohorts, we would add all 31 element by element.

Since there were 10 × 10 possible migrations from Cohort 1, and 6 × 6 possible migrations from Cohort 2, the total number of migrations or combinations would be 136. The resulting inter-industry DRTM matrix would be

		Industry 2		
		1	0	-1
Industry 1	1	15/136	15/136	0/136
	0	25/136	61/136	0/136
	-1	10/136	10/136	0/136

or

		Industry 2		
		1	0	-1
Industry 1	1	11.03%	11.03%	0.00%
	0	18.38%	44.85%	0.00%
	-1	7.35%	7.35%	0.00%

From the above example we see that the probability of an obligor in Industry 1 getting upgraded while an obligor in Industry 2 is being upgraded is 11.03%.

Deriving asset correlations from DRTMs

Non-parametric estimates of asset correlation can be calculated from a DRTM by using Greiner's equality, which can be presented as

$$\tau = \frac{2}{\pi}\arcsin\left(\rho\right)$$

where $\boldsymbol{\tau}$ is Kendall's tau and $\boldsymbol{\rho}$ is the estimate of asset correlation. Once $\boldsymbol{\tau}$ is obtained, using the equation above we can estimate the corresponding value of $\boldsymbol{\rho}$.

In turn, Kendall's tau can be computed in the following way

$$\tau = \frac{C_n - D_n}{\sqrt{C_n - D_n - E_x}\sqrt{C_n - D_n - E_y}}$$

where C_n is the number of concordant pairs, D_n is the number of discordant pairs, and E_x and E_y are the number of ties in x and y, which are the first elements of the pair.

We rewrite the inter-industry DRTM above in the following symbolic format:

M11	M12	M13
M21	M22	M23
M31	M32	M33

so that M11 corresponds to 11.03%, etc. We construct a matrix of pairs by taking the lower triangular matrix of all possible combinations of the above matrix with itself. In other words, the table of pairs would be the shaded areas on the table below:

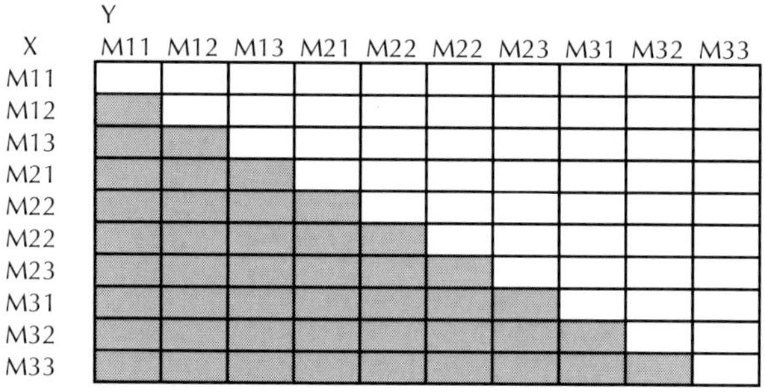

Note that each pair is a combination $\{(x_i, x_j);(y_i, y_j)\}$. The pair is concordant if $(x_i > y_i)$ and $(x_j > y_j)$ or $(x_i < y_i)$ and $(x_j < y_j)$. The pair is discordant if $(x_i > y_i)$ and $(x_j < y_j)$ or $(x_i < y_i)$ and $(x_j > y_j)$. The pair is a tie if it is neither concordant nor discordant.

The pair table for our example is reported as Table 6.3. We apply the concordant and discordant definitions using columns X_i, X_j, Y_i, and Y_j of the table to derive indicator variables for concordant, discordant, tie in X and tie in Y. These indicator variables are columns CON, DIS, TIEX and TIEY. For presentation purposes, we have created a column called P, which is X_P multiplied by Y_P. To calculate the concordant, discordant, etc probabilities, multiply the indicator variable with the column P. For example, in the first row of the table above the indicator variable TIEX is 1. Multiply this indicator variable with the column P to create the probability of TIEX or P_TIEX. Repeat this process for the entire table.

To get the probability of observing a concordant pair, we just sum all rows for the column P_CON, which is 7.1% in our example. Once we have computed probabilities for CON, DIS, TIEX, and TIEY we compute tau by using the formula above. Specifically

Table 6.3 Concordant pairs, discordant pairs and ties

X	X_P	Y	Y_P	P	X_i	X_j	Y_i	Y_j	CON	DIS	TIEX	TIEY	P_CON	P_DISC	P_TIEX	P_TIEY
M12	11.03%	M11	11.03%	1.22%	1	0	1	1			1				1.22%	
M13	0.00%	M11	11.03%	0.00%	1	−1	1	1			1				0.00%	
M13	0.00%	M12	11.03%	0.00%	1	−1	1	0			1				0.00%	
M21	18.38%	M11	11.03%	2.03%	0	1	1	1				1				2.03%
M21	18.38%	M12	11.03%	2.03%	0	1	1	0		1				2.03%		
M21	18.38%	M13	0.00%	0.00%	0	1	1	−1		1				0.00%		
M22	44.85%	M11	11.03%	4.95%	0	0	1	1	1				4.95%			
M22	44.85%	M12	11.03%	4.95%	0	0	1	0				1				4.95%
M22	44.85%	M13	0.00%	0.00%	0	0	1	−1		1				0.00%		
M22	44.85%	M21	18.38%	8.25%	0	0	0	1			1				8.25%	
M23	0.00%	M11	11.03%	0.00%	0	−1	1	1	1				0.00%			
M23	0.00%	M12	11.03%	0.00%	0	−1	1	0	1				0.00%			
M23	0.00%	M13	0.00%	0.00%	0	−1	1	−1				1				0.00%
M23	0.00%	M21	18.38%	0.00%	0	−1	0	1			1				0.00%	
M23	0.00%	M22	44.85%	0.00%	0	−1	0	0			1				0.00%	
M31	7.35%	M11	11.03%	0.81%	−1	1	1	1				1				0.81%
M31	7.35%	M12	11.03%	0.81%	−1	1	1	0		1				0.81%		
M31	7.35%	M13	0.00%	0.00%	−1	1	1	−1		1				0.00%		
M31	7.35%	M21	18.38%	1.35%	−1	1	0	1				1				1.35%
M31	7.35%	M22	44.85%	3.30%	−1	1	0	0		1				3.30%		
M31	7.35%	M23	0.00%	0.00%	−1	1	0	−1		1				0.00%		
M32	7.35%	M11	11.03%	0.81%	−1	0	1	1	1				0.81%			
M32	7.35%	M12	11.03%	0.81%	−1	0	1	0				1				0.81%
M32	7.35%	M13	0.00%	0.00%	−1	0	1	−1		1				0.00%		
M32	7.35%	M21	18.38%	1.35%	−1	0	0	1	1				1.35%			
M32	7.35%	M22	44.85%	3.30%	−1	0	0	0				1				3.30%
M32	7.35%	M23	0.00%	0.00%	−1	0	0	−1		1				0.00%		
M32	7.35%	M31	7.35%	0.54%	−1	0	−1	1			1				0.54%	
M33	0.00%	M11	11.03%	0.00%	−1	−1	1	1	1				0.00%			
M33	0.00%	M12	11.03%	0.00%	−1	−1	1	0	1				0.00%			
M33	0.00%	M13	0.00%	0.00%	−1	−1	1	−1				1				0.00%
M33	0.00%	M21	18.38%	0.00%	−1	−1	0	1	1				0.00%			
M33	0.00%	M22	44.85%	0.00%	−1	−1	0	0	1				0.00%			
M33	0.00%	M23	0.00%	0.00%	−1	−1	0	−1				1				0.00%
M33	0.00%	M31	7.35%	0.00%	−1	−1	−1	1			1				0.00%	
M33	0.00%	M32	7.35%	0.00%	−1	−1	−1	0			1				0.00%	
SUM													**7.1%**	**6.1%**	**10.0%**	**13.2%**

$$\tau = \frac{7.1-6.1}{\sqrt{7.1-6.1-10}\sqrt{7.1-6.1-13.2}} \cong 3.9\%$$ [5]

which, by Greiner's equation, implies that the corresponding asset correlation, $\boldsymbol{\rho}$ is 6.156%.

AN EMPIRICAL STUDY

In this section we apply the methodologies presented above to an empirical data sample. We use US corporate issuers that were rated between January 1970 and December 2007.[6] Accordingly, our dataset includes 89,220 yearly observations comprising 8,249 firms and 1,075 defaults. Consistent with previous studies, issuers were categorised by eight broad letter rating categories (AAA, AA, A, BBB, BB, B, CCC, default). In addition, issuers are classified into one of Fitch's 25 industry categorisations. We define default as the earliest date on which (a) a debt payment was missed, (b) the debtor filed for bankruptcy, (c) a distressed exchange was offered or (d) the rating was changed to default status.

Besides the approaches seen in the previous sections above on asset correlations based on default correlation estimates and asset correlations based on rating transitions, we will also compute asset correlations based on a formula introduced by the Basel Committee on Banking Supervision in June 2004 (Basel II), that is

$$Correlation(R) = 0.12 \times \frac{1-\exp(-50 \times PD)}{1-\exp(-50)} + 0.30 \times \frac{1-(1-\exp(-50 \times PD))}{1-\exp(-50)}$$

where PD is the marginal probability of default.

Comparison between models

Table 6.4 displays the average five-year asset correlation across all Fitch industries for the De Servigny and Renault (2002), the adjusted Frey and McNeil (2003), the RACM, the Gupton, Finger and Bhatia (1997) adjusted to incorporate the cohort method, and DRTM – the rating transition model. The results are also compared with the Basel II formula.

In the Table 6.5 we also provide the 95% confidence intervals for these estimates in order to illustrate the precision of the estimates presented above.

Based on these two tables, a few observations can be made. First, the average asset correlation estimates are close among different models, except for the rating transition model. The rating transition based model generates

Table 6.4 Asset correlation (five-year), 1970–2007

Model	**Intra** (%)	**Inter** (%)
De Servigny and Renault	22.89	17.99
Frey and McNeil (adjusted)	25.15	18.39
RACM	24.01	18.17
Gupton, Finger and Bhatia (adjusted)	25.56	20.33
Basel II formula	18.53	18.47
Rating transition model	7.72	3.39

Table 6.5 95% confidence interval of asset correlation 1970–2007

Model	Intra		Inter	
	Lower bound (%)	Upper bound (%)	Lower bound (%)	Upper bound (%)
De Servigny and Renault	20.65	25.14	17.06	18.92
Frey and McNeil (adjusted)	22.69	27.62	17.44	19.34
RACM	22.17	25.86	17.23	19.12
Gupton, Finger and Bhatia (adjusted)	23.08	28.00	19.31	21.31
Rating transition model	6.01	9.43	3.13	3.65

consistently low estimates in both intra- as well as inter-industry correlations. This may be due to the rating agencies' emphasis on rating stability, which may affect the speed at which ratings are revised.

Second, the intra-industry average asset correlation is always larger than the inter-industry asset correlation, as expected. Third, average asset correlation estimates of the De Servigny and Renault, the Frey and McNeil (adjusted version), the RACM, and the Gupton, Finger and Bhatia (adjusted version) fall into each other's 95% confidence interval, except for the Gupton, Finger and Bhatia (adjusted version) inter-industry average asset correlation. Hence, estimates of the De Servigny and Renault and the Frey and McNeil (adjusted) are not statistically different, and they are similar to Gupton, Finger and Bhatia (adjusted).

Finally, Basel II inter-industry correlation values seem to be at par with all the default-correlation-based methodologies. On the intra-industry correlations, however the Basel correlations yield lower estimates than those of other methodologies.

Comparison with Akhavein, Kocagil and Neugebauer (2005)

Next, it may be of interest to compare the more recent asset correlation findings with the findings of Akhavein, Kocagil and Neugebauer (2005), as this exercise may reveal information about the time sensitivity of the estimates as well as the general trends in the market.

Table 6.6 presents the results of the previous study by Akhavein, Kocagil and Neugebauer (2005), which is based on estimations between January 1970 and December 2004.

We note that almost all of the previous intra-industry average asset correlation estimates fall into the 95% confidence interval of our estimates (except for the De Servigny–Renault approach). That said, all of the previous inter-

Table 6.6 Asset correlation (five-year), 1970–2004

Model	Intra (%)	Inter (%)
De Servigny and Renault	19.73	14.44
Frey and McNeil (adj)	26.49	17.17
RACM	23.11	15.80
Gupton, Finger and Bhatia (adj)	26.39	15.48
Basel II formula 7	17.47	17.14
Rating transition model	7.85	4.56

Source: Akhavein, Kocagil and Neugebauer (2005)

industry average asset correlation estimates fall below the 95% confidence interval of our current estimates.

This can be thought to reflect the fact that inter-industry correlations have been rising since 2004, whereas on average intra-industry asset correlations have remained stable. This is an interesting finding, as it suggests that the changing factors over time must have increased the intra-industry correlations of those industries that co-vary with the other industries at a higher propensity.

In order to test differences at a more granular level, we carry out mean and distribution tests between previous and current asset correlation estimates at industry level. The conducted mean difference test is one-way ANOVA (the analysis of variance) and the distribution test is a two-sample Wilcoxon t-test. Accordingly, the reported p-values in Table 6.7 indicate that all models have statistically different estimates over the time periods for inter-industry correlations, except for the rating transition model. For intra-industry estimates, we again observe a statistical difference over the two time periods for almost all models except for the RACM, the Basel II formula, and the rating transition model.

When we examine the industries that exhibited the largest amount of intra-industry correlation increases between two findings of different time periods, we observe that the top three are banking and finance; leisure and entertainment; and lodging and restaurants. This is an interesting finding, as banking and finance is an industry that is known to have relatively higher systematic exposure. An increase in the banking industry's intra-correlations would trigger higher inter correlations. Note that this is consistent with the previous observation regarding the increase in inter-industry correlations with stable average intra-industry correlations.

Table 6.7 P-values for one-way ANOVA tests (mean test) and two-sample Wilcoxon tests (distribution test)

	P-value			
	Mean test		Distribution test	
Model	**Intra (%)**	**Inter (%)**	**Intra (%)**	**Inter (%)**
De Servigny and Renault	1.13	0.00	0.20	0.00
Frey and McNeil (adj)	0.68	0.00	1.89	0.00
RACM	90.85	0.00	54.15	0.00
Gupton, Finger and Bhatia (adj)	0.00	0.00	0.00	0.00
Basel II formula	14.93	0.06	17.44	0.10
Rating transition model	13.88	85.98	0.50	69.26

Finally, on a more technical note, the previous comparison between estimates of the De Servigny and Renault and the Frey and McNeil (adj) during 1970 and 2004 concludes that, for a majority of industries, the Frey and McNeil (adj) asset correlation estimate is above the De Servigny and Renault. This is consistent with current estimates during 1970 and 2007 (see Figures 6.5 and 6.6).

To help visualise the results, the intra and inter-industry correlations are graphed separately in Figures 6.7 and 6.8. Excluding the rating transition model and the Basel II formula, the intra-industry average asset correlations are contained within the De Servigny and Renault and the adjusted Gupton, Finger and Bhatia estimators. In other words, these estimators seem to define the lower and upper bound of the estimates. This is slightly different from the previous finding that the De Servigny and the adjusted Frey and McNeil estimators tend to define the lower and upper bond of the estimates based on 1970 to 2004.

As we noted earlier, Basel II formula estimates are within the bounds for the inter-industry correlations, whereas they tend to be lower on the intra-industry correlations.

Hypothesis testing

In this section, we present the test statistics on several hypotheses. In the benefit of space we report only the results based on RACM.[8]

We employ the bootstrap methodology to test hypotheses regarding intra-industry and inter-industry asset correlations. Specifically, we chose

Figure 6.5 Intra-industry five-year asset correlation, 1970–2007

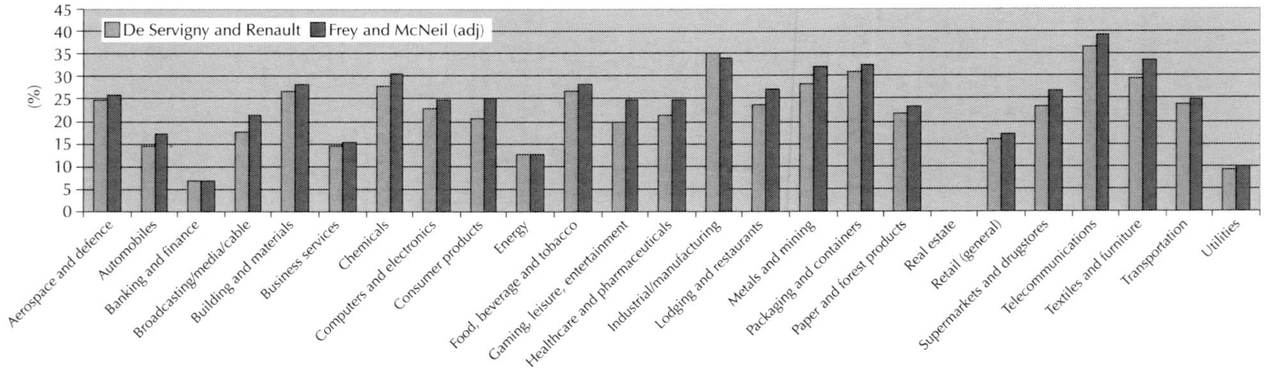

Figure 6.6 Inter-industry five-year asset correlation, 1970–2007

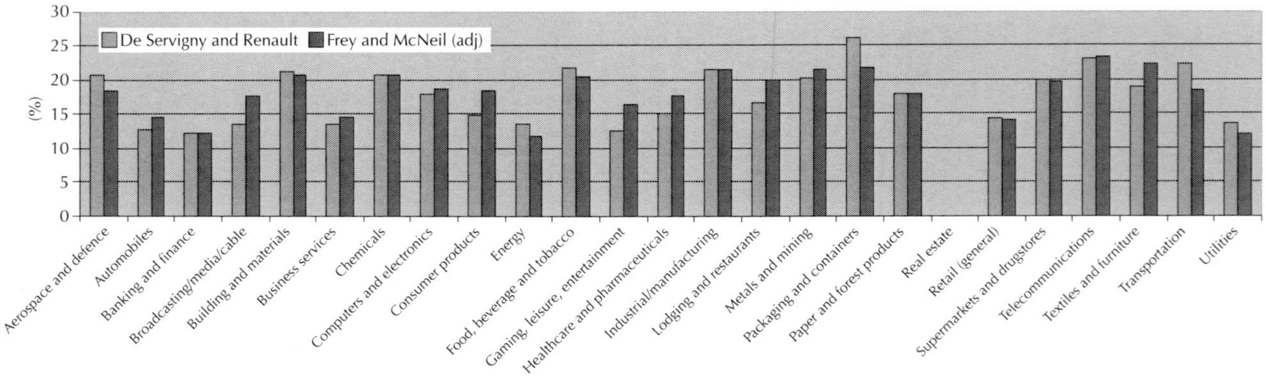

Figure 6.7 Intra-industry five-year asset correlations, 1970–2007

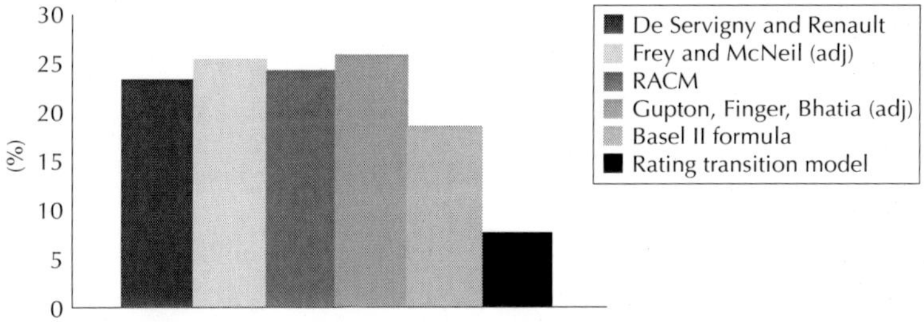

Figure 6.8 Inter-industry five-year asset correlations, 1970–2007

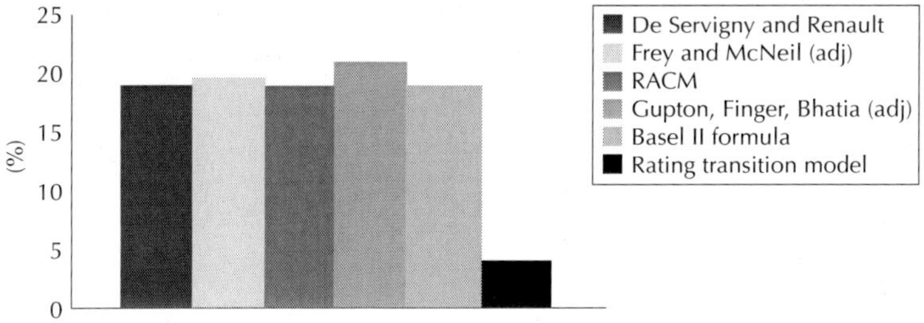

1,000 stratified random samples with replacement from our original historical ratings so that the overall rating distributions are preserved. For each sample, we created 34 cohorts for each of the 25 Fitch industry groups, re-estimated default correlations, converted these to asset correlations and then performed the testing.

In particular, the hypotheses we would like to test are the following:

1. How different are inter-industry correlations from zero?
2. Can time-invariant and/or constant asset correlations across sectors be assumed?

In order to answer the first question, the sensitivity of the estimates was tested by conducting a bootstrap exercise of 1,000 runs. Within these 1,000 bootstrap runs there was not a single occurrence for any industry where the inter-industry correlation was zero. In other words, even the smallest estimate was a positive number. The corresponding sigma based on the 1,000 bootstraps was calculated. We determined that approximately a five-sigma shock would be needed for any of the estimates to become zero, which probabilistically is an extremely small number.[9]

Our comparison of different sample windows in the previous subsection already has illustrated that time invariance in asset correlations does not hold. Thus, next we wanted to examine the cross-sectional behaviour: whether inter-industry asset correlations can be assumed to be constant across Fitch's 25 industry groupings. Bootstrapped samples were used along with the *t*-, Kolmogorov–Smirnov and Wilcoxon tests to conduct industry pairwise comparisons. There are 25 separate industries, therefore 25 × (25 – 1) / 2 = 300 pairs were compared. For example, inter-industry correlations between auto and aerospace, auto and utilities and so on were compared to determine if they were different. Table 6.8 reports the number of pairs out of 300 that could statistically have the same inter-industry correlations.[10] As the results indicate, statistically speaking it cannot be assumed that inter-industry correlations are constant across all industries.

Table 6.8 Inter-industry correlations: number of pairs that are not statistically different at the 0.01% level

	Inter
t-test	12
Kolmogrov-Smirnov	7
Wilcoxon	10

Similarly, the same pairwise testing routine was conducted on the intra-industry correlations. As before, out of 300 possibilities we identify how many pairs can be assumed to have a constant correlation. As Table 6.9 illustrates, probabilistically the likelihood of intra-industry correlation being constant is relatively small to allow such a blanket assumption.

Table 6.9 Intra-industry correlations: number of pairs that are not statistically different at the 0.01% level

	Inter
t-test	13
Kolmogrov-Smirnov	5
Wilcoxon	10

SUMMARY AND CONCLUSIONS

In this chapter we presented a number of techniques to estimate asset correlations using default-correlation-based and rating-transition-based formulas. We then empirically estimated correlations and compared them with each other, with the Basel II formula, and with the results of a previous study. These comparisons were on the intra- and inter-industry level defined according to the Fitch industry categories.

The empirical findings of the study are in line with (Akhavein, Kocagil and Neugebauer, 2005) and confirm that: (a) there is a statistically notable empirical difference between intra-industry and inter-industry asset correlations (inter-industry asset correlations are relatively smaller), (b) intra-industry as well as inter-industry asset correlations vary across different industries, (c) they also vary over time, and, finally (d), Basel II formula based inter-industry correlations seem to be in line with the other estimates on average, however Basel II estimates for intra-industry correlations seem be smaller than other estimates.

In the light of these findings we recognise that similar to other measures, such as probability-of-default (PD) and loss-given-default (LGD), correlation estimates can also vary significantly across industries as well as across time. Thus, we should be cognisant that in an empirical sense we are dealing with a given point in a distribution function, where historical averages can provide us only information about the mean of the distribution. Caution should be exercised in making inferences, because, especially if the observation window is not observed for very long, deviations from the historical averages can be rather large.

APPENDIX 6.1: COMPARISON OF DE SERVINGY AND RENAULT AND ADJUSTED FREY AND MCNEIL MODEL OUTPUTS

We compared the De Servigny and Renault and the adjusted Frey and McNeil estimators by industry. We observed that, for nearly all industries, the asset correlation estimate stemming from the adjusted Frey and McNeil estimator is larger than the estimates from the De Servigny and Renault in magnitude for intra-industry asset correlations (see Figure 6.9).

Again for a majority of industries, the Frey and McNeil asset correlation estimate is above the De Servigny and Renault for the inter-industry comparisons.

Figure 6.9 Intra-industry asset correlation comparison

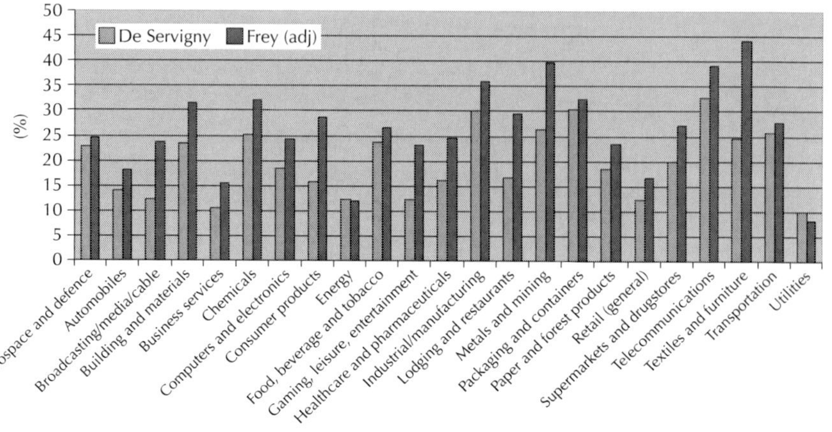

Figure 6.10 Inter-industry asset correlation comparison

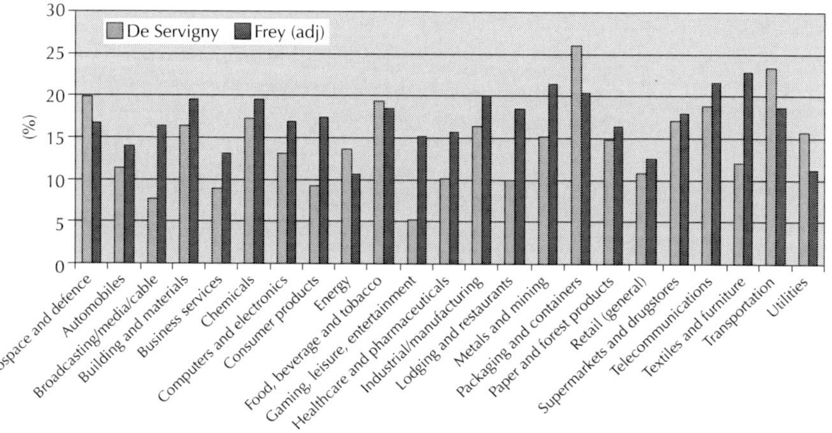

APPENDIX 6.2: STATISTICAL RESULTS

Two-tailed *T*-test results:

Examination of whether intra- and inter-industry asset correlations are the same in magnitude

T-test two-sided (unequal variances)
Intra-industry

	Industry	1	2	3	4	5	6	7	8	9	10	11	12	13	14	15	16	17	18	19	20	21	22	23	24	25
Aerospace and defence	1																									
Automobiles	2	0.000																								
Banking and finance	3	0.000	0.000																							
Broadcasting/media/cable	4	0.000	0.000	0.000																						
Building and materials	5	0.011	0.000	0.000	0.000																					
Business services	6	0.000	0.000	0.000	0.000	0.000																				
Chemicals	7	0.000	0.000	0.000	0.000	0.000	0.000																			
Computers and electronics	8	0.000	0.000	0.000	0.000	0.000	0.000	0.000																		
Consumer products	9	0.000	0.000	0.000	0.000	0.000	0.000	0.000	0.169																	
Energy	10	0.000	0.000	0.000	0.000	0.000	0.000	0.000	0.000	0.000																
Food, beverage and tobacco	11	0.242	0.000	0.000	0.000	0.000	0.000	0.000	0.000	0.000	0.000															
Gaming, leisure, entertainment	12	0.000	0.000	0.000	0.000	0.000	0.000	0.000	0.129	0.028	0.000	0.000														
Healthcare and pharmaceuticals	13	0.000	0.000	0.000	0.000	0.000	0.000	0.000	0.659	0.114	0.000	0.000	0.232													
Industrial/manufacturing	14	0.000	0.000	0.000	0.000	0.000	0.000	0.000	0.000	0.000	0.000	0.000	0.000	0.000												
Lodging and restaurants	15	0.000	0.000	0.000	0.000	0.000	0.000	0.000	0.001	0.041	0.000	0.000	0.000	0.000	0.000											
Metals and mining	16	0.000	0.000	0.000	0.000	0.000	0.000	0.000	0.000	0.000	0.000	0.000	0.000	0.000	0.000	0.000										
Packaging and containers	17	0.000	0.000	0.000	0.000	0.000	0.000	0.000	0.000	0.000	0.000	0.000	0.000	0.000	0.000	0.000	0.000									
Paper and forest products	18	0.000	0.000	0.000	0.000	0.000	0.000	0.000	0.000	0.000	0.000	0.000	0.000	0.000	0.000	0.000	0.000	0.000								
Real estate	19	0.000	0.000	0.000	0.000	0.000	0.000	0.000	0.000	0.000	0.000	0.000	0.000	0.000	0.000	0.000	0.000	0.000	0.000							
Retail (general)	20	0.000	0.797	0.000	0.000	0.000	0.000	0.000	0.000	0.000	0.000	0.000	0.000	0.000	0.000	0.000	0.000	0.000	0.000	0.000						
Supermarkets and drugstores	21	0.000	0.000	0.000	0.000	0.000	0.000	0.000	0.000	0.000	0.000	0.000	0.000	0.000	0.000	0.000	0.000	0.000	0.186	0.000	0.000					
Telecommunications	22	0.000	0.000	0.000	0.000	0.000	0.000	0.000	0.000	0.000	0.000	0.000	0.000	0.000	0.000	0.000	0.000	0.000	0.000	0.000	0.000	0.000				
Textiles and furniture	23	0.000	0.000	0.000	0.000	0.000	0.000	0.000	0.000	0.000	0.000	0.000	0.000	0.000	0.000	0.000	0.285	0.000	0.000	0.000	0.000	0.000	0.000			
Transportation	24	0.001	0.000	0.000	0.000	0.406	0.000	0.000	0.000	0.000	0.000	0.000	0.000	0.000	0.000	0.000	0.000	0.000	0.000	0.000	0.000	0.000	0.000	0.000		
Utilities	25	0.000	0.000	0.000	0.000	0.000	0.000	0.000	0.000	0.000	0.000	0.000	0.000	0.000	0.000	0.000	0.000	0.000	0.000	0.000	0.000	0.000	0.000	0.000	0.000	

T-test two-sided (unequal variances)
Inter-industry

	Industry	1	2	3	4	5	6	7	8	9	10	11	12	13	14	15	16	17	18	19	20	21	22	23	24	25
Aerospace and defence	1																									
Automobiles	2	0.000																								
Banking and finance	3	0.000	0.000																							
Broadcasting/media/cable	4	0.000	0.000	0.000																						
Building and materials	5	0.000	0.000	0.000	0.000																					
Business services	6	0.000	0.000	0.000	0.000	0.000																				
Chemicals	7	0.000	0.000	0.000	0.000	0.000	0.000																			
Computers and electronics	8	0.000	0.000	0.000	0.000	0.000	0.000	0.000																		
Consumer products	9	0.000	0.000	0.000	0.000	0.000	0.000	0.000	0.000																	
Energy	10	0.000	0.431	0.000	0.000	0.000	0.000	0.000	0.000	0.000																
Food, beverage and tobacco	11	0.000	0.000	0.000	0.000	0.000	0.000	0.000	0.000	0.000	0.000															
Gaming, leisure, entertainment	12	0.000	0.000	0.000	0.000	0.000	0.000	0.000	0.000	0.000	0.000	0.000														
Healthcare and pharmaceuticals	13	0.000	0.013	0.061	0.000	0.000	0.000	0.000	0.000	0.000	0.000	0.000	0.000													
Industrial/manufacturing	14	0.000	0.000	0.000	0.000	0.371	0.000	0.000	0.000	0.000	0.000	0.000	0.000	0.000												
Lodging and restaurants	15	0.000	0.000	0.879	0.000	0.000	0.000	0.000	0.000	0.000	0.000	0.000	0.000	0.050	0.000											
Metals and mining	16	0.000	0.000	0.000	0.000	0.000	0.000	0.000	0.000	0.000	0.000	0.000	0.000	0.000	0.000	0.000										
Packaging and containers	17	0.000	0.000	0.000	0.000	0.000	0.000	0.000	0.000	0.000	0.000	0.000	0.000	0.000	0.000	0.000	0.000									
Paper and forest products	18	0.000	0.000	0.000	0.000	0.000	0.000	0.000	0.000	0.000	0.000	0.000	0.000	0.000	0.000	0.000	0.000	0.000								
Real estate	19	0.000	0.000	0.000	0.000	0.000	0.000	0.000	0.000	0.028	0.000	0.000	0.000	0.000	0.000	0.000	0.000	0.000	0.000							
Retail (general)	20	0.000	0.000	0.000	0.000	0.000	0.000	0.000	0.000	0.028	0.000	0.000	0.000	0.000	0.000	0.000	0.000	0.000	0.000	0.000						
Supermarkets and drugstores	21	0.000	0.000	0.000	0.000	0.000	0.000	0.000	0.000	0.000	0.000	0.000	0.000	0.000	0.698	0.000	0.000	0.000	0.000	0.000	0.000					
Telecommunications	22	0.000	0.000	0.000	0.000	0.000	0.000	0.000	0.000	0.000	0.000	0.044	0.000	0.000	0.000	0.000	0.000	0.000	0.000	0.000	0.000	0.000				
Textiles and furniture	23	0.000	0.000	0.000	0.000	0.000	0.000	0.000	0.703	0.000	0.000	0.000	0.000	0.000	0.000	0.000	0.000	0.000	0.000	0.000	0.000	0.000	0.000			
Transportation	24	0.000	0.000	0.000	0.000	0.000	0.000	0.000	0.000	0.000	0.000	0.000	0.000	0.000	0.000	0.000	0.000	0.000	0.000	0.000	0.000	0.000	0.000	0.000		
Utilities	25	0.000	0.000	0.000	0.000	0.000	0.000	0.000	0.000	0.000	0.000	0.000	0.000	0.000	0.000	0.000	0.000	0.000	0.000	0.000	0.000	0.000	0.000	0.000	0.000	

Kolmogorov and Smirnov test results:

Testing equality of intra- and inter-industry correlations

Kolmogorov-Smirnov Two-sample test (asymptotic)
Intra-industry

	Industry	1	2	3	4	5	6	7	8	9	10	11	12	13	14	15	16	17	18	19	20	21	22	23	24	25
Aerospace and defence	1																									
Automobiles	2	0.000																								
Banking and finance	3	0.000	0.000																							
Broadcasting/media/cable	4	0.000	0.000	0.000																						
Building and materials	5	0.000	0.000	0.000	0.000																					
Business services	6	0.000	0.000	0.000	0.000	0.000																				
Chemicals	7	0.000	0.000	0.000	0.000	0.000	0.000																			
Computers and electronics	8	0.000	0.000	0.000	0.000	0.000	0.000	0.000																		
Consumer products	9	0.000	0.000	0.000	0.000	0.000	0.000	0.000	0.150																	
Energy	10	0.000	0.000	0.000	0.000	0.000	0.000	0.000	0.000	0.000																
Food, beverage and tobacco	11	0.000	0.000	0.000	0.000	0.000	0.000	0.000	0.000	0.000	0.000															
Gaming, leisure, entertainment	12	0.000	0.000	0.000	0.000	0.000	0.000	0.000	0.000	0.000	0.000	0.000														
Healthcare and pharmaceuticals	13	0.000	0.000	0.000	0.000	0.000	0.000	0.000	0.001	0.011	0.000	0.000	0.000													
Industrial/manufacturing	14	0.000	0.000	0.000	0.000	0.000	0.000	0.000	0.000	0.000	0.000	0.000	0.000	0.000												
Lodging and restaurants	15	0.000	0.000	0.000	0.000	0.000	0.000	0.000	0.000	0.029	0.000	0.000	0.000	0.000	0.000											
Metals and mining	16	0.000	0.000	0.000	0.000	0.000	0.000	0.000	0.000	0.000	0.000	0.000	0.000	0.000	0.000	0.000										
Packaging and containers	17	0.000	0.000	0.000	0.000	0.000	0.000	0.000	0.000	0.000	0.000	0.000	0.000	0.000	0.000	0.000	0.000									
Paper and forest products	18	0.000	0.000	0.000	0.000	0.000	0.000	0.000	0.000	0.000	0.000	0.000	0.000	0.000	0.000	0.000	0.000	0.000								
Real estate	19	0.000	0.000	0.000	0.000	0.000	0.000	0.000	0.000	0.000	0.000	0.000	0.000	0.000	0.000	0.000	0.000	0.000	0.000							
Retail (general)	20	0.000	0.960	0.000	0.000	0.000	0.000	0.000	0.000	0.000	0.000	0.000	0.000	0.000	0.000	0.000	0.000	0.000	0.000	0.000						
Supermarkets and drugstores	21	0.000	0.000	0.000	0.000	0.000	0.000	0.000	0.000	0.000	0.000	0.000	0.000	0.000	0.000	0.000	0.000	0.000	0.069	0.000	0.000					
Telecommunications	22	0.000	0.000	0.000	0.000	0.000	0.000	0.000	0.000	0.000	0.000	0.000	0.000	0.000	0.000	0.000	0.000	0.000	0.000	0.000	0.000	0.000				
Textiles and furniture	23	0.000	0.000	0.000	0.000	0.000	0.000	0.000	0.000	0.000	0.000	0.000	0.000	0.000	0.000	0.000	0.095	0.000	0.000	0.000	0.000	0.000	0.000			
Transportation	24	0.000	0.000	0.000	0.000	0.292	0.000	0.000	0.000	0.000	0.000	0.000	0.000	0.000	0.000	0.000	0.000	0.000	0.000	0.000	0.000	0.000	0.000	0.000		
Utilities	25	0.000	0.000	0.000	0.000	0.000	0.000	0.000	0.000	0.000	0.000	0.000	0.000	0.000	0.000	0.000	0.000	0.000	0.000	0.000	0.000	0.000	0.000	0.000	0.000	

Kolmogorov-Smirnov Two-sample test (asymptotic)
Inter-industry

	Industry	1	2	3	4	5	6	7	8	9	10	11	12	13	14	15	16	17	18	19	20	21	22	23	24	25
Aerospace and defence	1																									
Automobiles	2	0.000																								
Banking and finance	3	0.000	0.001																							
Broadcasting/media/cable	4	0.000	0.000	0.000																						
Building and materials	5	0.000	0.000	0.000	0.000																					
Business services	6	0.000	0.000	0.000	0.000	0.000																				
Chemicals	7	0.000	0.000	0.000	0.000	0.000	0.000																			
Computers and electronics	8	0.000	0.000	0.000	0.000	0.000	0.000	0.000																		
Consumer products	9	0.000	0.000	0.000	0.000	0.000	0.000	0.000	0.000																	
Energy	10	0.000	0.000	0.000	0.000	0.000	0.000	0.000	0.000	0.000																
Food, beverage and tobacco	11	0.000	0.000	0.000	0.000	0.000	0.000	0.000	0.000	0.000	0.000															
Gaming, leisure, entertainment	12	0.000	0.000	0.000	0.000	0.000	0.000	0.000	0.000	0.000	0.000	0.000														
Healthcare and pharmaceuticals	13	0.000	0.035	0.413	0.000	0.000	0.000	0.000	0.000	0.000	0.000	0.000	0.000													
Industrial/manufacturing	14	0.000	0.000	0.000	0.000	0.111	0.000	0.000	0.000	0.000	0.000	0.000	0.000	0.000												
Lodging and restaurants	15	0.000	0.002	0.460	0.000	0.000	0.000	0.000	0.000	0.000	0.000	0.000	0.000	0.069	0.000											
Metals and mining	16	0.000	0.000	0.000	0.000	0.000	0.000	0.000	0.000	0.000	0.000	0.000	0.000	0.000	0.000	0.000										
Packaging and containers	17	0.000	0.000	0.000	0.000	0.000	0.000	0.000	0.000	0.000	0.000	0.000	0.000	0.000	0.000	0.000	0.000									
Paper and forest products	18	0.000	0.000	0.000	0.000	0.000	0.000	0.000	0.000	0.000	0.000	0.000	0.000	0.000	0.000	0.000	0.000	0.000								
Real estate	19	0.000	0.000	0.000	0.000	0.000	0.000	0.000	0.000	0.000	0.000	0.000	0.000	0.000	0.000	0.000	0.000	0.000	0.000							
Retail (general)	20	0.000	0.000	0.000	0.000	0.000	0.000	0.000	0.000	0.000	0.000	0.000	0.000	0.000	0.000	0.000	0.000	0.000	0.000	0.000						
Supermarkets and drugstores	21	0.000	0.000	0.000	0.000	0.059	0.000	0.000	0.000	0.000	0.000	0.000	0.000	0.000	0.198	0.000	0.000	0.000	0.000	0.000	0.000					
Telecommunications	22	0.000	0.000	0.000	0.000	0.000	0.000	0.000	0.000	0.000	0.000	0.001	0.000	0.000	0.000	0.000	0.000	0.000	0.000	0.000	0.000	0.000				
Textiles and furniture	23	0.000	0.000	0.000	0.000	0.000	0.000	0.000	0.413	0.000	0.000	0.000	0.000	0.000	0.000	0.000	0.000	0.000	0.000	0.000	0.000	0.000	0.000			
Transportation	24	0.000	0.000	0.000	0.000	0.000	0.000	0.000	0.000	0.000	0.000	0.000	0.000	0.000	0.000	0.000	0.000	0.000	0.000	0.000	0.000	0.000	0.000	0.000		
Utilities	25	0.000	0.000	0.000	0.000	0.000	0.000	0.000	0.000	0.000	0.000	0.000	0.000	0.000	0.000	0.000	0.000	0.000	0.000	0.000	0.000	0.000	0.000	0.000	0.000	

Wilcoxon test results:

Testing equality of intra- and inter-industry correlations

Wilcoxon two-sample test – intra-industry
Two-sided Pr > |Z|

	Industry	1	2	3	4	5	6	7	8	9	10	11	12	13	14	15	16	17	18	19	20	21	22	23	24	25
Aerospace and defence	1																									
Automobiles	2	0.000																								
Banking and finance	3	0.000	0.000																							
Broadcasting/media/cable	4	0.000	0.001	0.000																						
Building and materials	5	0.000	0.000	0.000	0.000																					
Business services	6	0.000	0.000	0.000	0.000	0.000																				
Chemicals	7	0.000	0.000	0.000	0.000	0.000	0.000																			
Computers and electronics	8	0.000	0.000	0.000	0.000	0.000	0.000	0.000																		
Consumer products	9	0.000	0.000	0.000	0.000	0.000	0.000	0.000	0.602																	
Energy	10	0.000	0.000	0.000	0.000	0.000	0.000	0.000	0.000	0.000																
Food, beverage and tobacco	11	0.519	0.000	0.000	0.000	0.000	0.000	0.000	0.000	0.000	0.000															
Gaming, leisure, entertainment	12	0.000	0.000	0.000	0.000	0.000	0.000	0.000	0.000	0.000	0.000	0.000														
Healthcare and pharmaceuticals	13	0.000	0.000	0.000	0.000	0.000	0.000	0.000	0.194	0.077	0.000	0.000	0.000													
Industrial/manufacturing	14	0.000	0.000	0.000	0.000	0.000	0.000	0.000	0.000	0.000	0.000	0.000	0.000	0.000												
Lodging and restaurants	15	0.000	0.000	0.000	0.000	0.000	0.000	0.000	0.031	0.160	0.000	0.000	0.000	0.000	0.000											
Metals and mining	16	0.000	0.000	0.000	0.000	0.000	0.000	0.000	0.000	0.000	0.000	0.000	0.000	0.000	0.000	0.000										
Packaging and containers	17	0.000	0.000	0.000	0.000	0.000	0.000	0.000	0.000	0.000	0.000	0.000	0.000	0.000	0.000	0.000	0.000									
Paper and forest products	18	0.000	0.000	0.000	0.000	0.000	0.000	0.000	0.000	0.000	0.000	0.000	0.000	0.000	0.000	0.000	0.000	0.000								
Real estate	19	0.000	0.000	0.000	0.000	0.000	0.000	0.000	0.000	0.000	0.000	0.000	0.000	0.000	0.000	0.000	0.000	0.000	0.000							
Retail (general)	20	0.000	0.734	0.000	0.000	0.000	0.000	0.000	0.000	0.000	0.000	0.000	0.000	0.000	0.000	0.000	0.000	0.000	0.000	0.000						
Supermarkets and drugstores	21	0.000	0.000	0.000	0.000	0.000	0.000	0.000	0.000	0.000	0.000	0.000	0.000	0.000	0.000	0.000	0.000	0.000	0.104	0.000	0.000					
Telecommunications	22	0.000	0.000	0.000	0.000	0.000	0.000	0.000	0.000	0.000	0.000	0.000	0.000	0.000	0.000	0.000	0.000	0.000	0.000	0.000	0.000	0.000				
Textiles and furniture	23	0.000	0.000	0.000	0.000	0.000	0.000	0.000	0.000	0.000	0.000	0.000	0.000	0.000	0.000	0.000	0.554	0.000	0.000	0.000	0.000	0.000	0.000			
Transportation	24	0.000	0.000	0.000	0.000	0.242	0.000	0.000	0.000	0.000	0.000	0.000	0.000	0.000	0.000	0.000	0.000	0.000	0.000	0.000	0.000	0.000	0.000	0.000		
Utilities	25	0.000	0.000	0.000	0.000	0.000	0.000	0.000	0.000	0.000	0.000	0.000	0.000	0.000	0.000	0.000	0.000	0.000	0.000	0.000	0.000	0.000	0.000	0.000	0.000	

Wilcoxon two-sample test – inter-industry
Two-sided Pr > |Z|

	Industry	1	2	3	4	5	6	7	8	9	10	11	12	13	14	15	16	17	18	19	20	21	22	23	24	25
Aerospace and defence	1																									
Automobiles	2	0.000																								
Banking and finance	3	0.000	0.001																							
Broadcasting/media/cable	4	0.000	0.000	0.000																						
Building and materials	5	0.000	0.000	0.000	0.000																					
Business services	6	0.000	0.000	0.000	0.051	0.000																				
Chemicals	7	0.000	0.000	0.000	0.000	0.000	0.000																			
Computers and electronics	8	0.000	0.000	0.000	0.000	0.000	0.000	0.000																		
Consumer products	9	0.000	0.000	0.000	0.000	0.000	0.000	0.000	0.000																	
Energy	10	0.000	0.366	0.000	0.000	0.000	0.000	0.000	0.000	0.000																
Food, beverage and tobacco	11	0.000	0.000	0.000	0.000	0.000	0.000	0.000	0.000	0.000	0.000															
Gaming, leisure, entertainment	12	0.000	0.000	0.000	0.000	0.000	0.000	0.000	0.000	0.000	0.000	0.000														
Healthcare and pharmaceuticals	13	0.000	0.029	0.205	0.000	0.000	0.000	0.000	0.000	0.000	0.006	0.000	0.000													
Industrial/manufacturing	14	0.000	0.000	0.000	0.000	0.455	0.000	0.000	0.000	0.000	0.000	0.000	0.000	0.000												
Lodging and restaurants	15	0.000	0.000	0.553	0.000	0.000	0.000	0.000	0.000	0.000	0.000	0.000	0.000	0.068	0.000											
Metals and mining	16	0.000	0.000	0.000	0.000	0.000	0.000	0.000	0.000	0.000	0.000	0.000	0.000	0.000	0.000	0.000										
Packaging and containers	17	0.000	0.000	0.000	0.000	0.000	0.000	0.000	0.000	0.000	0.000	0.000	0.000	0.000	0.000	0.000	0.000									
Paper and forest products	18	0.000	0.000	0.000	0.000	0.000	0.000	0.000	0.000	0.000	0.000	0.000	0.000	0.000	0.000	0.000	0.000	0.000								
Real estate	19	0.000	0.000	0.000	0.000	0.000	0.000	0.000	0.000	0.000	0.000	0.000	0.000	0.000	0.000	0.000	0.000	0.000	0.000							
Retail (general)	20	0.000	0.000	0.000	0.000	0.000	0.000	0.000	0.000	0.001	0.000	0.000	0.000	0.000	0.000	0.000	0.000	0.000	0.000	0.001						
Supermarkets and drugstores	21	0.000	0.000	0.000	0.000	0.298	0.000	0.000	0.000	0.000	0.000	0.000	0.000	0.000	0.773	0.000	0.000	0.000	0.000	0.001	0.000					
Telecommunications	22	0.000	0.000	0.000	0.000	0.000	0.000	0.000	0.000	0.000	0.000	0.012	0.000	0.000	0.000	0.000	0.000	0.000	0.000	0.001	0.000	0.000				
Textiles and furniture	23	0.000	0.000	0.000	0.000	0.000	0.000	0.000	0.926	0.000	0.000	0.000	0.000	0.000	0.000	0.000	0.000	0.000	0.000	0.001	0.000	0.000	0.000			
Transportation	24	0.000	0.000	0.000	0.000	0.000	0.000	0.000	0.000	0.000	0.000	0.000	0.000	0.000	0.000	0.000	0.000	0.000	0.000	0.001	0.000	0.000	0.000	0.000		
Utilities	25	0.000	0.000	0.000	0.000	0.000	0.000	0.000	0.000	0.000	0.000	0.000	0.000	0.000	0.000	0.000	0.000	0.000	0.001	0.001	0.000	0.000	0.000	0.000	0.000	

1 There are no material differences in the empirical results for industry-level asset correlations whether we use initial rating of the firm or the last available rating. We will report the results using the initial rating.
2 For the rest of the chapter, p_{ii} and p_{ij} will denote the intra-industry and inter-industry joint default probabilities. All other notations will follow suit.
3 The superscripts SR, FM and so forth refer to the methodologies used. For example SR stands for De Servigny and Renault.
4 See De Servigny and Renault (2002).
5 The actual numbers are 7.10960%, 6.13650%, 10.002% and 13.246%.
6 We restrict our sample to the US in order to be consistent with previous studies and achieve an "apples-to-apples" comparison with other methodologies.
7 We also calculate asset correlation of 1970–2004 based on Basel II formula to facilitate the comparison.
8 These results are also consistent with De Servigny and Renault, Frey and McNeil, and Gupton, Finger and Bhatia adjusted.
9 Given normally distributed data, the two-sigma level should encompass 95.44997% of all occurrences, while a three-sigma measurement should encompass 99.73002% of all occurrences. The four- and five-sigma confidence limits are 99.99366% and 99.99994% respectively, which can be thought as an event with odds of 6 in 10,000,000.
10 The full matrix is reported in Appendix 6.2.

REFERENCES

Akhavein, J., A. Kocagil and M. Neugebauer, 2005, "An Empirical Assessment of Asset Correlations", Fitch QFR, URL: http://www.fitchresearch.com/creditdesk/reports/report_frame.cfm?rpt_id=244820

De Servigny, A. and O. Renault, 2002, "Default Correlation: Empirical Evidence", Risk Solutions, Working Paper.

Frey, R. and A. J. McNeil, 2003, "Dependent defaults in models of portfolio credit risk", *The Journal of Risk* 6(1), pp. 59–92.

Gordy, M. B., 2002, "A comparative anatomy of credit risk models", *Journal of Banking and Finance* 24, pp. 119–49.

Gupton. G, C. Finger, and M. Bhatia, 1997, "Credit Metrics – Technical Document" 1st edition, URL: http://www.riskmetrics.com

Lindskog, F., 2000, "Modeling Dependence with Copulas", RiskLab Report, ETH Zürich.

Lucas, D., 1995, "Default correlation and credit analysis", *Journal of Fixed Income*, March, pp. 76–87.

Nagpal, K., and R. Bahar, 2001, "Measuring Default Correlation", *Risk* 14, pp. 129–32.

Schoenbucher, P.J., 2003, *Credit Derivatives Pricing Models* (Chichester: John Wiley & Sons Ltd).

7

Modelling and Measuring Business Risk

Klaus Böcker

UniCredit Group

As can be seen for example by the cutting edge section of *Risk* magazine, research papers mainly focus on market risk, credit risk, and – with a little less attention – operational risk. Although these risk types are very important for financial institutions, the true landscape of risk is much more complex and far from being well explored and understood. There is a variety of "other" risks looming on the horizon, which seriously threaten a banks profitability or which can disrupt or even destroy its business completely. Moreover, such risks often reflect an under-researched area of financial risk management, and established and ready-to-use measurement techniques are rarely available. Also banking supervisors demand that more attention is being paid to such "hard-to-measure" risks as the following Pillar II passages of the new international regulatory framework of Basel II (Basel Committee on Banking Supervision 2004) show:

- 731: "… Sound capital assessment include … policies and procedures designed to ensure that the bank identities, measures, and reports all material risks."
- 742: "Although the Committee recognises that other risks […] are not easily measurable, it expects industry to further develop techniques for managing all aspects of these risks."

This view has also been confirmed by different European supervisors, confer for example, The Committee of European Banking Supervisors (2004).

Capturing all material risks of a financial institution requires a broad risk self assessment to find out which are the most relevant risk drivers for the bank. One of the most obvious variables to be monitored in this context are earning themselves. However, none of the Pillar I risks take earnings volatility directly as a primary driver into account, instead, they usually focus on aspects of the business environment that only indirectly affect the institution earnings by virtue of for example, failed processes, credit defaults, drop in share prices, or interest rate changes.

For an all-encompassing risk assessment it is therefore necessary to introduce an additional kind of risk that is directly linked to the uncertainty of specific earnings components not yet associated to other risk types. Usually, such an earnings-related potential loss, which can also threaten a banks market capitalisation, is referred to as business risk.

Evidence for the growing importance of business risk was recently also given in a survey undertaken by the IFRI/CRO Forum about economic capital practices in leading financial institutions (The Institute of the Chief Risk Officers (CROs) and Chief Risk Officers Forum (CRO Forum 2007)) where 85 % of the participants stated to include business risk in their aggregated economic capital assessment. Yet surprisingly, there is no common agreement on a precise definition, specific risk drivers, and measurement methodology for business risk, even though its absolute size in term of economic capital is comparable to that of operational risk, see again The Institute of the Chief Risk Officers (CROs) and Chief Risk Officers Forum (CRO Forum 2007). With this regard, we also performed a benchmark exercise on a sample of 15 international banks by analysing their risk management practise as disclosed in their official financial annual reports from 2004 to 2006. Again, we found that an increasing number of institutions are trying to quantify business risk in some way, even if different definitions and assumptions are adopted. Broadly speaking, approaches for business risk quantification can be divided into two main categories; top-down and bottom-up. Top-down techniques are linked to the general trend of the business environment and benchmark analysis based on external data is used for approximating business risk. In contrast to that, bottom-up approaches try to explicitly determine the volatility of particular, bank-internal economic time series (such as volumes, earnings, revenues, and expenses) at a more granular level, which is then transformed into a measure of business risk.

Here we we propose a bottom-up approach for modelling and measuring business risk where the dynamic of the underlying earnings is described in a continuous-time model. The remainder of this chapter is structured as follows. After some preliminaries such as formulating the discounted-cashflow method in continuous time, we introduce a first stochastic model for quantifying business risk later in the chapter where we also briefly point out how such a model could be implemented in practice. The results obtained are then used to investigate the relation between the earnings-at-risk (EaR) measure and the so-called capital-at-risk (CaR) measure in greater detail. Finally, we propose a possible extension of the simple business risk model.

MODELLING BUSINESS CAR: A SIMPLE APPROACH

Setting the scene

Overlap with other risk types

Of course, the concept of "revenues" and "expenses" as we used so far is too general for measuring business risk. In particular, in order to avoid double counting and risk overlap, revenue and cost components that enter the business risk model must not directly or indirectly be used for the quantification of other risk types. To give an example, as potentially relevant revenues it may be considered customer related provisions and net interest rate income, while on the cost side administrative expenses and depreciations may be included into business risk quantification. On the other hand, earnings related to trading activities would clearly cause an overlap with market risk, and should therefore not be included. Something similar holds for loan loss provisions, when they are captured within the banks credit portfolio model.

However, the question which revenue and cost components are really relevant for modelling a particular firms business risk, and which parts have to be excluded, is not an easy one. The answer crucially depends on the firms definition of others risk types and its economic capital framework in general, and therefore setting up a business risk model should always be an integral part of the banks overall risk-defining and assessment process. Moreover, it is necessary to be aware that the availability and granularity of revenue and cost data may also depend on the firms accounting rules, controlling standards, and IT infrastructure. As a consequence, the quality of data may differ from one legal entity to the other, and in order to achieve reliable results at aggregated level, great attention should be paid with regard to data selection and preparation. Hereafter, when we talk about earnings, we actually always mean non-credit and non-market earnings so that there is no double counting with other risk types that are already measured within a banks economic capital model.

EaR versus CaR

Business risk can be defined as the potential loss in the company's earnings due to adverse, unexpected changes in business volume, margins, or both. Such losses can result above all from a serious deterioration of the market environment, customer shift, changes in the competitive situation, or internal restructuring. On one hand, these effects can lead to a drop in earnings in the short-term, for example within the next budget year, and are often measured in terms of earnings volatility, more general by EaR. On the other hand, volume or margin shrinking probably leads to a longer-lasting weakening of the earnings situation, thereby seriously diminishing the company's market capitalisation, and this risk is often referred to as CaR. As pointed out by Saita (2004, 2007), the recognition of such negative long-term effects on earnings and the resulting impact on the market capitalisation is particular important for the shareholder perspective on capital and should also be used in the context of risk-adjusted performance measurement, for example by means of RAROC, EVA, or related concepts.

A convincing analysis proving this link between earnings related risk and a company's loss in market value is given in Morrison, Quella and Slywotzky (1999). They found out that during a period of five years, 10% of Fortune 1,000 companies lost (at least once) 25% of their shareholder value within a one-month period, and that nearly all of these stock drops were a result of reduced quarterly earnings or reduced expected future earnings. Moreover, the majority of these earnings-shortfalls (about 58%) were not owing to classical financial risks or operational losses but rather to what Quella *et al* refer to as strategic risk factors, such as raising costs and margin squeeze, emerging global competitors, and customer priority shift etc.

If business risk is considered as a matter of market capitalisation and therefore is measured by CaR, the uncertainty of (all) future earnings have to be taken into account. As mentioned above, such earnings fluctuations, ie, the deviations of the realised earnings from the planned earnings trajectory, may be the result of many different factors. However, for the model we suggest here, it is not necessary to explicitly link all these risk factors to future earnings. Instead we suppose that all risk factors together constitute some random "noise" effect, mixing with the expected earnings path; ie, for $t \geq 0$ future cumulated earnings $E(t)$ can be written as

$$E(t) = f(t) + \text{"noise"}, \qquad t \geq 0$$

where f is a nonrandom function describing the planned earnings trajectory. Consequently, further in the chapter we model future earnings as a stochastic process $(E(t))_{t \geq 0}$.

Discounted-cashflow method

Before we go on, however, it is worthwhile to recall some basic facts about company valuation, especially about the discounted-cashflow method where expected future earnings are discounted to obtain the company's market value (see for example Goedhart, Koller and Wessels (2005) or Pratt, Reilly and Schweihs (2000) for a more detailed description of this subject). Denote by $\Delta E_{t_i} \in \mathbb{R}$ the company's earnings that are planned to be realised in $\Delta t_i = t_i - t_{i-1}$, ie, between the future time periods t_{i-1} and t_i, defined for all $0 = t_0 < t_1 < \ldots < t_T$. The present value or market value of the company is usually defined as

$$V(T) = \sum_{i=1}^{T} \frac{\Delta E_{t_i}}{(1+r_i)^{t_i}} \tag{7.1}$$

where $r_i \in \mathbb{R}_+$ is a risk adjusted discount rate. Expression 7.1 simply says that a company's market value is just the sum of its discounted expected future earnings. For our purposes, however, a continuous-time setting of the present value 7.1 is more feasible.

Definition 7.1 (Present value in continuous time)

The present value of all earnings cumulated until the time horizon t is given by

$$P(t) = P(0) + \int_0^t e^{-r(s)} dE(s), \quad t \geq 0$$

with discount rate $r(t) = \int_0^t \hat{r}(\tau) d\tau$ for $t \geq 0$, where $\hat{r}(\cdot)$ is a nonrandom positive function, representing the short-term discount rate and

$$P(t) = P(0) + \int_0^t dE(s), \qquad t \geq 0$$

are the cumulated future earnings as they are expected to be realised up to a time horizon t. Furthermore, we define

$$P(\infty) := \lim_{t \to \infty} P(t)$$

provided that the limit exists.

Model definition and first results

We begin our analysis of business CaR with a simple model based on Brownian motion. Such a model allows for closed-form solutions for business CaR and is therefore particularly useful to understand the nature and general properties if this important risk type.

Stochastic modelling of future cashflows

We define our model in a multivariate fashion in that it takes the dependence between different cells into account. Each cell could simply reflect a legal entity, business division, geographical region, or a combination of them. If earnings are explicitly split up into revenues and costs, each of them are represented by different cells. Hence, for each cell, we can define a cashflow process describing the stochastic evolution of revenues, costs, or earnings. In the following we treat revenues as positive and costs as negative variables.

Definition 7.2 (Brownian motion cashflow (BMC) model)

Consider a d-dimensional standard Brownian motion $(W_1(t), \ldots, W_d(t))_{t\geq 0}$ on a probability space $(\Omega, \mathcal{F}, P)$. Then, the BMC model consists of:

(1) Cashflow processes

For each business risk cell, indexed by $i = 1, \ldots, m$, cumulated future cashflows $X_i(t)$ for $t \geq 0$ are described by a cashflow process, which is the strong continuous solution to the Itô-stochastic-diferential equation

$$dX_i(t) = \alpha_i(t)dt + \sum_{j=1}^{d} \sigma_{ij}(t)dW_j(t), \qquad t \geq 0 \tag{7.2}$$

The bank's total aggregated cashflow is given by the aggregate cashflow process

$$X(t) = \sum_{i=1}^{m} X_i(t) = \sum_{i=1}^{m} X_i(0) + \sum_{i=1}^{m} \int_0^t dX_i(s)$$

Here, $\alpha_i(\cdot) > 0$, $i = 1, \ldots, m$, and $\sigma_{ij}(\cdot)$, $i = 1, \ldots, m$; $j = 1, \ldots, d$, are non-random functions of time, satisfying the integrability conditions $\int_0^t |\alpha_i(s)|\, ds < \infty$ and $\int_0^t |\sigma_{ij}^2(s)|\, ds < \infty$.

(2) Value process

Let $r(\cdot) > 0$ be a non-random discount rate so that $\int_0^t (|\alpha_i(s)| e^{-r(s)} + \sigma_{ij}^2(s)e^{-2r(s)})ds < \infty$. Then, the aggregate value process $(P(t))_{t \geq 0}$ is defined by (setting $P(0) = 0$)

$$\begin{aligned} P(t) &= \sum_{i=1}^{m} \int_0^t e^{-r(s)} dX_i(s), \\ &= \sum_{i=1}^{m} \int_0^t \alpha_i(s)e^{-r(s)}ds + \sum_{j=1}^{d}\sum_{i=1}^{m} \int_0^t \sigma_{ij}(s)e^{-r(s)}dW_j(s), \qquad t \geq 0 \end{aligned} \tag{7.3}$$

Remark 7.3

(a) For every $t \geq 0$, the BMC model describes multivariate normally distributed cumulated cashflows $X_i(\cdot)$, $i = 1, \ldots, m$, with expectation

$$\mathbb{E}X_i(t) = X_i(0) + \int_0^t \alpha_i(s)ds, \qquad t \geq 0 \tag{7.4}$$

and cross-covariance function of $X_i(\cdot)$ and $X_k(\cdot)$, $i, k = 1, \ldots, m$, given by

$$\operatorname{covar}(X_i(t), X_k(t)) = \int_0^t \sum_{j=1}^{d} \sigma_{ij}(s)\sigma_{kj}(s)ds =: \int_0^t \Sigma_{ik}(s)ds, \quad t \geq 0$$

Here, $\Sigma := (\Sigma_{ik}(t))_{ik}$ is called instantaneous cashflow covariance matrix, which is assumed to be positive definite for all $t \geq 0$.

(b) The variance of future cashflows $X_i(\cdot)$, $i = 1, \ldots, d$, can be written as

$$\operatorname{var}(X_i(t)) = \int_0^t \Sigma_{ii}(s)ds =: \int_0^t \sigma_i^2(s)ds, \qquad t \geq 0 \tag{7.5}$$

where $\sigma_i(\cdot)$; $i = 1, \ldots, m$, are referred to as the instantaneous cashflow volatilities.

(c) For non-zero $\sigma_i(\cdot)$, the cross-correlation function between $X_i(\cdot)$ and $X_k(\cdot)$ is

$$\operatorname{corr}(X_i(t), X_k(t)) = \frac{\operatorname{covar}(X_i(t), X_k(t))}{\sqrt{\operatorname{var}(X_i(t))}\sqrt{\operatorname{var}(X_k(t))}}, \quad t \geq 0 \tag{7.6}$$

Informally, we denote the instantaneous correlation between $dX_i(\cdot)$ and $dX_k(\cdot)$ as

$$\operatorname{corr}(dX_i(t), dX_k(t)) = \frac{\Sigma_{ik}(t)}{\sigma_i(t)\sigma_k(t)} =: \rho_{ik}(t), \quad t \geq 0$$

(d) The value of the aggregate cashflow process $X(t)$ at time $t \geq 0$ gives the total earnings of the bank that have been realised between 0 and t (cumulated earning). Its variance is given by

$$\begin{aligned}
\operatorname{var}(X(t)) &= \int_0^t \sum_{j=1}^{d} \left(\sum_{i=1}^{m} \sigma_{ij}(s) \right)^2 ds \\
&= \int_0^t \sum_{j=1}^{d} \sum_{i=1}^{m} \sum_{k=1}^{m} \sigma_{ij}(s)\sigma_{kj}(s)ds \\
&= \int_0^t \sum_{i=1}^{m} \sum_{k=1}^{m} \Sigma_{ik}(s)ds =: \int_0^t \sigma^2(s)ds, \quad t \geq 0
\end{aligned} \tag{7.7}$$

where we call $\sigma(\cdot)$ the instantaneous aggregate cashflow volatility.

(e) Note that the number d of independent Brownian motions $W_i(\cdot)$ can be different from the number m of business risk cells. Therefore, our model also allows for such realistic scenarios where the number of risk factors (represented by different Brownian motions) is greater than the number of clusters; think for example of a bank with two legal entities that are exposed to three risk factors, which affect their non-credit and non-market earnings and thus business risk.

Example 7.4 (Bivariate BMC model with constant parameters)
Consider a simple bivariate BMC model with constant drift and diffusion parameters where the cashflow processes are given by

$$\begin{aligned} dX_1(t) &= \alpha_1 dt + \sigma_1 dW_1(t) \\ dX_2(t) &= \alpha_2 dt + \sigma_2\left(\rho dW_1(t) + \sqrt{1-\rho^2}\,dW_2(t)\right), \quad t \ge 0 \end{aligned} \tag{7.8}$$

From Remark 7.3 it follows that

$$\Sigma = \begin{pmatrix} \sigma_1^2 & \rho\sigma_1\sigma_2 \\ \rho\sigma_1\sigma_2 & \sigma_2^2 \end{pmatrix}$$

implying for the variance of the i-th cumulated future cashflow

$$\operatorname{var}\left(X_i(t)\right) = \sigma_i^2 t, \quad t \ge 0, \quad i = 1,2 \tag{7.9}$$

Moreover, the correlation between $X_1(\cdot)$ and $X_2(\cdot)$ and the instantaneous correlation are given for all $t \ge 0$ by

$$\operatorname{corr}\left(X_1(t), X_2(t)\right) = \operatorname{corr}\left(dX_1(t), dX_2(t)\right) = \rho$$

Since all parameters are time-independent, this model can be calibrated quite easily. After discretisation of 7.8 by using the Euler method, σ_1 and σ_2 can be calculated directly from the standard deviations of the discrete increments $\Delta X_1(\cdot)$ and $\Delta X_2(\cdot)$. Then, according to 7.9, volatilities at a larger time-scale t can be derived by using the $\sqrt{t}$-scaling law. Finally, α_1 and if α_2 can be estimated through the sample means of the discretisised incremental cashflows 7.8, or, alternatively, they can be obtained from the cumulated cashflows

$$\mathbb{E}X_i(t) = \alpha_i t + \text{const.}, \quad t \ge 0$$

for $i = 1, 2$ by regression analysis.

Example 7.5 (Bivariate BMC model with time-dependent parameters)
We use a similar set up as in 7.8 but with time-dependent parameters for $t \geq 0$ of $\alpha_i(t) = \alpha_i t^{\alpha_i}$ and $\sigma_i(t) = \sigma_i t^{b_1}$ for α_i, $b_i \geq 0$; $i = 1, 2$:

$$\begin{aligned} dX_1(t) &= \alpha_1 t^{\alpha_1} dt + \sigma_1 t^{b_1} dW_1(t) \\ dX_2(t) &= \alpha_2 t^{\alpha_2} dt + \sigma_2 t^{b_2} \left(\rho dW_1(t) + \sqrt{1-\rho^2} dW_2(t)\right), \quad t \geq 0 \end{aligned} \tag{7.10}$$

The expectations and variances of future cashflows can be calculated from 7.4 and 7.5; for $i = 1, 2$ we obtain

$$\mathbb{E}X_i(t) = \frac{\alpha_i}{1+\alpha_i} t^{1+\alpha_i}, \quad t \geq 0$$

and

$$\text{var}(X_i(t)) = \frac{\sigma_i^2}{2b_i+1} t^{2b_i+1}, \quad t \geq 0$$

The instantaneous correlation in this model is still ρ, however, using 7.6 we derive

$$\text{corr}(X_1(t), X_2(t)) = \frac{\sqrt{2b_1+1}\sqrt{2b_2+1}}{1+b_1+b_2} \rho, \quad t \geq 0$$

We now define the signal-to-noise ratio, also referred to as Sharpe ratio, for each cashflow process as the ratio of its expected growths to the fluctuations, ie, for $i = 1, 2$

$$\eta_i(t) = \frac{\mathbb{E}X_i(t) - X_i(0)}{\sqrt{\text{var}(X_i(t))}}, \quad t \geq 0 \tag{7.11}$$

Instead of constant volatilities $\sigma_i(\cdot) = \sigma_i$ as in the Example 7.4, we are now asking for constant Sharpe ratios $\eta_i(\cdot) = \eta_i$. Obviously, the Sharpe ratios of $X_1(\cdot)$ and $X_2(\cdot)$ are here constant for $b_i = a_i + \frac{1}{2}$. A typical situation as it may occour in practice is depicted in Figure 7.1, which shows the monthly earnings over five years for two hypothetical legal entities.

Calculating business CaR

For the purpose of CaR calculations we have to learn more about the value process $(P(t))_{t \geq 0}$. The following result is well-known and describes its distributional properties.

Proposition 7.6

Consider the BMC model of Definition 7.2 with value process $(P(t))_{t\geq 0}$. Then, for every $t > 0$, the value $P(t)$ has normal distribution function Φ_P with expected value

$$\mathbb{E}P(t) = \sum_{i=1}^{m} \int_0^t \alpha_i(s) e^{-r(s)}\, ds, \qquad t \geq 0 \tag{7.12}$$

and variance

$$\operatorname{var}(P(t)) = \int_0^t \sigma^2(s) e^{-2r(s)} ds, \qquad t \geq 0$$

where $\sigma(\cdot)$ is the instantaneous aggregate cashflow volatility defined in 7.7.

Proof

Note that on the right-hand side of Equation 7.3 the integrals in the first term are standard Riemann whereas those of the second term given by $I(t) = \int_0^t \sigma_{ij}(s)e^{-r(s)}dW_j(s)$ are Itô integrals with deterministic integrands. Then $I(t)$ is normally distributed with $\mathbb{E}(t) = 0$ and $\operatorname{var}(I(t)) = \mathbb{E}(I(t)^2)$, see for example Shreve (2004), Theorem 4.4.9. Using Itô's isometry we further obtain

$$\begin{aligned}
\operatorname{var}(P(t)) &= \sum_{j=1}^{d} \operatorname{var}\left(\sum_{i=1}^{m} \int_0^t \sigma_{ij}(s) e^{-r(s)}\, dW_j(s) \right) \\
&= \sum_{j=1}^{d} \mathbb{E}\left(\sum_{i=1}^{m} \int_0^t \sigma_{ij}(s) e^{-r(s)}\, dW_j(s) \right)^2 \\
&= \sum_{j=1}^{d} \int_0^t \left(\sum_{i=1}^{m} \sigma_{ij}(s) e^{-r(s)} \right)^2 ds \\
&= \int_0^t \sigma^2(s) e^{-2r(s)}\, ds, \qquad t \geq 0
\end{aligned}$$

Since we now know that in the BMC model the banks total market value $P(\cdot)$ is normally distributed with distribution function Φ_P, it is straightforward to calculate business CaR. Before, however, we want to precisely define business CaR for general distributions of $P(\cdot)$.

Definition 7.7 (Business CaR)

Consider different business risk cells with cashflow processes $X_i(\cdot)$, $i = 1, \ldots, m$, that are not attributable to other risk types, and define their corresponding market value process $P(\cdot)$ according to 7.3. For $t > 0$, suppose that F_t is the distribution function of the value $P(t)$ with mean value $\mathbb{E}P(t) < \infty$. Then, business CaR at time horizon t and confidence level $\kappa \in (0, 1)$ is given by

Figure 7.1 Illustration of monthly earnings of two different legal entities as described in Example 7.5.

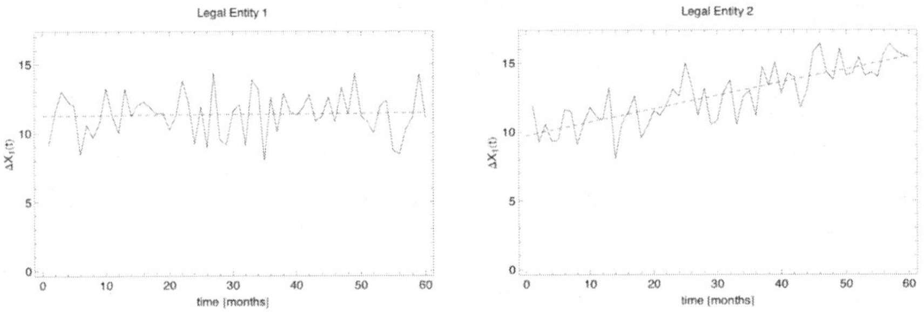

In contrast to legal entity 1, the monthly earnings of legal entitiy 2 seems to have a positive linear drift which eg, could be determined by linear regression (showed as dashed lines). Hence, $\alpha_1 = 0$ and $\alpha_2 = 1$ could be set in 7.10. Regarding the volatilities either $b_1 = b_2 = 0$ (constant absolute volatilities) or $b_1 = 0.5$ and $b_2 = 1.5$ (constant Sharpe ratios) can be used.

Figure 7.2 Business CaR is defined as the difference between the expected market value $\mathbb{E}P(t)$ of the bank's aggregate value process and a very low quantile of its market value distribution F_t.

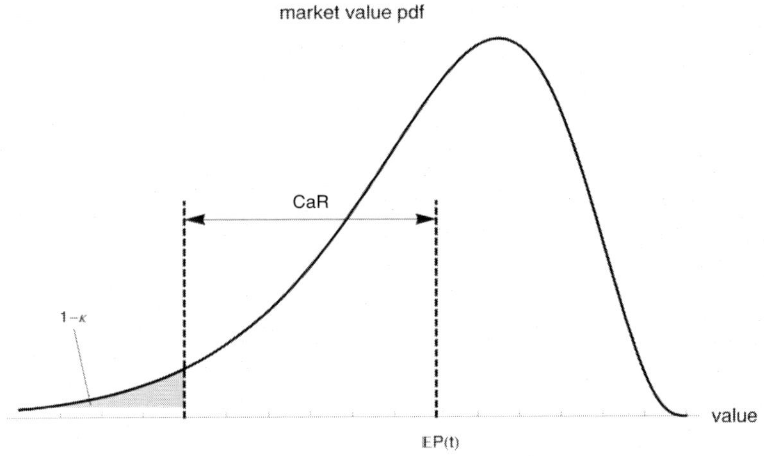

$$CAR_\kappa(t) = \mathbb{E}P(t) - F_t^{\leftarrow}(1-\kappa), \quad t \geq 0 \tag{7.13}$$

where $F_t^{\leftarrow}(\kappa) = \inf\{x \in \mathbb{R} : F_t(x) \geq \kappa\}$, $0 < \kappa < 1$, is the generalised inverse of F_t. If F_t is strictly increasing and continuous, we may write $F_t^{\leftarrow}(\cdot) = F_t^{-1}(\cdot)$.

In the context of economic capital calculations, the confidence level κ is a number close to 1, eg, $\kappa = 0.999$. In the case that the probability density function (pdf) of F_t exists, the definition of business CaR is illustrated in Figure 7.2. In general, F_t and thus business CaR cannot be calculated analytically. For the BMC model, however, a closed-form expression for business CaR is available.

Theorem 7.8 (Business CaR for the BMC model)
Assume that future cashflows are described by a BMC model with instantaneous aggregate cashflow volatility (see Equation 7.7)

$$\sigma(t) = \sum_{i=1}^{m}\sum_{j=1}^{d}\sum_{k=1}^{m}\sigma_{ij}(t)\sigma_{kj}(t), \quad t \geq 0 \tag{7.14}$$

and non-random discount rate $r(\cdot)$. Then, business CaR at time-horizon t and confidence level $\kappa \in (0, 1)$ is given by

$$CAR_\kappa(t) = \Phi^{-1}(\kappa)\sqrt{\int_0^t \sigma^2(s)e^{-2r(s)}\,ds}, \qquad t \geq 0 \tag{7.15}$$

where Φ is the standard normal distribution function.

Proof
The assertion follows directly from Proposition 7.6 together with the definition of business CaR 7.13.

This analytical expression for business CaR is mainly a consequence of using non-random discount rates. If instead $r(\cdot)$ is allowed to be some continuous adapted interest rate process, the distribution function F_t, $t \geq 0$, of the aggregate value process $(P(t))_{t\geq 0}$ is in general not normal anymore, and the result for business CaR will rarely be available in closed-form.

Note that 7.15 only depends on the cashflows covariance matrix and not on other model parameters such as drift parameters $\alpha_i(\cdot)$ or the initial values $X_i(0)$. As a consequence thereof, the BMC model can be calibrated easily, confer also Examples 7.4 and 7.5.

The Relationship Between EaR and CaR

Earnings-at-Risk

In the light of Definition 7.2 we now can qualify our notion of EaR, which we have already introduced. From Remark 7.3 (d) we know that var($X(t)$) is the volatility of the banks total aggregate cashflows accumulated between time 0 and t. It is also well-known that $X(t)$, $t \geq 0$, is normally distributed, see for example Shreve (2004), Theorem 4.4.9, so that EaR of the cumulated earnings $X(t)$ at $t \geq 0$ and confidence level $\kappa \in (0, 1)$ is simply given by

$$EAR_{\kappa}(t) = \Phi^{-1}(\kappa)\sqrt{\mathrm{var}(X(t))}$$
$$= \Phi^{-1}(\kappa)\sqrt{\int_0^t \sigma^2(s)ds}, \quad t \geq 0 \qquad (7.16)$$

where Φ is the standard normal distribution function. In contrast to 7.15, we see that in 7.16 the volatility is not discounted. Moreover, it should be mentioned that according to what we have said earlier in the chapter, the time parameter t in 7.16 should be chosen in a way that it reflects a short-term horizon so that discounting effects can be neglected. Finally, we define the instantaneous EaR as

$$\mathrm{ear}_{\kappa}(\cdot) = \Phi^{-1}(\kappa)\sigma(\cdot) \qquad (7.17)$$

EaR-CaR-transformation factors

An interesting question concerns the relation between EaR and CaR. Intuitively, CaR should be higher than EaR since CaR takes – in contrast to EaR – the long-term uncertainty of future cashflows into account. It has been suggested for example by Matten (1996) or Saita (2004, 2007) that CaR is a constant multiplier of EaR, and that the multiplication factor depends only on a (risk-adjusted) interest rate (discount factor) and the time horizon t. Saita based his analysis of the EaR-CaR relationship on a discrete-time cash-flow model similar to 7.1 where EaR reflects the uncertainty of the ΔE_{t_i}, and Saita (2007), section 5.8, gives a very readable overview about this topic.

In the case of the BMC model, we see by comparing 7.15 with 7.17 that such a proportionality between EaR(t) and CaR(t) does not hold for all $t \geq 0$ because of the time dependence of the instantaneous aggregate-cashflow volatility $\sigma(\cdot)$. However, the mean value theorem ensures that $\xi \in (0, t)$ can always be chosen so that 7.15 can be written as

$$\mathrm{CAR}_{\kappa}(t) = \Phi^{-1}(\kappa)\sigma(\xi)\sqrt{\int_0^t e^{-2r(s)}\,ds}$$
$$= \mathrm{ear}_{\kappa}(\xi)\sqrt{\int_0^t e^{-2r(s)}\,ds}, \qquad t \geq 0$$

and we can think of $\mathrm{ear}_{\kappa}(\xi)$ as an average EaR of the time interval $[0, t]$. The following two examples illustrate the relationship between EaR and CaR, in particular showing that – even in the quite simple framework of BMC models – EaR-CaR-transformation crucially depends on the specifications of the cashflow processes $X_i(t)$, $i = 1, \ldots, d$.

Example 7.9 (BMC model with constant diffusion parameters)
Consider a BMC model with $\sigma_{ij}(\cdot) = \sigma_{ij}$ = const. for $i = 1, \ldots, m; j = 1, \ldots, d$. Then also the aggregate-cashflow volatility 7.14 is constant and we obtain

$$\text{CAR}_\kappa(t) = k_1(r,t)\Phi^{-1}(\kappa)\sigma = k_1(r,t)\text{ear}_\kappa, \quad t \geq 0$$

with EaR-CaR transformation factor

$$k_1(r,t) = \int_0^t e^{-2r(s)}\, ds$$

where we indicated the explicit dependence of k_1 on the discount rate $r(t)$ by r. Hence, in this special case business CaR is proportional to the (constant) instantaneous EaR. If furthermore the short-term discount rate is constant, $\hat{r}(\cdot) = \hat{r}$ we have that $r(t) = \int_0^t \hat{r}\, ds = \hat{r}t$ and we arrive at

$$k_1(\hat{r},t) = \sqrt{\frac{1-\exp(-2\hat{r}t)}{2\hat{r}}} \tag{7.18}$$

which is a simple function of the time horizon t and the discount rate $\hat{r}$. The higher $\hat{r}$ is, the smaller k_1 will be because future cashflows (and so their fluctuations) tend to have lower impact on the market value (and so on its uncertainty). Similarly, longer time horizons t lead to a growing k_1 because more uncertain future cashflows are taken into account. In the limit $t \to \infty$ expression 7.18 simplifies to

$$\lim_{t\to\infty} k_1(\hat{r},t) = \frac{1}{\sqrt{2\hat{r}}} \tag{7.19}$$

Example 7.10 (BMC model with constant Sharpe ratio)
Consider a BMC model with cumulated cashflows $X_i(\cdot)$ for $i = 1, \ldots, m$. As in Example 7.5 we consider the Sharpe ratios $\eta_i(\cdot)$ given by 7.11. Adopting a linear-growth model with constant drift parameters $\alpha_i(\cdot) = \alpha_i > 0$, $i = 1, \ldots, m$, we know from Example 7.5 that constant Sharpe ratios require square-root-of-time scalings of the instantaneous cashflow volatilities, ie, $\sigma_i(t) = c_i\sqrt{t}$ for some constants c_i, $i = 1, \ldots, m$. This implies that the aggregate-cashflow volatility 7.14 for $t \geq 0$ can be written as $\sigma(t) = \sigma\sqrt{t}$, resulting in sample paths of $X_i(\cdot)$ that are in general more noisy than the one obtained in Example 7.9, a fact that is illustrated in the top chart of Figure 7.3.

Finally, using 7.15 we can calculate business CaR in the case of a constant short-term discounr rate $\hat{r}$ to

$$\text{CAR}_\kappa(t) = k_2(\hat{r},t)\Phi^{-1}(\kappa)\sigma, \quad t \geq 0$$

with EaR-CaR transformation factor

$$k_2(\hat{r},t)=\sqrt{\int_0^t se^{-2\hat{r}s}\,ds}=\frac{1}{2\hat{r}}\sqrt{1-(1+2\hat{r}t)\exp(-2\hat{r}t)}$$

and

$$\lim_{t\to\infty} k_2(\hat{r},t)=\frac{1}{2\hat{r}}$$

Comparing the different BMC-model specifications of Example 7.9 and 7.10, it could be expected that k_2 is greater than k_1 because in the previous example the Sharpe ratio was actually increasing with $\sqrt{t}$ (implying a decrease of future cashflow fluctuation) whereas here it is constant by construction. Hence, k_2 accumulates more future uncertainty than k_1. As we see in the bottom chart of Figure 7.3, this is indeed the case if t exceeds a certain threshold, ie, $t > t_0(\hat{r})$, which for $\hat{r} = 0.1$ is approximately given by $t_0(0.1) = 2.2$. Moreover, by comparing 7.19 and 7.21 it follows that for all $t \geq t_0(\hat{r})$ we have that

$$0\leq\frac{k_2(\hat{r},t)}{k_1(\hat{r},t)}\leq\frac{1}{\sqrt{2\hat{r}}}$$

A MODEL WITH LEVEL-ADJUSTED VOLATILITY

In the BMC model the absolute changes of future cashflows $X_i(\cdot)$ are directly modelled by a Brownian motion, see Equation 7.2, which in particular means that the uncertainty of a business cells cashflow is independent from its absolute level. There is, however, no rational for this behaviour and, intuitively, higher earnings should actually be more volatile than low earnings. As a possible remedy, future cashflows could be described by a geometric Brownian motion as it is used for example, for stock prices in the famous famous Black-Scholes-Merton setting. Then, for $t \geq 0$ cumulated cashflows $X_i(\cdot)$, $i = 1, \ldots, m$, would be given by

$$X_i(t)=X_i(0)\exp\left[\int_0^t\left(\alpha_i(s)-\frac{1}{2}\sum_{j=1}^{d}\sigma_{ij}^2(s)\right)ds+\sum_{j=1}^{d}\sigma_{ij}(s)dW_j(s)\right]$$

implying an expected exponential cashflow growth of

$$\mathbb{E}X_i(t)=X_i(0)\exp\left(\int_0^t\alpha_i(s)ds\right)$$

which, however, might be considered as too extreme and optimistic for most businesses. Alternatively, we suggest a model with still moderate growth but a kind of "cashflow level adjusted" volatility. More precisely, we have the following definition.

Figure 7.3 Cashflow paths for future earnings

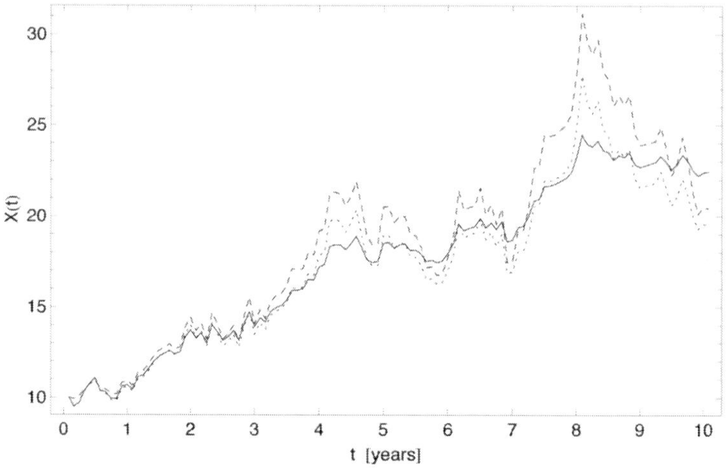

Top panel: Typical cashflow paths $X_i(t)$ with constant absolute cashflow volatility (solid line) and constant Sharpe ratio (dashed line) referring to Examples 7.9 and 7.10, respectively. The parameters are $X_i(0) = 10$, $\alpha_i = 1.2$ and $\sigma_i = 1.4$ with a time horizon of 10 years and monthly increments. Moreover, the dotted path is obtained by the advanced model discussed, especially Example 7.12, and we set $\sigma_i = \sigma_i / X_i(0) = 0.14$. We used the same seeds of normal random variables for all three paths.

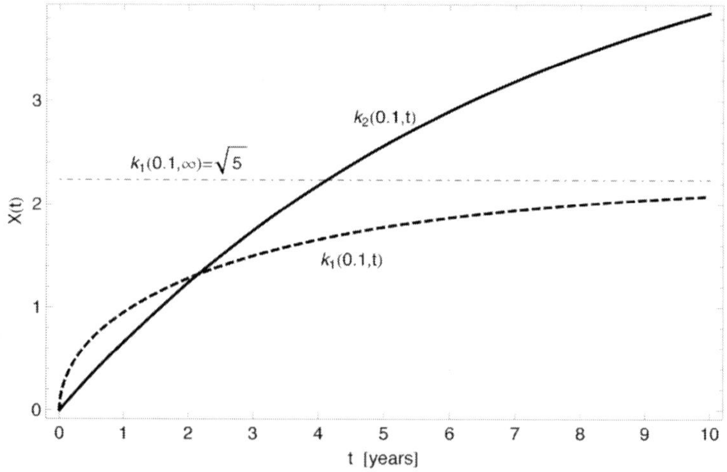

Bottom panel: EaR-CaR-transformation factors $k_1(\hat{r},t)$ and $k_2(\hat{r},t)$ according to (7.18) and (7.20), respectively, as a function of time for a short-term discount rate $\hat{r} = 0.1$. The dotted-dashed line indicates the asymptote of $k_1(\hat{r},t)$ when $t \to \infty$.

Definition 7.11 (Level-adjusted BMC model)
Consider a d-dimensional standard Brownian motion $(W_1(t), \ldots, W_d(t))_{t\geq 0}$ on a probability space $(\Omega, \mathcal{F}, \mathbb{P})$. Then, the level-adjusted BMC model consists of:

(1) Cashflow processes.
For each business risk cell, indexed by $i = 1, \ldots, m$, cumulated future cashflows $X_i(t)$ for $t \geq 0$ are described by a cashflow process, which is the strong continuous solution to the Itô-stochastic-diferential equation

$$dX_i(t) = \alpha_i(t)dt + X_i(t)\sum_{j=1}^{d}\tilde{\sigma}_{ij}(t)dW_j(t), \quad t \geq 0 \tag{7.20}$$

with aggregate cashflow process

$$X(t) = \sum_{i=1}^{m} X_i(t) = \sum_{i=1}^{m} X_i(0) + \sum_{i=1}^{m}\int_0^t dX_i(s)$$

Here, $\alpha_i(\cdot) > 0$, $i = 1, \ldots, m$, and $\tilde{\sigma}_{ij}(\cdot)$, $i = 1, \ldots, m$; $j = 1, \ldots, d$, are nonrandom functions of time, satisfying the integrability conditions $\int_0^t |\alpha_i(s)|\, ds < \infty$ and $\int_0^t \tilde{\sigma}_{ij}^2(s)\, ds < \infty$. The matrix $(\tilde{\sigma}_{ij}(t))_{ij}$ is assumed to be positive definite for all $t \geq 0$.

(2) Value process
Let $r(\cdot) > 0$ be a nonrandom function so that $\int_0^t (|\alpha_i(s)|\, e^{-r(s)} + \tilde{\sigma}_{ij}^2(s)e^{-2r(s)})\, ds < \infty$. Then, the aggregate value process $(P(t))_{t\geq 0}$ is definedby (setting $P(0) = 0$)

$$P(t) = \sum_{i=1}^{m}\int_0^t e^{-r(s)}\, dX_i(s), \qquad t \geq 0$$

Let us first consider the cashflow process and compare 7.20 with 7.2 of the BMC model. For the latter, the diffusion parameters σ_{ij} play the role of an absolute measure of uncertainty for the increments of $X_i(\cdot)$, whereas in 7.20 the $\tilde{\sigma}_{ij}$ describe the increment's fluctuations relative to the level of $X_i(\cdot)$. Furthermore, instead of 7.20 we may write

$$X_i(t) = X_i(0) + \int_0^t \alpha_i(s)ds + \sum_{i=1}^{d}\int_0^t X_i(s)\tilde{\sigma}_{ij}(s)dW_j(s), \quad t \geq 0 \tag{7.21}$$

and from the martingale property of the Itô integral it immediately follows that the expectation of $X_i(\cdot)$ *is* given by

$$\mathbb{E}X_i(t) = X_i(0) + \int_0^t \alpha_i(s)ds, \quad t \geq 0$$

ie, it is the same as for the BMC model, and, in particular, the model does not exhibit exponential growth as it would be the case when geometric Brownian motion is used. We close this section with an extended example that illustrates some properties of the level-adjusted volatility model.

Example 7.12 (Constant drift and diffusion parameters)
For the sake of simplicity we focus on the case of constant parameters $\alpha_i(\cdot) = \alpha_i$ and $\tilde{\sigma}_{ij}(\cdot) = \tilde{\sigma}_{ij}$. Note however, that the diffusion parameter of the process 7.20 is random and given by $X_i(\cdot)\tilde{\sigma}_{ij}$. In order to find a solution for 7.21 we define the function

$$F(t,W(t)) := \exp\left(-\sum_{j=1}^{d}\tilde{\sigma}_{ij}W_j(t)+\frac{1}{2}\sum_{j=1}^{d}\tilde{\sigma}_{ij}^2 t\right),\quad t\geq 0$$

Then, by using Itô's formula the differential of the product FX_i can be calculated as

$$d\big(F(t,W(t))X_i(t)\big)=\alpha_i F(t,W(t))dt$$

which after integration finally yields (setting $W_j(0) = 0$ for $j = 1, \ldots, d$),

$$X_i(t)=F(-t,-W(t))\left(X_i(0)+\alpha_i\int_0^t F(s,W(s))ds\right),\quad t\geq 0 \qquad (7.22)$$

According to 7.22, the cumulated cashflows $X_i(t)$ at time $t \geq 0$ are not normally distributed as they are in the BMC model. A one-dimensional example for a typical path of $X_i(\cdot)$ according to 7.22 is plotted as a dotted line in the top panel of Figure 7.3.

The Itô representation of the value process $(P(t))_{t\geq 0}$ is given by

$$P(t)=\sum_{i=1}^{m}\alpha_i\int_0^t e^{-r(s)}ds+\sum_{j=1}^{d}\sum_{i=1}^{m}\tilde{\sigma}_{ij}\int_0^t X_i(s)e^{-r(s)}dW_j(s),\quad t\geq 0, \qquad (7.23)$$

which cannot be calculated in closed form. Note, however, that the expectation of $P(\cdot)$ is again given by 7.12 and therefore is the same as for the BMC model. This can also be seen in Figure 7.4. In the top panel, we compare the distribution of the present value as obtained by 7.23 firstly to that of a normal distribution with the same mean and variance (dashed curve), and secondly to the normally distributed present value calculated from the BMC model of Example 7.9 (solid curve). It can be seen that 7.23 leads to a distribution that is more skewed to the right (positive skewness) and is more peaked and heavier-tailed than a normal distribution with the same variance (kurtosis larger than 3).

Figure 7.4 Value distribution of future earnings

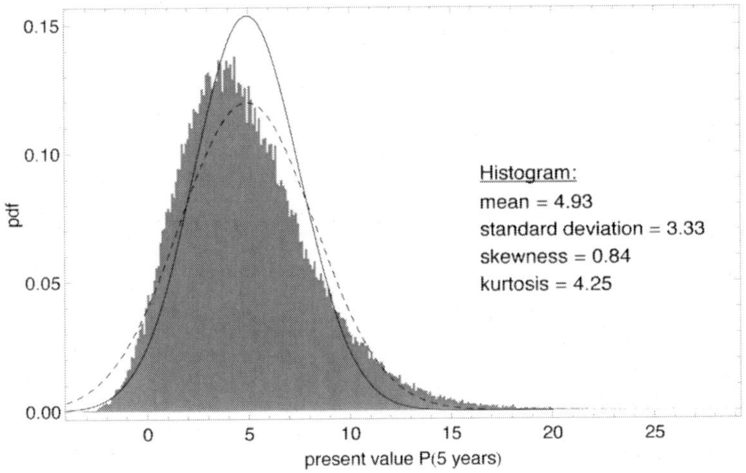

Top panel: The histogram shows the simulated present-value distribution for $t = 5$ years of the level-adjusted volatility model as discussed in Example 7.12 (with discount rate $r = \hat{r}t$) as well as the mean, standard deviation, skewness, and kurtosis parameters of the simulated data. This is compared to a normal distribution with the same mean and standard deviation as the simulated data, plotted as a dashed line. The solid curve represents the normally distributed present value as obtained from the BMC model of Example 7.9. We set $X_i(0) = 10$ and use the yearly parameters $\alpha_i = 1.2$, $\sigma_i = 1.4$, $\tilde{\sigma}_i = \sigma_i / X_i(0) = 0.14$, and a yearly interest rate of $\hat{r} = 0.08$.

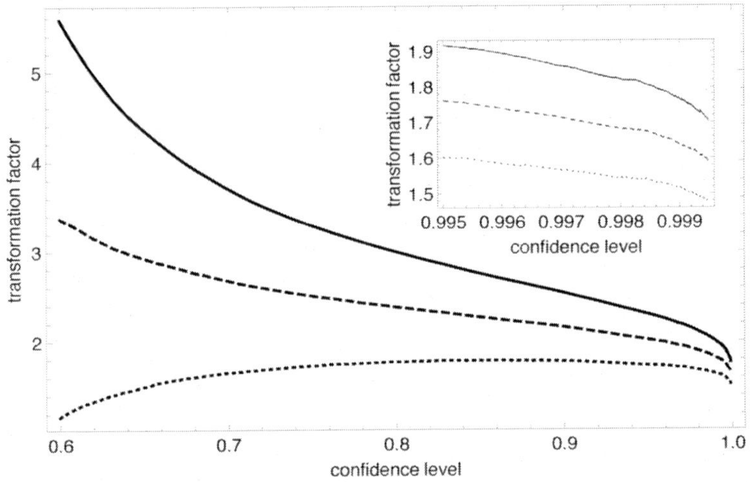

Bottom panel: EaR-CaR-transformation factor for the level-adjusted growth model of Example 7.12 as a function of the confidence level κ and different values $\alpha_1 = 1.0$ (solid line), $\alpha_2 = 1.2$ (dashed line), and $\alpha_3 = 1.4$ (dotted line) of the growth parameter. The other parameters are the same as used above.

EaR-CaR-transformation revisited

We have seen that for the BMC model both the cumulated cashflows $X_i(\cdot)$ and the present value $P(\cdot)$ are normally distributed. This has two important consequences. First, business CaR (and thus the EaR-CaR-transformation factor) of the BMC model is independent of the expected growth and thus of $\alpha_i(\cdot)$; $i = 1, \ldots, m$. Second, the transformation factor is invariant under changes of the confidence level and equals the ratio of the present value volatility and the earnings volatility (see Examples 7.9 and 7.10). This is a consequence of the well-known property of elliptically distributed random variables, which says that their quantiles can always be expressed in terms of their standard deviation.

However, such a behaviour cannot be expected for the level-adjusted BMC model because $P(\cdot)$ is not elliptically distributed. Figure 7.4 serves to illustrate this for the model of Example 7.12. It shows the results of a simulation study where the transformation factor between CaR and EaR (calculated at $t = 0$ where EAR is normally distributed with standard deviation $\sigma = \sigma_i X_i(0)$) is plotted as a function of their confidence level. The growth parameter is set to be $\alpha_i = 1.0$, 1.2, and 1.4. Note that the higher the growth rate is, the lower the transformation factor and therefore the ratio between CaR and EaR will be. In contrast, if we compare the ratio of the volatilities of the present value and EaR, ie, the volatility of the simulated histogram data to the initial absolute cashflow volatility $\sigma = \sigma_i X_i(0) = 1.4$, we obtain 2.29, 2.38, and 2.46 for $\alpha_i = 1.0$, 1.2, and 1.4, respectively. Moreover, we see that an increasing confidence level leads to a decreasing transformation factor.

Summing up we can conclude that in general the question of how a EaR can be converted into a CaR is not straightforward to answer. While for the BMC model this seems to be easier and intuitively easier to grasp (since independent of the confidence level and the expected growth rate) it becomes rather involved for more general models like the one discussed in this section.

CONCLUSION AND OUTLOOK

In this chapter we suggested a multivariate continuous-time setting for assessing business risk using stochastic models for the future cashflows of (non-credit, nonmarket, etc.) earnings. In contrast to scenario-based methods for estimating business risk, our model has the advantage that it results in a time-dependent probability distribution of future earnings, which allows for an accurate definition of VaR-like risk measures at any confidence level and time horizon.

We also investigated the relationship between EaR and CaR, which for general cashflow processes turns out to be not straightforward, and, in particular, a constant multiplier converting EaR into CaR is usually not available. However, a simple EaR-CaR-transformation factor only depending on the time horizon and the discount rate can analytically be derived for the simple BMC model. Such a result may be useful when a fast and approximative VaR estimation based on some EaR figure is needed.

Since in our model the dependence structure between different legal entities or business units is reflected by their correlation matrix, risk-reducing strategies such as known from stock portfolio analysis can be straightforwardly applied.

Several enhancements of the BMC model can be thought of. A particular interesting possibility would be to introduce jumps in the earnings processes representing sudden and sharp falls in a company's earnings caused by, for example, a change in the competitor environment or a customer shift. A particular important class of jump process are the Lévy processes, which have become quite popular also in financial modelling, see for example Cont and Tankov (2004). Then, in addition to the covariance structure of the multivariate Brownian motion we already discussed, jump dependence between future earnings could be modelled by so-called Levy copulas, see for example Böcker and Klüppelberg (2008) for an application of this technique to operational risk. However, since every model should be seen also in the light of the data needed for its calibration, it may be wise to start with a well-known and established Brownian approach.

In our opinion, the development of advanced business risk models will be an important task in quantitative risk management, despite the difficulties and complexity discussed above. Equally important is to work on a harmonised definition of this material risk type, which clearly requires a closer collaboration between practitioners and academics.

Disclaimer

The opinions expressed in this chapter are those of the author and do not reflect the views of UniCredit Group. Moreover, presented risk measurement concepts and risk control techniques are not necessarily used by UniCredit Group or any affiliates.

Acknowledgement
The author would like to thank Alessandra Crimmi from UniCredit Group for helpful discussions about business risk.

REFERENCES

Basel Committee on Banking Supervision, 2004, "International Convergence of Capital Measurement and Capital Standards", Basel.

Böcker, K. and C. Klüppelberg, 2008, "Modelling and Measuring Multivariate Operational Risk with Levy Copulas", *The Journal of Operational Risk*, 3(2).

Committee Of European Banking Supervisors (CEBS), 2004, "The Application Of The Supervisory Review Process Under Pillar 2". London.

Cont, R. and P. Tankov, 2004, *Financial Modelling With Jump Processes* (Boca Raton: Chapman & Hall).

Goedhart, M., T. Koller and D. Wessels, 2005, *Valuation: Measuring and Managing the Value of Companies* (New York: John Wiley & Sons).

The Institute of the Chief Risk Officers (CROs) and Chief Risk Officers Forum (CRO Forum), 2007, "Insights from the joint IFRI/CRO Forum survey on Economic Capital Practice and application" supported by Oliver Wyman.

Matten, C., 1996, *Managing Bank Capital, Capital Allocation and Performance Measurement* (Chichester: John Wiley & Sons).

Morrison, D.J., J.A. Quella and A.J. Slywotzky, 1999, "Countering strategic risk with pattern thinking", *Mercer Management Journal* 11.

Pratt, S.P., R.F. Reilly and R.P. Schweihs, 2000, *Valuing a Business: the Analysis and Appraisal of Closely Held Companies* (New York: McGraw-Hill).

Saita, F., 2004, "Risk Capital Aggregation: the Risk Manager's Perspective", Working Paper.

Saita, F., 2007, *Value at Risk and Bank Capital Management* (San Diego: Elsevier).

Shreve, E.S., 2004, *Stochastic Calculus for Finance II: Continuous-Time Models* (New York: Springer).

8

An Introduction to Liquidity Risk

Mario Anolli; Andrea Resti

Università Cattolica del S. Cuore; Bocconi University

Interest rate risk is not the only risk arising from the different maturity structure of a bank's assets and liabilities.[1] In fact the time mismatch between liabilities (mostly short-term) and assets (more geared towards long maturities) can also give rise to liquidity risk.

By liquidity of a security we mean the ease with which it can be cashed back or traded, even in large amounts, on a secondary market. An asset is said to be liquid[2] when market participants can trade any desired quantity quickly, at prices that are in line with those prevailing when they decided to trade (so that the trade itself does not affect the price).[3]

The liquidity of a market is that of the financial securities traded on that market. Liquidity indicators include the spread between bid and ask quotes (bid–ask spread), the traded volumes or the quoted volumes (in this latter case, not all the quotes are included, but only those close enough to the best price, that is, that lie within a range of some basis points from it); however, no universally accepted measure of liquidity exists.[4] The liquidity of a market is affected by several factors: the number of market participants, the size and frequency of trades, the degree of informational asymmetry existing among market participants, the time interval needed to carry out a trade.

The liquidity of a financial institution could be defined, loosely speaking, as the difference between the average liquidity of its assets and that of its liabilities; in practice, however, such a definition might prove unsatisfactory for several reasons. First, because liquid assets can be increased not only by selling (or cashing in) securities, but also by using those securities as a collateral to get new loans (or if the institution's reputation is good enough, by tapping the market for new unsecured loans); second, because what matters

– in the case of liabilities – is not the overall liquidity (both on the primary and on the secondary market) but only the possible reimbursement claims (as a sale on the secondary market would not affect the need for cash of the issuer); third, because off-balance-sheet items (such as loan commitments, derivatives and stand-by liquidity facilities) must be analysed, next to on-balance-sheet assets and liabilities, to get a complete and reliable picture of the financial institution's liquidity profile.

Liquidity risk is the risk that a financial institution may not be able to pay back its liabilities in a timely manner because of an unexpectedly high number or volume of claims; or that, more realistically, it may be able to meet those requests only by quickly selling large amounts of assets ("fire sale", at a price that is below their current market value, thereby suffering a loss.

Liquidity risk therefore depends on the different maturity of assets and liabilities. However, this does not refer only to the final maturity, but also to the maturity associated with each intermediate cashflow (eg, for financial contracts entailing an amortisation schedule, or for coupon-bearing bonds), including the early prepayment of loans or the unforeseen usage of credit lines.

Liquidity risk may be of two types: funding risk and market liquidity risk.[5]

By funding risk we mean the risk that a financial institution may not be able to face efficiently (that is, without jeopardising its orderly operations and its financial balance) any expected or unexpected cash outflows (due to the reimbursement of liabilities, to commitments to issue loans, to its creditors' request to increase collaterals). Market liquidity risk is the risk that a financial institution, to liquidate a sizable amount of assets, will end up affecting the price in a considerable (and unfavourable) manner, because of the limited depth (or of a momentary disruption) of the financial market where those assets are traded.

Although separate in principle, those two risk types are deeply connected. In fact, it is obvious that a financial institution wishing to face unexpected cash outflows may have to sell a large volume of securities on the secondary market. If that leads to a sharp fall in the selling price, then liquidity risk will hit twice.[6]

Liquidity risk is somehow intrinsic in banking, since it involves – among other things – the transformation into liquid liabilities (which can be used as means of payment) of a portfolio of loans issued to finance investments with long maturities and usually no secondary market. However, there are some factors that can make liquidity risk especially sharp, including some products that banks provide to savers and companies, as well as some circumstances that can significantly increase this type of risk.

Regarding bank products, a number of them give customers a high discretionality in deciding future cashflows. This includes: demand deposits, that are usually left with the bank for years and still can be withdrawn with no prior notice; guarantees issued by the bank, that could lead to a cash outflow if the beneficiary were to default on its obligations; irrevocable loan commitments issued to companies or special-purpose vehicles (including those associated with securitisations or commercial paper programmes); derivatives involving margin requirements, that could unexpectedly rise because of unfavourable market movements.

Circumstances that may lead to a sharper liquidity risk can be divided into bank-specific and systemic. The former involve events that, by distressing the confidence of third parties in a given bank, induce them to accelerate the repayment of the credits issued to the bank (eg, by withdrawing demand deposits or by not rolling over term loans).[7] This could be due, for example, to the release of bad news concerning the bank's management, the quality of its accounts or a rating downgrade. Rating downgrades may prove especially harmful when funds are provided to the bank on the wholesale market subject to covenants or triggers, whereby some minimum rating is required below which the funds must be immediately paid back, or considerable collaterals must be provided.

Systemic factors affecting liquidity risk may include a generalised confidence crisis which leads savers to claim back their bank deposits. Another example could be a market disruption leading to a temporary inactivity, so that listed financial securities cannot be liquidated or can only be traded with a wide bid–ask spread, which makes asset sales economically harmful.[8]

According to many experts (Institute of International Finance 2007), liquidity risk has increased, over the latest years, because of several factors. The globalisation of large financial groups has led them to have assets and liabilities in place with a large number of counterparties, also through their subsidiaries operating in emerging countries; this makes it harder to keep a complete and updated picture of all possible future cashflows. Technology has increased the speed with which funds can be moved away from banks; this is true not only for large, professional counterparties but also, due to internet banking, for retail customers. Securitisations make it possible for banks to turn into liquid funds those assets (such as mortgages or instalment loans) that could hardly be traded on a secondary market; yet, they often involve, for originating banks, the commitment to provide liquidity lines upon request. The increased role of investors, such as hedge funds, using leverage to carry out "arbitrage" strategies, makes it more likely for markets (especially less developed and more peripheral ones) to witness sudden liquidity crises. The mergers and acquisitions among large financial groups have created a small number of large institutions, accounting for a considerable share of the overall banking system; a default – or even a momentary withdrawal from trading and settlement systems – of these mega-banks would have deep implications for the whole financial system. The rise in competition on banking products and the shift from relationship banking to transaction banking have increased the role, on both sides of banks' balance sheets, of products that are sensitive to market conditions (such as interest rates and the banks' ratings) and therefore have quite volatile volumes.

This increase in the importance of liquidity risk has attracted interest from scholars, the financial industry and the supervisory authorities. Books such as Persaud (2003) and Matz and Neu (2007), as well as scientific papers, such as Acharya and Pedersen (2005) and de Jong and Driessen (2005), have investigated liquidity risk and its drivers.

Supervisors, too, having laid more emphasis, in the past, on market, credit and operational risks,[9] are now increasingly turning their attention to liquidity risk. This has led to documents discussing risk management principles and risk measurement schemes (the Joint Forum 2006; Financial Services Authority 2003) as well as surveys (European Central Bank 2007) aimed at getting a better insight on the relevance and nature of liquidity risks. Financial institutions, too, have released studies and analyses, intended to prompt regulators to define univocally (and uniformly across countries) rules and practices for dealing with this class of risks (Institute of International Finance 2007).

This chapter discusses some techniques for liquidity risk management, including a number of more sophisticated approaches on which no consensus has emerged, yet, as far as practical implementation is concerned.

We look at the main drivers of market liquidity risk and show how market risk measures for a bank's security portfolio may have to be adjusted to account for the liquidity premium paid on large sales. Then we focus on funding liquidity risk, suggesting ways to measure it and laying a special emphasis on balance-sheet items with no clear contractual maturity. We move on, then, to show how funding liquidity risk must be assessed not only under normal conditions, but also simulating the effect of possible liquidity shocks. Finally, we discuss organisational implications for banks wishing to implement a sound liquidity management policy.

MARKET LIQUIDITY RISK

"Liquidity is what markets are all about" (Amihud and Mendelson 1988): secondary markets exist to provide liquidity to the securities traded in them. This is the core of market liquidity risk, or, as stated earlier, the risk of loss incurred by companies when, in order to cope with their obligations, they are unable to convert (some of) their assets into cash at the current price.[10]

While the concept of liquidity is clear, the various possible measures of liquidity are difficult to quantify. Liquidity, however, can be alternately defined from an objective viewpoint, that is the viewpoint of the market (in terms of depth, breadth, resiliency[11]) or from a subjective viewpoint, that is the viewpoint of the individual willing to trade.

Market liquidity risk is of paramount importance for banks, as they hold on their books a significant portion of illiquid instruments. Unlike funding liquidity risk (which is often agent-specific, or tends to characterise all the activities of the bank as a whole[12]), market liquidity risk tends to be asset-specific, although influenced by the overall market conditions. For an intermediary, market liquidity risk can be twofold: exogenous, when it depends on the general characteristics of the market and therefore is outside the control of the intermediary itself; or endogenous, when it depends specifically on the intermediary's characteristics (eg, the particular composition and size of its portfolio). A security characterised by low exogenous risk may, however, involve a significant endogenous risk when held in significant amounts.

The common way to measure liquidity is to measure the lack, or scarcity, of it: that is, to measure transaction costs. These are defined as the sum of all costs (explicit and implicit) incurred by investors to trade. The higher the transaction costs incurred to trade an asset, the lower its liquidity.[13]

Transaction costs have two components: an explicit component (money paid for commissions and other operating costs borne by the party carrying out the transaction); and an implicit component (the suboptimal price conditions at which the transaction could have to be carried out). Implicit costs,[14] according to the classification of Keim and Madhavan (1998), have three components: quoted bid–ask spread, market impact and opportunity costs.

- The quoted bid–ask spread[15] pays for the market-making services.[16]
- The market impact (particularly relevant for large orders) stems from the fact that large transactions (compared with the current depth of the market) tend to adversely affect the price for the party initiating the trade (sales prompt a price decrease and vice versa). This cost component

(Arnott and Wagner 1990) can be defined as the difference between the actual transaction price and the price that would have prevailed if the transaction had not taken place. There is no perfect methodology for measuring the market impact, because it depends on the market, the time, and the trader's motives. It has a temporary component (stemming from order imbalance) and a permanent one (stemming from informational asymmetry); both components are a function of the volume traded and of the execution strategy.[17]

- The opportunity costs arising from a missed trade are typical of traders who have superior information, insofar as the value of such information declines with time. Opportunity costs can result from the fact that the trade is not executed, is only partially executed, or from the fact that it takes time to be completed (due to the choice to trade gradually or to the inability to do otherwise). Opportunity costs arise when the market price moves adversely (eg, the price declines pending a decision to sell); in this case the choice to trade gradually has opposite effects (see Figure 8.1) on opportunity costs and on market impact. Opportunity costs are hard to measure because it should be known when the decision to trade was taken.[18] Opportunity costs may also be negative if prices decline (rise) when the trader wants to buy (sell).

When traders trade large volumes quickly, they face transaction costs due to market impact; when they do so slowly, they face a higher risk of an adverse price change (Engle, Ferstenberg and Russell 2006). When a bank experi-

Figure 8.1 Market impact, opportunity costs and time

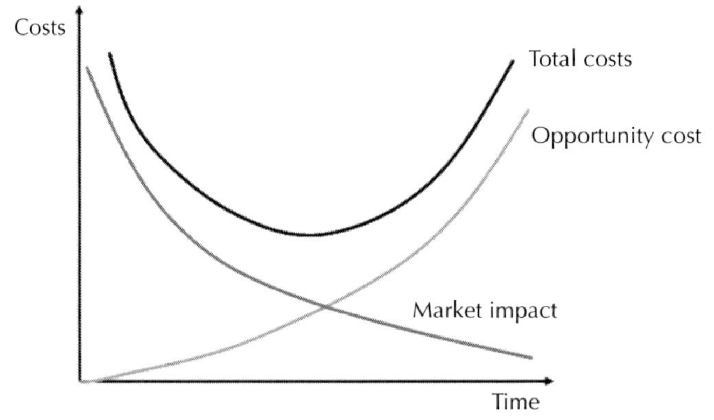

ences liquidity shortages, the analysis should be further qualified in two directions:

- when shortages are systematic (not idiosyncratic) in nature, a decline in the asset price is more likely than an increase; thus the expected opportunity cost is greater than zero (waiting involves a risk that the asset price may decrease); and
- a strategy of gradual liquidation is only partially feasible if the bank has immediate cash needs.

Given the uncertain nature of transaction costs, the liquidity supply curve can be seen as a stochastic function (Jarrow 2005).[19] In fact, in any time period between 0 and t (see Figure 8.2), there is not only a movement in the marginal price[20] of a given security, but also a change in the shape of its liquidity supply curve. Figure 8.2 shows that at time 0 liquidity conditions were tight (so large volumes could only be traded with large and increasing adverse effects on prices), while at time t they were more eased, so investors could buy/sell large quantities at prices close to the marginal one.[21]

The liquidity-adjusted value-at-risk

The traditional measures of risk (eg, value-at-risk (VaR)) can be adapted in order to take into consideration the effects of liquidity risk and transaction costs. When we account for transaction costs, in fact, positions cannot be

Figure 8.2 Liquidity supply curves

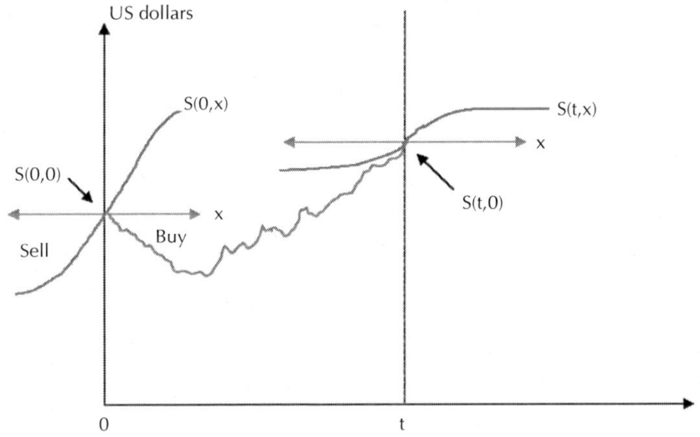

Source: R. A. Jarrow 2005

closed at the mid-price (at which VaR measures are usually computed), but at the price net of (explicit and implicit) transaction costs.

If there is no uncertainty about the impact of the trade on prices, then the liquidation value of a position is equal to the bid price, and thus the transaction cost is

$$C = \frac{1}{2} P_t \bar{S} \tag{8.1}$$

where P_t is the mid-quote of the liquidated asset at time t and $\bar{S}$ is the percentage bid–ask spread. However, if the price impact is uncertain, a somewhat more complex approach is required.

As a first approximation, the effect of liquidity risk could be included implicitly into VaR measures by simply increasing their time horizon, that is, the time required to liquidate the position (hence, also VaR itself). In this case, liquidity risk would be accounted for by "rescaling" VaR over a longer risk horizon, without a proper recalculation of variances and covariances.[22]

Alternatively, liquidity risk could be modelled explicitly, as in Bangia *et al* (1999), breaking up uncertainty into pure market risk (arising from the uncertainty about returns, measured at the mid-quote) and liquidity risk (due to the uncertainty about the actual liquidation value). This approach makes a distinction between the mark-to-market value (valued, as usual, at the marginal price) and the liquidation value (based on the expected actual liquidation price). The latter is a function of the size of the trade and of the evolution of market conditions, including the adverse selection effect triggered by the sale. The relationship between market and liquidity risk can be direct[23] or indirect.[24] In the former case, liquidity risk is exogenous, while in the latter liquidity risk is endogenous (Figure 8.3).

The uncertainty about the liquidation value of an asset would therefore depend on two factors:

- the variability of the mid-price (the midpoint of the bid–ask spread); and
- the variability (namely, the possible widening) of the bid–ask spread, as a result of changing market conditions (ie, exogenous liquidity risk).

As for the changes in the mid-price, if we assume that the logarithmic return of a security, $r_t = \ln\left[\frac{P_t}{P_{t-1}}\right]$ is normally distributed, then the worst price associated with a given confidence level (1-c) may be defined, using standard parametric VaR, as

Figure 8.3 Market risk and liquidity risk

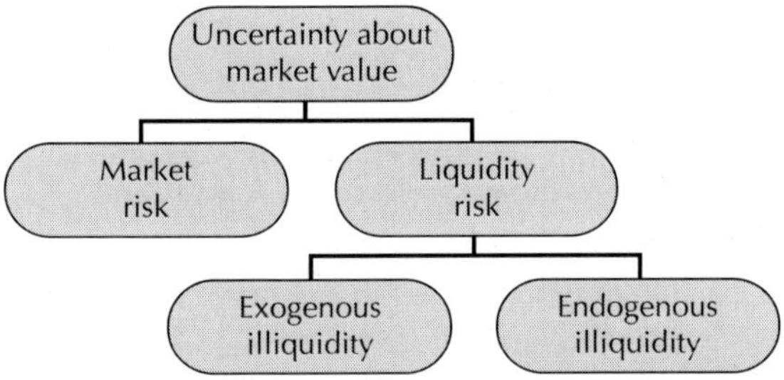

Source: Bangia *et al*, 1999.

$$P_{(1-c)} = P_t e^{[E(r_t)-\alpha\sigma_t]} \tag{8.2}$$

where (1-c) indicates the desired confidence level, σ_t the asset's return volatility and α is the corresponding percentile of the standard normal distribution.

Accordingly, the parametric VaR with confidence level (1-c) is

$$VaR = P_t[1-e^{-\alpha\sigma_t}] \tag{8.3}$$

Equation 8.3 considers the variability of the mid-quote only; as for the variability of the bid–ask spread, a stochastic version of Equation 8.1 can be written and the transaction costs *TC* estimated based on the mean percentage bid–ask spread and its volatility $\tilde{\sigma}$

$$TC = \frac{1}{2}P[\bar{S} + \alpha'\tilde{\sigma}] \tag{8.4}$$

However, unlike with market risk, the percentile α' ($\neq\alpha$) cannot be assumed to be normally distributed, as this would be an unrealistic assumption for the bid–ask spread.[25]

If the correlation between the volatility of the mid-price and that of the bid–ask spread is high, as we can expect especially in times of tight liquidity, the two effects can be added up, getting a liquidity-adjusted VaR (VaR_L)

$$VaR_L = P_t\left[1-e^{-\alpha\sigma_t} + \frac{S+\alpha'\tilde{\sigma}}{2}\right] \tag{8.5}$$

Equation 8.4 represents transaction costs in a simplistic way. In fact, as noted above, transaction costs can be expected to increase with the transaction size (see Figure 8.4), or, namely, with its impact in relation to market depth. Moreover, explicit transaction costs can be assumed to be inversely related to the time used to complete the transaction (even if this will lead to an increase in execution risk).

To (partially) accommodate for these remarks,[26] Dowd (2002) modifies Equation 8.4 as follows

$$TC = \left[1 + \frac{PS}{MS}\right]^{\lambda_1} (AL \cdot \frac{S}{2}) e^{-\lambda_2 hp} \tag{8.6}$$

where *PS* is the size of the position held by the bank, *MS* is the market size (for example, the average daily trading volume on the security), *AL* the amount to be liquidated before the end of the holding period (*hp*), λ_1 and λ_2 are positive parameters to be determined empirically, accounting respectively for the resiliency of transaction costs to the relative position size and for the decay rate of transaction costs over time.

In Equation 8.6, transaction costs increase with the relative position size and with their elasticity to the change in the position size (basically, the slope of curves in Figure 8.4), and decrease with the time available to close the position. The equation also measures the effect of the size of the bid–ask spread on transaction costs, weighted by the amount sold and accounting for the holding period.

Common factors in the liquidity of financial instruments

The correlations across the liquidity of various financial instruments play a crucial role in market liquidity risk. Recent studies in markets microstruc-

Figure 8.4 Traded volume and bid–ask spread

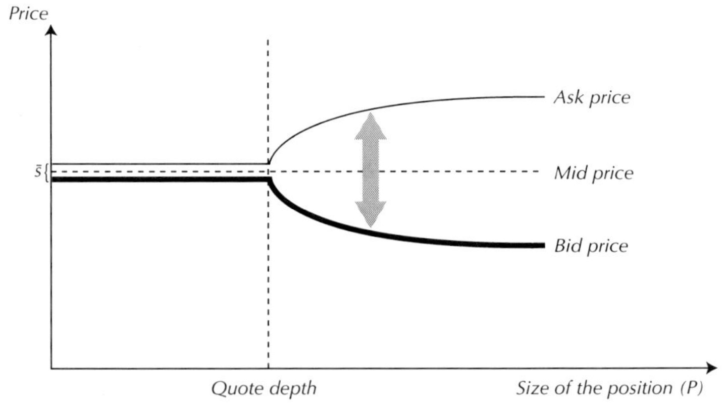

Source: Bangia *et al*, 1999.

ture deal with the identification of common factors explaining the co-movements in the liquidity of financial instruments. Significant correlations have emerged between the quoted spread for a given security and the liquidity observed on other ones.

Such common factors (ie, commonalities, see Chordia, Roll and Subrahmanyam 2000) may emerge for several reasons: trading typically shows common responses to the general level of securities' prices; furthermore, changes in volumes affect the inventory management by market makers and this generates adjustments leading to changes in the quoted bid–ask spreads and volumes. The volatility of returns may have market components as a result of trading patterns involving several related parties, and this is particularly true during liquidity shortages.

Acharya and Pedersen (2005) show that the expected return on a security depends on its expected liquidity and on the covariance of its return and liquidity with the return and liquidity of the market. Their pricing model expands the logic of the capital asset pricing model (CAPM) to take into account liquidity risk. They start from two considerations: the liquidity of a financial asset is risky and is driven by a number of common factors (commonalities). In their model the return required to hold a risky security depends on:

- the expected cost of illiquidity;
- the covariance between the overall market return (net of the expected cost of illiquidity) and the return on the security;
- the covariance between market illiquidity costs and the illiquidity costs of the security: this is because the return required by an investor to hold a security increases if it becomes illiquid when the market as a whole experiences liquidity shortages;
- the covariance between market illiquidity costs and the return on the security: the return required by an investor to hold a security decreases if it offers greater returns when the market as a whole becomes illiquid; and
- the covariance between the market return and the illiquidity cost of the security: the return required by an investor to hold a security decreases if it becomes more liquid when the market return is low.

According to the estimates by Acharya and Pedersen on the US stock market, the risk premium from commonalities in liquidity is equal to 0.08% (showing that investors require only a small premium to hold securities that are illiquid when market liquidity as a whole dries up). The risk premium due to the covariance between the return on the security and market illiquidity costs is estimated at 0.16%, so investors prefer securities with higher returns in phases of market illiquidity. The risk premium due to the covariance between market returns and the illiquidity cost of the security is definitely wider (0.82%): securities that stay highly liquid when market returns decrease are highly valued (ie, they require a lower return) since they act as liquidity reserves in adverse market phases. These results show that market participants are very sensitive to the liquidity of a security during difficult market phases.

Liquidity risk differs from illiquidity premium (that is the difference between the level of transaction costs associated with two investments characterised by different levels of liquidity). Acharya and Pedersen have estimated the difference between the expected return of two portfolios characterised by the same systematic risk, the same liquidity risk, but different transaction costs[27] at 3.5% on a yearly basis.

FUNDING LIQUIDITY RISK

As explained above, funding risk is the risk that a financial institution (eg, a bank) may not be able to face both expected and unexpected cash outflows without endangering its orderly operations and financial equilibrium.

According to the European Central Bank (2007), there are three approaches mainly used by banks to measure this type of risk: the stock-based approach, the mismatch-based approach and the hybrid approach.

The stock-based approach measures the stock of financial assets that can promptly be liquidated to face a possible liquidity shock; the mismatch-based approach (also known as cashflow-based approach) compares expected cash in- and outflows over the following months, grouping them into a number of maturity bands and checking that the former are enough to cover the latter; the hybrid approach is a combination of the other two, since expected cashflows are integrated with cashflows that could be obtained by selling financial assets that can be promptly liquidated (or by using those assets as a collateral to get new loans).

When applying these approaches, the emphasis is not on contractual cashflows, but rather on actual cashflows, that is, on estimated cashflows that account for the foreseeable behaviour of the bank's counterparties (for example, treating part of the demand deposits as associated with longer maturities) and for the bank's wish not to jeopardise its current business relationships (so that, for instance, some loans that in principle would be promptly revocable may be treated as committed). This kind of adjustment clearly changes depending on whether liquidity is estimated within a "normal" or a "stressed" scenario.

The stock-based approach and the cash capital position

The stock-based approach requires that the bank's balance sheet be restated in order to appreciate the contribution that each individual item gives to creating/hedging funding risks; namely, the following must be highlighted.

- Cashable assets[28] (CA): This includes all assets that can quickly be converted into cash. Besides short-term deposits and other liquidity sources, it includes part of the bank's loans and securities. As regards loans, these are those short-term credit lines (for example, overnight and other similar interbank facilities) than can be easily and effectively claimed back without endangering the bank's customer relationships and without causing trouble to the financial stability of its obligors; the actual ability to liquidate a position must therefore be looked at, rather than its contractual maturity. As concerns the security portfolio, only unencumbered positions should be included, that is, only those assets that are not being used, for example, as a collateral against loans or derivative contracts; such unencumbered positions should be subjected to a haircut, which serves two different purposes. First, it represents the possible loss, relative to the market mid-price, that the bank might be forced to face in order to liquidate the assets quickly on the secondary market; second (and more importantly), it measures the difference between the current value of the securities and the (lower) value of the short-term loans that could be obtained by pledging them as collateral. In fact, loans secured by securities are usually issued for an amount that is below that of the collateral (for example, the loan could be equal to 90% of the value of the securities); the haircut must therefore be subtracted from the value of the securities in order to get a reliable estimate of the loan they could give access to. Note that unencumbered assets are not necessarily short-term: instead, they may include long-term bonds and even shares. Of course, this type of securities, being more volatile in value, will need a higher haircut and therefore will lead, all other things being equal, to a lower amount of unencumbered assets. Besides applying haircuts, all those securities that are not traded on a liquid market and that are not "eligible", that is, that are not accepted as a collateral (for example, shares in private companies held for merchant banking purposes, unrated bonds) should be discarded.
- Volatile liabilities (VL): These are short-term funds (including demand

deposits) for which there is a risk that they may not be rolled over. They include wholesale funding (for example, overnight interbank loans, or very short-term repurchase agreements) and the portion of customer deposits that is considered volatile. In the case of customer deposits, too, it is not the contractual maturity that is looked at (in which case, all customer demand deposits would, by definition, be volatile), but rather to the actual behaviour of the counterparties. In fact, unless the market is experiencing panic and bank runs, it is highly unlikely that all the bank's customers will decide to withdraw their funds at the same time, as they need bank deposits as a means of payment for commercial transactions and as a liquid investment. Accordingly, some share of the customers' demand deposits (the so-called "core deposits") will have to be treated as stable and therefore be excluded from volatile liabilities.

- Commitments to lend (CLs): These are off-balance-sheet items that represent an irrevocable commitment to issue funds upon request. They can therefore cause cash outflows, above and beyond those associated with volatile liabilities being paid back.
- Steadily available credit lines (ALs): These are irrevocable commitments to lend issued to the bank by third parties (usually other financial institutions); thanks to those commitments, the bank should be able to rely on additional cash inflows when necessary, without having to pledge securities or other assets as a collateral.

The share of cashable assets that is not absorbed by volatile liabilities is sometimes called cash capital position (CCP = CA − VL). A large CCP signals the ability to withstand liquidity shortages due to a greater-than-expected volatility in funding sources, as well as by unexpected difficulties met in the management of cashable assets (say, a generalised increase in haircuts due to unfavourable financial markets). To control for the bank's size, the CCP is sometimes scaled by total assets.

When computing the CCP, most banks also include, next to VL, their commitments to lend. This leads to the following definition

$$CCP = CA - VL - CL \tag{8.7}$$

It might be wondered whether this equation should be completed by adding to CA all the steadily available credit lines (AL) that the bank could enjoy in the event of unexpected liquidity shortages. Many banks, however, prefer not to make such an adjustment, in order to be more conservative. In fact, if a bank were hit by a liquidity crisis, its counterparties might choose not to honour their commitments (facing penalties and other legal costs), rather than issue a loan that has a high probability of default. For this reason, credit lines may not be available in practice right when they are most needed, that is, when the bank is suffering from a confidence crisis; this justifies the choice of ignoring AL in Equation 8.7.

The *CCP* is not the only index based on stock-based approaches. Another example is the so-called long-term funding ratios, which give the portion of assets with a maturity greater than n years funded with liabilities having a corresponding maturity (for example, the share of assets with a maturity greater than five years that is funded with liabilities maturing in five years or more, or with capital and reserves). As banks usually transform short-term liabilities into medium-to-long-term loans to companies, long-term funding ratios are usually expected to be below 100%; however, very low values (or a deterioration over time) may indicate possible unbalances in the maturity structure of assets and liabilities.

The cashflow-based (or mismatch-based) approach

The slots into which assets and liabilities are sorted when computing the CCP look oversimplified. In fact, assets and liabilities are divided in a binary way, between "stable" and "unstable" ones (where by "unstable" we mean cashable in the case of assets, volatile in the case of liabilities). In practice, however, infinitely many "shades" of liquidity are possible: a demand deposit is certainly more liquid than an item that is due in one month, but the latter is, in turn, more flexible than a contract maturing in one year. It is then advisable to restate the balance sheet going beyond a binary logic, and using a whole maturity ladder that includes a more detailed set of time bands.

Furthermore, as mentioned earlier, the fact that assets or liabilities may have a long final maturity and yet produce intermediate cashflows due to interest payments has to be accounted for. Such intermediate flows must obviously be considered.

Such remarks have led to the mismatch-based approach (cashflow-based approach); here, the focus is no longer on stocks, but rather on all in- and outflows associated with assets and liabilities. These flows – including interest payments – are allocated to a "ladder" including N different maturity buckets (which could range, for example, from overnight to 10-year flows).

As in the stock-based approaches, demand deposits and loans are dealt with based on their expected actual maturity. Accordingly, only a share of the expected withdrawals from the customers' current accounts (as well as of the repayments on overdraft facilities) is associated with the "overnight" band, or with other short-term buckets.

More generally, cashflows are sorted across the different rungs of the ladder based on the bank's expectations and its past experience, and reflect a moderately constrained liquidity environment (any "shocked" scenarios – for example, the release of unfavourable news on the bank, or a situation of market disruption – are to be considered separately[29]). Based on past data, the bank also makes assumptions on the share of "commitments to lend" that will actually be used by its customers (as it is unlikely that all credit lines granted by the bank will be drawn jointly), as well as on their timing.

After sorting all expected cashflows across maturities, for each bucket in the maturity ladder the net unbalance between inflows and outflows can be computed (mismatch or liquidity gap, G_t). The unbalance between flows associated with a given band and all shorter maturities, that is

$$GC_t \equiv \sum_{i \leq t} G_t \tag{8.8}$$

is called cumulative liquidity gap;[30] to avoid ambiguity, the G_ts relative to just one time band are sometimes called marginal liquidity gaps. Negative cumulative liquidity gaps for the shortest time bands indicate that the bank cannot cover the foreseeable cash payments with the expected inflows; this is a severe warning, as it indicates that the bank – pending adequate corrective actions – is bound to suffer from a liquidity shortage.

In practice, however, the liquidity picture provided by this approach is made less reliable by the fact that cashflows associated with securities (including unencumbered assets), are based on contractual maturities and coupons, and hence do not account for the fact that those assets can be used as collateral to get new loans, also at a very short notice. The maturity ladder must therefore be rewritten taking into account the role played by unencumbered assets in facing liquidity risks, just as we do when computing a bank's cash capital position. This is what the hybrid approach does, as explained below.

The hybrid approach

In the cashflow-based approach, as mentioned above, all cashflows expected from securities are sorted into maturity buckets according to their contractual maturity. This means that, for example, a 10-year zero coupon bond with a face value of €10 million is totally associated with the "10-year" time band. In practice, however, the bank's treasurer might manage liquidity shortages by selling the bond or by using it to get funded through a collateralised loan or a repurchase agreement.[31] Of course, due to the haircut, the funds raised would not be €10 million, but only a share (say, 90%) of the bond's current value (which in turn would be less than the face value); for example, the funds may amount to €7 million. Accordingly, a share (70%) of the bond value might be cashed in quickly (although temporarily), while the remaining part (interest and haircut, amounting in this example to 30%) would be available only in 10 years.

This line of reasoning applies only to unencumbered eligible assets that the bank can freely sell or pledge as collateral. A significant share of those assets will therefore be ascribed to short-term time bands (including very short-term ones), while the rest will be left to buckets associated with their original maturities (and coupons).

Once we account for loans that can be raised (from the central bank or from other financial institutions) using unencumbered assets as collateral, we might find out that negative liquidity gaps (where outflows used to exceed inflows) become positive; accordingly, as the bank has enough liquidity reserves, no warning signal is triggered.

Figure 8.5 shows an example of marginal gaps (the difference between positive and negative bars) and cumulative gaps (the dashed line). It can be seen that cumulative net flows stay in the positive for the first three months. The bank therefore looks adequately equipped to face its expected liquidity claims.[32] Note that the time bands used in the figure are merely an example; in fact, large international banks are reported (European Central Bank 2007) to use a more fine-grained ladder for short and very short maturities (including several intra-day bands), while using a simplified structure for medium to long ones (for example, using one single bucket for all maturities beyond one week).

The results in the figure are clearly affected by the assumptions made when assigning expected flows to different time bands in the maturity ladder. This is especially relevant whenever it is expected that the actual time profile of the cashflows associated with an item will be different from contractual provisions (think of long-term mortgages being prepaid, demand deposits left with the bank for years and so forth). Some methodologies used to assess the uncertainty surrounding actual cashflows (amount, timing or both) will be discussed later.

The quantitative approaches reviewed above are usually used by banks together with more qualitative tools, aimed at controlling liquidity risk

Figure 8.5 Example of hybrid approach

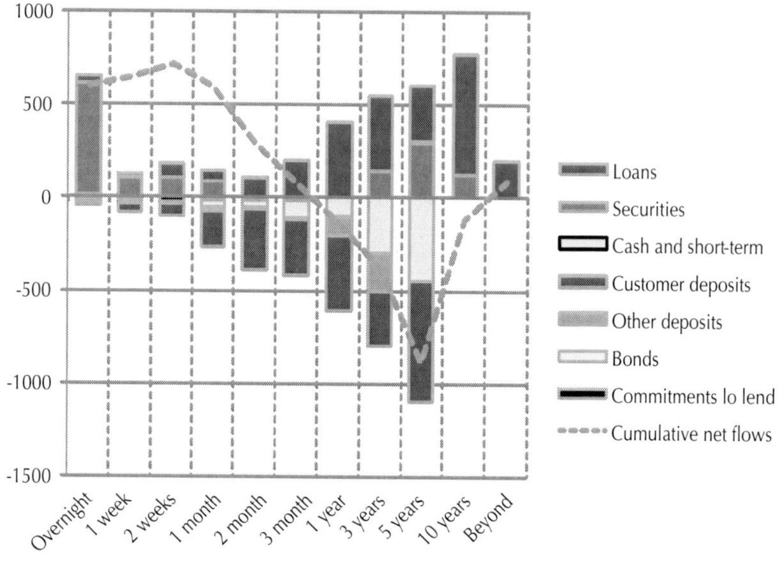

Source: Resti and Sironi, 2008.

through a set of periodic liquidity reports and an adequate structure of internal checks.

As concerns multinational banks, funding risk is never managed in a completely centralised way: instead, local subsidiaries are partially responsible for it. To summarise a range of rather heterogeneous practices, it could be said that principles, policies and limits for liquidity management are defined centrally, while the day-to-day management of liquidity (based on group-wide accepted principles) is left to local entities.[33] Such a choice is driven by several objectives: to increase responsibility and accountability of the local management, to comply with constraints posed by national supervisors, to account for local regulations (for example, rules on large exposures and deposit reserve requirements[34]) that in some countries make it too costly to shift large liquidity lines to and from the holding company.

THE TREATMENT OF NON-MATURING ASSETS AND LIABILITIES (NOMAL)

The management of liquidity risk requires the ability to predict the pattern of future cashflows arising from assets and liabilities. These flows are subject to two sources of uncertainty (Bardenhewer 2007):

- the replacement of expired contracts/instruments; and
- changes in the volume of products without contractual maturity (the so-called "non-maturing assets and liabilities" – "NOMAL").

In this section we focus on the latter. To see how complex this issue is[35] consider, for example, a plain deposit: the uncertainty in its cashflows – giving rise to liquidity risk – originates from three groups of interrelated variables:

- market interest rates (which drive the relative attractiveness of substitute products);
- the interest rate applied by the bank on the deposit (which, together with market interest rates, affects the clients' demand for deposits); and
- exogenous factors (eg, the customer's cash needs) driving the balance of the deposit.

Similar remarks apply to assets, for example, in the case of overdraft facilities.

When estimating the cashflow on NOMALs over an extended period of time, the problem is made more complex by the fact that the options available to the bank customers are "nested", which means that the amount of deposits that can be withdrawn at time *t*, also depends on the amount existing at time *t*-1, which in turn is affected by the amount at *t*-2 etc.

The possibility to withdraw funds from a bank account or to pay back an overdraft can be seen as an option held by the customer. However, the evaluation of this option is made complex by three circumstances:

- its value does not depend on a particular interest rate, but on the entire term structure;
- even though the options embedded in non-maturing contracts are American, the client does not necessarily exercise them as soon as they are in the money, given the known stickiness[36] of bank assets and liabilities in the event of changes in market rates; and
- the bank can influence the probability of exercise by adapting (fully or partially) the interest rates applied to customers to the new market conditions.

Moreover, while the options available to bank clients on both sides of the balance sheet are affected by the same underlying factors (market rates), those on the assets side cannot necessarily be expected to hedge those on the liabilities side, and vice versa. Indeed, options embedded in assets and liabilities tend to be exercised at different times; for example, a liquidity crisis could trigger a reduction in deposits but no early repayment of loans. Finally, different classes of customers will exercise their options at different times.

There are two main approaches to addressing liquidity risk of non-maturing products: the replicating portfolio approach and the option-based approach (also known as option adjusted spread, OAS).

The replicating portfolio approach

The replicating portfolio approach aims at transforming the products with indefinite maturity into an equivalent portfolio (in terms of cashflow generation) made of instruments – such as money-market instruments and plain vanilla bonds traded in liquid markets[37] – that involve no optionalities. According to this approach (Bardenhewer 2007), a indefinite-maturity liability (asset), is invested in (funded by) a replicating portfolio consisting of instruments with explicit and predetermined maturities, that generates cashflows that match the net outflows arising from the options embedded in the indefinite-maturity liability (asset).

The construction of the replicating portfolio can follow two approaches (Frauendorfer and Schurle 2007):

- static replication, which identifies the replicating portfolio based on historical data and keeps constant the weights of the assets in the portfolio; and
- dynamic replication, which identifies the weights of securities to be included in the replicating portfolio based on simulation models, and adjusts such weights continuously (as a matter of fact, with very high-frequency).

The static replication approach is based on the estimation of a relationship between the evolution of assets with indefinite maturity and that of several endogenous factors: market rates, rates charged/paid to customers, volumes of non-maturing products recorded in the past. This relationship identifies a replicating portfolio whose cashflows (inflows or outflows, including principal and interest) must equate those of the bank's NOMAL portfolio. This involves minimising the tracking error between the replicating portfolio and the NOMAL portfolio. Weights derived from the optimisation process are then left constant over time (or rather, are reviewed at discrete, wide time intervals).

While weights are kept stable, the possible NOMAL volumes may experience changes in the period between two weight revisions; to address this, the replicating static portfolio can be divided into a core portfolio (where weights are kept unchanged) and a volatile portfolio. The core portfolio is in turn divided into portions, invested across the different maturities of the replicating portfolio. Expired instruments are then renewed within the same maturity bucket. The volatile portfolio is invested on very short maturities and serves as a buffer for volume fluctuations (Frauendorfer and Schurle 2007). The segmentation of the core portfolio across a number of maturities means that the return on the portfolio is an average of many market rates and therefore experiences smooth changes over time, as it normally happens for deposits and loans with indefinite maturity.

The simplest (and less realistic) example of static replication assumes constant volumes for all indefinite-maturity items (eg, current account deposits). In this case, the replication portfolio is constructed by dividing the total amount across all buckets and by replacing expired contracts with equal ones (for example, if a three-month deposit expires, it is replaced by a contract of the same maturity). The return of this replicating portfolio is then given by the yields on the various maturities (eg, one, two, three months, five years and so on), weighted by the invested amount. In this context, changes in the volume of deposits can be seen as random fluctuations around the average, and the volume invested in the replicating portfolio is adjusted accordingly: if there is an unexpected deposits inflow, that amount is invested in the shortest maturity available (and vice versa in case of unexpected outflows). The one-month bucket acts as a buffer for unexpected[38] fluctuations in volumes.

This approach can be made more realistic by assuming a trend in the pattern of volumes. In this case, variations in volumes can be divided into a deterministic component, associated with the expected trend, and a stochastic component, given by the fluctuations around the trend. The shape of the trend function (linear,[39] quadratic, exponential) can be determined through ordinary regression techniques.

Dynamic replication (Frauendorfer and Schurle 2007) is a more advanced and complex approach, based on multistage stochastic programming. This methodology, instead of deriving investment (or refinancing) decisions from historical data, is based on the future probability distribution of risk factors (scenarios) and chooses portfolio weights through some optimisation criteria. This dynamic optimisation differs from the static one because it does not calibrate the model on one set of historical factors (that is, in practice, on one single scenario), but takes into account an entire tree of market rates, customer rates and volumes (calibrated according to past data).

The optimisation problem can be specified in a couple of ways: minimisation of the tracking error or maximisation of net interest margin under some risk constraint (eg, a minimum level of liquidity). Dynamic optimisation implies that, unlike for static optimisation, the weights according to which available amounts are reallocated to new maturities are variable. The optimisation process involves the following steps:

1. define the universe of investable items (including only the most liquid maturities – key maturities – and excluding all contracts that embed an option);
2. choose risk factors and collect data on them (for example market interest rates, customer interest rates, current volumes);
3. define a set of appropriate quantitative models to simulate the dynamics of risk factors[40] in subsequent periods;[41]
4. generate scenarios based on these quantitative models;
5. define any constraints to the optimisation process[42] (for example, a floor on net interest income, a cap on its volatility, risk limits, liquidity floors, a cap on the maximum number of recalibration transactions[43] etc); and
6. based on these generated scenarios and constraints, carry out the dynamic optimisation process for the replicating portfolio, usually by minimising the expected downside deviation,[44] or the risk that the replication portfolio fails to meet the total outflow, across all maturities (given the trend in volumes and interest rates), of the NOMALs.

The option-based approach (option adjusted spread – OAS)

The option-based approach (Bardenhewer 2007) tries to capture the value of the option embedded in products with indefinite maturity. Loosely speaking, the option value is given by the difference between the value of a straight bond and the value of an identical bond with an early repayment option. The analogy is not perfect, however, because the bond option may be exercised only at definite maturities (European or Bermudan option) and expires with the final maturity of the bond, while products with indefinite maturity never expire and the prepayment option may be exercised at any time (American option).

The approach of Jarrow and van Deventer (1998) is based on a term structure model and two equations that describe the evolution of deposit rates and volumes (both driven by the money market rate). The model admits closed-form solution, but involves the unrealistic assumption that money market rates are the only factor affecting volumes and rates with customers, hence does not provide an adequate insight of real-life NOMAL portfolios. In fact, banks do set their rates with customers based on market rates, but with some stickiness. Moreover, the volumes associated with indefinite-maturity products are partly insensitive to changes in market rates.

For this reason, more realistic versions of the model have been developed (Bardenhewer 2007), which, however, have no closed-form solution and require a simulation approach. For example, to take into account for the delay in the adjustment of bank rates to market rates, the former can be linked not just to current market rates, but to their past values (possibly, through a moving average). Volumes are partly driven by exogenous customer choices, and not only by market rates.[45] This can be done quite simply, for example, by assuming that retail demand deposits decrease steadily over each month and pick up at month end, and/or follow seasonal patterns (eg, higher withdrawals during the holiday season); typically, such models also include autoregressive terms.

In its more general version, the OAS approach requires a model for the term structure of interest rates, a model for the evolution of interest rates charged to customers and a model for the evolution of volumes. While there are many term-structure models available in the literature, modelling bank rates and volumes involves less-common techniques.

Regarding bank rates, it may be assumed that they are set according to market rates but, as mentioned above, with some stickiness. The model for customer rates could therefore include as explanatory variables the average Euribor rate in the last n months ($\bar{r}_t^s$) and the average, over the last n months, of the five-year swap rate ($\bar{r}_t^e$).

$$cr_t = \beta_0 + \beta_1 \bar{r}_t^e + \beta_1 \bar{r}_t^s \tag{8.9}$$

Alternatively, the model could be made autoregressive, or include polinomially distributed lags on market rates.

As for volumes, part of them may be considered insensitive to rate changes. This "stable" portion depends on the type of product (for example, it is higher for demand deposits, which are mostly held for transaction purposes, than it is for savings accounts). The model for rate-sensitive volumes (V_t) could instead include market rates $\bar{r}_t^e$ and $\bar{r}_t^s$ (eg, delayed by two months), and a series of quarterly dummies to account for seasonality effects:

$$V_t = \alpha_0 + \alpha_1 \bar{r}_t^e + \alpha_2 \bar{r}_{t-2}^s + \sum_{i=1}^{3} \alpha_i D_i \qquad (8.10)$$

This model, too, could be expressed in autoregressive form.

Once these models have been defined, an OAS model can be made operational through simulations, based on the following steps:

- estimate the term structure and simulate the evolution of interest rates (scenario generation);
- use market rates in each scenario as the independent variables to generate a value for customer rates and volumes;
- based on these volumes and rates at time t, estimate cashflows due to interest payments, withdrawals, prepayments, new deposits and new loans; and
- if the generated cashflows look unsatisfactory (and not consistent with past history), calibrate the models' parameters until the result becomes more realistic.[46]

SCENARIO AND STRESS ANALYSIS

A stress test is a simulation exercise aimed at quantifying the effects (in our case, on liquidity) of an especially-adverse scenario. Here, we try to assess how an adverse economic environment would affect the stochastic cashflows associated with NOMALs like those discussed earlier. In fact, actual cashflows may behave quite differently, compared with a "normal" scenario, if the bank or the financial system are experiencing a crisis. As liquidity risk – like any other risk – proves especially dangerous right when unexpected, extreme (hence, unlikely) situations materialise, one bank cannot content itself with checking its liquidity gaps under normal scenarios, but instead must check by how much liquidity could deteriorate – due to indefinite-maturity items – under an unfavourable scenario.

To estimate how cashflows would behave under stressed conditions, one or more of the following approaches can be used.

- The historical approach is based on scenarios that actually occurred in the past to the bank, to other financial institutions hit by individual risk factors (including, for example, data on the share of demand deposits that were unexpectedly withdrawn within, say, two or four weeks from the first alarming news reported in the press), or to financial markets (when liquidity crises were widespread and systemic in nature).

- The statistical approach uses historical data to extract, based on a suitable set of hypotheses on the probability distribution followed by the risk factors, a reasonable estimate of the shocks (say, on deposits, haircuts, interbank loans) that would follow from a liquidity shortage.
- The judgement-based approach is based on subjective appraisals carried out by the bank's top management (possibly with the support of the risk management department, the supervisors or some outside consultants).

These approaches can be used to simulate individual risk factors separately or, more often, to build worst-case scenarios where several risk factors are shocked jointly, giving rise to extreme liquidity risks. For example, the effects of a "bank run" on demand deposits, and those of a sudden increase in market volatility that drives up haircuts on unencumbered assets can be estimated separately; alternatively, those two circumstances can be simulated jointly.

Stressed scenarios are rather intuitive in principle, but their practical implementation can prove difficult (and involve a number of arbitrary choices) for the following reasons.

First, to keep complexity at a reasonable level and to make results more readable, the stress exercise is limited to a number of selected balance-sheet items, while the remaining ones are kept unchanged. For example, the effect of an extreme scenario on the time profile of cashflows associated only with securities may be simulated, ignoring other assets and liabilities (such as customer deposits). This approach, addressing only direct effects on some specific items and ignoring other indirect effects, may make the stress test results weaker and less reliable. A market turmoil leading to higher haircuts (and hence reducing the liquidity content of eligible securities) may in fact be accompanied by an increase in customer deposits, due to the fact that investors are postponing their asset allocation choices; this interaction would reduce liquidity risk. Accordingly, indirect effects should also be included in a simulation when assessing the effects of some exogenous shock.

Second, when more risk factors are considered jointly (for example, a bank run and an increase in market volatility) a simple "algebraic" summation of their effects may not be correct. On the one hand, a scenario involving two or more joint shocks might be overly pessimistic (hence, unnecessarily conservative) if the risk factors involved are not strongly correlated; on the other hand, if two unfavourable circumstances should really occur jointly, then the impact on liquidity risk might be more than additive, as the two shocks might be mutually reinforcing. Think of a confidence crisis hitting a bank in the midst of a market-wide currency crisis. Under such a scenario, even those depositors who would have resisted the panic, and left their savings with the bank, might want to get them back to convert them into foreign currency. The pressure on deposits might therefore be stronger than it would be in a "quiet" macroeconomic environment.

Notwithstanding these limits, which can be addressed through more sophisticated simulation techniques, stressed scenarios prove quite useful in that they help the bank to plan in advance those emergency plans ("contingency funding plans", CFPs) that could be triggered if an extreme scenario should indeed take place.

A CFP surveys all possible sources of extra funds that can/must be made available in the event of a liquidity shock (for example, temporary withdrawals of compulsory reserves, repos with the central bank, secured or unsecured interbank loans and so forth[47]), also setting the priority order in which they should be tapped. Such a ranking obviously depends on the cost and flexibility of the various available sources, but also on the type of liquidity shock to be faced: in fact, while it should be possible to rely on some volume of interbank loans (say, up to the value of the eligible unencumbered securities less the haircut) in the event of an institution-specific shock, a market-wide crisis would call for immediate intervention of the central bank providing extra discount facilities. The CFP also describes in detail people and structures responsible for implementing emergency funding policies, as well as those who must communicate and explain to outsiders (such as supervisors, rating agencies and the media) what went wrong and what actions have been undertaken to return to normality.

A CFP is not only a reaction to a liquidity crisis, but in turn affects its outcome and depth. A credible CFP, enabling an early and suitable response to the claims coming from depositors and wholesale investors, can quickly bring panic under control, limiting the duration and breadth of the liquidity shortage; similarly, a plan granting access to funding sources that are adequately diversified across countries and currencies can help the bank overcome a momentary lack of funds and enable it to act as a stabiliser on a disrupted local market.

ORGANISATIONAL ISSUES

As for other risks, liquidity risk management (LRM) requires organisational rules that ensure a systematic approach. In particular, the bank's organisation structure should incorporate an LRM unit and a funds management unit. In what follows we sketch some guidelines for the construction of organisational structures and processes for LRM. Needless to say, the identification of the best organisation structure for a particular institution must take into account its specific strategic objectives, risk appetite, size, etc.

The first step involves setting up an LRM policy (Office of the Comptroller of the Currency 2001). In this respect, the board of directors plays a key role and must be fully aware of the nature and consequences of liquidity risk, its peculiarities and its technical identification, evaluation, supervision and management. The board:

- is responsible for ensuring that liquidity risk is correctly identified, defined, measured, monitored and controlled;
- defines the risk tolerance of the whole bank and consequently the strategy for LRM;
- communicates and shares the strategy within the bank; and
- identifies roles and responsibilities of the LRM unit and provides it with the human and technological resources needed to operate correctly.

Banks must not only define policies, procedures and roles, but also review them periodically or when anomalies occur. Finally, the board must receive adequate reports on the liquidity situation and additional reports when needed (that is, in case of uncommon liquidity shortages).

The senior management is responsible for developing and implementing procedures and practices that translate the board's policies into operating standards and for achieving and maintaining systems that identify, measure, monitor and manage liquidity risk.

An effective management information system is a key factor in LRM. The reports produced on a regular basis should always put the bank in a position to manage liquidity in times of stress. When a trade-off between timeliness and accuracy occurs, the decision should be based on the fact that liquidity risk spreads very quickly and may soon become irreparable. It might therefore be more important to have timely information on major cashflows than a higher degree of detail.

Some examples of reports to be produced regularly are the following:

- analysis of the flow of funds;
- contingency funding plan;
- list of the largest providers of funds;
- analysis of the funding gap and of its maturity structure;

- list of episodes in which liquidity limits were exceeded;
- evolution of the bank's reputation in the market;
- evolution of asset quality;
- structure and composition of the bank's balance sheet; and
- size and cost of the more recent very short-term funding.

As for other categories of risk, LRM involves setting limits to the risk-taking units. These limits are subject to revision in case of changes in market conditions or in the bank's risk tolerance. They may involve indicators such as: the absolute maturity gap, the volume of overnight funding in relation to total assets; the gap between liquid assets and short-term liabilities; the amount of liquid and cashable assets net of the expected erosion in the event of stress; the concentration of liabilities across counterparties.

The internal audit department plays a crucial role in the LRM process. It is responsible for developing appropriate guidelines for the verification of the main aspects associated with liquidity risk: the conditions of the systems dedicated to LRM, the degree of consistency between the policies set by the senior management and day-by-day risk management, the adequacy of the processes followed and the soundness of the measures used, as well as of the policies to be implemented in case of crisis.

The ALM Committee (ALCO) includes representatives of all the business areas that affect liquidity risk and is responsible for establishing specific policies for LRM, ensuring that the measurement systems are adequate to identify and quantify the bank's liquidity risk and that the reporting systems convey accurate and relevant information about the level and origins of such risk (both on individual transactions and at the portfolio level, either on existing or on new products).

The LRM unit is responsible for identifying liquidity risks incurred by the bank, the methods for evaluating and monitoring the evolution of its liquidity profile, the policies for controlling and mitigating liquidity risk and the factors that may influence it. It also has to develop appropriate rules for LRM and to disseminate them within the organisational units and functions that can generate liquidity risk.[48] An important task of the LRM unit is to develop a liquidity contingency plan. This must comprise a clear definition of the circumstances that identify a crisis, the procedures for the release of "official information" about the crisis and the powers and responsibilities of the various subjects involved. The LRM unit is involved in the development of new products and provides consulting services and training. It is responsible for mitigating liquidity risk, and steps in with corrective actions in the event of risk-limit breaches.

The actual configuration of the LRM unit depends on the size, operating characteristics and complexity of the bank. Banks that rely extensively on wholesale funding must have comparatively more sophisticated measurement systems than traditional banks.

Particular attention should be paid to the liquidity management within banking groups: a correct analysis of the liquidity position must be carried out both on a consolidated basis (given the speed and ease with which liquidity spreads between subjects) and for individual banks.

An important role is also played by early warnings (internal and external), that is by events that signal liquidity shortages in advance, or with a very short delay. In case one or more indicators trigger an alert, an additional monitoring can be started, causes be investigated, the alarm spread to other units, and possibly a state of crisis be declared. Internal early warnings may include the following (Office of the Comptroller of the Currency 2001): increased concentration of assets or liabilities; reduction of asset quality and decline of profits; a rapid increase of assets financed by volatile funding. Examples of external indicators are: market rumours about the soundness of the bank; downgrades; requests for clarification from customers; sharp decline in the price of the shares (for listed banks); increase in the spread paid by the bank in the money market; increase in the trading volume of securities issued by the bank; drop in funding opportunities or increase in requests for guarantees; increase in the cost of funding; request for (additional) collateral by counterparties; reluctance by brokers to expose the name of the bank; reduction in the lines of credit by corresponding banks; reduction in the number of counterparties willing to trade with the bank; increased number of refusals; abandonment of the bank by counterparties sensitive to creditworthiness; reduction in the availability of long-term contracts; requests for early repayment; deterioration of key indicators (such as loans on deposits; short-term liabilities on total assets; liquidity available; increased dependence on wholesale funding).

The Basel Committee (Basel Committee on Banking Supervision 2000) has issued 14 principles (sound practices) for LRM. These comprise (see Table 8.1 for a summary): organisational measures (development of a structure for the management of liquidity; anticipation of emergency plans; systems for internal controls); measurement issues (systems for measuring and monitoring liquidity needs); management of market access, management of currency liquidity needs; role of transparency and of supervisors in the process of liquidity risk control.

Table 8.1 Liquidity risk management principles

Area	N.	Content
Developing a structure for managing liquidity	1	Each bank should have an agreed strategy for the day-to-day management of liquidity. This strategy should be communicated throughout the organisation.
	2	A bank's board of directors should approve the strategy and significant policies related to the management of liquidity. The board should also ensure that senior management take the steps necessary to monitor and control liquidity risk. The board should be informed regularly of the liquidity situation of the bank and immediately if there are any material changes in the bank's current or prospective liquidity position.
	3	Each bank should have a management structure in place to execute effectively the liquidity strategy. This structure should include the ongoing involvement of members of senior management. Senior management must ensure that liquidity is effectively managed, and that appropriate policies and procedures are established to control and limit liquidity risk. Banks should set and regularly review limits on the size of their liquidity positions over particular time horizons.
	4	A bank must have adequate information systems for measuring, monitoring, controlling and reporting liquidity risk. Reports should be provided on a timely basis to the bank's board of directors, senior management and other appropriate personnel.
Measuring and monitoring net funding requirements	5	Each bank should establish a process for the ongoing measurement and monitoring of net funding requirements.
	6	A bank should analyse liquidity utilising a variety of "what if" scenarios.
	7	A bank should review frequently the assumptions utilised in managing liquidity to determine that they continue to be valid.
Managing market access	8	Each bank should periodically review its efforts to establish and maintain relationships with liability holders, to maintain the diversification of liabilities, and aim to ensure its capacity to sell assets.

Contingency planning	9	A bank should have contingency plans in place that address the strategy for handling liquidity crises and include procedures for making up cashflow shortfalls in emergency situations.
Foreign currency liquidity management	10	Each bank should have a measurement, monitoring and control system for its liquidity positions in the major currencies in which it is active. In addition to assessing its aggregate foreign currency liquidity needs and the acceptable mismatch in combination with its domestic currency commitments, a bank should also undertake separate analysis of its strategy for each currency individually.
	11	Subject to the analysis undertaken according to Principle 10, a bank should, where appropriate, set and regularly review limits on the size of its cashflow mismatches over particular time horizons for foreign currencies in aggregate and for each significant individual currency in which the bank operates.
Internal controls for LRM	12	Each bank must have an adequate system of internal controls over its LRM process. A fundamental component of the internal control system involves regular independent reviews and evaluations of the effectiveness of the system and, where necessary, ensuring that appropriate revisions or enhancements to internal controls are made. The results of such reviews should be available to supervisory authorities.
Role of public disclosure in improving liquidity	13	Each bank should have in place a mechanism for ensuring that there is an adequate level of disclosure of information about the bank in order to manage public perception of the organisation and its soundness.
Role of supervisors	14	Supervisors should conduct an independent evaluation of a bank's strategies, policies, procedures and practices related to the management of liquidity. Supervisors should require that a bank has an effective system in place to measure, monitor and control liquidity risk. Supervisors should obtain from each bank sufficient and timely information with which to evaluate its level of liquidity risk and should ensure that the bank has adequate liquidity contingency plans.

Source: Basel Committee on Banking Supervision, 2000.

APPENDIX: REASONS FOR TRADING AND TRANSACTION COSTS

Some introductory notions of financial market microstructure may be useful to understand the causes of transaction costs, ie one of the key determinants of market liquidity risk.[49]

Traders act either for liquidity (that is to invest/divest) or for information reasons (that is, to exploit inefficiencies in the market price). The fundamental distinction is between:

- motives that are exogenous to trading, where the investment/disinvestment resulting from the trade is just a tool to achieve further objectives (for example, to transfer resources in time and space, to cover risks); and
- motives that are endogenous to trading, in which case the outcome of the trading (to earn a profit) coincides with the very objective of the trade.

In the former case, trading – carried out by liquidity traders – is utilitarian; in the latter, trading is speculative, and is put in place by informed traders who trade because they believe that by doing so they can earn profits.[50]

In order to understand the origin of transaction costs, the behaviour of the market maker should be focused on, who, ontologically, has to remain in the market and thus has to develop effective "survival strategies".

The market maker has a "preferred position" in terms of the inventory of securities and liquidity held, and tends to adapt his bid and ask prices in order to achieve that preferred position. Consequently, when the stock of securities in inventory tends to grow above the desired level, the market maker lowers both the bid and the ask prices (to avoid receiving further sale orders and to foster a gradual liquidation of the securities), until the desired level is achieved, and, when the inventory size is deemed too small, the opposite happens.

In this context, the inventory position of the market maker depends on the flow of orders on a given security and not on the true value attached to it by the market maker. Quoted bid and ask prices are not affected by the market maker's expectations about the fair price of the security, as they assume that the market "is right" (or, more simply, that it might be too expensive to go "against the market").[51] The behaviour of the market maker is summarised in Figure 8.6: the flow of orders (in this case, sell orders) from market participants does not change the market maker's assessment of the fundamental value of the security (which is the same in Sections A and B of the figure); they move the bid and ask prices only in order to have their inventory rebalanced.

Given that trading is generated both by liquidity and by information motives, a market maker must expect to trade both with liquidity and with informed traders. Inventory considerations must then be complemented by information considerations. The informed traders (who always make a profit) trade only when the prices quoted by the market maker are informationally inefficient.[52] Therefore they are willing to trade more (in terms of frequency and volume) the farther the price quoted by the market maker from the equilibrium value.[53] This increase in trading activity in turn signals to the market makers that their quotes are not informationally efficient; accordingly, they react promptly, updating quotes based on the order flow, that is, increasing (reducing) prices when buy (sale) orders arrive. In fact, when buy (sale) orders prevail, the market makers learn that their quoted prices underestimate (overestimate) the true value of the security (see Figure

Figure 8.6 The dynamics of bid–ask prices and inventory position

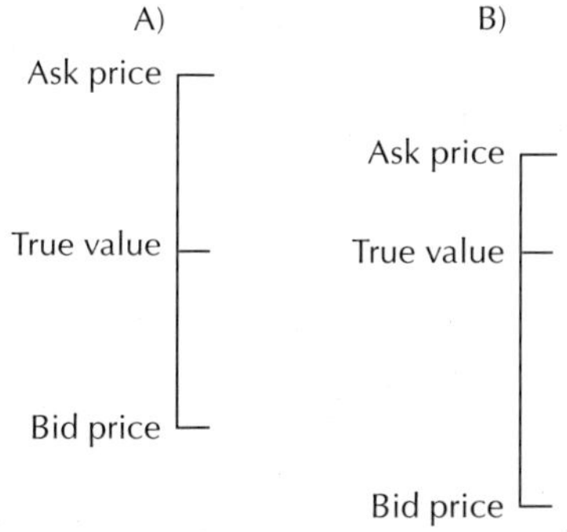

Figure 8.7 The dynamics of bid–ask prices and the information content of the order flow

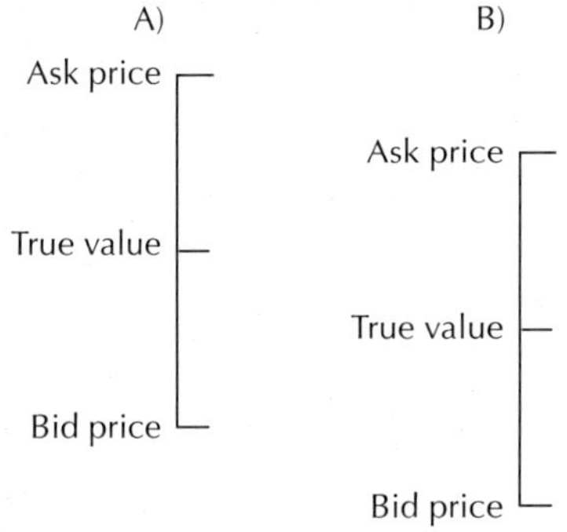

8.7). Unlike in Figure 8.6, bid and ask prices change because the market maker has changed their views about the fundamental value of the security (identified by the midquote).

1 See Chapter 11.
2 In this chapter we focus mainly on liquidity arising from trades, that is, on the so-called "artificial liquidity". "Natural liquidity", instead, arises from the fact that a security comes to its final maturity and therefore is paid back by the issuer.
3 The concept of liquidity is different from that of immediacy, which means that a trade at fixed prices can take place immediately.
4 "Liquidity is difficult to define and even more difficult to measure. Of the several dimensions of market liquidity, the two most important are tightness and depth. Tightness is a market's ability to match supply and demand at low cost (measured by bid–offer spreads). Market depth relates to the ability of a market to absorb large trade flows without a significant impact on prices (approximated by volumes, quote sizes, and the amount of liquidity available at the best spreads). A liquid market would exhibit "tight" bid–ask spreads, high volumes and little deterioration in the price or bid-offer spread as orders are filled beyond the best available price" (Persaud, 2007).
5 The Joint Forum (2006). Market liquidity risk is also known as asset risk or product risk, while funding risk is sometimes called cashflow risk (Jorion 2003).
6 In other words, "a fire-sale of assets can lead to severe market turmoil, if a sizeable amount of assets needs to be sold to overcome a liquidity shortage and market demand is not perfectly elastic. This links the liquidity of individual institutions to market liquidity" (European Central Bank 2007).
7 The crisis of Continental Illinois, in 1984, is a nice example of crisis due to individual circumstances. Having invested heavily in loans to oil and gas companies, the bank experienced increasing difficulties in raising funds on the domestic market, especially because of rumours spreading after another bank (Penn Square) had defaulted because of a similar industry mix. Funds were then raised on the wholesale international markets (mostly in Japan) underestimating the risk that, once the rumours on Continental would spread to those markets, lenders would quickly claim back their loans. After getting claims for reimbursements of about US$6 billion in 10 days (Crouhy, Galai and Mark 2006), the bank could survive only thanks to the prompt intervention of US supervisors.
8 In 1998, following the Russian financial crisis, investors moved their asset allocation towards "core" markets (mainly towards US and German T-bonds), while selling securities issued in emerging countries and corporate bonds. These asset classes therefore became more difficult and costly to liquidate; furthermore, the decrease in their market value caused banks to ask for extra margins from all borrowers that had pledged those securities as collateral against loans. This was the market setting which led to the default of Long Term Capital Management, a hedge fund that had bet on the convergence in yields between core markets and emerging markets.
9 As stated in 2004 by Paul Sharma, head of department at the UK Financial Services Authority, "We have been heavily engaged in negotiating and implementing the reforms to the regulation of credit, market and operational risk in Basle II … These reforms have been based on years of detailed work. A vast literature, both regulatory and academic, exists on these risks. In sharp contrast almost no attention has been given to liquidity risk."
10 The ability to liquidate positions at current market value is the main rationale behind market-price accounting, set by standards such as IAS 39 and by market practices based on the mark-to-market criterion.
11 A market is defined deep if there are orders at prices higher and lower than the current one, wide if such orders are of considerable size and resilient if price changes (transitory

volatility) due to the asynchrony in the order flow (order imbalance) quickly prompt new orders that revert the stock price to equilibrium values.

12 In some cases, funding liquidity risk originates from a generalised turmoil in the markets, and in such cases it qualifies as systemic risk.

13 To understand the causes of transaction costs, it may be useful to recall some topics of market microstructure theory; see the Appendix.

14 Implicit costs mainly affect large transactions. Retail trades cause neither market impact nor opportunity costs, as they are usually performed within a single transaction.

15 This is usually measured as a percentage of the mid-quote. The quoted bid–ask spread, however, tends to overestimate the real transaction cost for several reasons. First, many transactions are executed, in quote-driven markets, within the quoted bid and ask prices (as market makers can improve their quotations, at the request of the counterparty, when the deal is made); second, bid and ask prices tend to move as a result of trades being carried out, since a buy- (sell-) initiated trade tends to move up (down) both the bid and the ask price (regardless of the spread). For this reason, a round-trip transaction made of a purchase followed by a sale tends to be less expensive than indicated by the bid and ask prices quoted when the trade was initiated (as the purchase moves the price in a favourable way for the following sale).

16 Mid-quote, or mid-price, is the average between the best bid price and the best ask price.

17 The order execution strategy is based on the trader's utility function, which depends on the (total) cost incurred to liquidate the position.

18 Note that the real opportunity cost may be lower when considered dynamically (Keim and Madhavan 1998). The price movement can induce investors to reconsider the size and desirability of the transaction originally planned. For example, a trader who witnesses a price reduction while gradually executing their sale order could decide to stop it or to reduce it to a smaller quantity. Finally, the opportunity cost may not necessarily be harmful for the trader: if the probability of market price increases and decreases are equally likely, the expected opportunity cost could be deemed equal to zero.

19 The function $S(t, x)$ in Figure 8.2 describes the transaction price at time t for a volume x ($x>0$ for a purchase and $x<0$ for a sale while $x = 0$ represents the marginal trade). $S(t, 0)$ is therefore the classic transaction price, which suffers from no impact on the market. The supply curve of the security is positively inclined: when x rises, $S(t, x)$ rises as well, consistently with the informational asymmetry approach: the market responds to large transactions (potentially affected by informational asymmetry) showing increasing sell prices and decreasing buy prices.

20 The marginal trade is defined as an infinitely small one. Hence, the price of the marginal trade is shown in the figure as $S(\tau, 0)$, where τ (that is, 0 or t) is the moment when the price is observed and 0 is the amount to be traded. For finite values x of the amount (positive or negative depending on whether there is a purchase or a sale), an actual liquidity supply curve must be considered, see also Acerbi and Scandolo (2008).

21 Contrary to what Figure 8.2 suggests, liquidity supply curves may not be symmetric. In particular, in a disrupted market, increased liquidity demand may face steeper curves than increased supply.

22 However, the accuracy becomes progressively less acceptable as the market faces liquidity shortages (given the role played by opportunity costs).

23 For instance, the market for high-risk securities, such as structured securities, is normally thin, whereas the market for low-risk securities, such as Treasury bonds, tends to be wide and deep.

24 This is the case of high liquidity risk and low market risk; for instance, when low-risk securities are held in huge amounts, compared with the overall market size, and this causes a high potential impact on the liquidation price.

25 Empirical spread distributions (unlike return distributions) have shapes that differ significantly from known statistical distributions (Bangia *et al* 1999), and often are multi-modal.

26 The measure proposed by Dowd (2000), since it assumes a process of decay of the cost when the holding period lengthens, does not take into account the execution risk (opportunity cost).

27 Transaction costs measure the difference in the level of liquidity, not the liquidity risk.

28 We use the word "cashable" here, rather than "sellable", to emphasise that such assets are often turned into cash without a proper sale, but rather, serving as collateral for new loans.

29 See the section titled "Scenario and stress analysis".

30 Note that those indicators may look similar, at first sight, to the "gaps" used in the measurement of interest rate risk (see Chapter 10); however, when sorting assets and liabilities across time bands, we are considering cashflows (not stocks) and their actual expected maturity (not their repricing period, as is the case with interest rate risk).

31 Repurchase agreements (repos) are contracts whereby one party (A) sells a security to another one (B) while undertaking to repurchase it at a future date (usually, after a few months or days) at a fixed price (the sale price plus accrued interest). The European Central Bank provides liquidity to large financial institutions through repos, for which a wide array of low-risk securities (eligible securities) can be used.

32 In order to facilitate the comparison between different time periods and different banks the liquidity gap measures can be expressed in percentage of total assets or third-party liabilities, giving rise to gap ratios (Financial Services Authority 2003).

33 That seems to be the case for about two-thirds of the banks surveyed in European Central Bank (2007).

34 In fact, in some EU Member States' deposits with non-residents are subject to reserve requirements even if they are provided to a bank by its parent company; furthermore, loans issued by the parent company may be included in the computation of "large exposures" as defined by directive 92/121. For more details, see European Central Bank (2007).

35 The complexity of the problem often implies that their solution is based on numerous assumptions (often "nested") and this implies that banks (often somewhat unconsciously) expose themselves to model risk. The error due to model risk is also often amplified by hedging policies decided on the basis of incorrect models.

36 It is a well-known fact (see also Chapter 10) that interest rates charged by banks on assets and liabilities vary less frequently than market rates, and in an asymmetric way.

37 This liquidity is essential in models based on replication portfolios. The ability to compose replication portfolios is closely linked with the ability to buy and sell securities at any time.

38 Obviously, such a buffer cannot cope with extreme changes in the available amounts, but only with "normal" fluctuations.

39 An example of a linear function may be (Bardenhewer 2007)

$$V_t = \beta_0 + \beta_1 \Delta_t + \sum_i k_i (r_{i,t} - \bar{r}_i) + \delta \cdot (cr_t - \overline{cr}) + \varepsilon_t$$

where i represents maturity buckets, V_{ti} the total volume at time t, $r_{i,t}$ the market interest rate with maturity i observed at time t, $\bar{r}_i$ the average interest rate for maturity i in the valuation period, cr_t the rate applied to customers at time t, $\overline{cr}$ the average rate to customers during the valuation period, Δt the time elapsed between 0 and t, β, k e δ are parameters to be estimated. The same variables can be used to fit squared or exponential functions, respectively

$$V_t = \beta_0 + \beta_1 \Delta_t^2 + \sum_i k_i (r_{i,t} - \bar{r}_i) + \delta \cdot (cr_t - \overline{cr}) + \varepsilon_t$$

and

$$V_t = \beta_0 + e^{\beta_1 \Delta_t} + \sum_i k_i (r_{i,t} - \bar{r}_i) + \delta \cdot (cr_t - \overline{cr}) + \varepsilon_t$$

40 For example, market interest rates could be modelled based on Vasicek or Cox–Ingersoll–Ross models approaches; customer rates can be modelled assuming discrete and asymmetric changes, to account for their usual stickiness; volumes can be modelled based on volumes at t-1, a time trend as well as current and past interest rates.

41 The model of the term structure of returns affects all other stochastic variables: market interest rates, customer rates and volumes.

42 Constraints usually include some "sanity checks" (for example, the volume of a transaction cannot exceed the amount available at any time *t*; the sum of all positions in the replication portfolio equals the volume of the normal). There may also be limits on the volumes associated with some individual dates (concentration limits).

43 The number of transactions (Frauendorfer and Schurle 2007) may be affected by the fact that volumes to be traded at each maturity are split into several tranches, priced at increasing spreads, to account for their market impact.

44 As risk is asymmetrical, a skewed risk measure is used instead of variance.

45 The money held on a current-account deposit, in fact, is only partially intended as an investment, while most of it is held for liquidity/precautionary reasons.

46 Parameter calibration for customer rates and volumes requires the availability of reliable internal data, which could be more or less detailed in practice (for example, broad product categories such as mortgage loans, deposits and overdrafts, rather than data on individual product lines).

47 Available funding channels may also include he so-called "tri-party repurchase agreements", that is, repos on securities that were previously left with a third party (guaranteeing the loan and ensuring that the collateral is really available). Such schemes save the time and costs due to the delivery of the securities, while reassuring the lender, as the borrower does not remain in possession of the collateral.

48 The rules for the management of liquidity risk should specify, at least: roles, responsibilities and organisational structure for the management of liquidity risk; criteria for identifying and reporting the factors that may give rise to liquidity risk; criteria for evaluating the liquidity risk and for its monitoring; limits to liquidity risk; policies and formats for reporting to senior management.

49 See Harris (2003) and O'Hara (1995) for a more thorough treatment.

50 Superiority in the information set, however acquired, is in any case the only way to trade systematically with a profit. It may result from a superior analysis of public information (for speculators), from a more prompt reaction to the news (headline traders), from price-sensitive private information (insider traders), from opportunistic behaviour allowed by some special position (parasitic traders and order anticipators), or even by forged information (manipulators, bluffers).

51 The market maker moves thus in the Keynesian logic according to which, "markets can remain irrational longer, more than you can remain solvent".

52 That is when the market maker's quoted prices do not contain all the relevant information.

53 Value of equilibrium, which, by definition, they know, being informed traders.

REFERENCES

Acerbi, C. and G. Scandolo, 2008, "Liquidity Risk Theory and Coherent Measures of Risk", *Risk*, forthcoming.

Acharya, V.V. and L. H. Pedersen, 2005, "Asset Pricing with Liquidity Risk", *Journal of Financial Economics* pp. 375–410.

Amihud Y. and H. Mendelson, 1988, "Liquidity, volatility, and Exchange Automation", *Journal of Accounting, Auditing and Finance*, pp. 369–95

Arnott, R. D. and W. H. Wagner, 1990, "The Measurement and Control of Trading Costs", *Financial Analysts Journal*, November/December, pp. 73–80.

Bangia, A. ***et al*****,** 1999, "Modelling Liquidity Risk, With Implications for Traditional Market Risk Measurement and Management", Working Paper, 99–06, Wharton School, Philadelphia.

Bardenhewer, M. M., 2007, "Modeling Non-maturing Products", in di L. Matz and P. Neu, *Liquidity Risk. Measurement and Management. A practitioner's guide to global best practices* (Chichester: John Wiley & Sons).

Basel Committee on Banking Supervision, 2000, "Sound Practices for Managing Liquidity in Banking Organisations" mimeo, Bank for International Settlements.

Brunnermeier, M. K. and L. H. Pedersen, 2006, "Market Liquidity and Funding Liquidity", Working Paper.

Chordia, T., R. Roll and A. Subrahmanyam, 2000, "Commonality in liquidity", *Journal of Financial Economics* 56, pp. 3–28.

Crouhy, M., D. Galai and R Mark, 2000, *Risk Management* (New York: McGraw-Hill).

Crouhy, M., D. Galai and R. Mark, 2006, *The Essentials of Risk Management* (New York: McGraw-Hill).

de Jong, F. and J. Driessen, 2005, "Liquidity Risk Premia in Corporate Bond Markets", Working Paper, Tilburg University.

Dowd, K., 2002, *Measuring Market Risk* (Chichester: John Wiley & Sons).

Engle, R., R. Ferstenberg and J. Russell, 2006, "Measuring and Modeling Execution Cost and Risk", Working Paper.

European Central Bank, 2007, "EU Banking Structures", European Central Bank, Frankfurt.

Financial Services Authority, 2003, "Liquidity risk in the Integrated Prudential sourcebook: a quantitative framework", Discussion Paper 24, FSA, London.

Frauendorfer, K. and M. Schurle, 2007, "Dynamic Modeling and Optimisation of Non-maturing Accounts", in di L. Matz and P. Neu (eds), *Liquidity Risk: Measurement and Management: A practitioner's guide to global best practices* (New York: John Wiley & Sons).

Harris, L., 2003, *Trading and Exchanges. Market Microstructure for Practitioners* (New York: Oxford University Press).

Institute of International Finance, 2007, *Principles of Liquidity Risk Management* (Washington: Institute of International Finance).

Jarrow, R. A., 2005, "Liquidity Risk and Classical Option Pricing Theory", Working Paper.

Jarrow, R. A. and D. R. van Deventer, 1998, "The arbitrage-free valuation and hedging of demand deposits and credit card loans", *Journal of Banking and Finance* 22, pp. 249–72.

Joint Forum, 2006, "The Management of Liquidity Risk in Financial Groups" (Basel: Bank for International Settlements).

Jorion, P., 2003, *Financial Risk Manager Handbook* (New York: John Wiley & Sons).

Keim, D. B. and A. Madhavan, 1998, "The Cost of Institutional Equity Trades", *Financial Analysts Journal*.

Matz, L. and P. Neu, 2007, *Liquidity Risk. Measurement and Management: A practitioner's guide to global best practices* (Chichester: John Wiley & Sons).

O'Hara, M., 1995, *Market Microstructure Theory* (Cambridge, MA: Blackwell Publishing).

Office of the Comptroller of the Currency, 2001, *Liquidity Comptroller's Handbook* (Washington, DC: mimeo).

Persaud, A. D., 2003, *Liquidity Black Holes, Understanding, Quantifying and Managing Financial Liquidity Risk* (London: Risk Books).

Persaud, A. D., 2007, *Improving efficiency in the European Government Bond Market* (London: Intelligence Capital).

Resti, A. and A. Sironi, 2008, *Risk Management and Shareholders' Value in Banking* (Chichester: John Wiley & Sons).

9

Portfolio Theory in Illiquid Markets

Carlo Acerbi
Abaxbank

MOTIVATIONS AND OBJECTIVES

Liquidity risk is one of the most fundamental and ubiquitous characteristics of financial markets and yet, one for which no consensus mathematical formalisation has ever been achieved. If it is true that financial professionals understand liquidity risk in all of its aspects and that they also know how to manage it successfully in most circumstances, it is nevertheless true that a satisfactory quantitative approach to liquidity risk within modern portfolio theory is still missing. The mathematical notation we commonly use to handle portfolios and describe their risks and returns is not rich enough to allow us even to just formulate most of the problems we face every day when managing liquidity risk. And worse than this, the usual notation of portfolio theory, as we will try to show below, betrays hidden assumptions of perfect liquidity, proving therefore unappropriate in the general case when liquidity risk is not negligible at all. As a matter of fact, to date, liquidity risk management to a large extent is still a qualitative discipline whose scarce quantitative tools do not seem to emerge from a truly integrated risk-theoretical framework.

In this chapter we present the approach recently taken in Acerbi and Scandolo (2007) where instead of introducing *ad hoc* "liquidity risk measures" in the notation of ordinary portfolio theory, a new more general formalism for portfolio theory itself is defined, reconsidering the most basic concepts (such as asset, portfolio, value, price, risk, ...) and extending their notation to the case when the market is not perfectly liquid. In doing this, we will discover that some of the most primitive relationships among these concepts that we had always taken for granted, turn out to be wrong in the general illiquid case, unveiling a richer picture where liquidity risk finds a natural formalisation. And we will also discover that once this generalisation has been made, there is no need to introduce specific "liquidity risk measures" at all, as the effects of liquidity risk will automatically be captured by traditional measures of risk and reward in an integrated scheme.

When physicists describe the mechanics of a system, before studying its dynamics (which is the list of hypotheses they make on the forces acting on the system plus the study of their effects on its degrees of freedom) they need to clarify first its kinematics (which is nothing but the preliminary definition of the geometry of the system, of all its relevant degrees of freedom and of the constraints that bound them irrespectively of the forces that will be hypothesised). Borrowing this analogy from physics, we can say that to extend portfolio theory from the liquid to the general illiquid case, we will not yet make a new dynamics, but just a new kinematics, describing meticulously the variables that need to be considered and their interplay. And in fact, we will make no hypotheses at all on the dynamics of the market, leaving complete freedom to anybody who will want to make models out of what here is nothing but a formalism. The very fact that we do not make hypotheses, will give this approach wide generality.

Depending on the context, liquidity risk is sometimes understood as only one of the following three distinct phenomena,

1. Portfolio liquidity risk: the possibility that a portfolio runs dry of liquidity (cash money) necessary for the settlement of due payments
2. Market liquidity risk: the fact that the depth of prices is limited, so that a trade in a given asset for a given size hits second-best prices or turns out to be even unfeasible because the market is too shallow.
3. Systemic liquidity risk: the risk of drainage of the liquidity circulating in the whole economy

which are the major concerns of treasurers, portfolio managers and central bankers respectively. Liquidity risk is not simply one of these separate phenomena. It is a complex and somehow intangible reality which manifests itself through these phenomena altogether. Hence when we speak of liquidity risk, we will mean any situation in which either of the above eventualities are not assumed to be impossible *a priori*. And it is clear from what we have outlined in this section that we will not be satisfied with a descriptive model addressing only one of the above aspects separately. We have on the contrary the ambition to set up a unified language allowing us to formalise these issues altogether.

A foreword on the style adopted is in order. We tried to do our best to convey the financial insight to a wider audience still keeping a formally precise technical language. We deliberately skipped all technical proofs that can be found in Acerbi and Scandolo (2007). We added several concrete examples to illustrate the most important concepts instead.

TWO FUNDAMENTAL OBSERVATIONS

In this section we discuss two distinct observations that will turn out to be fundamental both in showing that the formalism of portfolio theory is unfit to describe liquidity risk and in giving us precious hints for building a more appropriate formalism.

A portfolio is a set, not a sum

We all know that a portfolio **p** is essentially a set whose elements are assets (ie, contracts, securities, goods, … exchanged on the market at a standardised size) A_i ($i = 1, \ldots, n$) each appearing with some multiplicity w_i. Portfolio theory however, does not use for portfolios a set notation such as

$$\mathbf{p} = \left\{ \underbrace{A_1, \ldots, A_1}_{w_1}, \underbrace{A_2, \ldots, A_2}_{w_2}, \ldots, \underbrace{A_n, \ldots, A_n}_{w_n} \right\}$$

but rather a notation such as

$$\mathbf{p} = \sum_{i=1}^{n} w_i A_i \qquad (9.1)$$

that is clearly an algebraic relation among the value of the portfolio and the values of its assets. In other words in portfolio theory we do not write that "a portfolio is a set containing its assets", but we rather write that "a portfolio is the sum of its assets", confusing formal objects (assets and portfolios) with their values. The union set operation among portfolios is implicitly identified with the algebraic operation of summation of their values.

We have seen Equation 9.1 so many times that it may seem harmless and even obvious. Such a relation is instead not at all necessary nor obvious. On the contrary it is pregnant with precise consequences and we will realise that it is simply meaningless in the presence of liquidity risk. Validity of 9.1 requires in fact the following assumption

- that there exists a unique value A_i to assign to the asset i

and bears the following consequences

- that portfolios live in a vector space spanned by assets
- that the "value" is a linear function in the space of portfolios.

We know however that in the presence of liquidity risk, markets display multiple prices for any given asset depending on the trade size and side (bid or ask). Hence, the assumption of the existence of a unique value A_i for every asset i is compatible only with an assumption of perfect liquidity of the market. In the presence of liquidity risk, assets do not have any definite value, and consequently we can not assume that the value of a portfolio is simply given by Equation 9.1. In fact, we soon realise that in the presence of liquidity risk we do not know what is the value of a portfolio at all.

The lesson we learn is that in a general illiquid situation, assets and portfolios will need to be kept as distinct concepts which no more live in the same vector space. An asset will be only characterised by a list of multiple prices quoted by market participants through supply and demand, but it will not possess any definite value. Portfolios on the contrary are not in general traded on the market and so they have no price, but they will be assigned a value, which however needs not be necessarily a linear function in the vector space of portfolios. Among other things, we also learn that in an appropriate formalism for liquidity risk, a portfolio $\mathbf{p}$ and its value $V(\mathbf{p})$ need to be considered as well distinct notions with different notations.

A hidden variable: the liquidity policy

The second important point we want to make is the following. We argue that both the liquidity risk and the value of a given portfolio can not be just a function of its assets. They must also depend on what the owner of the portfolio needs to do with it.

An example may help. Consider a portfolio $\mathbf{p}$ made of long-term very illiquid bonds (ie, traded on a very shallow market) quoting around par with face value of US$1 million. Now suppose the two distinct cases a) that $\mathbf{p}$ is held by Alan, a very rich man with other liquid assets for hundreds of million US dollars and small debts to repay and b) that the same $\mathbf{p}$ represents the total portfolio owned by a person, Ben, who has a lot of debts (say half a million) to pay back in the short term. Is $\mathbf{p}$ worth the same value for Alan and Ben?

Alan can afford to hold portfolio $\mathbf{p}$ until maturity, because he does not need to liquidate it on the market. Ben, on the contrary, will be forced to liquidate large portions of $\mathbf{p}$ experiencing (with pain) its illiquidity. We can fairly say that $\mathbf{p}$ is completely liquidity-risk-free for Alan while it bears significative liquidity risk for Ben.

Notice that the argument applies not only to the risk but also to the value of **p**. Alan can reasonably claim that his **p** is worth US$1 million, while Ben will soon discover that this is not the case for him, as the proceedings of forced sudden liquidation will bring in much less that the face value, and he should better be prepared for that right now. Alan would never sell **p** for much less than US$1 million while Ben could find it convenient to accept, say, a bid of US$800,000 spot cash for the whole portfolio (see Example 9.8).

When a function (here the liquidity risk or the value) assumes two different values on the same argument (here **p**) there must be a 'hidden variable that we are not considering. The hidden variable here is what we will call the "liquidity policy" ($\mathcal{L}$) to which the portfolio **p** is subject, and that turns out to be very different in the two cases of Alan and Ben. We will describe the different asset-liability situation of Alan and Ben by means of their respective liquidity policies, and we will say that Ben's portfolio is subject to a more restrictive liquidity policy than Alan's.

The valuation of a portfolio and the assessment of its risk in the presence of liquidity risk will therefore necessarily be also a function of some new formal concept $\mathcal{L}$ representing the liquidity policy to which the portfolio is subject. The appropriate definition of such a formal concept is maybe the most subtle step to take, and will represent the cornerstone of the formalism.

THE GENERAL FORMALISM

We set up the general formalism for portfolio theory in the presence of liquidity risk. Keeping in mind the observations raised earlier we will introduce formal definitions for basic objects that avoid any assumption of perfect liquidity, and describe the complexity of illiquid markets in full detail.

Assets

An asset A is any object quoted on the market through bid and offer prices. We assume that one unit (or contract) of an asset corresponds to a standardised amount (eg, one lot of a future, one stock, US$100 notional of a bond or of a swap, one ounce of gold, ...). In general many bid prices and many offer prices will be quoted simultaneously for the same asset at a given time, and each of these prices will be characterised by a maximum size bidded or offered. At time t therefore, the information structure characterising an asset is not only a single real number (the "value") and not even two real numbers (the bid and the offer prices), but the whole list of all bid and offer prices each one associated to a given maximum size. The only assump-

Table 9.1 A hypothetical list of prices for an asset

	Offer				Bid			
Price (US$)	100.90	100.50	100.30	**100.25**	**100.10**	100.00	99.75	99.55
Size (number of contracts)	1	5	2	4	2	7	2	5

tion we make is the natural no-arbitrage requirement that any bid price is lower than any offer price. An example of such a data structure is given in Table 9.1 where prices have been conventionally sorted in decreasing order. As a consequence, the best bid (offer) price turns out to be the leftmost bid (respectively rightmost offer), printed in bold.

We assume that when a trade is executed, best prices are exploited first, until the target size of the trade is reached. For instance in our example, selling 10 assets on the market we will receive $100.10 \times 2 + 100.00 \times 7 + 99.75 \times 1 =$ US\$999.95 while buying 10 assets we will pay $100.25 \times 4 + 100.30 \times 2 + 100.50 \times 4 =$ US\$1003.60. The market may display a limited "depth". In this example more than $2 + 7 + 2 + 5 = 16$ assets can not be sold and more than $4 + 2 + 5 + 1 = 12$ assets can not be bought.

The market information of an asset at a given time can be summarised by a single function that we call marginal supply-demand curve (MSDC). To build such a function consider a real variable s. A trade of size s will conventionally represent a sale of s units of the asset if $s > 0$ or a purchase of $|s|$ units if $s < 0$. The MSDC function $s \to m(s)$ will then be defined as the last (hence the word "marginal" in MSDC) price hit in a trade of size s and will therefore correspond to some bid or offer price depending on whether s is positive or negative. The MSDC built with the prices of the previous example is shown in Table 9.2 and plotted in Figure 9.1. In this case it is a piecewise constant function. This is always the case, by construction, when all the prices are quoted for a finite size. For modelling purposes, we will also consider general decreasing MSDCs such as strictly monotonic ones

Table 9.2 The marginal supply–demand curve of the example of Table 9.1

	Offer				Bid			
$m(s)$	100.90	100.50	100.30	100.25	100.10	100.00	99.75	99.55
$s \in$	[–12,–11)	[–11,–6)	[–6,–4)	[–4,0)	(0,2]	(2,9]	(9,11]	(11,16]

Figure 9.1 The plot of the MSDC of Table 9.1

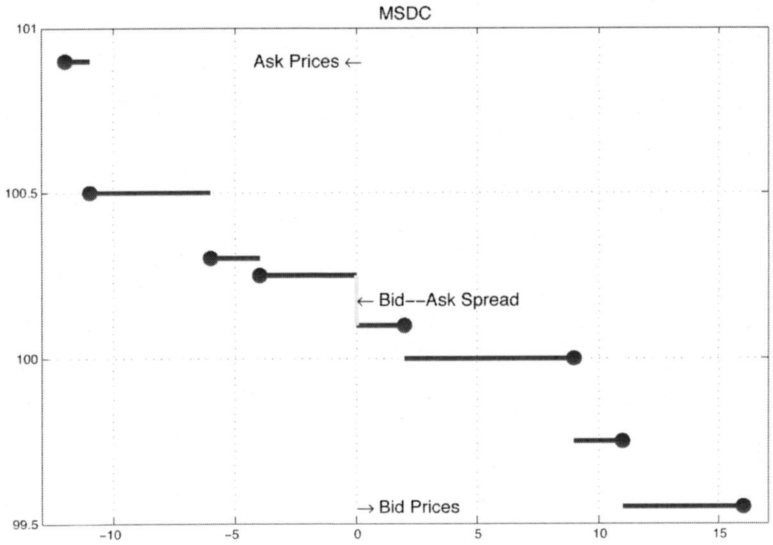

Figure 9.2 A stylised example of strictly decreasing MSDC

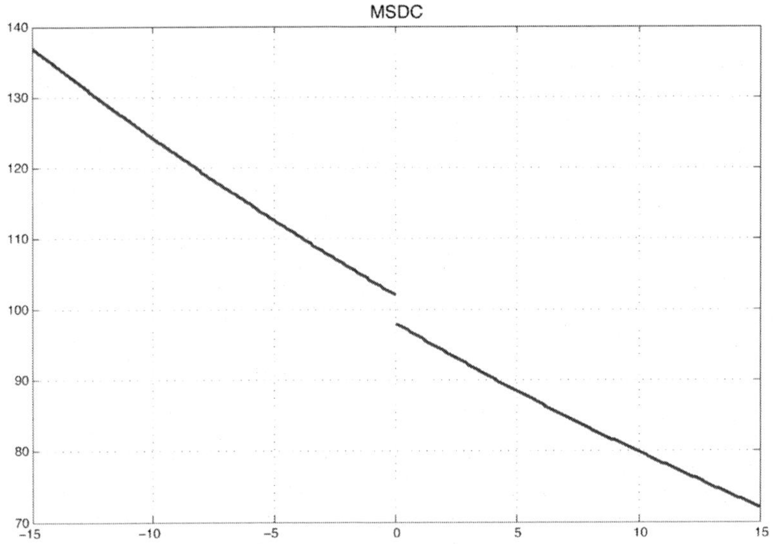

(see Figure 9.2 for example) that correspond to a continuum of prices quoted for infinitesimal size.

Notice that an MSDC is not defined in $s = 0$. This reflects the fact that no notion of "mid price" is introduced in the formalism. A MSDC just contains true prices expressed by market participants. Mid prices are mere abstractions which do not exist in any real market and so we will not consider them at all.

Outside the range of market depth (ie, outside the interval $s \in [-12, 16]$ in the above example), the MSDC is prolonged with fictitious worst-case quotes for both bids and offers, which are typically cast at minus and plus infinity respectively. In some cases MSDCs may however display natural finite upper or lower bounds. For instance the lower bound for the MSDC of any security (ie, a contract providing positive definite cashflows) or of any commodity is naturally floored at zero simply because instead of selling a security or a commodity at a negative price, its owner is always entitled to simply throw it away, which is essentially a zero price sale. So, the worst case bid for a security is zero. In the case of a swap, which gives its owner both rights and obligations, this will not be possible, and MSDCs will also display in general negative prices.

We will in fact call a security any asset whose MSDC is positive definite (eg, a stock, a option, a bond, a commodity, …), and a swap (*latu senso*) any asset whose MSDC can assume both positive and negative values (eg, an interest rate swap (IRS), a credit default swap (CDS), a repo, a forward rate agreement (FRA), …). Notice that assets with negative definite MSDCs can be excluded by redefining any such an asset as its opposite, which is a security (ie, inverting its conventional definition of long and short position).

Summarising the above reasoning, we therefore conclude the following:

Definition 9.1

An asset A is an object traded on the market in standardised units. At any given time t, it is characterised by a MSDC which is defined as any map m: $\mathbb{R} \setminus \{0\} \rightarrow [-\infty, +\infty]$ satisfying

1. m is decreasing, ie, $s_1 < s_2 \Rightarrow m(s_1) \geq m(s_2)$
2. $m(s)$ is cadlag (ie, $\lim_{x\downarrow s} m(x) = m(s)$) for $s < 0$ and ladcag (ie, $\lim_{x\uparrow s} m(x) = m(s)$) for $s > 0$,

The limits $m^+ := m(0^+)$ and $m^- := m(0^-)$ will be called best bid and best offer respectively and their difference $\delta m := m^- - m^+ \geq 0$ will be called the bid–offer spread. □

Condition 1 is not a restrictive hypotheses. MSDCs are decreasing by construction because we chose to organise quoted prices in decreasing order, placing better bids and offers closer to the origin $s = 0$. The only declared hypotheses is that we assume absence of arbitrage opportunities, so that any bid must be lower than any offer. The technical condition 2 strictly speaking is totally irrelevant. Financially relevant quantities will depend only on integrals of MSDCs for which such a condition has no effect. However, the way we construct MSDCs from market quotes systematically enforce this condition as may be seen from Table 9.2.

The reader who may find the jargon of Definition 9.1 too mathematical, may simply think of an MSDC as any possible decreasing function defined on any $s \neq 0$ and with values that can be real or infinity. A MSDC is nothing but the list of current prices plotted as horizontal segments of length equal to their trade size and organised in decreasing order (see Figure 9.1). Once we realise that an asset can be completely identified with its MSDC at time t it becomes clear that an asset does not possess any meaningful notion of 'value'. An asset has prices (plural), and no value.

It is also important to realise that the operation of addition of two assets is not defined in this formalism. In fact, given two assets A_1 and A_2, it is tempting to define $A_1 + A_2$ in the usual way as the package containing both contracts 1 and 2. But in general for such a package there will be no quoted prices and hence no MSDC. An owner of both A_1 and A_2, in order to liquidate them will need to find two separate bids. We do not exclude the possibility that in particular cases some package (eg, a "straddle" on a stock, whose payoff is the sum of a call = A_1 and a put = A_2 options) is indeed quoted on the market as a whole. But in a general case, say A_1 = "a GBP/JPY FX-swap" and A_2 = "a barrel of oil", this will not be the case. When a package is indeed an asset endowed with a MSDC like in the case of the straddle, we will simply call it say A_3 and the fact that its payoff is the sum of the payoffs of A_1 and A_2 will only entail no-arbitrage conditions that bound the MSDCs m_1, m_2 and m_3 together. But we will not write $A_3 = A_1 + A_2$ because the addition of two assets is generally undefined. Summing up, the set of all assets is not a vector space as it is not closed under the operation of linear combination.

Coming back to Equation 9.1 we now see why we said that it is meaningless in the presence of liquidity risk. It can not be interpreted as a relation between values because assets do not have any definite real value. It cannot be interpreted as a relation among formal objects because there is no notion of addition among assets.

A particular asset is the US dollar.

Definition 9.2

The US dollar is a particular asset A_0 representing the currency paid or received when trading any asset. It is characterised by a MSDC $m_0(s) = 1$, which is identically equal to 1 for any $s \in \mathbb{R} \setminus \{0\}$. □

The US dollar is the perfectly liquid asset by definition. Any asset with multiple prices of finite size will be called illiquid.

It is important to realise that the US dollar asset A_0 corresponds to spot cash money, namely pure banknotes. Debt instruments like loans, deposits or money market accounts, will instead correspond to some other assets A_1 with nontrivial MSDCs in general.

Definition 9.3

The market is a finite collection of assets $\mathcal{M} = \{A_0, A_1, \ldots, A_N\}$ containing in particular the US dollar. □

The dynamics of every asset of the market will be described by a process in time with values in the space of all possible MSDCs. We will not make any assumption on these dynamics in the general case. The historical series of an asset under illiquid conditions, is no more the history of a real number like we are used to know, but the history of an entire real-valued function.

The notation of MSDCs is very convenient because it provides a compact way of expressing the economic result of a trade of size s in a given asset.

Definition 9.4

The proceeds from a trade of size s in the asset A are defined as

$$P(s) := \int_0^s m(x)\,dx \tag{9.2}$$

and represent the number of US dollars received (or payed, if it is negative) in the trade. □

For instance, considering the MSDC m defined in Table 9.1, the sale of 10 assets generates US\$999.95 because

$$P(10) = \int_0^{10} m(x)\,dx = \text{US\$999.95}$$

while the purchase of 10 assets costs US\$1003.60 because

$$P(-10) = \int_0^{-10} m(x)\,dx = -\text{US\$1003.60}$$

For securities, the proceeds from a sale are always positive and the proceeds from a purchase are always negative. But notice that for swaps the proceeds $P(s)$ from a sale ($s > 0$) are not necessarily positive. For instance, selling off a swap with negative bids will determine an unwinding cost because $P(s) =$

$\int_0^s m(x)\,dx < 0$. Similarly, the proceeds of a swap purchase may be positive (ie, money is received) when offer prices happen to be negative.

The idea of using MSDCs to describe assets in illiquid markets is not new and is borrowed, for example, from Jarrow and Protter (2005), and Çetin, Jarrow and Protter (2004) where the concept of (non-marginal) supply demand curve (SDC) is introduced. The difference between MSDCs and SDCs is only a matter of convention as they may be shown to encode the same information. In our formalism we adopt MSDCs because they are easier to handle for the specific purpose of defining a value function for portfolios. The relationship between the SDC $S(s)$ of Jarrow and Protter (2005), and Çetin, Jarrow and Protter (2004) and our notation is

$$S(-s) = \frac{\int_0^s m(x)dx}{s}$$

$S(s)$ is therefore the average unit price hit in a trade of size s, and the convention on the sign of s (the trade size) is opposite to ours.

Portfolios

Portfolios are holdings of assets. A suitable notation for a portfolio is therefore just a vector of real numbers recording all the positions held in each of the markets assets, with positive numbers representing long positions and negative numbers representing short positions. So, for instance, in a market $\mathcal{M} = \{A_0, A_1, A_2, A_3\}$ containing A_0 = one US dollar, A_1 = one bond, A_2 = one stock, A_3 = one call on the stock, a portfolio p holding 10 US dollars, 3 stocks and 1 short position in the call will be denoted by $\mathbf{p} = (10, 0, 3, -1)$.

The operations of addition and scalar multiplication on portfolios is well defined. If $\mathbf{p}$ and $\mathbf{q}$ are two portfolios, the portfolio given by their union is represented as $\mathbf{p} + \mathbf{q}$ and is a perfectly legitimate portfolio as well as the portfolio obtained from $\mathbf{p}$ rescaling all its positions by some factor $\alpha \in \mathbb{R}$ which corresponds to the vector $\alpha\mathbf{p}$. In other words, given a market $\mathcal{M} = \{A_0, \ldots, A_N\}$, the space $\mathcal{P}$ of all portfolios is isomorphic to $\mathbb{R}^{n+1}$ and inherits a natural structure of vector space.

We can therefore give the following formal.

Definition 9.5

A portfolio is a vector $\mathbf{p} = (p_0, \vec{p}) = (p_0, \ldots, p_N) \in \mathbb{R}^{N+1}$, where p_0 is the "portfolio liquidity" and $\vec{p} := (p_1, \ldots, p_N) \in \mathbb{R}^N$ *is* the "assets' position". We will say that $\mathbf{p}$ is "long-", "flat-" or "short-asset A_k" if $p_k > 0$, $p_k = 0$ or $p_k < 0$ respectively. The space $\mathcal{P} \approx \mathbb{R}^{N+1}$ of all portfolios is endowed with a natural

Figure 9.3 The plot of *L*, *U* and *C* defined in Example 9.2 as functions of the portfolio weights p_1 and p_2

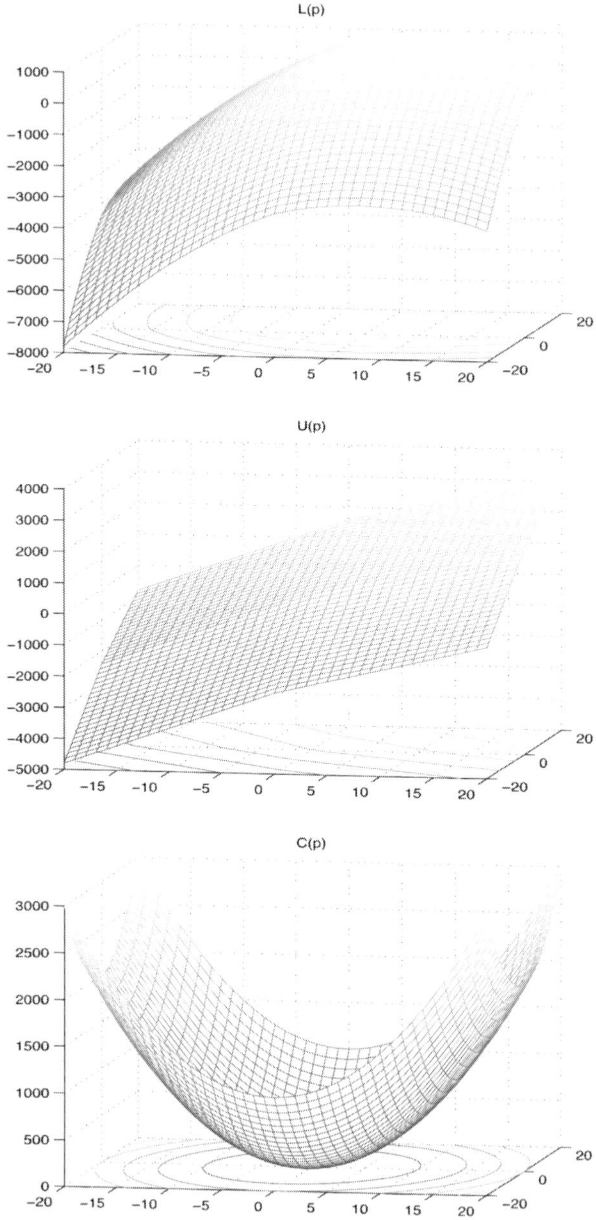

structure of vector space, with operations of addition and multiplication by scalars.

Portfolios will be denoted in bold ($\mathbf{p}$, $\mathbf{q}$, . . .) or by $(p_0, \vec{p})$ where p_0 is the liquidity component and $\vec{p}$ is the vector of illiquid components. Portfolios made of liquidity only $(a, \vec{0})$ will be also denoted with scalars a so that expressions like $\mathbf{p} + a$ will be meant as $\mathbf{p} + (a, \vec{0})$.

It is important not to confuse an asset (say A_1) with the portfolio made of a single unit of that asset (say (0, 1, 0, …, 0)). If this identification is made, it might be tempting to say that assets live in a vector space as well, missing a crucial distinction. When we sum two such portfolios we are not summing assets. A portfolio is a private holding of goods, while an asset is a public list of market prices.

At this point the natural question is: given a portfolio $\mathbf{p}$, what is now its value? Once understood that Equation 9.1 is of no help, however, it is soon clear that this question has no obvious answers. We will choose to answer this question by extending the notion of "mark-to-market" (MtM) to the general illiquid case confronting a portfolio with the structure of prices encoded in the MSDCs. A first attempt to do this is to compute the total proceeds obtained from the liquidation of the portfolio on the market. To this purpose we give the following

Definition 9.6

The liquidation of a portfolio $\mathbf{p} \in \mathcal{P}$, is the US dollar amount deriving from the proceeds of the sale of $\mathbf{p}$ and is given by

$$L(\mathbf{p}) := \sum_{i=0}^{N} \int_0^{p_i} m_i(x)\,dx \tag{9.3}$$

Interpreting $L(\mathbf{p})$ as the value of $\mathbf{p}$ is clearly a very drastic and prudential point of view. $L(\mathbf{p})$ is the amount of US dollars we can obtain immediately if we liquidate the portfolio and so this could be a necessary MtM policy to use in those cases when the portfolio could be forced, for some external reason, to close up all positions immediately.

An opposite point of view is taken when we use best prices (best bids for long positions and best offers for short positions) for marking a portfolio to market. This practice, which is indeed very widespread in the marketplace is much less prudent as it does not probe at all the depth of such best prices, irrespective of how big the position to mark is. To this purpose we define the operator $U(\mathbf{p})$.

Figure 9.4 The value of **p** for Ben as studied in Example 9.8. We plot it versus the number of bonds N and versus the cash level c

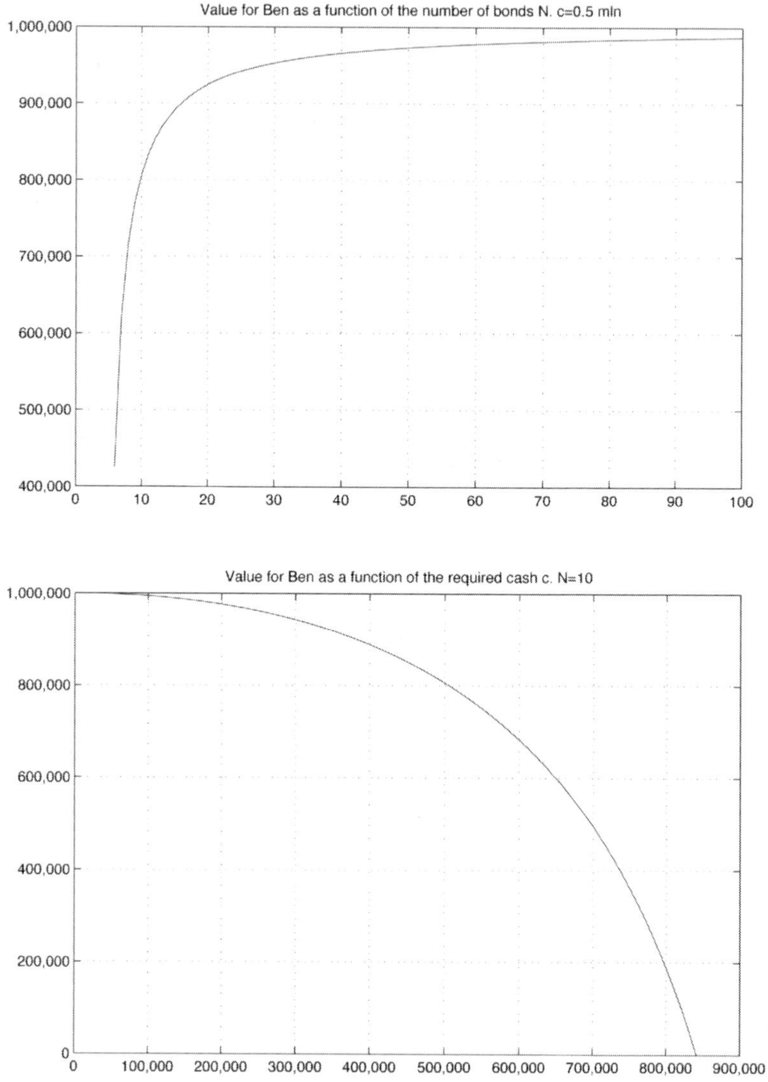

Definition 9.7

The uppermost mark-to-market of a portfolio $\mathbf{p} \in \mathcal{P}$, is defined by

$$U(\mathbf{p}) := \sum_{i=0}^{N} \left(m_i^+ (p_i)^+ - m_i^- (p_i)^- \right) \tag{9.4}$$

□

We have denoted $(\cdot)^+ := \max(\cdot, 0)$ and $(\cdot)^- := -\min(\cdot, 0)$ the positive and negative part functions respectively, not to be confused with m_i^+ and m_i^- which are the best bid and offer of A_i.

The operator U can also be considered a candidate value function for a portfolio, but it is clear that it is an appropriate one only in those cases when for some reason it is certain that no portion of the portfolio will ever be liquidated. If a partial liquidation is needed, worse prices would be hit showing that $U(\mathbf{p})$ was a too optimistic estimate.

It is easy to see that U is linear whenever there is no bid-offer spread, namely when $m_i^+ = m_i^-$ for all i, in which case it becomes trivially $U(\mathbf{p}) = \Sigma_i m_i^- p_i$. In all other cases, U is nonlinear.

An even more widespread MtM practice is to mark all assets to mid prices. To do this we could have for instance defined mid prices by $m(0) := (m^+ + m^-)/2$ and defined an operator

$$M(\mathbf{p}) := \sum_{i=0}^{N} m_i(0) p_i$$

which look pretty much as Equation 9.1. Of course, this would lead to an even more optimistic value than $U(\mathbf{p})$ and in fact it is not difficult to show in general that $M(\mathbf{p}) \geq U(\mathbf{p}) \geq L(\mathbf{p})$ for any $\mathbf{p}$. We consider this practice totally wrong, as mid prices do not exist on the market and so this is not MtM but marking-to-fictitious-figures. Long positions need to be marked on bids and short positions need to be marked on offers because these are the only true prices through which we can close a position. We will never adopt this approach and we will forget $M(\mathbf{p})$ and $m(0)$ as relics of an unappropriate old formalism unable to capture the basics of liquidity risk.

Example 9.1

Consider an asset A_1 with a linear MSDC given by $m(s) = N - ks - f\,\mathrm{sgn}(s)$ where $\mathrm{sgn}(s) = \pm 1$ is the sign of s (see Figure 9.2). The coefficient $k > 0$ (say $k = 0.01$) controls the slope of the MSDC, and hence the degree of illiquidity of the asset and the constant f (say $f = 0.1$) controls the bid offer spread. Choosing $N = 100$, the best bid is US\$99.9 and the best offer is US\$100.1.

The liquidation of a portfolio $\mathbf{p} = (0, p)$ holding p units of asset A_1 gives

$$L(\mathbf{p}) = \int_0^p m(x)\,dx = Np - f\,|\,p\,| - kp^2/2$$

while the uppermost MtM is

$$U(\mathbf{p}) = Np - f\,|\,p\,|$$

We see that while U grows linearly with p unaware of the market illiquidity, L has a market impact negative penalty $-kp^2/2$ which grows quadratically with the portfolio size. For instance, for $p = 100$ we easily obtain $U(\mathbf{p}) =$ US\$9.990 and $L(\mathbf{p}) = -$US\$9.940. For $p = -100$ we have $U(\mathbf{p}) = -$US\$10.010 and $L(\mathbf{p}) = -$US\$10.060. In any case $U > L$ as we expect from the fact that L is more prudential.

Had we used a mark-to-mid-market procedure, it is elementary to show that we would have simply found

$$M(\mathbf{p}) = Np$$

which is a completely misleading value, which is blind both to the steepness k of the MSDC and to the presence of a bid offer spread f. □

In the spirit of the preliminary discussion earlier in the chapter, we see that both L and U may represent reasonable "value" functions for a portfolio but each only under specific opposite circumstances. L is an extremely prudential attitude, considering the maximum possible impact of market illiquidity on a portfolio experienced in a sudden liquidation. U is an extremely permissive attitude that neglects the impact of liquidations at all. To build a more general value function, which is appropriate for general, less extreme circumstances, we need first of all to give a mathematical definition to the circumstances themselves, or in other words, to the possible constraints under which a portfolio is managed. This will lead to the concept of liquidity policy, the essential missing variable of a portfolio value function under liquidity risk.

The difference $C = U - L$ defines a positive function $C(\mathbf{p}) \geq 0$ which we interpret as a liquidation cost of the portfolio $\mathbf{p}$ because it measures the drop we experience if we need to liquidate a portfolio which was optimistically marked to market by U.

Definition 9.8

The liquidation cost of a portfolio $\mathbf{p} \in \mathcal{P}$, is defined by the positive function

$$C(\mathbf{p}) := U(\mathbf{p}) - L(\mathbf{p}) \geq 0 \tag{9.5}$$

□

Taking for instance the portfolio $\mathbf{p}$ of Example 9.1, it is easy to see that the liquidation cost is given by $C(\mathbf{p}) = kp^2/2 \geq 0$. It is quadratic in the portfolio size p and linear in the slope k of the MSDC.

Some properties of L, U *and* C

Before going on in our search for a general definition of portfolio value, we focus to analyse some important properties of the functions defined so far.

The operator L plays a fundamental role in our formalism and will be used not only to liquidate a whole portfolio, but any time we make a trade. If we own a portfolio $\mathbf{p}$ and at time t we sell a portfolio $\mathbf{r}$ it can easily be realised that we receive $L(\mathbf{r})$ US dollars. Then, immediately after the trade, our portfolio becomes

$$\mathbf{p}_{t+\varepsilon} = \mathbf{p}_t - \mathbf{r} + L(\mathbf{r})$$

redefining $\mathbf{q} = -\mathbf{r}$ we see that if we buy a portfolio $\mathbf{q}$ instead, we pay $B(\mathbf{q}) := -L(-\mathbf{q})$ US dollars

$$\mathbf{p}_{t+\varepsilon} = \mathbf{p}_t - (-\mathbf{q}) + L(-\mathbf{q}) = \mathbf{p}_t + \mathbf{q} - B(\mathbf{q})$$

The two cases above differ only for the sign choice of the traded portfolio because selling a portfolio $-\mathbf{q}$ is clearly the same as buying $\mathbf{q}$. The above relations establish a connection between the portfolio $\mathbf{p}_t$ and all portfolios $\mathbf{p}_{t+\varepsilon}$ that can be obtained from $\mathbf{p}_t$ by trading on the market (ie, selling $\mathbf{r}$ or buying $\mathbf{q}$). Hence it makes sense to give the following.

Definition 9.9

A portfolio $\mathbf{q}$ is said to be attainable from $\mathbf{p}$ if there exists some portfolio $\mathbf{r} \in \mathcal{P}$ such that

$$\mathbf{q} = \mathbf{p} - \mathbf{r} + L(\mathbf{r})$$

In this case we will also write $\mathbf{q} \in \mathrm{Att}(\mathbf{p})$. □

The functions L, U and C can be shown (see Acerbi and Scandolo (2007) for a proof) to have important convexity and scaling properties, holding in general under any market hypotheses, which are collected in the following proposition.

Proposition 9.1

Let $\mathbf{p}, \mathbf{q} \in \mathcal{P}$, $\alpha \in [0,1]$ and $\lambda \geq 1$.

- The function $L : \mathcal{P} \to \mathbb{R}$ is concave and positive sub-homogeneous

$$L(\alpha\mathbf{p} + (1-\alpha)\mathbf{q}) \geq \alpha L(\mathbf{p}) + (1-\alpha)L(\mathbf{q}) \tag{9.6}$$

$$L(\lambda\mathbf{p}) \leq \lambda L(\mathbf{p}) \tag{9.7}$$

- The function $U : \mathcal{P} \to \mathbb{R}$ is concave and positive homogeneous

$$U(\alpha\mathbf{p} + (1-\alpha)\mathbf{q}) \geq \alpha U(\mathbf{p}) + (1-\alpha)U(\mathbf{q}) \tag{9.8}$$

Figure 9.5 The plot of $V^{\mathcal{L}}(\mathbf{p})$ of Example 9.9

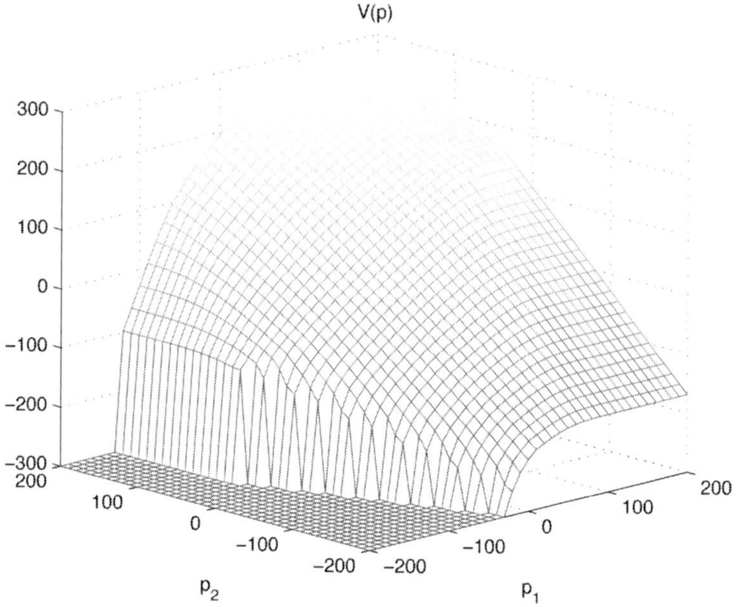

$$U(\lambda\mathbf{p}) = \lambda U(\mathbf{p}) \tag{9.9}$$

- The function $C : \mathcal{P} \to \mathbb{R}_+$ is convex and positive super thomogeneous

$$C(\alpha\mathbf{p}+(1-\alpha)\mathbf{q}) \le \alpha C(\mathbf{p})+(1-\alpha)C(\mathbf{q}) \tag{9.10}$$

$$C(\lambda\mathbf{p}) \ge \lambda C(\mathbf{p}) \tag{9.11}$$

□

The properties are quite intuitive. Under dilatation $\mathbf{p} \to \lambda\mathbf{p}$ of a portfolio, the uppermost MtM $U(\lambda\mathbf{p})$ grows proportionally, the liquidation $L(\lambda\mathbf{p})$ grows less than proportionally and the cost of liquidation $C(\lambda\mathbf{p})$ grows more than proportionally. If we blend two portfolios $\mathbf{p}$ and $\mathbf{q}$ into a convex combination $\alpha\mathbf{p} + (1 - \alpha)\mathbf{q}$ we see that both U and L are concave while C is convex. This means that each of these three cases displays the liquidity benefit of portfolios blending: the value (L or U) of the blend is higher than the blend of the values, and the liquidation cost of the blend is lower than the blend of the liquidation costs. We will interpret this benefit as a granularity effect. Blending two portfolios always reduces the granularity of large positions and this in turn has a positive effect in a illiquid market. This general principle is perfectly captured by this formalism and we will see that the above results turn out to be special cases of a more general result (theorem 1).

Example 9.2

Consider a market with only two illiquid assets A_1 and A_2 with MSDCs given by $m_i(s) = N_i - k_i s - f_i \operatorname{sgn}(s)$. For a portfolio $\mathbf{p} = (0, p_1, p_2) = (0, \vec{p})$ we have

$$L(\mathbf{p}) = \sum_{i=1}^{2} \left(N_i p_i - f_i \, | p_i | - k_i p_i^2 / 2 \right)$$

$$U(\mathbf{p}) = \sum_{i=1}^{2} \left(N_i p_i - f_i \, | p_i | \right)$$

$$C(\mathbf{p}) = \sum_{i=1}^{2} k_i p_i^2 / 2$$

The three functions are plotted in Figure 9.3 with parameters $\vec{N} = (100, 100)$, $\vec{k} = (5, 10), \vec{f} = (20, 20)$. The concavity of L and U and the convexity of C are easily appreciated by the plot as well as their scaling properties under portfolio dilatation. The parameters have been chosen in such a way to produce very illiquid MSDCs to enhance these visual features.

The plots of L and U would be simple identical planes in absence of liquidity risk (ie, with flat MSDCs, or in other words $k = 0, f = 0$) and C would be identically zero. □

Another important property is given by the following (Acerbi and Scandolo 2007)

Lemma 1. Let $\mathbf{q} \in \mathrm{Att}(\mathbf{p})$. Then $U(\mathrm{q}) \le U(\mathbf{p})$ □

This means that it is impossible to increase the U-value of a portfolio $\mathbf{p}$ by just trading on the market. Any time we attain a new portfolio $\mathbf{q} \in \mathrm{Att}(\mathbf{p})$ we necessarily impact the market reducing the final U-value. This lemma reminds us that the less we trade in a illiquid market the better it is.

Example 9.3

Consider again Example 9.1. Let $\mathbf{p} = (0, p)$. Any portfolio $\mathbf{q} \in \mathrm{Att}(\mathbf{p})$ is given by $\mathbf{q} = \mathbf{p} - \mathbf{r} + L(\mathbf{r})$ with $\mathbf{r} = (r_0, r_1) \in \mathbb{R}^2$. But $L(\mathbf{r}) = r_0 + Nr_1 - f|r_1| - kr_1^2/2$. Now, $U(\mathbf{q}) = q_0 + Nq_1 - f|q_1| = Nr_1 - f|r_1| - kr_1^2/2 + N(p - r_1) - f|p - r_1| = Np - kr_1^2/2 - f|r_1| - f|p - r_1|$ which attains its maximum value $U(\mathbf{q}) = Np - f|p| = U(\mathbf{p})$ when $r_1 = 0$. □

The liquidity policy

What is the level of market depth we need to probe when we mark a portfolio? There is no single answer to this question as we learned noticing that

Figure 9.6 The value of $\mathbf{p} + b$ for Ben as studied in Example 9.10.

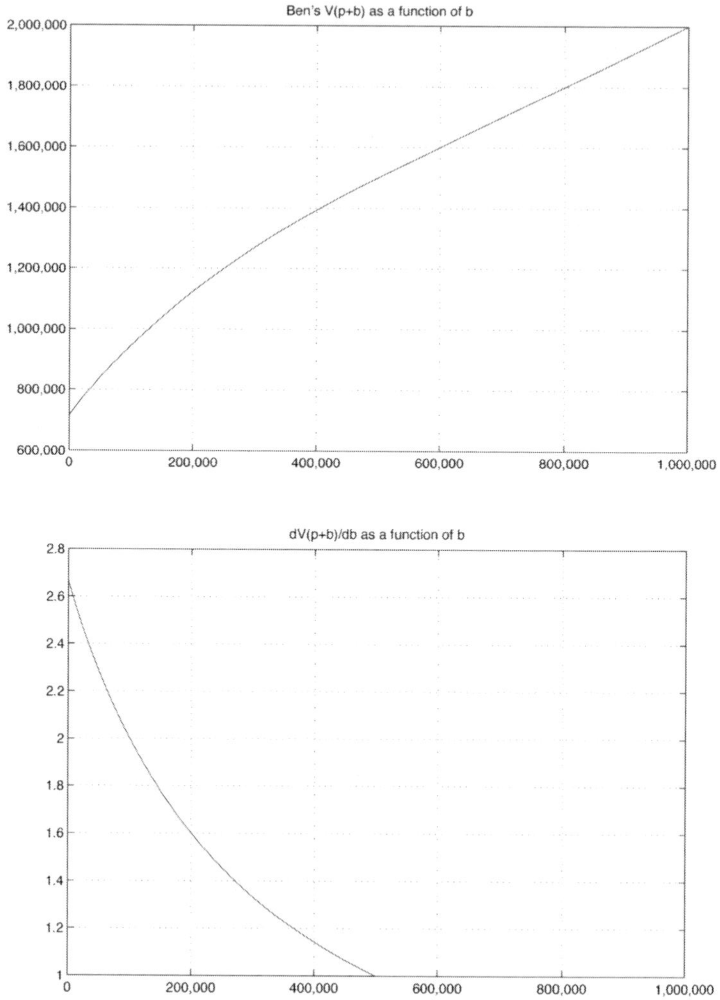

30

We have chosen $k = 10^{-5}$, $c =$ US\$500,000, $N = 10$. The first plot shows $V^{Ben}(\mathbf{p} + b)$ as a function of b. The second plot gives the marginal value of any added US dollar as a function of b. Notice that the first US dollar added is "worth" US\$2.6

the opposite cases of L and U may be appropriate in specific different circumstances. We believe that a sensible MtM of a portfolio should test the market up to some depth level imposed by the liquidity constraints the portfolio is subject to. To give a mathematical meaning to these constraints we introduce the concept of liquidity policy.

A liquidity policy in our formalism is a subset $\mathcal{L} \subset \mathcal{P}$ of the space of portfolios $\mathcal{P}$. If $\mathbf{p} \in \mathcal{L}$ we will say that $\mathbf{p}$ satisfies the liquidity policy $\mathcal{L}$ or that $\mathbf{p}$ is $\mathcal{L}$-liquid. Not all subsets of $\mathcal{P}$ however have the right shape. For a set to be a sensible liquidity policy we require that

- if a portfolio $\mathbf{p}$ satisfies $\mathcal{L}$, it will still satisfy $\mathcal{L}$ if we add more cash to it.
- if a portfolio $\mathbf{p}$ satisfies $\mathcal{L}$ and we shrink all its illiquid positions by a common factor, it will still satisfy $\mathcal{L}$
- any portfolio obtained by blending two portfolios that satisfy $\mathcal{L}$, also satisfies $\mathcal{L}$.

The above requirements are quite natural. We want a liquidity policy to establish minimum amounts of cash to be held to balance the size of illiquid positions. Therefore, this limit will never be breached by just adding cash to a portfolio or by just reducing the size of its illiquid assets proportionally. The third condition is a convexity requirement on $\mathcal{L}$: all portfolios in the "segment" drawn between two liquid portfolios, must be liquid as well for $\mathcal{L}$.

Formally we give therefore the following.

Definition 9.10

A liquidity policy $\mathcal{L} \subset \mathcal{P}$ *is* a closed and convex subset of the space of portfolios satisfying.

1. If $\mathbf{p} \in \mathcal{L}$, and $a \geq 0$, then $\mathbf{p} + a \in \mathcal{L}$
2. If $\mathbf{p} = (p_0, \vec{p}) \in \mathcal{L}$, then $(p_0, \vec{0}) \in \mathcal{L}$ □

Notice that given the convexity of $\mathcal{L}$, the requirement 2. is equivalent to require that if $\mathbf{p} = (p_0, \vec{p}) \in \mathcal{L}$ then any $(p_0, \mu\vec{p}) \in \mathcal{L}$ for $\mu \in [0, 1]$.

We will say that a liquidity policy $\mathcal{L}_1$ is more restrictive than another liquidity policy $\mathcal{L}_2$ if $\mathcal{L}_1 \subset \mathcal{L}_2$. Clearly, the least restrictive of all liquidity policies is

$$\mathcal{L}^U := \mathcal{P} \tag{9.12}$$

which will turn out to be related to the U operator. On the contrary, it is easy to check that there is not any most restrictive liquidity policy because for any liquidity policy $\mathcal{L}$, we can define $\mathcal{L}_a := \{\mathbf{p} + a \mid \mathbf{p} \in \mathcal{L}; a > 0\}$ which is another more restrictive liquidity policy $\mathcal{L}_a \subset \mathcal{L}$.

Another particular liquidity policy is defined by the "US dollar axis"

$$\mathcal{L}^L := \left\{ \mathbf{p} = (p_0, \vec{p}) \in \mathcal{P} \mid \vec{p} = \vec{0} \right\} \tag{9.13}$$

which will turn out to be related to the L operator.

Much more concrete examples of liquidity policies are easily found in the practice of financial risk management.

Example 9.4

Consider a market of bonds $A_1, \ldots, A_k$ and swaps $A_{k+1}, \ldots, A_N$. Suppose that a trader of a bank is allowed to trade in this market, but subject to risk limits given by

- the maximum notional of each long position in bond is M. The maximum notional in any short position in bond is S.
- the absolute value of the "DV01" (ie, sensitivity in US dollars to a basis point shift in the interest rate curve) of the portfolio must be less than D.

We normalise all assets units to have a notional of US$1 and we call $DV01_i$ the $DV01$ of one unit of asset i. The set of all portfolios satisfying these limits is

$$\hat{\mathcal{L}} = \left\{ \mathbf{p} \in \mathcal{P} \left| \begin{array}{ll} (p_i)^+ \leq M & \forall i = 1, \ldots, k \\ (p_i)^- \leq S & \forall i = 1, \ldots, k \\ \left| \sum_{i=1}^N p_i DVO1_i \right| \leq D & \end{array} \right. \right\}$$

It is easy to show that the set $\hat{\mathcal{L}}$ is a liquidity policy. In this case it is insensitive to the amount of cash p_0 held by the portfolio, and it only bounds the size of the illiquid components of the portfolio. Moreover it is elementary to show that $\hat{\mathcal{L}}$ is a convex set, because it is the intersection of the $2k + 1$ convex sets defined by each of the above inequalities. □

Example 9.5

Consider a member of a stock exchange trading on derivatives $A_1, \ldots, A_N$ (futures and options) with underlying a single equity index. The clearinghouse requires to keep a minimum margin amount (ie, cash p_0) basically computed as the negative part of the smallest possible value of the derivatives portfolio $(0, \vec{p})$ in k pre-specified scenarios of the underlying return and implied volatility. The derivatives prices here are clearly meant in the traditional sense, as theoretical Black–Scholes prices and the portfolio value is also computed in a traditional way. We denote these prices with β_i^ζ where $\zeta = 1, \ldots, k$ is the label of the specific scenario.

$$\bar{\mathcal{L}} = \left\{ \mathbf{p} \in \mathcal{P} \,\middle|\, p_0 \geq \max_{\zeta=1,\dots,k} \left(\sum_{i=1}^{N} p_i \beta_i^{\zeta} \right)^{-} \right\}$$

The set $\bar{\mathcal{L}}$ is easily shown to be a legitimate liquidity policy. In this case it establishes a minimum balance between the cash and the risky position. □

Example 9.6

A mutual fund with US$1 billion assets under management is fully invested in risky assets. Suppose that by prospectus the fund must be prepared to liquidate up to 20% of its assets immediately if it happens that a number of investors ask for their money back. Redemptions of larger fractions can be postponed instead to reduce market impact. In this case the liquidity policy is very simple. Liquid portfolios are all portfolios that contain c = US$0.2 billion of cash.

$$\mathcal{L}(c) = \{ \mathbf{p} \in \mathcal{P} \mid p_0 \geq c \} \tag{9.14}$$

Notice that in this case, the fund is not supposed to satisfy the liquidity policy all the time. It would be crazy to park one fifth of the assets in pure cash. The fund must only be prepared to satisfy the liquidity policy, in the sense that the evaluation of its "net asset value" (NAV) has to reflect the possibility of such a liquidation.

Liquidity policies of the form $\mathcal{L}(c)$ will be called cash liquidity policies with minimum required cash $c \in \mathbb{R}$. □

Example 9.7

The capital requirement of a bank is essentially a liquidity policy. Consider a bank with a portfolio $\mathbf{p} = \mathbf{p}_A \oplus \mathbf{p}_L$ where $\mathbf{p}_A$ are assets and $\mathbf{p}_L$ are liabilities. We use the "direct sum symbol" $\oplus$ to mean that $\mathbf{p}_A$ and $\mathbf{p}_B$ have mutually exclusive nonzero components, because they contain different assets. Liabilities in our simplified example, can be thought of as the short positions represented by the stocks and bonds issued by the company. The "capital" of the bank is essentially the liquidation value of $-\mathbf{p}_L$ namely $L(-\mathbf{p}_L)$. The requirement imposes that the capital must be larger than some "measure of risk" $\rho(\mathbf{p}_A)$ of the assets of the bank. If ρ is a convex measure of risk as it should be, then the requirement is easily shown to be a liquidity policy in the sense of Definition 9.10.

$$\mathcal{L}^{CR} = \{ \mathbf{p} = \mathbf{p}_A \oplus \mathbf{p}_L \in \mathcal{P} \mid L(-\mathbf{p}_L) \geq \rho(\mathbf{p}_A) \}$$

It is easy to show that this is in fact a liquidity policy thanks to the convexity of ρ and the concavity of L.

Notice that the Basel II capital accord actually does not define a liquidity policy because it adopts non-convex measures like value-at-risk. □

The examples above may seem somehow different. In some cases (for instance Examples 9.4 and 9.5), the portfolio usually has to be managed in such a way as to satisfy the liquidity policy all the time. In other cases, such as Example 9.6 the liquidity policy represents a constraint that the portfolio has to be prepared to satisfy instead. We stress that it is in this second more general sense that we will think of liquidity policies. A portfolio will be said to be subject to $\mathcal{L}$ if it is supposed to be ready to satisfy $\mathcal{L}$. This fact will in turn be reflected in the "value of the portfolio" in a way that will be made precise in the next section.

The value of a portfolio

We now want to answer the crucial question: what is the value of a given portfolio $\mathbf{p}$ in an illiquid market once we know the liquidity policy $\mathcal{L}$ it is subject to? To ask this question we simply define a MtM procedure which probes the liquidity of the market up to the depth imposed by the presence of the liquidity policy. In this way, the value of a portfolio will contain the potential effect of future liquidations needed to comply the liquidity policy, if necessary.

The MtM procedure can be outlined as follows. Let us therefore choose a portfolio $\mathbf{p}$ and suppose that it is subject to a certain liquidity policy $\mathcal{L}$.

- if a portfolio $\mathbf{p}$ already satisfies the liquidity policy ($\mathbf{p} \in \mathcal{L}$), it can be marked to market with no additional caution. Its value is therefore given by the least prudential choice $U(\mathbf{p})$.
- if instead $\mathbf{p} \notin \mathcal{L}$, we must consider all portfolios $\mathbf{q} \in \text{Att}(\mathbf{p}) \cap \mathcal{L}$ which are attainable from $\mathbf{p}$ and also satisfy the liquidity policy. If asked to comply $\mathcal{L}$ the owner of $\mathbf{p}$ can in fact choose to convert it in any such portfolio $\mathbf{q}$. We will therefore say that the value of $\mathbf{p}$ is given by the maximum of $U(\mathbf{q})$ taken among all $\mathbf{q} \in \text{Att}(\mathbf{p}) \cap \mathcal{L}$. The optimal portfolio $\mathbf{q}^*$ for which $U(\mathbf{q}^*)$ attains the maximum, will be interpreted as the most convenient choice for the owner to satisfy $\mathcal{L}$.
- if $\mathbf{p} \notin \mathcal{L}$ and there is no portfolio attainable from $\mathbf{p}$ that satisfies $\mathcal{L}$ (ie, if $\text{Att}(\mathbf{p}) \cap \mathcal{L} = \emptyset$) this means that the portfolio is not able to satisfy $\mathcal{L}$ unless some money is injected from outside sources. The portfolio is unfit for $\mathcal{L}$ and we will give it a formal value of minus infinity.

The strategy defined above is fully summarised in the following.

Definition 9.11

The value $V^{\mathcal{L}}(\mathbf{p})$ of a portfolio $\mathbf{p}$ subject to a liquidity policy $\mathcal{L}$ is a function $V^{\mathcal{L}} : \mathcal{P} / \mathbb{R} \cup \{-\infty\}$ defined by

$$V^{\mathcal{L}}(\mathbf{p}) = \sup\{U(\mathbf{q}) \mid \mathbf{q} \in \mathrm{Att}(\mathbf{p}) \cap \mathcal{L}\} \tag{9.15}$$

This definition encompasses all the three cases mentioned before. In fact, lemma 1 has the immediate consequence that $V^{\mathcal{L}}(\mathbf{p}) = U(\mathbf{p})$ if $\mathbf{p} \in \mathcal{L}$. Moreover, by conventional definition of sup, $V^{\mathcal{L}}(\mathbf{p}) = -\infty$ when $\mathrm{Att}(\mathbf{p}) \cap \mathcal{L} = \varnothing$. □

An important property that immediately descends from the above definition is.

Proposition 9.2

If $\mathcal{L}_1$ is more restrictive than $\mathcal{L}_2$ (ie, if $\mathcal{L}_1 \subset \mathcal{L}_2$) then $V^{\mathcal{L}_1}(\mathbf{p}) \leq V^{\mathcal{L}_2}(\mathbf{p})$ for all $\mathbf{p} \in \mathcal{P}$. As a consequence, $V^{\mathcal{L}}(\mathbf{p}) \leq U(\mathbf{p})$ for all liquidity policies $\mathcal{L}$ and portfolios $\mathbf{p}$. □

Therefore, the more restrictive are the constraints a portfolio is subject to, the more prudential its value will be, as we should expect.

It can be shown that apart from the case when $\mathrm{Att}(\mathbf{p}) \cap \mathcal{L} = \varnothing$ the sup is always attained by some portfolio $\mathbf{q}^*$, not necessarily unique. This portfolio represents the most convenient portfolio to attain when the liquidity policy must be satisfied. If our value function is built to account for the effect of possible future liquidations, we expect then whenever the owner of the portfolio is really forced to meet the liquidity policy and convert $\mathbf{p}$ into $\mathbf{q}^*$ then the value of the portfolio does not suffer any drop. This is in fact the case as stated by the following

Proposition 9.3

Let $\mathbf{q}^* \in \mathrm{Att}(\mathbf{p}) \cap \mathcal{L}$ be a solution of the sup in Equation 9.15, so that $U(\mathbf{q}^*) = V^{\mathcal{L}}(\mathbf{p})$. Then also $V^{\mathcal{L}}(\mathbf{q}^*) = V^{\mathcal{L}}(\mathbf{p})$. □

It is easy to show that the operators L and U defined earlier are nothing but very special cases of the value function $V^{\mathcal{L}}$.

The U operator is the value function associated with the least restrictive liquidity policy $\mathcal{L}^U = \mathcal{P}$. Any portfolio $\mathbf{p}$ satisfies this liquidity policy and therefore $V^{\mathcal{L}^U}(\mathbf{p}) = U(\mathbf{p})$ by definition. From Proposition 9.2 we see that in our formalism $U(\mathbf{p})$ represents the most optimistic value that a portfolio can assume. Hence the name uppermost MtM.

The L operator is the value function associated with the liquidity policy $\mathcal{L}^L$ (Equation 9.13) which imposes the liquidation of all positions of a portfolio.

To check that in fact $L(\mathbf{p}) = V^{\mathcal{L}^L}(\mathbf{p})$ it suffices to notice that $\text{Att}(\mathbf{p}) \cap \mathcal{L}^L$ contains only one portfolio $\mathbf{q} = L(\mathbf{p})$ made of cash only.

A particularly important issue to check is whether the optimality problem hidden in Equation 9.15 is in general a difficult task to solve or not. In practical situations, the evaluation of a portfolio should be a very fast operation. In ordinary portfolio theory this operation is simply a sum and we wonder whether now it is still an operation that does not pose serious computational obstacles. Were it not the case, this formalism would be a dead letter. A very reassuring answer comes from the following

Proposition 9.4

The optimality problem 9.15 is equivalent to

$$V^{\mathcal{L}}(\mathbf{p}) = \sup\{U(\mathbf{p}-\mathbf{r}) + L(\mathbf{r}) \mid \mathbf{r} \in \mathcal{P}, \mathbf{p}-\mathbf{r}+L(\mathbf{r}) \in \mathcal{L}\} \tag{9.16}$$

This problem is convex because the map $\mathbf{r} \to U(\mathbf{p} - \mathbf{r}) + L(\mathbf{r})$ is concave, and the domain $\{\mathbf{r} \in \mathcal{P} \mid \mathbf{p} - \mathbf{r} + L(\mathbf{r}) \in \mathcal{L}\}$ is convex. □

This result is very important, especially for large portfolios, where the dimensionality of the problem is high. In such cases, non-convex optimality problems often turn out to be very challenging, while convex problems are in any case computationally tractable and fast to solve. General references for convex optimisation and algorithms are Rockafellar (1970), Boyd and Vandenberghe (2004), and Hiriart-Urruty and Lemarechal (2004).

Notice that in general the solution of the optimality problem hidden in the definition of value does not lend itself to an analytical solution. Only selected stylised examples may be illustrated analytically. In general cases, and essentially in all financially concrete cases, the problem must be faced numerically, by optimisation routines. The convexity of the problem however, is of immense help for any computer implementation.

Example 9.8

Let us consider the case of Alan and Ben mentioned earlier. We write $\mathbf{p} = (0, \vec{p})$, with a number of illiquid bonds given by $\Sigma_{i=1}^{N} p_i = M = 10^6$. Let us suppose that the bonds have MSDCs given by

$$m_i = a_i e^{-k_i s}, \qquad i = 1, \ldots, N \tag{9.17}$$

with a_i = US\$1 and $k_i > 0$, so that the overall face value of the bonds in the portfolio is US\$1 million. The situation of Alan is very simple. He has (lucky him) no liquidity constraints at all. He will never liquidate the assets of portfolio $\mathbf{p}$. This means that his liquidity policy is simply $\mathcal{L}^{\mathcal{U}}$ and the portfolio value for him is

$$V^{Alan}(\mathbf{p}) = U(\mathbf{p}) = \sum_{i=1}^{N} a_i p_i = \$1\text{mln} \tag{9.18}$$

For Ben the situation is different. He has to be prepared to liquidate at least c = US\$0.5 million very soon. Neglecting other possible constraints he may have, he has a liquidity policy $\mathcal{L}(c)$ of cash type (see Equation 9.14) with level c. The portfolio value for Ben will therefore be given by $V^{\mathcal{L}(p)}(\mathbf{p})$ computed according to 9.15 or equivalently 9.16. To compute this value, we have to maximise $U(\mathbf{p} - \mathbf{r} + L(\mathbf{r}))$ with $\mathbf{r} = (0, \vec{r}) \in \mathcal{P}$ keeping $\mathbf{p} - \mathbf{r} + L(\mathbf{r}) \in \mathcal{L}(c)$, which means $L(\mathbf{r}) \geq c$. It is easy to compute

$$L(\mathbf{r}) = \sum_{i=1}^{N} \int_0^{r_i} m_i(s)\,ds = \sum_{i=1}^{N} \frac{a_i}{k_i}\left[1 - e^{-k_i r_i}\right]$$

A simple lagrangean approach to this constrained maximisation, give us the following equations

$$\begin{cases} a_i\left(e^{-k_i r_i} - 1\right) + \lambda a_i e^{-k_i r_i} = 0 \\ \sum_{i=1}^{N} (a_i / k_i)\left[1 - e^{-k_i r_i}\right] = c \end{cases}$$

to be solved in the variables r_i and λ, the Lagrange multiplier. The solution is given by

$$\begin{cases} \hat{r}^i = \log(1+\lambda)/k_i \\ \lambda = c \Big/ \left(\sum_{i=1}^{N} a_i / k_i - c\right) \end{cases}$$

which in turn give us a value

$$V^{Ben}(\mathbf{p}) = V^{\mathcal{L}(c)}(\mathbf{p}) = U(\hat{\mathbf{q}}) = c + M - \log\left(\frac{\sum_{i=1}^{N} a_i / k_i}{\sum_{i=1}^{N} a_i / k_i - c}\right) \sum_{i=1}^{N} (a_i / k_i) \tag{9.19}$$

Let us suppose for simplicity the symmetrical case where all bonds are indistinguishable, $k_i = k = 10^{-5}$ and the portfolio is equally weighted $p_i = M/N$. Then we have

$$V^{Ben}(\mathbf{p}) = c + M - (N/k)\log\left(\frac{N/k}{N/k - c}\right) \tag{9.20}$$

We plot this value as a function of N and as a function of c in Figure 9.4. Notice how this value is always below US\$1 mln. $V^{Ben}(\mathbf{p})$ is a pronounced increasing function in the number of bonds N reflecting the liquidity benefit of the granularity effect. The more concentrated the portfolio, the smaller is its value. $V^{Ben}(\mathbf{p})$ is of course a decreasing function in the required cash level c because this is the amount of short term debts that Ben is supposed to repay. Notice how in some circumstances (eg, $N = 8$, $c =$ US$0.5 million) the value is well below US$800,000 so that Ben would probably accept such a bid on the whole $\mathbf{p}$ as we anticipated earlier. Notice also how in some circumstances we have $V^{Ben}(\mathbf{p}) < c$. This may seem paradoxical but it is not. It happens when Ben is obliged to sell more bonds than he has, using the short selling of bonds as a financing facility. Had we imposed a stricter liquidity policy $\mathcal{L}$ forbidding also the short selling we would have found $V^{Ben}(\mathbf{p}) = -\infty$ in these circumstances, because Ben's portfolio would have been incompatible with $\mathcal{L}$ at all (ie, $\mathrm{Att}(\mathbf{p}) \cap \mathcal{L} = \varnothing$). □

A very important characterisation of the map $V^{\mathcal{L}}$ is provided by the following.

Theorem 1

Let $\mathcal{L}$ be any liquidity policy. Then the map $V^{\mathcal{L}} : \mathcal{P} \to \mathbb{R} \cup \{-\infty\}$

1. is concave, ie, for any $\alpha \in [0, 1]$ and for any $\mathbf{p}, \mathbf{q} \in \mathcal{P}$

$$V^{\mathcal{L}}\left(\alpha\mathbf{p} + (1-\alpha)\mathbf{q}\right) \geq \alpha V^{\mathcal{L}}(\mathbf{p}) + (1-\alpha)V^{\mathcal{L}}(\mathbf{q}) \tag{9.21}$$

2. is translationally supervariant, ie, for any $\mathbf{p} \in \mathcal{P}$ and for any $a \geq 0$

$$V^{\mathcal{L}}(\mathbf{p} + a) \geq V^{\mathcal{L}}(\mathbf{p}) + a \tag{9.22}$$

□

Both results tell us important things. The concavity of the value map is a very general feature of liquidity risk. In fact this simply means that when we blend two portfolios $\mathbf{p}$ and $\mathbf{q}$, the value of the blend portfolio $\alpha\mathbf{p} + (1 - \alpha)\mathbf{q}$ is higher than the blend of the two values. But this is nothing but the correct formalisation of the well-known practitioners thumb rule that suggests to reduce, when possible, portfolio granularity. The concavity of the value map in other words reminds us that in illiquid markets, assets concentration costs. It is important not to confuse this granularity effect with the traditional risk reduction that is obtained with portfolio diversification exploiting assets decorrelation. The granularity effect is something totally different, as it manifests itself in portfolio values and not in portfolio risks and has therefore nothing to do with assets correlation. It is something we can measure immediately, at current time, with no assumptions on future events, and it is a non vanishing effect also when the blended portfolios are perfectly correlated. We discover in other words that the 'diversification principle' has two neatly distinguished sides. A market risk side we already formalised long ago, related to the benefit produced on risk measures by a decorrelated portfolio. A liquidity risk side, related to the benefit produced on the value of the portfolio by a smaller granularity, which probably finds a correct formalisation here for the first time.

Example 9.9

Consider a portfolio $\mathbf{p} = (0, p_1, p_2)$ in a two assets market with exponential MSDCs $m_i(s) = e^{-k_i s}$ $i = 1, 2$ and suppose that the portfolio is subject to a liquidity policy of the type

$$\mathcal{L} = \left\{ \mathbf{q} \in \mathcal{P} \middle| q_0 \geq \sum_{i=1}^{2} a_i \, | \, q_i \, | \right\}$$

which requires a certain amount of cash to be held asset proportional to the absolute value of the position. The computation of $V^{\mathcal{L}}(\mathbf{p})$ needs to be done numerically. We plot this function in Figure 9.5 versus p_1 and p_2. We have chosen $k = (0.05, 0.1)$ so that the second asset is more illiquid and $a = (0.08, 0.2)$ so that the liquidity policy is more prudential with respect to the second asset. The plot is manifestly concave in the chosen range displaying the granularity effect. The flat region represents portfolios for which $V^{\mathcal{L}} = -\infty$ because in those cases there are no attainable portfolios satisfying $\mathcal{L}$. □

The translationally supervariance of the value map also formalises something that practitioners perfectly know already. It explains why a single US dollar sometimes may be worth millions of US dollars. Adding liquid money to a portfolio not only adds nominal value, but also improves the liquidity properties of the portfolio. Therefore, on the edge of a liquidity crisis, a single US dollar can make a huge difference and avoid the market liquidation of illiquid assets.

Example 9.10

Consider again Example 9.8. Suppose we add b US dollars to the portfolio $\mathbf{p}$ of Ben. Repeating the calculations in the symmetric case it is easy to obtain

$$V^{Ben}(\mathbf{p}+b) = \begin{cases} c + M - (N/k)\log\left(\dfrac{N/k}{N/k - c + b}\right) & \text{if } b < c \\ b + M & \text{if } b \geq c \end{cases} \tag{9.23}$$

We see that for $b < c$ the value increases non-linearly with b as can be shown in the first plot of Figure 9.6. The second plot shows that for small b the marginal gain in the value produced by any added US dollar is much higher than one. The very first added US dollar in this example has a marginal value of around US$2.6. □

In defense of banalities

We observe that both the results of theorem 1 are sheer banalities. Every practitioner having a basic experience of liquidity risk perfectly knows these things. The fact that it is better to fragment a portfolio into small pieces than having large portions invested in the same asset is just marketplace commonsense. Realising that the benefit of a money injection is not just its notional value but also the liquidity improvement it provides is nearly obvious. But this is exactly the point with liquidity risk. Things that people have known for a long time had never been convincingly expressed by an appropriate notation. Mathematics has long been of no help to confirm and support human insight. This is why, liquidity risk was treated as an exception, to be faced qualitatively when the hidden hypotheses of portfolio theory's formalism ceased to be valid. We would have been worried if we had devised a formalism that displays surprising and unexpected results. We strongly wished to find a formalism that indeed produces sheer banalities in the first place because this is exactly what we needed.

CONCLUSIONS

In the above sections we have proposed a formalism for portfolio theory in illiquid markets and in particular a new definition of portfolio value $V^{\mathcal{L}}(\mathbf{p})$ starting from two main observations stated at the beginning of the chapter. Let us summarise the achievements obtained and how they fit the observations.

As for the first observation, we now have a formalism that perfectly distinguishes between what is a portfolio $\mathbf{p}$ and what is its value $V^{\mathcal{L}}(\mathbf{p})$. The portfolio $\mathbf{p}$ is no more confused with a "sum" of assets. The value map $V^{\mathcal{L}}$ is not simply a linear combination of assets values, but a generally non-linear map. It is exactly this non-linearity and in particular its general concavity, the peculiar fingerprint of liquidity risk. Any formalism that does not account for this concavity, misses the fundamental aspect of portfolio theory in illiquid markets represented by the granularity effect. We stress that the formalism we propose, to the best of our knowledge is the first convincing one which clearly provides a general description of this effect. Equation 9.1 is wrong when liquidity is not perfect, and can be thought of as a limiting case, when liquidity risk tends to zero, namely when MSDCs can be assumed to be essentially flat on all $\mathbb{R}$.

As for the second observation, we notice that now, in this formalism, the value of a portfolio is not defined *per se* unless a liquidity policy has been specified. In our formalism there is no paradox in discovering that the same portfolio **p** may be worth a different value in the hands of two different persons. There is no mystery in this. The value of a portfolio is now a subjective assessment of its usefulness within specific asset-liability constraints, which may vary enormously from person to person. That is why, a new variable $\mathcal{L}$ which was hidden before, now appears as a crucial ingredient in the value function $V^{\mathcal{L}}$. This is also a fundamental aspect of liquidity risk. Were all people as lucky as Alan, who may forget about any potential liquidation, there would be no liquidity risk at all. But people are more generally faced with liquidity constraints which force them to confront their portfolio with the illiquid structure of the market. The MtM procedure defined earlier and embedded in Definition 9.11 simply does this job and probes the value of a portfolio confronting its assets to market prices up to a market depth given by the liquidity policy $\mathcal{L}$ it is subject to.

In this note, we focused on portfolio value only, without dealing with risk measures due to space limits. The subject is treated for instance in Acerbi and Scandolo (2007) and Jarrow and Protter (2005). It is however important to realise that no specific liquidity risk measures need to be devised once the effect of liquidity risk is already taken into account in portfolio values. Risk measures are statistics of future portfolio values under specific hypotheses of the market dynamics. Therefore, the adoption of a common measure of risk $\rho(\cdot)$ (say the standard deviation of a portfolio value at future time $T > t$) is a perfectly legitimate choice provided the value of the portfolio has been correctly computed as the liquidity-adjusted value $V^{\mathcal{L}}(\mathbf{p})$. In this way, $\phi^{\mathcal{L}}_{t,T}(\mathbf{p}) := \rho_t(V^{\mathcal{L}}_T(\mathbf{p}))$ is obtained as a measure of risk which necessarily depend on the liquidity policy $\mathcal{L}$ showing that also liquidity risk (and not only portfolio values) is subjective in the sense that it depends on the liquidity constraints the portfolio is subject to. This is the strategy adopted in both Acerbi and Scandolo (2007) and Jarrow and Protter (2005), in the particular (but extremely interesting) case when the measure of risk is chosen to be a coherent measure of risk.

The real difficulty in entering the realm of liquidity-adjusted measures of risk is not conceptual, but of model type. In fact, when modelling the probabilistic distribution of future events in a illiquid market, we will need to model the stochastics of a real-valued function (the MSDC) for any asset of the market, and no more the stochastics of a single real number (its value) as we are used to do. The modelling freedom is huge and the need for reasonable assumptions in order to end up with a tractable framework is vital. The modelling increase of complexity however must be seen as a necessary complication to face if we want to look at illiquid markets in an appropriate manner. Illiquid markets have indeed such complexity, and neglecting these additional degrees of freedom means closing our eyes in front of liquidity risk at all, which is what in our opinion portfolio theory has done up to date.

REFERENCES

Acerbi, C. and G. Scandolo, 2007, "Liquidity Risk Theory and Coherent Measures of Risk", *Quantitative Finance* forthcoming.

Boyd, S. and L. Vandenberghe, 2004, *Convex Optimization* (Cambridge University Press).

Çetin, U. R., R. A. Jarrow and P. Protter, 2004, "Liquidity Risk and Arbitrage Pricing Theory", *Finance and Stochastics*, 8, pp. 311–341.

Hiriart–Urruty, J.B. and C. Lemarechal, 2004, *Fundamentals of Convex Analysis* (Berlin: Springer Verlag).

Jarrow, R. A. and P. Protter, 2005, "Liquidity Risk and Risk Measure Computation", *Review of Futures Markets*, 11(1).

Rockafellar, R. T., 1970, *Convex Analysis* (Princeton University Press).

10

Interest Rate Risk on the Banking Book

Andrea Resti, Andrea Sironi

Bocconi University

DEFINING INTEREST RATE RISK ON THE BANKING BOOK

Interest rate risk can be defined as the risk that changes in market interest rates reduce the profitability and the economic value of a portfolio of assets and/or liabilities (for example, of a bank).

This risk is due to the fact that bank assets and liabilities have different durations and/or repricing periods. Typically, a bank may raise short-term deposits and use them to finance long-term loans. This means that a shift in market rates could severely affect the bank's profitability, for example, if market rates go up and deposits have to be rolled over at higher costs, while the return on long-term, fixed-rate loans remains unchanged. Such a shift in market rates would cause the bank's net interest margin to shrink; also, as the value of a bank's equity is given by the discounted value of all future profits, the decrease in the spread between the return on loans and the cost of funds would adversely affect the net value of the bank.

In the case of tradable assets and liabilities, interest rate risk can be seen as a special case of market risk. Consider, for example, a 10-year, fixed-rate Treasury bond: if market rates go up, the bond's fair price will fall, causing a loss when the bank sells (or marks-to-market) its securities portfolio. However, there are many assets and liabilities in a bank's balance sheet for which no secondary market is available, and therefore no market price can be observed; these include typical bank items, such as loans or deposits, which constitute a bank's "banking book". Since the interest rate risk on the banking book cannot be measured through market prices, the methodologies developed for market risk prove inappropriate, and *ad hoc* approaches need to be devised and put in place.

Another difference between interest rate risk on the banking book and market risk (due to interest rates) on tradable securities relates to the so-called "indirect effects" of interest rate risk. A shift in market rates, while changing the unit price of a T-bond, does not, *per se*, affect the number of bonds held by a bank; instead, the volume of bank deposits and/or of loans with customers may change (as well as their unit value) because of interest rate movements. Consider, for example, fixed-rate mortgages: in the event of a decrease in market rates, customers are likely to pay back their debt, to get a new one at cheaper conditions; in the same market scenario, the amount of demand deposits held with the bank is likely to rise, as the opportunity cost of liquid investments decreases.

This chapter aims to provide a basic framework for the measurement of interest rate risk that is consistent with the provisions of Pillar II. It first describes how interest rate risk on the banking book is regulated in the new Basel Accord and in other Basel Committee documents; it then presents the main approaches used to measure interest rate risk in banks, distinguishing between methods that rely on the earnings-at-risk (EaR) paradigm and on the value-at-risk (VaR) one, and showing how they can be used to quantify the effect, on the bank's value, of a 2% shift in market rates (as required by Pillar II). We then discuss extensively the treatment of non-maturing assets and liabilities, that is, of balance-sheet items that, while being formally on demand, react to market rate changes only partially and with delay. We next concisely provide a general framework for dealing with the indirect effects of interest rate risk on the banking book, and finally we review and conclude.

INTEREST RATE RISK IN PILLAR II AND OTHER BASEL COMMITTEE GUIDELINES

Basel II does not call for a specific capital requirement against interest rate risk on the banking book, but rather requires that banks have in place appropriate risk measurement procedures, and that the results of such procedures be disclosed to supervisors. Accordingly, Sections 762–4 of the new Basel Accord (Basel Committee on Banking Supervision 2006) include interest rate risk on the banking book under Pillar II. As with other Pillar II risks, there are no fixed formulas or weights for its quantification: rather, the capital required to face interest rate risk must be assessed primarily by the banks' internal systems.

Such systems (as indicated in Section 739) must include all material interest rate positions of the bank and consider all relevant repricing and maturity data, including contractual interest rate ceilings or floors for floating-rate items. As usual, the system's assumptions and techniques must be well documented and thoroughly shared with supervisors.

While relying on the banks' internal tools, the measurement of interest rate risk follows a slightly more structured framework than other Pillar II risks,[1] as the banks' systems have to be used to carry out a standard risk-measurement exercise, that is, to simulate the change in the banks' net value following a 2% parallel shift in the term structure of interest rates.

If, following such a rate shock, the bank's value falls by more than 20% of its overall regulatory capital (including both Tier 1 and Tier 2), then the bank is called an "outlier bank" and will be monitored with particular attention by the supervisors. Such monitoring may include a request to the bank to reduce its risky assets, to hold an additional amount of capital, or some combination of the two. However, the discretionary nature of Pillar II implies that a bank may be subjected to such requests even if it does not formally qualify as an outlier.

The choice of a 2% shift as the benchmark against which interest rate risk must be measured has been explained by the Basel Committee as follows. The Committee wanted to choose a rate shock reflecting a fairly uncommon and stressful scenario; furthermore, the shock had to be strong enough to highlight the effects of any embedded options (such as the customers' option to pay back fixed-rate loans after a decrease in rates) and any non-linearities (that is, effects that cannot be captured by simplified risk measures based on first-order derivatives[2]). The shock also had to be simple and easy to implement. In this sense, while a non-parallel shift might have proven more realistic (given that short-term rates tend to be more volatile than long-term ones), the Committee felt that it may have made the banks' risk assessments less readable and therefore less effective. Finally, the shock had to be based on a methodology that, while being appropriate for G10 countries, could be easily generalised to non-G10 currencies

With these targets in mind, the Basel Committee analysed six years of interest rate data for various maturities and G10 currencies. Six years were considered enough to provide a wide array of market conditions that was not unduly affected by any specific state of the cycle. Rate changes over a one-year rolling window (for example, between January 1, 2001, and January 1, 2002) were computed and ranked, and the 1st and 99th percentiles were singled out. For most currencies and most maturities (especially for longer ones), those percentiles indicated a rate change of about 2% (either negative or positive).[3] Accordingly, a 2% (200 basis points) shift was considered adequate to serve as a benchmark to assess a bank's vulnerability to adverse interest rate movements.[4]

Besides the few paragraphs included in the Accord, the Basel Committee has also dictated a set of guidelines to banks on how to measure interest rate risk on the banking book. Namely, a list of 12 fundamental principles was drawn up in 1997 and extended to 15 in 2004 (Basel Committee on Banking Supervision 1997; Basel Committee on Banking Supervision 2004). These principles, rather than focusing on merely methodological issues, address mainly the role of the board and the top management in ensuring that proper policies and procedures for managing interest rate risk are in place; accordingly, for example, Principle 2 lays a considerable emphasis on the involvement of senior management. According to the Basel Committee, instead, top managers should participate in the definition of objectives, criteria and procedures of the risk management system. Although this may appear obvious, such an involvement still represents a critical issue for many banks, where interest rate risk measurement systems were introduced by the "technicians" in the treasury department, without a clear and strong mandate by the top executives.

Another crucial issue (Principle 3) is that interest rate risk management is to be assigned to an independent unit (put at arm's length from departments, such as the treasury department, where risks are originated and "bets" on the future movements of the yield curve are made). Such a unit must support the senior management from a technical point of view; its duties and responsibilities include the definition of a suitable set of criteria for measuring risk; the validation of risk measures provided by individual business units in the bank; and the updating of parameter estimates needed to feed the system. The risk management unit has to be independent, in order to be authoritative and credible.

Principle 4 highlights the importance of measuring and managing interest rate risk at a consolidated level. This means that interest rate risk can be adequately appraised and managed only by taking into account a banking group as a whole, instead of focusing on individual areas. In fact, two legal entities in the same group might offset each other's risks, so that the group as a whole is roughly hedged against market rate changes; alternatively, small specialised companies could take on a considerable amount of interest rate risks, so that a risk measurement system focused only on the mother company, and its main subsidiaries could significantly underestimate risk.

Another remarkable principle stated by the Basel Committee is that the system for interest rate risk measurement should be integrated into the bank's day-to-day management. Accordingly, any criteria developed for measuring interest rate risk have to be used in practice, as a means to steer corporate policy, and must not be seen as purely abstract measures used only by the risk management unit.

Interest rate risk measures must not only be escalated to the bank's top management, but also have to be communicated to the public (consistent with Basel's Pillar III) and reported to supervisors (consistent with Pillar II).

THE MAIN APPROACHES TO INTEREST RATE RISK MEASUREMENT

Models based on EaR and VaR

Bearing this regulatory framework in mind, we now introduce the two main approaches to interest rate risk measurement used by banks. Before we begin, however, a distinction must be made between models based on EaR and VaR.

As mentioned in the first section, in fact, a shift in the yield curve can affect both a bank's earnings (for example, by reducing the spread between the weighted average return on financial assets and the weighted average cost of financial liabilities) and its net value (for example, by reducing the market value of the fixed-rate securities held by the bank). Note that these two effects are just different ways of representing the same event: on one hand, each time a decrease in (current and possibly future) earnings occurs, shareholders are worse off and that must be reflected in the value of their investment; on the other hand, a decline in the value (price) of a fixed-rate asset just mirrors the fact that its coupon rate has become less attractive, so its (current and future) earnings have fallen, compared with its opportunity costs.[5]

While from a purely theoretical point of view it is quite equivalent to focus on earnings or value, in practice this choice significantly affects the type of measures used by banks to assess interest rate risk. Indeed, while Basel II requires evaluating the impact on the bank's net value following a 2% parallel shift in the term structure, many banks still prefer to quantify interest rate risk in terms of missed earnings (for example, in the following 12 months), using the so-called repricing gap approach. This means that risk measures based on the repricing gap (that is, measures of EaR) have to be converted into a VaR figure in order to be compliant with the criteria introduced by Pillar II.

In the next section we will briefly review the repricing gap approach and discuss ways to make it consistent with the VaR perspective; in the subsection "Models based on VaR: the duration gap", instead, we present an alternative approach, based on the so-called duration gap, which is intrinsically consistent with the VaR perspective.[6]

Models based on earnings: the repricing gap

A bank's net interest income (NII) can be computed as follows

$$NII = II - IE = \sum_i r_i a_i - \sum_j r_j l_j \tag{10.1}$$

where II is interest income, IE are interest expenses, r_i is the rate earned the i-th asset, held for an amount a_i, r_j is rate paid on the j-th liability l_j.

Suppose we want to measure the effect of a shift in market rates on the NII expected between now and some future date t (say, one year[7]). Assuming that the amounts of assets and liabilities stay constant (that is, that there are no indirect effects as defined in the first section above), this would be

$$\Delta NII_t = \sum_i \Delta r_i a_i - \sum_j \Delta r_j l_j \tag{10.2}$$

Note that, for all assets and liabilities that are to be replaced or repriced after t, the Δr will be zero; they can therefore be omitted from Equation 10.2, getting

$$\Delta NII_t = \sum_{i \in I_t} \Delta r_i a_i - \sum_{j \in J_t} \Delta r_j l_j \tag{10.3}$$

where I_t and J_t are two subsets of the bank's assets and liabilities, including only rate-sensitive assets and liabilities. By rate-sensitive, we mean assets and liabilities that will be rolled over or repriced (for example, in the case of indexed bonds) at some date $t_i < t$ ($t_j < t$), that is, before the end of the gapping period.

Furthermore, consider the following: the new rate conditions will affect the net interest margin only after the rate-sensitive assets and liabilities have been rolled over or repriced, that is, only for a fraction of the gapping period. Accordingly, Equation 10.3 can be made more precise by writing

$$\Delta NII_t = \sum_{i \in I_t} \Delta r_i \left(t - t_i\right) a_i - \sum_{j \in J_t} \Delta r_j \left(t - t_j\right) l_j \tag{10.4}$$

For example, if we set t=1 (gapping period of one year) and consider a loan that will be rolled over in three months (t_i = 0.25), the rate change on the loan, Δr_i, is going to affect the bank's net interest margin for only three quarters (0.75).

Finally, suppose that we have estimated a relationship between the rates r_i and r_j on one hand, and some benchmark market rate r (eg the three-month Libor rate) on the other hand, and that for each rate earned or paid on the bank's assets and liabilities, a sensitivity coefficient β exists, linking its movements to the changes in the benchmark rate. This means that we can write

$$\Delta r_i \cong \beta_i \Delta r \tag{10.5}$$

and

$$\Delta r_j \cong \beta_j \Delta r \tag{10.6}$$

for any i and j.

For example, in the case of retail deposits (which are held by the public not only as an investment, but also as a liquidity buffer), a sensitivity coefficient β_j below one would be expected. Assuming, for instance, $\beta_j = 0.5$, that would imply that a 1% increase in market rates would only cause the cost of deposits to rise by 50 basis points.

Based on Equations 10.5 and 10.6, the change in NII can be rewritten as

$$\Delta NII_t = \sum_{i \in I_t} \beta_i \Delta r (t - t_i) a_i - \sum_{j \in J_t} \beta_j \Delta r (t - t_j) l_j = \left(\sum_{i \in I_t} \beta_i \Delta r (t - t_i) a_i - \sum_{j \in J_t} \beta_j \Delta r (t - t_j) l_j \right) \Delta r = G_t \Delta r \tag{10.7}$$

where

$$G_t \equiv \sum_{i \in I_t} \beta_i (t - t_i) a_i - \sum_{j \in J_t} \beta_j (t - t_j) l_j \tag{10.8}$$

is the bank's repricing gap associated with the gapping period t.

To understand the logic behind the repricing gap measure, consider the case of a bank with a considerable amount of assets to be repriced/rolled over in a few days, while most of its liabilities are fixed-rate and will not expire before two years. Also, assume that the bank's assets are with professional counterparties, so that their β_is are close to 100%, while its liabilities are retail and show low sensitivities (that is, low β_js) to changes in market rates. In such a situation, the one-year gap G_1 would clearly be positive and large; this means that the bank's net interest margin increases if market rates go up (in a few days, the bank is able to roll over its loans at higher rates, while keeping its funding costs almost unchanged), but conversely suffers if market rates fall (because interest income quickly adjusts to new market conditions, while interest expenses for the following year will stay roughly constant).

Now, consider the rate change chosen, as a benchmark, by the Basel Committee: the loss associated with a 2% shift (either up or down) in r would be

$$L_t = \left| \sum_{i \in I_t} \beta_i (t - t_i) a_i - \sum_{j \in J_t} \beta_j (t - t_j) l_j \right| 0.02 = |G_t| 0.02 \tag{10.9}$$

Note that:

1. we took the absolute value of the gap because we want to obtain a positive value for the loss; in other words, we want to make sure that we consider an unfavourable shift, not a favourable one (in the example above, that would be a 2% decrease, not an increase, in rates); and
2. this loss is a measure of EaR, as it represents the decline in the earnings expected by the bank between today and time t; it must therefore be converted into a VaR measure.

To convert this EaR into a VaR, let us proceed as follows. First, we consider two different possible lengths for the gapping period, say t_1 and $t_2 > t_1$ (eg, one year and two years). By appropriately choosing rate-sensitive assets and liabilities, Equation 10.7 can be used to quantify the change in *NII* expected for the first period (that is, the first year) only

$$\Delta NII_1 = \left(\sum_{i \in I_1} \beta_i (t_1 - t_i) a_i - \sum_{j \in J_1} \beta_j (t_1 - t_j) l_j \right) \Delta r = G_1 \Delta r \qquad (10.10)$$

(where I_1 and J_1 denote risk-sensitive assets and liabilities that are rolled over or repriced before time t_1). By appropriately extending the sets I and J, the same can be done for t_2, that is, for the next two years

$$\Delta NII_2 = \left(\sum_{i \in I_2} \beta_i (t_2 - t_i) a_i - \sum_{j \in J_2} \beta_j (t_2 - t_j) l_j \right) \Delta r = G_2 \Delta r \qquad (10.11)$$

Comparing Equations 10.10 and 10.11, we see that the change in *NII* for the second year only is given by

$$\Delta NII_2' = \Delta NII_2 - \Delta NII_1 = G_2' \Delta r \qquad (10.12)$$

where G_2' denotes the marginal gap associated with the interval (t_1, t_2), that is

$$G_2' = \left(\sum_{i \in I_2} \beta_i (t_2 - t_i) a_i - \sum_{i \in I_1} \beta_i (t_1 - t_i) a_i \right) - \left(\sum_{j \in J_2} \beta_j (t_2 - t_j) l_j - \sum_{j \in J_1} \beta_j (t_1 - t_j) l_j \right) \qquad (10.13)$$

Equations 10.12 and 10.13 can easily be generalised to get the change in *NII* expected in any period (t_{y-1}, t_y). Without loss of generality, we can think of $\Delta NII_y'$ as the change in the *NII* expected for year y and write

$$\Delta NII_y' = G_y' \Delta r \qquad (10.14)$$

Now consider a bank expecting changes in its net interest margin of ΔNII_1, $\Delta NII'_2$, …, $\Delta NII'_y$, …, $\Delta NII'_N$ for the next N years. The change in the bank's value is clearly equal to the net present value of those changes

$$\Delta V = \sum_{y=1}^{N} \frac{\Delta NII'_y}{\left(1+r_e+\Delta r\right)^y} = \Delta r \sum_{y=1}^{N} \frac{G'_y}{\left(1+r_e+\Delta r\right)^y} \tag{10.15}$$

Note that, to compute the net present value, we use the bank's current cost of capital (Saita 2007),[8] r_e, adjusted to account for the shift in market rates.

Finally, to find the change in value associated with a 2% shift, as requested by the Basel Committee, we compute the ΔV associated both with a 2% increase and a 2% decrease, and choose the worse one[9]

$$VaR = -\min\left[0.02\sum_{y=1}^{N}\frac{G'_y}{\left(1+r_e+0.02\right)^y}; -0.02\sum_{y=1}^{N}\frac{G'_y}{\left(1+r_e+0.02\right)^y}\right] \tag{10.16}$$

To sum up, the approach based on the repricing gap requires that:

1. the bank knows the rollover/repricing schedule of all its assets and liabilities, as well as their sensitivities to market rates, in order to be able to compute marginal repricing gaps for a number N, large enough, of future years; and
2. the bank knows its cost of equity.[10]

If this information is available, the next step is computing marginal gaps based on Equation 10.13), and then using Equation 10.16 to transform them into a VaR estimate that is consistent with the benchmark shift in market rates chosen by the Basel Committee.

Note, however, that the construction of the rollover/repricing schedule is far from being trivial. In fact, a number of assets and liabilities exist for which maturity and repricing period are uncertain. More details on how to deal with such items will be provided later.

Models based on VaR: the duration gap

From standard finance theory, we know that the change in the value of an asset, a_i, following a shift Δr_i in the term structure, can be approximated based on its modified duration, MD_i

$$\Delta a_i \cong -a_i \cdot MD_i \cdot \Delta r_i \tag{10.17}$$

The same applies to the value of a liability, l_j

$$\Delta l_j \cong -l_j \cdot MD_j \cdot \Delta r_j \tag{10.18}$$

As the net value of a bank, V, is given by the total value of assets minus the total value of liabilities, the change in value for the bank following a shift in market rates can be estimated as

$$\Delta V = \sum_i \Delta a_i - \sum_j \Delta l_j \cong -\left(\sum_i a_i \cdot MD_i \cdot \Delta r_i - \sum_j l_j \cdot MD_j \cdot \Delta r_j \right) \tag{10.19}$$

Assume, as we did in the previous subsection, that the bank has estimated a set of sensitivity coefficients, β, linking changes in the rates earned and paid on its assets and liabilities to some benchmark market rate Δr; then we can write

$$\Delta V = \sum_i \Delta a_i - \sum_j \Delta l_j \cong -\left(\sum_i a_i \cdot MD_i \cdot \beta_i - \sum_j l_j \cdot MD_j \cdot \beta_j \right) \Delta r = -DG \cdot \Delta r \tag{10.20}$$

where

$$DG \equiv \sum_i a_i \cdot MD_i \cdot \beta_i - \sum_j l_j \cdot MD_j \cdot \beta_j \tag{10.21}$$

is the bank's duration gap. A bank with a positive duration gap (long-term assets funded through short-term liabilities) will increase in value if market rates go down ($\Delta r < 0$), as its investments will appreciate while the value of its liabilities stays unchanged (as they quickly adapt to the new, lower rates); however, it will be vulnerable to increases in market rates, as they would bring forth losses on the assets side, without any material benefits for its liabilities.

Now, consider the benchmark shift chosen by the Basel Committee: the loss in value associated with a 2% change in r is simply

$$VaR = |DG| \cdot 0.02 \tag{10.22}$$

Note that, since we are interested in the absolute value of the loss, we take the modulus of DG.

Unlike the repricing gap, the duration gap does not require any transformation of EaR into VaR, since it is already based on a value-at-risk framework. However, since it uses modified durations, it requires that all assets and liabilities are marked-to-market and all future cashflows associated with each of them are known.

Furthermore, equations such as Equation 10.17 provide only an approximation of the change in value experienced by an asset/liability following a shift in market rates. Such an approximation may prove acceptable if the rate shift is small or if the function linking values and rates is almost linear; if, instead, the function is highly nonlinear, the duration gap approach can be made more precise by including a second-order effect, based on the convexity of the individual assets and liabilities held by the bank. This refinement, known as the convexity gap approach, ensures that interest rate risk is measured more accurately, but also increases the complexity of the computations required and makes the final output less understandable for the bank's top management.[11]

DEALING WITH NON-MATURING ASSETS AND LIABILITIES

The practical application of the approaches seen in the previous section is made especially complex by the presence, in the banking book, of many assets and liabilities that could be paid back before their contractual maturity (eg, mortgage loans for which the borrower has a prepayment option) or that do not even have a contractual maturity or repricing period (eg, demand deposits, overdrafts).

Prepayment risk on mortgages and other long-term exposures can be measured and managed through option-pricing models, since this type of loan can be seen as embedding a call option, which the borrower can use to buy back the debt at a fixed price. A well-known model to estimate the value of this option and its probability of exercise is due to Fischer Black, Emanuel Derman and Bill Toy (1990); this and other similar models have become standard practice in most banks, since accounting standards today require financial institutions to estimate and update the value of the prepayment option.

Assets and liabilities that do not have a contractual maturity (eg, demand deposits) could in principle be considered as instantly repriced: each time market rates increase, customers could ask for the rate on deposits to be updated accordingly; in case their request is not met, they could withdraw their funds at no notice and look for a better investment opportunity elsewhere.

However, to ask for a rate update each time market yields move, customers would have to spend time and face costs; also, the threat to withdraw funds and take them to another bank could not be credible if deposits are used as a means of payment, so that their transfer would entail significant switching costs. This is especially true for retail deposits, where the average account size does not justify the costs inherent in the bargaining process required to get a rate increase.

Furthermore, while rate changes on retail deposits and loans tend to be quicker when they benefit the bank (rate cuts on deposits, rate increases on loans), they are usually slower to occur if they are favourable to customers (rate increases on deposits, rate cuts on loans); this is because banks can renegotiate rates unilaterally for large numbers of accounts and exposures, but of course do so only if such a renegotiation originates a profit.

In short, rates on many non-maturing assets and liabilities (NOMALs) might prove sticky and asymmetrical: they follow market moves only partially, with delay, and with a speed that depends on the direction in which benchmark rates have moved.

In the rest of this section, we see how this stickiness and asymmetry can be modelled. More precisely, we show how to estimate a set of parameters that can be used to input NOMAL data into the repricing gap and duration gap models seen in the previous section.

To begin, consider the example shown in Figure 10.1: here, we can see the link between market rates (the interbank rate) and the rates earned and paid by a bank on its overdrafts and demand deposits. Notice that, while the latter somehow mimic the behaviour of the interbank rate, their response to its movements is rather slow.

One way to describe such a behaviour is to estimate an equation like the following one, where the level of the rate $r_{j,t}$ currently paid on the j-th liability (or earned on i-th asset) is assumed to be a function not just of the benchmark rate's current value (r_t), but also of the lagged values of both rates ($r_{j,t-1}$ and r_{t-1})

Figure 10.1 An example of sticky and asymmetrical rate adjustments

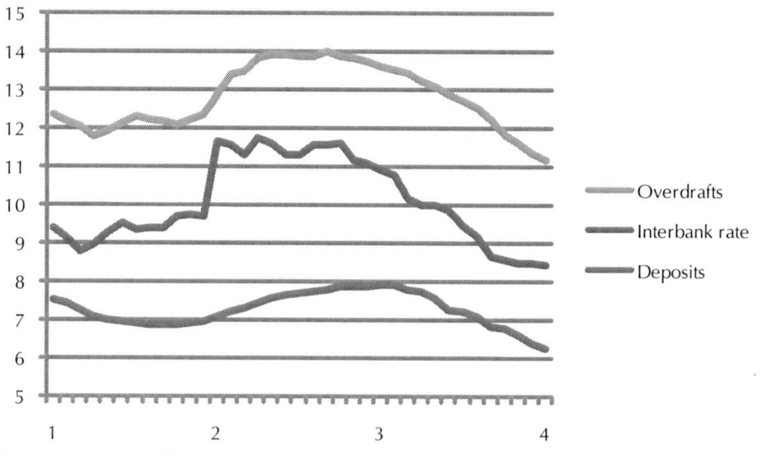

$$r_{j,t} = k + \alpha_1 r_{j,t-1} + \beta_0 r_t + \beta_1 r_{t-1} \tag{10.23}$$

Equation 10.23 represents a model with autoregressive distributed lags of order 1 (in r_j) and 1 (in r); in short, ADL(1,1). The model can be estimated, for example, by ordinary least squares using a standard statistical software application (or a simple office automation tool such as Microsoft Excel). By recursively substituting in Equation 10.23 expressions such as the following

$$r_{j,t-1} = k + \alpha_1 r_{j,t-2} + \beta_0 r_{t-1} + \beta_1 r_{t-2} \tag{10.24}$$

you get

$$r_{j,t} = k\sum_{i=0}^{\infty} \alpha_1^i + \beta_0 r_t + \sum_{i=1}^{\infty}\left(\alpha_1^i \beta_0 + \alpha_1^{i-1}\beta_1\right) r_{t-i} = \frac{k}{1-\alpha_1} + \beta_0 r_t + \sum_{i=1}^{\infty} \delta_i r_{t-1} \tag{10.25}$$

where

$$\delta_i \equiv \alpha_1^i \beta_0 + \alpha_1^{i-1}\beta_1$$

Based on Equation 10.25 the following parameters can be computed:

1. an impact coefficient, β_0, showing what portion of a change in r is reflected without delay by r_j; and
2. a set of increasing intermediate multipliers, $I_k \equiv \beta_0 + \sum_{i=1}^{k} \delta_i$, showing the cumulated effect on r_j of a movement in r occurred k periods before.

In the long run, it can be assumed that any shock on r_j and r has been fully absorbed, so that

$$r_{j,t} = r_j; \quad r_t = r \text{ for any } t$$

and the equilibrium version of Equation 10.25 becomes

$$r_j = \frac{k}{1-\alpha_1} + \frac{\beta_0 + \beta_1}{1-\alpha_1} r \tag{10.26}$$

Accordingly, $\frac{\beta_0+\beta_1}{1-\alpha_1}$ represents the total adjustment in r_j after a change in the benchmark rate r.

The model in Equations 10.23–26 can be made slightly more complex to account for the fact that the rates in Figure 10.1 tend to respond differently to movements in the benchmark rate, depending on whether it experiences a rise or a fall. To capture this asymmetry, the time series for the benchmark rate has to be "split" into two time series, with the former driven only by rate increases and the latter only by rate decreases. This can be done by constructing the following two variables (note that $r_t^+ + r_t^- \equiv r_t$ for any t)

$$r_t^+ = r_0 + \sum_{i \le t \wedge \Delta r > 0} \Delta r_i; \qquad r_t^- = \sum_{i \le t \wedge \Delta r_t < 0} \Delta r_i$$

The asymmetric ADL(1,1) model then becomes

$$r_{i,t} = k + \alpha_1 r_{i,t-1} + \beta_0^+ r_t^+ + \beta_1^+ r_{t-1}^+ + \beta_0^- r_t^- + \beta_1^- r_{t-1}^- \qquad (10.27)$$

Using this model, it is possible to differentiate between rate cuts and rate rises, and separately compute the impact coefficient, the intermediate multipliers and the total adjustment factor as described above (after replacing β_0 and β_1 with the specific coefficients associated with positive/negative changes in the benchmark rate).

However, as the model now includes a higher number of (possibly multicollinear) variables, coefficient estimates may become less precise, compared with the ones in Equation 10.23.

Tables 10.1 and 10.2 report the coefficients estimated, based on Equation 10.27, for the rates on deposits and overdrafts in Figure 10.1. Although not

Table 10.1 Values of the asymmetric ADL(1,1) model for the rate on deposits

Coefficient	Value	Standard error	*T*-statistic	*P*-value
k (constant term)	0.852336	0.387137	2.201642	0.0329
α_1 (lagged rate on deposits)	0.717524	0.048463	14.80573	0.0000
β_0^+ (one-month interbank rate, r_t^+)	0.045721	0.052118	0.877255	0.3850
β_1^+ (lagged one-month interbank rate, r_{t-1}^+)	0.097816	0.058474	1.672812	0.1013
β_0^- (one-month interbank rate, r_t^-)	0.274831	0.063485	4.329049	0.0001
β_1^- (lagged one-month interbank rate, r_{t-1}^-)	–0.101707	0.065306	–1.557393	0.1264
R-squared	0.985739			
Adjusted *R*-square	0.984154			

Table 10.2 Values of the asymmetric ADL(1,1) model for the rate on overdrafts

Coefficient	Value	Standard error	*T*-statistic	*P*-value
k (constant term)	1.643966	0.333146	4.934668	0.0000
α_1 (lagged rate on deposits)	0.656195	0.026363	24.89042	0.0000
β_0^+ (one-month interbank rate, r_t^+)	0.254141	0.045282	5.612373	0.0000
β_1^+ (lagged one-month interbank rate, r_{t-1}^+)	0.044555	0.052982	0.840942	0.4048
β_0^- (one-month interbank rate, r_t^-)	0.194424	0.056653	3.431821	0.0013
β_1^- (lagged one-month interbank rate, r_{t-1}^-)	0.118196	0.062099	1.903356	0.0634
R-squared	0.996126			
Adjusted *R*-square	0.995696			

all coefficients are strongly significant, the model as a whole has an excellent goodness-of-fit and the link between market rates and bank rates behaves as expected.

Based on the values in Table 10.1, the impact factor and the intermediate multipliers for the rate on deposits have been computed and are shown in Figure 10.2. It can be seen that the total adjustment factor is different in the event of rate increase (about 0.5 – see the total of the black and grey bars on the left) or decrease (about 0.6 – see bars on the right). This means that the bank is more effective in passing on rate movements to depositors when those movements lead to lower funding costs. Not only the total, but also the structure of the grey bars in the figure tends to be quite different for rate increases and decreases: when market rates go down, almost half of the total adjustment in deposit rates takes place within one month (as opposed to about one-tenth in the case of a rate increase).

Results for overdrafts (Figure 10.3) are similar, but work in the opposite direction: in this case, the bank is faster in updating lending rates when the cost of money has increased, while it is somehow slower in the event of a rate cut; also, note that the total adjustment factor is much closer to one than it was for deposits.

The results in Figures 10.2 and 10.3 can be used to allocate deposits or overdrafts to different time bands in the bank's repricing/rollover schedule,

Figure 10.2 Impact factors (black), intermediate multipliers (grey) and total adjustment factor (black and grey) for the rate on deposits

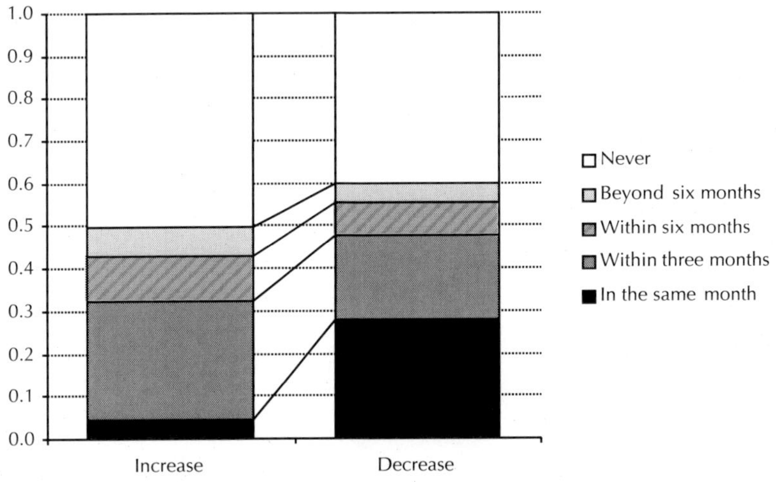

Figure 10.3 Impact factors (black), intermediate multipliers (grey) and total adjustment factor (black + grey) for the rate on overdrafts

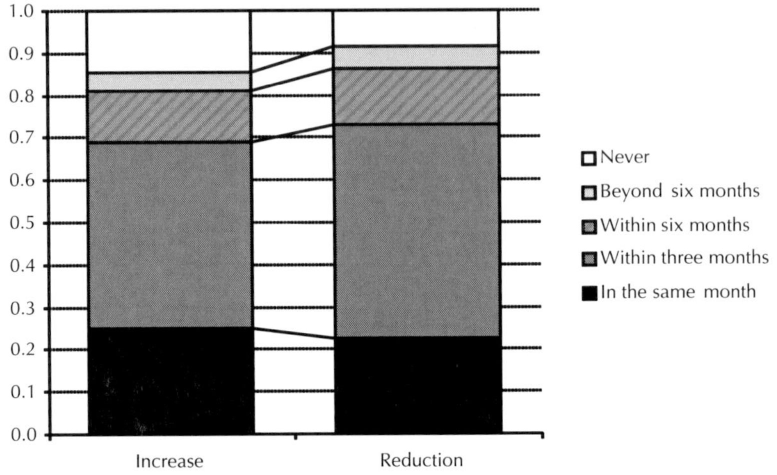

which serves as an input for both the repricing gap and the duration gap approach; this is shown through an example in Table 10.3.

Here, we consider a bank with €1 million of deposits, for which the coefficients in Table 10.1 have been estimated. Based on the impact factor and the intermediate multipliers, the deposits can be allocated as indicated in the table; the repricing gap or duration gap approach can then be applied to demand deposits using this adjusted repricing/maturity schedule.

Note that, since the asymmetric ADL(1,1) model generates two different repricing/rollover schedules for rate increases and decreases, the repricing gap G and the duration gap *DG* discussed above will have to be computed twice, getting two different values (for example, G^+ and G^- respectively for repricing gaps associated with positive and negative changes in market rates). To assess the effect of the 2% shift chosen as a benchmark by the Basel Committee, a bank will then have to use G^+ (or DG^+) when simulating the impact of $\Delta r = +2\%$ and use G^- (DG^-) when considering a $\Delta r = -2\%$. As usual, the worse of the two results will be chosen to assess the risks associated with interest rate movements.

MODELLING INDIRECT EFFECTS DUE TO RATE/QUANTITY INTERACTIONS

In previous sections we have chosen to ignore the indirect effects of interest rate risk, that is, we have assumed that moves in market rates, while

Table 10.3 Repricing/rollover schedule for demand deposits derived from the asymmetric ADL(1,1,) model

Time bands	In the event of a rate increase			In the event of a rate decrease		
	Coefficient	Value (%)	Deposits (€)	Coefficient	Value (%)	Deposits (€)
Immediate	β_0^+	4.6	45,721	β_0^-	27.5	274,831
1 month	δ_1^+	13.1	130,622	δ_1^-	9.5	95,491
2 months	δ_2^+	9.4	93,724	δ_2^-	6.9	68,517
3 months	δ_3^+	6.7	67,249	δ_3^-	4.9	49,163
4–6 months	$\sum_{t=4}^{6}\delta_t^+$	10.8	107,719	$\sum_{t=4}^{6}\delta_t^-$	7.9	78,747
7–12 months	$\sum_{t=7}^{12}\delta_t^+$	5.4	54,492	$\sum_{t=7}^{12}\delta_t^-$	4.0	39,836
13–24 months	$\sum_{t=13}^{24}\delta_t^+$	0.8	8,451	$\sum_{t=13}^{24}\delta_t^-$	0.6	6,178
Rate-insensitive	$1-\frac{\beta_0^+ + \beta_1^+}{1-\alpha_1}$	49.2	492,022	$1-\frac{\beta_0^- + \beta_1^-}{1-\alpha_1}$	38.7	387,237
Total		100.0	1,000,000		100.0	1,000,000

changing the returns and unit costs of a bank's assets and liabilities, do not affect their volumes. This approach is sometimes referred to as a "static simulation" approach (Basel Committee on Banking Supervision, 2004).

In practice, however, the demand for bank loans, deposits and other products is likely to be affected by a change in market conditions. To try to account for such indirect effects, a "dynamic simulation" approach must be adopted: instead of being kept unchanged, quantities must be somehow updated, based on a set of equations that capture their past reactions to changes in market rates.

The estimation of such equations, however, is far from straightforward. In fact, rate changes are usually the consequence of a given macroeconomic scenario involving several tens of variables; the demand for bank products is likely to be affected not only by the level of market rates, but also by all other variables in the scenario (eg, stock-market returns, house prices, demand for durable goods). Indeed, the analysis of the past behaviour of the demand for bank deposits or loans could lead to counterintuitive results, when carried out in a strictly univariate framework. For example, it might be found that the demand for loans slows down when rates decrease, just because cuts in benchmark rates are usually associated with phases of economic sluggishness, when retail loan applications decline and companies postpone investments. Similarly, customer deposits may be found to decrease as short-term rates go up, as higher rates could be the central bank's response to a buoyant stock-market that drives funds away from more liquid investments.

Besides considering a whole set of macroeconomic variables that might affect the demand for bank products, an econometric analysis of indirect effects should also capture time lags in the rate/volumes relationship. As seen in the previous section, the reaction of bank loans and deposits tends to be sticky, especially in the retail market, so the demand for bank products cannot be expected to respond instantaneously to new rate conditions. This introduces a further degree of complexity in the statistical analyses of the past behaviour of bank products and risks, making their results highly fragile and unstable over time.

For these reasons, rather than setting up an econometric model that tries to forecast the indirect effects associated with any given shift in rates, a bank might feel more comfortable with a stress-testing approach, where a set of arbitrary scenarios are simulated for quantities, and their effects on the repricing gap or duration gap separately quantified.

For example, when assessing the effects of a 2% increase in the level of interest rates, a bank may alter the amounts on its balance sheet in the following way:

1. a 10% decrease in overdrafts, to take effect gradually over the following 12 months;
2. a 30% decrease in the issuance of new term loans, to take effect gradually, as current term loans are rolled over;
3. a 5% increase in demand deposits, to take effect gradually over the following 12 months;
4. a 20% increase in the demand for new certificates of deposit, to take effect gradually, as current certificates of deposit expire; and/or
5. an increase in interbank lending (or a decrease in interbank borrowing) to account for the new funds raised, that are not used for customer loans.

A 2% decrease in market rates could instead be accompanied by a shock in quantities that is similar to the one described above, but with all signs reversed (ie, an increase in loans with a decrease in funds from customers).

Such simulated scenarios would not be grounded on any formal econometric analysis, but simply on the bank managers' experience and expectations; yet, while being less rigorous and more subjective, they would also be more readable and transparent in their structure and implications.

A more formal approach could instead be used to assess changes in volumes due to prepayment risk. As mentioned in the previous section, prepayment risk is the risk that the borrowers will pay back their debt in advance, because new market conditions make it advisable to replace that debt with a cheaper one. This could be the case for fixed-rate mortgages issued by the bank, but also for callable bonds on the liabilities side, if present. When simulating the effects of a given shift in market rates, it is relatively easy to compute the gain that the borrower would get from paying back an "old" exposure and getting funded at the "new" rates, as this is like checking whether an option is in the money, given a change in the price for the underlying asset.

Obviously, in order for an exposure to be paid back in advance, the gain from exercising the prepayment option must be material enough to cover exercise costs (including the cost of raising new funds on the market, that is, to negotiate a new mortgage or to set up a new bond issue); furthermore, in the case of retail exposures, it is necessary to account for informational inefficiencies that cause customers to react imperfectly and with delay.

FINAL REMARKS

In this chapter, we provided a general framework for the measurement of interest rate risk on the banking book that is broadly consistent with the provisions of the Pillar II in the new Basel Accord.

To that end, we first summarised how interest rate risk on the banking book is regulated in the new Basel Accord and in other Basel Committee documents, and explained the economic rationale behind the choice of a 200 basis-point shift, as the benchmark shock against which individual banks must check their exposure to interest rate risk.

We also discussed the main approaches used by banks to measure interest rate risk, namely the repricing gap and the duration gap approach; we stressed the fact that the repricing gap approach, while being still widely used by banks, is not fully consistent with the VaR perspective chosen by the Basel Committee, and therefore must be appropriately adjusted to fit into the Pillar II framework. We then turned to NOMALs and introduced an ADL(1,1) model that can be used to slot them into the repricing buckets required, as an input, by the repricing and duration gap approaches. Finally, we discussed the pros and cons of the use of econometric estimates when dealing with the indirect effects of interest rate risk on the banking book, and suggested an approach based on stress tests that are consistent with the top management's experience and judgement.

Putting together these different steps, it should be possible to set up a suitable framework for the measurement of interest rate risk on the banking book that can be further enhanced and customised based on each bank's peculiarities and the top management's priorities.

Before we conclude, however, we would like to point out that the approach presented in this chapter (and, more generally speaking, the approach suggested by the Basel Accord) is likely to prove somehow conservative, because of a gap between the risk horizon adopted by the repricing/duration gap measures discussed in the section "The main approaches to interest rate risk measurement" and that of the rate shifts used by the Basel Committee in the empirical analysis (see the section "Interest rate risk in Pillar II and other Basel Committee guidelines") that led to choosing a 200 basis-point change as a standard benchmark.

In fact, the 200 basis-point shift was chosen based on a time series of one-year rate changes. This means that, in real life, a 2% change in interest rates is possible but requires, on average, 12 months to take effect fully. On the other hand, both measures presented in this chapter (the repricing gap and the duration gap) assume that the change in market rates Δr will take place immediately and therefore overestimate the effects of a rate move that, based on past empirical data, should occur more gradually over time. Hence, the approach described above can be thought to provide a sort of maximum ceiling for the actual decrease suffered by a bank's value and profits.

1 The framework for interest rate risk measurement can be made even further structured by national supervisors. In fact, under Basel II, they are entitled to establish a mandatory minimum capital requirement; this, in practice, amounts to moving interest rate risk much closer to Pillar I.

2 See, for example, the duration-gap approach presented in the section "Models based on value at risk: the duration gap".

3 Note that this result holds for G10 currencies. Banks holding exposures in non-G10 currencies, are invited to compute the 1st and 99th percentile of one-year rate changes following the same approach used by the Committee, and to share their results with their supervisors.

4 The Committee admits that the 2% shift rule could be replaced if future market rate changes were to differ significantly from those of the last six years.

5 The link between EaR and VaR is thoroughly discussed, in the context of business risk, in Chapter 7 of this book.

6 For a more detailed presentation of the repricing and duration gap, with examples and Excel files, see Resti and Sironi (2007).

7 The period over which the change in net interest margin is simulated is usually called the "gapping period".

8 A similar formula has been proposed by Matten (2000), but using the risk-free rate, r, in place of the cost of capital, r_e.

9 From Equation 10.16 it can be seen that, when we look at the effects of a 2% increase in rates on the bank's value (that is, in VaR terms), any increase or fall is mitigated, to some extent, by the fact that future events are evaluated with a more severe discount factor.

10 The estimation of a bank's fair cost of equity is far from being trivial. Alternative approaches are discussed in Resti and Sironi (2007).

11 See Resti and Sironi (2007) for further details on the convexity gap approach.

REFERENCES

Basel Committee on Banking Supervision, 1997, "Principles for the Management of Interest Rate Risk", Bank for International Settlements.

Basel Committee on Banking Supervision, 2004, "Principles for the Management and Supervision of Interest Rate Risk", Bank for International Settlements.

Basel Committee on Banking Supervision, 2006, International Convergence of Capital Measurement and Capital Standards – A Revised Framework", Comprehensive Version, Bank for International Settlements.

Black, F., E. Derman and W. Toy, 1990, "A One-Factor Model of Interest Rates and Its Application to Treasury Bond Options", *Financial Analysts Journal*, January–February, pp. 24–32.

Matten, C., 2000, *Managing Bank Capital* second edition (New York: John Wiley & Sons).

Resti, A., and A. Sironi, 2007, *Risk Management and Shareholders' Value Creation in Banks* (Chichester: John Wiley & Sons).

Saita, F., 2007, *Value at Risk and Bank Capital Management*. (Amsterdam: Academic Press – Elsevier).

Part 3

Risk Integration and Capital Management

11

Principles of Risk Aggregation

Francesco Saita

Bocconi University

When assessing capital adequacy of a financial institution, risk aggregation – ie, the aggregation of economic capital estimates linked to different risks into a single measure, accounting for potential diversification benefits – is clearly very important. In fact, risk aggregation could be seen as the final step of a process starting with the identification of the material risks for a financial institution and with an effort to quantify economic capital for each of them. This explains its relevance both for supervisors and, more so, for senior bank managers.

From the supervisors' point of view, there has been a considerable debate about whether diversification benefits among risk types should be taken into consideration when setting capital requirements, as suggested by part of the industry during the process leading to the final Basel II document (see, for instance, Kuritzkes, Schuermann and Weiner 2001, 2002; Joint Forum 2003). The final outcome of this debate was that, while minimum capital requirements in Pillar I do not take into account potential intra-risk diversification benefits, risk aggregation plays an important role in the internal capital adequacy assessment process (ICAAP) carried out by the bank when assessing its overall economic capital, and hence should carefully be scrutinised under Pillar II. Pillar II is therefore prompting an increased interaction between financial institutions and regulators, to discuss what risks should be aggregated and how, and acts as a key driver for most banks' efforts to improve their risk aggregation process.

However, risk aggregation would be quite important for bank managers even without the ICAAP and the need to prove to supervisors the soundness of the overall capital adequacy assessment process; in fact, risk aggregation plays a crucial role in supporting top management decisions about the overall capital required by a bank to run its businesses, and therefore drives the aggressiveness/cautiousness of the bank in its risk-taking decisions, given its current and future risk capacity (ie, available capital) and risk appetite.

At the same time, another – often understated – aim of risk aggregation is to improve a bank's understanding of the interaction among risk types and/or business lines in generating diversification benefits. In other words, risk aggregation should ideally enable top managers to measure the risk-adjusted performance of each business and its contribution to the bank as a whole, by comparing its profits not only to its "standalone" (that is, "undiversified") risk capital, but rather its "diversified" risk capital, ie, to its contribution to the overall economic capital of the bank. This would, for example, allow the identification of those businesses that, while having a relatively low risk-adjusted profitability in terms of standalone risk capital, enjoy a low correlation with the rest of the bank's portfolio and therefore produce a significantly higher risk-adjusted profitability when internal diversification benefits are taken into account.

While risk aggregation is theoretically important, its implementation poses several problems. Below we will briefly discuss the following issues: (a) what risk measure should be aggregated; (b) what risks should be considered for risk aggregation; (c) how to harmonise the risk measures for different risks; and (d) what are the possible approaches to risk aggregation and how their key parameters can be estimated. When discussing these issues we must keep in mind that aggregation may occur across either risk types or business units; while the first approach is ideally the better one, aggregating across business units may also be important to estimate the contribution of each business unit to the bank's overall economic capital and hence to support the top managers' decision-making process.

WHAT RISK MEASURE SHOULD BE AGGREGATED?

Risk aggregation should obviously be able to summarise the overall economic capital needed by a bank. However, depending on how economic capital is calculated for an individual risk type or business unit, several problems may arise. In particular, since most banks use a value-at-risk (VaR) approach when calculating economic capital, we should remember that, as shown by Artzner *et al* (1999), VaR is not always subadditive, ie, given two portfolios X and Y it is not always true that $VaR(X+Y) \leq VaR(X) + VaR(Y)$.

Consequently, it could be questioned whether it is appropriate to aggregate VaRs, especially since most banks currently use a simplified approach to aggregate risks, based on the "square-root formula" (see below) taken from the variance–covariance approach, that would always produce a subadditive aggregated VaR. It could therefore be claimed that only those banks that do not adopt a VaR-based approach to estimate economic capital (eg, those adopting a stress-test approach) can reasonably aggregate economic capital across divisions.

In practice, while the subadditivity issue is well known, it must be recalled that, while for some special portfolios VaR is not subadditive, there is no clear evidence that this may happen when aggregating large portfolios' VaR by risk types or business units. Furthermore, by using aggregation techniques that are more sophisticated than the usual square-root formula, a bank may be able to aggregate VaR correctly (even if it found that overall economic capital is larger than the sum of standalone economic capital values). In other words, using VaR-based economic capital estimates does not necessarily lead to wrong aggregate economic capital estimates. This could occur only if VaR were combined with an inadequate risk aggregation technique. These remarks may explain why most banks, while being aware of the non-subadditivity problem, still feel confident in aggregating VaR-based economic capital estimates.

WHICH RISK TYPES SHOULD BE INCLUDED?

While market, credit and operational risk (as defined in Pillar I) should obviously be considered in estimating aggregated economic capital, views may differ as far as other risks are concerned. Most banks apparently treat some risks as already included in their internal models; this could be the case, for example, for concentration risk, if an adequate internal credit risk model is available. Furthermore, some risks should not necessarily be included in the risk aggregation process. Some of them, in fact, should be managed mostly through risk monitoring, risk mitigation and suitable contingency plans in cases of crisis, rather than by setting aside capital. This could be the case, for instance, of liquidity risk and strategic risk.

An increasing number of large banks are also including business risk in their economic capital estimates, at least for internal purposes. Business risk can be defined as the risk deriving from revenue and cost volatility that is not generated by market, credit and operational risks, and by its impact on the P&L account and on the value of the bank. Such a risk is particularly relevant for fee-generating businesses such as asset management, advisory and payment services, since for these business units it represents – together with operational risk – the main risk faced by the bank. Unfortunately, definitions of business risk still vary among banks, and measurement methodologies are still in their early stages.[1] However, 85% of the banks participating to the IFRI/CRO Forum (2007) survey included business risk in their economic capital estimates, and the average weight of business risk over aggregate economic capital was around 10%, with a remarkable dispersion in individual estimates that confirms the problems still existing in definition and measurement.

HARMONISING RISK MEASURES

When aggregating economic capital measures for different risks, one critical issue is the harmonisation between individual risk measures, since they can differ in terms of (a) the confidence level, (b) the time horizon over which the potential loss is estimated, and (c) the concept of "capital" at risk adopted.

The confidence level

The first problem is to harmonise the confidence level considered for each risk when calculating economic capital. Since there are different approaches to risk aggregation, this may not be an issue, depending on the approach followed. If, for instance, aggregated economic capital is found by simulation, that is, by estimating the full distribution of the whole bank's P&L through the generation of a high number of scenarios, then there is no need to harmonise individual economic capital measures, since the final results are directly observable. Harmonisation may instead be required if standalone economic capital for individual risk types (or business units) is an explicit component in the formula for aggregated economic capital.

For most banks that adopt a 99.97% confidence level as the target for economic capital estimate, the main problem is to scale up market risk VaR from 99% to 99.97%. This is not straightforward when 99%-confidence VaR is calculated through historical simulation (as it is often the case) since the 99.97% confidence level can hardly be estimated directly. As a consequence, a bank could either resort to extreme-value theory (to fit the left tail of the loss distribution so to estimate properly the 99.97th percentile), or accept some strong simplification, for example, by adopting the multiplier that would be required to transform the 99% into the 99.97% percentile if the return distribution were normal, even when this is not the case.

Remarkably, some banks have disclosed to outsiders the simplifications inherent in their approaches. For instance, UBS (2007, p. 73) states that "conversions between different confidence intervals typically rely on assumption of statistical 'normality', which is generally not fully valid …

Comparison of VaR levels between institutions can therefore be misleading and must be treated with caution".

Time horizon harmonisation

The typical problem for time horizon harmonisation is the translation of market risk VaR, which is usually measured over short horizons (one to 10 days), into a one-year VaR. Some financial institutions address this issue directly, by using VaR for day-by-day risk limits only and then resorting to stress and scenario analyses to define one-year economic capital for market risk.

However, banks using market risk VaR both for risk limits and for economic capital measurement have to define a rule to rescale daily VaR into annual VaR. The typical solution is to apply a fixed multiplier, which is frequently equal to the square root of the number of trading days in one year; this multiplier is usually kept constant across all types of market risk, while only a few banks adopt more sophisticated solutions differentiating that scale factor across different desks (see IFRI/CRO Forum 2007).

This approach may be reasonable when rescaling a point-in-time VaR estimate, for example, market risk VaR on December 31. However, the estimate of one-year economic capital for market risk should not be based on a single point-in-time value, but rather on the "average" capital absorbed throughout the year. In this case, the daily average VaR for market risk, scaled up by the square root of the number of trading days looks a sensible estimate but provides only a lower bound for yearly economic capital.

In fact, the yearly P&L for market risk can be seen as the sum of n independent daily P&Ls; then its standard deviation is equal to

$$\sigma_{yearly\ P\&L} = \sqrt{\sum_{i=1}^{n} \sigma^2_{daily\ P\&L,i}}$$

Assuming VaR can be expressed as a constant multiple of the standard deviation, we would have

$$VaR_{yearly} = \sqrt{\sum_{i=1}^{n} VaR^2_{daily,i}}$$

where, again, n is the number of trading days. From this equation, we see clearly that assuming that VaR_{yearly} is equal to the average daily VaR times the square root of n provides a lower bound for yearly VaR; in fact, this approach would produce a correct estimate only if all daily VaRs were identical (and hence equal to average VaR as well), as we would have:

$$VaR_{yearly} = \sqrt{\sum_{i=1}^{n} VaR^2_{daily,i}} = \sqrt{\sum_{i=1}^{n} \overline{VaR}^2_{daily}} = \overline{VaR}_{daily}\sqrt{n}$$

If instead daily VaRs fluctuate over time, then (even leaving the average daily VaR unchanged) the risk for the bank increases. Intuitively, the bank would be exposed to the risk that a large negative market move may occur at the point when its VaR is higher: for example, over one week, a trader with a VaR of 50 on one single day and zero on the other four faces more risk than a trader with a constant VaR of 10 every day. Hence, the difference between the two formulas for yearly VaR reported above is acceptable when VaR is sufficiently stable through time, while differences become larger if daily VaR fluctuates remarkably.

The harmonisation of the time horizon is relevant also for financial conglomerates that must harmonise economic capital measures for insurance divisions, where risk may be measured over a multi-period framework. In long-dated life insurance policies, profits, market movements or actuarial/demographic risks (such as longevity risk) may affect more than one period. In this case, when computing economic capital on a yearly basis, whether to assess the consequences of an adverse event (eg, a shift in the term structure) only on the P&L for the first year, or instead on the whole value of the insurance business must be chosen. This choice depends on the concept of "capital at risk" used by a financial institution (see below) and can lead to very different estimates.

The notion of "capital" at risk

When we define economic capital as the amount that can be lost under some "severe adverse event" by a given business unit (or because of a given risk type), we have to consider that the concept of "capital" we refer to can be substantially different.

In particular, we may consider book capital or market capitalisation (ie, the value of the bank on the stock market). For some risks, the difference is close to zero; this is the case, for instance, for market risk positions that are fully marked-to-market. However, this is not true for most other risks. For business risk, for example, a bank announcing an unexpected profit reduction of €10 million in, say, its asset management business, will experience moderate consequences in terms of book capital (in principle, as long as the profit reduction does not lead to losses, no book capital would be destroyed). However, the market may react negatively to the bank's underperformance and the loss in its market capitalisation will then be even larger than €10 million.

Similarly, for operational risk, Cummins, Lewis and Wei (2004) and Perry and de Fontnouvelle (2005) have pointed out (respectively for insurance companies and for banks) that the reduction in the market capitalisation as a consequence of announcements of operational losses typically exceeds the size of the disclosed loss. Again, this provides evidence that losses may affect differently the various concepts of "capital" used.

As far as internal capital adequacy assessment in Pillar II is concerned, it would be natural to focus mostly on book capital, since this is more consistent with supervisors' concerns to prevent a bank from failure; also, a capital-at-risk based on book capital could be more easily compared with available book capital (which in turn is more stable than the bank's market capitalisation). However, the choice between "book capital-at-risk" and "market capitalisation-at-risk" is relevant for two reasons: first, to preserve consistency in the risk aggregation process (for example, measuring business risk in terms of market capitalisation at risk, other risks in terms of book capital-at-risk, and then comparing the aggregated result with some measure of available book capital can not be done); second, the "market capitalisation at risk" perspective may be extremely important for risk managers and senior managers since it is provides the shareholders' point of view (shareholders are likely to be most concerned with market capitalisation) rather than the supervisory one; this improves internal decision making and helps gain a better perception of units originating risk for the bank.

RISK AGGREGATION TECHNIQUES

Once risk measures have been harmonised, a bank has to choose a methodology to aggregate them. When choosing the "best" methodology, consider the following.

- The problem is not only in defining which methodology is superior in theory, but which one may produce the best results given the costs of producing an estimate and, namely, the potential problems in parameterising the model, so that the joint effect of model risk and input uncertainty risk will be minimised when estimating aggregated economic capital.
- The risk manager may aim at producing both an aggregated risk measure and a set of measures expressing the contribution of each business (or risk type) to the overall economic capital; that would provide senior managers with information about the business lines that most contribute

to diversification benefits. This second set of measures is not equally easy to produce under all possible alternative aggregation methodologies.

Apart from a very naïve approach (the simple summation of all standalone economic capital estimates for each risk type or business lines, which would clearly ignore diversification benefits), the main approaches available are the variance–covariance approach, copulas and multi-factor simulation approaches.

The first (and simpler approach) is to aggregate capital-at-risk using the usual formula for portfolio CaR (CaR_p) under the variance–covariance approach, ie,

$$CaR_p = \sqrt{\sum_{i=1}^{n} CaR_i^2 + \sum_{i=1}^{n}\sum_{j\neq i} CaR_i CaR_j \rho_{ij}}$$

where CaR_i, CaR_j represent standalone capital-at-risk (economic capital) for the different business lines/risk types, and ρ_{ij} is the correlation coefficient between the returns of i and j. This simple approach, also known as normal CaR or hybrid CaR approach (see Rosenberg and Schuermann 2006) can be used whenever CaR is a fixed multiple of standard deviation, and that multiple is the same for the portfolio as a whole and for each business line/risk type that has to be aggregated. While this assumption is clearly far from trivial, this methodology is largely used in practice: according to the joint survey by the Institute of the Chief Risk Officers and the Chief Risk Officer Forum (IFRI/CRO Forum 2007), involving a selected group of very large financial institutions, more than 60% said they used a simple variance–covariance approach (while, for instance, none claimed to use copulas).

There are many intuitive reasons why this solution is still largely appreciated in practice, despite its theoretical pitfalls. First, it is easy to calculate and to explain to senior managers and outsiders. Secondly, correlation coefficients are the only parameters required (although this is not an easy task, many banks assume that, as long as correlation estimates are conservative enough, the overall economic capital should be reasonable); having correlations as the key input also makes it easier for supervisors to compare alternative assumptions used by different banks and to assess their conservatism when assessing economic capital.

A third advantage of this methodology is that the calculation of the contribution of each business line to overall economic capital can be derived in a straightforward way.[2]

Copulas represent an incredibly attractive solution (at least, in theory), since they allow us to combine returns with completely different marginal distributions in a very flexible way. However, the choice of the optimal copula function and of copula parameters (see Nelsen 1999; Cherubini, Luciano and Vecchiato 2004) is nontrivial when, as is often the case in risk aggregation, empirical data about the relationship among different risks are scarce. While it may be relatively easier to use copulas to model the relationship among other instrumental variables that affect risks (for example, joint shocks of macroeconomic factors in the simulation-based approach discussed below), for which reliable time series are available, their calibration is trickier when the variables to be aggregated are the losses originated by different risk types.[3] This is true even when, as is quite usual, the copula function is chosen between only two common and easier alternatives, the Gaussian copula and the t-Student copula (with some number of degrees of freedom that must be determined empirically). Furthermore, depending on the chosen copula, the aggregate economic capital estimate can vary materially (see Rosenberg and Schuermann 2006).

Also, copulas may make it more complex to estimate the contribution of an individual risk type (or business line) to the overall aggregated economic capital; this may be an issue, given the importance that those estimates play in the bank's internal risk-adjusted profitability assessment.[4] The greater sophistication of the copula approach and of its calibration may also make results harder to communicate to the bank's senior managers and to relevant outsiders (equity analysts, rating agencies and so forth).

A third approach, encompassing different alternatives, is represented by simulation bottom-up approaches. Such approaches often model individual components through a multi-factor model; for example, Alexander and Pezier (2003) first proposed to model business units' P&Ls ($P_1, P_2, \ldots, P_n$) as

$$P_i = \alpha_i + \beta_{i,1}x_1 + \beta_{i,2}x_2 + \ldots + \beta_{i,n}x_n + \varepsilon_i$$

where α_i represents the expected profit, $\beta_1, \beta_2, \ldots \beta_n$ are the coefficients (to be estimated empirically) linking the business unit's P&L to its relevant risk factors $x_1, x_2, \ldots x_n$ and ε_i is a specific risk that is not explained by common factors. Alexander and Pezier's multi-factor approach has some clear advantages:

- it can easily include business units that are mainly exposed to business risk; and
- it does not require us to model correlation/dependence among business

unit returns directly, since it is implied in the correlation/dependence among risk factors and in the beta coefficients.

The model also allows us to derive analytically the standard deviation of the bank's returns, while estimating percentiles typically requires simulation. The main concern with this multi-factor approach is related to the potential oversimplification in credit risk modelling; while nonlinear relationships between the P&L of business lines and credit risk factors may be modelled as nonlinear, the relatively simple structure of the model may create simplifications as opposed to the more sophisticated internal credit risk models available within the bank. This may result in inaccurate estimates of overall economic capital. Considering that, on average, credit risk accounted for as much as 60% of economic capital for banks surveyed by IFRI/CRO Forum (2007), approximations in modelling this risk may have a remarkable impact on the accuracy of the aggregated economic capital.

To address this issue, one may resort to a "mixed multi-factor approach" (Saita 2004) combining an internal credit risk model (based, for example, on the simulation of a set of correlated risk drivers) to simulate the behaviour of the credit portfolio, with Alexander and Pezier's multi-factor approach for remaining business units/risk types. In this way, economic capital would necessarily have to be derived through simulation (simulating jointly the risk factors required by the credit risk model and the extra factors affecting P&Ls of other business units/risk types). While computationally burdensome, this approach would ensure perfect consistency between the overall economic capital estimate and the credit risk VaR of the bank, ie, the portion of economic capital modelling that typically accounts for the larger share of overall economic capital. Furthermore, this approach could identify economic capital directly, by identifying the desired percentile of the bank's overall P&L simulated distribution. The correlation/dependence structure among risk types would mainly derive from the choice of the risk factors and from the estimated sensitivity of each business unit/risk type (as well as of the credit portfolio) to each factor. This would make it easier to document assumptions to supervisors, and may also help confining concerns for improper estimates in those businesses whose P&L history is shorter, while allowing better estimates whenever a longer P&L time series is available.[5]

In various forms, bottom-up simulation-based approaches are getting more attention and many interesting variants and extensions have been proposed, especially in the case of credit and market risk integration. Aas, Dimakos and Øksendal (2005) aggregate market, credit and insurance risk by simulating them simultaneously, while Medova and Smith (2005) propose a framework in which credit risk is a function also of market variables, so that credit risk is simulated conditional on the state of those variables. Böcker and Hillebrand (2007) use a combination of a Merton-like factor model for credit risk and a linear factor model for market risk, that can be used both in a simulation and in an analytical setting; Fiori and Iannotti (2008) suggest using a factor-augmented vector autoregressive (FAVAR) approach to efficiently model the effect of a large set of real and financial variables for the purposes of risk aggregation. This suggests that, while banks are still generally favouring simple top-down methods, simulation-based methods are growing in sophistication and flexibility and might become more widespread in the industry through time.

PARAMETER ESTIMATION FOR RISK AGGREGATION

One of the main advantages of simulation-based bottom-up approaches (such as those just discussed above) is that they do not need explicit estimates for the correlation or dependence among risk types or business lines. This dependence follows on from the dependence between common risk factors as well as from the relationship between risk factors and each business unit's (risk type's) P&L. This often allows the use of longer and "cleaner" data series to estimate the interaction among risk factors and – as regards the interaction with supervisors – may offer better empirical evidence to support the bank's estimates.

If, on the other hand, a bank decides to use other approaches, for example, the widespread variance–covariance approach, then it will have to estimate a correlation matrix among risks. A similar exercise will be required also for banks using copulas.

To estimate correlation matrices, the most common alternatives are the following:

- subjective estimates/expert opinions;
- estimates derived from the time series of stock market returns for listed financial institutions; and
- estimates derived from the (internal) time series of the business units' earnings.

The first solution is clearly the simplest one. Potentially, correlation estimates may be derived either by interviewing the bank's managers, resorting to external independent experts and surveys, or adopting the estimates

Table 11.1 Correlation estimates among market, credit and operational risk in three different research papers

Risk types	Kuritzkes, Schuermann and Wiener (2001)	Ward and Lee (2002)	Dimakos and Aas (2003)
Credit – Market	0.80	0.20	0.30
Credit – Operational	0.40	0.20	0.44
Market – Operational	0.40	0.20	0.13

Source: Saita (2007)

produced in some research papers (see, for example, Kuritzkes, Schuermann and Wiener 2001; Ward and Lee 2002). Some banks also choose to combine historical and subjective data (Joint Forum 2003). Yet, the dispersion among the estimates published in the few papers providing explicit correlation estimates is striking (see Table 11.1)

The second solution is to derive correlations from stock-market returns of competitors. This would be appropriate if a number of specialised, single-business competitors existed for each business line/risk type, but clearly this is typically not the case. A more sophisticated alternative solution would be to infer correlations across risk types or business lines from the correlations among stock-market returns of listed banks with a known portfolio mix in terms of risk type and/or business line. This would be like deriving correlation among individual stocks with unobservable returns but included, with known weights, in a number of portfolios with observable returns. However, if the mix in terms of risk type and/or business line is not well known by outsiders, then implementing this methodology could be considerably less straightforward.

The third solution is to use correlation parameters estimated on the time series for the business units' past earnings. These could be used directly when economic capital is aggregated among business lines, or as proxies for risk-type correlations when capital is aggregated across risk types (although only to some extent: while there are business units whose returns are mostly driven by market or credit risk, no single unit can, for example, be used to proxy operational risk). Internal earnings data apparently represent the best source of information (as they are objective data grounded in the bank's empirical history), however a number of caveats apply.

- Available data series include earnings rather than returns. This implies for instance that changes in the size of the business unit (eg, due to sustained growth or acquisitions) may affect earnings even if profitability is unchanged. Depending on the business unit, it must be decided whether such an effect should be included in the analysis and whether and how it could bias correlation estimates.
- Available time series are typically short, and data quality may be harmed by acquisitions or divestures (for example, the acquisition of smaller banks would increase the size of the credit portfolio).
- As few years' worth of data is available, quarterly or monthly data is often used to increase the number of available data points. Unfortunately, using such infra-annual data does not adequately capture the correlation among business units whenever there is positive cross-autocorrelation between earnings or returns ie, whenever there are events that impact on a business unit's earnings immediately and on other business units' earnings gradually through the time (Saita 2007).[6]

HOW BANKS DISCLOSE THEIR RISK AGGREGATION OUTCOMES

To conclude, we briefly comment on the banks' current level of disclosure (in their official reports) about aggregated economic capital. In fact, while most large banks have a risk aggregation methodology in place, with different degrees of sophistication, the disclosure on aggregated economic capital is still limited. This happens even if (see again IFRI/CRO Forum 2007) most banks consider economic capital as a crucial component of external communication and expect more disclosure to be done in the future.

While it is obviously hard to measure how many banks disclose internal capital estimates (and to what extent) in private meetings with equity analysts or rating agencies, only a few banks operate a significant disclosure to the general public of investors through the risk management section of their annual report. Among those disclosing more, for example, Citigroup, Credit Suisse and Deutsche Bank can be mentioned, although they, too, provide very little or no information on the risk-aggregation methodology used to derive overall economic capital. This is unsurprising, given that aggregation techniques are still at an early stage and even the most advanced methodologies still need to be properly calibrated.

Regarding parameter calibration, the wide range of variation in the inter-risk correlation estimates emerging from the above-mentioned IFRI/CRO Forum (2007) survey (which confirmed the difficulties in finding adequate empirical data supporting correlation estimates that were highlighted by the Joint Forum in a 2003 study) clearly explains why most banks are so cautious in disclosing data on aggregated risk capital. However, given the increasing relevance of this data for all external analysts (and not only for supervisors), it should be expected in the short term that substantial efforts to improve the quality of data and methodologies and for greater disclosure (especially by those banks who think they have a superior risk-aggregation methodology). The pressure from the market will therefore reinforce supervisory efforts to make banks further improve their ability to assess and monitor their integrated economic capital.

1 For a more detailed discussion on business risk measurement see Matten (2000), Saita (2007).

2 See, for example, Resti and Sironi (2007), Saita (2007) for further details.

3 Of course, when modelling dependence among risk types, copula parameters can be estimated by using (rather than a past joint distribution of the effects of credit, market, operational and business risk) a simulated joint distribution derived from the bank's internal risk models. However, once a similar distribution has been built in a reliable way (see simulation approaches later), it could be used to estimate aggregated economic capital directly, and there would be no need to resort to copulas.

4 While in theory the bank should try to understand the true contribution of a business line/risk type to overall economic capital taking into consideration the correlation or dependence among risks or business lines, in a number of banks diversification benefits – see Joint Forum (2003) – are allocated back to business lines or risk types by simply multiplying their standalone economic capital by the ratio between aggregated economic capital and the sum of standalone business capital (the so-called "splitting" or "haircut" method). Of course this is possible with copulas as well, but unfortunately this solution to calculate "diversified" economic capital for individual business lines totally fails to identify which business lines are really contributing to diversification benefits more than others.

5 Note that in a simpler way the idea of modelling market and operational risk outcomes conditional on credit risk outcomes had already been proposed in Dimakos and Aas (2003), even if credit risk outcomes were summarised by simpler variables such as the default rate.

6 A simple example of such a situation is a very negative return on the stock market in month t that would impact immediately on the earnings of a capital markets and trading division with long stock exposure, and would impact gradually but persistently on the earnings of an asset management division as a consequence of decreased asset under management and hence lower fees in the subsequent months.

REFERENCES

Aas, K., X. K. Dimakos and A. Øksendal, 2005, "Risk Capital Aggregation", working paper, Norwegian Computing Center, December.

Alexander, C. and J. Pezier, 2003, "On the Aggregation of Market and Credit Risks", ISMA Centre Discussion Papers in Finance 2003–13, University of Reading, October.

Artzner, P. *et al*, 1999, "Coherent Measures of Risk", *Mathematical Finance* 9, pp. 203–28.

Böcker, K. and M. Hillebrand, 2007, "Interaction of Market and Credit Risk: An Analysis of Inter-Risk Correlation and Risk Aggregation", working paper.

Cherubini, U., E. Luciano and W. Vecchiato, 2004, *Copula Methods in Finance* (Chichester: John Wiley & Sons).

Cummins, D. J., C. M. Lewis and R. Wei, 2004, "The Market Value Impact of Operational Risk Events in US Banks and Insurers", Wharton School working paper, December.

Dimakos, X. K. and K. Aas, 2003, "Integrated Risk Modelling", working paper, Norwegian Computing Center, December.

Fiori, R. and S. Iannotti, 2008, "Channels for Interaction of Market and Credit Risk: A FAVAR Approach", working paper presented at the European Banking Symposium, Università Bocconi.

IFRI/CRO Forum, 2007, "Insights from the joint IFRI/CRO Forum Survey on Economic Capital Practice and Applications", Institute of the Chief Risk Officers, Chief Risk Officer Forum, working paper.

Joint Forum, 2003, "Trends in Risk Integration and Aggregation", Bank for International Settlements, Basel, August.

Kuritzkes, A., T. Schuermann and S. M. Weiner, 2001, "Study on the Risk Profile and Capital Adequacy of Financial Conglomerates", Oliver, Wyman & Co, URL: http://www.dnb.nl/publicaties/pdf/study_Risk_profile.pdf.

Kuritzkes, A., T. Schuermann and S. M. Weiner, 2002, "Risk Measurement, Risk Management and Capital Adequacy in Financial Conglomerates", Wharton Financial Institutions Center Working Papers Series, n. 03–02.

Matten, C., 2000, *Managing Bank Capital. Capital Allocation and Performance Measurement* (New York: John Wiley & Sons).

Medova, E. A. and R. G. Smith, 2005, "A framework to measure integrated risk", *Quantitative Finance* 5, pp. 105–121.

Nelsen, R. B., 1999, *An Introduction to Copulas* (New York: Springer-Verlag).

Perry, J., P. de Fontnouvelle, 2005, "Measuring Reputational Risk: The Market Reaction to Operational Loss Announcements", working paper, Federal Reserve Bank of Boston.

Resti, A. and A. Sironi, 2007, *Risk Management and Shareholders' Value in Banking* (Chichester: John Wiley & Sons).

Rosenberg, J. V. and T. Schuermann, 2006, "A General Approach to Integrated Risk Management with Skewed, Fat-Tailed Risks", *Journal of Financial Economics* 79, pp. 569–614.

Saita, F., 2004, "Risk Capital Aggregation: The Risk Manager's Perspective", Newfin Research Center Working Papers, November.

Saita, F., 2007, *Value at Risk and Bank Capital Management. Risk Adjusted Performances, Capital Management and Capital Allocation Decision Making* (Burlington, MA: Elsevier Academic Press, Advanced Finance Series).

UBS, 2007, *Handbook 2005/2006*, UBS, Zurigo.

Ward, L. S. and D. H. Lee, 2002, "Practical Application of the Risk-Adjusted Return on Capital Framework", working paper, CAS Forum Summer, URL: http://www.casact.org/pubs/forum/02sforum/02sftoc.pdf

12

Aggregation by Risk Type and Inter-Risk Correlation

Klaus Böcker[1]

UniCredit Group

With the new Basel Accord "Basel II" a new chapter of regulatory supervision has begun, setting risk-adjusted standards for a bank's minimum capital requirement as well as demanding a better and more comprehensive internal risk measurement framework. Basel II is structured in three Pillars. Here we focus on Pillar II, which introduces the so-called internal capital adequacy assessment process (ICAAP) and also contains guidance for the supervisory review process.

Besides the treatment of "other" risks not covered under Pillar I (such as interest rate risk or credit concentration risk) the ICAAP also deals with an institution's risk exposure as a whole. According to the Committee of European Banking Supervisors (2005), banks shall derive a reasonable, overall capital number as a part of their ICAAP, which should cover all material risks of different businesses, products and so forth of the financial institution. Although the ICAAP does not explicitly require a firm to use economic capital techniques, many banks have such models in place, and in this case the overall capital number can be regarded as the group-wide aggregated economic capital of the institution.

So far no standard procedure for risk aggregation has emerged, but according to several surveys, eg, the Joint Forum (2003) or more recently the IFRI/CRO Forum (2007), the most prominent one in practice is a kind of aggregation-by-risk type approach where standalone risk figures of different risk types are combined in some way to obtain the desired aggregated economic capital.

Aggregation by risk type is performed in two steps. First, for every risk type, a group-wide, preaggregated economic capital is calculated on a stand alone basis, ie, without interaction with other risk types. Second, these preaggregated economic capital figures are further integrated in order to obtain the final aggregated economic capital. The popularity of this approach is mainly for two reasons. First, it fits very well with a typical organisational structure of a bank's CRO area where different risk types are measured and managed separately in different departments, such as market risk, credit risk and operational risk. Therefore, in the first step above, for each risk type, the existing methodology and IT infrastructure can be used to calculate preaggregated risk-type figures. Second, when further aggregating preaggregated risk figures, most banks adopt a simple, analytical aggregation technique, namely the well-known square-root formula or variance–covariance approach. Though only mathematically justified in the case of elliptically distributed risk types (with the multivariate normal or t distribution as prominent examples), this approach is often used as a first approximation because aggregated economic capital can be determined without simulation. In doing so, let us describe preaggregated losses associated with the ith risk type by a random variable X_i, $i = 1, \ldots, m$, and define the associated economic capital at confidence level $\alpha \in (0, 1)$ by (for the sake of clarity we drop the time-horizon index t)

$$\mathrm{EC}_{X_i}(\alpha) = F_i^{-1}(\alpha) - \mathbb{E}X_i$$

where $\mathbb{E}X_i$ is the expected loss of risk type i and $F_i^{-1}(\cdot)$ is the inverse of the distribution function $F_i(\cdot) = P(X_i \leq \cdot)$, which here, and in the sequel, is always assumed to be strictly increasing and continuous. Moreover, if the linear correlations between risk types are denoted by $\rho_{ij} = \mathrm{corr}(X_i, X_j)$ for $i, j = 1, \ldots, m$, then aggregated economic capital $\mathrm{EC}^{+}(\alpha) := \mathrm{EC}_{X_1+\ldots+X_m}(\alpha)$ for elliptically distributed $(X_1, \ldots, X_m)$ is given by

$$\mathrm{EC}^{+}(\alpha) = \sqrt{\sum_{i=1}^{m}\sum_{j=1}^{m} \mathrm{EX}_{X_1}(\alpha)\rho_{ij}\mathrm{EX}_{X_j}(\alpha)} \qquad (12.1)$$

Hence, a typical problem of risk aggregation is the calculation of the inter-risk correlation matrix $\boldsymbol{C} := (\rho_{ij})$, $i, j = 1, \ldots, m$, and its estimation and calibration is a core problem for implementing aggregation by risk type in practice.

An aggregation-by-risk type technique, which is more advanced compared with the variance–covariance approach, is based on copulas. In the past few years, copulas have become very popular in basically all areas of quantitative financial modelling. In the context of bank-wide risk aggregation, copula techniques are discussed by Dimakos and Aas (2004), Rosenberg and Schuermann (2004) or Ward and Lee (2002) for example.

Another valuable resource is Brockmann and Kalkbrener (2008) where also a multiperiod model for risk aggregation is proposed. The importance of copulas for financial risk management is essentially a result of Sklar's now famous theorem, saying that every multivariate distribution function can be separated into their marginal distribution functions and a copula. As a consequence thereof, copulas allow for a separate modelling of marginal distribution functions of preaggregated risk types on one hand and their dependence structure (ie, the copula) on the other. However, the choice and parameterisation of a copula is not straightforward, specifically in the context of risk aggregation where the lack of reliable data makes a sound statistical estimation more difficult.

In this chapter we confine ourselves to some specific aspects in the context of the aggregation-by-risk type approach, a more general overview about risk aggregation and a discussion about different industry practices can be found in Chapter 12 or in Saita (2007). The next section considers the aggregation-by-risk type approach in more detail. Following that, we review some important properties of the (pairwise) linear correlation coefficient, followed by a discussion of alternative dependence measures such as copulas, Kendall's tau and tail dependence, and finally of the inter-risk-correlation matrix as a whole. We also investigate how the estimation of inter-risk correlation can be supported by means of expert judgements, an exciting field that so far has received only a little attention in the context of risk aggregation. We go on to illustrate our results with an extended numerical example, which describes a typical aggregation-by-risk type problem as it may also occur in practice. We move on to concentrate on the interaction between credit risk and another, normally distributed risk type, say market risk. Based on Böcker and Hillebrand (2007) and Böcker and Klüppelberg (2008), we calculate closed-form expressions for their inter-risk correlation and, moreover, suggest how their Gaussian copula can be estimated.

AGGREGATION BY RISK TYPE

Inter-risk dependence measures

A crucial question in the context of aggregated economic capital is the recognition of diversification effects. Banks are usually diversified as a result of their business mix or, especially large international banks, due to different geographical regions they are operating in. This results in a diversification benefit, which, according to the survey of the IFRI/CRO Forum (2007), most banks take into consideration when analysing their internal capital adequacy. However, in order to determine diversification affects across different risk types the interaction between them has to be analysed first. Therefore, we start by considering some important dependence measures and how they can be used in the context of aggregation by risk type.

Inter-risk correlation

As already stated, the variance–covariance method is currently the dominant approach for risk aggregation and, consequently, dependence between different risk types is described in terms of linear (Pearson) correlation, which for two random variables X and Y is defined as

$$\rho = \text{corr}(X,Y) = \frac{\text{cov}(X,Y)}{\text{var}(X)\text{var}(X)}$$

where $\text{cov}(X, Y) = \mathbb{E}(XY) - \mathbb{E}X\ \mathbb{E}Y$ is the covariance between X and Y and $\text{var}(X)$, $\text{var}(Y)$ the variances of X and Y.

It is important to understand how inter-risk correlation is usually determined in practice. First, it can be derived from a purely statistical analysis based on empirical data. However, since data in sufficient volumes and quality is often hard to come by, a second approach relies on expert judgements, and in our estimation expert-based inter-risk correlations are widely used when risk aggregation is performed in practice. Therefore, evaluation of expert knowledge merits closer examination and this will be done later. In any case, quantifying inter-risk correlation, or even an entire inter-risk-correlation matrix, is a non-trivial task and it is useful to recall some of its statistical properties.

Linear correlation, which is frequently used by both practitioners and academics, is a very important concept in statistics and describes the linear dependence between different random variables. Yet it is just one dependence measure among many others, and for most multivariate problems it is not even the most natural one to use. Only for elliptical distributions is linear correlation the natural measure of dependence because in this case the dependence between the marginals is uniquely determined by the correlation matrix. In all other cases, Embrechts, McNeil and Straumann (2002) pointed out several "correlation fallacies" and some of them are especially important in the context of risk aggregation. Let us consider two real-valued risk types X and Y with finite variance and distribution functions F_X and F_Y. Then:

- Liner correlation $\text{corr}(X, Y)$ depends on the specific form of the marginals F_X and F_Y. Therefore, linear correlation can only be interpreted with respect to the specific distribution functions adopted for X and Y.

- In general, not all correlations in the interval of [–1, 1] can be attained but the range of possible correlations is actually a subinterval of [–1, 1], where the upper bound corresponds to comonotonicity (perfect positive dependence) and the lower bound to counter monotonicity (perfect negative dependence). Comonotonicity is the strongest positive dependence possible for two random variables, meaning that all risks move in lockstep. Since the upper bound can be arbitrarily low, correlation itself is only a poor indicator for comonotonicity and thus the diversification within a portfolio.
- Although independence between X and Y implies that corr(X, Y) = 0, it is not true that a correlation of zero implies independence of two random variables. For instance, within the important class of elliptical distribution functions, uncorrelatedness is only equivalent to independence in the multivariate normal case.

However, despite such shortcomings and the resulting potential confusion, linear correlation is unquestionably a valuable concept provided that anyone engaged in practical risk management is better equipped to encounter the problems associated with it.

The standard estimator for linear correlation ρ is the Pearson product-moment correlation. For sample data (x_i, y_i), $i = 1, \ldots, n$, it is given by

$$\hat{\rho} = \frac{\sum_i^n (x_i - \bar{x})(y_i - \bar{y})}{\sqrt{\sum_i^n (x_i - \bar{x})^2}\sqrt{\sum_i^n (y_i - \bar{y})^2}} \tag{12.2}$$

where $\bar{x}$ and $\bar{y}$ are the sample means of X and Y, respectively. There are many other estimators for linear correlation available that are often superior to 12.2, but a deeper discussion would lead us beyond the scope of this chapter. Overviews about statistical properties of different estimators can be found in Devlin, Gnanadesikan and Kettering (1981) or Lindskog (2000).

The major obstacle in calculating inter-risk correlation, however, is not usually that of finding an appropriate statistical estimator $\hat{\rho}$. Recall that we are interested in correlations between yearly losses of different risk types, and therefore we should in principle try to base our correlation estimate on yearly sample data $(x_1, \ldots, x_n)$ and $(y_1, \ldots, y_n)$ corresponding to risk types X and Y, respectively. Needless to say, this is hardly feasible in practice because time series will either be too short or they will not represent the actual risk of the portfolio properly. As a consequence thereof, estimations of inter-risk correlation are frequently based on quarterly or monthly data instead of yearly ones. To give an example, in order to determine the correlation between operational and business risk, bank-internally collected operational loss data in combination with business-risk relevant revenues/cost components (as proposed in Chapter 7 of this book for example) may guide the way. However, it is not necessarily the case that such a monthly or quarterly correlation estimate adequately reflects the yearly correlation between the two risk types because, in general, their correlation may be time dependent. This problem is similar to the univariate one of scaling a 10-day volatility (or VaR) of market risk to a longer time-horizon, say one year. Such important questions can only be answered by adopting a dynamic framework for risk aggregation, which is certainly a very fruitful area for future research, yet beyond the scope of this chapter. In the meanwhile, estimates based on monthly or quarterly data has to be used cautiously, may be complemented by methods discussed in the following section "Elicitation of expert knowledge".

Copulas and tail dependence

Besides the variance–covariance approach where inter-risk dependence is completely captured by linear correlation, different risk figures can alternatively be aggregated by means of a distributional copula, which has become a standard concept for characterising the dependence structure between different distribution functions. General, readable introductions about this subject that focus on financial applications are Embrechts, Lindskog and McNeil (2001) or Cherubini, Luciano and Vecchiato (2004).

Distributional copulas are multivariate distribution functions with uniform marginals. They are used for dependence modelling within the context of Sklar's theorem, which says that any multivariate distribution with continuous marginals can be transformed into a multivariate distribution with uniform marginals, called the copula. Copulas have the important property that they are invariant under monotonously increasing transformations. As a consequence thereof, for a multivariate distribution function $F(x_1, \ldots, x_m)$, the copula is the part that does not depend on its margins $F_1(x_1)$, $\ldots$, $F_m(x_m)$. Put another way, the term copula is just another word for dependence structure.[2]

In general there are many different copulas that could, in principle, be used for modelling dependence between a set of preaggregated risk types, and there is no obvious answer which one is best to use. Nevertheless, copula techniques are an appropriate way to deal with model risk and to train a risk manager's awareness concerning the impact of different inter-risk dependence structures on the final aggregated economic capital. With this respect, we should be wary of interpreting too much aggregated economic capital in absolute rather than relative terms, and owing to the many uncertainties involved, the final figure should be taken as an approximation rather than a number with arbitrary precision.

Among all copulas discussed in the literature, maybe those most frequently used for risk aggregation are the Gaussian copula and the t copula, and both allow for natural extensions of the variance–covariance approach. Recall that Equation 12.1 holds only for multivariate elliptically distributed risk types, ie, having elliptical marginals and an elliptical dependence structure. Now, because both the Gaussian copula and the t copula describe elliptical dependence, they allow modelling of the same dependence structure as in Equation 12.1, however, in combination with more general, non-elliptical marginal distributions for each risk type.

For basically all practically relevant cases, the Gaussian copula and t copula can be parameterised by means of a correlation matrix $\mathbf{R}$, and, in the case of the t copula, by an additional degree-of-freedom parameter $\nu > 0$, which controls the degree of extreme dependence between the tails of the marginal distribution functions. More generally, one can define the important concept of (upper) tail dependence, which for two random variables X and Y with distribution functions F_X and F_Y is given by

$$\lambda := \lim_{u \to 1} P\left(Y > F_Y^{-1}(u) \mid X > F_X^{-1}(u)\right) \tag{12.3}$$

where $F_X^{-1}(\cdot)$ and $F_Y^{-1}(\cdot)$ denote the quantiles of the distribution function of X and Y, respectively. Hence, focusing on risk aggregation, tail dependence λ between two risk types is the conditional probability that an (asymptotically) high loss in risk type Y occurs, given that another (asymptotically) high loss in risk type X has already been observed. If $\lambda = 0$, then X and Y are called tail independent. Moreover, it can be shown that, in contrast to linear correlation, λ is solely a property of the underlying copula, ie, tail dependence does not depend on the specific marginals F_X and F_Y. For instance, for a bivariate t copula with correlation parameter R and degree-of-freedom parameter ν it has (see Embrechts, Lindskog and McNeil 2001)

$$\lambda_t(R, \nu) = 2 - 2F_{\nu+1}\left(\sqrt{\nu+1}\sqrt{1-R} / \sqrt{1+R}\right) \tag{12.4}$$

where F_ν is the Student t distribution function with ν degrees of freedom. Note that the tail dependence 12.4 is not vanishing even for $R = 0$. As a matter of fact, bivariate t distributed random variables are still dependent even if they are uncorrelated.

Figure 12.1 Scatter plot of a simulation of joint losses in market and credit risk

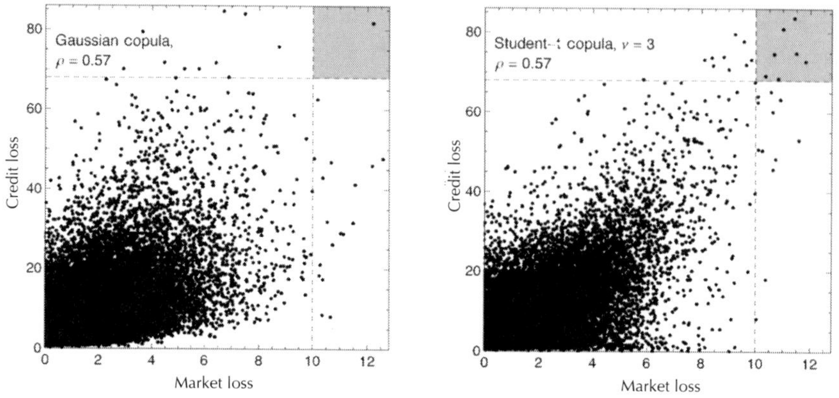

Market risk losses are described by a Student t distribution with 10 degrees of freedom and a 99.95% quantile of 10 (indicated by the vertical dashed line). Credit risk follows a Vasicek distribution with average default probability $p = 0.3\%$, uniform asset correlation $\varrho = 8\%$ and a 99.5% quantile of about 68 (indicated by the horizontal dashed line). The correlation parameter of both copulas is set to $R = 0.66$ and for the t copula we further have $\nu = 3$. Note that the linear correlation between both risk types is different from R and for both copulas estimated to be about $\rho = 0.57$.

The different dependence structures of a Gaussian copula on one hand and a t copula with $\nu = 3$ on the other hand are depicted in Figure 12.1. For each scatter plot of joint losses (defined as positive values), we assume a Student t distribution for market risk, a Vasicek distribution for credit risk (see Vasicek (2002) and Table 12.1 in this chapter for details about the parameterisation we use here) and a correlation parameter of R =0.66 for both copulas. While the bodies of both plots (ie, the area of small or medium-sized losses of market and credit risk) are quite similar, we see that with increasing loss sizes the t copula causes less scattering and more points that are concentrated around the 45-degree line compared to the Gaussian copula. Consequently, losses in market and credit risk are more likely to occur simultaneously if their dependence is given by a t copula instead of a Gaussian one. Especially, there is a significant amount of extreme joint losses above each risk type's 99.95% quantile (indicated by the gray-shaded region in the upper right edges of the figures) in the case of the t copula, whereas for the Gaussian copula only very few extreme joint losses can be observed. This observation is not just a random effect but can be explained systematically. It can be shown that a Gaussian copula with correlation parameter $R < 1$ does not have tail dependence, ie, $\lambda_{\text{Gauss}} = 0$, and therefore very extreme losses do not tend to occur simultaneously. In contrast the t copula has a non-zero tail dependence (even for $R = 0$), and λ_t is increasing in the correlation parameter R and decreasing in ν. Furthermore, with growing ν the t copula fades into the Gaussian copula so that in the limit $\nu \to \infty$ we obtain $\lambda_t = 0$. This property is useful for practical applications such as stress-testing inter-risk aggregation because the t copula can be used to explore the impact of different degrees of tail dependence on the aggregated economic capital.

It is worthwhile mentioning that the correlation matrix **R** of the Gaussian or t copula does not equal the usual inter-risk correlation matrix **C** calculated from empirical loss data as described earlier. In particular, for pairwise correlations R_{ij}, $i, j = 1, \ldots, m$, all values of the interval [0, 1] can be attained in principle, which we know is in general not true for ρ_{ij}, $i, j = 1, \ldots, m$, and comonotonicity (counter monotonicity) between risk types X_i and X_j is reached for $R_{ij} = 1 (R_{ij} = -1)$. However, as we will see in the next section, there are algebraic boundary conditions for the whole matrix **R**, which again may restrict some R_{ij} to a subinterval of [0, 1]. As an example, consider again Figure 12.1 where the copula parameter between market and credit risk is set to $R = 0.66$. The corresponding linear correlation can be estimated by applying 12.2 to the sample data shown in the scatter plots, yielding for both copulas a value of about $\rho = 0.57$. In a later section we will give an analytical expression for the relation between R and the actual correlation coefficient ρ, which confirms this result.

A useful estimator for **R** is based on Kendall's tau rank correlation τ, which is defined as the probability of concordance minus the probability of discordance, ie

$$\tau(X,Y) = P\left[(X - X')(Y - Y') > 0\right] - P\left[(X - X')(Y - Y') < 0\right]$$

where (X', Y') is an independent copy of (X, Y). If $(x_1, \ldots, x_n)$ and $(y_1, \ldots, y_n)$ are two samples of X and Y, then the standard estimator for Kendall's tau is given by

$$\hat{\tau} = \frac{n_c - n_d}{\sqrt{(n_c + n_d + n_x)(n_c + n_d + n_y)}}$$

Here, n_c is the number of concordant pairs of observations and n_d is the number of discordant pairs, where a concordant pair (x_i, y_i) and (x_j, y_j) is one such that both $x_i > x_j$ and $y_i > y_j$ or both $x_i < x_j$ and $y_i < y_j$. A discordant pair is one such that $x_i > x_j$ and $y_i < y_j$ or $x_i < x_j$ and $y_i > y_j$. Moreover, n_x denotes the number of so-called ties where $x_i = x_j$, and similarly, n_y counts the ties in y in which $y_i = y_j$.

It was pointed out by Embrechts, Lindskog and McNeil (2001), and Lindskog, McNeil and Schmock (2003) that Kendall's tau can be used to construct a robust and efficient estimator for the correlation parameters R_{ij} and thus the matrix **R** of a Gaussian or t copula. In doing so, we note that for essentially all elliptical distributions Kendall's tau is linked to the linear correlation coefficient by

$$R = \sin\left(\pi\tau / 2\right) \tag{12.5}$$

Now, since copulas are invariant under monotonously increasing transformations, Relationship 12.5 also holds true for basically all marginal risk type distributions and can therefore be used as an estimator for R.

Inter-risk correlation matrix

We now assume that for given risk types X_i, $i = 1, \ldots, m$, we have estimated their linear correlations ρ_{ij}, or, alternatively, the correlation parameters R_{ij} of a Gaussian or t copula (eg, by using such methods as described in the previous section). By definition, in order to be a proper correlation matrix, the pairwise correlation estimates must satisfy several conditions: the matrices **C** and **R** must be symmetric and all their diagonal elements must be equal to 1, moreover, they have to be positive semi-definite. The first two conditions can be checked easily, and for the latter there exist several mathematically equivalent ways of testing it. Using modern computer algebra systems, a particular convenient method is to calculate the eigenvalues of the matrix; then, if all eigenvalues are non-negative, the matrix is positive semi-definite and hence a proper correlation matrix. If some eigenvalues are negative, a positive semi-definite matrix has to be generated from the raw data before risk aggregation can be performed. Algorithms for doing this are discussed, eg, in Higham (2002), Rebonato and Jäckel (1999) or Lindskog (2000), who came to the conclusion that the best technique is the eigenvalue method, where negative eigenvalues of the raw matrix are replaced by a small positive constant $\delta > 0$, and the new matrix is then calculated invoking standard results from linear algebra.

In order to illustrate the potential impact of the positive semi-definiteness requirement on calculating an inter-risk correlation matrix, let us consider the following four-dimensional symmetric matrix based on average industry data according the survey of the IFRI/CRO Forum (2007) (see "An aggregation exercise" for further details)

$$\mathbf{R} = \begin{pmatrix} & \text{market} & \text{credit} & \text{oprisk} & \text{business} \\ \text{market} & 1 & 0.66 & 0.30 & R \\ \text{credit} & 0.66 & 1 & 0.30 & R \\ \text{oprisk} & 0.30 & 0.30 & 1 & R \\ \text{business} & R & R & R & 1 \end{pmatrix} \qquad (12.6)$$

where we assume that business risk has an unknown but uniform correlation parameter R with other risks. What can we say about the possible values of R, for instance, would it be possible to adopt the conservative assumption of $R = 1$? A look at Figure 12.2 reveals that $\mathbf{R}$ is a proper correlation matrix only if R is smaller than 0.78, which therefore is the correct upper bound (instead of $R = 1$) to be used for a conservative calculation of aggregated economic capital. Though the property of positive semi-definiteness is in general difficult to grasp, consider the following intuitive argument: Assume that R in 12.6 is set to the extreme value of $R = 1$, implying that business risk comonotonously depends on market risk, credit risk and operational risk, ie, their loss variables always move in lock steps. This, however, implies at least a medium degree of comovement also between, eg, operational risk and market risk, or between operational risk and credit risk, since their random variables are coupled by virtue of the

Figure 12.2 Plot of $\min(\lambda_1, \lambda_2, \lambda_3, \lambda_4)$ of all eigenvalues λ_i of the symmetric matrix 12.6 as a function of the unknown correlation parameter R of business risk

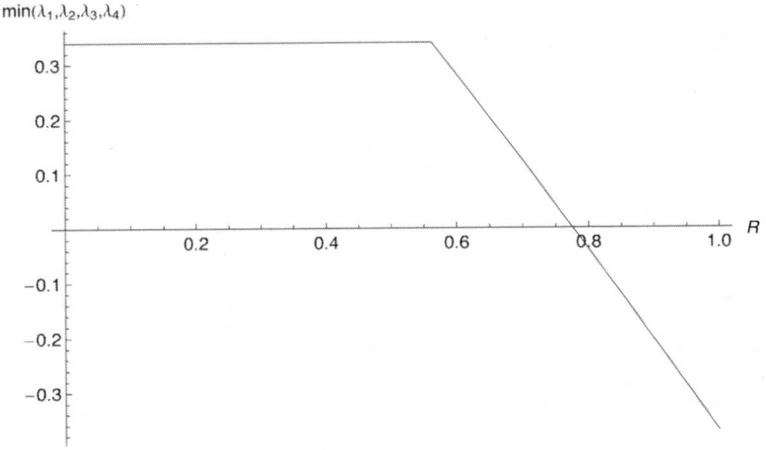

For $R < 0.78$ all eigenvalues are positive and R becomes a well-defined correlation matrix.

business risk random variable. This is, however, in contradiction to their relatively low correlation of 0.3 in 12.6. Consequently, the coupling of business risk to the other risk types must be less strong, implying an inter-risk correlation that is somewhat smaller than 1.

Elicitation of expert knowledge

Introduction

Because of the often scarce empirical data, it is usually not guaranteed that statistical estimators like 12.2 yield reliable and robust results for the inter-risk correlation, and in this case it is necessary to draw on expert opinions. This has also been acknowledged by the Committee of European Banking Supervisors in their recent consultation paper (CEBS 2008), where they explicitly distinguish statistical techniques versus expert judgements. However, because elicitation of expert knowledge is not an easy task, supervisors are usually concerned about how the subjectivity of expert estimates can be addressed and controlled.

Therefore, in this section we try to shed some light on this subject matter and review some basic concepts and key results about expert judgements. A reliable elicitation of expert probabilities requires knowledge both in statistics and in psychology of judgements under uncertainty. Excellent overviews about the methodological framework of elicitation of probabilities are O'Hagan *et al* (2006) or Jenkinson (2005), and they were the source of inspiration for the following brief presentation on this intriguing subject.

To understand how experts construct probability judgements it is important to distinguish "frequency probability" versus personal or "subjective probability". Simply stated, frequency probability of an event is the relative proportion of its occurrence in an ideally infinitive, series of repetitions. Think, for example, of the relative number of "heads" in a (obviously repeatable) coin-tossing game. Indeed, the strong law of large numbers ensures that the sample average converges in probability towards the expected value, ie, for the coin-tossing game we have that

$$P\left(\lim_{n\to\infty}\frac{H_n}{n}=\frac{1}{2}\right)=1$$

where H_n denotes the number of "heads" in a series of n trials. Hence, frequency probability can be used to describe the statistical uncertainty (also referred to as aleatory uncertainty) in one or more instances of a random process. On the other hand, if there is also systematic uncertainty (also referred to as epistemic uncertainty) due to imperfect knowledge, or if the "game" cannot be repeated, the definition of frequency probability does not suffice. Put another way, we then have to associate the notion of probability with the uncertainty of knowledge rather than with the results of repeatable experiments. This leads to the definition of subjective probability as a person's degree of belief in an uncertain proposition.

Given the frequency interpretation of probability, it is clear that also the personal probability should not contradict some formal laws of probability, such as the multiplication law $P(A \cap B) = P(A)\,P(B)$ for independent events A and B. However, empirical research revealed that, in practice, people's judgement of probabilities is often biased and non-coherent, ie, violating formal axioms of probability. The reasons for that are manifold, eg, the expert's statement of probability crucially depends on the facilitator's questions but also on the response scale on which the expert is asked to express his personal probability. Another reason is that the information on which the respondent's judgement is built may be based only on a sub-sample or subjective selection of what is potentially relevant. A groundbreaking work regarding the psychological foundation that governs the heuristics that are employed in making judgements of probabilities was the heuristics and biases research programme by Tversky and Kahneman (1974).[3] According to this, people rely their judgements of probability on some heuristic principles instead of a more complex assessment that requires more effort. In general, such approximative heuristics work sufficiently well "but sometimes they lead to severe and systematic errors." (Tversky and Kahneman 1974, p. 1124). By way of illustration, let us consider the following frequently cited experiment, see Tversky and Kahneman (1983):

> Linda is 31 years old, single, outspoken and very bright. She majored in philosophy. As a student she was deeply concerned with issues of discrimination and social justice and also participated in antinuclear demonstrations. Respondents were asked to tick the most likely alternative between:
>
> - Linda is a bank teller; and
> - Linda is a bank teller and is active in the feminist movement.

The majority of people (typically more than 80%) rate the second opinion as more likely than the first one; a result, which is obviously in contradiction to the laws of probability because the conjunction of two events (Linda is a bank teller and an active feminist) can never be greater than either of the standalone events (eg, Linda is a bank teller).

Eliciting inter-risk dependence measures

What are the implications of this research for estimating inter-risk correlation based on experts' opinion? First, we mention that judging correlations between two random variables contains the complexity of multivariate elicitation. Hence, one can expect to encounter similar or even bigger problems compared to those found when assessing means, medians or variances of univariate distributions. It has therefore been suggested that in order to elicit association (such as linear correlation) in a joint distribution, it is more reliable to elicit joint probabilities or conditional probabilities rather than the association measure directly. With this respect, O'Hagan *et al* (2006, p. 110), suggest a method for estimating the correlation between two random variables X and Y by means of their positive quadrant probability, which is defined as $P(X > x_{\text{med}}, Y > y_{\text{med}})$ where x_{med} and y_{med} are the medians of X and Y, respectively. For example, if X and Y are bivariate normally distributed with correlation ρ and standard deviations σ_x and σ_y, then their positive quadrant probability can be analytically calculated as (see Lindskog 2000, Example 2.2)

$$\begin{aligned} P(X > x_{\text{med}}, Y > y_{\text{med}}) &= \frac{1}{2\pi\sigma_x\sigma_y\sqrt{1-\rho^2}} \int_0^\infty \int_0^\infty \exp\left[-\frac{1}{2(1-\rho^2)}\left(\frac{x^2}{\sigma_x^2} - \frac{2\rho xy}{\sigma_x\sigma_y} + \frac{y^2}{\sigma_y^2}\right)\right] \\ &= \frac{1}{4} + \frac{\arcsin(\rho)}{2\pi} \end{aligned} \quad (12.7)$$

Solving 12.7 for ρ, an elicited positive quadrant probability can be transformed into a measure for the linear correlation coefficient.

Naturally, in the context of risk aggregation, two risk types are seldom bivariate normally distributed and 12.7 can not be used directly. However, the basic idea can be easily generalised to elicit the parameters of a given bivariate copula. It is worth mentioning that in order to extract the parameters of a bivariate copula by estimating a joint probability such as 12.7, any assumptions about the marginal distribution functions need to have been solved already as well as for the copula. We now exemplify this technique for the Gaussian and t copula.

We now already adopt the notation we will use later and denote the credit risk and market risk random variables by L and Z, respectively. Let us consider the joint probability that market risk loss and credit risk loss exceed certain thresholds of x_L and x_Z , ie, $P(Z > x_Z, L > x_L)$. From Figure 12.3 we immediately obtain

$$\begin{aligned} P(Z > x_Z, L > x_L) &= 1 - P(Z \le x_Z) - P(L \le x_L) + P(Z \le x_Z, L \le x_L) \\ &= 1 - F_Z(x_Z) - F_L(x_L) + C_R(F_Z(x_Z), F_L(x_L)) \end{aligned} \quad (12.8)$$

where F_L and F_Z are the marginal distribution functions of preaggregated credit and market risk, and $C_R(\cdot, \cdot)$ is a bivariate Gaussian or t copula,

Figure 12.3 Joint probability $P(Z > x_Z, L > x_L)$ that credit loss is above x_L and market loss is above x_Z

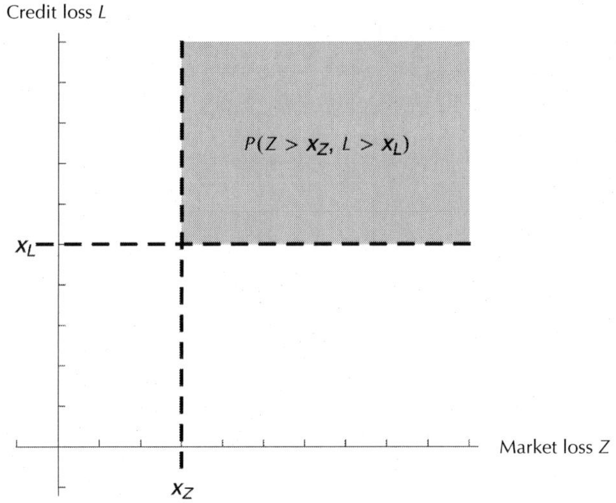

As described in the text, this probability can be used to estimate the correlation parameter R of a bivariate Gaussian or t copula.

depending on the unknown parameter R to be estimated. Expression 12.8, which can be understood as a generalisation of 12.7 to arbitrary marginals and bivariate copulas, cannot usually be solved analytically for the copula parameter, here R. However, numerical techniques or a graphical analysis may help to infer R from an elicited value for $P(Z > x_Z, L > x_L)$.

It has been argued by several authors such as O'Hagan *et al* (2006) or Gokhale and Press (1982) that people usually have more quantitative feeling about one-dimensional probabilities instead of (bivariate) joint probabilities. Hence, to diminish the bias of an expert estimate, they suggest to reduce a joint probability to a conditional probability, which is a statement regarding only one random variable. In our example of market and credit risk, we therefore could do better in eliciting

$$P(L > x_L \mid Z > x_Z) = \frac{P(Z > x_Z, L > x_L)}{P(Z > x_Z)} \tag{12.9}$$

ie, the probability that credit losses will be above x_L given that a market risk loss greater than x_Z has already occurred. In order to illustrate this with a numerical example, let us first specify x_L and x_Z by the expectations $\mathbb{E}L$ and $\mathbb{E}Z$ of the marginal credit risk and market risk distributions. We use the same Student t and Vasicek distribution for marginal market and credit risk as in Figure 12.1, and moreover we set without loss of generality $\mathbb{E}Z = 0$, whereas expected credit loss is roughly about 7.0 as described in the following subsection "An aggregation exercise". From 12.8 and 12.9 we then obtain

$$\begin{aligned} P(L > \mathbb{E}L \mid Z > 0) &= 2P(Z > 0, L > \mathbb{E}L) \\ &= 1 - 2F_L(\mathbb{E}L) + 2C_R\left(\frac{1}{2}, F_L(\mathbb{E}L)\right) \end{aligned} \tag{12.10}$$

The left-hand side of Figure 12.4 shows the conditional probability $P(L > \mathbb{E}L \mid Z > 0)$ as a function of the copula parameter R both for a Gaussian and a t copula with three degrees of freedom. It can be seen that there is essentially no difference between both copulas, implying that extreme dependence between two risk types cannot be assessed by means of 12.10. This is mainly a consequence of the fact that we have chosen such moderate values for the thresholds x_L and x_Z, namely the expected losses of L and Z, respectively. If we set both x_L and x_Z in 12.8 to more extreme values, eg, to high quantiles such as 99%, one can graphically differentiate both cpoulas as it is shown in the right-hand side of Figure 12.4. The conditional probabilities derived from a Gaussian or a t copula are now different because, as we explained in the subsection "Copulas and tail dependence", both copulas differ in the way they reflect extreme dependence. In particular, recall that $\lambda_{\text{Gauss}} = 0$, and therefore, in order to achieve a certain level of extreme joint loss probability $P(L > x_L \mid Z > x_Z)$, the correlation parameter of the Gaussian copula must be higher compared to the one of a t copula. Since in the right-handside of Figure 12.4 the thresholds x_L and x_Z are chosen as high quantiles (99%) of the marginal loss distributions, the plot effectively is a numerical approximation of the tail dependence 12.3 for different values of R. The exact tail dependence parameter for a t copula was given in 12.4 and is illustrated in Figure 12.4 as a dotted line, specifically, for $R = 0$ and $\nu = 3$ we have $\lambda_t = 0.12$.

Based on several expert estimates for different thresholds x_L and x_Z, one could, in principle, use the described method to determine both R and the degree-of-freedom parameter ν of a t copula. However, because such procedure would require expert knowledge about high-quantile losses such as used in the right-hand side of Figure 12.4, one might expect a high degree of uncertainty when they are assessed by expert judgement.

Let us again consider the left-hand side of Figure 12.4. Statistically it is clear from 12.9 that the conditional probability $P(L > \mathbb{E}L \mid Z > 0)$ always takes values in a subinterval of [0, 1], in particular, we have in the case of independent

Figure 12.4 Plot of the conditional probability $P(L > x_L | Z > x_Z)$ as a function of the parameter R of a Gaussian copula (solid line) and a t copula with three degrees of freedom (dashed line) according to 12.9

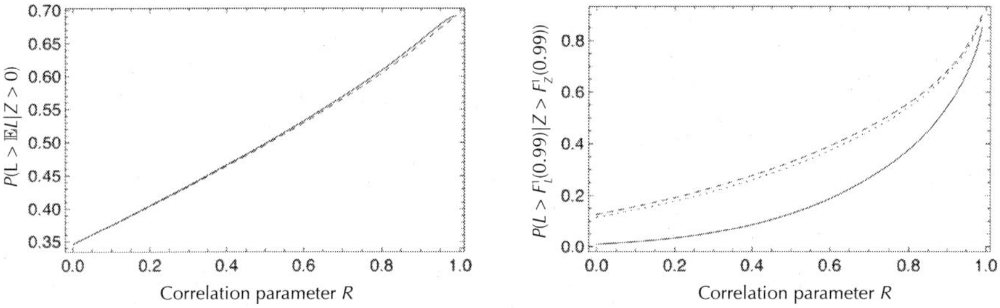

In the case of the Gaussian copula, independence between market and credit risk is reached for $R = 0$, and the joint probability is then equal to the probability that credit losses are above x_L. Moreover, marginal market and credit risk follow the same Student t and Vasicek distributions as used in Figure 12.1. Left: Here $x_L = \mathbb{E}L$ and $x_Z = \mathbb{E}Z = 0$. Right: $x_L = F_L^{-1}(0.99)$ and $x_Z = F_Z^{-1}(0.99)$. As explained in the text, this plot can therefore be interpreted as a numerical approximation of the tail dependence λ, which for the t copula is additionally shown as a dotted line.

market and credit risk $P(L > \mathbb{E}L \mid Z > 0) = P(L > \mathbb{E}L) > 0$. Assuming a Gaussian copula, this is equivalent to $R = 0$[4]. However, since humans cannot be guaranteed to act according to the rules of probability theory, we cannot take it for granted that this is also clear for the expert. The facilitator should therefore carefully explain the underlying statistical concept to the expert at the beginning of the elicitation exercise and maybe use the lower boundary $P(L > \mathbb{E}L)$ as an anchor that helps to calibrate the expert's estimate of $P(L > \mathbb{E}L \mid Z > 0)$. Finally, a possible question to the expert could be this one:

> Suppose you were told that the actual yearly loss in market risk is above its expected value. Can you now determine the probability that also yearly credit loss is above the expected one?

The expert's estimate for $P(L > \mathbb{E}L \mid Z > 0)$ can then be transformed into an estimate for R either graphically by Figure 12.4 or numerically by solving 12.10. Moreover, if we are interested in the linear correlation coeffcient ρ between both risk types, we can calculate it from simulated random variates obtained from the copula C_R together with the assumed marginal distributions, just as we did in Figure 12.1.

Needless to say, the described elicitation approach can be used to assess associations between almost every kind of risk-type marginals and, in principle, also in combination with other copulas. However, as we have already

Table 12.1 Marginal distributions for market, credit, operational and business risk, where F_v is the Student t distribution function with v degrees of freedom and Φ is the standard normal distribution function

Risk	Distribution function	Parameters
Market	$F(x)=F_v\left(\frac{x-\mu}{\sigma}\right), \quad x\in\mathbb{R}$	$\mu = 0$, $\sigma = 2.18$, $v = 10$
Credit	$F(x)=\Phi\left[\frac{1}{\sqrt{\varrho}}\left(\sqrt{1-\varrho}\,\Phi^{-1}\left(\frac{x}{X}\right)-\Phi^{-1}(p)\right)\right], \quad x>0$	$X = 2338.64$, $p = 0.3\%$, $\varrho = 8\%$
Operational	$F(x)=\Phi\left[\frac{\ln x-\mu}{\sigma}\right], \quad x>0$	$\mu = -0.893$, $\sigma = 1.089$
Business	$F(x)=\Phi\left[\frac{x-\mu}{\sigma}\right], \quad x\in\mathbb{R}$	$\mu = 0$, $\sigma = 4.54$

Market risk follows a scaled Student t and credit risk is described by a Vasicek distribution with total exposure X, uniform asset correlation ϱ and average default probability p. Operational risk is assumed to be lognormally distributed and business risk is modelled by a normal distribution. The parameters for the distribution functions are chosen so that market, credit, operational and business risk absorb 10, 61, 14 and 15 units of econmic capital at 99.95% confidence level. Finally, only credit and operational risk have non-zero expected losses of about 7.0 and 0.7, respectively.

seen by comparing the Gaussian copula and the t copula in Figure 12.4, this method cannot (straightforwardly) be used to assess a possible extreme dependence between two risk types, without touching the thorny issue of extreme value estimation based on expert opinions.

If a bank has decided to build its inter-risk correlations (partially) on expert judgements, elicitation of expert knowledge as described above can add additional value to the whole risk aggregation exercise. Moreover, once an expert estimate for inter-risk correlation is obtained, it can be combined with observed empirical data by using Bayesian methods, and the interested reader may refer to Congdon (2007) as a readable introduction on Bayesian modelling techniques.

An aggregation exercise

After the inter-risk correlation matrix **C** or the matrix **R** of an elliptical copula is determined, one can begin with the aggregation of the different risk types. This section is devoted to illustrating this aggregation procedure by considering a bank-typical example. We assume that preaggregated economic capital for each risk type has already been determined at a confidence level of 99.95% with a time horizon of one year, and that the portfolio composition based on these preaggregated risk-type figures is given by 10% market risk, 61% credit risk, 14% operational risk and 15% business risk.

Table 12.2 Aggregated economic capital at a confidence level of 99.95% with a one-year time horizon for the portfolio consisting of market, credit, operational and business risk as specified in Table 12.1

Aggregated economic capital			
Sum	**Gaussian copula**	***t* copula (ν = 5)**	**Upper bound EC^{+}_{max}**
100	79.57 (82.39)	85.95 (83.10)	122.48

The correlation matrix **R** used for the Gaussian and *t* copula is given by 12.11. The values in brackets are obtained by the variance–covariance formula 12.1 where we have used the simulated inter-risk correlations 12.12 and 12.13, respectively. The calculation of the upper bound ψ^{-1} is described in the text.

These values represent an industry average obtained from large banks that participated in a survey of the IFRI/CRO Forum (2007, Figure 16). For the different risk types we assume distributions and parameterisations as widely used in practice, see Table 12.1. In particular, the Vasicek distribution for credit risk will be further explained in the later subsection "One-factor approximations". Also regarding the specification of the inter-risk correlation matrix we stick to the IFRI/CRO survey and use average benchmark results reported in (2007, Figure 10). This is not, however, so straightforward since we know from the subsection "Inter-risk correlation" above that these correlations not only describe dependence between different risk types but also are impacted by the marginal risk distributions. Hence, to simplify matters we interpret these benchmark correlations as the correlation matrix **R** of a Gaussian or *t* copula as described earlier, and we write

$$\mathbf{R} = \begin{pmatrix} & \text{market} & \text{credit} & \text{oprisk} & \text{business} \\ \text{market} & 1 & 0.66 & 0.30 & 0.58 \\ \text{credit} & 0.66 & 1 & 0.30 & 0.67 \\ \text{oprisk} & 0.30 & 0.30 & 1 & 0.60 \\ \text{business} & 0.58 & 0.67 & 0.60 & 1 \end{pmatrix} \tag{12.11}$$

Note that this matrix is positive semi-definite and thus a proper correlation matrix. Before we go on with our aggregation exercise, let us have a look at the corresponding correlation matrix **C** of linear correlation coeffcients ρ_{ij}, i, j =1, 2, 3, 4. As linear correlation depends on the dependence structure, we get different results for different copulas. Using the marginal distributions of Table 12.1 together with a Gaussian copula, a simulation yields

$$\mathbf{C}_{\text{Gauss}} = \begin{pmatrix} & \text{market} & \text{credit} & \text{oprisk} & \text{business} \\ \text{market} & 1 & 0.57 & 0.30 & 0.42 \\ \text{credit} & 0.57 & 1 & 0.26 & 0.55 \\ \text{oprisk} & 0.30 & 0.26 & 1 & 0.43 \\ \text{business} & 0.42 & 0.55 & 0.43 & 1 \end{pmatrix} \tag{12.12}$$

whereas in the case of a *t* copula with five degrees of freedom we obtain

$$C_{\text{Student}} = \begin{pmatrix} & \text{market} & \text{credit} & \text{oprisk} & \text{business} \\ \text{market} & 1 & 0.58 & 0.30 & 0.44 \\ \text{credit} & 0.58 & 1 & 0.26 & 0.61 \\ \text{oprisk} & 0.30 & 0.26 & 1 & 0.43 \\ \text{business} & 0.44 & 0.61 & 0.44 & 1 \end{pmatrix} \tag{12.13}$$

The results of the aggregation analysis are shown in Table 12.2. It can be seen that total aggregated economic capital in the case of a Gaussian dependence structure is slightly below the result obtained from the variance–covariance approach. However, because these results depend on the relative importance of the different risk types as well as the specific forms of the marginal distributions, this observation should not be generalised without investigation.

Assessing superaddivity of risks when using VaR

Value-at-risk attracted lots of criticism because it lacks the property of subadditivity and therefore is not a coherent risk measure in the sense of Artzner *et al* (1999). This also has consequences for the aggregation-by-risk type approach since the sum of the preaggregated economic capital figures is not necessarily an upper bound for aggregated economic capital. Put another way, it is not guaranteed that even a comonotone (ie, complete positive) dependence provides a risk manager with the worst-case scenario they may be looking for. In our example of the four risk types, this means that aggregated economic capital could be even higher than 100. How can a risk manager account for this uncertainty when assessing the capital adequacy of a bank?

In more general terms, the problem as follows. We know the marginal probability distributions of two or more (real-valued) random variables X_i, $i = 1, \ldots, m \geq 2$ with distribution functions F_i, but we have no, or only incomplete, information about their dependence structure. If we denote the distribution function of their sum $Z = \sum_i^m X_i$ by

$$F^{+}(z)=P(Z\leq z)=P\left(\left\{(x_1,\ldots x_m)\in\mathbb{R}^m:\sum_{i=1}^{m}x_i\leq z\right\}\right),\quad z\in\mathbb{R}$$

it is then possible for a given $z \in \mathbb{R}$ to compute an interval $[F^{+}_{\min}(z), F^{+}_{\max}(z)]$ of possible distribution functions $F^{+}(z)$ that can be attained under any kind of dependence structure? In principle, it is clear that $F^{+}_{\min}(z)$ is the infimum of possible values for $F^{+}(z)$ over all joint distributions of $(X_1, \ldots, X_m)$ for which the marginal distributions coincide with the given marginal distribution functions F_i. Similarly, $F^{+}_{\max}(z)$ corresponds to the supremum of all such distribution functions. However, a precise answer to this question, which was originally raised by Kolmogorov, is, in general, difficult to obtain and was for $m = 2$ eventually given by Kolmogorov's student Makarov (1981). This result was later restated by Frank, Nelsen and Schweizer (1987) using the copula framework, and finally an algorithm for computing $F^{+}_{\min}(z)$ and $F^{+}_{\min}(z)$ for $z \in \mathbb{R}$ was suggested by Williamson and Downs (1990), who also proved that these bounds are pointwise best possible, ie, cannot be improved.

In our terminology of risk aggregation, an important implication of these findings is that for two risk types X and Y a bound for aggregated VaR at confidence level $\alpha \in (0, 1)$ is given by

$$\mathrm{VAR}_{X+Y}(\alpha)\leq\left(F^{+}_{\min}\right)^{-1}(\alpha)=\inf_{C_L(u,v)=\alpha}\left\{F_X^{-1}(u)+F_Y^{-1}(v)\right\}=:\psi^{-1}(\alpha)\quad(12.14)$$

where $F_X^{-1}(\cdot)$ and $F_Y^{-1}(\cdot)$ are the inverse of the distribution functions of X and Y, and $(F^{+}_{\min})^{-1}(\cdot)$ is the inverse of $F^{+}_{\min}(\cdot)$. Moreover, $C_L(u, v) = \max(u + v - 1, 0)$ is the bivariate lower Fréchet copula. Practical calculations usually build on a suitable discretisation of 12.14, eg

$$\psi^{-1}(\alpha)=\min_{\alpha\leq t\leq 1}\left\{F_X^{-1}(t)+F_Y^{-1}(1+\alpha-t)\right\}\quad(12.15)$$

which can then be computed by calculating a finite number of values of $t \in [\alpha, 1]$. In order to obtain an upper bound for aggregated economic capital, one just has to subtract the total expected loss from 12.14, ie

$$EC^{+}(\alpha)\leq\psi^{-1}(\alpha)-\mathbb{E}X-\mathbb{E}Y\quad(12.16)$$

By way of illustration, let us again consider the numerical example of above where credit and market risk sum up to 71 units of economic capital. In contrast, the upper bound for their aggregated economic capital derived from 12.16 is approximately given by 75.89.

Formula 12.14 has been extended to $m \geq 3$, however, it can be shown that in this case the upper bound on $\mathrm{VaR}_{X_1+\ldots+X_m}(\alpha)$ is usually not best possible anymore, and that numerically calculating such a best-possible bound is in general computationally intractable, see Denuit, Genest and Marceau (1999), Embrechts and Puccetti (2006) or Kreinovich and Ferson (2006) for further details. In general, the multivariate analogons in 12.14 and 12.15 involve finding minima over a hyperplane. However, as pointed out by Denuit *et al* (1999) and Frank *et al* (1987), the computation of VaR bounds for $m > 2$ risks can actually be done iteratively. Starting with the first two risk types X_1 and X_2, evaluating 12.15 for different vales of α gives by inversion the minimum distribution function $F^{\min}_{X_1+X_2}$. This can than be used together with F_{X_3} to determine $F^{\min}_{X_1+X_2+X_3}$ by means of 12.15, and so on and so forth.

We have calculated such bounds on aggregated economic capital for the example portfolio of Table 12.1. We found a worst-case aggregated economic capital that is about 22% higher than the simple-sum economic capital of 100, see also Table 12.2. Though the simulated bound for more than two risk types is in general overconservative, such an analysis could be useful when assessing the risk taking capacity of a bank in practice. At any case, given proper estimates of the marginal risk types, calculating upper bounds for aggregated economic capital reduces model risk, especially when non-subadditive VaR measures are used.

INTER-RISK CORRELATION OF CREDIT RISK

In this section we focus our analysis on the correlation between a credit portfolio and another risk type, which we henceforth refer to as market risk. In doing so we follow Böcker and Hillebrand (2007) and Böcker and Klüppelberg (2008) and combine a Merton-like factor model for credit risk with a linear factor model for market risk. Within this setup one can calculate inter-risk correlation between market and credit risk analytically, and also derive inter-risk correlation bounds.

Preliminaries and main results

We assume that credit risk is modelled by a classical structural model[5] where default of a single obligor $i \in \{1, \ldots, n\}$ is modelled by a Bernoulli random variable L_i with $P(L_i = 1) = p_i = 1 - P(L_i = 0)$ and default probability p_i. A single default is triggered if the asset value log-return A_i falls below the default point D_i, ie

$$L_i = 1_{\{A_i < D_i\}}, \qquad i = 1, \ldots, n$$

If we denote the exposure at default (perhaps enriched by discounting factors and/or net of recovery rates) of an individual obligor by e_i, portfolio loss is given by

$$L^{(n)} = \sum_{i=1}^{n} e_i L_i$$

Let $Y = (Y_1, \ldots, Y_K)$ now be a random vector of factors with multivariate standard normal distribution, and assume that each of the standardised asset value log-returns A_i for $i = 1, \ldots, n$ linearly depends on Y as well as on a standard normally distributed idiosyncratic factor ε_i (modelling the performance of counterparty i) independent of Y, ie

$$A_i = \sum_{k=1}^{K} \beta_{ik} Y_k + \sqrt{1 - \sum_{k=1}^{K} \beta_{ik}^2}\, \varepsilon_i, \qquad i = 1, \ldots, n \tag{12.17}$$

The factor loadings β_{ik} satisfy $R_i^2 := \sum_{k=1}^{K} \beta_k^2 \in [0, 1]$, which is the part of the variance of A_i that can be explained by the systematic factors Y. Such a model will henceforth be called the normal factor model for credit risk.

In a credit risk factor model, default correlation $\text{corr}(L_i, L_j)$ between different obligors can be attributed to the correlation of their asset value log-returns $\text{corr}(A_i, A_j)$, which again can be explained by their common dependence on the factors Y. Now, in the context of inter-risk correlation it is intuitively clear that the correlation $\text{corr}(L^{(n)}, Z)$ between a credit portfolio $L^{(n)}$ and market risk, represented by a random variable Z, is attributable to the n correlations $\text{corr}(L_i, Z)$, and therefore to $\text{corr}(A_i, Z)$, $i = 1, \ldots, n$. Needless to say, for a general risk type Z with arbitrary distribution function, $\text{corr}(L^{(n)}, Z)$ cannot be calculated in closed-form. However, in the important cases that Z is normally distributed or t distributed, analytical results can be found. To achieve this, it is convenient to describe Z by a factor model similar to 12.17, but which moreover allows to account for possible heavy tails of Z. Let $Y = (Y_1, \ldots, Y_K)$ therefore be the same set of multivariate standard normal factors as used in the normal factor model for credit risk and let η be a standard normally distributed idiosyncratic factor, independent of Y. Further, let W be a positive random variable, independent of Y and η. Then, the multiplicative shock model for preaggregated market risk is given by

$$Z = -\sigma W \left(\sum_{k=1}^{K} \gamma_k Y_k + \sqrt{1 - \sum_{k=1}^{K} \gamma_k^2}\, \eta \right) \tag{12.18}$$

with scaling factor σ and factor loadings γ_k satisfying $\sum_{k=1}^{K} \gamma_k^2 \in [0, 1]$, representing systematic market risk, which can be explained by the systematic factor Y. The interpretation of 12.18 is that the mixing variable W represents a "global shock" that simultaneously drives the variance of all factors Y. An important example is if $W = \sqrt{\nu/S_\nu}$ and S_ν is a χ^2_ν distributed random variable with ν degrees of freedom, implying that Z follows a scaled t distribution with distribution function $F(\cdot) = F_\nu(\cdot/\sigma)$ as also specified in Table 12.1, hereafter referred to as the t_ν model.

Combining the normal factor model for credit risk and the multiplicative shock model for market risk above, allows to calculate their inter-risk correlation in closed form. According to Böcker and Klüppelberg (2008, Theorem 3) the following is then obtained

$$\operatorname{corr}\left(L^{(n)}, Z\right) = g(W) \frac{\sum_{i=1}^{n} r_i e_i \exp\left[-\frac{1}{2}\left(\Phi^{-1}(p_i)\right)^2\right]}{\sqrt{2\pi \sum_{i,j=1}^{n} e_i e_j \left(p_{ij} - p_i p_j\right)}} \tag{12.19}$$

with

$$g(W) = \frac{\mathbb{E}W}{\sqrt{\mathbb{E}\left(W^2\right)}}$$

Here, $\Phi^{-1}(\cdot)$ is the inverse of the standard normal distribution function and p_{ij} is the joint default probability of two obligorsϱ

$$p_{ij} := P\left(A_i \le D_i, A_j \le D_j\right) = \begin{cases} \Phi_{\varrho_{ij}}\left(\Phi^{-1}(p_i), \Phi^{-1}(p_j)\right), & i \neq j, \\ p_i, & i = j \end{cases}$$

where $\Phi_{\varrho_{ij}}$ denotes the bivariate normal distribution function with standardised marginals and asset correlation $\varrho_{ij} := \operatorname{corr}(A_i, A_j) = \sum_{k=1}^{K} \beta_{ik}\beta_{jk}$, $i, j = 1, \ldots, n$. Furthermore

$$r_i := \operatorname{corr}\left(A_i, Z\right) = \sum_{k=1}^{K} \beta_{ik}\gamma_k, \quad i = 1, \ldots, n \tag{12.20}$$

denotes the correlation between the obligors' asset value log-returns A_i and market risk Z. Some remarks are appropriate. First, note that r_i in 12.20 becomes negative if (some) factor loadings β_{ik} and γ_k have a different sign, hence also negative inter-risk correlations can be achieved. Second, in 12.19 the terms $e_i \exp[-(\Phi^{-1}(p_i))^2/2]$, $i = 1, \ldots, n$, which are increasing in p_i, can be interpreted as rating-adjusted exposures. Consequently, for two obligors with equal exposure sizes e_i, the one with the better rating has less impact on inter-risk correlation than the low-rated creditor. Third, in the special case of the t_ν model with $\nu > 2$ one can further evaluate $g(W)$ to

$$g(W)=\sqrt{\frac{\nu-2}{2}}\frac{\Gamma\left(\frac{\nu-1}{2}\right)}{\Gamma\left(\frac{\nu}{2}\right)}=:f(\nu)$$

In this case, Equation 12.19 gives the inter-risk correlation between a credit risk portfolio and a t distributed market risk with variance $\sigma^2\nu/(\nu-2)$. Moreover, since for $\nu\to\infty$ the t distribution approaches the normal distribution and because $\lim_{\nu\to\infty} f(\nu)=1$, Equation 12.19 together with $g(W)\equiv 1$ also gives the inter-risk correlation for normally distributed market risk. Finally, from $\mathbb{E}W>0$ it follows by the Cauchy–Schwarz inequality that

$$0<g(W)\leq 1$$

and therefore, given a positive inter-risk correlation for normally distributed market risk, introducing a global shock that diminishes inter-risk correlation.

In the section "Inter-risk correlation", we have already stated that linear correlation is usually bounded to a subinterval of [–1, 1], and 12.19 perfectly exemplifies this in the case for the inter-risk correlation of market and credit risk. Let us assume that the only information we have about market risk is that Z follows a scaled Student t distribution. In other words, Z can be described by the factor model 12.18 but with yet unknown factor weights γ_k, $k=1,\ldots,K$. Because of $0\leq\sum_{k=1}^{K}\gamma_k^2\leq 1$ it then follows from 12.20 by the Cauchy– Schwartz inequality that

$$|r_i|=\left|\sum_{k=1}^{K}\beta_{ik}\gamma_k\right|\leq\left(\sum_{k=1}^{K}\beta_{ik}^2\right)^{1/2}\left(\sum_{k=1}^{K}\gamma_k^2\right)^{1/2}\leq\left(\sum_{k=1}^{K}\beta_{ik}^2\right)^{1/2}=|R_i|\leq 1$$

and from 12.19 we finally obtain the following upper inter-risk correlation bound

$$\left|\mathrm{corr}\left(L^{(n)}\right)\right|=g(W)\frac{\sum_{i=1}^{n}e_i\sqrt{\sum_{k=1}^{K}\beta_{ik}^2}\exp\left[-\frac{1}{2}\left(\Phi^{-1}(p_i)\right)^2\right]}{\sqrt{2\pi\sum_{i,j=1}^{n}e_ie_j\left(p_{ij}-p_ip_j\right)}}\leq 1 \quad (12.21)$$

One-factor approximations

The results so far can be used to estimate inter-risk correlation between a Student t distributed, preaggregated market risk Z and credit risk $L^{(n)}$, which is modelled by a classical Merton approach. For the purpose of illustration, and to gain deeper insights into the interaction between $L^{(n)}$ and Z, it is helpful to consider the one-factor versions of 12.17 and 12.18 as well as for the corresponding inter-risk correlation.

Especially for credit risk, one-factor approximations are very popular because they deliver the theoretical foundation for the calculation formulas for regulatory capital charges in the internal-ratings-based approach of Basel II. Within such a one-factor framework, the credit portfolio is assumed to be homogeneous; ie, for $i = 1, \ldots, n$, we have exposures $e_i = e$, default probabilities $p_i = p$ and factor loadings $\beta_{ik} = \beta_k$ for $k = 1, \ldots, K$, ie, these quantities are the same for all credits of the portfolio. Then, credit risk is systematically explained only by one single factor $\tilde{Y} := \sum_{k=1}^{K} \beta_k Y_k / \sqrt{\varrho}$, which is a compound of all Y_k for $k = 1, \ldots, K$, where $\varrho := \sum_{k=1}^{K} \beta_k^2$ is the uniform asset correlation of the credit portfolio. The situation further simplifies for very large portfolio sizes, finally resulting in the large homogeneous portfolio *(LHP)* approximation, also known as the asymptotic single-risk factor model, see Chapter 5, and is usually formulated as

$$\frac{L^{(n)}}{ne} \underset{}{\overset{a.s.}{\longrightarrow}} \Phi\left(\frac{\Phi^{-1}(p) - \sqrt{\varrho}\tilde{Y}}{\sqrt{1-\varrho}} \right) =: L, \quad n \to \infty \tag{12.22}$$

This asymptotic expression for the credit loss random variable L finally leads to the now well-known Vasicek distribution, which is often chosen as an analytical approximation to describe credit portfolio loss, and which we have also used in our previous aggregation exercise, see Table 12.1.

As shown in Böcker and Hillebrand (2007), such a one-factor framework can consistently be extended to include also market risk, which is then also systematically described by the single factor $\tilde{Y}$, and 12.18 simplifies to

$$\tilde{Z} = -\sigma W\left(\tilde{\gamma}\tilde{Y} + \sqrt{1-\tilde{\gamma}^2}\tilde{\eta}\right) \tag{12.23}$$

where we wrote $\tilde{Z}$, $\tilde{\gamma}$ and $\tilde{\eta}$ to distinguish them from the parameters used in the general factor model 12.18. Then, inter-risk correlation in the case of the t-model is given by

$$\operatorname{corr}\left(L, \tilde{Z}\right) = f(\nu) \frac{r e^{-\left(\Phi^{-1}(p)\right)^2/2}}{\sqrt{2\pi\left(p_{12} - p^2\right)}} \tag{12.24}$$

and the bound 12.21 simplifies to

$$\left|\operatorname{corr}\left(L, \tilde{Z}\right)\right| \le f(\nu) \frac{\sqrt{\varrho} r e^{-\left(\Phi^{-1}(p)\right)^2/2}}{\sqrt{2\pi\left(p_{12} - p^2\right)}} =: B(p, \varrho, \nu) \tag{12.25}$$

Figure 12.5 LHP approximations of the inter-risk correlation bound as a function of the average portfolio rating according to 12.25

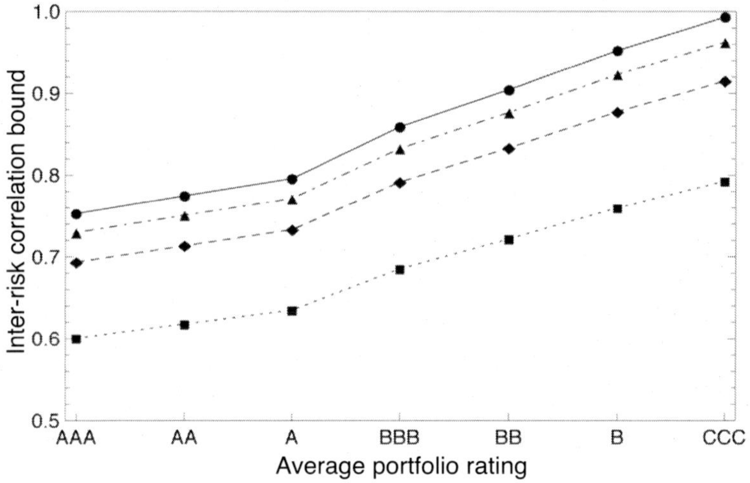

The solid line corresponds to the normal factor model (formally $\nu \to \infty$) and the t model is illustrated for $\nu = 3$ (dotted line), $\nu = 5$ (dashed line) and $\nu = 10$ (dotted-dashed line). The uniform asset correlation is assumed to be $\varrho = 8\%$.

where $p_{12} = \Phi_\varrho(\Phi^{-1}(p), \Phi^{-1}(p))$ is the joint default probability and $r = \sum_{k=1}^{K} \beta_k Y_k$. Moreover, note that normally distributed market risk corresponds to $f(\nu) = 1$.

In Figure 12.5 the inter-risk correlation bound $B(p, \varrho, \nu)$ is plotted as a function of the average portfolio rating (and thus average default probability p) for different degrees of freedom ν of the t distribution of market risk. As already mentioned before, we see that introducing global shocks in market risk effectively reduces the inter-risk correlation. However, in the light of the correlation fallacies presented earlier, we should be wary of interpreting such results as this in terms of an increasing correlation.

Applications

Since actual credit portfolios are rarely homogeneous, Expressions 12.24 and 12.25 are not exactly true in practice. However, similar to the victory march of the credit risk one-factor model of Basel II, our formulas can be useful for investigating and approximating inter-risk correlation also for real credit portfolios. This shall be illustrated with some selected examples.

Inter-risk correlation bound for general credit portfolios

Except of the degree of freedom parameter v of the market risk distribution, Expression 12.25 for the inter-risk correlation bound only depends on a few standard parameters of the credit portfolio like the uniform asset correlation ϱ and the average default probability p. Both variables can easily be estimated also for a general credit portfolio, eg, using Monte Carlo simulation. In doing so, assume that the actual credit portfolio has an expected loss μ and a total exposure of e_{tot}. If the variance of the actual, simulated loss distribution is calculated to be $\hat{s}^2$, then estimators $\hat{p}$ and $\hat{\varrho}$ for the unknown parameters p and ϱ can be found by moment matching

$$\mu = e_{\text{tot}}\hat{p}$$
$$\hat{s}^2 = e_{\text{tot}}^2\left[\Phi_{\hat{\varrho}}\left(\Phi^{-1}(\hat{p})\right) - \hat{p}^2\right]$$

and from 12.25 we finally obtain the following moment estimator for the upper inter-risk correlation bound

$$\hat{B}(\hat{p},\hat{\varrho},\hat{v}) = f(\hat{v})\frac{e_{\text{tot}}}{\hat{s}}\frac{\sqrt{\hat{\varrho}}\exp\left[-\left(\Phi^{-1}(\hat{p})\right)^2/2\right]}{\sqrt{2\pi}} \tag{12.26}$$

where $\hat{v}$ has to be determined from the preaggregated market risk distribution. For example, adopting the distributions for market and credit risk given in Table 12.1, $\hat{B}$ (0.3%, 8%, 10) = 0.83 is obtained. Furthermore, we can ask which value for the average correlation r between the creditors' asset value log-returns A_i and market risk Z matches an observed inter-risk correlation, and from 12.24 and 12.25 we see that

$$r = \frac{\operatorname{corr}(L,\tilde{Z})}{B(p,\varrho,v)}\sqrt{\varrho}$$

For instance, the simulated market–credit correlation in 12.13 of 0.58 implies an r of about $r = (0.58/0.83)\sqrt{0.08} = 0.20$. Such a calculation provides a new interpretation of the inter-risk correlation, hence, it can be used for double-checking a given correlation estimate for corr(L, $\tilde{Z}$), which has been obtained by statistical methods or expert judgement.

Estimating the correlation parameter *R* of a Gaussian copula

A problematic issue with copula techniques in general is that it is not straightforward to decide which copula is appropriate for a given situation. As we mentioned before, in the context of risk aggregation it is often assumed that the dependence structure between different risk types is properly reflected by a Gaussian or a t copula, however, for no apparent reason.

The joint LHP approximation for credit and market risk, however, naturally suggests a Gaussian dependence structure, see Böcker and Hillebrand (2007, Proposition 5.1). To show this, let us consider the case of normally distributed market risk, ie, Expression 12.23 with $W \equiv 1$

$$\tilde{Z} = -\sigma\left(\tilde{\gamma}\tilde{Y} + \sqrt{1-\tilde{\gamma}^2}\tilde{\eta}\right) \tag{12.27}$$

Now, since copulas are invariant under monotonously increasing transformations, and credit portfolio loss L in the LHP approximation is given by 12.22

$$L(Y) = \Phi\left(\frac{\Phi^{-1}(p) - \sqrt{\varrho}\tilde{Y}}{\sqrt{1-\varrho}}\right)$$

is a monotonously increasing function of $-\tilde{Y}$, it follows that L and $\tilde{Z}$ have the same copula as $-\tilde{Y}$ and $\tilde{Z}$. For the latter we infer from 12.27 that they are bivariate normally distributed with $\text{corr}(-\tilde{Y}, \tilde{Z}) = \tilde{\gamma}$ implying that L and $\tilde{Z}$ are associated by a Gaussian copula with parameter $R = \tilde{\gamma}$.

The argumentation above only works for the LHP approximation and not for general credit portfolios for which the parameter $\tilde{\gamma}$ is not defined. However, in Böcker and Hillebrand (2007) we also suggest two different estimators for the copula parameter R, which can be applied to general, non-homogeneous credit portfolios. One of them is given by

$$\hat{R} = \frac{\text{corr}\left(L^{(n)}, Z\right)}{\hat{B}(\hat{p}, \hat{\varrho}, \infty)} \tag{12.28}$$

where $\text{corr}(L^{(n)}, Z)$ is the inter-risk correlation of credit and market risk, which can be calculated from 12.19 with $g(W) = 1$ but also by other methods mentioned in this chapter. Furthermore, $\hat{B}(\hat{p}, \hat{\varrho}, \infty)$ is the moment estimator 12.26 for the inter-risk correlation bound in the case of normally distributed market risk.

CONCLUSION

In this chapter we examined different aspects of the popular aggregation-by-risk type approach, which is represented by the square-root formula 12.1. Assuming that risk figures for different risk types have already been preaggregated, a core problem is the estimation of reliable inter-risk correlations.

Besides standard statistical methods based on historical data expert judgments can be used, and we looked in more detail on how this could be done in a rigorous and reliable way.

One problematic issue with the square-root formula 12.1 is that the diversification between different risk types is directly linked to the concept of inter-risk correlation. Having in mind the various potential fallacies of linear correlation as a dependence measure, one should be very careful when specifying inter-risk correlations. There are many examples in financial literature about how things may go awry if linear correlation is directly interpreted as a dependence measure (see Embrechts *et al* (2002) or Böcker and Klüppelberg (2008) for example) with applications to operational risk.

Therefore, and being aware that square-root aggregation is theoretically justified only for multivariate elliptically distributed risk types, it may be wise to perform risk aggregation also by means of other techniques, such as the copula aggregation approach. Copula aggregation can be regarded as a natural extension of the square-root formula approach because it allows for more realistic distribution functions representing the preaggregated risk types. The example presented gives a feeling of how aggregated risk figures may change if different copulas are used, in particular, when tail dependence is switched on. Moreover, we mentioned some methods, which allow risk managers to calculate upper bounds of the aggregated economic capital that cannot be exceeded.

Finally we looked in more detail at the interaction between a credit portfolio and another risk type, eg, market risk. We calculated inter-risk correlations and inter-risk correlation bounds analytically and showed how they depend on parameters of the credit portfolio. The presented model can also be used to estimate the correlation parameter of a Gaussian copula.

1 The opinions expressed in this chapter are those of the author and do not reflect the views of UniCredit Group. Moreover, presented risk measurement concepts and risk control techniques are not necessarily used by UniCredit Group or any affiliates.

2 Despite the fast growing popularity of copulas in finance, some authors are more sceptical about the concept of couplas. First to mention in this way Thomas Mikosch, who's criticism initiated a discussion involving different experts and which is now documented in (Mikosch 2006).

3 Kahneman was awarded the 2002 Nobel Prize in Economic Sciences for this and related work, and Tversky, who died in 1996, was acknowledged in the announcement because the Royal Swedish Academy of Sciences does not award prizes posthumously.

4 We want to stress again that this is not in general true, confer the third correlation fallacy mentioned in the subsection "Inter-risk correlation".

5 See also chapter 5 where a similar model is presented in the context of concentration risk.

REFERENCES

Artzner, P., F. Delbaen, J. Eber and D. Heath, 1999, "Coherent measures of risk", *Mathematical Finance*, 9(3), pp. 203–228.

BCBS, IOSCO, IAIS (The Joint Forum), 2003, "Trends in Risk Integration and Aggregation", August.

Böcker, K. and M. Hillebrand, 2007, "Interaction of market and credit risk: an analysis of inter-risk correlation and risk aggregation", Submitted for publication, URL: http://www.ma.tum.de/stat/.

Böcker, K. and C. Klüppelberg, 2008, "Economic Capital Modelling and Basel II Compliance in the Banking Industry", in W. Jäger and H.-J. Krebs (eds), *Mathematics – Key Technology for the Future* (Berlin: Springer).

Böcker, K. and C. Klüppelberg, 2008, "Modeling and Measuring Multivariate Operational Risk with Lévy Copulas", *The Journal of Operational Risk*, 3(2), pp. 3–27.

Brockmann, M. and M. Kalkbrener, "On the Aggregation of Risk", Working Paper, Deutsche Bank.

Cherubini, U., E. Luciano and W. Vecchiato, 2004, *Copula Methods in Finance* (Chichester: John Wiley & Sons).

Committee of European Banking Supervisors (CEBS), 2005, "Application of the Supervisory Review Process under Pillar 2", Consultation Paper.

Committee of European Banking Supervisors (CEBS), 2008, "Consultation paper on technical aspects of diversification under Pillar 2", Consultation Paper.

Congdon, P., 2007, *Bayesian Statistical Modelling* (Chichester: John Wiley & Sons).

Denuit, M., C. Genest and E. Marceau, 1999, 'Stochastic bounds on sums of dependent risks', *Insurance Math. Econ.*, 25(1), pp. 85–104.

Devlin, S. J., R. Gnanadesikan and J. R. Kettering, 1981, "Robust estimation of dispersion matrices and principal components", *Journal of the American Statistical Association*, 76, pp. 354–362.

Dimakos, X. K. and K. Aas, 2004, "Integrated Risk Modelling", *Statistical Modelling*, 4, pp. 265–277.

Embrechts, P., F. Lindskog and A. McNeil, 2001, "Modelling Dependence with Copulas and Applications to Risk Management", in S. Rachev (ed), *Handbook of Heavy Tailed Distributions in Finance* (Elsevier), pp. 329–384.

Embrechts, P., A. McNeil and D. Straumann, 2002, "Correlation and dependence in risk management: properties and pitfalls", in M. A. H. Dempster (ed), *Risk Management: Value at Risk and Beyond* (Cambridge University Press), pp. 176–223.

Embrechts, P. and G. Puccetti, 2006, "Bounds for functions of dependent risks", *Finance and Stochastics*, 10, pp. 341–352.

Frank, M. J., R. B. Nelsen and B. Schweizer, 1987, "Best-possible bounds for the distribution of a suma problem of Kolmogorov", *Probab. Theory Related Fields*, 74, pp. 199–211.

Gokhale, D. V. and S. James, 1982, "Press Assessment of a Prior Distribution for the Correlation Coefficient in a Bivariate Normal Distribution", *Journal of the Royal Statistical Society A*, 145(2), pp. 237–249.

Higham, N. J., 2002, "Computing the Nearest Correlation Matrix – a Problem From Finance", *IMA Journal of Numerical Analysis*, 22(3), pp. 329–343.

The Institute of the Chief Risk Officers/Chief Risk Officer Forum, 2007, "Insights from the joint IFRI/CRO Forum survey on Economic Capital practice and applications".

Jenkinson, D., 2005, "The Elicitation of Probabilities – A Review of the Statistical Literature", Working Paper BEEP, URL: http://www.shef.ac.uk/beep/publications.html.

Kreinovich, V. and S. Ferson, 2006, "Computing best-possible bounds for the distribution of a sum of several variables is NP-hard", *International Journal of Approximate Reasoning*, 41(3), pp. 331–342.

Lindskog, F., 2000, *Linear correlation estimation*, Preprint, ETH Zürich, url: {http://www.risklab.ch/Papers.html}.

F. Lindskog, A. J. McNeil and U. Schmock, 2003, "Kendall's Tau for Elliptical Distributions", in G. Bol *et al* (eds), *Credit Risk-Measurement, Evaluation and Management* (Heidelberg: Physica-Verlag), pp. 149–156.

Makarov, G. D., 1981, "Estimates for the distribution function of the sum of two random variables with given marginal distributions", *Theory Probab. Appl.*, 26, pp. 803–806.

Mikosch, T., 2006, "Copulas: tales and facts", *Extremes*, 9(1), pp. 3–20, Discussion 21–53, Rejoinder 5562.

O'Hagan, A., C. E. Buck, A. Daneshkhah, J. R. Eiser, P. H. Garthwaite, D. J. Jenkinson, J. E. Oakley amd T. Rakow, 2006, *Uncertain Judgements: Eliciting Experts' Probabilities* (Chichester: John Wiley & Sons).

Rebonato, R. and P. Jäckel, 1999, "The most general methodology to create a valid correlation matrix for risk management and option pricing purposes", *The Journal of Risk*, 2(2), pp. 17–24.

Rosenberg, J. V. and T. Schuermann, 2004, "A General Approach to Integrated Risk Management with Skewed, Fat-Tailed Risk", Working Paper no. 185, Federal Reserve Bank of New York Staff Reports.

Saita, F., 2007, *Value at Risk and Bank Capital Management* (San Diego, CA: Elsevier).

Tversky, A. and D. Kahneman, 1974, "Judgment under Uncertainty: Heuristics and Biases", *Science*, 185, pp. 1124–1131.

Tversky, A. and D. Kahneman, 1983, "Extensional vs. intuitive reasoning: The conjunction fallacy in probability judgment", *Psychological Review*, 90, pp. 293–315.

Vasicek, O., 2002, "Loan portfolio value", *Risk*, December, pp. 160–162.

Ward, L. and D. Lee, 2002, "Practical application of risk-adjusted return on capital framework", Dynamic Financial Analysis Discussion Paper, CAS Forum.

Williamson, R. C. and T. Downs, 1990, "Probabilistic arithmetic: numerical methods for calculating convolutions and dependency bounds", *International Journal of Approximate Reasoning*, 4(2), pp. 89–158.

13

Risk Aggregation in a Large International Financial Group: a Case Study

Ruben Olieslagers, Patrick Acx[1]

Fortis

In this chapter we review a number of risk aggregation criteria and techniques based on the real-life experience of a large financial conglomerate. Our case-study focuses on Fortis, an international financial services provider engaged in banking and insurance, and represents the methods that have been applied for the 2007 annual financial statements.

Fortis offers personal, business and institutional customers a comprehensive package of products and services through its own channels, in collaboration with intermediaries and through other distribution partners.

Fortis is a large conglomerate that faces a wide range of risks across its various banking, insurance and investment activities. Risk management is a core part of Fortis' business and has an impact on all areas of management. Since its inception in 1989, Fortis has undergone explosive growth, both organically and through acquisitions. Its banking and insurance operations have been strengthened by several mergers and acquisitions. Therefore, given the different origins of the banking and insurance pool entities, these entities developed very different terminology and approaches for risk assessment and, as a result, these risks were only measured separately to support local decision-making.

Given the consequential inconsistencies in risk measurement methodologies, it was difficult to identify the main areas of risk and an adequate objective and unitary comparison of risks taken was not possible. An overall view on risks necessary to determine capital adequacy did not exist.

In 1999,[2] the executive committee decided to launch the Fortis Capital

Adequacy Project (ForCAP), aimed at developing a group-wide and consistent risk measurement framework to determine capital adequacy for banking and insurance. This integrated approach would allow the board to understand the general distribution of economic capital consumption across risk types and business activities, and maximise group advantages of scale, diversification benefits and knowledge sharing within Fortis entities.

Within Fortis we drew a distinction among three types of capital.

1. Regulatory capital: minimum amount of capital you must have as specified by the regulator (eg, Capital Adequacy Directive of European Union, Solvency Requirements).
2. Rating agency capital: the amount of capital the rating agencies expect you to have based on their rules in order to feel comfortable for a given rating (eg, AA in the case of Fortis).
3. Economic capital: The amount of capital you should have based on requirements calculated on an economic basis.

At that time, the regulatory requirements (Basel I and Solvency I) were often standardised and simplified while not reflecting the true economic risks and fully recognising risk diversification.

Initially, ForCAP was not meant to replace any other risk metric developed through the various initiatives supported by either the bank or the insurance pool. Rather, it was aimed at developing an additional risk metric to improve Fortis's risk management capabilities and support stakeholder discussions (eg, rating agencies, analysts, investors, regulators).

The project was organised in two phases: a top-down phase and a bottom-up phase. The aim of the top-down phase was to arrive at robust relative results using a pragmatic approach based on the available risk measures from local risk management departments in the operating entities. Where necessary, some benchmarks and assumptions had to be inserted to fill possible gaps while at the same time maintaining consistency in the whole process. In the second phase, bottom-up refinements have been constantly implemented to replace existing benchmarks, to improve methodologies and to increase the granularity of the calculations.

This chapter will present in detail the main methodologies and outcomes in the ForCAP project; although, for comprehensiveness and competitive reasons, some issues have been simplified and outdated figures are presented, we feel that this does not affect the underlying argument.

The chapter unfolds as follows: in the next section, the risk taxonomy, the choice of confidence interval, time horizon and economic capital aggregation process are explained; we then present a number of alternative risk aggregation techniques that were carefully analysed and tested, as well as a set of results based on such techniques; the final two sections focus on the regulatory recognition of risk diversification and provide some final remarks.

CAPITAL AGGREGATION AT FORTIS

The Fortis capital aggregation and disaggregation approach (Henrard and Olieslagers 2004) encompasses five main aspects:

1. definition of the risk taxonomy;
2. metric for measuring risk: economic capital within banking and insurance;
3. calibration: confidence level and time horizon;
4. aggregation of economic capital; and
5. disaggregation of economic capital.

Definition of the risk taxonomy

Before calculating the group-wide risk, the risk taxonomy should be defined. Many different ways of classifying risk are possible, and no single taxonomy is inherently better than another. Within Fortis, the risk taxonomy has been designed to ensure that all material risks are adequately captured according to the relative importance of the various risk types (see Figure 13.1). A more detailed description of the various risk types is provided in the Appendix.

Note that liquidity risk is not incorporated into the economic capital calculations. Fortis, like almost all of its peers, does not calculate economic capital for liquidity risk, as capital is not a palliative for liquidity events. Liquidity risk is managed in a qualitative way and controlled through limits, gap analysis and stress-testing. A liquidity policy framework (strategic principles, reporting, limit setting, early warning signals and accountability) has been put in place.

Metric for measuring risk: economic capital within banking and insurance

Several alternative metrics for measuring risks are possible. Within Fortis it has been decided to use economic capital as the key measure.

Economic capital is defined as the capital Fortis needs to hold to protect its net asset value from falling below zero after the event of a worst-case fair-

Figure 13.1 Fortis risk taxonomy

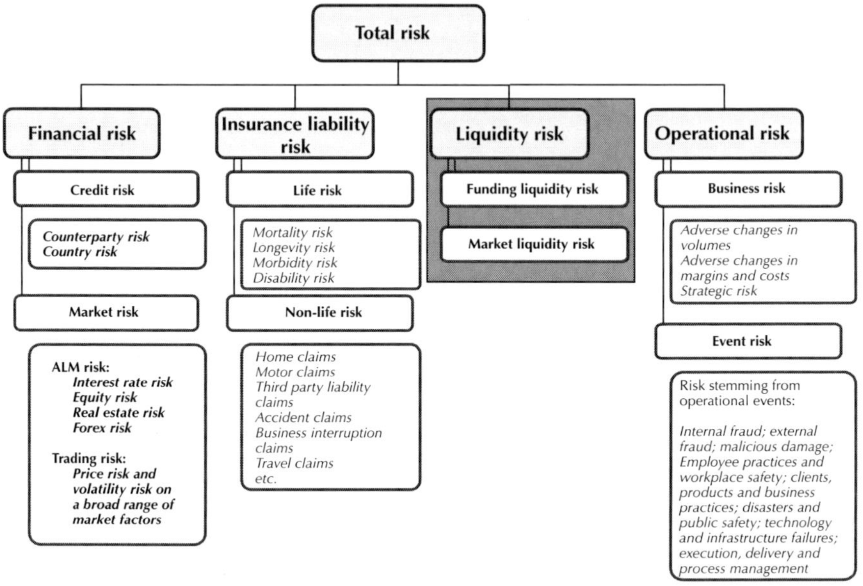

value loss over one year, worst case being associated with a tail probability of 0.03%, reflecting the one-year probability of default of an AA debt rating. In other words, economic capital corresponds to the amount of capital needed to cover unexpected economic losses during extreme events. It is measured as the difference between potential unexpected economic losses over a one year time period at a 99.97% confidence level and its expectation (see Figure 13.2).

A critical issue in Fortis's case is the difference in terminology and focus within the risk management units of the banking and insurance divisions (see Table 13.1). The differences are substantial, mainly because of the differences in the dominant risk type. Mapping had to be done in order to allow an "apples-to-apples" comparison.

Calibration: time horizon and confidence level

The "economic capital" measure has been developed within Fortis in order to provide a consistent and comparable measure of risk across all risk types and geographies. Therefore, all economic capital measurements within Fortis are calibrated to the same time horizon and confidence interval. The

Figure 13.2 Economic capital calculation within Fortis (AA rating)

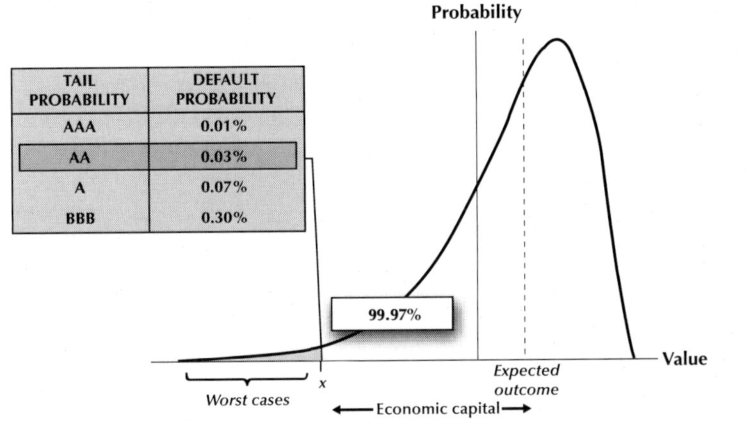

choice of the time horizon (one year) and confidence interval (99.97%) is explained in detail below.

Time horizon

Capital requirements need to be expressed over a set time horizon. The local risk managers in Fortis's banking and insurance activities measure risks over various time horizons. For the purpose of aggregating all capital requirements across the Group, ForCAP needed to set a common time horizon for the calibration of risk. Within Fortis it was decided to use a one-year horizon as a compromise between conventions typical in the banking

Table 13.1 Various approaches used in banking and insurance

	Banking	Insurance
Terminology	Expected loss Rating master scale VaR Economic capital RAROC	Claims Mortality tables Embedded value Reserves/solvency/risk-based capital Various performance measures
Focus	Expected and unexpected losses One-year asset risks	Prudent estimates Multi-year liability risks
Historical weaknesses	Over simplified modelling of customer behaviour	Insufficient use of modern financial theory Little use of transfer pricing (ALM)

pool (eg, relatively short-term) and the insurance pool (eg, relatively long-term).

There are a number of aspects that have been considered when setting the one-year time horizon.

- The time horizon should be long enough to increase capital or reduce risk through loss-mitigating action if needed. This action could include raising new capital, selling assets, or restructuring the bank.
- It should be long enough to include normal business cycles of strategic planning, capital budgeting, and the publishing of accounts.

If we look at current practice[3] outside Fortis, the one-year time horizon for both capital budgeting and group risk monitoring purposes is the market standard (see Figure 13.3), as one year is considered the amount of time necessary to recapitalise an institution. For trading risk, often measured in shorter time horizons (one to 10 days), the horizon has been extrapolated using the square-root-of-time rule and a stop-loss factor was modelled into the calculation to take account of the effect of management intervention.

It should be noted that this one-year time horizon is intended for group risk reporting purposes only. The operating companies should continue to apply different time horizons and planning scenarios for their own risk measurement, pricing and management purposes.

Confidence level

One of the purposes of ForCAP is to evaluate Fortis Group's overall capital adequacy to ensure that it maintains the current rating agency target group

Figure 13.3 Time horizon used for economic capital calculation

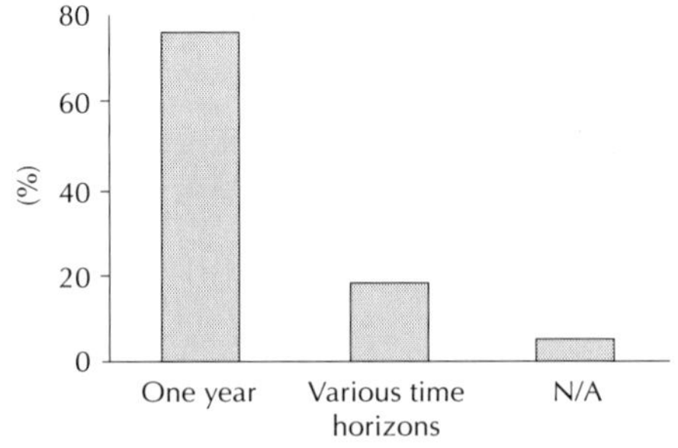

Source: Mercer, Oliver & Wyman 2006

debt rating, eg, an S&P rating of AA (99.97% of confidence interval equivalent to a probability of default of 0.03%). All economic capital measurements are therefore calibrated to the capital held to support economic risks by an average AA-rated financial institution. In Figure 13.2, the link of the tail probabilities of failure with S&P ratings is shown in function of the desired rating.

Economic capital figures are based on a very high confidence interval (99.97%) and reflect potential large losses with a very low probability. The economic capital figures are therefore hard to interpret for senior management. To show management that their economic capital provides a reasonable outcome, which is in line with intuition, economic capital is also calculated for other confidence intervals, eg, 90% probability. These 90% economic capital figures, which can occur once in 10 years, are referred to as earnings-at-risk (EaR) and provide a better idea of the size of the potential losses. They are very useful for top management to get an idea of the volatility of P&L.

Aggregation of economic capital

Current aggregation technique

After estimating the economic capital separately for each type of risk and per business, the total economic capital is calculated for Fortis as a whole. Since it is extremely unlikely that all risk events will take place at the same time, an allowance is made for diversification when combining the individual risks.

Within Fortis, three different levels of diversification are considered (see also Figure 13.4).

- The first level focuses on the "standalone" risks within a single risk type, eg, credit risk in a commercial banking portfolio.
- The second level regards diversification across the different business lines and forms the "inter-business view", eg, between commercial banking and private banking.
- The third level considers diversification between the different risk types and consists in the "inter-risk view", eg, between credit risk and event risk

Note that the three different diversification levels correspond neither to successive aggregation steps nor to cumulative diversification levels. They should be envisaged as "structures" where diversification effects occur.

The difference between the mere algebraic sum of standalone economic

Figure 13.4 Various aggregation levels considered within Fortis

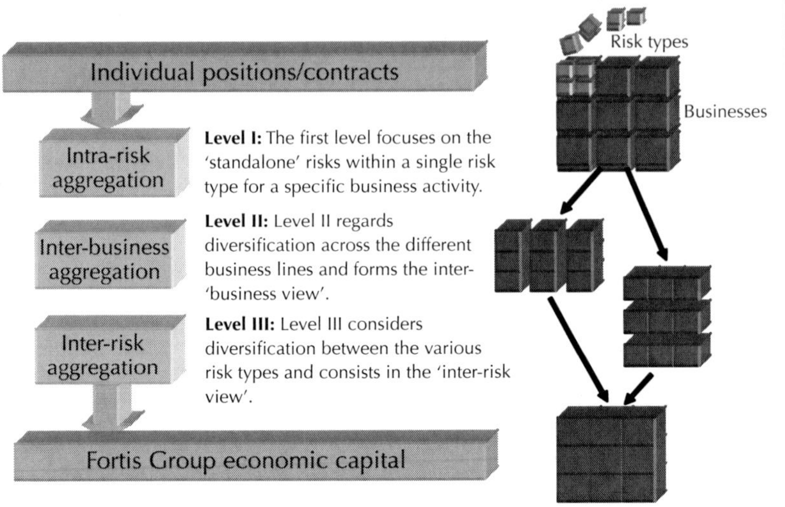

capital figures and final fully diversified economic capital represents the "diversification benefits". These are the benefits Fortis gets from the diversification of its activities. Stated differently, benefits are derived from netting risks (ALM bank and insurance) or accumulating risks that are not fully correlated instead of treating each of these risks separately and individually. *Post facto*, these benefits are "redistributed" to single-risk-type figures.

This results in a total economic capital at group level that is significantly lower than it would be if the individual risks were simply added together. Within Fortis, diversification benefits amount to more than 30%[4] (see also Figure 13.5) when comparing the standalone economic capital for each business and per risk type with the total aggregated capital figure.

The major part of the diversification benefit is due to the fact that Fortis is a large international group with activities in investment, banking (wholesale and retail) and insurance (life and non-life).

For the ForCAP calculations, it was decided early to use the variance-covariance (var-covar) approach for aggregating economic capital across risk types for various businesses.[5] Most leading financial conglomerates that have implemented group-wide risk frameworks have typically adopted this kind of approach initially (see also Figure 13.6).

Fortis computes its total economic capital by first calculating the standalone economic capitals per business and risk type (eg, credit risk in

Figure 13.5 Fortis diversification benefit

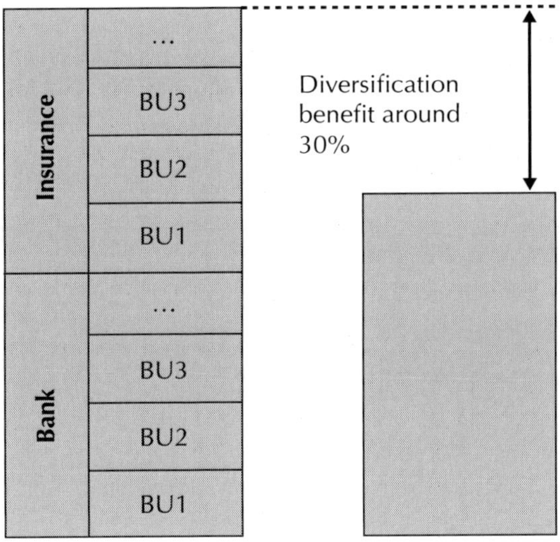

Figure 13.6 Results survey, IFRI/CRO Forum[6] on aggregation approaches

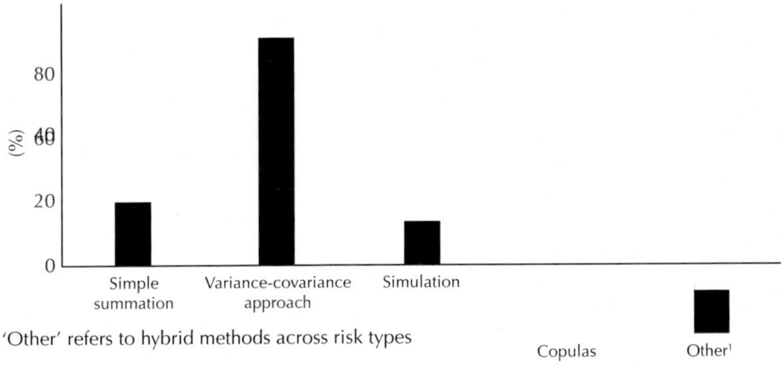

[1] 'Other' refers to hybrid methods across risk types

Source: IFRI – Institute of the Chief Risk Officers and Chief Risk Officer Forum (CRO Forum), 2007

business line BL1). These economic capitals are then aggregated in one step by using a standard var-covar approach with a predefined correlation matrix (to be further discussed). Figure 13.7 shows an overview of the aggregation process.

Figure 13.7 Economic capital calculation within Fortis (one-step approach

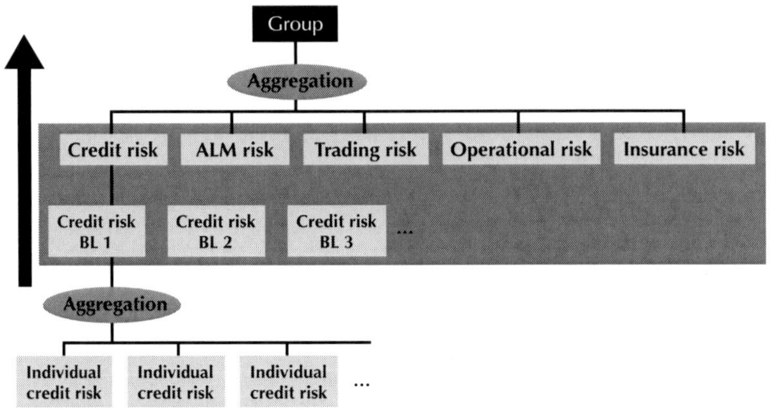

The underlying rationale behind this var-covar approach is its ease of calculation. The sum of variables with various distributions is cumbersome to work with and it is generically not possible to know the overall distribution of the aggregated loss. When assuming a multivariate normal distribution, the loss distribution can be directly analytically determined without making further assumptions or sophisticated computations. Also, the var-covar approach is very flexible for adding new businesses. Given the number of mergers and acquisition at Fortis over the past years, the latter is certainly an issue.

Choice of the correlation matrix

Empirically, correlations among various risk types and businesses can be measured by observing the long-term relationship between two data series. In practice, there is a limited amount of relevant data currently available for measuring correlations besides the fact that correlations tend to be unstable in crises.[7] To assume a 100% correlation between all risks is very conservative and does not allow for the incorporation of the diversification benefits that accrue by being a large financial conglomerate.

Fortis has opted for a rather pragmatic approach to compute correlations in the aggregation process of economic capital, by using a partially judgemental methodology, blending empirical coefficients with pure judgemental ones. The economic capital correlation matrix focuses mainly on risk types (geographical correlation aspects are taken into account only implicitly) and is based on the following assumptions:

- risk types are 100% correlated to themselves;
- the correlation of financial risks (credit, ALM and trading) is assumed to be high (between 60% and 100%) because in times of high volatilities (ie, high-confidence intervals), the systematic risk factors move financial risks in the same direction;
- property and casualty (P&C) risk, life and health risk are lowly correlated (between 0% and 20%) with any other risk types because there is no reason to believe that at times of high credit losses, for example, claims and mortality rates should also rise sharply;
- event risk is lowly correlated (between 0% and 40%) with any other risk type with the exception of business risk (closer to 50%); and
- business risk is medium-correlated (between 50% and 70%) with financial risks because in financial crises typically business volumes and the ability to cover expenses have fallen.

The economic capital is calculated as follows

$$Ecap^2_{Total} = \begin{bmatrix} EC_1 & EC_2 & \cdots & EC_M \end{bmatrix} P \begin{bmatrix} EC_1 \\ EC_2 \\ \cdots \\ EC_M \end{bmatrix}$$

where P is the correlation matrix and EC_i the "standalone" capital for a given risk type within a certain business ($i = 1 \ldots M$ with M = number of risk types * number of businesses).[8]

These EC_i are obtained following more advanced methodologies (loss and value approaches). For example, the calculation of credit risk is based on a bottom-up credit value-at-risk (VaR) approach taking into account the individual probability of default, loss given default and exposure at default. These individual parameters are used to calculate the expected and unexpected loss figures and then aggregated at portfolio level via a credit VaR loss approach (with a default correlation matrix clustered by asset size, sector, geography and rating class). To link the unexpected loss at portfolio level with the economic capital (99.97% confidence interval for an AA rating), Fortis makes use of Monte Carlo simulations.[9]

Credit risk, ALM risk for insurance and ALM risk for bank are the major risks, representing more than 70% of all risks within Fortis.

The var-covar approach has its merits because it is a simple approach and is relatively easy to apply. However, it rests on a number of simplifying assumptions and shortcuts. Before discussing more advanced aggregation techniques in combination with the sensitivity of the correlation matrix, we conclude this section by briefly describing the disaggregation techniques considered within Fortis.

Disaggregation of capital

Once the correct group-wide capital figure has been computed, it must be reallocated back to risk types and business lines. Clearly, if the capital aggregation process is inadequate, so will be the resulting disaggregated output.

The disaggregation process consists in redistributing the diversification benefits. There are many different ways of allocating these benefits among the individual business units (or to the individual sources of risk). Note, however that no single approach is correct – rather the choice amounts to a trade-off between various desirable properties.

Disaggregation methods (Koyluoglu and Stoker 2002) typically used are as follows.

- The haircut method: this is the simplest method, which evenly redistributes the diversification benefit according to the weight of the standalone capitals only.
- Discrete marginal contribution: this is a two-step process that calculates the economic capital of the entire group including the business line in question and then the economic capital of the group excluding the business line. The difference represents the capital to assign to the business line.
- Continuous marginal contribution: each component should receive a share in the diversification benefit in relation to its marginal contribution to the total group economic capital. Most commonly used for reallocating diversification.
- Shapley method: this contemplates the benefits of joining a group. All possible orders and the benefits resulting from it are sequentially computed. The average of all possible allocations will be considered as diversified capital.

All methods have their advantages and disadvantages. Various criteria to be considered are as follows.

- Transparency of calculation: figures should be easily computed and self-explanatory.
- Stability of results at the level of the entity: absence of volatility due to external events ensuring a "consistent" link between outcome and incentives, across time and compared to budget.
- Consistency between results of entity and impact at total group level (static and dynamic)
- Independence of the group's structural changes: the outcome should be independent of a split or merger of business lines/businesses/activities

Table 13.2 provides an overview of the various disaggregation methods and the Fortis assessment based on the various criteria. Given the growth of Fortis characterised by a series of mergers and acquisitions, the organisational structure has been subsequently optimised. Therefore, the independence criteria for structural changes are very important and have outweighed the other criteria in the choice of the disaggregation method. Discrete marginal contribution and the Shapley method do not of themselves provide consistent results in case of organisational changes. The haircut and discrete-marginal-contribution methods have been selected for the Fortis disaggregation process.

For consistency reasons, it is important subsequently to compare the models at different levels: methodology, information technology (data, systems), scope, coverage and operational issues (eg, impact on people and processes). These steps are necessary before full integration and when using alternative aggregation techniques such as the two-step aggregation approach (see below).

In the following section, the aggregation methodology and underlying assumptions are analysed in more detail. More advanced aggregation

Table 13.2 Assessment of various disaggregation methods

	Score on criteria			
Method	**Transparency**	**Stability**	**Consistency**	**Independence**
Haircut	☺☺	☺☺	☹	☺
DMC	☹	☹☹	☹	☹☹
CMC	😐	☹	☺☺	☺☺
Shapley	☹☹	☺	☺	☹☹

methodologies for computing economic capital are proposed and discussed.

ALTERNATIVE AGGREGATION TECHNIQUES

In this section we describe a number of potential improvements in the aggregation methodology described above. First, we introduce a two-step approach in dealing with the aggregation of risk types and business lines; then we turn to a number of advanced aggregation techniques such as comonotonicity, Monte Carlo simulations and copulas, which can deal with different loss distributions instead of requiring that all distributions be normal. Finally, we test the sensitivity of the correlation matrix for the different aggregation methods.

Our purpose is not to describe complex techniques in detail. The focus will be on providing a feeling for these approaches, some derived characteristics and the possible application of these approaches within Fortis.[10]

Different aggregation level: the two-step approach

In the section entitled "Capital aggregation at Fortis" (see Figure 13.7) the aggregation of risk capitals via the correlation matrix was assumed to take place in one step, moving from a standalone situation per risk type and per business to a fully diversified total. Fortis has reviewed this aggregation method and aims to use a different aggregation order, namely, first aggregating all individual risks of a certain risk type (Step 1) and then aggregating the various risk types (Step 2). Figure 13.8 provides an overview of the two-step approach.

The advantages of this method are:

- it considerably reduces the dimensional complexity in correlations (leading to a smaller size of the correlation matrix);
- it takes advantage of the integrated way risk models have been developed by taking advantage of the embedded cross business lines/entities correlations/dependencies (inter-business view);
- it permits the more accurate inclusion and computation of the possible different correlations/dependencies structures between business lines/entities in function of the risk types; and
- it indirectly relaxes the multivariate normal constraint.

As each risk type economic capital calculation for a specific business is based on a specific approach with specific underlying distributional

Figure 13.8 Aggregation of economic capital (two-step approach)

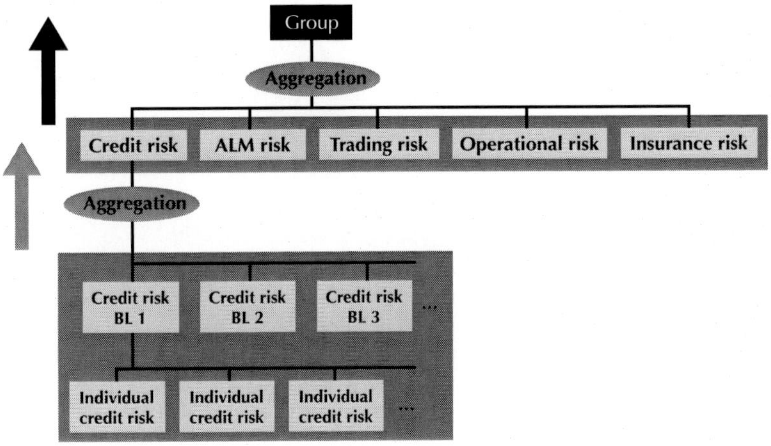

assumptions, the inter-business view allows the partial reduction of the bias introduced by the departure from the multivariate normality assumption.

However, even if the differences in tail behaviour are taken into account when computing the risk type (diversified) economic capital (inter-business view), this is not the case in the aggregation across risk types (inter-risk view), where all risks are considered normal.

The use of the comonoticity concept allows a slight relaxation of the normality assumption and gives closed-form results for an approximate aggregated capital. An approximation obtained from comonoticity considerations allows using both normal and lognormal distribution assumptions.

The use of the copula theory completely relaxes the normality assumption and allows for various type of dependence structure between risks, but needs numerical simulation. An extension of the correlation concept through the use of copulas would allow for any distributional assumption.

These techniques (and Monte Carlo simulation) are discussed in more detail on the following page.

Comonotonicity

The theory of comonotonicity (Dhaene *et al* 2002a and b) is an elegant and accurate alternative to solving financial and actuarial problems such as option valuation, estimation of provisions and calculation of economic capital. The idea behind the comonotonic approach consists of replacing the dependency structure of the variables by another dependency structure that allows us to simplify the calculations. This new dependency structure could be chosen in such a way that the result is more conservative than the exact calculation (more fat-tailed distribution). Based on the theory of comonotonicity an upper bound can be calculated. Mathematically, it is also possible to calculate a lower bound that is less conservative and very often close to the exact result based on extensive simulations.

The main advantages of the comonotonic methods developed by KUL (Dhaene *et al* 2006) are twofold:

- the analytical approach is almost as easy to implement as the current standard method; and
- the approximation of the credit risk by a lognormal variable makes more sense than to approximate it by using a normal variable.

Monte Carlo simulations

Monte Carlo simulations have had a great impact in many different fields of computational science and use random numbers to model some sort of a process. This technique works particularly well when the process is one where the underlying probabilities are known but the results are more difficult to determine. Accuracy can be improved by simulating more scenarios and is proportional to the square root of the number of scenarios used.

Within Fortis, in order to evaluate the economic capital, a large number of scenarios of the aggregated loss are simulated (eg, one million simulations). The mean and the p-quantile of this large sample are computed, from which an estimate of the economic capital can be deduced.

The advantage of using Monte Carlo simulations is that neither the marginal distributions (eg, Beta distribution) nor the dependency structure is modified. On the other hand, a large number of samples are necessary to obtain a fair estimation of the 99.97% confidence interval of the aggregated loss, which requires considerable computation time and capacity.

Copulas

Although the definition of a copula dates from 1959 (Sklar 1959) its merits have long been disregarded in insurance, finance and risk management applications. In 1999, Embrechts, McNeil and Straumann (1999) applied the copula framework to financial data. Meanwhile, the copula theory has been developed to textbook level. Today, copulas enjoy an increasingly large fan base among the financial fraternity.[11]

The term "copula" (Dowd and Fackler 2004) is derived from Latin, and refers to connecting or joining together. It is closely related to more familiar English words such as "couple". But the "copulas" we are concerned with here are statistical concepts that refer to the way in which random variables relate to each other.

We take the marginal distributions, each of which describes the way in which a random variable moves "on its own" and the copula function tells us how they "come together" to determine the multivariate distribution. Suppose we have two risky variables X and Y, and we want to model the relationship or dependency between them. Most people would model this by means of linear correlation (we assume two risky variables for the sake of convenience, but everything we postulate may be generalised). However, there is a tendency in risk measurement to use correlation as if it were an all-purpose dependency measure, resulting in the correlation often being misused and applied to problems for which it is not suitable. To quote the 1999 paper by P. Embrechts, A. McNeil, and D. Straumann:

> … as well as being one of the most ubiquitous concepts in modern finance and insurance, [correlation] is also one of the most misunderstood concepts. Some of the confusion may arise from the literary use of the word to cover any notion of dependence. To a mathematician correlation is only one particular measure of stochastic dependence among many. It is the canonical measure in the world of multivariate normal distribution functions, and more generally for spherical and elliptical distributions. However, empirical research in finance and insurance shows that the distributions of the real world are seldom in this class.

In short, although the terms "correlation" and "dependency" are often used interchangeably, correlation is actually a rather imperfect measure of dependency, and there are many circumstances where correlation should not be used. We therefore need an alternative dependency measure that is reliable when correlation is not – and the answer is to use copulas.

The main advantage of this approach is that the marginal distributions are preserved, which makes it the best approach from a theoretical point of view. For example, if credit risk is beta-distributed, it is not necessary any longer to approximate the beta distribution by a lognormal or a normal distribution.

On the other hand, the copula must be correctly estimated, which is extremely difficult in practice. An infinite number of copulas that preserve the correlation exist and these may give completely different results (Frey, McNeil and Nyfeler 2001). Some frequently used copulas are the Gaussian copula and the Student copula. The difference between both is that the tail correlation is higher in a bivariate t distribution than in a bivariate normal distribution. As there is no tractable analytical expression of the economic capital with this framework, Monte Carlo simulations are necessary as well, which gives rise to the same disadvantages as mentioned in the previous method.

AN APPLICATION OF ALTERNATIVE AGGREGATION METHODS

A calculation example using various aggregation techniques

When applying the alternative risk aggregation methods (comonotonicity, simulations and copulas) presented in the preceding section to estimate the economic capital of Fortis, we assumed that the risks have already been aggregated across the various business lines. For each risk type (seven in total), the standalone economic capital, exposure and standard deviation are known elements.

Furthermore, we assumed credit risk to be beta-distributed (characterised by two parameters). All the other risks are, for the time being, assumed to be normally distributed. A 99.97% confidence interval is applied.

Table 13.3 shows the correlation matrix used in our experiment. Note that:

- to evaluate the impact of a change in the correlation matrix, the correlation between credit, ALM and trading risk is represented by a parameter α, which will vary between 0 and 100%; and
- the other correlations have been arbitrarily set at 0%, 50% or 100%.

Based on the correlations in Table 13.3, the following aggregated economic capital figures have been computed:

1. $ECAP^{upper}$ = when summing up all the standalone economic capitals;
2. $ECAP^{Fortis}$ = the economic capital of the aggregated loss with the current Fortis methodology where the beta distribution of credit risk is approximated by a normal distribution and a var-covar calculation is applied;
3. $ECAP^{com}$ = the economic capital of the aggregated loss with the analytical approximation using the comonotonicity theory (credit risk approximated by a lognormal);
4. $ECAP^{sim}$ = the economic capital of the aggregated loss computed using Monte-Carlo simulations (credit risk is beta distributed); and
5. $ECAP^{cop}$ = the economic capital of the aggregated loss computed using a Gaussian copula and Monte Carlo simulations (credit risk is beta-distributed).

Table 13.3 Correlation matrix with parameter "alpha"

	Credit	ALM	Trading	Business	Event	P&C	Life
Credit	1	α	α	0.5	0	0	0
ALM	α	1	α	0.5	0	0	0
Trading	α	α	1	0.5	0	0	0
Business	0.5	0.5	0.5	1	0	0	0
Event	0	0	0	0	1	0	0
P&C	0	0	0	0	0	1	0
Life	0	0	0	0	0	0	1

The results are shown in Figure 13.9.

When taking parameter $\alpha = 100\%$ (see the right end of the x-axis) and comparing the economic capital figures for the various approaches, the following conclusions can be drawn.

- As expected, the largest economic capital is $\text{ECAP}^{\text{upper}}$ when summing up all the standalone economic capitals. This upper bound overestimates the other economic capital figure by more than 20%. This clearly shows the importance of the diversification effect.
- When α is set at 100%, all the other economic capitals are quite close to one another (with a variation of less than 1%). This is due to the very high correlation between credit, ALM and trading risk. Indeed, since the correlation among these three risks is 100%, this means that for any of the methods the economic capital related to the sum of these risks will be close to the sum of the three standalone economic capitals. The difference between the various methods can become apparent on only a small portion of the total economic capital. Given these small differences between the var-covar approach currently used at Fortis and the more advanced aggregation methods, the value-added of the latter approaches could be questioned.

However, if values below 100% are tested for α (that is, if we assume lower correlations between financial risks), we notice that the following conclusions can be drawn.

- The results of the economic capital calculation decrease and this is especially so for alternative, more advanced aggregation methods. In general, it turns out that $\text{ECAP}^{\text{Com}}(\alpha) \approx \text{ECAP}^{\text{Sim}}(\alpha) < \text{ECAP}^{\text{copula}}(\alpha) < \text{ECAP}^{\text{Fortis}}(\alpha)$.

Figure 13.9 Economic capital as a function of the "alpha" correlation parameter

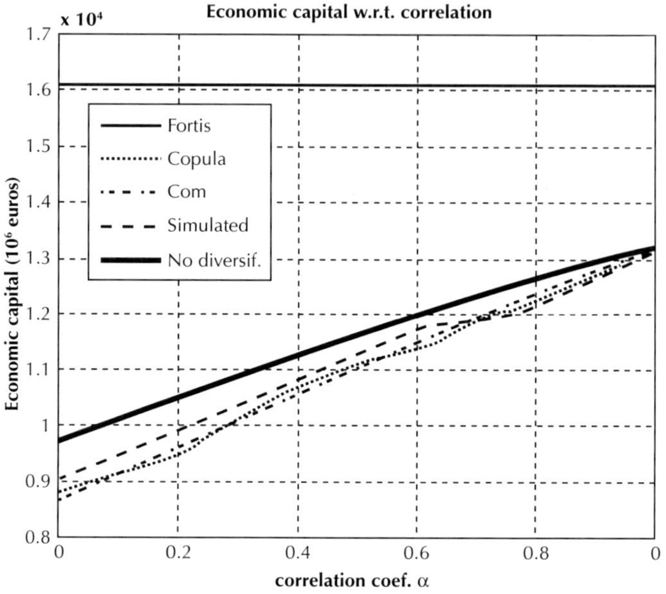

- In other words, $ECAP^{Fortis}(\alpha)$ is always greater than all the other economic capitals. Moreover, the smaller the correlation coefficient α, the greater the difference.
- Finally, the upper bound $ECAP^{Upper}$ is not altered by any modification of the correlation matrix.

A similar exercise is possible to test the sensitivity of the correlation of event risk with the other financial risks (credit, ALM and trading risk). Since the 9/11 terrorist attacks on the World Trade Center in New York and the Pentagon in Washington, fairly low correlations between event risk and other risks are under discussion. As might be expected, the economic capital figure is higher for higher correlation values but the impact is rather limited given the smaller size of the standalone economic capital of event risk.

Conclusions and next steps

From a theoretical point of view the copula approach, which is the only one to preserve marginal distributions, is probably the best choice. However, other considerations such as complexity of calculations, transparency and acceptance by supervisors and rating agencies should be taken into account to make a choice among the various approaches.

- The copula approach requires the correct estimation of the copula, which is very difficult and currently an important topic for further research. Given its limited transparency (due to the lack of an analytical expression), it will be difficult to persuade supervisors to accept this approach (eg, under Pillar II of Basel II) in the coming years.
- Monte Carlo simulations are a good alternative, but might become very heavy for a larger number of risks.
- The approximation based on comonotonicity, which can deal with sums of normal and lognormal distributions, is a good alternative that does not seem to have the above-mentioned disadvantages.

REGULATORY RECOGNITION OF DIVERSIFICATION

Based on a survey (Joint Forum 2003a), the Joint Forum's[12] Working Group on Risk Assessment and Capital has observed two important trends: a greater emphasis on the management of risk on an integrated firm-wide basis and related efforts to aggregate risks through mathematical models. In their report (Joint Forum 2003b), a number of clear statements and intentions were formulated.

- Financial institutions should be strongly encouraged to use firm-wide approaches to risk management.
- Supervisors should understand the new approaches, monitor the results and support where appropriate the firms' efforts.
- The Working Group does not recognise diversification benefits and emphasises a strong and conservative regulatory capital framework in relation to the largest financial firms because of, among other things, limitations on available data.

Regulatory requirements for banking (Basel II) and insurance (Solvency I) do not adequately recognise (or only in a very simplified way) diversification. However, in order to promote more advanced risk management practices in the financial world, the Basel II Pillar II (supervisory review) allows banks to hold dialogue with the supervisor about their more advanced risk management approaches (eg, economic capital framework).

Some industry associations have taken the initiative to combine industry views and coordinate input on the topic of diversification and to make suggestions on how diversification should be treated within the prudential regulatory framework. It is clear that this approach, representing the view of the main industry stakeholders, has had a significant impact on the design of the Solvency II, where diversification has been explicitly recognised.

CONCLUSIONS AND FOOD FOR THOUGHT

In the financial world, requirements in the fields of risk management, corporate governance, accounting and internal auditing are becoming more extensive and challenging in their implementation, in order to cope with the external investor, regulatory and rating agency environments.

In 2000, Fortis designed and implemented an advanced economic capital framework. Over the past few years, the computation of economic capital has been continually refined and improved. The implementation of the economic capital framework allows the Fortis board and the businesses to have a better understanding of the true underlying risks and to take diversification benefits into account.

Two key aspects that have been assessed are the aggregation method and the correlation matrix. Alternative aggregation methods (comonotonicity/simulations/copula) have been tested in cooperation with the Actuarial Research Group of the University of Leuven. The sensitivity of the correlation matrix has been analysed for lower values of correlation between the financial risk and higher values of correlation for event risk. The calculations show that these alternative aggregation approaches give lower capital requirements (a small difference of 1%) but that the impact is more significant in case the correlations between the financial risks are lowered.

In the years to come Fortis will continue to fine-tune the models, to make risk and governance structures work in practice and to improve the consistency of risk/return performance measures. Other challenges will be to prepare for Solvency II in 2012 and to continue to seek better alignment between external constraints and economic reality.

We strongly believe that joining forces at industry level is key to having an impact on the design of regulatory frameworks. Dialogue has a positive impact on the exchange of views, improves coordination of approaches where desirable, increases the availability of data and promotes better understanding of these processes by regulators and supervisors.

In our opinion, in the coming years, momentum should be maintained and additional research should be undertaken, especially perhaps concentrating on the following issues:

- definition and measurement of correlations and relationship between risk factors;
- understanding of diversification and aggregation methods: var-covar, comonotonicity, Monte Carlo simulations, copulas; and
- fungibility and capital support: the ability of a group to provide capital support to its subsidiaries is currently limited by the fungibility of physical capital held.

Furthermore, we are convinced that the diversification aspect that has been analysed mainly from the perspective of an insurance company (most members of the CRO Forum are insurance companies) should be extended to the banking world, where smaller initiatives regarding diversification and aggregation have already been applied in the past. The interaction between banking and insurance is increasingly important in the field of risk management (actuarial profession and bank risk managers) but also at the regulator level (eg, the recent merger of banking and insurance regulators and supervisors, the Joint Forum). We need a more rational regulatory framework to respond in an appropriate manner to the issues and opportunities raised by the convergence of the banking and insurance communities. Financial conglomerates such as Fortis are keen to play a role in bringing both worlds more closely together.

It is not exclusively the financial institutions developing an economic capital approach that are faced with a multiplicity of challenges to overcome. Regulators and rating agencies also have to cope with new trends, complicated by "events". It is only in a spirit of cooperation and willingness to learn from each other that we will reap the full benefits of convergence in order to measure risks in the most accurate and efficient way. Maybe some topics are too hot to handle today but we are convinced that with the current commitment of the industry and openness of the regulator this could quickly change over time.

APPENDIX: DESCRIPTION OF RISK TYPES

- Credit risk is defined as the risk to earnings or capital arising from an obligor's failure to meet the terms of any contract or to otherwise fail to perform as agreed.
- Market risk is the potential for loss resulting from unfavourable market movements, which can arise from trading or holding positions in financial instruments. Market risk is divided into two types, ALM risk and trading risk, depending on the purpose of the position taken. All positions

taken within the trading book, which refers to transactions (buying and selling) of marketable securities and related instruments aimed at making a profit from short-term price variations, pertain to trading risk. Other positions (banking book) are addressed under ALM risk.

- Liquidity risk is the risk that actual and potential payment and collateral posting obligations cannot be met when due. Liquidity risk has two components: funding liquidity risk and market liquidity risk.
- Property and casualty (P&C) risk is the variability in future claims paid and the variability in the liabilities for outstanding claims over time.
- Life risk is the risk exclusively associated with a life insurer (mortality, longevity).
- Health risk is the risk due to variation in claims levels and timing due to fluctuations in policyholders' morbidity.
- Operational risk encompasses all other risks (not being financial risk, insurance risk or liquidity risk) that Fortis Bank faces. Operational risk is encountered by all companies, not just financial institutions, due to the uncertainty inherent in all business situations and decisions. A distinction is made between event risk and business risk.
- Event risk is the risk of incurring an extreme loss, due to single, one-off events such as systems failure, errors and omissions, fraud, etc.
- Business risk is the risk of loss due to changes in the competitive environment that damage the franchise or operating economics of a business.

1 Our gratitude goes to all those who have helped us in carefully reading this article and providing comments. We would like to thank in particular Fred Bos (chief risk officer of Fortis), Alexander Gräwert (general manager, Integrated Risk) and Peter Ullman (managing director, Risk and Portfolio Management Energy, Commodities and Transportation).

2 In 2000, Fortis published economic capital figures in the *Fortis Annual Review 2000*, pp. 46–57.

3 See Filopovic and Rost 2005. This study has been carried out on behalf of the CRO Forum. Fortis participated in this study.

4 This figure is higher than a lot of our peers due to the additional diversification between banking and insurance activities, which most of our peers do not have.

5 See Chapters 12 and 13 of this book for further details on the var-covar approach.

6 The Chief Risk Officers (CRO) Forum comprises risk officers from major European insurance companies and financial conglomerates.

7 It must be borne in mind that economic capital is calculated with a 99.97% confidence interval. The needed correlations are those of a once-in-a-3,333-year crisis.

8 If we consider around 20 business units and seven risk types, more than 10,000 correlations have to be calculated.

9 Copulas have also been used in close collaboration with the Actuarial Research Group of KU Leuven University (Professor J. Dhaene and M. Goovaerts). The interested reader is referred to Dhaene *et al* (2003).

10 These calculations have been undertaken together with the University of Leuven (Department of Applied Economics). See Research Activities (2005).

11 For an introduction, see Embrechts, Hoïng and Juri (2003).

12 Joint Forum consists of three parties: Basel Committee on Banking Supervision, International Organization of Securities Commissions and International Association of Insurance Supervisors

REFERENCES

Brealey, R. A. and S. C. Myers, 2005, *Principles of Corporate Finance,* Eighth Edition, (New York: McGraw Hill Irwin).

CRO Forum, 2005, "A framework for incorporating diversification in the solvency assessment of insurers", June.

Dhaene, J. *et al*, "Aggregating economic capital", *Belgian Actuarial Bulletin* 5, KU Leuven Research Center Insurance, pp. 14–25.

Dhaene, J. *et al*, 2002a, "The concept of comonotonicity in actuarial science and finance: Theory", *Insurance: Mathematics and Economics* 31(1), pp. 3–33.

Dhaene, J. *et al*, 2002b, "The concept of comonotonicity in actuarial science and finance: Applications", *Insurance: Mathematics and Economics*, 31(2), pp. 133–61.

Dhaene, J. *et al*, 2003, "On the Computation of the Capital Multiplier in the Fortis Credit Economic Capital Model", *Belgian Actuarial Bulletin* 3(1).

Dowd, K. and P. Fackler, 2004, "Estimating VaR with Copulas", *Fenews*, March/April.

Embrechts, P., A. Hoïng and A. Juri, 2003, "Using copulae to bound the value-at-risk for functions of dependant risks", *Finance and Stochastics* 7(2) pp. 145–67.

Embrechts, P., F. Lindskog and A. McNeil, 2003, "Modeling dependence with copulas and applications to risk management", in *Handbook of Heavy Tailed Distributions in Finance*, pp. 329–84 (Amsterdam: Elsevier North Holland).

Embrechts, P., A. McNeil and D. Straumann, 1999, "Correlation and Dependence in Risk Management: Properties and Pitfalls" Preprint ETH Zürich.

Filopovic, D. and D. Rost, 2005, "Benchmarking study of internal models", University of Munich, July, p. 45.

Fortis, 2000, "Fortis Annual Review 2000", pp. 46–57.

Frey, R., A. J. McNeil and M. Nyfeler, 2001, "Copulas and credit models", *Risk Magazine*, October, pp. 111–14.

Henrard, L. and R. Olieslagers, 2004, "Risk Management of a Financial Conglomerate", *Financieel Forum*, Bank en Financiewezen 2004.

IFRI – Institute of the Chief Risk Officers and Chief Risk Officer Forum (CRO Forum), 2007, "Insights from the joint IFRI/CRO Forum survey on Economic Capital practice and applications".

Joint Forum, 2003a, "Survey of 31 Financial Institutions in 12 jurisdictions.

Joint Forum, 2003b, "Trends in risk integration and aggregation".

Koyluoglu, U. and J. Stoker, 2002, "Honour your contribution", *Risk Magazine*, April, pp. 90–4.

Mercer, Oliver & Wyman, 2006, "Economic capital survey: Presentation of results for Fortis", December.

Oliver, Wyman and Company, 2001, "Study on the risk profile and capital adequacy of financial conglomerates", commissioned by the Dutch Central Bank, February.

Research Activities, 2005, Catholic University of Leuven, Department of Applied Economics, p. 37.

Saunders, A. and M. Cornett, 2005, *Financial Institutions Management: A risk management approach*, Fifth Edition (New York: McGraw Hill Irwin).

Sklar, A., 1959, "Fonctions de répartition à *n* dimensions et leurs marges", *Publications Statistiques Université de Paris* 8, pp. 229–31.

14

Compounding Effects between Market and Credit Risk: the Case of Variable-Rate Loans

Thomas Breuer, Martin Jandačka and Klaus Rheinberger; Martin Summer

PPE Research Centre FH Vorlarlberg; Austrian Central Bank

Pillar II of the Basel II framework requires banks to assess their risk comprehensively, and to set internal target levels of capital so as to reflect the full range of material risk faced by the bank. Thus banks face the question by which amount the total risk of their loan portfolios is smaller or larger than the sum of credit and market risk capital calculated under Pillar I. If market and credit risk interact negatively a compounding effect can occur: economic capital for total risk can be higher than the sum of pure market risk capital plus pure credit risk capital. We specify a credit risk model for variable rate loans in which the interaction between market an credit risk can be analysed. The compounding effect is more pronounced for loans with bad ratings and high loan to value ratio (LTV). Market risk enhances credit risk more violently if LTV is high.

Industry and regulators are used to thinking about the risks borne by banks in a compartmentalised way. Market risk is defined as the risk that a financial position changes its value due to the change of an underlying market risk factor, like a stock price, an exchange rate or an interest rate. Credit risk is defined as the risk of not receiving the promised payment on an outstanding claim. In Pillar I of the Basel II framework these risks are treated separately and the risk capital is determined by adding up capital across risk categories. While it is acknowledged that this is only a rough approximation it is widely believed that this approach will always provide a safe upper bound for the necessary risk capital. It is believed total risk should be smaller or at most equal to the sum of credit and market risk. By this diversification intuition, integrated modelling of risks is seen as ultimately desirable but of second order importance.

For the case of variable rate loans it is obvious that the diversification intuition does not work: interest rate risk and credit risk are direct substitutes. It may seem to the bank that by issuing a loan with a variable rate and refinancing it in the same repricing period, it bears no market risk on this position. But the risk may materialise as a credit risk instead. If interest rates rise it may be increasingly difficult for obligors with variable rate loans to meet their payment obligations. Rising interest rates drive up probabilities of default and exposure at default. Therefore interest rate risk, although itself zero if loans are refinanced in the same repricing period, enhances credit risk.[1]

In this chapter we argue that diversification between risk categories occurs only under very special circumstances. In many standard risk management problems different risks can reenforce each other and lead to compounding rather than diversification effects. We show that these effects can be quantitatively significant even for very simple standard products like variable rate loans.

INTERACTION CHANNELS BETWEEN MARKET AND CREDIT RISK

Standard credit risk models are constructed from four central parameters, namely the probability of default (PD), the exposure at default (EAD), the loss given default (LGD), and default correlations. Market price movements play no role in standard credit risk models. There are, however, important channels across which market and credit risk interact.

- *PDs may depend on market prices.* Often payment obligations depend on market prices like interest rates, exchange rates or commodity prices. A counterparty with given payment ability is more likely to default if its payment obligation increases. This phenomenon was key at the onset of the subprime crisis in 2007, when rising interest rates payanble on adjustable rate mortgages (ARMs) drove up default frequencies.
- *EAD may depend on market prices.* The discounted value of an outstanding loan depends on the interest rate at which future payments are discounted. If the loan is in a foreign currency, its value additionally depends on the exchange rate.
- *LGD may depend on market risk factors.* Collateral values are subject to market price changes. For mortgages loss given default increases if real estate prices drop.
- *Feedback from PD to LGD.* If default frequencies increase and banks liqui-

date collaterals, this increased supply on the real-estate market will reduce collateral values. For example the current drop in US real estate prices was caused partially by banks selling real estate which served as collateral to defaulted mortgages.

- *Defaults may increase exposure to market risk.* Positions hedged against market risk might suddenly be exposed because one side of the hedge defaults. For example in the Russian crisis of 1998 some Western banks suffered severe losses from US dollar/rouble futures. They held opposite future positions with Russian and with Western counterparties. These hedged positions suddenly became unhedged when Russian counterparties defaulted, and the open exposure was severely hit by the simultaneous devaluation of the rouble.

This discussion can be put into a more general context. Breuer *et al* (2008) discuss in an abstract framework the argument of approximating total economic capital by adding capital for market risk and credit risk calculated separately. They show that for a portfolio in which the value of positions depends on both market and credit risk factors, such an approximation is exact if and only if the portfolio value is separable into a market and a credit subportfolio. If some positions depend on both market and credit risk factors, such a separation is not possible. In this case, compounding effects can occur and they can be quantitatively significant.

Breuer *et al* (2008) introduce an index I of market and credit risk interaction that measures the estimation errors for a given portfolio. Values of I above 1 indicate underestimation of risk in a traditional separate calculation contrasted with an integrated approach, values below 1 indicate overestimation of risk in the tradtional calculation.

A MODEL FOR MARKET AND CREDIT RISK INTERACTION IN VARIABLE RATE LOANS

In the rest of the chapter we analyse the interaction of market and credit risk in variable rate loans. For variable rate loans risks arise from the interaction between market and credit risk. A rise in the interest rate increases payment obligations of obligors and thus triggers additional defaults. It also increases EAD and LGD. In order to quantify the size of these interaction effects we need a model which can describe the dependence of PD, EAD, and LGD on interest rates. We use a structural credit risk model assuming that an obligor defaults if his payment ability is smaller than his payment obligation.

Interaction channels involving collaterals will not be considered here, although this is a very important topic.

The loan portfolio

Consider a portfolio with N obligors indexed by $i = 1, \ldots, N$. All loans are underwritten at initial time $t = 0$. The loan amount is l_i and we assume that the bank refinances in the interbank market at the same repricing intervals. After one period, at time $t = 1$, which we take to be one year, the loan expires and the bank repays its liability on the interbank market with an interest rate r and it claims from the customer the amount $l_i(1 + r + s_i)$, which is the original loan plus interest r rolled over from four quarters plus a spread s_i. The customer's payment obligation to the bank at time 1 is

$$o_i = l_i(1+r) + l_i s_i \tag{14.1}$$

The first term on the right hand side is what the bank has to repay on the interbank market, the second term is the spread profit of the bank.

We assume loans to have variable interest rates. The loan period is split into four quarters. At the initial time bank and customer know the interest rate for the first quarter. After each quarter the new interest rate is fixed as the interbank rate plus the fixed spread. The interest rate r in Equation 14.1 is the average of the interbank rates over the four quarters. The average is not known initially.

Whether an obligor will be able to meet this obligation depends on his payment ability a_i. Obligors default in case their payment ability a_i at the expiry of the loan is smaller than their payment obligation o_i. In case of default the customer pays a_i instead of o_i. The profit of the bank with obligor i is therefore

$$v_i := \min(a_i, o_i) - l_i(1+r) \tag{14.2}$$

where the first term is what the bank actually receives from the obligor and the second term is what the bank has to pay on the interbank market.

In the numerical examples we will consider portfolios of $N = 100$ loans of $l_i =$ €10 000 by customers in the rating class B+, corresponding to an annual default probability of $p_i = 2\%$, or in rating class BBB+, corresponding to a default probability of $p_i = 0.1\%$.

Our portfolio is of course still stylised because it assumes that all loans are underwritten at the initial time 0 and simultaneously expire at time 1. This simplification is however not essential to focus on the key question we have in mind here: can we expect negative risk interaction to be quantitatively negligible or not?

A simple integrated credit and market risk model

We model the ability of an obligor to meet their obligations as a function of macroeconomic conditions and an idiosyncratic risk component. The form of our payment ability process resembles the firm value process in the model of Merton (1974) but it is adapted to incorporate the macroeconomic influence as in Pesaran *et al* (2005).

Assumption 1

The payment ability at final time 1 for each single obligor i is distributed according to

$$a_i(1) = a_i(0)\left(\beta_i\left(\frac{GDP(1)}{GDP(0)} - 1\right) + 1\right) \cdot \in_i \tag{14.3}$$

$$\log(\in_i) \sim N(\mu_i, \sigma_i) \tag{14.4}$$

where $a_i(0)$ and β_i are constants, and $\mu_i = -\sigma_i^2/2$ ensuring $\mathbb{E}(\in) = 1$. For different obligors the realisations $\in_i$ are independent of each other and of GDP and r.

GDP(0) is the known GDP at time zero, GDP(1) is a random variable. The distribution of $\in_i$ reflects obligor specific random events. The support of $\in_i$ is $(0, \infty)$ reflecting the fact that the amount a_i available for repayment of the loan cannot be less than zero.

The initial payment ability $a_i(0)$ is related to the initial loan to value ratio (LTV) by

$$LTV := \frac{l_i}{a_i(0)}.$$

Assuming that for different customers the realisations of $\in_i$ are independent is the doubly stochastic hypothesis.[2] Conditional on the path of macro and market risk factors which determine the default intensities of all customers, customer defaults are independent.

The constants β_i are obligor specific. They describe the elasticity of payment ability changes reacting to GDP changes. For $\beta = 1$ an 2% increase in GDP will translate into a 2% increase in the expected payment ability. For $\beta = -2$ a 2% increase in GDP will translate into a 4% reduction in the expected payment ability, describing an obligor in an anticyclical industry. Denote by r_i the relative payment ability change of obligor i, $r_i := a_i(1)/a_i(0) - 1$, and by r_G the growth rate of real GDP, $r_G :=$ GDP(1)/GDP(0) −1. Then we have

$$\beta_i = \frac{\mathrm{Cov}(r_i, r_G)}{\mathrm{VaR}(r_G)}.$$

So the β_i really are betas.

Our model is related to single factor credit risk models in that firm value changes are correlated because of common dependence on GDP changes. The correlation coefficient between payment ability changes of obligors i, j is given by

$$\mathrm{Corr}(r_i, r_j) = \beta_i \beta_j \frac{\mathrm{VaR}(r_G)}{\sqrt{\mathrm{VaR}(r_i)\mathrm{VaR}(r_j)}}.$$

In contrast to single factor credit risk models, default correlations are caused not just by the macroeconomic factor impacting firm values, but additionally by the stochastic default barriers being driven by a common factor, namely the interest rate.

Calibration

We use ratings which are intended to reflect PDs. Given the present payment ability, PDs will depend on the loan amount (respectively LTV higher PD for higher loan amount respectively higher LTV) and the obligor-specific standard deviation σ_i of idiosyncratic payment ability changes (higher PD for higher σ_i). In practice the initial payment ability, the initial LTV and σ_i would be determined in the loan approval procedure, and the model then delivers the resulting PDs. In this chapter, instead, we start from rating classes (PDs) and LTVs (initial payment ability), and then work out the corresponding σ_i from the model.

As the model involves a default threshold o_i that depends on the spread s_i, σ_i has to be estimated jointly with the loan spread. This is done as follows. The payment ability distribution must satisfy the following condition

$$p_i = P\left[a_i(1) < o_i\right] \tag{14.5}$$

$a_i(1)$ is a function of σ_i and o_i is a function of the spread s_i. We assume that the spread is set to achieve some target expected profit for each loan

$$\mathbb{E}\left(v_i(\sigma_i, s_i)\right) = \mathrm{EP}_{\mathrm{target}} \tag{14.6}$$

where v_i is the profit with obligor i and $\mathrm{EP}_{\mathrm{target}}$ is some target expected profit. The two free parameters σ and s are determined from these two conditions.

Specifically, the spread s_i for each rating class was set in such a way that a target expected profit of €160 on each loan is achieved, which amounts to

Table 14.1 Calibration results

Rating	LTV	σ	Spread (bp)
B+	0.17	0.73	205.1
B+	0.25	0.58	197.2
B+	0.50	0.30	181.1
B+	0.83	0.07	165.6
B+	0.91	0.03	162.5
B+	0.95	0.004	160.9
BBB+	0.17	0.53	161.3
BBB+	0.25	0.41	161.1
BBB+	0.50	0.21	160.6
BBB+	0.83	0.05	160.2
BBB+	0.91	0.02	160.1
BBB+	0.95	impossible	

For given rating classes with corresponding PDs, σ and spreads are determined for different initial LTV so as to achieve the required PDs and the target expected profit. If LTV is too high, some rating classes are not achievable, even with $\sigma = 0$.

a 20% return on an assumed capital charge of €800 for a loan of €10,000. The resulting spreads are given in Table 14.1. We observe what we expect: to be in one rating class, obligers with high LTVs need low σ_i. Spreads may vary considerably within the low rating class B+, with higher spreads being required for higher σ. Within the high rating class BBB+, spreads hardly vary with σ.

The distribution of the macro risk factors r and GDP was estimated from a global vector auto regressive (VAR) time series model adapted in Breuer *et al* (2008). Parameters were estimated from quarterly data 1989–2005. Nominal GDP data for Austria was from the IFS of the International Monetary Fund. The logs of risk factors, mean and covariance matrix of the estimated distribution are as follows:

	log(GDP)	$\log(r_{EUR})$
Mean	5.446	1.246
Std. dev.	0.0097	0.1870
Correlations	1.000	0.291
		1.000

The distribution of the profit V, which is the sum over all loan profits V_i in Equation 14.2, was calculated by a Monte Carlo simulation of 100,000 draws from the distribution of the market risk factor r and the macro risk factor GDP. In each macro scenario defaults of the customers' payment abilities were determined by draws from the distribution of the payment ability process of Equation 14.3.

SIZE OF MARKET AND CREDIT RISK INTERACTION IN VARIABLE RATE LOANS

We compare integrated risk to the sum of market and credit risk by analysing expected shortfall (ES) of market, credit, and integrated loss distributions. The market loss distribution ΔM arises from value changes caused by market risk factor moves, assuming no defaults are possible. The only relevant market risk factor is the interest rate r. The credit loss distribution ΔC reflects the value changes due to changes in the credit risk factors (GDP and the idiosyncratic $\in_i$) disregarding the possibility that interest rates could vary stochastically. The integrated loss distribution ΔV describes the value changes caused by simultaneous moves of all risk factors.

In order to exclude non-subadditivity of the risk measure as a possible explanation for the the negative inter-risk compounding effect, we calculate risk capital intended to cover unexpected losses as measured by ES. For a loss distribution X, our definition of risk capital is

$$\mathrm{RC}_\alpha(X) := \mathbb{E}(X) - ES_\alpha(X) \tag{14.7}$$

where ES_α is ES beyond some quantile α, as defined for example in Acerbi and Tasche (2002, Def. 2.6). Standard deviations of approximation errors of expected shortfall are calculated using the method of Manistre and Hancock (2005).

Results

Table 14.2 displays the risk capital for market, credit, and integrated risk for $\beta = 1$ and initial LTV at 25% in class BBB+ and 50% in B+, which are the median values in those classes. The key results are the integration indexes I in the last column of the tables. These indexes indicate that integrated risk capital is higher than the sum of credit and market risk capital by 4% to 14%.

What is the reason for total risk being larger than the sum of market and credit risk? One main risk of variable rate loans is the danger of increased defaults triggered by adverse interest rate moves. This is captured neither by pure market risk nor by pure credit risk models, but only by the integrated risk model.

Table 14.2 Risk capital for market, credit, and integrated risks of the loan portfolios

α	(a) MR no CR RC(ΔM)		(b) CR no MR RC(ΔC)		(c) Integrated MR and CR RC(ΔV)		c/(a+b) interaction *I*
BBB+							
10%	0	(0)	862	(14)	979	(15)	1.14
5%	0	(0)	1588	(20)	1721	(20)	1.08
1%	0	(0)	3042	(35)	3187	(36)	1.05
0.1%	0	(0)	4675	(87)	4859	(92)	1.04
B+							
10%	0	(0)	3906	(24)	4178	(26)	1.07
5%	0	(0)	4851	(31)	5177	(32)	1.07
1%	0	(0)	6863	(59)	7301	(63)	1.06
0.1%	0	(0)	9679	(171)	10319	(168)	1.07

The final column calculates the inter-risk diversification index *I*. Standard deviations are shown in brackets. The initial income $a_i(0)$ was assumed to be €40,000 in rating class BBB+ and €20,000 in B+, corresponding to an initial LTV of 25% in BBB+ and 50% in B+. Elasticity of the expected payment ability to GDP changes in $\beta = 1$. Standard deviations of risk capital numbers are in brackets.

Note that for variable rate loans in home currency pure market risk is zero. Under the assumption that no customer defaults and loans are refinanced in the same repricing period, profits of the bank are certain and do not depend on interest rates.

How does risk interaction depend on LTV?

Remember that in our model the rating of an obligor depends on both the initial payment ability (which is inverse to LTV) and on the standard deviation σ of idiosyncratic payment ability changes. Obligors with higher LTV can be in the same rating class only if they have less variation in idiosyncratic payment ability changes. We compare in the same rating class obligors with low LTV and high σ to obligors with higher LTV and lower σ.

Negative risk interaction gets stronger as LTV increases

Table 14.3 and the top plot of Figure 14.1 show how negative risk interaction strengthens with increasing initial LTV. For an LTV of 95% integrated risk is almost 60 times higher than the sum of market risk and credit risk.

Figure 14.1 Strength of negative integration effect in dependence of LTV

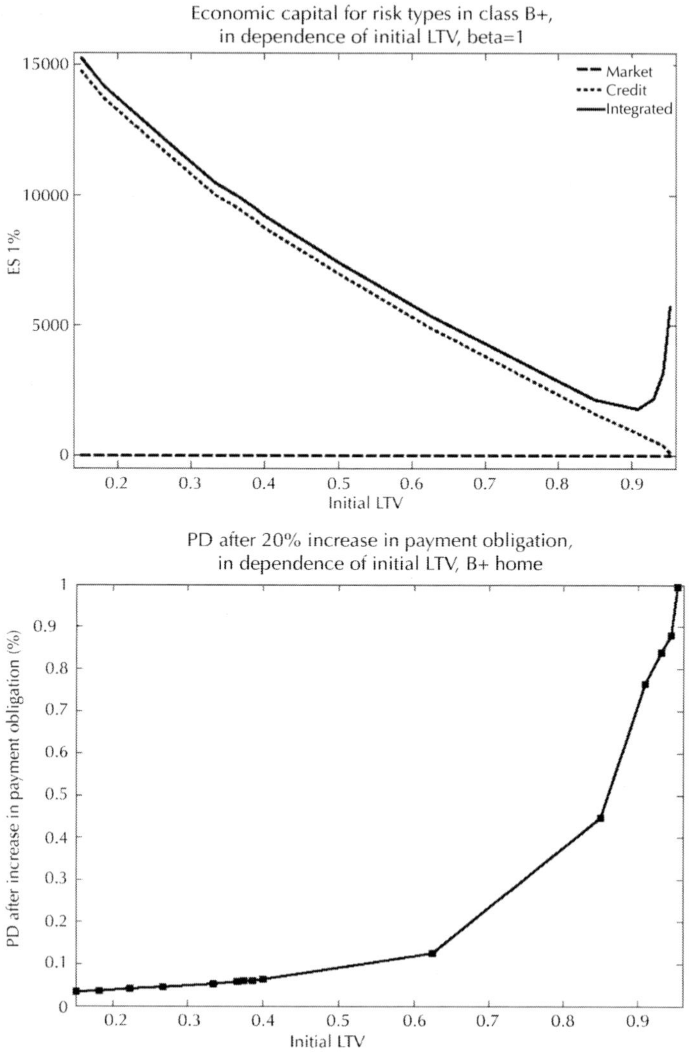

Top: Market, credit and integrated risk capital within one rating class in dependence of initial LTV. The strength of the malign interaction effect is reflected by the difference between integrated risk and the sum of market and credit risk. It increases with increasing LTV. *Bottom*: PD increase triggered by a 20% increase in the payment obligation due to an interest rate increase, within one rating class in dependence of initial LTV. For a loan with initial LTV of 95% a 20% increase in payment obligation leads to virtually certain default. A 20% increase in the payment obligation drives up PDs in rating class B+ from 2% to levels between 2% and 100%, depending on initial LTV. B+ rating, $\beta = 1$.

What is the reason for this dramatic effect? For the loan with higher LTV an increase in the payment obligation will lead to a sharper increase of PD. Market risk enhances credit risk more violently if initial LTV is high. This effect is displayed in the bottom plot of Figure 14.1. For a loan with initial LTV of 95% a 20% increase in payment obligation leads to virtually certain default.

This effect has an intuitive explanation. Compare two loans with the same PD, but with different LTV. The loan with higher LTV has a lower initial payment ability and therefore needs a lower σ to achieve the same PD. For this loan the payment ability distribution of Equation 14.3 will have lower expected value and smaller variance. The slope of the density function at the expected payment obligation will be steeper. Now an interest rate shock drives up the payment obligation. This will increase the probability that the payment ability is below the increased payment obligation. This probability increase will be more acute for the loan with higher LTV.

The same mechanism implies that integrated risk within a rating class is not monotone in LTV. With increasing LTV integrated risk decreases up to a point, but then increases again. But both market risk and credit risk within a rating class always decrease with rising LTV, as is evident from Table 14.3 and Figure 14.1. For high LTV the increase in integrated risk is caused by the increasing strength of the negative interaction effect. The difference between integrated risk and the sum of market and credit risk reflects the interaction effect. It increases with increasing LTV. The reason is that market risk enhances credit risk more violently if initial LTV is high.

Table 14.3 Strength of interaction within rating classes in dependence of initial LTV

Initial LTV	MR no CR		CR no MR		Integrated MR and CR		*I*
0.17	0	(0)	14059	(113)	14545	(116)	1.03
0.25	0	(0)	11896	(100)	12345	(103)	1.04
0.50	0	(0)	6863	(59)	7301	(63)	1.06
0.83	0	(0)	1810	(17)	2334	(22)	1.29
0.91	0	(0)	835	(10)	1772	(22)	2.12
0.95	0	(0)	96	(13)	5721	(149)	59.45

B+ rating, $\beta = 1$, quantile $\alpha = 1\%$. Standard deviations are in brackets.

Sensitivity on ß

In our macroeconomic model the correlation between GDP changes and interest rate changes is slightly positive, reflecting a tendency of the central bank to cut rates when the economy is slowing down. Therefore, positive GDP changes, which at high β tend to improve the payment ability, are accompanied by rising interest rates, which increase the payment obligation. High positive values for β should improve risk diversification across risk types. Indeed, Table 14.4 shows that negative risk interaction is slightly alleviated for larger β.

CONCLUSIONS

In this chapter we challenge the traditional view that because of "diversification" effects total economic capital will be smaller than the sum of market risk capital plus credit risk capital. Negative interaction between market and credit risk can require additional economic capital on top of pure market risk and pure credit risk capital. Only if a portfolio is separable into market and credit subportfolio, we can be sure that calculating economic capital independently for market and credit risk and adding up we will always get more than the necessary risk capital.

The value of a variable rate loan depends simultaneously on market and credit risk factor. For such loans a comprehensive assessment of risk under Pillar II will often have to set internal target capital levels higher than the sum of market and credit risk capital, even after accounting for traditional interest rate risk in the banking book. Neglecting the compounding effect between market and credit risk will often underestimate the material risk faced by the bank. The underestimation is more serious for loans with high loan to value ratios.

Table 14.4 Sensitivity of results on the elasticity β of expected payment ability on GDP changes

β	MR no CR		CR no MR		Integrated MR and CR		Risk Interaction
–2	0	(0)	6471	(57)	7044	(61)	1.09
–1	0	(0)	6515	(56)	7017	(59)	1.08
0	0	(0)	6691	(58)	7164	(62)	1.07
1	0	(0)	6863	(59)	7301	(63)	1.06
2	0	(0)	7287	(60)	7717	(64)	1.06

Rating class B+, initial LTV = 0.5, quantile α = 1%.

We do not claim that integrated risk will always be higher than the sum of market and credit risk. The strength of the compounding effect varies with correlations between market and credit risk factors (see Table 14.4), with the relative size of market and credit risk, and with the confidence level at which risk capital is calculated. We therefore do not propose a universally valid add-on to account for the compounding effect. Whether the compounding effect is present, and how large it is for a specific portfolio should be determined individually with an integrated risk model. Vendor models of credit risk are not sufficient if they do not allow for stochastic interest rates.

An alternative interpretation of our results is possible. Increased PDs, EADs, and LGDs triggered by rising interest rates are a novel form of interest rate risk in the banking book. Interest rate moves trigger additional counterparty risk. Accordingly, the Pillar II treatment of interest rate risk in the banking book cannot only be based on the rules set out by the Basel Committee on Banking Supervision (2001). It might be appropriate to enhance these rules to account for such additional counterparty risk.

1 This effect is not covered by the regulatory treatment of interest rate risk in the banking book, as set out by the Basel Committee on Banking Supervision (2001), which restricts to risk arising from the following sources. Repricing risk arises from timing differences in the maturity (for fixed rate) and repricing (for floating rate) of bank assets, liabilities and off-balance-sheet positions. Yield curve risk results from repricing mismatches exposing a bank to changes in the slope and shape of the yield curve. Basis risk arises from imperfect correlation in the adjustment of the rates earned and paid on different instruments with otherwise similar repricing characteristics. Optionality risk arises from the options embedded in many bank assets, liabilities and off-balance-sheet portfolios.

2 See Duffie and Singleton (2003). Note also that there is some empirical evidence that the doubly stochastic hypothesis might be violated, see Das *et al* (2007).

REFERENCES

Acerbi, C. and D. Tasche, 2002, "On the coherence of expected shortfall", *Journal of Banking and Finance*, 26, pp. 1487–1503.

Basel Committee on Banking Supervision, 2001, "Principles for the management and supervision of interest rate risk". Technical Report, Bank for International Settlemens, URL: http://www.bis.org/publ/bcbsca09.pdf.

Breuer, T., M. Jandačka, K. Rheinberger and M. Summer, 2008, "Regulatory capital for market and credit risk interaction: Is current regulation always conservative?", discussion Paper, Series 2: Banking and Financial Studies 14/2008, Deutsche Bundesbank, URL: http://217.110.182.54/download/bankenaufsicht/dkp/200814dkp_b_.pdf.

Das, S., D. Duffie, D. Kapadia and N. Saita, 2007, "Common failings: How corporate defaults are correlated", *Journal of Finance*, LX(11), pp. 93–117.

Duffie, D. and K. Singleton, 2003, *Credit Risk* (Princeton University Press)

Manistre, B. J. and G. H. Hancock, 2005, "Variance of the CTE estimator", *North American Actuarial Journal*, 9(2), pp. 129–156.

Merton, R. C., 1974, "On the pricing of corporate debt: The risk structure of interest rates", *Journal of Finance*, 29, pp. 449–470.

Pesaran, M. H., T. Schuermann and B. J. Treutler, 2005, "Global business cycles and credit risk", technical report NBER working paper No. W11493, NBER. Available at SSRN: http://ssrn.com/ abst ract=762771.

15

Credit Portfolio Stress Testing and Scenario Analysis

Brian Dvorak

Moody's KMV

With their recent focus on Pillar II of Basel II, banks are increasingly interested in implementing sound credit portfolio stress testing and scenario analysis practices. In addition, financial institutions of all types have found credit portfolio stress testing and scenario analysis to be useful tools for helping management quantify credit portfolio risks, plan responses to stress scenarios, and communicate those risks and mitigating plans both internally and externally. Unfortunately, ambiguities in terminology and challenges in designing useful stress tests and scenario analyses have complicated meaningful discussions among risk professionals, senior management and regulators.

This chapter will first define the term "stress testing" in a credit portfolio context, relating it to scenario analysis. It will then present the purpose and uses of credit portfolio stress testing and scenario analysis, discuss some of the key issues and challenges, and conclude with some practical recommendations.

DEFINING "STRESS TESTING" IN A CREDIT PORTFOLIO CONTEXT

"Stress testing" has at least two very different meanings in a credit portfolio context. To a credit portfolio model builder and user, "stress testing" means subjecting the model's inputs to extreme values on a standalone basis and in combination, in order to determine limitations in the predictive capabilities of the model. For example, how would the model perform if all exposures were concentrated into the same country and industry, or empirical correlations were replaced with near-perfect correlations? These types of stress test are important, and can provide useful insights on model limitations to both model builders and users.

However, this is not what "stress testing" means to most credit portfolio risk professionals and their senior management and regulators. To them, "stress testing" means analysing the impact on the portfolio of stress scenarios consisting of shocks to macroeconomic factors or some other adverse event that causes stressed conditions for one or a combination of input parameters. These parameters might include default probabilities, loss-given-default estimates, or default correlations. Such stress tests might also include specifications of interest rates, exchange rates or other market risk parameters in order to provide consistency in stress testing across different risk types or to test for portfolio interactions among market and credit risk parameters, such as "wrong-way" exposures. Stress testing in this context is therefore a special type of scenario analysis, where the latter is a more general term that may apply not only to input parameters, but also to assumptions about the portfolio itself. Examples of scenario analyses that are not stress tests include (1) a pre-deal analysis of the marginal portfolio economic capital required for a proposed new loan and (2) the economic capital implications of a business line's alternative medium-term portfolio growth and composition projections. This chapter will focus on this second definition of "stress testing", which may be more precisely defined as "stress scenario analysis".

PURPOSE AND USES OF CREDIT PORTFOLIO STRESS TESTING

Economic capital models (included those based on simulation) are designed to measure the extreme credit losses resulting from correlated defaults or migrations to distress under severe scenarios, as Figure 15.1 illustrates. Since credit portfolio stress testing also involves assessing the portfolio under severe scenarios, does an economic capital model perform portfolio stress testing? If so, why would any additional stress testing need to be implemented?

While it is true that a simulation-based economic capital model can stress-test a credit portfolio, there are three primary reasons why financial institutions complement their standard economic capital modelling with additional stress scenario analyses:

1. to extend the analytical framework for measuring portfolio risk, loss, and capital adequacy
2. to help management plan responses to stress scenarios

Figure 15.1 Does an economic capital model perform stress testing?

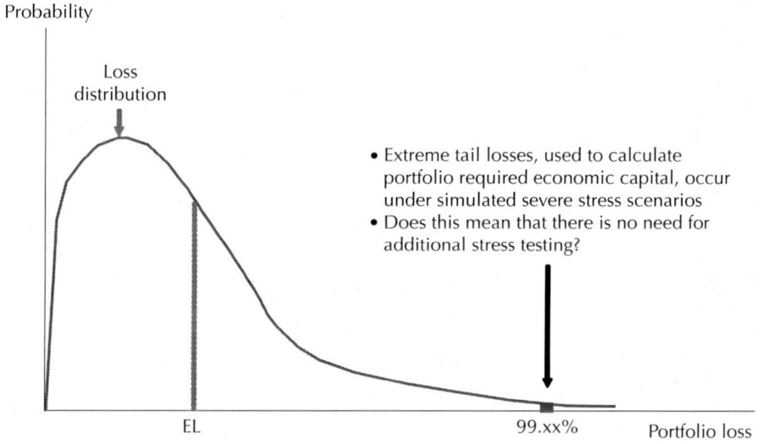

3. to facilitate communication of management responses to stress scenarios internally and to regulators

Extending the risk measurement analytical framework

Not all institutions have a good economic capital model for credit (Moody's KMV 2008). For these institutions, stress-testing can help identify obligor, industry, and country concentrations that may not be apparent based on exposure amounts or measured with a simplistic economic capital model.

The economic capital model may not enable analysis of certain types of risks or exposures, such as liquidity shocks, loan pipeline risk, loan covenant breaches by individual obligors, or "wrong-way" exposures. Stress testing may be able to fill these analysis gaps.

Also, the economic capital model may not enable rich analysis of the modelled scenarios giving rise to tail losses. While it may be easy to identify individual obligors, countries, and industries that have significant losses in tail scenarios, it may not be easy to determine which stress scenarios create problems for those obligors, countries, and/or industries. This makes planning remedial actions more difficult. Further stress testing may help illuminate tail risk scenarios and inform management responses.

Many institutions perform comparative static simulation-based stress tests, ie, altering input parameters (such as correlations) that are normally held constant in economic capital models. For example, using a different set of input correlation parameters allows an institution to assess the effects of potentially higher correlations that may occur in a financial crisis on the institution's economic capital requirements.

A more sophisticated simulation-based stress test is a conditional simulation, ie, constructing a conditional loss distribution based on constraining simulation scenarios to those consistent with defined stress scenarios. For example, one or more correlation factors (such as specific country and/or industry factors) might be constrained to be within a given range of negative returns over the simulation horizon, allowing other factors to move without such constraints. Only scenarios that passed such constraints would be represented in the conditional loss distribution. The result would be portfolio and obligor losses conditional on those constraints, for example, downturns in that set of countries and/or industries.

Figure 15.2 shows an example of such a conditional simulation. The "original" curve is the unconditional credit loss distribution from a Monte Carlo simulation of 10,000 trials on a sample credit portfolio consisting of 800 large corporate exposures diversified across several dozen industries and countries. The underlying systematic risk factors are orthogonal global, regional, country, sector and industry asset return factors from the Moody's KMV Global Correlation Model. The curve designated "Stressed" shows the conditional loss distribution where the US country and banking industry factors were stressed by specifying that both of these factors have large negative asset returns. Monte Carlo simulation trials were removed that did

Figure 15.2 Conditional simulation example

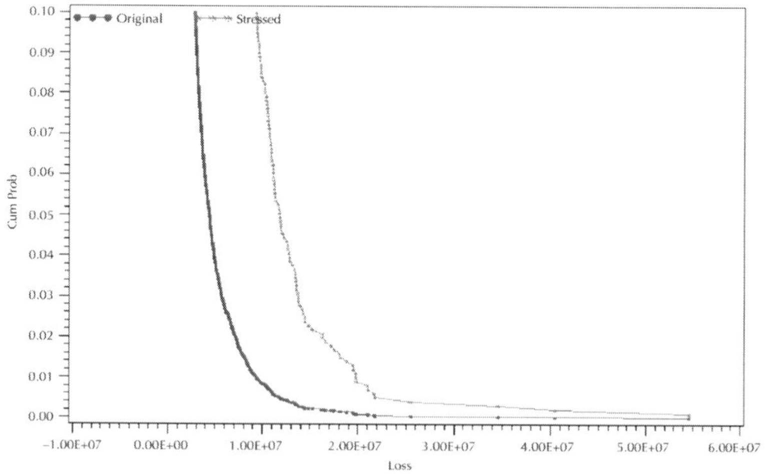

not have the requisite negative returns of these two factors. In this example, 8,989 of the original 10,000 Monte Carlo trials were removed, and the conditional loss distribution was derived from only the 1,011 simulation trials that had the requisite negative returns for the US country and banking industry factors. As expected for this stress scenario, the conditional loss distribution is shifted to the right of the unconditional loss distribution.

Figure 15.3 illustrates that there are at least three interesting questions that may be answered by conditional simulation, plus one question that probably should not be of much interest. The interesting questions include the following.

1. What level of losses would be expected in the stress scenario? This is indicated by the expected losses from the conditional distribution, EL_C.
2. What is the unconditional probability that losses would exceed EL_C? This is the shaded area under the unconditional loss distribution. While this cannot provide the probability of the stress scenario occurring, it can indicate the unconditional probability of having the equivalent loss severity that would be expected in the stress scenario.
3. What is the probability that stress scenario losses would exceed unconditional required economic capital? This is the shaded area under the conditional loss distribution. If the institution held capital equal to unconditional required economic capital, then this would be the probability of capital being wiped out if the stress scenario were to occur. For example, although the required economic capital tail probability might be 5 basis points (bp), if the stress scenario were to occur, there might be a 1% probability of losses exceeding capital.

It is probably not interesting to measure losses under the conditional loss distribution at the same extreme tail probability normally used for required economic capital, since that level of losses would occur with probability equal to the product of the tail probability and the stress scenario probability. For example, if the normal required economic capital tail probability were 5bp, and the stress scenario probability were 10%, then the unconditional probability of that extreme level of losses would be only 0.5bp. Some institutions and their regulators may be interested in this quantity, arguing that it represents economic capital required under a stressed scenario. However, recalling that required economic capital is normally measured from the extreme tail of the loss distribution, which already represents

Figure 15.3 Conditional simulation questions

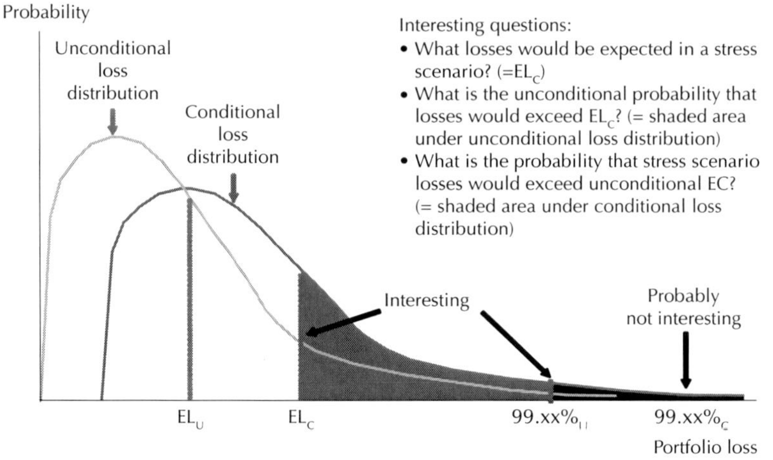

extremely stressed scenarios, this conditional required economic capital amount should be interpreted carefully. It represents a set of much more extreme stress scenarios, and hence a higher standard for capital adequacy.

Stress-testing may also help a financial institution to determine whether it is adequately capitalised. This could be performed in the following manner. Suppose the institution were to create a set of stress scenarios, estimate the joint probability of these stress scenarios occurring and measure the portfolio losses that would result from the stress scenarios. If the joint probability of those stress scenarios equalled or exceeded the institution's target insolvency probability (usually derived from its desired debt rating), then the present value of the resulting portfolio losses could be considered a measure of the stress scenario required economic capital. This could be compared directly with available financial resources to determine capital adequacy. Furthermore, if the stress scenario required economic capital exceeded the required economic capital measured from the institution's official economic capital model, then the stress scenario required economic capital could be considered the minimum required economic capital for the institution, replacing the required economic capital measured from the economic capital model.

For example, consider an institution that has a target insolvency probability of 5bp, required economic capital from its economic capital simulation model of US$8 billion, US$10 billion in available financial resources and a risk-free discount rate of 5%. That institution conceives of a stress scenario that would cause losses in one year of US$9 billion with probability of 5bp. The institution could consider its stress scenario required economic capital at that 5bp level to be US$8.57 billion (US$9 billion/1.05). Since this exceeds the US$8 billion required economic capital from the economic capital simulation model, the institution would consider its true economic capital requirement to be US$8.57 billion. Because its US$10 billion in available financial resources exceeded this required economic capital, the institution would consider itself to be adequately capitalised.

Note that most likely there would be considerable challenges estimating the portfolio losses and the probabilities, which would be necessary in order to make this approach feasible. In particular, portfolio losses would need to be calculated in some direct manner, analogous to calculating portfolio losses for a single Monte Carlo scenario in a credit portfolio model, which would require specifying both systematic and obligor-specific shocks in the scenario. Also, it may be very difficult to estimate the probabilities of the scenarios accurately. These challenges will be discussed further below.

Finally, similar to helping an institution determine whether it is adequately capitalised, stress-testing may help the institution's senior management determine the probability that losses would exceed some less extreme loss amount consistent with the institution's loss tolerance over some horizon. This would help senior management establish or reassess the institution's loss tolerance or risk appetite.

Helping management plan responses to stress scenarios

Stress-testing can facilitate senior management's planning of actions that might be taken in the event of severe loss scenarios, especially if such outcomes exceeded the institution's risk appetite or loss tolerance. Stress-testing and scenario analysis can also be used to design and test institutional responses to stress scenarios. This can assist the institution with its business continuity planning, especially if the stress scenarios involve not just macroeconomic or financial factors, but also the effects on personnel, systems and property. Examples include terrorist threats, pandemics and natural disasters such as earthquakes and floods.

Facilitating communication of management responses to stress scenarios internally and externally

Stress-testing may facilitate communication with regulators, rating agencies, investors, senior management or others in the firm who may not understand or trust the economic capital model. Alternatively, these parties may want to evaluate the potential impact of a topical hypothetical crisis on portfolio expected or unexpected loss or required economic capital, or on specific obligor, industry or country exposures.

Stress-testing and scenario analysis may be required by regulators, who demand that financial institutions understand the effects of credit migration on their risk-based capital requirements and ensure that sufficient economic and regulatory capital is maintained during all phases of economic cycles, including downturns. As a supplement to economic capital models, regulators consider stress scenario analysis as a means of understanding how economic cycles, especially downturns as described by stress scenarios, affect portfolio risk and required capital. This assessment helps financial institutions better understand the potential increase of risk in their credit portfolios and enables them to be better prepared to raise any necessary capital. For example, under Pillar II, one European regulator requires banks to stress-test all of their risks over a three- to five-year horizon under a hypothetical severe economic downturn such as might occur once in 25 years. This is in order to assess whether the banks can maintain their Pillar I minimum capital requirements over that horizon.

Since regulators have a vested interest in the institutions they regulate having higher capital, they will have a tendency to require tougher tests or more extreme scenarios. However, the objective should be to be realistic, not overly conservative, so management may need to negotiate appropriate stress tests with regulators.

To summarise, stress tests and scenario analyses are best considered complementary tools to an institution's standard economic capital modelling in order to extend the analytical framework for measuring risk and capital adequacy, plan management responses to crises and facilitate internal and external communication.

ISSUES AND CHALLENGES IN DESIGNING STRESS TESTS

Designing useful and meaningful stress tests and scenarios can be challenging. There are two broad methods used: historical stress scenarios, based on scenarios that have actually occurred historically; and hypothetical stress scenarios, based on scenarios that might occur and that are of concern to senior management or regulators.

Historical stress scenarios would appear to have the virtue of being plausible, assuming history may repeat itself. However, this assumption is more likely to be true in a generic than in a specific sense. Specific historical stress scenarios, such as a financial crisis in a specific country, are like airline security: the authorities tend to focus on preventing past disasters from recurring and rarely anticipate the scenario that turns out to be the cause of the next disaster. This is not surprising, since if the scenario were anticipated, it would be much more likely to be circumvented or ameliorated. Conversely, generic stress scenarios, such as a moderately severe recession, would be expected to recur, though the frequency or probability may be uncertain.

History can and should be considered in designing stress tests. Historical time series can be very useful for econometric analysis of both the magnitude of historical shocks to macroeconomic and financial factors and the correlation of risk drivers, which can lead to better-designed stress scenarios.

Hypothetical stress scenarios are often based on topical issues and concerns. Examples include oil price shocks; liquidity shocks based on recent market events that may affect the institution, as well as its key counterparties; adverse legal outcomes such as failure of a contract to be deemed valid in a key jurisdiction; sudden deterioration in reputation or competitiveness; and political or military crises in specific countries. Such stress scenarios may be more *ad hoc* in nature, as distinguished from those stress scenarios that may be performed on a more regular basis, such as a standardised recession scenario.

Whichever method is used to create stress scenarios, it is important to obtain broad agreement among the institution's senior management, risk professionals, economists and regulators on: (1) the stress scenarios to be used, (2) the purpose of each stress scenario and (3) likely management responses to each stress scenario. This reflects that primary purposes of stress-testing are to be a communication tool for sharing an understanding of the risks faced by the institution and for planning mitigating responses by the institution's management. Management reports should relate the likely losses resulting from each stress scenario to the institution's loss tolerance or risk appetite, flagging those scenarios where the resulting loss would exceed the institution's tolerance for losses over that analysis horizon so that mitigating responses could be planned.

There are at least three key challenges in designing stress scenarios. The first challenge is to create stress scenarios that are both plausible and stressful enough for their intended purpose. This can be particularly challenging when the purpose is to create an extreme stress scenario that could threaten the capital of the institution, which are the types of stress test that regulators tend to favour. Even if the institution were able to conceive of such stress scenarios, it might be very difficult for them to accept these scenarios as being plausible. In fact, one regulator has observed that it rarely sees stress scenarios in the financial institutions it regulates that would even result in dividend cuts, rating cuts, or annual losses, let alone in capital shortfalls or failure of the institution.

The second challenge is to calculate the obligor and portfolio losses that would result from the stress scenario. Most stress scenarios tend to be macroeconomic in nature. In such cases, the stressed macroeconomic factors need to be related explicitly to the portfolio risk drivers in order to calculate obligor and portfolio losses. Generally, financial institutions use Merton-style credit portfolio models where the correlated asset processes of individual firms are driven by systematic global, regional, sector, country and industry factors of asset return indexes. The macroeconomic factors describing the stress scenario therefore need to be related to these systematic risk factors in order to estimate the resulting obligor and portfolio losses. This can be done through direct calculation of the impact on obligors based on their factor loadings, or through conditional simulation as previously described.

If the stress scenario is not inherently macroeconomic in nature, such as a pandemic or natural disaster, the effects need to be cast in macroeconomic terms in order to enable the calculation of obligor and portfolio losses. This requires economic and econometric expertise. In addition, senior management and business unit responses to the crisis scenario need to be considered in order to quantify losses properly. This recasting of a crisis in macroeconomic terms and quantifying the impact on losses therefore requires broad involvement of economists, business units, senior management and risk management staff.

The third key challenge in designing stress scenarios lies in estimating the probability of the scenario occurring. This can be especially problematic for hypothetical stress scenarios, but is also an issue for historically based stress scenarios. Creating 10 stress scenarios and declaring that each has a 10% probability of occurring is not justifiable. The probability can be estimated if the scenario can be described in terms of macroeconomic factors and if the joint distribution of future realisations of those factors can be estimated. Unfortunately, this is challenging, and many financial institutions seem content to attach probabilities to stress scenarios based on guesses or blind faith.

Unless the institution can rigorously estimate the probabilities of its stress scenarios occurring, the usefulness of the stress tests plummets and it would not be appropriate to use the stress tests to determine whether the institution is sufficiently capitalised. Regulators are concerned that an institution might underestimate the probability of severe scenarios or overestimate the institution's ability to take timely and effective mitigating actions. However, the converse situation, where an institution might overestimate the probability of severe scenarios, is perhaps equally likely. As a result, despite the desires of regulators, it is questionable whether stress testing will prove useful in helping financial institutions accurately assess whether they are adequately capitalised.

SOME PRACTICAL RECOMMENDATIONS

Simulation-based economic capital models are designed to measure the effects of severely stressed scenarios creating extreme losses that could impair the institution's economic capital and potentially lead to failure of the institution. Major financial institutions have invested significant resources in deploying sound economic capital models that utilise consistent and rigorously estimated input parameters for probability of default, loss-given default, credit quality migration and obligor asset correlation. These institutions can and should rely on such models to perform the primary stress tests used by the institution. Stress scenario analysis as described in this chapter should be considered a complementary tool for augmenting the institution's economic capital model, particularly for analysing and planning management responses to stress scenarios not yet handled well by the economic capital model. Examples cited in this chapter include liquidity shocks, pandemics, natural disasters and political crises in specific countries.

Stress scenario analysis should be considered a tool for communication both externally and internally where, among senior management, it can facilitate a shared understanding of the risks faced by the institution. This is particularly in relation to the institution's loss tolerance and to the planning of mitigating responses. It is essential to obtain broad agreement both internally (among the institution's senior managers, risk managers and economists) and externally (eg, with its regulators) on both the purpose of and likely management responses to each stress scenario.

Finally, since regulators are requiring that institutions perform stress-testing, but often do not specify what stress tests to perform, and may not even provide clear guidance on what stress tests would be acceptable, it is important that the institution's management discuss with regulators the challenges in designing stress scenarios. These challenges include creating stress scenarios that are both plausible and stressful enough for their intended purpose, calculating the obligor and portfolio losses that would result from each stress scenario, and estimating the probability of each scenario occurring. Only by overcoming these challenges will stress testing prove useful in helping financial institutions accurately assess whether they are adequately capitalised, as desired by regulators.

REFERENCE

Moody's KMV, 2008, *RiskFrontier Release Notes Version 2.0,* (San Francisco: mimeo)

16

Towards Comparable Basel II Ratios: Standard & Poor's Risk-Adjusted Capital Framework

Bernard de Longevialle, Élie Hériard-Dubreuil, Thierry Grunspan

Standard & Poor's[1]

In our view, the Basel II methodology represents a clear improvement on Basel I. It is risk-sensitive and more comprehensive. It has also provided an incentive for improved risk identification, measurement and management across financial institutions. In addition, market constituents should benefit from enhanced disclosure of key risks and methodologies employed to measure and manage these risks.

A number of trade-offs have been made, however, in implementation timing, Basel II risk-measurement techniques and national discretions, which together are likely to impede comparability of results across and within countries. The technical challenges associated with migration to advanced measurement methodologies and using a mix of methodologies simultaneously will also likely raise comparability issues. Finally, the potential lack of robustness and consistency of banks' internal estimates, which are still relatively recent and have been mostly developed in a benign environment, will add another layer of complexity.

We expect that some banks will still communicate for several years on Basel I ratios, others on Basel II ratios calculated according to the standardised methodology, and others on a combination of Basel II methodologies. On top of that, the impact of floors and grandfathering options will likely distort results further. Published regulatory ratios will become very complex to assess and compare. Also, in our view, Basel II has not fully addressed the shortfalls of Basel I. In particular, regulatory treatment for the trading book has not changed materially and still understates to a significant extent the underlying risks in a stress environment. We believe that in-depth analysis and adjustments are needed to facilitate interpretation and international comparisons.

This is why Standard and Poor's Rating Services has developed a new measure, the risk-adjusted capital ratio (RAC). We expect it to provide a consistent risk-adjusted measure that will facilitate the assessment and comparability of capital adequacy, particularly during the long and complex transition period to Basel II.

The RAC will serve as the basis for our analysis of banks' capital adequacy. It will provide our analysts with a relatively simple measure of risk-adjusted assets that we intend to be globally comparable and able to neutralise the largest effects of differences in national application, regulatory options, and banks' internal risk measurement systems. This measure will also reflect the difference in our approach to risk assessment compared with that of Basel II and should be less volatile across the cycle than the Basel II internal ratings-based (IRB) calculations.

This chapter presents the motivations behind the RAC, as well as its backbone and the various steps underlying its computation. The next section discusses the need for a risk-adjusted capital measure and the reasons that lead S&P to introduce its own methodology. Then we show how the RAC is computed, introducing benchmark adjustments for Pillar I and Pillar II risks. The final section concludes and presents a table reporting an actual example of RAC estimation. The RAC methodology presented below has been presented to the market in 2008 as part of a vast consultation process involving banks, regulators and investors around the world. It is still a draft methodology under review, which may evolve before its final publication expected towards March 2009.

THE MOTIVATIONS BEHIND THE RISK-ADJUSTED CAPITAL RATIO

Everybody in the market agrees that banks need to have an appropriate level of capital in relation to risks, but measuring it is much more complicated and sometimes controversial. With the implementation of Basel II, market constituents face conflicting choices. Which is the more appropriate measure: Basel I or Basel II? What are appropriate assumptions for unexpected losses in lending and trading? What about the leverage ratio, which simply compares a bank's assets with its equity, which equity analysts are increasingly readopting? Are banks' internal economic capital models more appropriate? What about when these measures send conflicting messages?

Indeed, share prices for many banking groups in mature markets have declined over the past year, reflecting – besides expectations of higher losses and weaker earnings – high leverage ratios and expectations that financial institutions are going to raise capital, which would dilute equity for existing shareholders. On the other hand, most banks in developed markets are expected to report a decline in their regulatory risk assets, which would suggest that they need potentially less regulatory capital now that they have adopted Basel II. What are we to understand by this?

We do not expect the move from Basel I to Basel II ratios, by changing the measuring stick, to change our opinion about banks' capital adequacy. We have always focused on underlying economic leverage – how much capital a bank really needs to avoid default and run its business well – not regulatory measures. A change of thermometer from celsius to fahrenheit does not mean that the temperature has increased and you can remove your jacket!

Despite a number of caveats, we still believe that Basel II is a major move in the right direction. It is a more comprehensive and risk-sensitive framework than Basel I. The new framework is also more aligned with economic reality, which should reduce banks' ability and willingness to window-dress their published regulatory ratios. It has pushed banks to improve their risk-management systems, even if recent risk-management failures show that there is a lot of room for improvement. It will also likely represent a quantum leap, in terms of market disclosure, if implemented thoroughly. We believe that, over time, Basel II ratios will turn out to be better measures of capital adequacy than their Basel I counterparts.

A return to the old and crude leverage ratio is not a valid alternative, in our view. Indeed, this apparently conservative ratio fails to differentiate between very low-risk assets such as T-bills and high-risk assets. It also fails to capture off-balance-sheet risks, such as undrawn liquidity lines, which have been among those factors mainly responsible for the recent rise in risk profiles for banks.

Although it has many advantages, one of our main concerns about Basel II has been inconsistency. First public disclosure from banks that implemented Basel II ratios in 2007 confirms that. We are seeing inconsistencies among banks depending on which of Basel II's different methodologies they choose: the standard approach or the IRB approaches (see Figure 16.1).

Moreover, inconsistencies are also cropping up among banks that choose the same IRB approach. The findings show that Swedbank's corporate loan book would require almost twice as much regulatory capital as Swedish peer Svenska Handelsbanken. We believe this gap arises just as much from

Figure 16.1 Retail risk weightings under Basel II's standard and IRB approaches

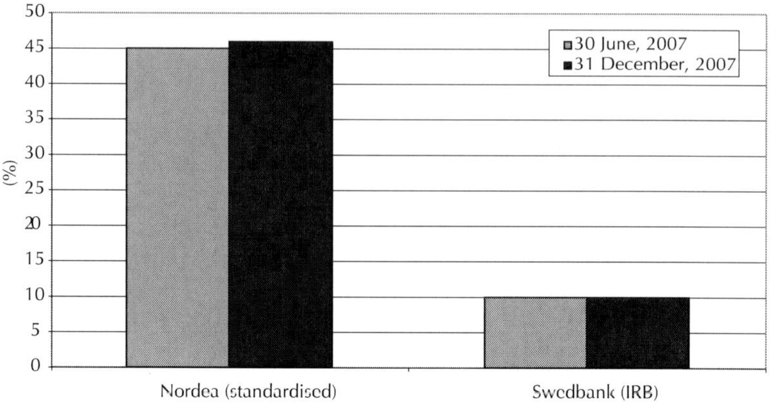

IRB – Internal ratings-based approach

Source: Bank data

differences in the banks' internal risk-measurement systems and asset classification as in their real risk profiles (see Figure 16.2). Discrepancies like these will likely occur when Basel II is implemented. Unfavourable economic conditions have yet to test calculations, which will probably evolve and improve over time. Most countries that are adopting Basel II have experienced few defaults for a number of years, amid an extended period of rosy credit conditions, which may have distorted the calibration of through-the-cycle probabilities of default. Indeed, most banks moving to Basel II have developed their internal risk-measurement systems in the past five years, despite their efforts to recalibrate the output to a recessionary scenario. The best test of their internal systems will be how they hold up to a real economic cycle.

During the transition from Basel I to Basel II, banks are likely to get inconsistent results for the amounts of regulatory capital they will need. In our view, the impact of regulatory floors and grandfathering options, combined with banks' gradual move towards the most advanced methodologies, will mean that for a number of years measurements of regulatory capital will reflect methodological changes and seasoning of measurement systems as much as, if not more than, changes in underlying economic leverage (see Figure 16.3). On top of that, countries will continue to have wide discretion over both the definition of regulatory capital and the computation of risk

Figure 16.2 Corporate risk weightings under Basel II's FIRB approach

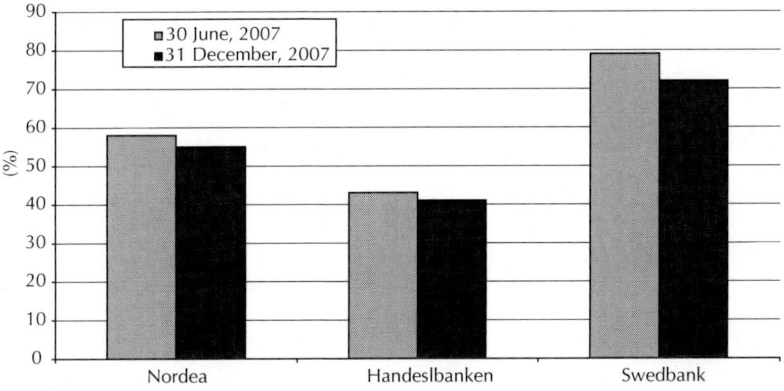

FIRB – Foundation internal ratings-based approach

Source: Bank data

Figure 16.3 The effect on Tier 1 ratios of change in methodologies under Basel II

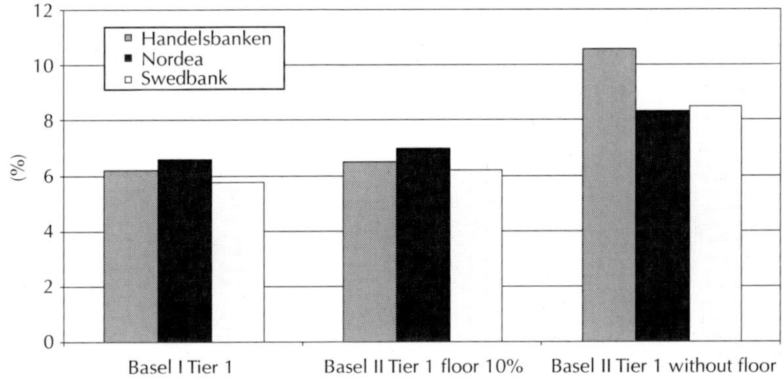

Note: The Tier 1 ratio is equal to regulatory original own funds divided by risk-weighted assets. The Basel II Tier 1 floor 10% is the ratio including the transitory regulatory complement that sets the capital requirement at a minimum 90% of Basel I in 2008.
Data as of 31 December, 2007

assets. Comparisons of regulatory capital ratios are likely to be a complex exercise.

For that reason, Standard & Poor's (S&P) has developed the RAC, which is intended to neutralise the biggest effects of differences in national application, regulatory options and banks' internal risk-measurement systems. It will be a relatively simple measure of risk-adjusted assets, but is meant to be globally comparable.

We do not expect rating changes as a consequence of the implementation of this new risk-adjusted measure, which does not reflect a change in opinion. We also emphasise that capital is only one rating factor among many – such as business profile, strategy, risk management, profitability and risk profile. The RAC is simply the formal and transparent quantification of our existing qualitative opinion on banks' risk-adjusted profiles. S&P has long been adjusting Basel I to address inconsistencies in calculating Tier 1 capital across regions and to reflect our own risk assessment. Under Basel I, we adjusted a bank's reported capital to calculate our measures of adjusted total equity (ATE) and adjusted common equity (ACE), which we believe are more consistent internationally than the regulatory Tier 1 capital definition. The move to Basel II, which provides a globally consistent risk disclosure for the first time, is allowing us to refine our methodology and begin adjusting risk-weighted assets (RWAs) to make them more comparable across institutions and countries. We intend to formally adjust regulatory RWAs in countries under both the Basel I and Basel II frameworks to make them more comparable and consistent with our own assessment of underlying risks (see Table 16.1).

Our primary objective is to develop a globally consistent risk-adjusted capital-measurement tool for financial institutions that we rate. We also expect to roll out the new measure in countries still under Basel I to promote a level playing field and enhance comparability of capital ratios. To promote transparency, the RAC quantitatively formalises all the main qualitative assessments we already routinely carry out in our analysis. We believe that it will help market constituents to understand better the way in which S&P views banks' capital levels.

Table 16.1 Comparison of regulatory and Standard & Poor's measures of bank capitalisation

	Regulatory	**Standard & Poor's (current)**	**Proposed RAC**
Available capital	Tier 1/total capital	Adjusted total equity	Adjusted total equity
Risk measure	RWA	Qualitatively adjusted RWA	Standard & Poor's RACF RWA

RACF – Risk-adjusted capital framework. RWA – Risk-weighted assets. RAC – Risk-adjusted capital ratio.
Source: Standard & Poor's

The main feature of the RAC is that it applies globally consistent benchmark charges, calibrated at the industry level for each Basel II risk type, to banks' published exposures. We will use these benchmark charges instead of the charges set out in the Basel II standardised approach, or Basel I when still applied. For banks that use IRB approaches, we will also substitute the benchmark charges. In our view, these adjustments under the RAC should help restore comparability by neutralising the impact of methodologies used to compute regulatory ratios.

The RAC will also go beyond Pillar I risks (credit, market and operational) by introducing quantitative adjustments to key Pillar II risks – such as concentration, diversification and interest-rate risk in the banking book (IRRBB) – into the adjusted RWA measure.

S&P's benchmark charges may differ in some instances from Basel II calibrations. For trading risk, equity risk and securitisation treatment in particular, S&P's charges are higher than Basel II requirements. This is not always the case for the majority of other risk types, for which our benchmark charges will sometimes be lower than Basel II standardised capital charges in low-risk countries and higher in high-risk countries (see, for instance, our benchmark risk weights for prime mortgages in Figure 16.4). When compared with risk-sensitive charges processed under the IRB approaches, we believe our benchmark charges, which are calibrated to

Figure 16.4 Example of Standard & Poor's benchmark risk weights for prime mortgages

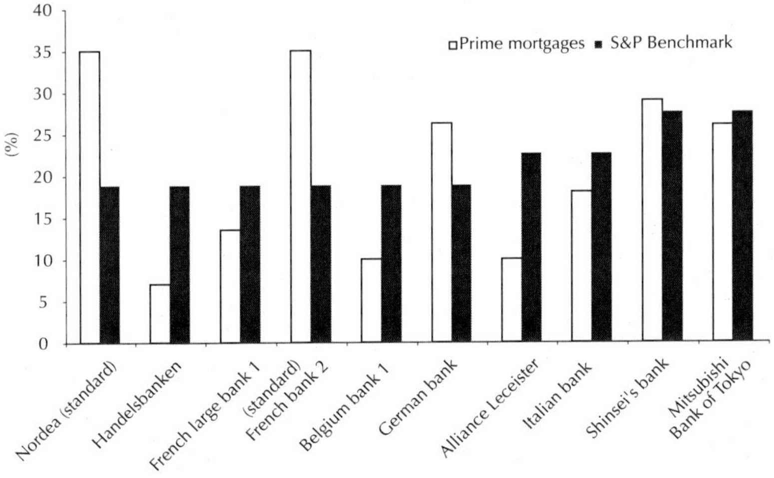

Source: Bank data, Standard & Poor's

capture capital needs at the bottom of the cycle, should be on average more conservative in benign environments but also much less volatile in stressed periods.

The RAC will support our assessment of a financial institution's capital adequacy. It will do this by producing a capital adequacy ratio that compares ATE with the combined risk charges expressed in terms of adjusted RWAs. We expect to be able to compare this adjusted ratio over time for a particular institution, among financial institutions, and across countries and types of institutions.

HOW RAC IS CALCULATED

S&P will base its risk-adjusted capital analysis on the benchmark charge approach (BCA), which will produce a capital adequacy ratio based primarily on public and readily available information calibrated at the industry level.

We intend to publish a single risk-adjusted capital ratio.

Our two main goals remain international comparability and factoring S&P's opinion on risk into the RACF, where it differs from regulatory requirements.

Fundamental principles

S&P believes that capital should be available to meet an unexpected loss, which is consistent with the Basel II philosophy. To support this expectation, we have embedded a level of stress in the industry risk benchmark, equivalent to a 99.9% confidence level over a one-year time horizon, which is also aligned with Basel II. However, we also believe that capital requirements should be detached from the business cycle as much as possible and that they should take into account the need to absorb losses over a more extended period; for these reasons we also look at complementary scenarios.

S&P defines capital available to absorb losses according to globally consistent measures: ACE and ATE. We note that the definition of regulatory Tier 1 capital differs significantly among countries. In an increasing number of countries, Tier 1 capital includes significant amounts of hybrid securities.

Our approach differs to some extent from Basel II in the treatment of expected loss because we believe that earnings should also be taken into consideration. Basel II requires banks using IRB approaches to deduct the shortfall of provisions compared with expected loss from their regulatory capital. But we will not systematically adjust our ATE because we believe that expected losses should be met from earnings, which provide an initial buffer for absorbing losses. For this reason, we believe that capital adequacy measures should be considered in the context of an institution's earnings power.

The S&P RACF follows the same building block approach as Basel II. It aggregates risks by asset class and risk category. We intend to go one step further than Basel II, however: we will also reflect in RWAs the extent of diversification/concentration in an institution's operations, as well as interest-rate risk in the banking book. These two important risk factors are captured by Basel II, Pillar II, but potential regulatory capital add-ons will not be disclosed and, in our opinion, are unlikely to be consistent.

The RAC will primarily use regulatory Pillar III disclosure requirements as a starting point for its adjustments. Its rollout will rely on the effective implementation of consistent and extensive risk disclosure by individual banks as required under Pillar III. On a temporary basis in the US, as well as in a number of countries where Basel II will be implemented with some delays, our starting point will be published accounts.

Benchmark capital adjustments (BCA) for Pillar I risks

Calibration of the RAC, while often consistent with Basel II methodology, brings to light differences in risk assessment. Given the lack of consistent good data available on a global scale, as well as the need to avoid reliance on a single quantitative number at a given confidence interval, we have not derived our benchmark charge from a single quantitative measure and believe that statistical analytics should be subject to qualitative overlay.

The review has typically included analysis of 99.9% one-year loss scenarios and 99% three-year cumulative loss scenarios on industry data and actual and/or theoretical portfolios. Samples of banks' internal estimates as well as Bank for International Settlements (BIS) quantitative impact studies have also been discussed. In addition, we have examined historical peak losses over one year and three years, as well as forward-looking scenarios.

We believe that our benchmark charges, which are top-down measures calibrated against stress scenarios, should be higher on average than banks' internal estimates in benign environments. We expect them, however, to be less cyclical than IRB regulatory measures. In particular, while some IRB calculations could experience high double-digit volatility over an economic cycle (Bank of England 2007), this should not be the case for the RAC.

In the following, we outline how the main Pillar I risk types are dealt with when estimating BCAs.

Credit risk

Our starting point is the exposure at default (EAD) expected to be published by banks because it will be available for all Basel II institutions whatever the options chosen. In the US, we plan to use on-balance-sheet and off-balance-sheet assets in published accounts.

We intend to apply our benchmark charge to banks' EAD, which would be independent of the risk weights that it calculates under Basel II.

A limitation of our approach is that we do not quantitatively differentiate risks within the same asset class in a country except for credit risk mitigation. However, under our RACF we intend to continue differentiating qualitatively in the rating process.

Sovereign exposures

Banks are expected to publish their sovereign exposure broken down by geographic location. We have calibrated some benchmark risk weights for each S&P ratings level. Based on a breakdown of sovereign exposure by rating and geographic location, we should be able to roll out the risk weights in Table 16.2. If geographic disclosure is not precise enough, we expect to apply a risk weight reflecting the average of the region.

We have derived our charges from historical data, using in particular S&P's long-term averaged historical cumulative default rates observed over three years.

Financial institutions, corporate, and retail exposures

Our approach to determining credit risk weights for these major Basel II asset classes is to establish three main risk categories for each asset class (low, intermediate and high) according to our estimate of risk within different groups of countries. For example, mortgage assets in Japan have different characteristics from those in Brazil. We then assign a risk weight against these three risk categories for each asset class.

The next step is to establish 10 groups into which we classify each country in accordance with our existing Banking Industry Country Risk Assessment (BICRA) methodology, which acts as a broad proxy for the relative strengths and weaknesses of a country's banking system. For the corporate and retail asset classes, following a consultation process with market constituents, we decided to develop an internal economic risk score instead of using the BICRA. The latter reflects indeed both economic risk and banking system industry risk, and is in some cases heavily influenced by the latter and not always well correlated to domestic corporate and retail credit risk. We are

Table 16.2 Standard & Poor's proposed risk weights for sovereign exposures

Standard & Poor's rating	BCA (%)	Basel II standardised approach (%)
AAA	3	0
AA+	3	0
AA	3	0
AA–	3	0
A+	4	20
A	10	20
A–	18	20
BBB+	27	50
BBB	38	50
BBB–	50	50
BB+	63	100
BB	78	100
BB–	95	100
B+	113	100
B	133	100
B–	154	100
CCC+	177	150
CCC, CCC–, CC, and C	201	150
Not rated	201	100

BCA = benchmark charge approach
Source: Standard & Poor's

finalising the development of a new economic risk-scoring system and expect to make it public when we introduce the RACF. The economic risk score will be used as a scaling factor to compute our country charges for corporate and retail asset classes.

As country classification per economic risk scores is not yet finalised and disclosed to the market, we publish in Figure 16.5, for illustration purpose only, the benchmark risk weights classified per BICRA scores.

We then map these groups to the three risk categories using a quadratic function (see Figure 16.5).

In this way, the lowest risk charges are applied to countries in BICRA or Economic Risk Group 1, the highest to those in BICRA or Economic Risk Group 10.

Figure 16.5 Standard & Poor's benchmark charge approach risk weights

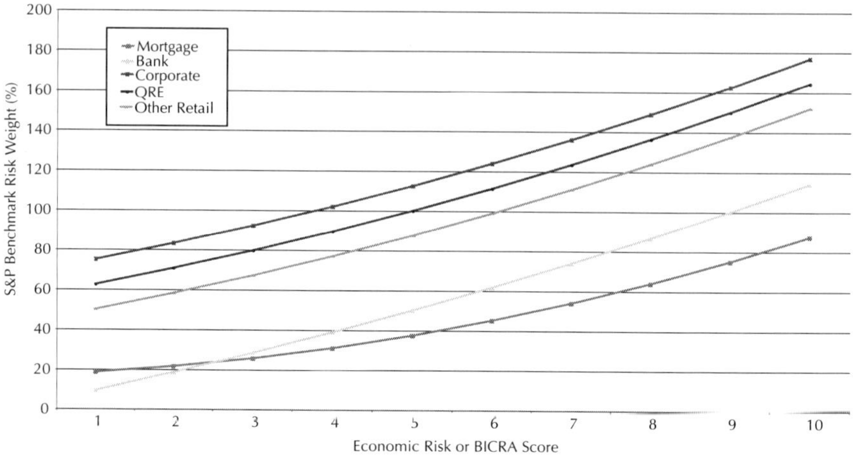

Source: Standard & Poor's

Table 16.3 provides the scale of benchmark risk weights agreed in S&P's global committees for the RAC.

The table shows that RAC benchmark risk weights may be below Basel II standardised risk weights for most asset classes in low-risk countries and much above in high-risk countries. As noted above, we expect them to be higher in benign periods, but less volatile than IRB regulatory capital requirement estimates.

In order to improve the risk sensitivity of our approach, we intend to use more granular asset class definitions and define new benchmark risk weights at the outset of the RACF rollout. We will also seek to better recognise credit risk mitigation factors. For example, we expect the RACF to be able to differentiate for portfolios such as commodities finance, funds, Lombard loans, leasing or those hedged with credit derivatives. However, we will aim to stick as much as possible to Basel II sub-asset-class definitions, in order to maintain consistency in definition and minimise any extra workload for credit institutions.

Other items

In line with Basel II treatment, we assign a 100% risk weight to other items not specifically captured by our framework. This risk weight is equivalent to an 8% capital charge.

Table 16.3 Standard & Poor's proposed benchmark risk weights for major exposure classes

Risk category	Sovereign	Bank	Corporate	Residential mortgage	Credit card	SME retail	Other retail
Low	3.1	9.4	75.0	18.8	62.5	75.0	50.0
Medium	62.5	50.0	112.5	37.5	100.0	112.5	87.5
High	125.0	100.0	162.5	75.0	150.0	162.5	137.5
Basel I*	0.0	20.0	100.0	50.0	100.0	100.0	100.0
Basel II standardised approach	100.0	50.0	100.0	35.0	75.0	75.0	75.0

*These charges reflect the most common treatment under Basel I for exposures in OECD countries. For exposure classes where the Basel II standardised approach relies on external ratings, only the charge corresponding to unrated exposures is indicated. SME = small and medium-sized enterprise.
Source: Standard & Poor's

Counterparty risk

As part of Pillar III requirements, banks are expected to disclose counterparty risk within the trading book (EAD) separately. When the breakdown between the different types of counterparties (financial institutions, hedge funds, monoline insurers, others) is not available, we will consider as a starting point that 80% of exposure is towards financial institutions and 20% towards corporations, based on empirical analysis. We are aware that banks' methodologies for calculating EAD will vary, as some banks will develop internal expected positive exposure models while others will continue to use the current exposure method. In this respect, we may perform some adjustments.

Credit risk mitigation

S&P's benchmark charge will be adjusted to reflect the impact of credit risk mitigation factors at the individual bank level. The starting point for this adjustment will be publicly available information. We will also factor in credit risk mitigation based on confidential data provided by individual banks.

Concerning financial collateral, banks adopting the standardised approach and the foundation IRB approach will disclose (under Pillar III) covered exposure. S&P will deduct the disclosed secured exposure from the corporate EAD. For banks adopting the advanced IRB approach, if no disclosure is available, we expect to factor financial collateral based on confidential information.

We assume that, without any precise breakdown, reported nonfinancial collateral concerns mainly real estate collateral on commercial real estate. Since our benchmark charge calibration already reflects the typical collateralisation of real estate activities, no additional benefit should be given in the BCA.

Our approach regarding credit derivatives and guarantees follows the Basel II treatment (for standardised and foundation banks), consisting of substituting the probability of default (PD) of the credit protection provider for the PD of the obligor (assuming direct exposure on the credit protection provider).

Treatment of securitisations

S&P's risk-based capital charge is aligned with the Basel II standardised treatment when the underlying tranche exposure is rated "BBB–" or above. We apply more conservative capital treatment for tranches rated below "BBB–" than that required by Basel II.

Unlike under Basel II, we will not recognise risk transfer for revolving securitisations with early amortisation features. We intend to treat exposures as if they had not been securitised. We consider that this type of securitisation, while very useful from an asset-liability management (ALM) viewpoint, does not change a bank's underlying economic exposure to the performance of the securitised assets. Moreover, if a real stress occurs and an early amortisation trigger takes place, the likelihood of the new drawings not being transferred off balance sheet will be high.

Concerning liquidity facilities, the Basel II framework imposes credit conversion factors that are higher than under Basel I. We will reflect this in the RAC.

Concerning unrated exposures, we propose to apply a lower capital risk weight to unrated senior exposures and unrated liquidity facilities associated with asset-backed commercial paper (ABCP) programmes.

Market risk of equity portfolios in the banking book

The listed equity portfolio in the banking book is subject to variability of price and liquidity, and can contain unrealised gains. We consider Basel II treatment of equity portfolios to be on average too lenient. While both model computation and historical track records clearly show that stock market fluctuations of 30% to 50% over a one-year period can take place (see Figure 16.6), regulatory measures propose a range of risk weights equivalent to capital charges of between 8% and 32% depending on the regulatory options chosen. However, S&P acknowledges that a simple unique benchmark would likely fail to capture the diverse composition of the world's stock markets, as well as the differences in diversification and concentration of portfolios that institutions hold. All other things being equal, we consider that a portfolio composed of one single line of €100 million is riskier than a portfolio composed of 100 lines of €1 million each.

S&P intends to differentiate equity risk weights according to the volatility of each market, granularity of the portfolio and geographic diversification.

We will offset 100% of unrealised gains against the capital charge. Such recognition of unrealised gains is sometimes present in banks' IRB models for equity portfolios and sometimes not; it is not part of standardised methodologies. Besides having the advantage of being implemented consistently across countries, this approach also neutralises the impact of differences in accounting treatments between banks that account their portfolios at fair value, and account 100% of unrealised gains under equity, and those who do not account them at fair value.

Market risk in the trading book

Assessing capital requirements for market risk in the trading book is difficult due to weak disclosure of underlying risks, the large size of nominal positions and a growing industry trend towards including assets in the trading book that are subject to fat tails – for example, credit risk assets. Recent events demonstrate that losses can be very large in relation to regu-

Figure 16.6 One-year S&P 500 index cumulative return

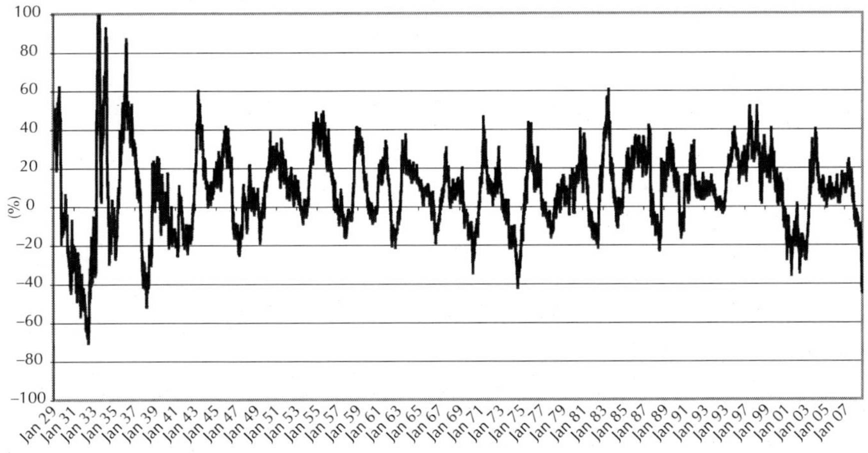

Source: Standard & Poor's

latory capital requirements, and S&P has for many years considered capital requirements to be small relative to risk. We will therefore measure risks in the trading book through a combination of measures – including a scaled value-at-risk (VaR) measure and a revenue-based measure.

We will scale up the regulatory VaR capital charge by a factor of three and incorporate specific risk VaR if this is disclosed separately. The purpose of the scaled VaR is to align with our one-year horizon and to adjust reported exposures to ensure a 99.9% confidence interval. This adjustment also takes into account some of the fat-tail events that have been estimated on the basis of a hypothetical trading portfolio consisting of equities, interest rates, commodities and foreign exchange. Also consistent with the one-year horizon, we will use average reported exposure as a reference for the typical exposure maintained by an institution. Such a scaled VaR should better reflect the magnitude of market risks, including illiquidity risks, which can increase sizably in times of stress.

For banks applying the standardised approach, we will apply only a 1.5 multiplier. This reflects our opinion that the standardised approach is more conservative than the regulatory approved VaR, in particular for the treatment of concentration/diversification.

We are aware that this methodology may in some cases underestimate specific risk, in particular incremental default risk in the trading book, given the trend towards greater exposure to credit risk and illiquid assets. We believe that the BIS current consultation and data-collection exercise in this area may shed some light on this issue and help us to enhance our approach in the coming years (BIS 2007).

In our view, the Basel II regulatory "incremental default charge", which banks are expecting to implement in 2010, should cover not only default risk but also event risk, such as unexpected rating downgrades over the horizon of the VaR or credit spread changes that are unrelated to the credit quality of the issuer (such as liquidity issues and downgrades of guarantors).

We anticipate that banks with large capital market operations are likely to consider preparing themselves for increased regulatory capital requirements for market risk flowing from the IERC. Preliminary estimates show that they could rise by 3x to 6x in January 2010, when the IERC and the modelling of default and migration risk take effect. These extra capital risk weights, we believe, could rise even further in January 2011 if the IERC is extended to other risks (such as equity or spread risks).

S&P will consider adapting the RACF to these changes in the regulatory treatment of the trading book. The RAC ratio, which we expect to introduce in 2009, will include a multiple to regulatory capital requirements for the trading book that may no longer be needed once the IERC fully takes effect. We will continue to closely monitor regulatory developments and update our RACF accordingly as we consider appropriate.

We also accept that the VaR-based approach to regulatory capital embeds some model risk within our framework. For this reason we would urge greater disclosure of risk factors within banks' trading books and in particular an extensive disclosure on specific risk. We also intend to capture some of this model risk via an operational risk charge for trading activities, which will be considerably greater than the regulatory requirement.

Operational risk

The Basel II framework introduces a capital charge for operational risk, with the basic indicator approach applying a flat 15% charge on revenue across all business units. The standardised approach allows for some degree of granularity, with varying percentages of revenue required across eight business lines. Basel II also authorises the calculation of a charge based on an internal model methodology: the advanced measurement approach.

We have decided to work primarily with a single indicator, revenue, and apply risk charges in a manner similar to that of the Basel II standardised approach, with some adjustments.

One of our main adjustments to the Basel II standardised approach is to revise upward to 25% from 18% the risk charges relating to both "corporate finance" and "trading and sales" business activities (see Table 16.4). The adjustment for these business lines reflects our belief that large losses can be influenced by heightened/above-average legal risk, model risk and fraud-related risk. The significance of such risks has been amply demonstrated over time. We have also related the risk-based capital charge to the highest revenue base of the past three years, rather than the average of the past three, as in the standardised approach. This is to accommodate recent activities and growth momentum and to avoid providing capital relief to banks having experienced a recent drop in revenues as a consequence of operational or trading losses.

We do not wish to rely extensively on operational risk models at this stage. We believe there is a lot of value in developing operational risk measurement frameworks, which are helpful for operational risk management and measurement. However, we consider that quantitative operational risk models are on average still relatively recent and therefore unlikely to be a reliable guide to capital requirements.

Table 16.4 Standard & Poor's proposed benchmark risk weight for operational risk (%)

	Benchmark charge approach	Basel II standardised approach
Highest of past three years' gross revenues	187.5	187.5
Corporate finance	312.5	225
Trading and sales	312.5	225
Commercial banking	187.5	187.5
Payment and settlement	225	225
Agency services	187.5	187.5
Asset management	150	150
Retail banking	150	150
Retail brokerage	150	150

Source: Standard & Poor's

Benchmark capital adjustments (BCA) for Pillar II risks

We have sought to enhance the transparency and comparability of capital adequacy by including some items classified under the Pillar II framework within our RACF, such as diversification and asset-liability management. There remain, however, a number of risks that will not affect S&P's evaluation of capital adequacy, including funding risk, which we consider more related to risk management than to capital adequacy; and reputation and strategic risk, which are very difficult to quantify. While there is a relationship between solvency and access to funding – banks that are well capitalised are less likely to experience a funding shock – as the Basel Committee pointed out in a recent paper, "recent events demonstrate that even well-capitalised banks can face severe liquidity problems" (Basel Committee 2008). For this reason, funding risk is not a factor in our RACF. However, although we have excluded these risk types from the current version of the RACF, they comprise important components of the rating process and the evaluation of business and financial risks. We distinguish funding risk from asset illiquidity risk, which is an important risk factor affecting market risk and specific risk in the trading book. We consider that, unlike funding risk, asset illiquidity risk requires a capital charge.

Diversification and concentration are two of the most difficult risk attributes to recognise consistently. S&P's RACF recognises diversification by name and sector, country, across asset classes, and by risk type. The basis of our methodology varies depending on the type of diversification analysed.

We recognise that asset-liability risk calculation is inherently difficult to perform. For this reason, we intend to apply to a quantitative measure an overlay of analytical views concerning risk appetite, quality of enterprise risk management (ERM) and volatility of the interest-rate environment.

In the following, we provide more details on adjustments for diversification risk and interest-rate risk on the banking book.

Diversification adjustments

S&P considers diversification to be a very important factor in capital adequacy. While Basel II uses standard diversification assumptions, the RAC will introduce quantitative measures of diversification aiming to capture its benefits (where diversification is substantial) and additional risks (where there is little or no diversification). The overall impact of these diversification/concentration adjustments is expected to range from a minus 20–30% adjusted risk weight for the most diversified financial institutions around the globe to plus 20–40% for the most concentrated. We are aware that diversification benefits appear moderate compared with most of the results of banks' internal economic capital models, which suggest much larger figures. We have deliberately decided not to go beyond this order of magnitude, however, given what we view as the potential lack of robustness of correlation assumptions in very stressed environments.

We assess the level of diversification within a financial institution in five categories – single-name concentration, industry-sector concentration/diversification, geographic diversification, exposure-class diversification, and finally risk-type diversification – as follows.

- A credit or charge is calculated for each diversification adjustment within the portfolio. Where we consider that diversification is evident across any or all of these categories relative to the benchmark there will be a downward adjustment to the credit risk charge (for the first four) and total capital charge (for the latter). Conversely, if we observe a high degree of concentration relative to the benchmark, we will adjust the benchmark capital charges as we consider appropriate.
- Single-name concentration is captured through a granularity adjustment add-on, calibrated to correct the assumption of infinite granularity embedded in the Basel II formula.
- Sector, geographic, asset class and risk-type diversification adjustments are all computed using the same methodology: the individual risk weights are aggregated using a correlation matrix. This is a top-down

approach to diversification, consistent with disclosure available in regulatory reports.
- Regarding risk type diversification, S&P currently factors in diversification among credit, market, operational, insurance and ALM risks only.

We now discuss in more detail the various adjustments outlined in the list above.

The Basel II framework, as well as our benchmark charges, assumes that portfolios are "infinitely granular", in other words, that there is no large exposure concentration. We observe that this assumption is not verified in practice and believe the charge needs to be adjusted using an add-on to the corporate book capital charge (see Figure 16.7).

S&P derives the add-on from reporting provided by rated institutions detailing their largest exposures. Unlike most of the other BCA adjustments, this granularity add-on is based on confidential information. The methodology used is derived from Gordy and Lutkebohmert (2007).

Figure 16.7 How Standard & Poor's adjusts for single-name and industry sector concentration

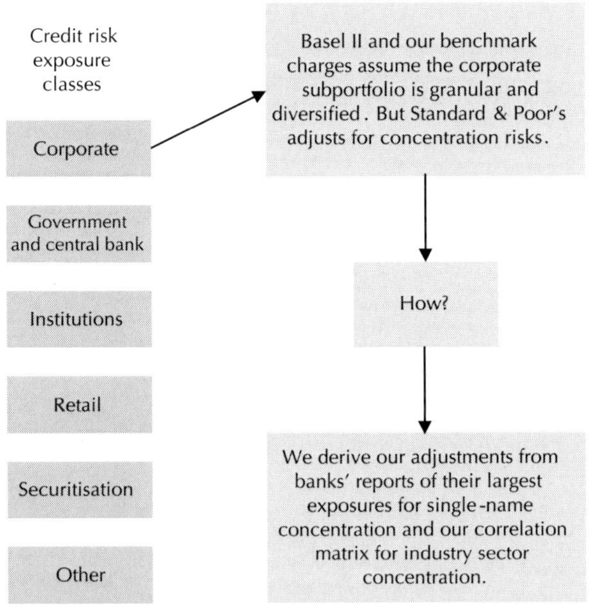

Source: Standard & Poor's

S&P proposes to employ a top-down approach to industry sector diversification of the corporate portfolio, based on a breakdown of benchmark capital requirements by sector, using the EAD measure obtained from Pillar III.

S&P has made the assumption of a diversified portfolio for the purposes of deriving its benchmark. Consequently, we intend to adjust each individual industry sector by a concentration factor (currently set at 5%, the risk weight is multiplied by 1.05). The subportfolios are then aggregated using a Markowitz formula, that is, using a correlation matrix between sectors calibrated on MSCI (Morgan Stanley Capital International) stock indexes.

In order to assess geographic diversification for each credit risk exposure class, S&P again uses a top-down approach.

In a first step we assume that, on average, the degree of concentration within a single country or geographic region varies with size of area. Consequently, the benchmark concentration factor applied to each subportfolio by country and/or geographic region depends on the GDP of this economy, though we may overlay specific adjustments for certain economies. This function is currently calibrated to be neutral for the world's largest economies (the US obtains 1% relief) and to adjust downward the smaller economies (Colombia by 33%, for example).

In a second step the subportfolio capital charges are aggregated using a correlation matrix as for industry sector diversification (see Figure 16.8). As under the Basel II framework, these correlations should reflect the dependence between the asset values driving the solvency of counterparties under a Merton framework. Under the BCA, we have used MSCI stock indexes as a proxy to calculate these correlations.

In a manner similar to that used for industry sector and geographic diversification, S&P aggregates the various exposure classes within credit risk, according to a correlation matrix.

Diversification between the equity portfolio in the banking book and market risk in the trading book is captured using the same methodology as above, with a correlation of 85%.

Finally, S&P recognises diversification among risk types (market risk, operational risk, credit risk, interest-rate risk in the Banking Book, insurance risk) using a correlation matrix.

Figure 16.9 summarises the adjustments for concentration and diversification performed under the BCA.

With regard to insurance risk, the adjustment reflects a refinement of our prior practice, whereby, in order to evaluate the capital strength of banks

Figure 16.8 How Standard & Poor's adjusts for geographic diversification

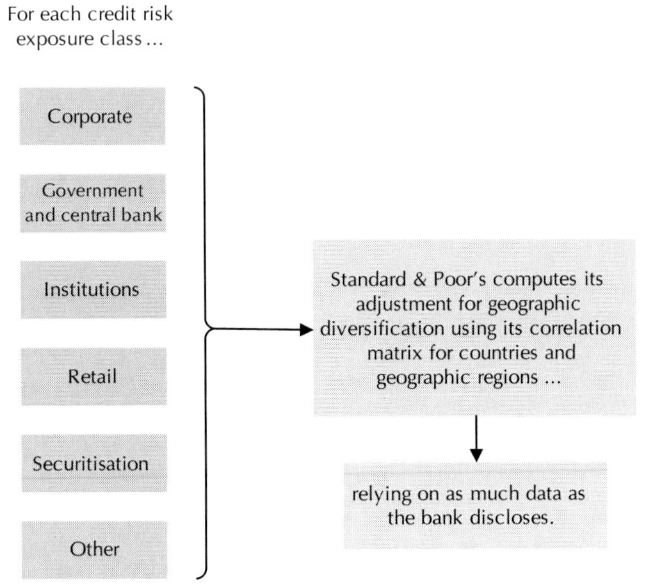

Source: Standard & Poor's

that had insurance subsidiaries, we deducted the net equity of these subsidiaries from ATE. The refinement has resulted in exposure to an insurance subsidiary being included within the total BCA risk-weighted assets with a one-for-one capital charge, rather than as a deduction from capital. This treatment should benefit financial conglomerates by factoring in the model risk-type diversification between banking and insurance activities.

A potential next step we are considering is the substitution of the capital charge computed according to S&P's insurance capital model for the net equity invested in the insurance company. We believe this option would provide a more risk-sensitive view of the magnitude of the risks stemming from insurance subsidiaries than net equity. It would have the value of avoiding an underweighting of undercapitalised insurance subsidiaries and overweighting of well-capitalised ones.

Another potential next step is that instead of adjusting for diversification across asset classes and risk types, we intend to adjust for concentration and diversification across business lines (such as corporate, retail, trading, insurance). This is more in line with our analytical reasoning.

Figure 16.9 Summary of Standard & Poor's adjustments for diversification and concentration

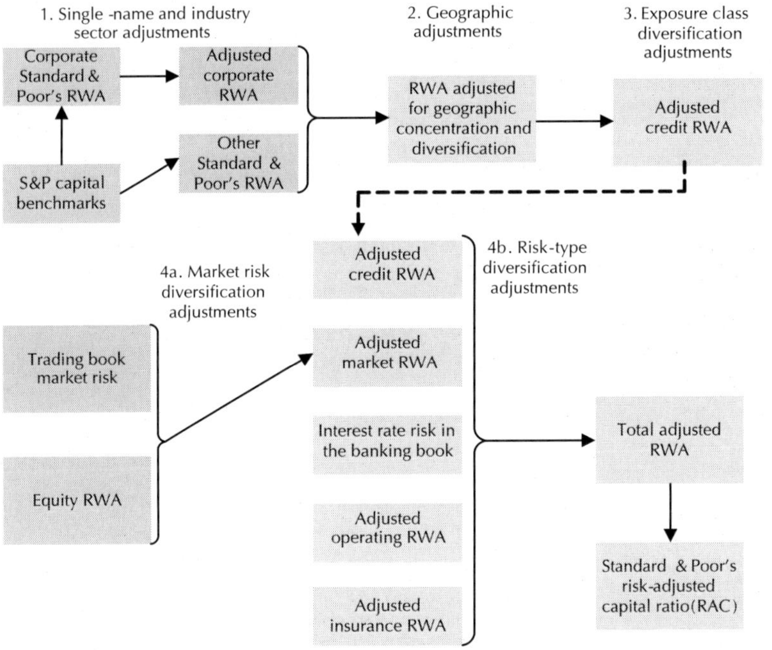

RWA – Risk-weighted assets
Source: Standard & Poor's

Interest-rate risk in the banking book

S&P believes that interest-rate risk in the banking book is an important risk factor for a large number of banks. It can typically attract a low double-digit proportion of banks' economic capital requirements. We also recognise that it is a complex risk type to measure because the diversity of ALM assumptions and interest-rate risk management practices makes it difficult to implement the Basel II standardised approach. While this has led regulators not to quantify any charge for interest-rate risk in the banking book, we're considering integrating this risk into our computation of banks' RWAs.

The approach we suggest is a top-down one, considering that, on average, interest-rate risk should attract a low double-digit proportion of banks' overall capital requirements. We anticipate that our methodology will include some important judgement calls from our analytical committees. In particular, it will use a combination of the following three indicators:

Table 16.5 Illustrative example of S&P's detailed RAC results

	Exposure[1]	Basel II RWA[2]	% of Exposure	S&P's RWA	% of Exposure
Credit risk					
Government and central banks	4,828	550	11	297	6
Institutions	9,706	2,053	21	2,155	22
Corporate	46,523	44,675	96	40,321	87
Retail	38,418	8,753	23	11,728	31
of which mortgage	32,096	4,225	13	7,712	24
Securitisation	0	0	0	0	0
Other assets	525	525	100	525	100
Credit risk total	100,000	56,555	57	55,026	55
Market risk					
Equity in the banking book	251	260	104	1,568	625
Trading book market risk	–	3,042	–	4,563	–
Interest-rate risk in the banking book	–	–	–	0	–
Market risk total	–	3,302	–	6,131	–
Insurance risk					
Insurance risk RWA	–	–	–	7,377	–
Operational risk					
Operational risk RWA	–	3,114	–	3,325	–
Total before diversification					
RWA before diversification	–	62,972	–	71,859	–
		Basel II RWA	**% Of RWA**	**S&P's RWA**	**% Of RWA**
Diversification and Concentration					
Single name (on corporate portfolio)	–	–	5,815	14.4	
Sector (on corporate portfolio)	–	–	(1,569)	(3.9)	
Geographic	–	–	6,223	11.3	
Business and risk type	–	–	(5,236)	(4.8)	
Total RWA adjustment	–	–	6,914	9.6	
Total after diversification					
RWA after diversification	62,972	–	78,773	–	
Capital ratio					
Tier 1	4,770	7.6	–	–	
ATE (RAC ratio)	–	–	4,650	5.9	

[1] In order to preserve anonymity, data has been rebased to US$100,000 total credit risk exposure

[2] RWA: risk-weighted assets

- interest-rate volatility;
- risk appetite/relevance of interest-rate risk for a given institution through a qualitative score; and
- adequacy of risk management.

These indicators would be looked at in conjunction with the results of the 200-basis-point (bp) standardised shock (parallel shock of the yield curve) exercise that banks will have to display as part of the Pillar III disclosure (either the change in economic value or the change in earnings).

FINAL REMARKS

We aim to provide a high level of transparency in calculation of the RAC for individual banks. In line with the publication of the adjustments we make to calculate ATE for individual banks we envisage publishing a table comparing Basel II RWAs with S&P's benchmark RWAs before and after concentration/diversification impacts. Such a table will make it possible to identify the main differences for each risk factor driving the difference in the overall published ratio.[2]

We view our RAC ratio as a complement to and not a substitute for Basel II. All approaches generally lead to a simplification of the underlying economic reality. In addition to, in our view, minimising model risk, having several quantitative indicators of capitalisation gives us a more nuanced opinion about financial institutions' capitalisation. We will use our RAC ratio as a starting point for analysing a bank's Basel II ratio output and its internal Pillar II assessment. By analysing the differences among this data, we believe that we shall be able to reach a more informed opinion about a bank's capital adequacy. S&P will continue to refer to regulatory capital ratios in its analysis and publications. In particular, the Basel II ratios constitute key inputs for many aspects of our analysis, especially our assessment of a bank's enterprise risk management (ERM), risk profile and capital.

Table 16.4 presents detailed results illustrating how we derive the RAC from our benchmark risk weights and Basel II capital charges for financial institutions from around the world. Our results are mostly based on public disclosures from banks, but we have adjusted the data to be representative of our proposed adjustments and protect anonymity. In particular, the exposure amounts have been rebased to a total EAD of 100,000. The case study is therefore for demonstration purposes only; actual results may vary.

1 Chapter 16 kindly contributed by Standard & Poor's – McGraw-Hill International (UK) Limited (2008) – All rights reserved.

2 We have developed a US GAAP version of the RAC. It is available from the authors upon demand.

REFERENCES

Bank of England, 2007, "Monitoring Cyclicality of Basel II Capital Requirements", Financial Stability Paper No 3, December.

Basel Committee, 2008, "Liquidity Risk Management and Supervisory Challenges", February.

Bank for International Settlements, 2007, "Guidelines for Computing Capital for Incremental Default Risk in the Trading Book", Consultative Document, October.

Gordy, M. and E. Lutkebohmert, 2007, "Granularity adjustment for Basel II", Deutsche Bundesbank discussion paper, January.

17

Capital Allocation to Business Units and Sub-Portfolios: the Euler Principle

Dirk Tasche[1]

Lloyds TSB Bank

In many financial institutions there is a well-established practice of measuring the risk of their portfolios in terms of economic capital (see for example, Dev 2004). Measuring portfolio-wide economic capital, however, is only the first step towards active, portfolio-oriented risk management. For purposes such as identification of concentrations, risk-sensitive pricing or portfolio optimisation, it is also necessary to decompose portfolio-wide economic capital into a sum of risk contributions by sub-portfolios or single exposures (Litterman 1996).

Overviews of a variety of different methodologies for this so-called capital allocation were given for example, by Koyluoglu and Stoker (2002) and Urban *et al* (2004). McNeil *et al* (2005, Section 6.3) discuss in some detail the Euler allocation principle. The goal with this chapter is to provide more background information on the Euler allocation, in particular with respect to the connection of Euler's theorem and risk diversification and some estimation issues with Euler risk contributions. We furthermore investigate a new application of Euler's theorem to the problem of how to identify the contributions of underlying names to expected losses of collateralised debt obligation (CDO) tranches. Martin and Tasche (2007) suggested applying Euler allocation to measure the impact of systematic factors on portfolio risk. In the last section of the chapter, we illustrate this approach with another example and compare its results with the results of an alternative approach. The presentation of the subject is largely based on work by the author but of course refers to other authors where appropriate.

The section named "Theory" is mainly devoted to a motivation of the Euler allocation principle by taking recourse to the economic concept of risk adjusted return on capital (RORAC) compatibility. Additionally part of that section demonstrates that Euler risk contributions are well-suited as a tool for the detection of risk concentrations. The next section "Practice" presents the formulas that are needed to calculate Euler risk contributions for standard deviation based risk measures value-at-risk (VaR) and expected shortfall (ES). Some VaR-specific estimation issues are discussed in that section. Furthermore, it is shown that there is a quite natural relationship between Euler contributions to VaR and the Nadaraya–Watson kernel estimator for conditional expectations. As a further practical application of Euler's theorem, we analyse the decomposition of CDO tranche expected loss into components associated with the underlying names and illustrate the results with a numerical example. Later in that section this example is re-used for illustrating different concepts of measuring the impact of single risk factors or sets of risk factors on portfolio risk. The chapter concludes with a brief summary. The Appendix provides some useful facts on homogeneous functions.

THEORY

The Euler allocation principle may be applied to any risk measure that is homogeneous of degree 1 in the sense of Definition A.1 (see Appendix) and differentiable in an appropriate sense. After having introduced the basic setting for the chapter, we discuss the economic motivation for the use of Euler risk contributions. The fact that the Euler allocation principle can be derived by economic considerations may constitute as the most appealing feature of this principle. We then show that the economic foundation of the Euler allocation becomes even stronger in the case of subadditive risk measures because it can then be used for efficient detection of risk concentration.

Basic setting

Suppose that real-valued random variables $X_1, \ldots, X_n$ are given, which stand for the profits and losses with the assets (or some sub-portfolios) in a portfolio. Let X denote the portfolio-wide profit/loss

$$X = \sum_{i=1}^{n} X_i \tag{17.1}$$

The economic capital (EC) required by the portfolio (ie, capital as a buffer against high losses caused by the portfolio) is determined with a risk measure ρ, ie

$$\mathrm{EC} = \rho(X) \tag{17.2}$$

In practice, usually, ρ is related to the variance or a quantile of the portfolio loss distribution. See the section on "Practice" for some examples of how ρ can be chosen.

For some kinds of risk (in particular credit risk), for risk management traditionally only losses are considered. Let $L_i \geq 0$ denote the loss with (credit) asset i and assume that $L = \sum L_i$ stands for portfolio-wide loss. Then this loss perspective on portfolio risk can be reconciled with the profit/loss perspective from equations 17.1 and 17.2 by considering

$$X_i = g_i - L_i \tag{17.3}$$

where g_i denotes the lender's stipulated gain with credit asset i if the credit is repaid regularly. In the following as a general rule we will adopt the profit/loss perspective from 17.2.

It is useful to allow for some dynamics in model 17.1 by introducing weight variables $u = (u_1, \ldots, u_n)$

$$X(u) = X(u_1, \ldots, u_n) = \sum_{i=1}^{n} u_i X_i \tag{17.4}$$

Then we have obviously $X = X(1, \ldots, 1)$. The variable u_i can be interpreted as the amount of money invested in the asset that underlies X_i or just as the credit exposure if X_i is chosen as a default indicator. For the purpose of this chapter we assume that the probability distribution of the random vector $(X_1, \ldots, X_n)$ is fixed. We will, however, consider some variations of the variable u. It is then convenient to introduce the function

$$f_{\rho,X}(u) = \rho(X(u)) \tag{17.5}$$

For the same risk measure ρ the function $f_{\rho,x}$ can look quite different for different distributions of X. As we assume that the distribution of X is fixed we can nevertheless drop the index X and write f_ρ for $f_{\rho,x}$.

In this chapter, we focus attention to (positively) homogeneous risk measures ρ and functions f_ρ (see Appendix for some important properties of such functions).

Defining risk contributions

When portfolio-wide economic capital is measured according to Equation 17.2, it may be useful to answer the question: how much contributes asset (or sub-portfolio) i to EC = $\rho(X)$? Some potential applications of the answer to this question will be given below. For the time being, we denote the (still to be defined) risk contribution of X_i to $\rho(X)$ by $\rho(X_i \mid X)$.

Definition 17.1

Let $\mu_i = \mathrm{E}[X_i]$. Then

- the total portfolio RORAC[2] is defined by

$$\mathrm{RORAC}(X) = \frac{\mathrm{E}[X]}{\rho(X)} = \frac{\sum_{i=1}^{m} \mu_i}{\rho(X)},$$

- the portfolio-related RORAC of the ith asset is defined by

$$\mathrm{RORAC}(X_i \mid X) = \frac{\mathrm{E}[X_i]}{\rho(X_i \mid X)} = \frac{\mu_i}{\rho(X_i \mid X)}.$$

Based on the notion of RORAC as introduced in Definition 17.1, two properties of risk contributions can be stated that are desirable from an economic point of view.

Definition 17.2

Let X denote portfolio-wide profit/loss as in Equation 17.1.

- Risk contributions $\rho(X_1 \mid X), \ldots, \rho(X_n \mid X)$ to portfolio-wide risk $\rho(X)$ satisfy the full allocation property if

$$\sum_{i=1}^{n} \rho(X_i \mid X) = \rho(X)$$

- Risk contributions $\rho(X_i \mid X)$ are RORAC compatible if there are some $\varepsilon_i > 0$ such that

$$\mathrm{RORAC}(X_i \mid X) > \mathrm{RORAC}(X) \Rightarrow \mathrm{RORAC}(X + hX_i) > \mathrm{RORAC}(X)$$

  for all $0 < h < \varepsilon_i$

It turns out that in the case of a "smooth" risk measure ρ, requiring the RORAC compatibility property of Definition 17.2 completely determines the risk contributions $\rho(X_i \mid X)$.

Proposition 17.1

Let ρ be a risk measure and f_ρ be the function that corresponds to ρ according to Equations 17.4 and 17.5. Assume that f_ρ is continuously differentiable. If there are risk contributions $\rho(X_i \mid X), \ldots, \rho(X_n \mid X)$ that are RORAC compatible in the sense of Definition 17.2 for arbitrary expected values $\mu_1, \ldots, \mu_n$ of $X_1, \ldots, X_n$, then $\rho(X_i \mid X)$ is uniquely determined as

$$\rho_{\text{Euler}}\left(X_i \mid X\right)=\frac{d\rho}{dh}\left(X+hX_i\right)\big|_{h=0}=\frac{\partial f_\rho}{\partial u_i}\left(1,\ldots,1\right). \tag{17.6}$$

See Theorem 4.4 of Tasche (1999) for a proof of Proposition 17.1. It is easy to see that risk contributions defined by 17.6 are always RORAC compatible.

Figure 17.1 demonstrates the concept of Definition 17.2 and Proposition 17.1 with a two-sub-portfolios example.[3] As long as RORAC($X_1 \mid X$) $\neq$ RORAC(X) or RORAC($X_2 \mid X$) $\neq$ RORAC(X), the portfolio-wide RORAC (when considered as function of the weight of the first sub-portfolio) does not reach its optimum. Only at a weight of about 70% of sub-portfolio 1 when all the three RORAC-curves intersect the portfolio-wide RORAC obtains its maximum because no further improvement by shifting the portfolio weights is possible.

What about the full allocation property of Definition 17.2? Assume that the function f_ρ corresponding to the risk measure ρ is continuously differentiable. Then, by Euler's theorem on homogeneous functions (see Theorem A.1 in Appendix), f_ρ satisfies the equation

$$f_\rho\left(u\right)=\sum_{i=1}^{n} u_i \frac{\partial f_\rho\left(u\right)}{\partial u_i} \tag{17.7}$$

for all u in its range of definition if and only if it is homogeneous of degree 1 (see Definition A.1). Consequently, for the risk contributions to risk measures ρ with continuously differentiable f_ρ the two properties of Definition 17.2 can obtain at the same time if and only if the risk measure is homogeneous of degree 1. The risk contributions are then uniquely determined by 17.6.

Remark 17.1

If ρ is a risk measure that is homogeneous of degree 1 (in the sense of Definition A.1), then risk contributions according to Equation 17.6 are called Euler contributions. Euler contributions satisfy both properties of Definition 17.2, ie, they are RORAC compatible and add up to portfolio-wide risk. The process of assigning capital to assets or sub-portfolios by calculating Euler contributions is called Euler allocation.

The use of the Euler allocation principle was justified by several authors with different reasonings:

- Patrik *et al* (1999) argued from a practitioner's view emphasising mainly the fact that the risk contributions according to the Euler principle by Equation 17.6 naturally add up to the portfolio-wide economic capital.
- Litterman (1996) and Tasche (1999, as mentioned previously) pointed out

Figure 17.1 Illustration of Definition 17.2 and Proposition 17.1

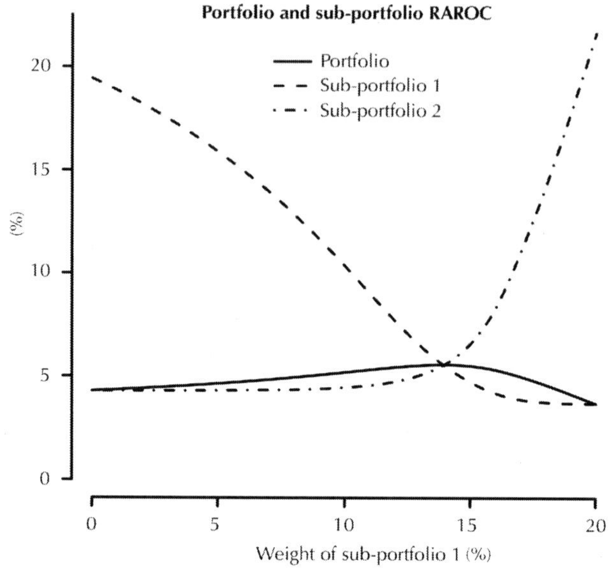

Sub-portfolio profit/loss variables $X_1 = 0.015 - L_1$, $X_2 = 0.04 - L_2$ with L_1, L_2 as defined by Equation 17.42a. Portfolio-wide profit/loss $X = X(u) = uX_1 + (1 - u)X_2$, where $u \in [0,1]$ is the weight of sub-portfolio 1. $\rho(X) = \mathrm{UL}_{\mathrm{VaR},\alpha}(X)$ as defined by 17.22a. Parameter values as in 17.43.

that the Euler principle is fully compatible with economically sensible portfolio diagnostics and optimisation.

- Denault (2001) derived the Euler principle by game-theoretic considerations.
- In the context of capital allocation for insurance companies, Myers and Read (2001) argued that applying the Euler principle to the expected "default value" (essentially E[max(X, 0)]) of the insurance portfolio is most appropriate for deriving line-by-line surplus requirements.
- Kalkbrener (2005) presented an axiomatic approach to capital allocation and risk contributions. One of his axioms requires that risk contributions do not exceed the corresponding stand-alone risks. From this axiom in connection with more technical conditions, in the context of subadditive and positively homogeneous risk measures, Kalkbrener concluded that the Euler principle is the only allocation principle to be compatible with the "diversification" axiom (see also Kalkbrener *et al* 2004; Tasche 2002; and the section below).
- More recently the Euler allocation was criticised for not being compatible

with the decentralised risk management functions of large financial institutions (Schwaiger, 2006). Gründl and Schmeiser (2007) even find that capital allocation is not needed at all for insurance companies.

Contributions to subadditive risk measures

As risk hedging by diversification plays a major role for portfolio management we briefly recall the observations by Kalkbrener (2005) and Tasche (1999) on the relation between the Euler allocation principle and diversification.

It is quite common to associate risk measures that reward portfolio diversification with the so-called subadditivity property (Artzner *et al* 1999). A risk measure ρ is subadditive if it satisfies

$$\rho(X+Y) \leq \rho(X)+\rho(Y) \qquad (17.8)$$

for any random variables X, Y in its range of definition. Assume the setting of the section "Basic setting" and that ρ is a risk measure that is both homogeneous of degree 1 and subadditive. By Corollary A.1 then the function f_ρ, that corresponds to ρ via 17.5 fulfills the inequality

$$\sum_{i=1}^{n} u_i \frac{\partial f_\rho(u+v)}{\partial u_i} \leq f_\rho(u), \qquad i=1,\ldots,n. \qquad (17.9a)$$

With $u = (0, \ldots, 0, 1, 0, \ldots, 0)$ (1 at ith position) and $v = (1, \ldots, 1) - u$, (17.9a) implies

$$\rho_{\text{Euler}}(X_i \mid X) \leq \rho(X_i), \qquad i=1,\ldots,n, \qquad (17.9b)$$

where $\rho_{\text{Euler}}(X_i \mid X)$ is defined by 17.6. Hence, if risk contributions to a homogeneous and subadditive risk measure are calculated as Euler contributions, then the contributions of single assets will never exceed the assets' standalone risks. In particular, risk contributions of credit assets cannot become larger than the face values of the assets.

Actually Corollary A.1 shows that for continuously differentiable and risk measures ρ homogeneous of degree 1 property 17.9b for the Euler contributions and subadditivity of the risk measure are equivalent. This is of particular relevance for credit risk portfolios where violations of the subadditivity property are rather observed as violations of 17.9b than as violations of 17.8 (see Kalkbrener *et al* 2004).

Recall the notion of the so-called marginal risk contribution[4] for determining the capital required by an individual business asset or sub-portfolio. Formally, the marginal risk contribution $\rho_{\text{marg}}(X_i \mid X)$ of asset i, $i = 1, \ldots, n$, is defined by

$$\rho_{\text{marg}}\left(X_i \mid X\right)=\rho\left(X\right)-\rho\left(X-X_i\right) \tag{17.10}$$

ie, by the difference of the portfolio risk with asset i and the portfolio risk without asset i. In the case of continuously differentiable and subadditive risk measures that are homogeneous of degree 1, it can be shown that marginal risk contributions are always smaller than the corresponding Euler contributions (Tasche 2004a, Proposition 2).

Proposition 17.2

Let ρ be a subadditive and continuously differentiable risk measure that is homogeneous of degree 1. Then the marginal risk contributions $\rho_{\text{marg}}(X_i \mid X)$ as defined by 17.10 are smaller than the corresponding Euler contributions, ie,

$$\rho_{\text{marg}}\left(X_i \mid X\right)\leq \rho_{\text{Euler}}\left(X_i \mid X\right) \tag{17.11a}$$

In particular, the sum of the marginal risk contributions underestimates total risk, ie,

$$\sum_{i=1}^{n}\rho_{\text{marg}}\left(X_i \mid X\right)=\sum_{i=1}^{n}\left(\rho\left(X\right)-\rho\left(X-X_i\right)\right)\leq \rho\left(X\right). \tag{17.11b}$$

As a workaround for the problem that marginal risk contributions do not satisfy the full allocation property, sometimes marginal risk contributions are defined as

$$\rho^{*}_{\text{marg}}\left(X_i \mid X\right)=\frac{\rho_{\text{marg}}\left(X_i \mid X\right)}{\sum_{j=1}^{n}\rho_{\text{marg}}\left(X_j \mid X\right)}\rho\left(X\right) \tag{17.12}$$

This way, equality in Equation 17.11b is forced. In general however, marginal risk contributions according to Equation 17.12 do not fulfil the RORAC compatibility property from Definition 17.2.

Measuring concentration and diversification

In BCBS (2006 paragraph 770) the Basel Committee on Banking Supervision states:

> A risk concentration is any single exposure or group of exposures with the potential to produce losses large enough (relative to a bank's capital total assets or overall risk level) to threaten a bank's health or ability to maintain its core operations. Risk concentrations are arguably the single most important cause of major problems in banks.

In BCBS (2006, paragraph 774) the Basel Committee then explains:

> A bank's framework for managing credit risk concentrations should be clearly documented and should include a definition of the credit risk concen-

trations relevant to the bank and how these concentrations and their corresponding limits are calculated.

We demonstrate in this section that the Euler allocation as introduced in the subsection "Defining risk contributions" is particularly well suited for calculating concentrations.

The concept of concentration index (following Tasche, 2006) we will introduce is based on the idea that the actual risk of a portfolio should be compared to an appropriate worst-case risk of the portfolio in order to be able to identify risk concentration. It turns out that "worst-case risk" can be adequately expressed as maximum dependence of the random variables the portfolio model is based on. In actuarial science, the concept of comonotonicity is well-known as it supports easy and reasonably conservative representations of dependence structures (see, for example, Dhaene *et al* 2006). Random variables V and W are called comonotonic if they can be represented as non-decreasing functions of a third random variable Z, ie

$$V = h_V(Z) \quad \text{and} \quad W = h_W(Z) \tag{17.13a}$$

for some non-decreasing functions h_V, h_W. As comonotonicity is implied if V and W are correlated with correlation coefficient 1 it generalises the concept of linear dependence. A risk measure ρ is called comonotonic additive if for any comonotonic random variables V and W

$$\rho(V + W) = \rho(V) + \rho(W) \tag{17.13b}$$

Thus comonotonic additivity can be interpreted as a specification of worst-case scenarios when risk is measured by a subadditive (see 17.8) risk measure: nothing worse can occur than comonotonic random variables, which seems quite natural.[5] These observations suggest the first part of the following definition.

Definition 17.3

Let $X_1, \ldots, X_n$ be real-valued random variables and let $X = \sum_{i=1}^{n} X_i$. If ρ is a risk measure such that $\rho(X), \rho(X_1), \ldots, \rho(X_n)$ are defined, then

$$\mathrm{DI}_\rho(X) = \frac{\rho(X)}{\sum_{i=1}^{n} \rho(X_i)} \tag{17.14a}$$

denotes the diversification index of portfolio X with respect to the risk measure ρ. If Euler risk contributions of X_i to $\rho(X)$ in the sense of Remark 17.1 exist, then the ratio

$$\mathrm{DI}_\rho(X_i \mid X) = \frac{\rho_{\mathrm{Euler}}(X_i \mid X)}{\rho(X_i)} \tag{17.14b}$$

with $\rho_{\mathrm{Euler}}(X_i \mid X)$ being defined by Equation 17.6 denotes the marginal diversification index of sub-portfolio X_i with respect to the risk measure ρ.

Note that without calling the concept "diversification index" Memmel and Wehn (2006) calculate a diversification index for the German supervisor's market price risk portfolio. Garcia Cespedes *et al* (2006) use the diversification indexes as defined here for a representation of portfolio risk as a "diversification index"-weighted sum of stand-alone risks.

Remark 17.2

Definition 17.3 is most useful when the risk measure ρ under consideration is homogeneous of degree 1, subadditive, and comonotonic additive. Additionally, the function f_ρ associated with ρ via 17.7 should be continuously differentiable. Expected shortfall, as considered in the subsection of that name later, enjoys homogeneity, subadditivity and comonotonic additivity. Its associated function is continuously differentiable under moderate assumptions on the joint distribution of the variables X_i (Tasche 1999 and 2002).

Assume that ρ is a risk measure that has these four properties. Then

(i) by subadditivity, $\mathrm{DI}_\rho(X) \leq 1$
(ii) by comonotonic additivity, $\mathrm{DI}_\rho(X) \approx 1$ indicates that $X_1, \ldots, X_n$ are "almost" comonotonic (ie, strongly dependent)
(iii) by 17.9b, $\mathrm{DI}_\rho(X_i \mid X) \leq 1$
(iv) by Proposition 17.1, $\mathrm{DI}_\rho(X_i \mid X) < \mathrm{DI}_\rho(X)$ implies that there is some $\epsilon_i > 0$ such that $\mathrm{DI}_\rho(X + h\,X_i) < \mathrm{DI}_\rho(X)$ for $0 < h < \epsilon_i$.

With regard to conclusion (ii) in Remark 17.2, a portfolio with a diversification index close to 100% might be considered to have high risk concentration whereas a portfolio with a low diversification index might be considered well diversified. However, it is not easy to specify how far from 100% a diversification index should be for implying that the portfolio is well diversified.

Conclusion (iv) in Remark 17.2 could be more useful for such a distinction between concentrated and diversified portfolios because marginal diversification indexes indicate rather diversification potential than "absolute" diversification. In this sense a portfolio with high unrealised diversification potential could be regarded as concentrated.

PRACTICE

On principle, formula 17.6 can be applied directly for calculating Euler risk contributions. It has turned out, however, that for some popular families of risk measures it is possible to derive closed-form expressions for the involved derivative. In this section, results are presented for standard deviation based risk measures, VaR and ES.[6] We then discuss in some detail how to implement Equation 17.6 in the case of VaR when the underlying distribution has to be inferred from a sample. A related but somehow different application of Euler's theorem to the calculation of single name contributions to the expected loss of CDO tranches is then discussed before we present another application of Euler allocation to the measurement of risk impacts on non-linear portfolios. In the following the notation of the subsection "Basic setting" is adopted.

Standard deviation based risk measures

We consider here the family of risk measures σ_c, $c > 0$ given by

$$\sigma_c(X) = c\sqrt{\text{var}[X]} = c\sqrt{\text{E}\left[\left(X - \text{E}[X]\right)^2\right]} \tag{17.15}$$

It is common to choose the constant c in such a way that

$$\text{P}\left[X \le \text{E}[X] - \sigma_c(X)\right] \le 1 - \alpha \tag{17.16}$$

where α denotes some large probability (like 99% or 99.95%). Sometimes this is done assuming that X is normally distributed. A robust alternative would be an application of the one-tailed Chebychev-inequality

$$\text{P}\left[X \le \text{E}[X] - \sigma_c(X)\right] \le \frac{1}{1 + c^2} \tag{17.17}$$

Solving $1/(1 + c^2) = 1 - \alpha$ for c will then ensure that 17.16 obtains for all X with finite variance. Note that however, this method for determining c will yield much higher values of c than the method based on a normal-distribution assumption.

The risk measures σ_c, $c > 0$ are homogeneous of degree 1 and subadditive, but not comonotonic additive. For $X = \sum_{i=1}^{n} X_i$ the Euler contributions according to Remark 17.1 can readily be calculated by differentiation

$$\sigma_c(X_i \mid X) = c\frac{\text{cov}\left[X_i \mid X\right]}{\sqrt{\text{var}[X]}} \tag{17.18a}$$

In case that X_i is given as $g_i - L_i$ (see Equation 17.3), we have $\sigma_c(X) = \sigma_c(L)$ and

$$\sigma_c\left(X_i \mid X\right) = c\frac{\operatorname{cov}\left[L_i \mid L\right]}{\sqrt{\operatorname{var}\left[L\right]}} \tag{17.18b}$$

Value-at-risk

For any real-valued random variable Y and $\gamma \in (0, 1)$ define the γ quantile of Y by

$$q_\gamma\left(Y\right) = \min\left\{y : \mathrm{P}\left[Y \leq y\right] \geq \gamma\right\} \tag{17.19a}$$

If Y has a strictly increasing and continuous distribution function $F(y) = \mathrm{P}[Y \leq y]$ quantiles of Y can be expressed by the inverse function of F

$$q_\gamma\left(Y\right) = F^{-1}\left(\gamma\right). \tag{17.19b}$$

For a portfolio-wide profit/loss variable $X = \sum_{i=1}^{n} X_i$ the VaR of X at confidence level α (α usually close to 1) is defined as the α-quantile of $-X$:

$$\mathrm{VaR}_\alpha\left(X\right) = q_\alpha\left(-X\right) \tag{17.20}$$

Value-at-risk as a risk measure is homogeneous of degree 1 and comonotonic additive but not in general subadditive. Under some smoothness conditions (see Gouriéroux *et al* 2000 or Tasche 1999, Section 5.2), a general formula can be derived for the Euler contributions to $\mathrm{VaR}_\alpha(X)$ according to Remark 17.1. These smoothness conditions, in particular, imply that X has a density. The formula for the Euler VaR contributions reads

$$\mathrm{VaR}_\alpha\left(X_i \mid X\right) = -\mathrm{E}\left[X_i \mid X = -\mathrm{VaR}_\alpha\left(X\right)\right] \tag{17.21a}$$

where $\mathrm{E}[X_i \mid X]$ denotes the conditional expectation of X_i given X. In case that X_i is given as $g_i - L_i$ (see 17.3), we have $\mathrm{VaR}_\alpha(X) = q_\alpha(L) - \sum_{i=1}^{n} g_i$ and

$$\mathrm{VaR}_\alpha\left(X_i \mid X\right) = \mathrm{E}\left[L_i \mid L = q_\alpha\left(L\right)\right] - g_i. \tag{17.21b}$$

Often, it is not VaR itself that is of interest but rather unexpected loss

$$\mathrm{UL}_{\mathrm{VaR},\alpha}\left(X\right) = \mathrm{VaR}_\alpha\left(X - \mathrm{E}\left[X\right]\right) = \mathrm{VaR}_\alpha\left(X\right) + \mathrm{E}\left[X\right] \tag{17.22a}$$

In terms of $X_i = g_i - L_i$ Equation 17.22a reads

$$\mathrm{UL}_{\mathrm{VaR},\alpha}\left(X\right) = \mathrm{VaR}_\alpha\left(\mathrm{E}\left[L\right] - L\right) = q_\alpha\left(L\right) - \mathrm{E}\left[L\right] \tag{17.22b}$$

Having in mind that the Euler contribution of X_i to $\mathrm{E}[X]$ is obviously $\mathrm{E}[X_i]$, the formulas for the Euler contributions to $\mathrm{UL}_{\mathrm{VaR},\alpha}(X)$ are obvious from Equations 17.21a to 17.22b.

In general, the conditional expectation of X_i given X cannot easily be calculated or estimated. For some exceptions from this observation see Tasche (2004b, 2006). As the conditional expectation of X_i given X can be interpreted as the best prediction of X_i by X in a least squares context, approximation of $\mathrm{VaR}_\alpha(X_i \mid X)$ by best linear predictions of X_i by X has been proposed. Linear approximation of the right-hand side of 17.21a by X and a constant yields

$$\mathrm{VaR}_\alpha(X_i \mid X) \approx \frac{\mathrm{cov}[X_i, X]}{\mathrm{var}[X]} \mathrm{UL}_{\mathrm{VaR},\alpha}(X) - \mathrm{E}[X_i]. \tag{17.23}$$

The approximation in 17.23 can be improved by additionally admitting quadratic or other non-linear transformations of X as regressors (see Tasche and Tibiletti 2004, Section 5). All such regression-based approximate Euler contributions to VaR satisfy the full allocation property of Definition 17.2 but are not RORAC compatible. See the subsection "Risk measures for sample data" for an approach to the estimation of 17.21a that yields RORAC compatibility.

Expected shortfall

For a portfolio-wide profit/loss variable $X = \sum_{i=1}^{n} X_i$ the ES[7] of X at confidence level α (α usually close to 1) is defined as an average of VaRs of X at level α and higher

$$\mathrm{ES}_\alpha(X) = \frac{1}{1-\alpha} \int_\alpha^1 \mathrm{VaR}_u(X)\,du \tag{17.24a}$$

Expected shortfall as a risk measure is homogeneous of degree 1 comonotonic additive and subadditive. Under some smoothness conditions (see Tasche 1999, Section 5.3) a general formula can be derived for the Euler contributions to $\mathrm{ES}_\alpha(X)$ according to Remark 17.1. These smoothness conditions in particular, imply that X has a density. In that case ES can equivalently be written as

$$\mathrm{ES}_\alpha(X) = -\mathrm{E}[X \mid X \le -\mathrm{VaR}_\alpha(X)] \tag{17.24b}$$

The formula for the Euler ES contribution reads

$$\begin{aligned}\mathrm{ES}_\alpha(X_i \mid X) &= -E[X_i \mid X \le -\mathrm{VaR}_\alpha(X)] \\ &= -(1-\alpha)^{-1} E\left[X_i \mathbf{1}_{\{X \le -\mathrm{VaR}_\alpha(X)\}}\right]\end{aligned} \tag{17.25a}$$

Note that $\mathrm{E}[X_i \mid X \le -\mathrm{VaR}_\alpha(X)]$ in contrast to $\mathrm{E}[X_i \mid X]$ from 17.21a, is an elementary conditional expectation because the conditioning event has caused a positive probability to occur. In case that X_i is given as $g_i - L_i$ we have $ES_\alpha(X) = \frac{1}{1-\alpha}\int_\alpha^1 q_u(L)\,du - \sum_{i=1}^n g_i$ and

$$ES_\alpha(X_i \mid X) = E[L_i \mid L \geq q_\alpha(L)] - g_i \qquad (17.25b)$$

Often, it is not ES itself that is of interest but rather unexpected loss

$$UL_{ES,\alpha}(X) = ES_\alpha(X - E[X]) = ES_\alpha(X) + E[X] \qquad (17.26a)$$

In terms of $X_i = g_i - L_i$, Equation 17.26a reads

$$UL_{ES,\alpha}(X) = ES_\alpha(E[L] - L) = \frac{1}{1-\alpha}\int_\alpha^1 q_u(L)du - E[L]. \qquad (17.26b)$$

Having in mind that the Euler contribution of X_i to E[X] is obviously $E[X_i]$, the formulas for the Euler contributions to $UL_{ES,\alpha}(X)$ are obvious from Equations 17.25a to 17.26b.

In contrast to Euler contributions to VaR thanks to representation 17.25a, estimation of Euler contributions to ES is quite straightforward.

Risk measures for sample data

In most circumstances portfolio loss distributions cannot be calculated analytically but have to be estimated from simulated or historical sample data. For a portfolio of n assets as specified earlier in the section on "Basic setting", the sample data might be given as n-dimensional points

$$(x_{1,1}, \ldots, x_{n,1}), \ldots, (x_{1,N}, \ldots, x_{n,N}) \qquad (17.27)$$

where $X_{i,k}$ denotes the profit/loss of asset i in the kth observation (of N). Each data point $(x_{1,k}, \ldots, x_{n,k})$ would be interpreted as a realisation of the profit/loss random vector $(X_1, \ldots, X_n)$. The portfolio-wide profit/loss in the kth observation would then be obtained as $x_k = \sum_{i=1}^n x_{i,k}$. If the sample is large and the observations can be assumed independent, by the law of large numbers the empirical measure

$$\hat{P}_N(A) = \frac{1}{N}\sum_{k=1}^N \delta_A(x_{1,k}, \ldots, x_{n,k}), \quad A \subset \mathbb{R}^n \text{ measurable},$$
$$\delta_A(x_{1,k}, \ldots, x_{n,k}) = \begin{cases} 1, & \text{if } (x_{1,k}, \ldots, x_{n,k}) \in A; \\ 0, & \text{otherwise} \end{cases} \qquad (17.28)$$

will approximate the joint distribution $P[(X_1, \ldots, X_n) \in A]$ of the assets' profits/losses X_i.

Denote by $(\hat{X}_1, \ldots, \hat{X}_n)$ the profit/loss random vector under the empirical measure $\hat{P}_N$. Let $\hat{X} = \sum_{i=1}^n \hat{X}_i$ be the portfolio-wide profit/loss under the empirical measure $\hat{P}_N$. In the cases of standard deviation based risk measures and ES, then statistically consistent estimators for the risk contributions according to 17.18a and 17.25a respectively can be obtained by simply substituting $\hat{X}$, $\hat{X}_i$ for X, X_i. This naive approach does not work for Euler contributions to VaR according to 17.21a, if X has a continuous distribution. In this case, smoothing of the empirical measure (kernel estimation) as described in the following can help.

Let ξ be a random variable which is independent of $(\hat{X}_1, \ldots, \hat{X}_n)$ and has a continuous density (or kernel) φ (ξ standard normal would be a good and convenient choice). Fix some $b > 0$ (the bandwidth). Then $\hat{X} + b\xi$ has the density

$$\widehat{f_b}(x) = \widehat{f}_{b,x_1,\ldots,x_N}(x) = \frac{1}{bN}\sum_{k=1}^{N}\varphi\left(\frac{x - x_k}{b}\right) \tag{17.29}$$

Actually, Equation 17.29 represents the well-known Rosenblatt–Parzen estimator of the density of X. If the kernel φ and the density of X are appropriately "smooth" (see, for example, Pagan and Ullah 1999, Theorem 2.5 for details), it can be shown for $b_N \to 0$, $b_N N \to \infty$ that $\hat{f}_{b_N}(x)$ is a point-wise mean-squared consistent estimator of the density of X. Whereas the choice of the kernel φ, subject to some mild conditions, is not too important for the efficiency of the Rosenblatt–Parzen estimator, the appropriate choice of the bandwidth is crucial. Silverman's rule of thumb (see (2.52) in Pagan and Ullah 1999)

$$b = 0.9 \min(\sigma, R / 1.34) N^{-1/5} \tag{17.30}$$

is known to work quite well in many circumstances. In Equation 17.30, σ and R denote the standard deviation and the interquartile range respectively of the sample $x_1, \ldots, x_N$. In the case where X is not heavy tailed (as is the case for credit portfolio loss distributions) another quite promising and easy-to-implement method for the bandwidth selection is pseudo likelihood cross validation. See for instance, Turlach (1993) for an overview of this and other selection methods.

In the context of the Euler allocation, a major advantage with the kernel estimation approach is that the smoothness conditions from Tasche (1999, Section 5.2) are obtained for ξ, $\hat{X}_1, \ldots, \hat{X}_n$. As a consequence, it follows from Tasche (1999, Lemma 5.3) that

$$\begin{aligned}\text{VaR}_\alpha(X_i \mid X) &\approx \text{VaR}_\alpha\left(\widehat{X}_i \mid \widehat{X} + b\xi\right)\\ &= \frac{d\text{VaR}_\alpha}{dh}\left(\widehat{X} + b\xi + h\widehat{X}_i\right)\Big|_{h=0}\\ &= -E\left[\widehat{X}_i \mid \widehat{X} + b\xi = -\text{VaR}_\alpha\left(\widehat{X} + b\xi\right)\right]\\ &= -\frac{\sum_{k=1}^{N} x_{i,k}\varphi\left(\dfrac{-\text{VaR}_\alpha\left(\widehat{X} + b\xi\right) - x_k}{b}\right)}{\sum_{k=1}^{N}\varphi\left(\dfrac{-\text{VaR}_\alpha\left(\widehat{X} + b\xi\right) - x_k}{b}\right)}\end{aligned} \tag{17.31}$$

The right-hand side of Equation 17.31 is just the Nadaraya–Watson kernel estimator of $E[X_i \mid X = -\text{VaR}_\alpha(X)]$. Note that it is clear from the derivation of 17.31 in the context of the empirical measure 17.28 that the bandwidth b in 17.31 should be the same as in 17.29. By construction, we obtain for the sum of the approximate Euler contributions to VaR according to 17.31

$$\begin{aligned}\sum_{i=1}^{n}\text{VaR}_\alpha\left(\widehat{X}_i \mid \widehat{X} + b\xi\right) &= \text{VaR}_\alpha\left(\widehat{X} + b\xi\right) - \text{VaR}_\alpha\left(\xi \mid \widehat{X} + b\xi\right)\\ &= \text{VaR}_\alpha\left(\widehat{X} + b\xi\right) + \text{E}\left[\xi \mid \widehat{X} + b\xi = -\text{VaR}_\alpha\left(\widehat{X} + b\xi\right)\right]\end{aligned} \tag{17.32}$$

The sum of the approximate Euler contributions therefore differs from natural estimates of $\text{VaR}_\alpha(X)$ such as $\text{VaR}_\alpha(\hat{X})$ or $\text{VaR}_\alpha(\hat{X} + b\xi)$. Practical experience shows that the difference tends to be small. Some authors (for example, Epperlein and Smillie, 2006) suggest to account for this difference by an appropriate multiplier. Another way to deal with the issue could be to take the left-hand side of Equation 17.32 as an estimate for $\text{VaR}_\alpha(X)$.

Yamai and Yoshiba (2002) found that estimates for ES and VaR Euler contributions are very volatile. See Glasserman (2005) and Merino and Nyfeler (2004) for methods to tackle this problem for expected shortfall by importance sampling and Tasche (2007) for an approach to Euler VaR contribution estimation by importance sampling.

Expected loss decomposition for CDO tranches

In the case of a credit portfolio with loss variable $L \geq 0$ given as

$$L = \sum_{i=1}^{n} L_i \tag{17.33a}$$

or in a dynamic setting with exposure sizes u_i

$$L(u) = \sum_{i=1}^{n} u_i L_i \tag{17.33b}$$

the loss variables $L_i \geq 0$ for single assets represent a natural vertical decomposition of the portfolio-wide loss L. If the portfolio serves as the underlying of a CDO the normalised (ie, percentage) portfolio-wide loss $0 \leq L \leq 1$ is decomposed into tranches in a horizontal manner, via

$$L = \sum_{j=1}^{m} Y_j \tag{17.34a}$$

with

$$Y_j = \min(L, c_j) - \min(L, c_{j-1}), \quad j = 1, \ldots m \tag{17.34b}$$

where $0 = c_0 < c_1 < \ldots < c_{m-1} < c_m = 1$, $m \geq 2$ denote the so-called credit enhancement levels of the CDO.[8] Hence, the random variable Y_j is associated with the loss suffered with the jth tranche of the CDO and is characterised by the credit enhancement levels c_{j-1} and c_j.

According to 17.33a and 17.34a, in particular, the portfolio expected loss E[L] can be decomposed in two ways namely as

$$\mathrm{E}[L] = \sum_{i=1}^{n} \mathrm{E}[L_i] \tag{17.35a}$$

and

$$\mathrm{E}[L] = \sum_{j=1}^{m} \mathrm{E}[Y_j] \tag{17.35b}$$

Is there any reasonable way to further decompose the vertical and horizontal expected loss components E[L_i] and E[Y_j] respectively into sub-components E_{kl} such that

$$\mathrm{E}[L_i] = \sum_{l=1}^{m} E_{il} \tag{17.36a}$$

and

$$\mathrm{E}[Y_j] = \sum_{k=1}^{n} E_{kj} \tag{17.36b}$$

This question is of particular interest in the case where a portfolio of assets may contain names both directly as bonds or loans owed by the names or indirectly by the involvement of the names via CDO tranches. A decomposition of portfolio expected loss as indicated by 17.36a and b can then yield at least a rough measure of a single name's impact on the portfolio loss distribution. Interestingly enough, Euler's theorem A.1 also proves very useful for answering this question.

Observe first that it suffices to find a decomposition of E[min(L, c)] where c stands for any credit enhancement level. If then the decomposition procedure is applied consistently for all enhancement levels c_j, $j = 1, \ldots, m - 1$, property 17.36a will be satisfied thanks to definition 17.34b. Consider then the problem in the dynamic setting as indicated by 17.33b and assume that the enhancement level c also depends on the exposure sizes $u = (u_1, \ldots, u_n)$, ie, $c = c(u)$. We are then studying the function $F(u)$ with

$$F(u) = E\left[\min\left(L(u), c(u)\right)\right] \tag{17.37}$$

From 17.33b follows that F is homogeneous of degree 1 in the sense of Definition A.1 if c as a function of u is homogeneous of degree 1. Two such choices of c are common in practice: c as a quantile (see 17.19a) of the loss distribution, ie

$$c(u) = q_\alpha\left(L(u)\right) \tag{17.38a}$$

for some $\alpha \in (0, 1)$, or c as some multiple $b > 0$ of the portfolio expected loss ie,

$$c(u) = b\sum_{i=1}^{n} u_i \mathrm{E}\left[L_i\right] \tag{17.38b}$$

Homogeneity of degree 1 implies the following solution to the decomposition problem as stated by 17.36a and b.

Proposition 17.3

Let the credit enhancement levels $c_j = c_j(u)$, $j = 1, \ldots, m - 1$ be functions that are homogeneous of degree 1 in the sense of Definition A.1. Let the portfolio loss variable $L(u)$ and the tranche loss variables $Y_j = Y_j(u)$, $j = 1, \ldots, m$ be given by 17.33b and 17.34b respectively. Assume that the functions $F_j(u) = \mathrm{E}[\min(L(u), c_j(u))]$, $j = 1, \ldots, m - 1$ are partially differentiable with respect to all components of $u = (u_1, \ldots, u_n)$. Then the functions $E_{kl}(u)$, $k = 1, \ldots, n$, $l = 1, \ldots, m$ with

$$E_{kl}(u) = \begin{cases} u_k \dfrac{\partial F_1}{\partial u_k}(u), & l = 1; \\ u_k\left(\dfrac{\partial F_l}{\partial u_k}(u) - \dfrac{\partial F_{l-1}}{\partial u_k}(u)\right), & 2 \le l \le m-1; \\ u_k\left(\mathrm{E}\left[L_k\right] - \dfrac{\partial F_{m-1}}{\partial u_k}(u)\right), & l = m, \end{cases} \tag{17.39}$$

satisfy Equations 17.36a and b. In the following, the quantities $E_{kl}(u)$ will be called tranche loss components. Of course, what makes Equation 17.39 attractive as the solution to 17.36a and b is the fact that by inclusion of partial derivatives the resulting contributions to tranche expected losses reflect the potential dynamics from changes in the weights of the underlying names. This fact is illustrated by the following proposition.

Proposition 17.4

Assume the setting of Proposition 17.3. If for some $j \in \{1, \ldots, m\}$ there is a portfolio weight vector u^* such that $\frac{E[Y_j(u^*)]}{E[L(u^*)]}$ is a local minimum or maximum, then for all $i = 1, \ldots, n$ follows that

$$\frac{E_{ij}(u^*)}{u_i^* E[L_i]} = \frac{E[Y_j(u^*)]}{E[L(u^*)]}$$

By Proposition 17.4 in particular, there cannot be a local minimum or maximum of the ratio of tranche expected loss and portfolio expected loss as long as not all of the corresponding ratios of tranche loss components and expected losses of underlying assets are equal.

Note that $F(u) = E[\min(L(u), c(u))]$ from Proposition 17.3 can be represented as follows

$$F(u) = c(u)P[L(u) > c(u)] + E\left[L(u)1_{\{L(u)\le c(u)\}}\right] \tag{17.40a}$$

$$= c(u)P[L(u) > c(u)] + P[L(u) \le c(u)]E[L(u) \mid L(u) \le c(u)] \tag{17.40b}$$

Equation 17.40a is suitable for the calculation of the partial derivatives of F in many cases, eg, when $c(u)$ is given by 17.38b. If c is given by 17.38a, ie, as a quantile, and the distribution of $L(u)$ is continuous at $q_\alpha(L(u))$ for all u, 17.40b is more useful.

Remark 17.3

If the distribution of $L(u)$ is smooth enough with respect to the variable u, and c from 17.40a is partially differentiable, then the partial derivatives of F can be calculated as follows

$$\frac{\partial F}{\partial u_k}(u) = \frac{\partial c}{\partial u_k}(u)P[L(u) > c(u)] - c(u)\frac{\partial P[L(u) \le c(u)]}{\partial u_k} + \frac{\partial E\left[L(u)1_{\{L(u)\le c(u)\}}\right]}{\partial u_k} \tag{17.41a}$$

In case of $c(u) = q_\alpha(L(u))$ with $q_\alpha(L(u))$ being the quantile function as defined in 17.19a, we have $P[L(u) \le c(u)] = \alpha$ for all u if the distribution of $L(u)$ is continuous in $q_\alpha(L(u))$ for all u. Taking into account 17.21a and 17.25a then leads to the following simplified version of 17.41a

$$\frac{\partial E[\min(L(u), q_\alpha(L(u)))]}{\partial u_k} = (1-\alpha)E[L_k \mid L(u) = q_\alpha(L(u))] + \alpha E[L_k \mid L(u) \le q_\alpha(L(u))] \tag{17.41b}$$

Figure 17.2 Ratios of tranche loss components and sub-portfolio expected losses (tranche EL ratios) as a function of weight of first sub-portfolio

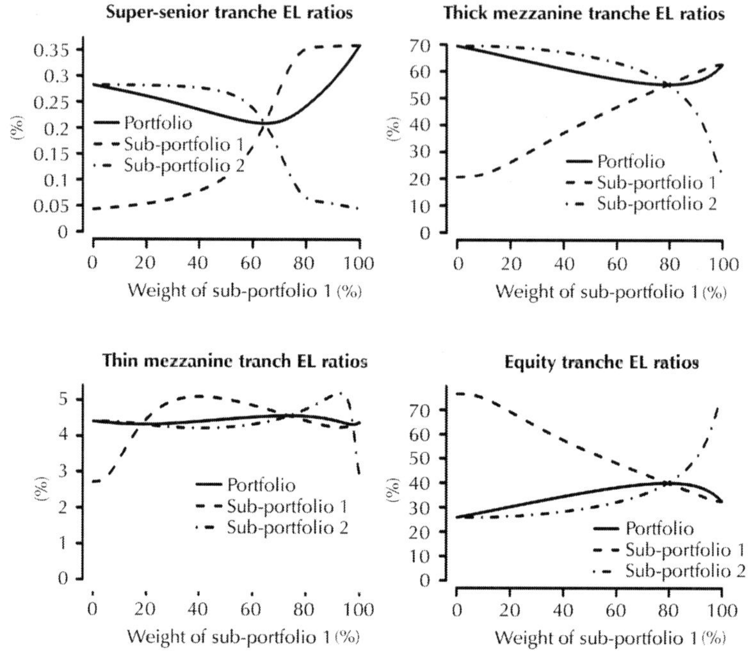

Definitions of loss variables as in 17.42a and 17.42b. Parameter values as in 17.43. Tranches defined by 17.44

We illustrate[9] the notion of tranche loss component and Proposition 17.4 with an asymptotic two-factor model as in Example 1 of Tasche (2006). Define L_i, $i = 1, 2$ as Vasicek-distributed random variables by

$$L_i = \Phi\left(\frac{t_i + \sqrt{\Omega_i} S_i}{\sqrt{1-\Omega_i}}\right) \tag{17.42a}$$

with asset correlations $\Omega_i \in (0, 1)$, default thresholds $t_i \in \mathbb{R}$ and systematic factors S_1, S_2 jointly standard normal such that corr$[S_1, S_2] = \tau \in [0, 1]$. Let

$$L(u) = uL_1 + (1-u)L_2, \quad u \in [0,1] \tag{17.42b}$$

$L(u)$ can then be interpreted as the loss (expressed as fraction of total exposure) in a credit portfolio that consists of two homogeneous sub-portfolios with corresponding loss variables L_1 and L_2. The parameters in Equations 17.42a and b are chosen as follows

$$t_1 = \Phi^{-1}(0.01), \qquad \Omega_1 = 0.2$$
$$t_2 = \Phi^{-1}(0.0025), \quad \Omega_2 = 0.3 \qquad (17.43)$$
$$\tau = 0.4$$

We define four tranche loss variables $Y_1(u)$, $Y_2(u)$, $Y_3(u)$, $Y_4(u)$ according to 17.34b by

$$\begin{aligned} c_0(u) &= 0, \\ c_0(u) &= q_{50\%}(L(u)), \\ c_2(u) &= q_{55\%}(L(u)), \\ c_3(u) &= q_{99.9\%}(L(u)), \\ c_4(u) &= 1 \end{aligned} \qquad (17.44)$$

For obvious reasons in the following we call tranche 1 the "equity tranche", tranche 2 the "thin mezzanine tranche", tranche 3 the "thick mezzanine tranche" and tranche 4 the "super senior tranche". Figure 17.2 displays, for each of the four tranches, the ratio of the expected losses of the whole tranche and the whole portfolio as well as the ratios of the tranche loss components and the expected losses of the two sub-portfolios. Note the different scales of the four charts. Not surprisingly the EL ratios are quite small for the super-senior and thin mezzanine tranches. Compared to the thicknesses of the tranches as measured by the differences of the defining confidence levels the expected loss ratios of the super senior and the thick mezzanine tranches are over-proportional. As stated in Proposition 17.4, in each chart the three curves intersect in the local extremes of the ratios of whole tranche and whole portfolio expected losses. The charts demonstrate that both local minima and maxima may occur and that even both kinds of extremes can be observed in one curve (in the case of the thin mezzanine tranche).

Measuring non-linear risk impact

Earlier we discussed the problem of how to meaningfully define risk contributions in the case of a linear portfolio as given by 17.1 or 17.33a. By considering the dynamic modification 17.4 of the problem, we argued that only Euler risk contributions 17.6 can be applied for determining optimal weights for the assets in the portfolio and, at the same time, making sure that the risk contributions add up at portfolio-wide risk. The reasoning for this, however, is heavily based on linearity of the portfolio profit/loss variable with respect to the profit/loss variables of the included assets and on homogeneity of the risk measure. At first glance, we dealt with a non-linear portfolio in the subsection on "Expected loss decomposition for CDO tranches" when we looked at the tranche loss variables Y_j as defined by 17.34b which are clearly not linear in the exposure sizes u_i from 17.33b. But we did not solve in full generality the problem of tranche loss decomposition. Instead we confined ourselves to the case where the credit enhancement levels are defined by functions homogeneous in the exposure sizes. This way, we essentially restated the problem in a shape similar to the setting in the section on "Theory" and accessible by means of Euler's theorem.

In order to analyse non-linear impact of a single factor or a set of factors on portfolio-wide risk, Martin and Tasche (2007) suggested to apply Euler allocation to the decomposition of the portfolio-wide profit/loss variable into the expectation of portfolio-wide profit/loss conditional on the factor (or set of factors) and its orthogonal complement. In the rest of this section, we will present this approach in some detail and illustrate it by an example based on the toy portfolio model as specified by Equations 17.42a and b.

Definition 17.4

Let L be a loss variable with finite expectation and ρ be a risk measure that is homogeneous of degree 1 in the sense of Definition A.1. Consider a set of risk factors $S = (S_1, \ldots, S_k)$ and the expected value $\mathrm{E}[L \mid S]$ of L conditional on S. Assume that the Euler contribution $\rho(\mathrm{E}[L \mid S] \mid L)$ of $\mathrm{E}[L \mid S]$ to $\rho(L)$ in the sense of Remark 17.1 is well defined and that $\rho(L) > 0$. Then the risk impact of the factor set S on L (with respect to ρ) is defined as

$$\mathrm{RI}_\rho(L \mid S) = \frac{\rho\big(\mathrm{E}[L \mid S] \mid L\big)}{\rho(L)}$$

A key property of conditional expectation is the uncorrelatedness of conditional expected value and residual. Applied to the situation of Definition 17.4, this means

$$\mathrm{corr}\big[\mathrm{E}[L \mid S], L - \mathrm{E}[L \mid S]\big] = 0 \tag{17.45a}$$

By the factorisation lemma (see, for example, Stannat 2008, Remark 1.3 (v)), there is a deterministic function $f(s_1, \ldots, s_k)$ such that

$$\mathrm{E}[L \mid S] = f(S_1, \ldots, S_k) \tag{17.45b}$$

Hence the first step in determining the risk impact $\mathrm{RI}_\rho(L \mid S)$ essentially means decomposing the portfolio-wide loss variable L into a deterministic function of the factors in S and some uncorrelated residual. Doing so by calculating the expectation of L conditional on S ensures that this decomposition works in an exhaustive manner that also covers non-linear effects.

Figure 17.3 Risk impacts according to Definition 17.4 for factors S_1 and S_2 of the model given by 17.42a, 17.42b, and 17.43, as functions of the weight of the first sub-portfolio.

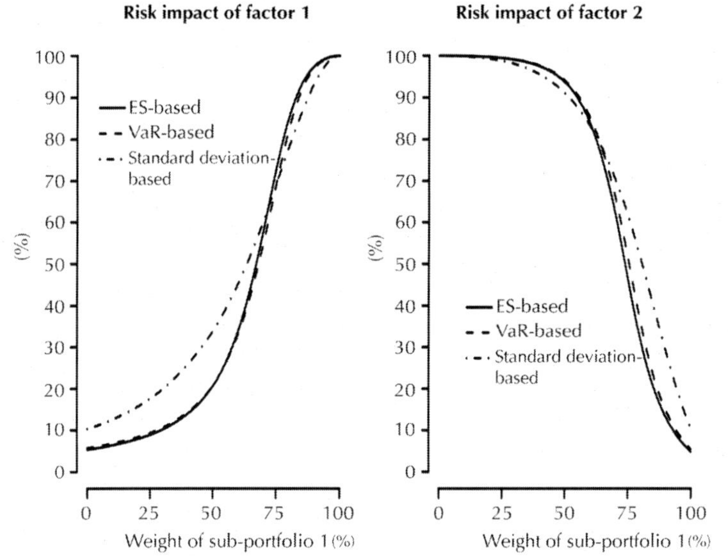

Results for risk impacts based on VaR and ES at 99.9% confidence level and standard deviation

What is the relationship between the notion of risk impact from Definition 17.4 when applied to the components of a linear portfolio as in 17.1 or 17.33a and the notion of Euler contribution in the sense of Remark 17.1, ie, what is (in the context of 17.33a) the connection between $\mathrm{RI}_\rho(L \mid L_i)$ and $\rho(L \mid L)$?

Let us assume without loss of generality that $i = 1$. It is instructive to consider the case where L_1 and $L_2, \ldots, L_n$ are stochastically independent. Then we obtain

$$\mathrm{E}\left[L \mid L_1\right] = L_1 - \mathrm{E}\left[L_1\right] + \mathrm{E}\left[L\right] \tag{17.46a}$$

and hence

$$\rho\left(\mathrm{E}\left[L \mid L_1\right] \mid L\right) = \rho\left(L_1 - \mathrm{E}\left[L_1\right] + \mathrm{E}\left[L\right] \mid L\right). \tag{17.46b}$$

If ρ is a risk measure such that the risk is not changed by adding constants, ie,

$$\rho\left(X + \alpha\right) = \rho\left(X\right), \quad \alpha \in \mathbb{R} \tag{17.46c}$$

then from 17.6 follows that $\rho(L_1 - \mathrm{E}[L_1] + \mathrm{E}[L] \mid L) = \rho(L_1 \mid L)$ and therefore

$$\frac{\rho(L_1 \mid L)}{\rho(L)} = \mathrm{RI}_\rho(L \mid L_1). \tag{17.46d}$$

Hence, in the case of an independent asset the risk impact coincides with the relative contribution of the asset to portfolio-wide risk. In general, without an assumption of independence, $\leq$ would intuitively be expected instead of $=$ in 17.46d. Showing this, however, seems non-trivial and presumably would require additional assumptions. We will not enter into this discussion here but just conclude that for reasons of compatibility of the definitions of risk contributions and risk impact, it makes sense to impose property 17.46c on the underlying risk measure or even to require that it is a general deviation measure in the sense of Rockafellar *et al* (2002).

σ_c from Equation 17.15 is a risk measure with property 17.46c. In this case

$$\mathrm{RI}_{\sigma_C}(L \mid S) = \mathrm{RI}_\sigma(L \mid S) = \frac{\mathrm{var}\left[E\left[L \mid S\right]\right]}{\mathrm{var}\left[L\right]} \in \left[0,1\right] \tag{17.47}$$

According to Equation 17.47, therefore, risk impact as introduced in Definition 17.4 is a generalisation of the notion of "coefficient of determination" or "R^2" from regression analysis. As regression models can be ranked with respect to their R^2 values with values closer to 100% indicating a better predictive power, also risk factors related to a portfolio can be ranked with respect to their associated risk impacts. A higher risk impact will then reflect a higher impact of the corresponding factor or set of factors that might require stronger attention from risk managers.

Thinking of the risk impact in similar terms as of the coefficient of determination could suggest defining risk impact simply by

$$\mathrm{qRI}_\rho(L \mid S) = \frac{\rho\left(\mathrm{E}\left[L \mid S\right]\right)}{\rho(L)} \tag{17.48}$$

with "qRI" standing for quasi-risk impact. This notion, however, is not compatible with Euler contributions in the sense of 17.46d. We will show by example that quasi-risk impact tends to emphasise the impact of a risk factor, when compared to risk impact risk impact.

Unexpected loss with respect to VaR and ES as defined in 17.22b and 17.26b are further examples of risk measures that satisfy property 17.46c and thus define risk impact measures compatible with Euler contributions in the sense of 17.46d. Based on 17.21b and 17.25b, we obtain the following formulas for risk impact with respect to VaR and ES respectively[10]

$$\mathrm{RI}_{\mathrm{VaR},\alpha}(L \mid S) = \frac{\mathrm{E}\left[\mathrm{E}[L \mid S] \mid L = q_\alpha(L)\right] - \mathrm{E}[L]}{q_\alpha(L) - \mathrm{E}[L]},$$

$$\mathrm{RI}_{\mathrm{ES},\alpha}(L \mid S) = \frac{\mathrm{E}\left[\mathrm{E}[L \mid S] \mid L \geq q_\alpha(L)\right] - \mathrm{E}[L]}{\mathrm{E}\left[L \mid L \geq q_\alpha(L)\right] - \mathrm{E}[L]} \tag{17.49}$$

Martin and Tasche (2007, Equation (7)) proved that $\mathrm{RI}_{\mathrm{ES},\alpha}(L \mid S) \leq 1$. To the authors' knowledge, no other general bounds to $\mathrm{RI}_{\mathrm{ES},\alpha}(L \mid S)$ or $\mathrm{RI}_{\mathrm{VaR},\alpha}(L \mid S)$ can be derived. Note that

$$\mathrm{RI}_{\mathrm{ES},\alpha}(L \mid S) = 0, \quad \mathrm{RI}_{\mathrm{VaR},\alpha}(L \mid S) = 0, \quad \text{and} \quad \mathrm{RI}_{\sigma}(L \mid S) = 0 \tag{17.50}$$

if L and S are independent.

For the two-factor example from the section on "Expected loss decomposition for CDO tranches", the expectations $\mathrm{E}[L(u) \mid S_i]$ $i = 1, 2$ of the portfolio loss variable $L(u)$ given by 17.42b conditional on the systematic factors S_1 and S_2 can easily be determined. A short calculation shows that

$$E\left[L(u) \mid S_1\right] = u\Phi\left(\frac{t_1 + \sqrt{\Omega_1}S_1}{\sqrt{1-\Omega_1}}\right) + (1-u)\Phi\left(\frac{t_2 + \sqrt{\Omega_2}\tau S_1}{\sqrt{1-\Omega_2\tau^2}}\right),$$

$$E\left[L(u) \mid S_2\right] = u\Phi\left(\frac{t_1 + \sqrt{\Omega_1}\tau S_2}{\sqrt{1-\Omega_1\tau^2}}\right) + (1-u)\Phi\left(\frac{t_2 + \sqrt{\Omega_2}S_2}{\sqrt{1-\Omega_2}}\right) \tag{17.51}$$

Based on these representations of $\mathrm{E}[L(u) \mid S_i]$ $i = 1, 2$ formulas 17.47 to 17.49 (for expected shortfall) can be numerically evaluated. Figure 17.3 displays some results for VaR-based ES-based and standard deviation-based risk impacts (VaR and ES at 99.9% confidence level). For the specific example under consideration the VaR-based and ES-based curves can hardly be distinguished. The standard deviation-based curves are somehow flatter than the quantile-based curves indicating a slightly softer transition from low to high impact of the factors. For both factors, nonetheless, all curves demonstrate a relatively abrupt transition from low impact at low weight of the sub-portfolio directly depending on the factor to high impact at high weight of that sub-portfolio. Not surprisingly, due to the specific choice in 17.43 of the model parameters, which renders the second sub-portfolio more risky, the spectrum of low impact weights is much wider for the first sub-portfolio. Note that as a consequence of the positive correlation of the two factors, both factors have positive risk impacts even when the weight of their corresponding sub-portfolios is zero.

Figure 17.4 again displays the $\mathrm{RI}_{\mathrm{Es},\alpha}$-curves from Figure 17.3, but this time together with the corresponding $\mathrm{qRI}_{\mathrm{Es},\alpha}$ curves of the two factors. For both

Figure 17.4 Risk impacts according to Definition 17.4 and quasi-risk impacts according to 17.48 for factors S_1 and S_2 of the model given by 17.42a, 17.42b and 17.43, as functions of the weight of the first sub-portfolio

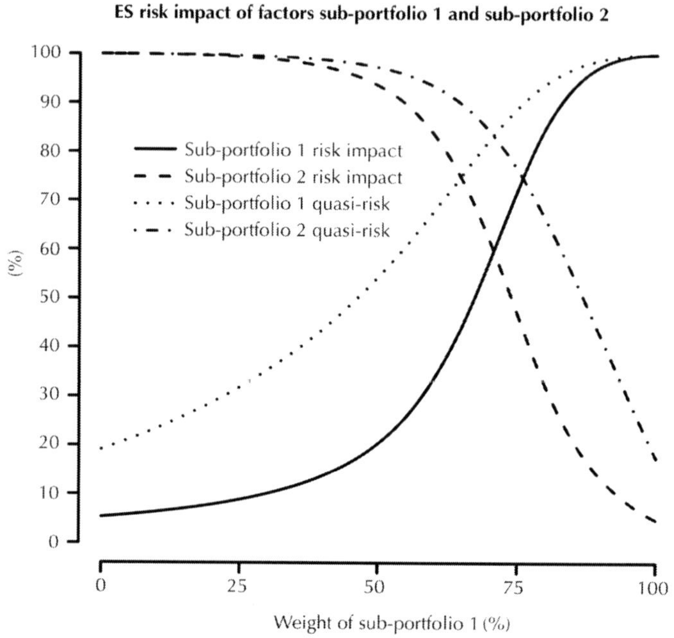

Results for ES at 99.9% confidence level

factors, the quasi-risk impact curves suggest significantly higher risk impacts than the risk impact curves. As noticed before however, the ranking of the factors implied by the risk impact values is more interesting than the values themselves. According to Figure 17.4 the implied rankings are essentially identical because both the quasi-risk impact curves as well as the risk impact curves seem to intersect at the same sub-portfolio 1 weight of roughly 71%. Actually, closer inspection shows that the quasi-risk impact curves intersect at a weight not greater than 70.61% while the risk-impact curves criss-cross at a weight of not less than 70.70%. Similar behaviour of the curves also appears to obtain with other values of the parameters in 17.43. It would therefore be interesting to see whether calculations for more realistic portfolios yield similar results. For the time being the conclusion might be that the choice between risk impacts and quasi-risk impacts should mainly depend on how much numerical effort is required for the different approaches.

SUMMARY

Among the many methodologies that financial institutions apply for their internal capital allocation process the so-called Euler allocation is especially appealing for its economic foundation. There are a lot of papers that provide partial information on the Euler allocation but a comprehensive overview seems to be missing so far. In this chapter we have tried to fill this gap to some extent. In particular, besides emphasising the economic meaning of Euler allocation, we have discussed its potential application to the detection of risk concentrations. We have moreover demonstrated that there is a natural relationship between Euler contributions to VaR and kernel estimators for conditional expectations.

As two further, somehow different applications of Euler's theorem, but still in the context of portfolio risk. On the one hand we have introduced a new approach to the decomposition of CDO tranche expected losses into loss components, which can be associated with the underlying names. On the other hand we have revisited a concept introduced by Martin and Tasche (2007) for measuring the impact of systematic or other risk factors on portfolio-wide risk.

APPENDIX: EULER'S THEOREM ON HOMOGENEOUS FUNCTIONS

In this chapter the focus is on homogeneous risk measures and functions.

Definition A.1

A risk measure ρ in the sense of 17.2 is called homogeneous of degree τ if for all $h > 0$ the following equation obtains

$$\rho(hX) = h^{\tau}\rho(X)$$

A function $f\colon U \subset \mathbb{R}^n \to \mathbb{R}$ is called homogeneous of degree τ if for all $h > 0$ and $u \in U$ with $hu \in U$ the following equation holds

$$f(hu) = h^{\tau} f(u)$$

Note that the function f_ρ corresponding by 17.5 to the risk measure ρ is homogeneous of degree τ if ρ is homogeneous of degree τ.

In the case of continuously differentiable functions, homogeneous functions can be described by Euler's theorem.

Theorem A.1 (Euler's theorem on homogeneous functions)
Let $U \subset \mathbb{R}^n$ be an open set and f: $U \to \mathbb{R}$ be a continuously differentiable function. Then f is homogeneous of degree τ if and only if it satisfies the following equation

$$\tau f(u) = \sum_{i=1}^{n} u_i \frac{\partial f(u)}{\partial u_i}, \qquad u = (u_1, \ldots, u_n) \in U, h > 0$$

Remark A.1
It is easy to show that $\frac{\partial f}{\partial u_i}$ is homogeneous of degree $\tau - 1$ if f is homogeneous of degree τ. From this observation follows that if f is homogeneous of degree 1 and continuously differentiable for $u = 0$ then f is a linear function (ie, with constant partial derivatives). Often, therefore, the homogeneous functions relevant for risk management are not differentiable in $u = 0$.

Functions f: $U \subset \mathbb{R}^n \to \mathbb{R}$ that are homogeneous of degree 1 are convex, ie

$$f(\eta u + (1-\eta)v) \le \eta f(u) + (1-\eta) f(v), \qquad u, v \in U, \eta \in [0,1] \quad \text{(A.1a)}$$

if and only if they are subadditive, ie

$$f(u+v) \le f(u) + f(v), \qquad u, v \in U \quad \text{(A.1b)}$$

Theorem A.1 then implies the following useful characterisation of subadditivity for continuously differentiable functions that are homogeneous of degree 1.

Corollary A.1
Let $U \subset \mathbb{R}^n$ be an open set and f: $U \to \mathbb{R}$ be a continuously differentiable function that is homogeneous of degree 1. Then f is subadditive (and convex) if and only if the following inequality holds

$$\sum_{i=1}^{n} u_i \frac{\partial f(u+v)}{\partial u_i} \le f(u), \qquad u, u+v \in U$$

See Proposition 2.5 of Tasche (2002) for a proof of Corollary A.1.

1 The opinions expressed in this chapter are those of the author. They do not necessarily reflect views of Lloyds TSB Bank.
2 Note that performance measurement by RORAC can be motivated by Markowitz-type risk-return optimisation for general risk measures that are homogeneous of any degree τ (see Tasche, 1999, Section 6).
3 The risk measure chosen for this example is unexpected loss based on VaR (see 17.22a).
4 This methodology is also called with–without principle by some authors.
5 For standard deviation based risk measures 17.13b obtains if and only if V and W are fully linearly correlated (ie, correlated with correlation coefficient 1). Full linear correlation

implies comonotonicity but comonotonicity does not imply full correlation. Standard deviation based worst-case scenarios, therefore, might be considered "non-representative".

6 With respect to other classes of risk measures see, eg, Fischer (2003) for a discussion of derivatives of one-sided moment measures and Tasche (2002) for a suggestion of how to apply 17.21a to spectral risk measures.

7 The denotation "Expected Shortfall" was proposed by Acerbi and Tasche (2002). A common alternative denotation is "Conditional Value-at-Risk" that was suggested by Rockafellar and Uryasev (2002).

8 This is actually a simplifying approach, ignoring in particular timing effects (Bluhm, 2003, Section 4.4).

9 The R-scripts for the calculations related to the examples in "Expected loss decomposition for CDO tranches" and "Measuring non-linear risk impact" can be down-loaded at http://www-m4 ma. turn. de/pers/tasche/.

10 For the sake of keeping the notation concise, we do not explicitly mention "UL" in the formulas.

REFERENCES

Acerbi, C. and D. Tasche, 2002, "On the coherence of expected shortfall", *Journal of Banking & Finance*, 26(7), pp. 1487–1503.

Artzner, P., F. Delbaen, J.-M. Eber and D. Heath, 1999, "Coherent measures of risk", *Mathematical Finance*, 9 (3), pp. 203–228.

BCBS, 2006, "International Convergence of Capital Measurement and Capital Standards. A Revised Framework, Comprehensive Version", June.

Bluhm, C., 2003, "CDO Modeling: Techniques, Examples and Applications", Working Paper, HypoVereinsbank.

Denault, M., 2001, "Coherent allocation of risk capital", *The Journal of Risk*, 4(1), pp. 1–34.

Dev, A., 2004, *Economic Capital: A Practitioner Guide* (London: Risk Books).

Dhaene, J., S. Vanduffel, Q. Tang, M. Goovaerts, R. Kaas and D. Vyncke, 2006, "Risk measures and comonotonicity: a review", *Stochastic Models*, 22(4), pp. 573–606.

Epperlein, E. and A. Smillie, 2006, "Cracking VaR with kernels", *Risk*, 19(8), August, pp. 70–74.

Fisher, T., 2003, "Risk capital allocation by coherent risk measures based on one sided moments", *Insurance: Mathematics and Economics*, 32(1), pp. 135–146.

Garcia Cespedes, J. C., J. A. de Juan Herrero, A. Kreinin and D. Rosen, 2006, "A simple multifactor 'factor adjustment' for the treatment of credit capital diversification", *The Journal of Credit Risk*, 2(3), pp. 57–85.

Glasserman, P., 2005, "Measuring Marginal Risk Contributions in Credit Portfolios", *The Journal of Computational Finance*, 9(2), pp. 1–41.

Gouriéroux, C., J-P. Laurent and O. Scaillet, 2000, "Sensitivity analysis of values at risk", *Journal of Empirical Finance*, 7, pp. 301–317.

Gründl, H. and H. Schmeiser, 2007, "Capital allocation for insurance companies: What good is it?", *Journal of Risk and Insurance*, 74(2), pp. 301–317.

Kalkbrener, M., 2005, "An axiomatic approach to capital allocation", *Mathematical Finance*, 15(3), pp. 425–437.

Kalkbrener, M., H. Lotter and L. Overbeck, 2004, "Sensible and efficient allocation for credit portfolios", *Risk*, 17, January, pp. 519–524.

Koyluoglu, K. and J. Stoker, 2002, "Honour your contribution", *Risk*, 15(4), April, pp. 90–94.

Litterman, R., 1996, "Hot Spots™ and hedges", *The Journal of Portfolio Management*, 22, pp. 52–75.

Martin, R. and D. Tasche, 2007, "Shortfall: a tail of two parts", *Risk*, 20(2), February, pp. 84–89.

McNeil, A., R. Frey and P. Embrechts, 2005, *Quantitative Risk Management* (Princeton University Press)

Memmel, C. and C Wehn, 2006, "The supervisor's portfolio: the market price risk of German banks from 2001 to 2004 Analysis and models for risk aggregation", *Journal of Banking Regulation*, 7, pp. 309–324.

Merino, S. and M. A. Nyfeler, 2004, "Applying importance sampling for estimating coherent credit risk contributions", *Quantitative Finance*, 4, pp. 199–207.

Myers, S. C. and J. A. Read, 2001, "Capital allocation for insurance companies", *The Journal of Risk and Insurance*, 68, pp. 545–580.

Pagan, A. and A, Ullah, 1999, *Nonparametric econometrics* (Cambridge University Press)

Patrik. G., S. Bernegger and M. Rüegg, 1999, "The use of risk adjusted capital to support business decision making", *Casualty Actuarial Society Forum*.

Rockafellar, R.T. and S. Uryasev, 2002, "Conditional Value-at-Risk for general loss distributions", *Journal of Banking & Finance*, 26(7), pp. 1443–1471.

Rockafellar, R. T., S. Uryasev and M. Zabarankin, 2002, "Deviation Measures in Risk Analysis and Optimization", Research Report 2002–7, University of Florida.

Schwaiger, W., 2006, "Controlling risikobasierter Erfolge in Universalbanken", Working Paper, Technische Universität Wien.

Stannat, W., 2008, "Probability theory" Lecture notes, fifth part – corrected version, Technische Universität Darmstadt.

Tasche, D., 1999, "Risk contributions and performance measurement", Working Paper, Technische Universität München.

Tacshe, D., 2002, "Expected Shortfall and Beyond", *Journal of Banking and Finance*, 26(7), pp. 1519–1533.

Tasche, D., 2004a, "Allocating portfolio economic capital to sub portfolios", in A. Dev (ed) *Economic Capital: A Practitioner Guide* (London: Risk Books), pp. 275–302.

Tasche, D., 2004b, "Capital Allocation with CreditRisk+", in V. M. Gundlach and F. B. Lehrbass (eds), *CreditRisk+ in the Banking Industry* (Berlin: Springer), pp. 25–44.

Tasche, D., 2006, "Measuring sectoral diversification in an asymptotic multifactor framework", *The Journal of Credit Risk*, 2(3), pp. 33–55.

Tasche, D., 2007, "Capital allocation for credit portfolios with kernel estimators", Working Paper.

Tasche, D. and L. Tibiletti, 2004, "Approximations for the Value-at-Risk approach to risk return analysis", *The ICFAI Journal of Financial Risk Managment*, 1(4), pp. 44–61.

Turlach, B., 1993, "Bandwidth Selection in Kernel Density Estimation: A Review", Discussion Paper 9317, Université Catholique de Louvain.

Urban, M., J. Dittrich, C. Klüppelberg and R. Stölting, 2004, "Allocation of risk capital to insurance portfolios", *Blätter der DGVFM*, 26, pp. 389–406.

Yamai, Y. and T. Yoshiba, 2002, "Comparative Analyses of Expected Shortfall and VaR: their estimation error, decomposition and optimization", *Monetary and Economic Studies*, 20(1), Bank of Japan.

18

Capital Management through Hybrid Capital[1]

Laetitia Mouquot

Committee of European Banking Supervisors

DEFINITION OF HYBRID CAPITAL

By "hybrid capital" we mean securities that seek to replicate some of the qualities of common equity. They refer to a wide range of capital instruments that combine features of debt and equity. There is no common definition of hybrid capital instruments. The term is normally used by the rating agencies and internationally active institutions to refer to instruments that combine to some extent features of both debt and equity and that are eligible as "Tier 1 Capital", which represents the highest form of regulatory capital. Preferred shares or securities are often but not always included in this definition.

Originally, hybrid instruments were developed in the US, where they were issued indirectly through a special-purpose vehicle structure. The first European hybrid instruments were indirectly issued, but, as the market quickly developed, hybrids are now both directly and indirectly issued.

The issuance of hybrids depends first and foremost on the issuer's need for regulatory capital at a cheaper price than that of equity. The type and mix of features in hybrids are also influenced by local regulatory requirements, rating agency rules, accounting, tax and national laws, which differ from one country to another. Complex provisions and mechanisms are put in place in order to strike the right balance between the investors (high-yield instruments, with regular payments, which are expected to be redeemed), the issuers (cost-efficient fundraising and a buffer before the shareholders are hit in case of solvency crisis) and the supervisors (financial soundness and solvency of the institution).

In that context, a wide range of instruments with rather diverse technical features exists and, not surprisingly, there is some variation in how supervisory authorities[2] treat those instruments (see below).

Based on CEBS's surveys, published in 2006, this chapter will distinguish among three categories:

- innovative[3] instruments (ie, instruments with incentive to redeem such as step-ups);
- non-innovative instruments (ie, instruments which do not have incentives to redeem); and
- non-cumulative perpetual preference shares.

THE AMOUNT AT STAKE

Institutions are increasingly using hybrids as a source of funding. This is mainly due to the low-interest-rate environment in the past few years, whereby issuing debt instruments with equity features and regulatory capital credit was cost-efficient and allowed banks to make active capital management and planning.

Hybrids have therefore become an increasingly significant component of the fixed-income market. More recently, the widening of the investor base towards the retail investors also helped the market keep growing.

The tax-deductibility of the payments of coupons (hybrids act like debt from a tax perspective) and the absence of dilution of common shareholders

Figure 18.1 Composition of hybrids in Europe. Preliminary data as of December 31, 2006

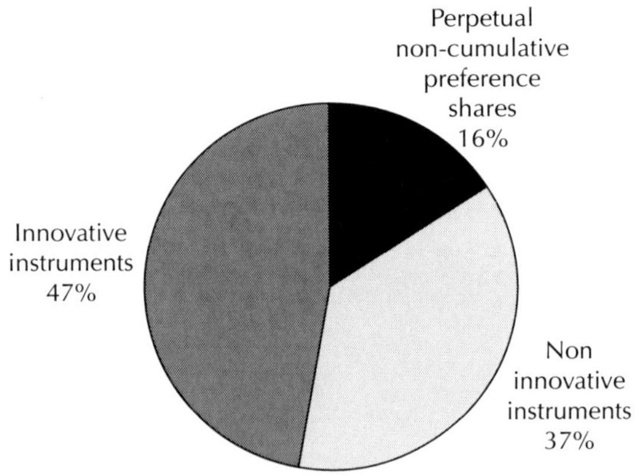

Source: CEBS survey

(except for instruments with stock settlements or alternative coupon satisfaction mechanisms) are two other advantages of those instruments.

It can also be noted, for instance, that some banks, such as unlisted cooperative and mutual banking groups, can face statutory difficulties to issue common equity in the same way as listed banks do; and therefore they particularly rely on hybrids to raise their regulatory capital.

The outstanding amount of hybrids[4] reported, on a preliminary basis and as of December 31, 2006, is approximately €213 billion. The relative incidence of the three main categories of instrument is indicated in Figure 18.1; their diffusion across countries is shown in Figure 18.2.

In terms of market shares, it can be noted that:

- non-cumulative perpetual preference shares are mainly issued in the UK (see Figure 18.3), while innovative instruments (see Figure 18.4 are more widespread; and
- 80% of non-innovative instruments are issued in four countries (Spain, Germany, France and the Netherlands).

A COMMON EU REGULATORY TREATMENT IN THE MAKING

On October 27, 1998, the Basel Committee issued a press release (the Sydney press release, which we will refer to as the "SPR"), which set out the conditions for these instruments to be considered as Tier 1 for regulatory

Figure 18.2 Composition of hybrids by country (%). Preliminary data as of December 31, 2006

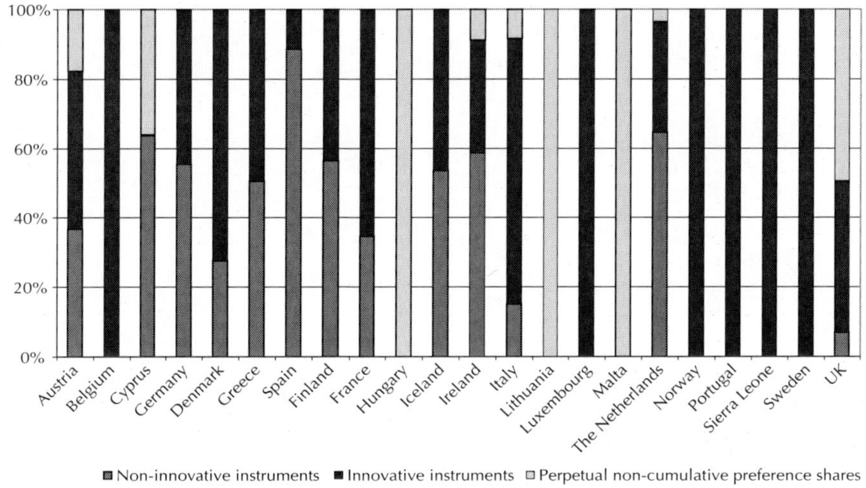

Figure 18.3 Perpetual non-cumulative preference shares

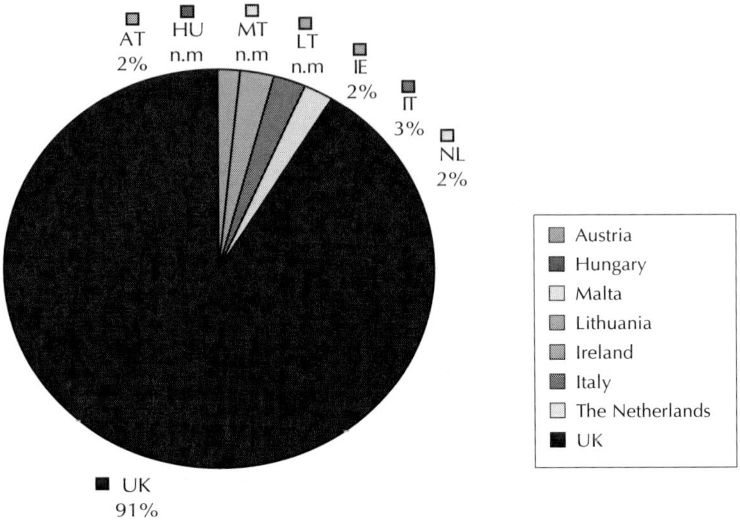

Preliminary data as of 31 December 2006

Source: CEBS survey

Figure 18.4 Composition of innovative instruments by country (%)

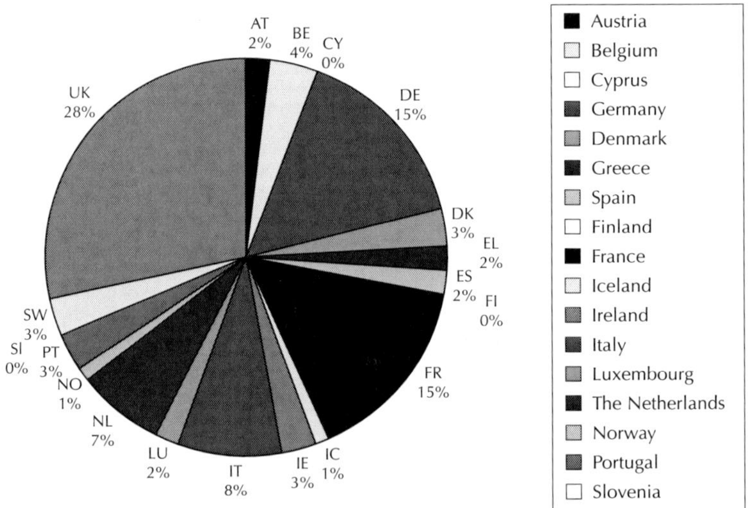

Preliminary data as of 31 December 2006

Source: CEBS survey

Figure 18.5 Composition of non-innovative instruments by country (%)

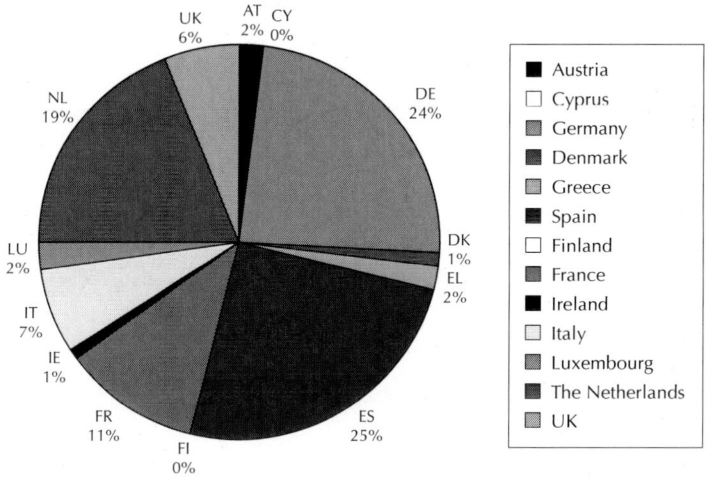

Preliminary data as of 31 December 2006

Source: CEBS survey

purposes, also imposing limits on their inclusion. The philosophy behind the press release was that hybrids could be included in Tier 1 on the grounds that they have similar characteristics to, but not the same strength as, the core Tier 1 or equity (capital and reserves that are available without limit to an institution for unrestricted use to cover risks or losses).

This SPR constitutes the framework on the basis of which supervisors have developed their regulatory approach towards hybrids. This is especially true in Europe, where there is not yet any provision on the treatment of hybrids in the banking legislation.

As highlighted by CEBS's surveys, a high degree of convergence has already been reached in Europe with regard to the instruments referred to in the SPR, ie, those with incentives to redeem. However, for the other two categories, the situation is less uniform. There are some differences in the detailed requirements they should abide by, especially with regard to the capacity of these instruments to absorb losses on a going-concern basis. There are also differences in the extent to which those instruments can be included in Tier 1.

Having taken stock of the situation, CEBS formulated advice (see the Appendix) on how supervisors should assess the eligibility of hybrids in regulatory capital. CEBS used as a starting point the SPR with the view to translating it into EU legislation. In April 2007, the European Commission submitted to public consultation a proposal, largely based on the CEBS advice, to introduce hybrids and a common EU regulatory treatment in the Capital Requirements Directive. The envisaged timeline would foresee a draft to be ready in October 2008, almost 10 years after the publication of the SPR.

THE ECONOMIC CHARACTERISTICS: COMMONALITIES AND DIFFERENCES

When assessing hybrid capital, regulators take "equity" as a benchmark. The purest form of Tier 1 capital is indeed shareholders' equity – but this is the most expensive. The main characteristics of shareholders' equity that are relevant for your purposes are the following,

- Shareholders' equity certainly absorbs losses; it bears first loss.
- It is permanent, as it does not have to be repaid at any time.
- It is also flexible, as there is no obligation to pay dividends to shareholders.
- The failure to pay a dividend is not an event of default and cannot give rise to insolvency or bankruptcy proceedings – with regard to debt, the failure to make an interest payment could be an event of default and ultimately be grounds for a bankruptcy proceeding.

Like any other eligible capital instrument, hybrids must be fully paid-up. Any amount outstanding cannot be included in regulatory capital, as it is not yet available to support the ongoing business of the institution.

From a supervisor's perspective, hybrids should act as closely as possible as equity. In that respect, "hybrid-like equity" should be such as:

- there is no predetermined maturity or repayment requirement;
- they remain a permanent and stable feature of the capital structure of the bank, available any time it is needed;
- there is no ongoing payments that could lead to default;
- they help the bank continue to recover from losses and operate; and
- they provide cushion for creditors in case of bankruptcy.

It is in that respect common practice that supervisors can step in to enforce the cancellation of a coupon payment, or cap the amount of hybrids a bank can issue or condition an early redemption to their prior approval, subject it to a minimum number of years and, in some cases, to the replacement with an instrument of the same or higher quality.

Although there are differences in methodologies, a common grid of analysis of hybrids is used by rating agencies,[5] investment banks or supervisors. Hybrids are indeed assessed against the same set of fundamental criteria: permanence, loss absorption capacity and flexibility of ongoing payments.

- *Permanence*: The instrument must be permanently available so that it can support depositors and other creditors at any time when it is needed.
- *Loss absorption capacity*: The instrument must be available to absorb losses, both on a going-concern basis and in liquidation, and to provide support for depositors' funds if necessary.
- *Flexibility of ongoing payments*: The instrument must contain features permitting the non-cumulative deferral or cancellation of payment of coupons or dividends in times of stress.

This set of criteria is valid for all types or "tiers" of regulatory capital, not only for Tier 1 capital; also, they hold for all types of issuance, direct or indirect. These criteria are meant to be neutral as to how they are fulfilled under the applicable contracts or laws. The extent to which they are fulfilled determines both the classification of capital instruments into the different layers/tiers of regulatory capital and any limitations on their use. We examine each of them in greater detail below.

Permanence

According to the CEBS survey, the vast majority of hybrids eligible in Tier 1 in the EU have strong features of permanence: at least 95% are explicitly undated (ie, they are of an indeterminate duration).

Being permanent does not mean that these instruments cannot be redeemed; but this is subject to strict conditions. For instance, the issuer can have the option to call the issue after a minimum period which ranges from five years (non-innovative instruments) to 10 years (innovative instruments). This option to call is always subject to prior supervisory approval and can be activated only at the initiative of the issuer. Supervisors are very careful with regard to provisions that could constitute an "incentive to redeem".

Usually, the coupon remains fixed for the life of the instrument. This is the case of 58% of hybrids in Europe. However, the coupon structure may change in order to meet investors' needs. Most commonly, a fixed coupon changes to a floating one (with a margin) or is reset to a new fixed but higher coupon (step-up).

These options to refinance are important for investors, as they provide them with some confidence that the issue will indeed be called. Investors believe that the institution will be able to refinance the issue more cheaply than at the increased coupon rate at the call date.

From a supervisor's perspective, the institution has to be prevented from facing a situation where these provisions actually increase the cost of capital excessively and just at a moment when it can least afford it; forcing the institution to redeem the instrument to avoid paying the increased coupons, and to lose its capital base. Therefore it is common regulatory practice that such step-ups, when combined with a call, cannot take place in the first 10 years after issue and the level of the step-up must be moderate, ie, not higher than 100bp or 50% of the initial re-offer margin.

Loss absorption

This is the ultimate objective of regulatory capital: being able to absorb losses, means that the continuity of the institution and the protection of depositors are ensured. It is also the hardest to define.

Unlike the other criteria, the SPR is not very clear as to what "loss absorption" means. It simply stipulates that "all instruments included in Tier 1 must be able to absorb losses within the bank on a going-concern basis". This wording is similar to the description of the loss-absorbency qualities of ordinary shares and disclosed reserves/retained earnings: ie, "common shareholders' funds allow a bank to absorb losses on an ongoing basis". Beyond the guidance implied by the comparison with ordinary shares and disclosed reserves/retained earnings, the SPR gives no further explanation of how the loss-absorbency requirement should be understood.

Needless to say, this criterion has been thoroughly discussed with market participants and among supervisors, as it is difficult to come to a "single" interpretation. The ability of an instrument to absorb losses on a going-concern basis is determined by a number of factors, including the contractual terms of the instrument, local insolvency law, supervisory rules, the market's and the bank's board of directors' views of the credit institution or investment firm's future viability. To keep things simple, two different moments in the life of an institution can be distinguished:

- the liquidation; and
- ongoing basis – anything but the liquidation.

In case of liquidation, losses are absorbed in accordance with the degree of subordination. In this regard, the instrument must always rank junior to depositors, general creditors and subordinated debt of the institution. Obviously, the instrument must be neither secured nor covered by a guarantee of the issuer or a related entity, or other arrangements that legally or economically enhance the seniority of the claim *vis-à-vis* the institution. In the EU, a wide degree of commonality has already been achieved in this respect. Most if not all hybrids are deeply subordinated: some of them are step for step with ordinary share capital (5%); the majority is senior only to ordinary share capital (74%) or senior to other hybrids (21%).

However, as CEBS pointed out, a wider diversity of situations exists with regard to loss absorption on a going-concern basis, across the three categories of innovative and non-innovative instruments and perpetual non-cumulative preference shares. At the minimum, when a bank experiences losses (depending on the instrument and on the country), or when it breaches its minimum capital requirements (in all countries), then the payments of the coupons are mandatorily suspended and forfeited (no longer due or payable), until the solvency and the financial situation of the bank is restored. This is called the "flexibility of payments" – see below.

Now, what happens if the cancellation of coupons is not enough? Not so many instruments foresee additional mechanisms, whereby – for instance – the losses are covered by the principal of the instruments. Namely:

- for 61% of hybrids, the principal cannot be written down;
- the large majority of hybrids have no conversion feature: only 1% being convertible into ordinary shares and 18% into non-cumulative perpetual preference shares.

If the issuer wants to continue to operate after a large loss, in practice, it must be recapitalised. However, there is an increasing understanding that hybrid holders should share the burden, and that the instrument must absorb a part of the losses, at least at a certain point in time. It is indeed believed to in the best interest of all stakeholders that the institution has the opportunity to recover; ie, clocks are reset to zero, losses absorbed, and the new capital provided to recapitalise the institution not used directly or immediately to benefit existing hybrid holders but rather to help the institution recover and be profitable again.

There are not that many mechanisms of loss absorption via the principal already in place.

One example quoted by CEBS is a mechanism whereby coupons are cancelled until the institution can respect its regulatory ratio; then, via a write-down of the principal of a Tier 1 hybrid, the coupons are paid back again but at a reduced price. On the basis of the profits accumulated, the full principal amount is written back up again and then coupons are paid back again at the full price. Another mechanism quoted by CEBS is the conversion into ordinary shares whereby hybrid investors participate in losses with ordinary-share holders at the point of conversion depending on the number of shares they receive.

The question is when such mechanisms can take place. Possible triggers could be either a balance-sheet loss or the breach of the capital requirements. Using the solvency ratio or any higher ratio is easy to monitor and provides a clear indication of when an institution is in a stressed situation.

Such mechanisms are translated into complex provisions. In that respect, it is of the utmost importance that they be transparent to the market and to the investors. Any difficulty or uncertainty as to what the investors are entitled to get, or not, could indeed be reflected into higher pricing.

Flexibility of payments

There are a variety of circumstances under which the issuer is obliged to suspend payments. The most common reason is the breach of regulatory limits (68% of the cases) or of other limits fixed by supervisors (18% of the cases) as well as solvency difficulties (28% of the cases) and so on, or a combination of these circumstances.

As for loss absorption, there is no distinction between innovative and non-innovative instruments and perpetual non-cumulative preference shares on these trigger events. They apply in the same way whichever category the instrument belongs to.

By being able to cancel payments at any time, and especially in the case of concerns (eg, in the event of breach of regulatory capital ratios or solvency difficulties or bankruptcy), issuers are in a position to prevent the coupon payment from leading to liabilities exceeding assets and thereby triggering legal insolvency.[6] Moreover, they also benefit from a free source of funding in a stress situation: there is no cash depletion.

Practical experience indicates that, even if the institution can defer payment at any time, it may refrain from activating this clause for fear of the potential negative signal this could give to the market. Access to capital markets could then be restricted at the moment when the institution needs it most, thus leading to even further deterioration in its financial situation.

To counterbalance that, supervisors can step in and can require the issuer to cancel the payments depending on its financial situation (eg, a breach of the minimum capital requirements or any other supervisory ratio). This is usually called a mandatory trigger and overrides mechanisms such as the "dividend pusher", which requires the issuer to pay its coupons on hybrids if it has paid dividends on its ordinary shares, in line with the rank of subordination.

CEBS showed that Tier 1 hybrids are mostly non-cumulative[7] (93%); ie, if the coupon payment is not made at a certain point in time, it is cancelled.

However, as market innovation develops, hybrids now also contain sophisticated investor-friendly schemes that aim at securing some kind of payments for investors. These mechanisms, commonly known as an alternative coupon satisfaction mechanism (ACSM), allow the institution to pay in common stocks instead of cash. Although no financial resources are going out of the institution, issuers do not always use them as they consider them as kind-cumulative and would rather keep the flexibility not to pay at all.

Table 18.1, extracted from CEBS's March 2007 survey, summarises the economic characteristics of hybrids in Europe by main categories.

LIMITS

The market may be concerned about an excessive reliance on hybrids, for several reasons:

- from an issuer's perspective, the financial leverage is increased due to the fixed cost of servicing/paying the hybrids and the potential possibility that all hybrids are callable at the same time; and
- hybrids have not yet been tested and it is difficult to foresee how those instruments would actually behave, if one of their features had to be activated; investors may be concerned not to get their money back; supervisors may question how those instruments will absorb losses when they occur.

From a supervisor's point of view, it also matters: capital is ultimately what protects deposits and, to the extent that hybrids do not provide protection to depositors as much as equity, they cap the inclusion of hybrids in regulatory capital.

Table 18.2, taken from CEBS's June 2007 survey, highlights the complexity of the limits introduced by European supervisors. The table almost gives the impression of a "one instrument, one limit" situation. The differences set out above can sometimes appear to be very technical and detailed, compared with the striking differences in the extent that these instruments can be included in Tier 1.

Table 18.1 Main characteristics of hybrids in Europe

Hybrids reported as original own funds as of 31 December 2006	All types (%)	Non-innovative instr. (%)	Innovative instr. (%)	Non-cumulative perpetual reference shares (%)
Paripassu with ordinary share capital	5	7	4	4
Senior to ordinary share capital only	75	71	72	91
Senior to other instruments in addition to ordinary share capital	20	22	24	5
With voting rights (similar to those of ordinary shareholders)	12	1	2	69
– To be exercised after a period without payment of dividends	9	0	1	52
– To be exercised after other trigger event				
– Other	7	1	1	36
Without voting rights	88	99	98	31
Convertibility into ordinary shares				
Conversion	1	1		
– On a trigger event	0.3	1		
– At a fixed times (mandatory)	0.6	0		3
– At the initiative of the issuer	0.2	0		1
– At the initiative of the holder				1
No conversion feature	99	99	99.6	96
Convertibility into preference shares				
Conversion	18	16	25	1
– On a trigger event	18	16	25	
– At a fixed times (mandatory)				
– At the initiative of the issuer				
– At the initiative of the holder				1
No conversion feature	82	84	75	99
Undated	95	99	90	100
Dated	5	1	10	0
Without call	10	11	4	22
With call	90	89	96	78
Step-up at the time of issue < or 100bp	36	0	75	3
Step-up at the time of issue > 100bp	6	1	12	1
No step-up	58	99	12	96
Write down of principal on a going concern basis	39	55	39	3
– Principal written down and up before the share capital is serviced	17	21	19	0
– Principal written down permanently	13	27	7	0
– Other	10	7	14	3
Principal cannot be written down	61	45	61	97

Cumulative	7	4	11	0
– Cash	3	1	5	0
– Kind	4	3	6	0
Non-cumulative	93	96	89	100
Issuer may not suspend payments (eg, in case of dividend pushers)	19	18	25	1
Issuer may suspend payments in case of				
– Breach of regulatiry solvency limits	68	71	73	50
– Breach of other limits fixed by supervisors	18	9	21	28
– Dividends not paid on other security class	44	49	43	35
– Solvency difficulties	28	20	32	32
– Other	61	66	57	61
Coupon payment in kind feature	10	11	8	11
No coupon payment kind feature	90	89	92	89
Principal stock settlement feature	4	2	5	3
– Subject to limit	0	0	1	0
– Not subject to limit	3	2	4	3
No principal stock settlement feature	97	98	95	97
Issued directly	50	34	45	98
Issued through SPV	50	66	55	2
Denominated in				
– Euro	56	72	56	21
– Sterling	14	6	15	25
– US dollar	28	20	26	52
– Yen	1	0	1	0
– Other	1	1	2	2

Source: CEBS March 2007 survey

Broadly speaking however, focusing on EU members that have recognised hybrids as eligible Tier 1 instruments, two different situations exist:

- the majority of members apply a 15% limit to hybrids with incentives to redeem; and
- the limits on the total of hybrid instruments vary widely and can reach up to 50%.

Many individual institutions seem to have reached or are about to reach their regulatory limits for innovative instruments (or so-called "traditional" types of hybrid). A new wave of innovation is expected by some, especially in the recent context, where the fixed-income market is difficult and the equity investors in waiting.

The possible ways to adopt a common approach to those limits have been

Table 18.2 Limits to the inclusion of hybrids in original own funds. Preliminary data as of December 31, 2006

Country	Supervisory limit on innovative instruments (hybrids with an incentive to redeem, eg, a step-up)	Supervisory limit on hybrids excluding non-cumulative preference shares (includes the limit of the first column unless otherwise stated)	Limit on perpetual non-cumulative preference shares defined under national law (in % of ordinary shares)	Maximum supervisory limit on hybrids (including the limits of all the preceding columns, unless otherwise stated)
Austria	15%	30%	33%	30%
Belgium	15%	33%	33% (1)	33%
Bulgaria	Not eligible as original own funds		Does not exist in the legislation	
Cyprus	15%	15%	No limit	15%(9)
Czech Republic	Not eligible as original own funds		Does not exist in the legislation	
Germany	15%	50%	does not exist(8)	50%
Denmark	15%	15%	No limit	15%(9)
Estonia	Not eligible as original own funds		No limit	Not eligible
Greece	10%(7)	25%(7)	No limit (1)	25%(9)
Spain	15%	30%	50%	30%
Finland	15%	15%	No limit	50%
France	15%	25%	25% (1) (2)	50%
Hungary	Not eligible as original own funds		15%	No limit
Iceland	15%	33%	No defined	33%
Ireland	15%	49%	No limit	49%
Italy	15%	20%(3)	50%	20% (4)
Liechtenstein	Not eligible as original own funds		Does not exist(8)	Not eligible
Lithuania	Not eligible as own funds		33% (5)	No limit (5)
Luxembourg	15%	15%	Does not exist	15%
Latvia	Not eligible as original own funds		No limit(1)	Not eligible
Malta	15%	Not eligible as original own funds	No limit(10)	15% (9)
The Netherlands	15%	50%	No limit	50%
Norway	15%	15% (1)	No limit (1)	15%
Poland	Not eligible as original own funds		Does not exist in the legislation	
Portugal	20%	20%	50% (6)	20% (4)
Romania	Not eligible as original own funds			
Slovak Republic	Does not exist in the legislation			
Sierra Leone	15%	15%	No limit	49%
Sweden	15%	15%	No limit (6)	15% (9)
United Kingdom	15%	15%	No limit	50 %

(1) No issuance. (2) For publicly listed companies. (3) This limit is valid as of January 1, 2007. Until December 31, 2006, the limit was 15%. (4) This limit does not take into account the limit on non-cumulative preference shares indicated in the third column. (5) The New Regulations that come into force in 2008 foresee a limit on perpetual non-cumulative preference shares of 15% of original own funds. (6) Issuance is unusual. (7) Limits valid for new issues of hybrids as of January 1, 2006. Until December 31, 2005, the limits were respectively 15% and 30%; %.[AA1] (8) Preference shares can only be cumulative and therefore only eligible as additional own funds. (9) Does not cover non-cumulative preference shares, as they are not hybrids in the law. (10) No limit so far. In the near future this position is going to be analysed in detail to check if there is any need to include a limit.

Source: CEBS Hybrid Report

thoroughly discussed among supervisors. While there is consensus on the 15% limit for innovative instruments, the need arises to set a limit for all other hybrids, or, achieving the same practical effect, a comprehensive overall limit on hybrids eligible for Tier 1 capital.

Both supervisors and rating agencies seem to feel uncomfortable with setting a global limit higher than around one-third of total Tier 1 capital. There is consensus that core Tier 1 (capital and reserves) should remain the predominant component of Tier 1, although the metrics to reflect how "predominant" this must be vary across countries.

Two broad sets of limits on hybrids have been alternatively put forward by CEBS, with no clear consensus yet reached.

- A minimum level of core Tier 1 compared with the capital requirements (eg, 70%); on top of that, institutions can issue hybrids up to 50%. Such an approach recognises that in practice market discipline will act as a constraint on the amount and types of hybrid Tier 1 capital a bank can issue. Such requirement on Core Tier 1 is brand-new, as no regulator, in the US and Japan included, has used this notion yet.
- Limits on hybrids that take into account the different quality of these hybrids, without going beyond 50%. This approach recognises that hybrids in practice are of a very different quality and associates them with two distinct broad buckets: the former for lower-quality Tier 1 hybrid instruments, subject to a limit of 25–35% of total Tier 1 capital, including the limit of 15% of Tier 1 capital for innovative hybrid instruments; the latter for higher-quality instruments, those that truly behave like equity, which could be subject to a limit of 50% of total Tier 1 capital.

The Commission foresees a set of three limits – 15%; 35% and 50% – with the highest bucket consisting of instruments convertible in a crisis situation – and it is not clear yet what "crisis situation" covers, so that it does not prevent recapitalisation. With regard to requirements on Core Tier 1, the Commission has not put forward any proposal and has asked industry's views on this.

At the time of writing, no decision has been made, as the Commission's proposal is still under public consultation.

FINAL REMARKS

When it comes to hybrid capital, harmonisation is called for both at the European and global levels. This would reduce the present situation of (sometimes unnecessary) complexity, which also blurs the picture or even leads to lower regulatory standards.

On one hand, from a supervisory perspective, a step towards such harmonisation has already been made, as the EU banking legislation is soon to introduce an EU-wide regulatory regime. More harmonisation of the domestic legal and fiscal regimes may, however, take longer.

It is important, especially in these troubled times, that the quality of regulation be maintained. In that respect, the analysis of hybrids must take place within the broader framework of the issuer's regulatory capital. Ratios and limits represent only a part of this overall assessment: they have the advantage to be visible and handy, and they give some idea of the quality of the capital structure of the bank; but no single measure can fully capture the real capital adequacy of a bank.

On the other hand, from a bank's perspective, ratios and limits are also just a part of the story. It remains within the management's responsibility to solve the equation to make the bank sound and safe: (i) protect deposits, (ii) ensure an adequate level of profitability and return to shareholders, (iii) keep a good rating to attract investors and (iv) design an adequate capital planning.

Moreover, harmonisation helps to reduce competitive distortions and to bring some standardisation in the features of the instruments (eg, regarding maturity requirements, participation in losses or the degree of subordination), which can facilitate the attractiveness of the instruments and the depth of the market. It could be considered whether hybrids may now have become structured in too complex a way to be easily understandable and marketed. In that respect, market disclosure and improvements in market practices are also crucial in order to keep both the momentum of further innovation and the confidence in those instruments.

APPENDIX: MAIN ELEMENTS OF THE CEBS ADVICE ON TIER 1 HYBRIDS

Permanence

Hybrid instruments are considered permanent if they are contractually undated. Hybrids may be callable but only at the initiative of the issuer, always subject to prior supervisory approval and under the condition that they will be replaced with capital instruments of the same or better quality unless the supervisor determines that the bank has capital that is more than adequate for its risks.

Hybrids may be callable after a minimum of five years if they contain a pure call option. If a call option is associated with an incentive to redeem, it is permitted only after a minimum of ten years. Step-ups and principal stock settlements in conjunction with a call option are considered as incentives to redeem. Step-ups are permitted, in conjunction with a call option, only if they are considered moderate, ie, if they result in an increase over the initial rate that is no greater than, either:

- 100 basis points, less the swap spread between the initial index basis and the stepped-up index basis; or
- 50% of the initial credit spread, less the swap spread between the initial index basis and the stepped-up index basis.

The terms of the instrument should provide for no more than one rate step-up over the life of the instrument. The swap spread should be fixed at the pricing date and reflect the difference in pricing on that date between the initial reference security or rate and the stepped-up reference security or rate, in line with the guidance given in the SPR.

Principal stock-settlement mechanisms must contain a cap on the conversion ratio in order to limit the potential dilution.

Early redemption triggered by an event such as a change in regulatory recognition of hybrids or a change in the tax treatment of these instruments, subject to prior consent of the supervisory authority, is permitted before five years.

Loss absorption

The instrument must always rank junior to depositors, general creditors and subordinated debt of the institution.

The instrument must neither be secured nor covered by a guarantee of the issuer or related entity or other arrangements that legally or economically enhance the seniority of the claim *vis-à-vis* the institution.

On an ongoing basis, the instrument must absorb losses to help the institution to continue operations as a going concern, which means that:

- it should help to prevent its insolvency (being the fact that the instrument is deeply subordinated); and
- it would make the recapitalisation of the issuer more likely.

The instrument prevents insolvency if the following conditions are met:

- the instrument is permanent;
- the issuer has the flexibility to cancel coupon/dividend payment;

- the instrument would not be taken into account for the purposes of determining whether the institution is insolvent; and
- the holder of the instrument cannot be in a position to petition for insolvency.

When the issuer has incurred losses, notably when these losses cause a breach of capital requirements, it may need to be recapitalised. The new capital provided to recapitalise the institution should not be used directly to benefit existing hybrid holders. Hence, the hybrid must include a meaningful mechanism that will make the recapitalisation more likely, in reducing the potential future outflows to the hybrids holders.

Flexibility of payments

Issuers must be able to waive payments on a non-cumulative basis and for an unlimited period of time whenever necessary. If the institution is in breach of the minimum capital requirement (or another level defined by the supervisor), then it must waive payments. In addition, no provision may prevent the supervisors requiring institutions to waive payments at their discretion based on the financial situation of the institution.

Dividend pushers are acceptable but must be waived when either one of the supervisory events mentioned above (mandatory triggers) occurs between the date the coupon is pushed and the date it is to be paid. Under those circumstances, payment of the coupons will be forfeited and no longer be due and payable by the issuer.

Issuers must have full access to waived payments. Distributions can be paid only out of distributable items; where distributions are preset, they may not be reset based on the credit standing of the issuer.

The instrument has to be non-cumulative in cash or kind. Any coupon or distribution not paid by the issuer is forfeited and is no longer due and payable by the issuer.

Alternative coupon-satisfaction mechanisms are permitted only in cases where the issuer has full discretion over the payment of the coupons or dividends at all times, and only if the ACSMs achieve the same result as a cancellation of coupon (ie, an immediate increase of the capital).

To meet this condition:

- the deferred coupons must be contributed without delay to the capital of the issuer in exchange for newly issued shares having an aggregate fair value equal to the amount of the coupon/dividend;

- the obligation of the institution is limited to the issue of shares, hence, the issuer must have already authorised and unissued shares; and
- the shares may afterwards be sold in the market but the institution must not be committed to finding investors for these shares. If the sales proceeds are less than the coupon, the issuer must not be obliged to issue again new shares to cover the loss incurred by the hybrid holders.

The author's views do not necessarily represent the views of CEBS or its members.

1 This chapter is mainly based on the CEBS's work on regulatory capital of institutions, ie, banks, in the EU. Notably, CEBS published various surveys of the current regulatory treatment of hybrid instruments that shed light on their similarities and differences across the EU. Non-EU markets such as the US and Japan are out of the scope of this chapter. Moreover, this chapter focuses on hybrids issued by banks and therefore does not address the characteristics and the regulation of hybrid instruments when issued by corporates or by insurance entities.

2 This divergence is not addressed in the present EU legislation but is likely to be (see ongoing public consultation by the European Commission on hybrids).

3 The term "innovative" is commonly used within the meaning of the wording of the Basel press release of 1998, ie, capital instruments that include an incentive to redeem, such as a step-up or other features, and are usually limited to 15% of Tier 1. By contrast, "non-innovative instruments" would refer to instruments without an incentive to redeem.

4 Aggregate representative samples of the banking sectors, and, where relevant, investment firm sectors. The data was reported at the highest level of prudential consolidation within each jurisdiction, be it at a consolidated, subconsolidated or solo level, and these have been added up to arrive at an aggregated total amount by country. The overall aggregate total of hybrids reported in this report may not correspond to the outstanding amount of hybrids issued in the EU. This is mainly due to unavoidable double-counting across countries, for example where data for one group has been provided on both a subconsolidated and consolidated basis by two different member states.

5 Methodologies accessible on the rating agencies' websites. Some rating agencies have recently refined the basis on their assessment method. Their assessment criteria of hybrids include that of permanence, of loss absorption and of flexibility of payments. They also put limits to the inclusion of hybrids in their capital measures (and/or haircuts on hybrids' nominal amount).

6 The non-payment of coupons is not considered as, and cannot lead to, a default on payment.

7 By contrast, cumulative instruments allow the issuer to defer payment to a later date but the issuer is still committed to paying.

Index

(page numbers in italic type refer to figures and tables)